Microsoft® Office 6 in 1

Microsoft® Office 6 in 1

alpha books

A Division of Prentice Hall Computer Publishing

11711 North College Avenue, Carmel, Indiana 46032 USA

International Standard Book Number: 1-56761-268-7
Library of Congress Catalog Card Number: 93-71676

95 94 93   9 8 7 6 5 4 3 2 1

Interpretation of the printing code: the rightmost number of the first series of numbers is the year of the book's printing; the rightmost number of the second series of numbers is the number of the book's printing. For example, a printing code of 93-1 shows that the first printing of the book occurred in 1993.

Screen reproductions in this book were created by means of the program Collage Plus from Inner Media, Inc., Hollis, NH.

Printed in the United States of America

Trademarks

All terms mentioned in this book that are known to be trademarks or service marks are listed below. In addition, terms suspected of being trademarks or service marks have been appropriately capitalized. Alpha Books cannot attest to the accuracy of this information. Use of a term in this book should not be regarded as affecting the validity of any trademark or service mark.

AutoCAD is a registered trademark of Autodesk, Inc.

Micrografx is a registered trademark of Micrografx, Inc.

Microsoft Windows, Microsoft Write, Microsoft Paintbrush, Microsoft Word, Microsoft Mail, Microsoft Access, Windows, Windows for Workgroups, PowerPoint, Toolbar, Toolbox, MS-DOS, Excel, and TrueType are registered trademarks of Microsoft Corporation.

WordPerfect for Windows is a registered trademark of WordPerfect Corporation.

Publisher
Marie Butler-Knight

Associate Publisher
Lisa A. Bucki

Managing Editor
Elizabeth Keaffaber

Acquisitions Editor
Stephen R. Poland

Development Editor
Seta Frantz

Production Editors
Linda Hawkins
Michelle Shaw

Cover Designer
Scott Fullmer

Designer
Roger Morgan

Indexer
Craig Small

Production Team
Diana Bigham, Katy Bodenmiller, Scott Cook, Tim Cox, Mark Enochs, Linda Koopman, Tom Loveman, Beth Rago, Carrie Roth, Tonya Simpson, Greg Simsic

Special thanks to Hilary Adams, Ed Guilford, Michael Hanks, and Kelly Oliver for ensuring the technical accuracy of this book.

CONTENTS

INTRODUCTION

"There aren't enough hours in the day." It's a common complaint. Time is a commodity everyone can use more of. The Microsoft Corporation has packaged six of their most powerful and useful software products into one impressive package called the Microsoft Office. With these software products, you can save time as you create impressive business documents, financial statements, and presentations, and use electronic mail for fast, convenient communication with colleagues.

The six software packages in Microsoft Office include:

- **Windows 3.1** A graphical user interface (GUI) that allows you to organize and run your software packages in a graphical operating environment, instead of using prompts and obscure commands (DOS). Windows comes with several useful applications, including a word processor (Write), a graphics painting program (Paintbrush), and a communications program (Terminal). It also features many accessories—such as a clock, a calendar, and a card file—that will help organize and simplify your work.
- **Word for Windows 2.0** A word processing program that's a premier program in the Windows operating environment. Word has features to let you create a one-page memo, a newsletter with graphics, or even a 500-page report.
- **Excel 4.0** A powerful yet easy-to-maneuver spreadsheet program. Excel can be used to generate impressive financial statements, charts and graphs, and databases, and to share the information with other software packages.
- **PowerPoint 3.0** An easy-to-use presentation program that lets you create impressive slides and overheads or print out presentations.
- **Mail 3.0** An electronic mail program that lets you share information (data and files) and exchange electronic mail with colleagues.
- **Access 1.1** A database program that's quickly become a leader in the industry because of its powerful capabilities and ease of use.

Using This Book

Microsoft Office 6 in 1 is designed to help you learn these six programs quickly and easily. You don't have to spend any time figuring out what to learn. All of the most important tasks are covered in this book. There's no need for long classes or thick manuals. Learn the skills you need in short, easy-to-follow lessons.

The book is organized into six parts—one for each software package—with approximately 23 lessons in each part. Because each of these lessons takes 10 minutes or less to complete, you can quickly master the basic skills needed to navigate Windows, create documents, financial statements, or slide shows, or send and reply to mail messages.

A bonus section discusses the sharing of information from one software package to another. This sharing is called Object Linking and Embedding (OLE).

If this is the first time you've ever used Windows or a Windows product, begin with the Windows part of this book. What you learn in this part will help you navigate your way through the other software packages.

Conventions Used in This Book

Each of the short lessons in this book includes step-by-step instructions for performing specific tasks. The following icons are included to help you quickly identify particular types of information:

Tip icons offer ways to save time when you're using any of the Microsoft Office products.

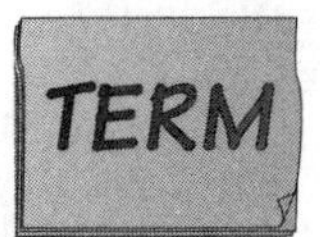

Term icons help you learn the terms you'll need to know in order to understand a software package.

Caution icons help you avoid making mistakes.

In addition to the above icons, the following conventions are also used:

On-screen text	On-screen text will appear in boldface type.
What you type	Information you type will appear in boldface type.
Items you select	Items you select or keys you press will appear in boldface type.

WINDOWS 3.1

Kate Miller

Starting Windows

In this lesson, you will learn what Windows is and how to start Windows and to recognize what you see when you get there.

The What and Why of Windows

Windows is a Graphical User Interface (GUI). This GUI comes with useful applications, including a word processor (Write), a graphics program (Paintbrush), and a communication program (Terminal). It also contains some nifty accessories that no work area should be without, such as a calendar, calculator, and notepad.

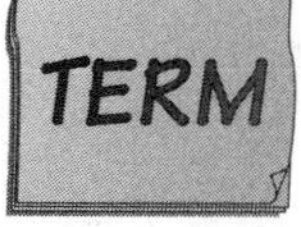

Graphical User Interface A GUI (pronounced "gooey") is a way to interact with your computer. You usually use a mouse to point at and select icons (small pictures that most often represent files or applications programs) as well as choose operations (commands from menus) on those icons. A GUI is an alternative to a *command-line interface*, where text commands are entered from the keyboard.

Why use Windows? Windows makes using your computer faster and easier in the following ways:

- You can work on more than one file at a time within a single application program. This allows you to copy information from one file to the other, without wasting time retyping information.

- You can also work in more than one application at a time. By choosing a simple menu command, you can switch between applications without having to close one to open the other. You can also copy information from one application to the other.
- Windows' graphical user interface is easy to figure out and remember, so you'll be up and running quickly. Once you get started, you'll be surprised how quickly your "educated guesses" become correct ones.
- All application programs designed for Windows use similar keyboard and mouse operations to select objects and choose commands. To a great extent, when you've learned one application, you've learned part of them all.

Windows' GUI provides a common approach to using a variety of applications for your computer. With just a little effort, Windows is fast, easy, and fun to learn.

Starting Windows

To start Windows, follow these steps:

1. Begin at the C prompt (or the prompt for the drive where Windows is installed). If you are not at the correct prompt, type the drive designation (such as C:) and press **Enter**.
2. Once you are at the correct prompt, type **win** and press **Enter**.

If Nothing Happens If you type **win** and get a message like **Bad command or file name**, Windows is probably not installed on your computer. Consult the *Windows Users Guide* to install Windows.

Once you have successfully started Windows, the Windows Title screen (including the version number) briefly appears. Next, the opening screen appears (see Figure 1.1).

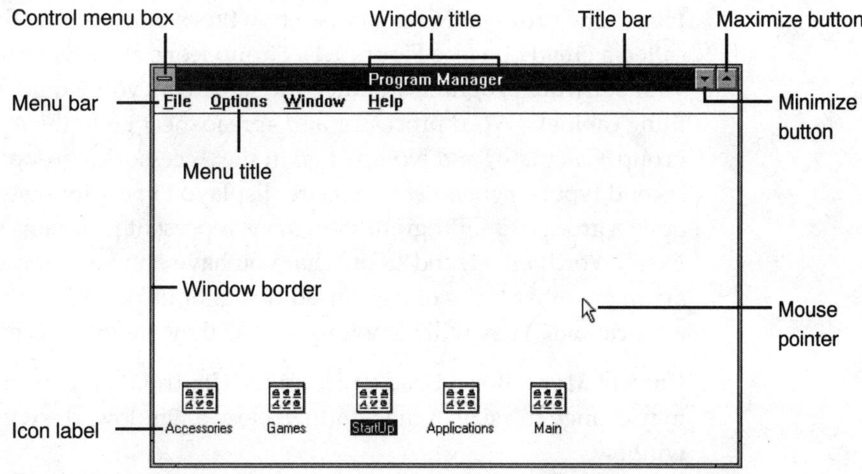

Figure 1.1 The opening screen showing the Program Manager window.

The Opening Screen

As you can see in Figure 1.1, the opening screen is made up of several components. These components are used throughout Windows and Windows applications to make it easy for you to get your work done.

The components of a window include:

Border Identifies the edge of the window.

Window Title Identifies the window and (often) suggests the use of the window.

Title Bar Gives added information, such as a document name if you are working with a document in the window.

Desktop This is the area outside the window.

Mouse Pointer The pointer (usually an arrow) on-screen that allows you to select items and choose commands. Move the mouse pointer and select items by clicking the mouse button. See Lesson 2 for more information about using the mouse.

Minimize and Maximize Buttons Click on these buttons to make the active window smaller or larger. Once the window is full-screen size, a button called the *Restore button* allows you to restore the window to its previous (smaller) size.

Icon The Program Manager uses two types of icons. The first type is called a *group icon* (see Figure 1.1). Group icons allow you to organize your software programs in much the same way you would organize a filing cabinet. (Word processor and spreadsheet go in the Applications group, Calculator and Notepad go in the Accessories group, etc.) The second type, *program-item icons,* are displayed in a window when you open a group icon. Program-item icons represent programs (Microsoft Excel, WordPerfect, and so on) that you have on your computer. There are many other types of icons used throughout Windows and Windows applications. They will be pointed out as they are introduced in the book.

Control Menu Box Used to access the Control menu, from which you may change the size of the window, close a window, or switch to another window.

Menu Bar Displays the menu titles you select to access the commands contained in the menu. Each application might have different menu titles, but you access the menus in the same fashion. For more on menus, see Lesson 4. Figure 1.2 shows the menu commands available in the **File** menu.

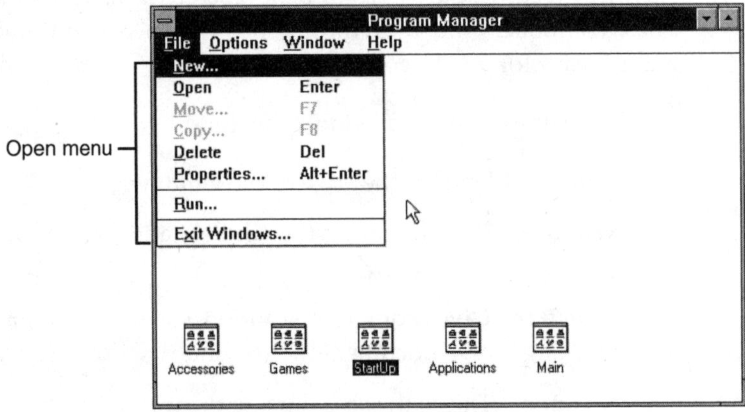

Figure 1.2 The Program Manager File menu.

How Windows Is Organized

It is no accident that the Program Manager appears when you start Windows. The Program Manager is the heart of Windows. From here you may access any of the applications that came with Windows or any applications you have installed.

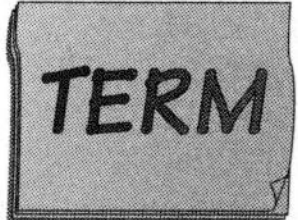

What Is a Program Manager Group? A Program Manager *group* is nothing more than a window containing a collection of related program-item icons.

When you first install Windows, several groups are created automatically. The Main group contains the following Windows applications:

Control Panel Contains the controls for the Windows environment. From the Control Panel, you can change the colors of the screen, control the sensitivity of the mouse and keyboard, and access many other features of Windows.

File Manager Helps you manage the files and directories on your disk. You can use File Manager to move or copy files to a different directory or disk, delete files, open applications and print files.

Print Manager Acts as the middleman between your application and the printer. When you print a file in Windows, it is sent to the Print Manager, which in turn sends it to the printer.

Windows Setup Allows you to add components to Windows that were not included when Windows was installed. Setup also allows you to add applications to run in Windows.

Tutorial Offers a guided tour of Windows. This icon will be present if you choose to include the Tutorial in the installation process.

PIF Editor PIF files contain information used by Windows to run non-Windows applications. This includes file names, memory requirements, and soon Windows 3.1 provides PIF files for more non-Windows applications than ever before and the PIF Editor allows you to configure them.

Clipboard Viewer Allows you to view and save Clipboard images. The Clipboard serves as a temporary storage area when you copy something from one application to be pasted into another.

DOS Shell For you diehard DOS prompt (C:>) lovers, the DOS Shell lets you jump out of Windows to the DOS prompt without actually exiting Windows.

Other groups include Accessories (containing Write, Paintbrush, and other helpful tools), Games, StartUp, and Applications.

Leaving So Soon? Just in case you want to take a break before starting Lesson 2, here is how you can exit Windows. From the Program Manager window (see Figure 1.1), press and hold down the **Alt** key, and press **F4**. Windows will ask you to confirm that you want to exit the program. Press **Enter** to confirm and exit or **Esc** to cancel and remain in Windows.

In this lesson, you learned how to start Windows, and you learned the major components of the opening screen. In the next lesson, you'll learn how to use the mouse.

Navigating the Desktop with the Mouse

In this lesson, you will learn how to use the mouse to make selections and change the appearance of the screen.

Mouse Basics

The mouse is often favored over the keyboard by both novice and experienced computer users. You can use the mouse to select objects, change the appearance of the screen and choose commands for Windows to perform. You don't *have* to use a mouse. All mouse operations have keyboard equivalents. Instructions for using both the keyboard and mouse are included in this book.

You'll see certain terms used throughout this chapter as well as the remainder of the book (such as *point, drag,* and *click*). Now is the time to become thoroughly familiar with these terms.

Selecting or Choosing Objects

You can use the mouse to quickly select an icon, window, or menu command. This is a two-step process:

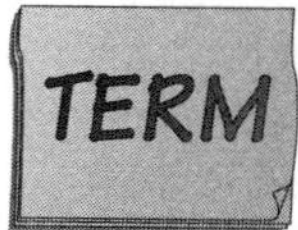

Point To point at an object (icon, menu title or command, window title bar, and so on), move the mouse across your desk or mouse pad so the mouse cursor (usually a pointer) touches the object. You may have to pick up the mouse and reposition it if you run out of room on your desk.

Simply pointing at an object doesn't give Windows enough information to do anything. To select an object or choose a command, click the left mouse button on the object you are pointing at.

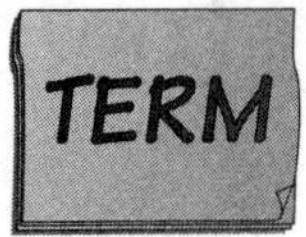

Click to Select After pointing at an object (menu title, icon, and so on) you can click on it to select it. Quickly press and release the left mouse button once. If the object is an icon or window, it will become highlighted. If you click on a menu title, the menu will open.

Try clicking the mouse. Click once on the **Control Menu** box in the upper left corner of the Program Manager window. You'll see menu options for sizing the Program Manager window, closing the Program Manager, and switching applications. You can make the menu disappear by clicking outside the menu. If you prefer to use the keyboard, press **Esc** to close the menu.

Opening or Closing a Window

Double-clicking an object is a shortcut to opening a group window or program-item from an icon. Double-clicking on the window control box is a shortcut to closing a window.

Double-Click to Open or Close Some operations require that you *double-click* on an object. As the name suggests, a double-click is simply two clicks of the left mouse button in rapid succession.

For example, point at the Accessories icon and double-click. If you do it correctly, the Accessories icon opens up to the Accessories window. You can double-click to open an icon to its window. You can also double-click on a windows Control Menu box. This is a shortcut to closing the window.

To close a window with the mouse:

1. Click on the **Control Menu** box to display the Control menu.
2. Choose (click on) the **Close** command to close the window.

The Quick Close Using the Mouse To close a window with the mouse, simply double-click on the Control Menu box.

Quitting Windows If you double-click on the Program Managers Control Menu box, you will exit Windows.

Moving Objects On-screen

You can also use the mouse to drag an object (usually a window, dialog box, or icon) to a new position on-screen.

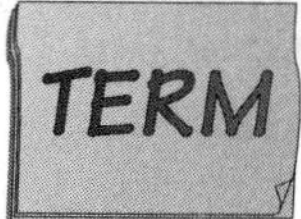

Drag To drag an object to a new location on-screen, point to the object, hold down the left mouse button, and move the mouse to a new location. The object is dragged along with the mouse cursor.

Resizing a Window

You can also drag a window border to change the size of a window. Try dragging a window border. Point at the right-hand border of the Program Manager window.

The mouse pointer changes into a double-headed arrow. As you become more familiar with Windows and Windows applications, you will learn that the shape of the mouse pointer can tell you a lot. In this example, by changing into the double-headed arrow, the pointer is telling you that you can now drag the border to a new position.

Drag the window border to the left or right making the window smaller or larger. When the window is the desired size, release the mouse button. Dragging any one border allows you to increase or decrease the size of the window in only one direction.

Point the mouse pointer at the lower right corner of the Program Manager window. When the pointer is properly placed on the border corner, the pointer changes to a diagonal, double-headed arrow. Drag the border down and to the right. The border changes position as shown in Figure 2.1. When the window is the desired size, release the mouse button.

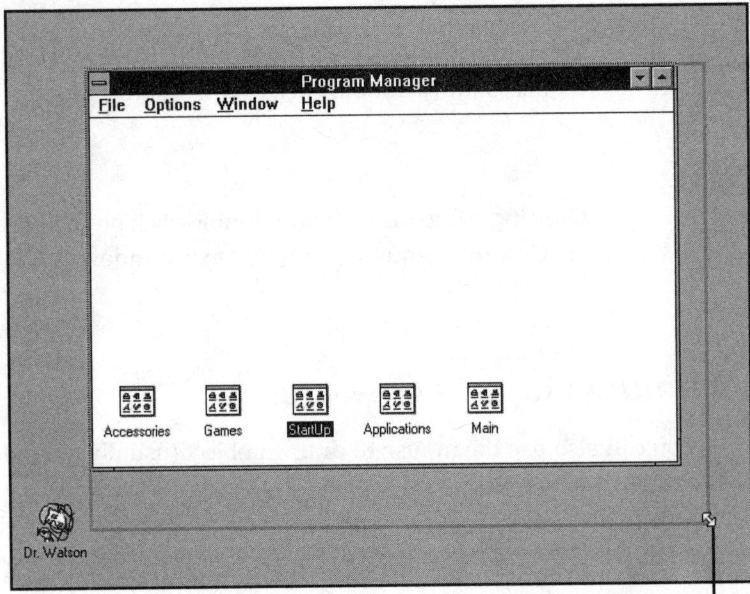

Figure 2.1 Dragging the window border.

Using Scroll Bars

Scroll bars appear when text, graphics, or icons in a window take up more space than the area shown. Using scroll bars, you can move up, down, left, or right in a window.

Figure 2.2 illustrates an example. If you drag the Applications icon outside the lower right of the Program Manager window area and release the mouse button, the scroll bars immediately appear. To use the scroll bars to view items outside the window, use the following technique:

1. To see an object that is down and to the right of the viewable area of the window, point at the down arrow located on the bottom of the vertical scroll bar.
2. Click on the arrow. The window's contents scroll up.
3. Click on the scroll arrow on the right side of the horizontal scroll bar. The window's contents move left.

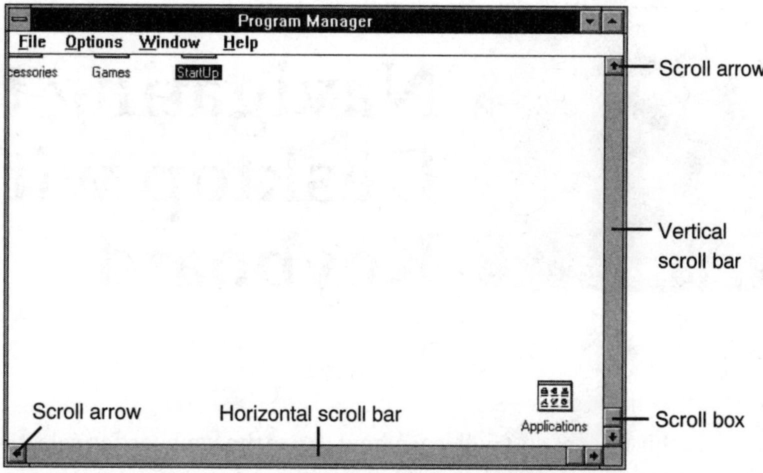

Figure 2.2 Scroll bars.

You can also drag the scroll box to move quickly to a distant area (top or bottom) of the window. To drag a scroll box:

1. Point to the scroll box in the scroll bar and hold down the mouse button.
2. Drag the scroll box to the new location.
3. Release the mouse button.

Window by Window You can move the contents of a window one windowful at a time. To do so, just click in the scroll bar on either side of the scroll box.

Empty Window? Don't worry if text or graphics don't appear in a window. Use the scroll bars to bring the text or graphic into view.

In this lesson, you learned how to navigate the Windows desktop using the mouse. In the next lesson, you will learn how to navigate the desktop using the keyboard.

3 Navigating the Desktop with the Keyboard

In this lesson, you will learn how to use the keyboard to select objects and change the appearance of the screen.

More About Icons

An icon is a small picture in Windows that may represent:

- A document, directory, or disk drive.
- An application program (such as WordPerfect for Windows).
- A group of applications (such as Accessories).

Most icons have labels (some are more descriptive than others). Figure 3.1 shows the window which appears after opening the Games group icon. Notice that there are program-item icons for two games: Solitaire and Minesweeper. To play either game, open the appropriate icon.

Opening an Icon into a Window

To open a group icon with the keyboard, follow these steps:

1. From the Program Manager window, press **Ctrl+Tab** as needed to select the group icon you want to open. The icon label appears highlighted when it's selected.
2. Press **Enter** to open the group window. See Figure 3.2.
3. Use the arrow keys to select the appropriate program-item icon within the group window.
4. Press **Enter** to open the program-item icon.

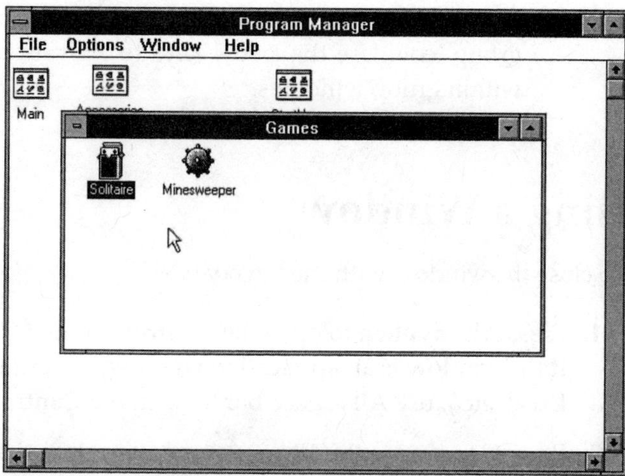

Figure 3.1 Game icons and their labels.

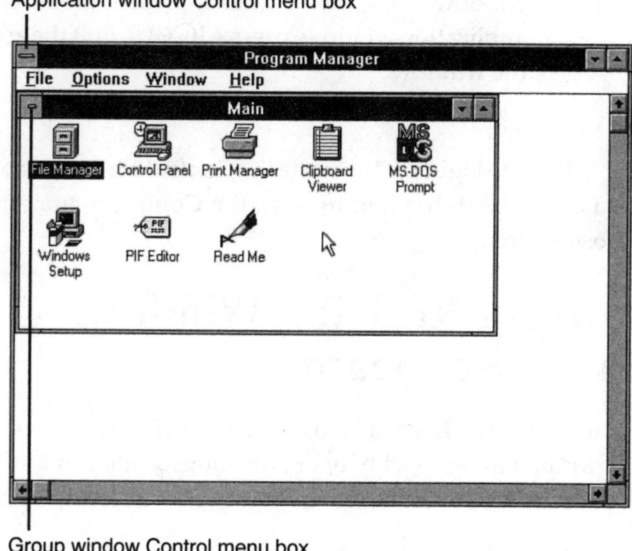

Figure 3.2 After opening the Main icon.

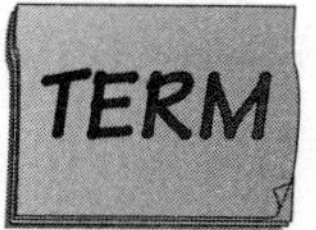

Active Window or Icon The active window (or icon) is the one with the highlighted title bar (or label). Any commands you choose will affect the active window or icon. To use the keyboard, press

Ctrl+Tab as often as is necessary to highlight the group window or group icon. Use the arrow keys to activate program-item icons within group windows.

Closing a Window

To close the window with the keyboard:

1. Press **Alt+hyphen** to open the **Control Menu** (for group or file windows). If the window is an application window (for instance, Program Manager, Excel, etc.), use **Alt+space bar** to open the **Control Menu**.
2. Press **C** to choose the **Close** command to close the window.

The Quick Close Using the Keyboard To close a group or file window using the keyboard, press **Ctrl+F4**. If the window is an application window, press **Alt+F4** to quit the application and close the window.

Refer to Figure 3.2 to locate the **Control Menu** box for the **Main** window. You could press **Alt+hyphen** to open the **Control menu** and press **C** to choose the **Close** option.

Moving or Resizing Windows with the Keyboard

You can use the keyboard to move and resize windows. These operations can be performed more quickly using the mouse, but you have more control using the keyboard. To use the keyboard to move a window to a new location on the screen:

1. Open the window's **Control** menu.
2. Press **M** to choose the **M**ove command. The mouse pointer turns into a four-headed arrow (see Figure 3.3) positioned over the title bar.
3. Use the arrow keys to move the window to a new location.
4. Press **Enter** to accept the new location. **Esc** cancels the operation and returns the window to its original location.

Control Menu Options Unavailable The **Control Menu Move** and **Size** commands are not active if the window is maximized. The **Size** command is also unavailable if the window is minimized.

To resize a window using the keyboard:

1. Open the window's **Control** menu.
2. Press **S** to choose the **Size** command. The mouse pointer will turn into a four-headed arrow.
3. Use the arrow keys to move the mouse pointer to the border or corner of the window you wish to resize. The four-headed arrow becomes a two-headed arrow, indicating the directions you can move the border.
4. Use the arrow keys to resize the window.
5. Press **Enter** to accept the new window size. **Esc** cancels the operation and returns the window to its original size.

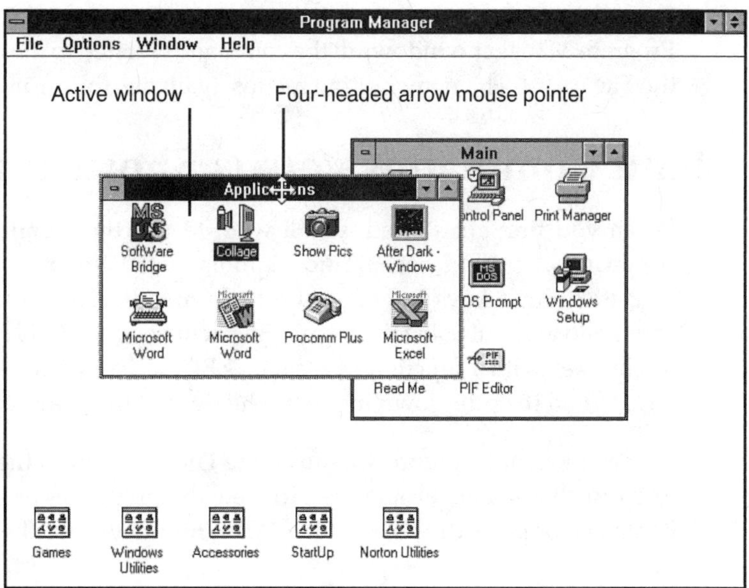

Figure 3.3 Moving a window using the keyboard.

In this lesson, you learned how to manipulate the Windows environment using the keyboard. In the next lesson, you'll learn how to make selections with the menus.

Using Menus

In this lesson, you will learn how to select and open menus, choose menu commands, and how to quit Windows.

What Is a Menu?

A menu is a group of related commands from which you can choose a command to perform. Menus are organized in logical groups. For example, from the Program Manager window, all the commands related to files may be accessed via the **F**ile menu. The names of the menus available appear in the menu bar.

Menu Commands versus Shortcut Keys

When you first get started, you'll want to use the menus to view and select commands. Once you become more familiar with Windows, you'll probably want to use shortcut keys for often-used commands. They allow you to access a command without using the menus. Shortcut keys typically combine the Alt, Ctrl, or Shift key with a function key (such as F1). If a shortcut key is available, it will be listed on the pull-down menu, to the right of the command.

For example, Figure 4.1 shows the **F**ile menu from the Program Manager. You can choose **F**ile, **P**roperties... to view the properties of a group or program-item icon, or press the shortcut key **Alt+Enter** to bypass the **F**ile menu.

Choosing Menu Commands This book uses the format *menu title, menu command* to tell you what menu commands to choose. In the above example, "choose **F**ile, **P**roperties..." is equivalent to "open the **F**ile menu and select the **P**roperties... command."

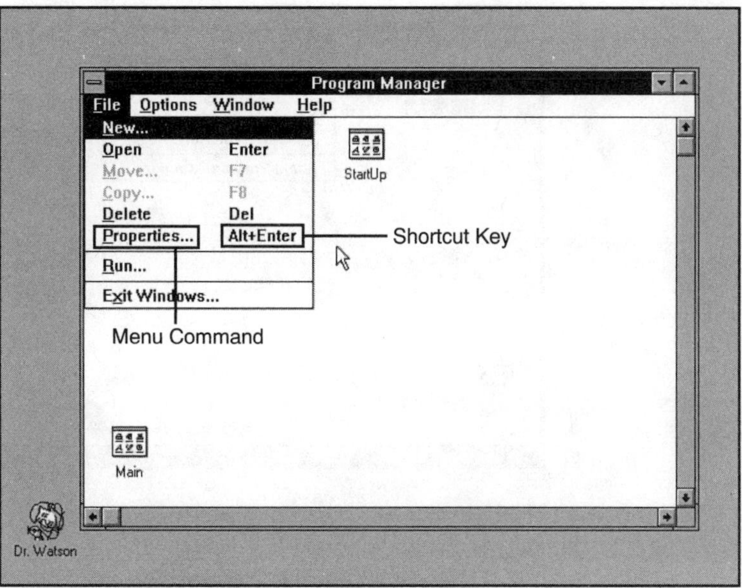

Figure 4.1 The Program Manager File menu.

Choosing Menu Commands with the Mouse

You can choose a menu command with the mouse or the keyboard. To use the mouse, click on the menu title in the menu bar. The menu opens to display the available commands. To choose a particular command, click on it with the mouse pointer.

Here's an example. To see the **H**elp options available for the Program Manager, just click on the **H**elp menu title in the Program Manager menu bar (see Figure 4.2).

To see the contents of the Program Manager Help facility, choose **C**ontents. The Program Manager Help window shown in Figure 4.3 appears. Notice that when the mouse pointer is positioned over a specific Help topic, it becomes a pointing finger. You can move the finger to any option and click on that option for specific Help information. (Remember, to close this or any window, double-click on the Control Menu box.)

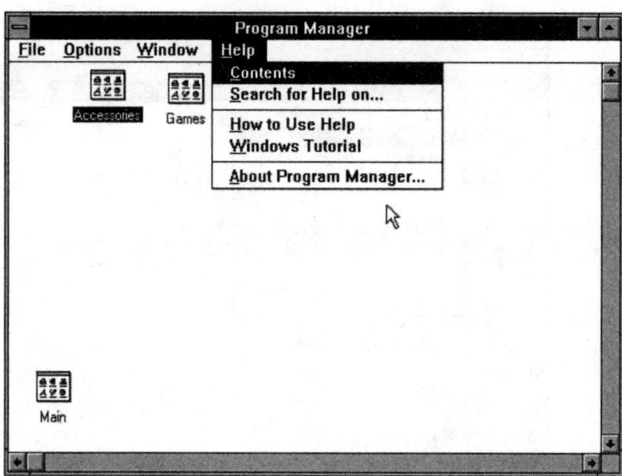

Figure 4.2 The Help menu.

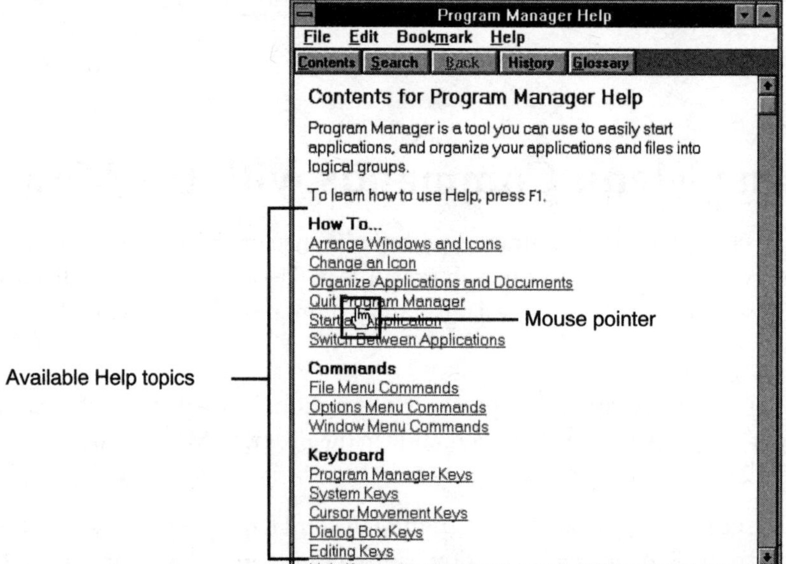

Figure 4.3 The Program Manager Help window.

Choosing Menu Commands Using the Keyboard

You can also select menus with the keyboard. Press **Alt** to activate the menu bar of the active window. Notice that the first menu title becomes highlighted. Once the menu bar is active, you may choose between two methods to select a menu:

- Use the arrow keys to highlight the menu title you want and press **Enter**.
- Press the underlined letter of the menu. (For example, to open the **H**elp menu, you would press **H**.)

To open the Control Menu with the keyboard, press **Alt+space bar** if the window is an application window (such as Microsoft Word or Pro-gram Manager) or **Alt+hyphen** if the window is a document or group window. You can then highlight your selection using the arrow keys and press **Enter**, or you can press the underlined letter of the command.

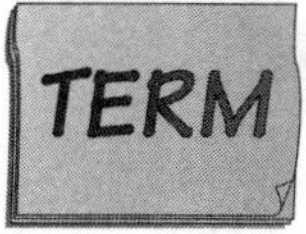

Commands, Options, or Selections? Commands, menu options, and menu selections all refer to the same thing—items you choose from a menu. Further, commands may be performed, executed, or selected. This simply means that the computer carries out the instructions associated with the command (whether it is to display another menu or perform an operation).

To close the Control menu (or any menu for that matter), press **Esc**.

Reading a Menu

Common conventions are used throughout Windows menus. Figure 4.4 illustrates the Program Manager **File** menu. Selection letters (letters you press to choose a command) are underlined. Also, shortcut keys (where available) are listed to the right of the command. Use these to bypass menus.

Unavailable Commands Some commands may appear grayed-out. These commands can only be used under certain circumstances. For example, you cannot copy an icon before you first select one to be copied.

Another menu convention shown in Figure 4.4 is the use of the ellipsis (...) after a command. The ellipsis indicates that more information is needed before the command is completed. Windows usually employs a *dialog box* to gather this information from you. For more on dialog boxes, see Lesson 5.

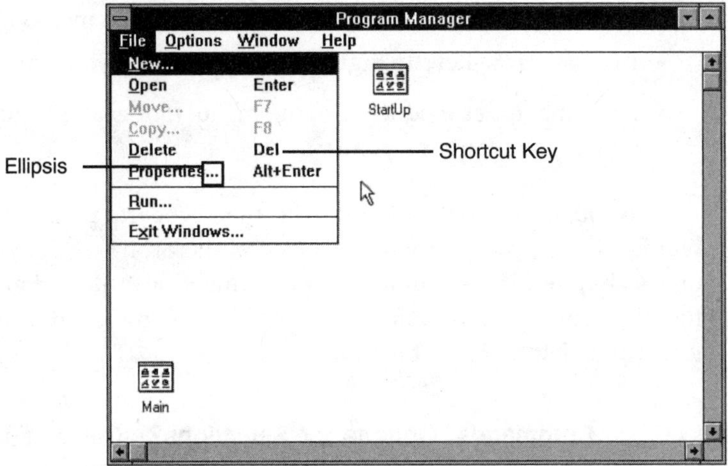

Figure 4.4 The Program Manager File menu.

For example, suppose you want to exit Windows. Follow these steps. (Notice the ellipsis following the Exit Windows command.)

1. Open the **F**ile menu using either the mouse or the keyboard.
2. Choose E**x**it Windows.... A dialog box appears.
3. If you want to exit Windows, click on the **OK** command button or press **Enter**. To abort the exit process, click on the **Cancel** command button or press **Esc**.

Another common menu symbol is the check mark. The check mark indicates that a menu option is currently active. Each time you choose the menu command, the option is turned on or off (like a light switch).

In this lesson, you learned how to choose menu commands using the mouse and keyboard and how to read a menu. In the next lesson, you will learn how to use dialog boxes.

5 Using Dialog Boxes

In this lesson, you will learn how to use dialog boxes to access and enter information.

What Is a Dialog Box?

Windows uses dialog boxes to exchange information with you. Most often, dialog boxes ask you to provide more information so that an operation can be completed. A menu command followed by an ellipsis (...) indicates that a dialog box will be used to gather more information. Dialog boxes are often used to warn you about a problem (for example, "File already exists, Overwrite?") or confirm that an operation should take place (for example, the Exit Windows dialog box).

Components of a Dialog Box

Dialog boxes vary in complexity. Some ask you to confirm an operation before it is executed—for example, a dialog box that asks you if you want to format a disk. In this case, you would select **OK** to confirm or **Cancel** to abort the operation. Other dialog boxes are quite complex, asking you to specify several options.

The following list briefly explains the components of a dialog box. The following sections describe the components and how to use them in greater detail.

Text Box A text box allows you to type in an entry; for example, a name for a file you want to save or a label for an icon you've just added to a group.

List Box A list box presents a list of possible choices from which you may choose. Scroll bars often allow you to scroll through the list. Often, a text box is associated with a list box. The list item that you select appears in the text box associated with the list.

Drop-Down List Box A single-line list box that opens to display a list of choices when you click on the down-arrow button on the right side of the list box.

Option Buttons Option buttons present a group of related choices from which you may choose one. Option buttons are sometimes (and incorrectly) referred to as radio buttons.

Check Boxes Check boxes present a single option or group of related options. The command option is active if an X appears in the box next to it.

Command Buttons Command buttons carry out the command displayed on the button (Open, Quit, Cancel, OK, and so on). If there is an ellipsis on the button, choosing it will open another dialog box (Options...).

Text Box

A text box allows you to enter information needed to complete a command. This is typically a file name or directory name. Figure 5.1 displays the Move dialog box (accessed from the File Manager **File** menu).

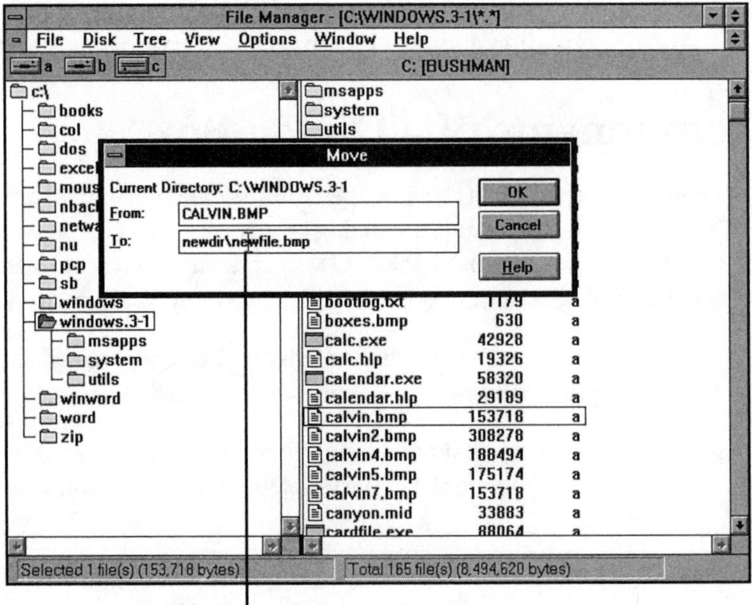

Figure 5.1 The Move dialog box from the Windows File Manager.

To activate a text box using the mouse:

1. Point at the text box you wish to activate. Notice that the mouse pointer changes to an I-beam when you point at the text box.
2. Click the left mouse button to activate the text box.

To activate a text box using the keyboard:

- Use the selection key sequence to activate the text box. For example, to activate the **To:** text box in Figure 5.1, press **Alt+T**.

Once you have activated a text box, you can use several keys to edit the text you enter. Table 5.1 outlines these keys.

Table 5.1 Editing Keys for Text Boxes

Key	*Description*
Del	Deletes the character to the right of the insertion point.
Backspace	Erases the character to the left of the insertion point.
End	Moves the insertion point to the end of the line.
Home	Moves the insertion point to the beginning of the line.
Arrow keys	Moves the insertion point one character in the direction of the arrow.
Shift+End	Selects the text from the insertion point to the end of the line.
Shift+Home	Selects the text from the insertion point to the beginning of the line.
Shift+Arrow	Selects the next character in the direction of the arrow.
Ctrl+Ins	Copies selected text.
Shift+Ins	Pastes selected text.

List Boxes

A list box is designed to allow you to make a selection from a list of available options. For example, the list box displayed in the Browse dialog box (shown in Figure 5.2) allows you to select a file to open.

Notice the scroll bar along the right-hand side of the list box displayed in Figure 5.2. You can use the scroll bar to bring items in the list into view.

To select an item from a list box using the mouse, click on the appropriate list item. Notice that in the Browse list box, the item you select is automatically displayed in the linked text box above the list box. Press **Enter** or click on **OK** to accept the selection; press **Esc** or click on **Cancel** to close the dialog box without making the selection.

To select an item from a list box using the keyboard:

1. Use **Alt+selection letter** to activate the list box. For example, to activate the **File Name** list box displayed in Figure 5.2, press **Alt+N**.

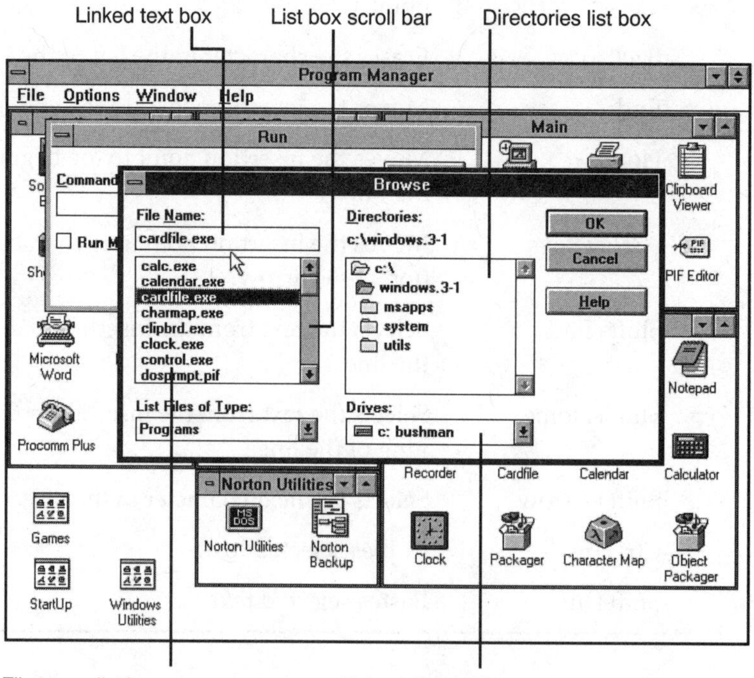

Figure 5.2 The Browse dialog box.

2. Use ↑ and ↓ or **PageUp** and **PageDown** to move through the list. Each list item will become highlighted as you come to it.
3. Press **Enter** to accept the selection and close the dialog box.

To select an item from a drop-down list box using the mouse, open the list box by clicking on the down-arrow button and then click on the appropriate list item. To select a drop-down list box item using the keyboard:

1. Use **Alt+selection letter** to activate the list box.
2. Use ↓ to open the drop-down list box.
3. Use ↑ and ↓ or **PageUp** and **PageDown** to scroll through the list.
4. Press **Enter** to make your selection and close the dialog box.

Option Buttons

Option buttons allow you to make a single choice from a list of possible command options. For example, the Print Range options displayed in Figure 5.3 allow you to select which pages of your document to print. The active option is indicated by the small, filled-in circle (the **All** option in Figure 5.3 is currently active).

To select an option button with the mouse, click on the circle for the option you want. To use the keyboard, press **Alt** plus the selection letter for the option you want. For example, press **Alt+A** to activate the **All** option in Figure 5.3.

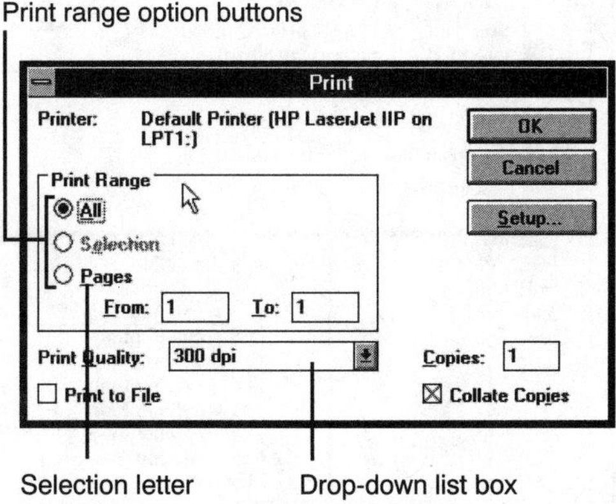

Figure 5.3 The Print dialog box from Windows Write.

Check Boxes

Command options you can select (activate) or deselect (deactivate) are usually presented as check boxes. When a check box is selected, an X appears in the box, and the associated command option is active (see Figure 5.4).

To select or deselect a check box option, click on its box with the mouse pointer. To use the keyboard, press **Alt+selection letter** to select or deselect a check box. For example, press **Alt+S** to activate the **S**ystem option in Figure 5.4.

Command Buttons

Command buttons are used to perform operations. In Figure 5.4, three common command buttons appear. The **OK** command button is used to accept the information you have entered or verify an action and close the dialog box. Pressing **Enter** is equivalent to selecting the **OK** button. **Cancel** is used to leave the dialog box without executing the information you provided in the dialog box. Pressing **Esc** is the keyboard equivalent to selecting the Cancel button. **Help** is another common command button that provides you with help specific to the dialog box you are working in. **Alt+H** and **F1** are the keyboard equivalents to selecting the **Help** button.

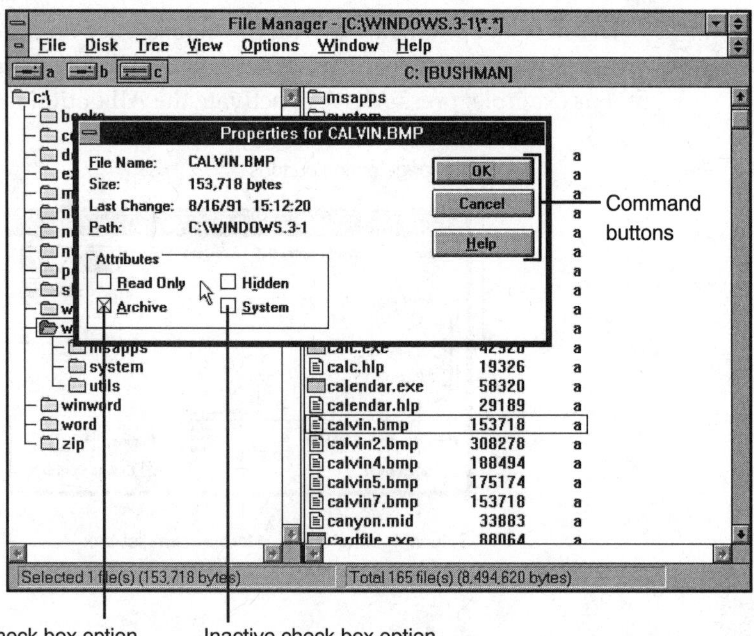

Figure 5.4 The Properties dialog box from the Windows File Manager.

Accidents Happen If you accidentally select the Cancel command button, don't worry. You can always reenter the dialog box and continue. Be careful when you select OK. The instructions you have entered in the dialog box are executed.

In this lesson, you learned how to use dialog boxes. In the next lesson, you will learn how to exit Windows and, perhaps more importantly, what to do before you exit.

Exiting Windows

So far, you have learned several ways to exit Windows. In this lesson, you will learn the steps to take before you leave Windows as well as other ways to exit Windows.

Methods to Exit Windows

Three methods are available to quit Windows:

- Through the Program Manager **F**ile menu.
- Through the Program Manager Control menu.
- With a shortcut key.

Exit Using the File Menu

You may exit Windows using the **F**ile menu (see Figure 6.1).

To use the mouse, follow these steps:

1. Choose **File, Exit Windows** from the Program Manager window.
2. Exit Windows by selecting the **OK** command button in the Exit Windows dialog box.

To use the keyboard, follow these steps:

1. Press **Alt** to activate the Program Manager menu bar.
2. Open **File** by pressing **F** or **Enter**.

3. Select **Exit Windows** by pressing **X** or use ↓ to highlight **Exit Windows** and press **Enter**. The Exit Windows dialog box appears, as shown in Figure 6.2.

4. Exit Windows by selecting the **OK** command button in the Exit Windows dialog box.

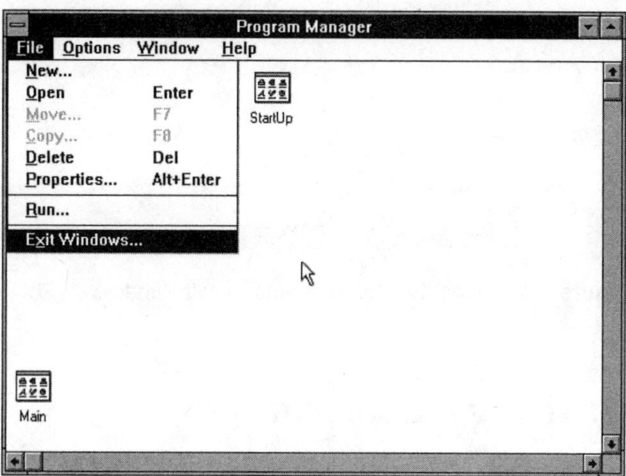

Figure 6.1 Using the File menu to exit Windows.

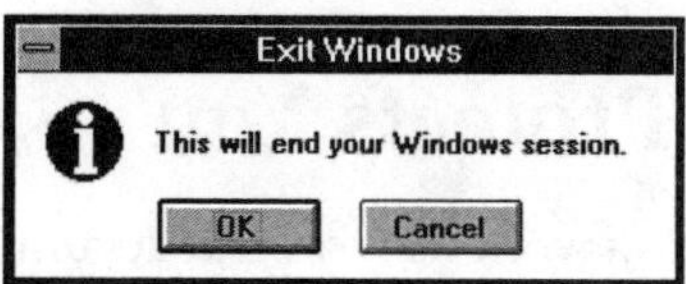

Figure 6.2 The Exit Windows dialog box.

Exit Using the Control Menu

To exit Windows using the Control menu, double-click the Program Manager Control Menu box. If you prefer to use the keyboard (see Figure 6.3), follow these steps:

1. Press **Alt+space bar** to open the Program Manager Control menu.

2. Select **Close** by pressing **C** or use ↓ to highlight **Close** and press **Enter**.

3. Exit Windows by selecting the **OK** command button in the Exit Windows dialog box.

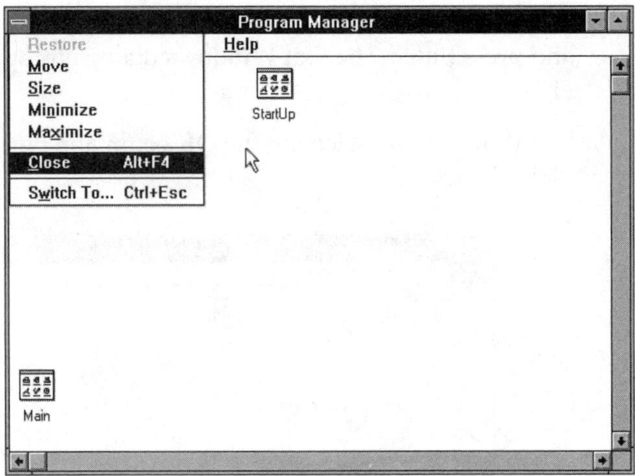

Figure 6.3 Using the Control menu to exit Windows.

Exit Using a Shortcut Key

As you may have noticed in Figure 6.3, a shortcut key is available to exit Windows. Once you have closed any open documents and applications and returned to the Program Manager window, press **Alt+F4**.

Windows Protects You

Because you can work with several documents and applications at one time, you may get carried away and forget to save a document before you exit Windows. Fear not; Windows protects you. For example, if you're working on a Write document and try to exit Windows without saving the document, the dialog box shown in Figure 6.4 prompts you to save your changes.

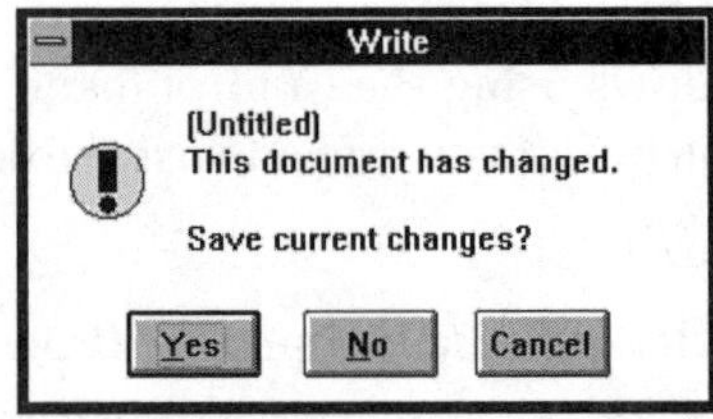

Figure 6.4 The Write: Save Current Changes? dialog box.

Select **Yes** to save the changes, **No** to discard any changes you made, or **Cancel** to stop exiting Windows. This dialog box helps you avoid losing document changes.

Forget To Save? This message is your only warning. If you accidently respond **No** to saving current changes, the changes made in the document are lost.

Leaving Applications Before Exiting Windows

Even though Windows provides the protection described, it is safest to get in the habit of closing documents and applications yourself before quitting Windows.

In most Windows applications, choose **File, Save** to save a document. Then, exit the application. If it is a Windows application, you can exit just as you would exit Windows (press **Alt+F4** or choose **File, Exit**).

The Way Things Were

If you've made any changes to the Program Manager window during your Windows session, you may want to save them so they will appear the next time you start Windows. The changes might include moving icons around within group windows, moving windows around within the Program Manager window, or even changing which windows will be open when you next start Windows.

To activate this option using the mouse, choose **Options, Save Settings on Exit**. A check mark appears when this option is active. To use the keyboard, from the Program Manager window:

1. Press **Alt** to activate the menu bar.
2. Press **O** to open the **O**ptions menu.
3. Press **S** to activate the **S**ave Settings on Exit command.

Save a Step If you want a particular application to start automatically every time you start Windows, place its program-item icon in the Program Manager group named StartUp.

In this lesson, you learned different ways to exit Windows. In the next lesson, you will learn how to start and exit applications.

7 Starting and Exiting Applications

In this lesson, you will learn how to start and exit Windows applications.

Starting Windows Applications

A Windows application is a program designed to take advantage of the Graphical User Interface built into Windows. By definition, a GUI provides a common interface between you and your programs. In the context of this lesson, this means that you are able to start (and exit) most Windows applications using the same procedures. If you are using a non-Windows (DOS) application through Windows, you will need to consult the manual for that application to learn how to start and exit.

There are several ways to start a Windows application; two that are discussed in this chapter are:

- Using the program-item icon associated with the application.
- Using the Program Manager **File**, **Run** command.

In Lesson 17, you will learn how to use the File Manager to start an application.

Using the Application Icon

You most often will use the program-item icon to start an application. When a Windows application is added to a Program Manager group, a program-item icon for the application is created. To use the program-item icon to open the application, you must first locate it in one of the Program Managers groups. For example, if you want to use Write, you would need to open the Accessories group icon to access the Write program-item icon. Figure 7.1 shows the Accessories group window and the program-item icons that might appear in it.

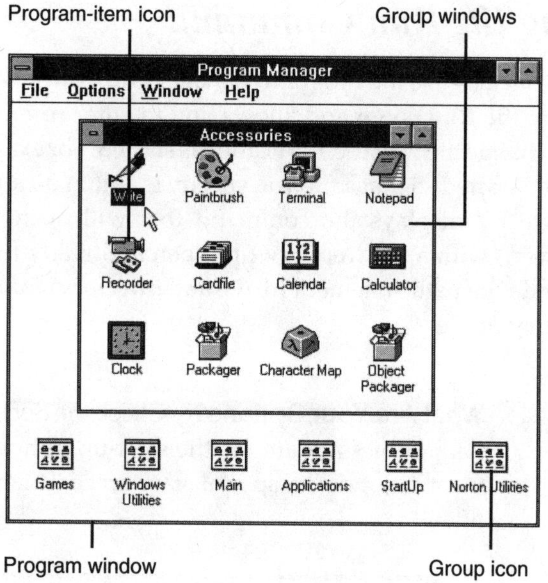

Figure 7.1 Program-item icons in the Accessories group.

To use the mouse to start an application from the program-item icon, follow these steps:

1. Open (double-click on) the Program Manager group that contains the program-item icon for the application you want to use.
2. Double click on the program-item icon for the application. The application window appears.

To start an application using the keyboard:

1. From the Program Manager window, press **Ctrl+Tab** to highlight the desired program group icon.
2. Press **Enter** to open the group window.
3. Use the arrow keys to highlight the program-item icon for the application you want to use.
4. Press **Enter** to start the application. The application window appears.

Using the Run Command

You can also use the Program Manager **File, Run** command to start applications. Using the **Run** command allows you to enter command parameters or options that change the way the application is started. For example, most word processors can be started so that a file you specify is automatically opened and ready to edit. Figure 7.2 displays the command that will open WordPerfect for Windows (wpwin) with a file (report.wpp) open and ready to edit. If necessary, you can include the path statement (drive and directory) for the program file and/or the document file.

What Are Your Options? Check the documentation that comes with your software for the start-up options available. You may want to jot down special start-up commands you plan on using often.

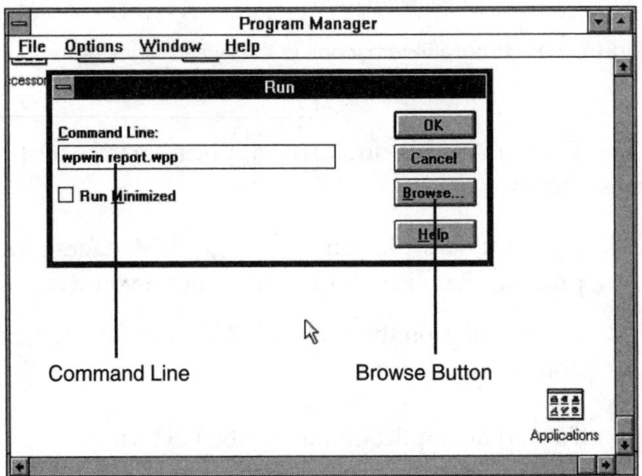

Figure 7.2 Loading WordPerfect for Windows and a document file using the Windows File, Run command.

To use the **Run** command, follow these steps:

1. From the Program Manager window, choose **File, Run**. The Run command dialog box appears (see Figure 7.3).

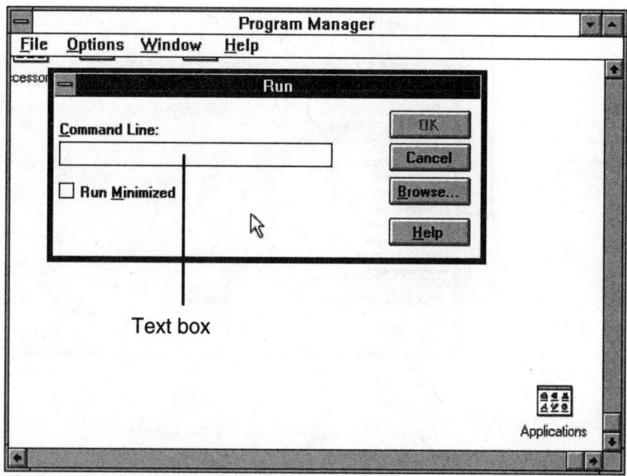

Figure 7.3 The Run dialog box ready for your command.

2. Type the command in text box. Examples of possible commands are as follows:

   WPWIN
   C:\WPWIN\WPWIN
   C:\WPWIN\WPWIN REPORT.WPP
   C:\WPWIN\WPWIN C:\MYFILES\REPORT.WPP

3. When the command is complete, select **OK**. (If you decide not to use the Run command, select **Cancel**.)

If You Don't Remember the Command Suppose you don't remember the command that will run the application. There are two routes to a solution. The most direct route is to use the **Browse** button on the Run dialog box. The Browse dialog box shown in Figure 7.4 appears. From it, you can see files which may be selected. Or you may select files to run from the File Manager (see Lesson 17).

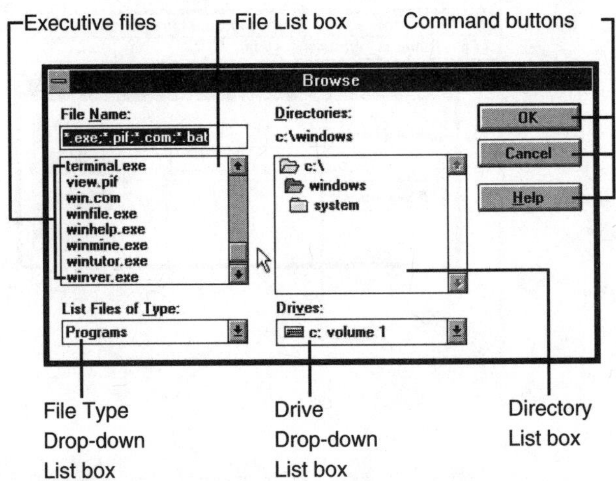

Figure 7.4 The Browse dialog box.

Using a Document Window

When you use specific applications with Windows, you will create documents. For example, a letter you create with WordPerfect for Windows will be contained in a document. These documents are sometimes called files or document files. When you are working on a document, it appears in a window.

Creating and Opening a Document Window

When you start up an application, a window for a new document is created for you. If you want to create another document window, you may choose the **File**, **New** command from that applications menu bar. A new window is created for you to start a new document and the document you were working on is still available.

Save Your Work Always save your documents using the **File**, **Save** command. You should give each document file a unique name. That way, you can use the **File**, **Open** command later to open the document file and continue working.

Closing a Document Window

When you are done with a document, always save your changes and close the document window. Choose **File, Save** and then choose **File, Exit,** or simply double-click on the **Control Menu** box. This ensures the document will not be lost or damaged accidently.

Exiting Windows Applications

Before you exit an application, make sure the open documents for that application are saved and closed through the **File** menu.

Forget to Save Your Changes? If you attempt to close a document window or exit an application before you save changes, Windows will ask you if you want to save before closing. (See Figure 7.5 for an example.) This is a safety feature built into Windows. To save your work, click on the **Yes** command button. To exit without saving your work, click on the **No** command button. To remain in the application, click on the **Cancel** command button.

Figure 7.5 The Write: Save Changes? dialog box.

There are three ways to exit a Windows application:

- With the Control menu.
- With the applications Exit command.
- With the shortcut key.

Close or Exit? The term *close* is used in reference to document windows. When you are finished working on a document, save your changes and close the document window. The application will still be open. The Exit command will close your document window(s) *and* exit the application.

Using the Application Control Menu

To exit an application using its Control menu, double-click on the Control Menu box. If you prefer the keyboard:

1. Press **Alt+space bar** to open the Applications Control menu.
2. Press **C** to choose the Close command.

Using the Applications Exit Command

You may exit an application by choosing **File, Exit**. You can click on the commands with the mouse or press **Alt** to activate the menu bar and proceed with the keyboard.

Using the Shortcut Key

The quick route to exiting is to use the shortcut key. Press **Alt+F4** and you're on your way.

In this lesson, you learned how to start and exit applications, and you learned common methods for creating, saving, and exiting a document window. In the next lesson, you will learn how to resize and move windows.

Resizing and Moving Windows

In this lesson, you will learn more about moving windows and changing their size.

Sizing with Maximize, Minimize, and Restore

You may want to increase the size of a window to see its full contents. Or, you may want to decrease the size (even down to icon form) to make room for other windows. One way to resize a window is to use the **Maximize**, **Minimize**, and **Restore** commands. If you use the mouse, you will use the Maximize, Minimize and Restore buttons located on the right side of the window title bar. If you use the keyboard, you can use the menu commands through the Control menu. Table 8.1 displays the Maximize, Minimize, and Restore buttons and defines the purpose of each one.

Figure 8.1 shows the Program Manager window maximized to full-screen size. At full size, the minimize and restore buttons are available. Figure 8.2 displays the Program Manager window with the Minimize and Maximize buttons.

Table 8.1 Window Sizing Command Buttons

Command Button	*Description*
▲	Select the Maximize button to enlarge the window to its maximum size.
▼	Select the Minimize button to reduce the Window to its icon form.

continues

Table 8.1 Continued

Command Button	*Description*
	The Restore button is only available after a window has been maximized. Select it to return a window to the size it was before it was maximized.

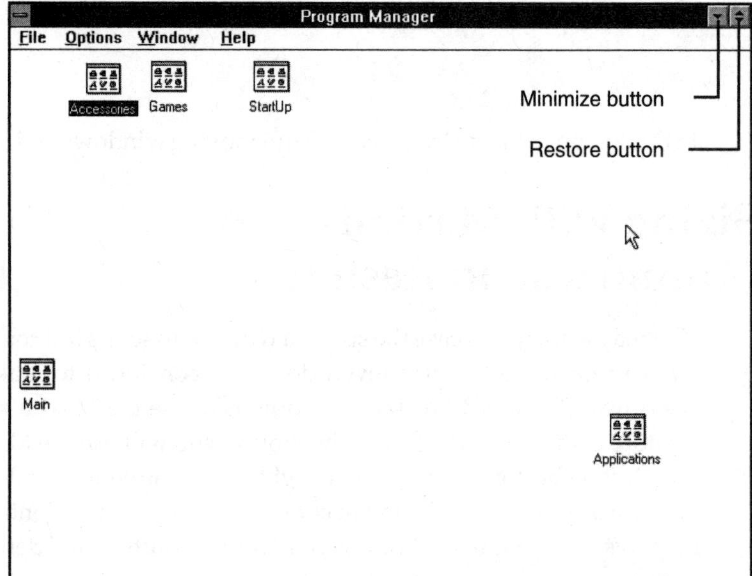

Figure 8.1 The Program Manager window maximized to full-screen size.

To maximize, minimize, or restore a window with the mouse, click on the appropriate button. To maximize, minimize, or restore a window with the keyboard, follow these steps:

1. Open the windows **Control menu** (see Figure 8.3).
2. Select the **Restore**, **Minimize**, or **Maximize** command from the menu.

Can't Choose Restore? Remember that some menu items will not be available under certain circumstances. Notice that the **R**estore command is unavailable (grayed-out) in Figure 8.3. This is because the window is not maximized.

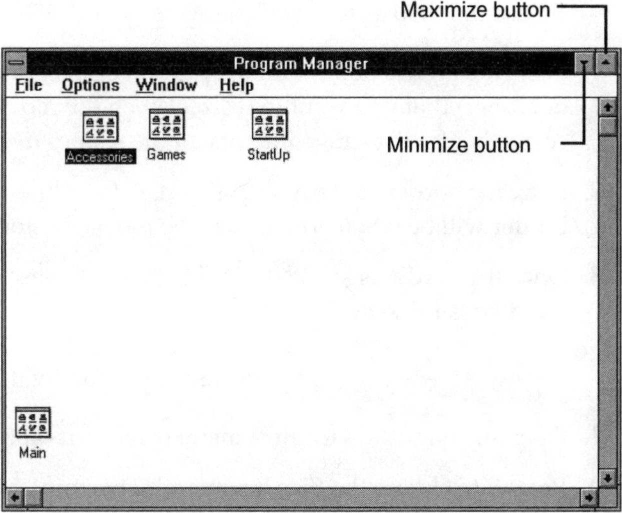

Figure 8.2 Program Manager window at regular size.

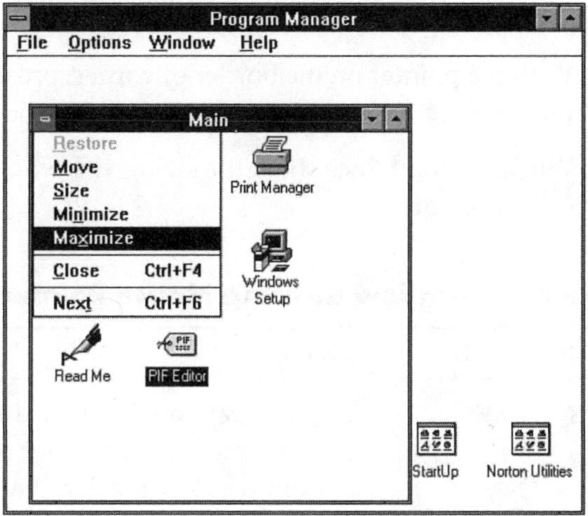

Figure 8.3 The Main group window Control menu.

Sizing the Borders

A particular size of window may be required to suit your needs. If so, simply drag the window border to change the size of the window. This may be done with the mouse or the keyboard.

To use the mouse, follow these steps:

1. Place the mouse pointer on the portion of the border (vertical, horizontal, or corner) that you want to resize. When the mouse pointer is positioned correctly, it will change into one of the shapes displayed in Table 8.2.
2. Drag the border to the new position. A faint line appears where the border will be when you release the mouse button.
3. Once the border is in the desired location, release the mouse button. The window is resized.

To resize a window using the keyboard, follow these steps:

1. Open the window's Control menu (press **Alt+space bar** or **Alt+hyphen**).
2. Press **S** to choose the **Size** command. The pointer becomes a four-headed arrow.
3. Use the arrow keys to move the pointer to the border or corner you wish to resize. The mouse pointer turns into one of the shapes displayed in Table 8.2.
4. With the pointer on the border or corner, press the arrow keys to resize the window. A faint line appears showing the new border location.
5. When the faint lines show the sizing you want, press **Enter**. To cancel the operation, press **Esc**.

Table 8.2 Window Resizing Mouse Pointers

Mouse Pointer	*Description*
⇳	The vertical double-headed arrow appears when you position the mouse pointer over either the top or bottom window border. It allows you to resize the window by dragging the border up or down.
⬄	The horizontal double-headed arrow appears when you position the mouse pointer over either side of the window border. It allows you to resize the window by dragging the border left or right.
⬂	The diagonal double-headed arrow appears when you position the mouse pointer over any of the four corners of the window border. It allows you to resize the window by dragging the corner diagonally.

Missing Some Icons? When you reduce the size of a window, some of the contents may not be visible in the resulting window size. Remember that you can use the scroll bars to see the contents of the window.

Moving a Window

When you start working with multiple windows, moving a window becomes as important as sizing one. You will want to move windows to make room for other work on your desktop. You may move a window with the mouse or keyboard.

To move a window using the mouse, point at the Windows title bar and drag it to a new location. To use the keyboard:

1. Open the window Control menu (press **Alt+space bar** or **Alt+hyphen**).
2. Press **M** to choose the **M**ove command. The pointer will appear as a four-headed arrow.
3. Use the arrow keys to move the window to a new location.
4. When the window is in the new location, press **Enter**. To cancel the operation and return the window to its original location, press **Esc**.

In this lesson, you learned how to change the appearance of your desktop by changing the size of or moving a window. In the next lesson, you will learn how to open, arrange, and move among multiple windows.

9 Working with Multiple Windows

In this lesson, you will learn how to open and arrange multiple windows. You will also learn how to move between windows.

Multiple Windows

Windows allows you to use more than one application at a time, and each Windows application supports multiple document windows. As you can imagine, opening multiple applications with multiple windows can make your desktop pretty busy! That's why it's important to be able to arrange and switch between windows easily.

As you learned in Lesson 7, you can open a program-item window by double-clicking on the icon or using the **Run** command. To open a new document window within an application, choose the **File**, **New** command associated with the application.

Arranging Windows

Once you have multiple open windows, you can use the commands under the **Window** menu to arrange the windows. Figure 9.1 shows several windows open at the same time. These are windows created from the group icons on the Program Manager screen, but they could be various program-item or document windows as well. The screen is confusing and, as you'll see, one window is hidden by the others.

Cascading Windows

A good way to get control of a confusing desktop is to choose the **Window**, **Cascade** command. Choosing this command causes Windows to lay all the open windows on top of each other so the title bar of each is visible. The resulting cascaded window arrangement is shown in Figure 9.2.

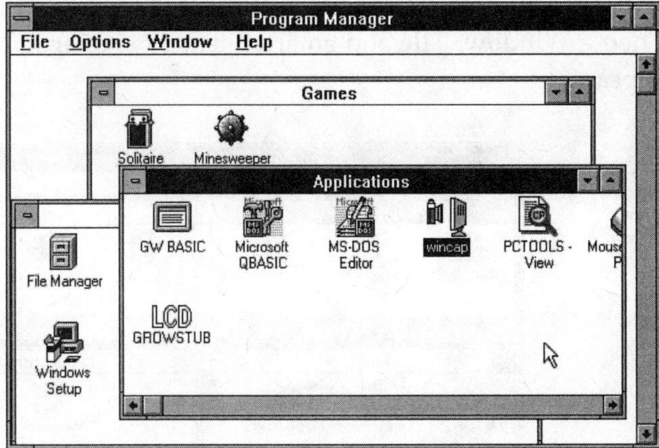

Figure 9.1 The Program manager with multiple windows open.

TIP

Cascade Quickly Press the shortcut key combination **Shift+F5** to cascade your windows without using the **Window** menu.

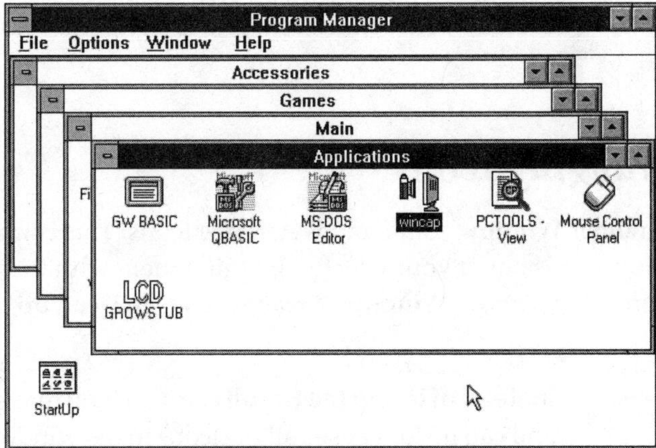

Figure 9.2 The windows after selecting Window, Cascade.

Tiling Windows

Another arrangement is referred to as *tiled*. When you choose this command, Windows resizes and moves each open window so they appear side-by-side. Choose **Window, Tile** and an arrangement similar to that shown in Figure 9.3 appears.

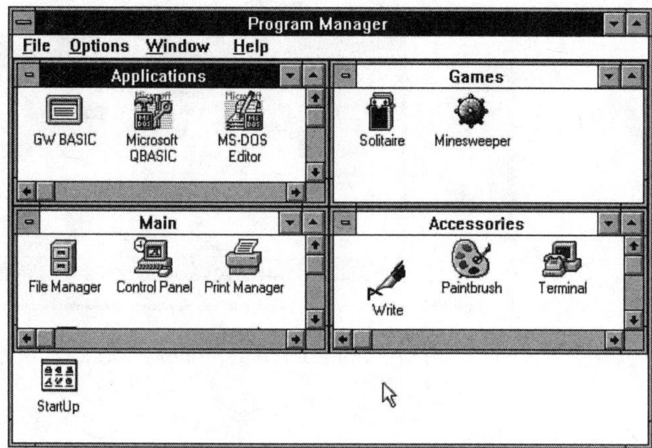

Figure 9.3 The windows after selecting Window, Tile.

Timely Tiling Press the shortcut key combination **Shift+F4** to cascade your windows without using the **Window** menu.

Arranging Icons

Another **Window** command is **Arrange** Icons. This command is handy after you move icons out of your way by dragging them with the mouse. When things get confusing, choose **Window, Arrange** Icons to clean up after yourself.

Instead of Using the Scroll Bars If you make a window smaller and can no longer see all the icons in the window, select **Window, Arrange Icons** to bring the icons into the new, smaller window area.

Moving Between Windows

Another common dilemma when using multiple windows is how to move between windows. The application (and document window if available) currently in use has a highlighted title bar. That's how you know which window is active.

Now Where Was I? The window currently in use is called the active window. Moving to a new window means you are changing the window that is active.

If you are using a mouse, click on any part of the window you want to use (make active). The title bar is highlighted, and you may work in the window.

To use the keyboard, open the **Window** menu by pressing **Alt+W**. Figure 9.4 shows the Program Manager's **Window** menu. Notice that the available windows appear in a numbered list. Simply press the number next to the window title you wish to activate. Most Windows applications make use of the **Window** menu.

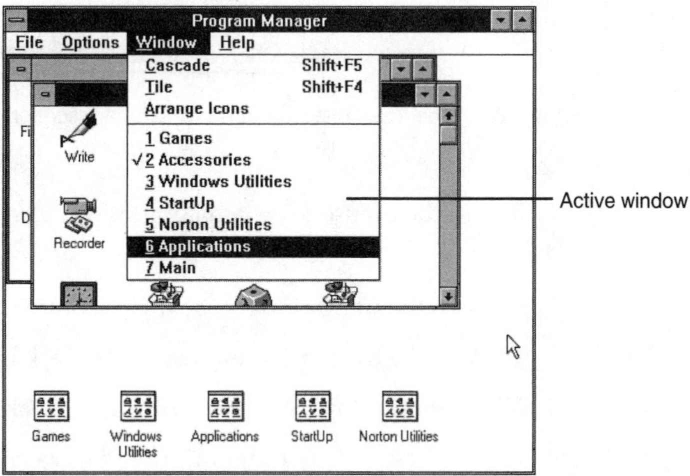

Figure 9.4 The Program Manager's Window menu.

Make sure you are able to move between windows before proceeding.

Moving Between Applications

Remember that Windows allows you to have multiple windows open within an application *and* have multiple applications open at the same time. The last section taught you how to move between windows in the same application. This section will tell you how to move between applications.

Using the Task List

A dialog box called the Task List can be used to switch between applications. A sample Task List is shown in Figure 9.5. There are three applications running. Notice that the entry for Write (Windows word processor application) is followed by the name of the active document window (RPT2.WRI).

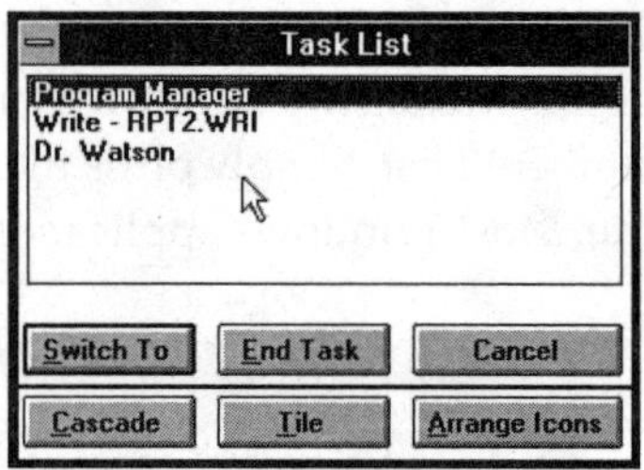

Figure 9.5 The Task List with three running applications.

To use the mouse to switch applications using the Task List, follow these steps:

1. Click on the **Control Menu** box. The Control menu appears.
2. Click on the **Switch To** command. The Task List appears.
3. Highlight the application to switch to by clicking it on.
4. Click on the **Switch To** button and you are taken to the application.

The keyboard can also be used with the Task List. These are the steps:

1. Press **Ctrl+Esc** to display the Task List.
2. Press ↑ or ↓ until the application you want is highlighted.
3. Press **Enter**.

Bypass the Task List Hold down the **Alt** key and press the **Tab** key. (Keep the **Alt** key down.) A dialog box appears displaying the name of one of the open applications. Each time you press the **Tab** key, a new (open) application is displayed. When you see the application you want, release the **Alt** key and you will switch to that application. If you decide you don't want to switch tasks after all, press **Esc** and release the Alt key. This technique works with both Windows and non-Windows applications.

In this lesson, you learned how to control your desktop by opening and arranging windows. You also learned how to move between multiple windows and applications. In the next lesson, you will learn how to move information between windows with the **Cut**, **Copy**, and **Paste** commands.

Copy, Cut, and Paste Text Between Windows

In this lesson, you will learn how to move information between windows using Copy, Cut, and Paste in conjunction with the Clipboard.

What Is the Clipboard?

One of the handiest features of the Windows environment is that information (both text and graphics) can be copied or moved from one window to another. This includes windows (documents) in the same application as well as between applications. When information is copied or cut, it is placed in an area called the Clipboard.

The Clipboard holds only the most recent information copied or cut. When you copy or cut something else, it replaces what was previously on the Clipboard.

Cut, Copy, and Paste When you *cut* information, it is removed from its original location and placed on the Clipboard. When you *copy* information, it is copied to the Clipboard without disturbing the original. When you *paste*, the information on the Clipboard is duplicated at the location you specify, without disturbing the copy on the Clipboard.

You can see the contents of the Clipboard at any time by following these steps:

1. Open the **Main** group icon.
2. From the Main window, open the **Clipboard Viewer** program-item icon.
3. The contents of the Clipboard appear in the Clipboard Viewer window. In Figure 10.1, an address was copied or cut to the Clipboard.

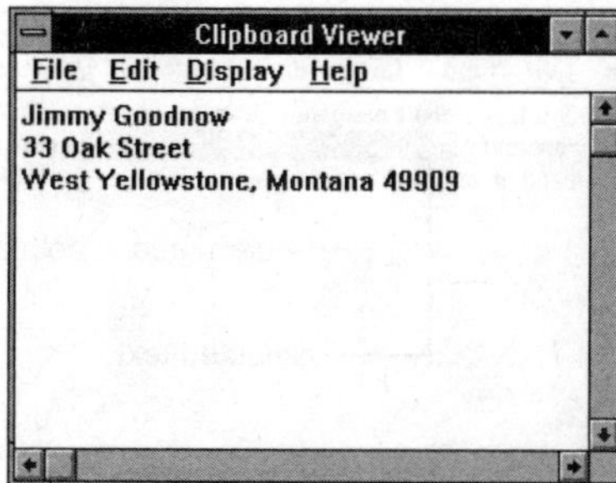

Figure 10.1 The contents of the Clipboard seen through the Clipboard Viewer.

Without a Trace When you turn off your computer or exit Windows, the contents of the Clipboard are lost.

Take a look at the contents of your Clipboard. Unless you have recently cut or copied information, the Clipboard will be empty.

Selecting Text

Before you can cut or copy text, you must identify which text is to be cut or copied. This is called *selecting* text.

Selected text is highlighted so you can quickly distinguish it. Figure 10.2 illustrates selected text in a Write document.

To select text with the mouse:

1. Position the I-beam pointer just before the first character to be selected.
2. Hold down the left mouse button and drag the I-beam pointer to the last character to be selected.
3. Release the mouse button. The selected text is highlighted.

To select text with the keyboard:

1. Use the arrow keys to position the insertion point (blinking vertical line) just before the first character to be selected.
2. Hold down the **Shift** key and use the arrow keys to move the highlight to the last character to be selected.

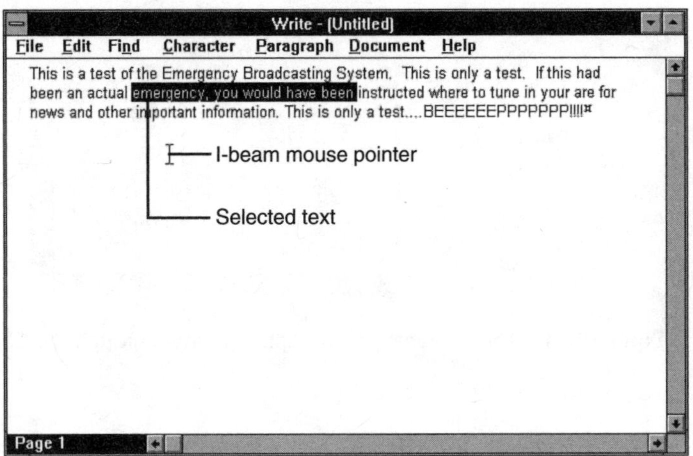

Figure 10.2 Selected text in a Write document.

3. Release all keys. The selected text is highlighted.

Deselecting Text To get rid of the highlight on the selection, click anywhere in the document with the mouse. To get rid of the highlight with the keyboard, press an arrow key.

Text Selection Shortcuts To select a single word using the mouse, double-click on the word. To select text word-by-word (instead of character-by-character), hold down both the **Shift** and **Ctrl** keys while using the arrow keys.

Selecting Graphics

The procedure for selecting graphics depends on the Windows application program you are using. In a word processing program such as Write, graphics are selected the same way as text. In a program like Paintbrush, there are special tools for cutting and copying either rectangular or irregular shapes. Since the procedure varies, it is best to refer to the documentation for each application.

Using Copy, Cut, and Paste Between Windows

Once you have selected the text or graphics, the procedures for cutting, copying, and pasting are the same in all Windows applications. To cut or copy and paste information between windows of the same application as well as between windows of different applications:

1. Select the text or graphic to cut or copy (following the instructions earlier in this lesson).
2. Open the **Edit** menu.
3. Choose **Edit, Copy** to keep the original selection in place or **Cut** to remove the original selection. The selected material is placed in the Clipboard.
4. Position the I-beam or insertion point where you want to insert the selection. (You may need to open another application or document.)
5. Open the **Edit** menu.
6. Choose **Edit, Paste**. The selection is copied from the Clipboard to your document. A copy remains on the Clipboard until you cut or copy something else.

Multiple Copies Because items remain on the Clipboard until you cut or copy again, you can paste information from the Clipboard multiple times. You can also perform other tasks before you paste.

Try it. Enter your address in Write and select it. Choose **Edit, Copy** to copy it to the Clipboard. Choose **File, New** to open a new Write window. Then, choose **Edit, Paste** to paste the address in the new window. When you're done, choose **File, Exit** to exit the Write program.

In this lesson, you learned how to copy, cut and paste information between windows. In the next lesson, you will learn how to manage your programs using the Program Manager.

Managing Programs with the Program Manager

In this lesson, you will learn about groups and how they keep track of your applications. You'll learn how to add new groups and new program-item icons to those groups, delete groups and program-item icons you don't need, and move program-item icons from group to group.

What Is a Group?

Imagine how it would be if all the icons for all of your programs were contained in one group window. You would have to search through them all every time you wanted to run a program! Luckily, Windows offers groups to help organize the program-item icons into logical categories.

A group is a window within the Program Manager window. When it's closed, it appears as a group icon on the desktop; when it's open, it reveals program-item icons for various applications you can run.

Windows sets up several useful groups for you automatically, such as Accessories, Main, and Games. You are not stuck with just these, however; you can create your own groups, move program-item icons to different groups, delete icons, and even delete groups.

Creating a Group

As you begin to use Windows, you may find that you want additional groups. For example, if there are a few applications that you use every day, you may want to set up a group for them. You may also wish to create separate groups for Windows and non-Windows applications.

To create a group, follow these steps:

1. From the Program Manager windows, choose **File**, **New**. The New Program Object dialog box appears (see Figure 11.1).
2. Make sure Program **G**roup is selected.
3. Select **OK**. The Program Group Properties dialog box appears.
4. Type the **D**escription (which will become the group icon label and the group window title).
5. Select **OK**. The group window is now created. A window with the description you entered appears.

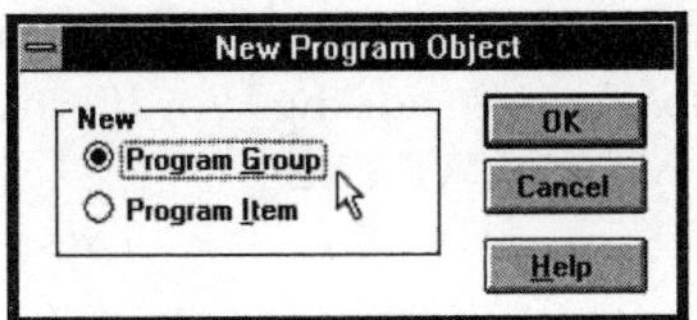

Figure 11.1 The New Program Object dialog box.

Try creating a group window for your own application. Once the group window is created, you can either drag applications into it from other groups or add applications by choosing **File**, **New**.

Adding an Application to a Group

Applications Must Be Installed Adding an application to a group is *not* the same as installing the application on your computer. The application must already be installed on your computer before you can add it to a group.

Adding an application to a group links the execution of the application to a program-item icon displayed in the group. When you add an application to a group, you really do two things:

- Set up a program-item icon to launch the application.
- Tell Windows what file to execute when the icon is opened.

Applications may be added to any group, including the ones that were created when Windows was installed. Follow these steps:

1. Open the group window that you want the new program-item icon to reside in.
2. From the Program Manager, choose **File**, **New**. The New Program Object dialog box appears.
3. Select the **Program Item** option button and then select **OK**. The Program Item Properties dialog box appears (see Figure 11.2).
4. Enter a **D**escription for the icon. This description will appear as the icon label and the group window title.
5. Enter the **C**ommand Line to the executable file including the path. For example, if you're adding WordPerfect 5.1 from the C:\WP51 directory, enter **C:\WP51\WP.EXE**.

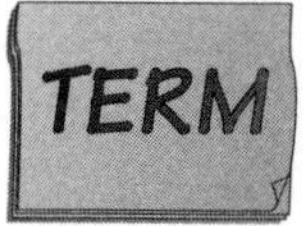

What's an Executable File? The *executable file* is the file name you normally type at the DOS prompt to start the application. If you don't know what it is, look in the applications documentation. Executable files usually end in .EXE. You can select the Browse command button to open the Browse dialog box. From here, you can search for and select the executable file you want included as the **C**ommand line.

6. If you want a different default directory while you're running the application, enter a **W**orking Directory. In most cases, you can skip this step.
7. To start the application as a desktop icon (instead of in a window), check **R**un Minimized.
8. Select **OK** when the Program Item Properties dialog box is complete.

Figure 11.2 illustrates a completed Program Item Properties dialog box. This is to set up an application called Collage Plus Version 3.2 within the Screen Utilities group.

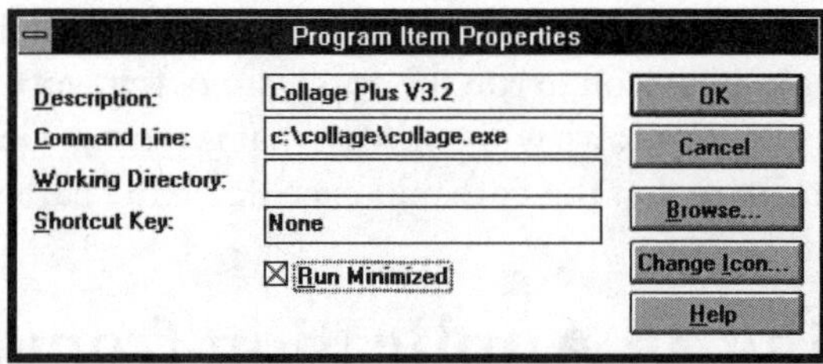

Figure 11.2 The completed Program Item Properties dialog box.

Figure 11.3 shows the Screen Utilities group window with the program-item icon just created. In this case, the icon was supplied by the application manufacturer, and referenced in the COLLAGE.EXE file. If an icon is not found by Windows, it assigns an icon for you.

Changing Icons If you don't like the looks of a program-item icon, you can assign a different one to the application. Choose **File, Properties...** from the Program Manager window. Select the **Change Icon...** command button and specify a new icon file. Windows 3.1 provides a host of new icons; the file MORICONS.DLL in the Windows directory contains these icons.

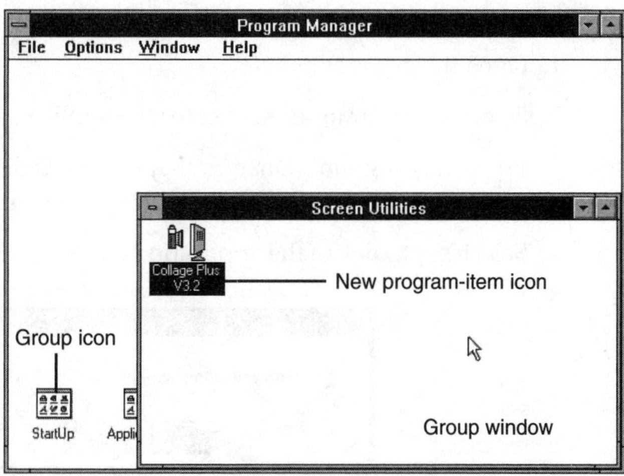

Figure 11.3 The Screen Utilities group window with the Collage Plus program-item icon.

After you have added an application, test it by double-clicking on the program-item icon to run the application. If it works, you're ready to move on. If it doesn't, Windows will tell you what is wrong. Go back and try the steps again, making sure that the path and executable file name are correct.

Deleting an Application from a Group

In rearranging the groups to best meet your needs, you may want to delete an application from a group. For example, if your system doesn't have any sound recording or playback capabilities, you may want to delete the Sound Recorder application that Windows installed in the Accessories group.

What Am I Really Deleting? Deleting an application from a group does not remove that application from your computer—it just makes Windows forget that it's there. Should you ever need to run it through Windows, you can add the application again using the steps you learned earlier in this lesson or simply run it from the File Manager (see Lesson 17).

To delete a program-item icon for an application from a group, follow these steps:

1. Open the group window.
2. Select the program-item icon for the application you wish to delete.
3. From the Program Manager, choose **File**, **Delete**. A message appears asking you to confirm the deletion (see Figure 11.4).
4. Select **Yes** to delete the application or **No** to cancel.

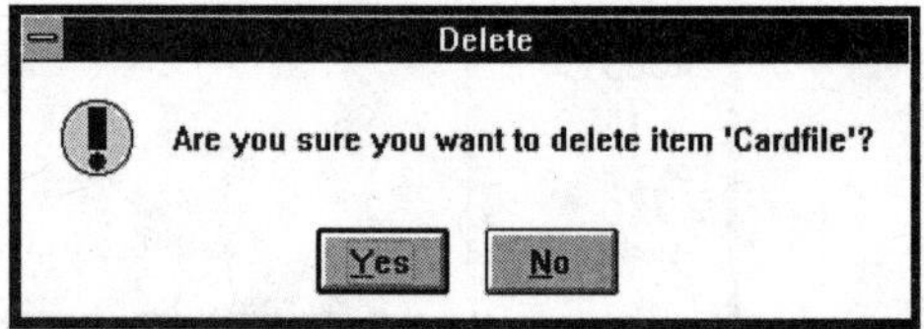

Figure 11.4 The Delete program-item icon confirmation dialog box.

Deleting a Group

You can also delete a whole group and all its associated program-item icons. When you do, the program files related to those program-items remain on your computer—Windows just forgets where they are located.

To delete a group, follow these steps:

1. From the Program Manager screen, select the group icon you wish to delete.
2. Choose **File, Delete**. A message (similar to Figure 11.4) appears asking for confirmation.
3. Select **Yes** to delete the group or **No** to cancel.

In this lesson, you learned how to control access to the software installed on your computer through the addition of groups and program-item icons. You also learned how to delete both program-item icons and groups. In the next lesson, you'll learn how to view drives and directories with the File Manager.

Viewing Drives and Directories with the File Manager

In this lesson, you will learn how to control disk drives and directories with the File Manager. You'll learn some basics about drives, directories, and files, and you'll learn how to manipulate them through the File Manager program.

What Are Drives?

A *drive* is the hardware that makes a disk function (seek, read, and write). A hard disk and its drive are considered one inseparable unit, while a floppy disk can easily be removed from its drive and replaced with a different disk.

Drives are given letter names. Drives A and B for most computers are floppy disk drives, used to store and retrieve data from diskettes. The designation for the hard disk inside the computer is typically drive C. (Since hard disks and their drives are not easily separated, the terms *disk* and *drive* are often used interchangeably when referring to hard disks.) If the computer has more than one hard disk, or if the hard disk has been divided into multiple partitions, or *logical drives*, the additional drives are usually labeled D, E, F, and so on.

What Are Directories?

Because so much information can be stored on a disk, hard disks are usually divided into directories. For example, drive C typically has a separate directory for DOS (the Disk Operating System), a directory for Windows, and so on. Floppy disks can contain directories too, but usually don't. (Because of their limited capacity, it is easy to keep track of files on a floppy disk without using directories.)

Disk space is not set aside for individual directories; in fact, directories take up hardly any disk space at all. If you think of a disk as a file drawer full of papers, directories are like tabbed folders used to organize the papers into manageable groups.

What Are Files?

Directories hold files, just as folders hold pieces of paper. A file may contain the instructions for the computer to perform (typically called *program* or *executable files*). Or, a file may contain a text document that you can read (often referred to as a *document file*).

Regardless of the type of file, you can use Windows' File Manager to view and control them.

Starting the File Manager

To start the File Manager, follow these steps:

1. Open the **Main** group icon from the Program Manager window.
2. Open the **File Manager** program-item icon. The File Manager appears.

Figure 12.1 shows the File Manager window. The directory window's title bar shows the drive for the information displayed (in this case, drive C).

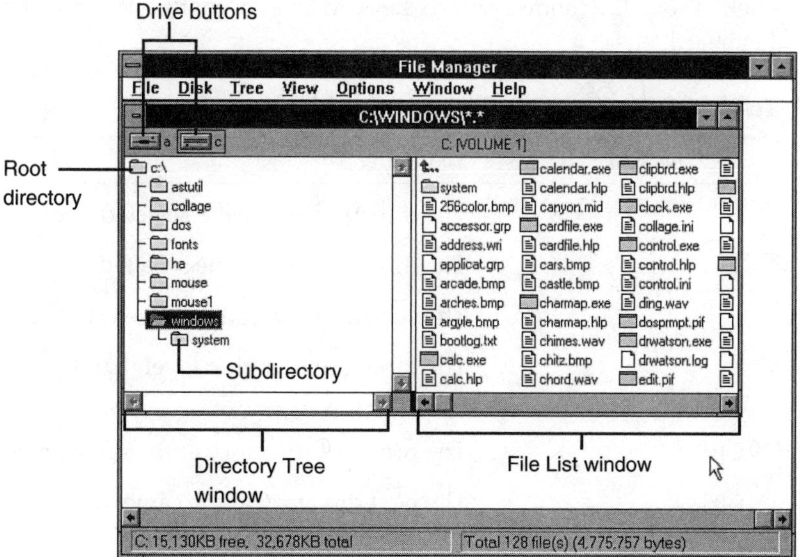

Figure 12.1 The File Manager window displaying a directory window.

The Directory Tree

The left side of the directory window contains the directory tree, a graphical representation of the directories and subdirectories on your system. (The directory tree on your screen will probably contain different directories from the one shown in Figure 12.1.)

In Figure 12.1, you can see that drive C contains a directory called *windows*. The Windows directory has a subdirectory: *system*. The right side of the window contains a list of the files in the directory currently highlighted on the directory tree. Notice that the folder icon next to the Windows directory (highlighted directory) appears as an open folder. In this example, the files in the Windows directory appear in the right half of the File manager window.

Changing Directories

When you change directories using the directory tree, it shows you the files in each directory. This is helpful if you are searching for a particular file to open, move, or copy.

To change the directory with the mouse, point to the directory you want and click. Table 12.1 shows which keys to use to change the directory with the keyboard.

Table 12.1 Keys to Change the Directory

Use This Key	*To Change To*
↑	The directory above the selected one.
↓	The directory below the selected one.
←	The subdirectory under the selected one.
→	The directory at higher level than the selected one.
Ctrl+↑	The previous directory at the same level.
Ctrl+↓	The next directory at the same level.
Home	The root directory.
End	The last directory in the tree.
First letter of name	Any specific directory.

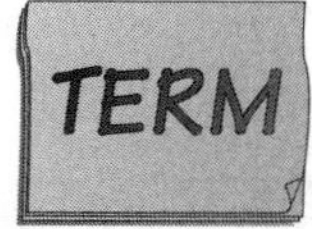

The Root Directory The directory that leads to all other directories (much like the root of a tree leads to all branches and leaves) is the *root directory*. In Figure 12.1, the root directory is shown as C:\.

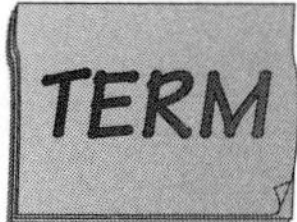

Subdirectories Any directory can have a subdirectory. You can think of it as having file folders within file folders; they help you organize your files. In Figure 12.1, *system* is a subdirectory of *windows*.

Notice that when you change to a new directory, the names of the files in the directory appear.

Expanding and Collapsing Directory Levels

As you noticed before, the directory tree shows the subdirectory of the Windows directory. You can *collapse* (decrease the detail of) the directory tree, so that the subdirectory does not appear. You can also *expand* (increase the detail of) the directory tree, so that subdirectories many levels deep will *all* show. Table 12.2 lists methods used to expand or collapse the directory levels.

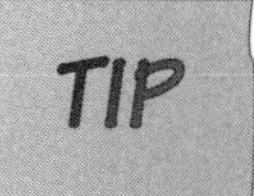

Expand and Collapse Quickly Use the File Manager **Tree** menu to speed expanding and collapsing of multiple directories. Select **Tree Expand Branch** to expand all levels for the selected directory. Select **Tree Expand All** to expand the entire tree. Select **Tree Collapse Branch** to collapse the levels for the selected directory.

Table 12.2 Methods of Expanding or Collapsing Directory Levels

Activity	*Action*
Expand with the mouse	Double-click on the directory icon.
Expand with the keyboard	Use the arrow keys to select the directory and press + (plus).

continues

Table 12.2 Continued

Activity	*Action*
Collapse with the mouse	Double-click on the directory icon.
Collapse with the keyboard	Use the arrow keys to select the directory and press - (hyphen).

It's Only for Show Collapsing and expanding affects only this display; it doesn't alter your directories in any way.

Changing Drives

You can change drives to see the directories and files contained on a different disk. To change drives with the mouse, click on the drive icon in the upper left corner of the Directory Tree window. To use the keyboard, press **Ctrl+***drive letter* (for example, press **Ctrl+A** for Drive A).

Can't Change Drives? Make sure there is a disk in the drive you are selecting. If there is not, a warning message will appear instructing you to try again.

Returning to the Program Manager

Each directory window can be minimized and maximized within File Manager, or closed altogether. If you have more than one directory window open at once, you may want to minimize all but the one you're working with.

You can also minimize or close the File Manager window itself to return to the Program Manager. If you're not going to use File Manager again right away, it is better to close it rather than minimize it, to conserve system resources.

To close the File Manager, double-click on the **Control Menu** box. Or, press **Alt+F** (for **File**), then **X** (for **Exit**).

In this lesson, you learned how to view the contents of drives and directories using the File Manager. In the next lesson, you'll learn how to create and delete directories with the File Manager.

Create or Delete a Directory with the File Manager

In this lesson, you will learn how to create and delete directories to organize your files.

Create a Directory

There are several reasons you may want to create a directory. Many application installation programs create a directory when you install the application on your computer. If one of your application installation programs does not, you will want to create a directory for the application.

A more common reason to create a directory is to store document files. For example, you may want to create a directory to store documents you create with Write. That way, the document files will not be scattered among the more than a hundred Windows program files in the Windows directory. Having a separate directory for Write documents can make it much easier to find and manipulate the documents you create.

To create a directory, follow these steps:

1. Open the **File Manager**. The directory window appears showing the directory tree and the files in the highlighted directory.
2. Highlight the directory under which you want the new directory to reside. (The directory you create will be a subdirectory of the directory you highlight.) If you don't want the new directory to be a subdirectory of another directory, highlight the root directory (C:\).
3. Choose **File**, **Create Directory**. The Create Directory dialog box appears.
4. Type the Name of the new directory, up to eight characters.
5. Select **OK**. The new directory is created.

Figure 13.1 illustrates the Create Directory dialog box for a new directory called WRITEDOC, a subdirectory of the Windows directory. Figure 13.2 shows the WRITEDOC directory added to the directory tree.

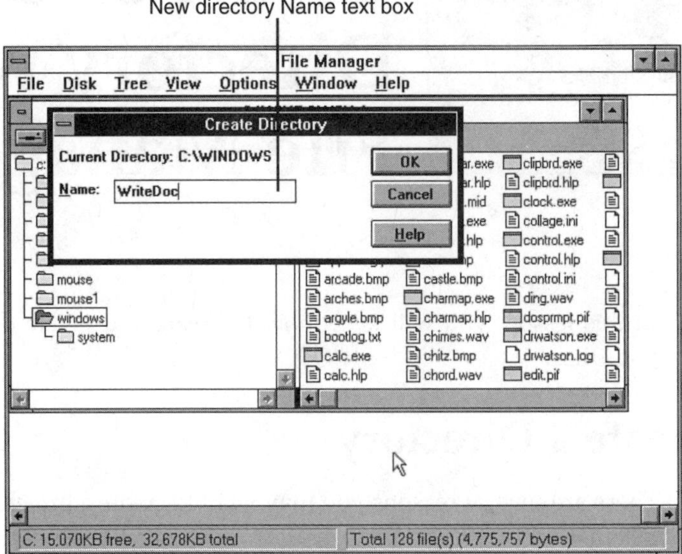

Figure 13.1 The Create Directory dialog box for the WRITEDOC directory.

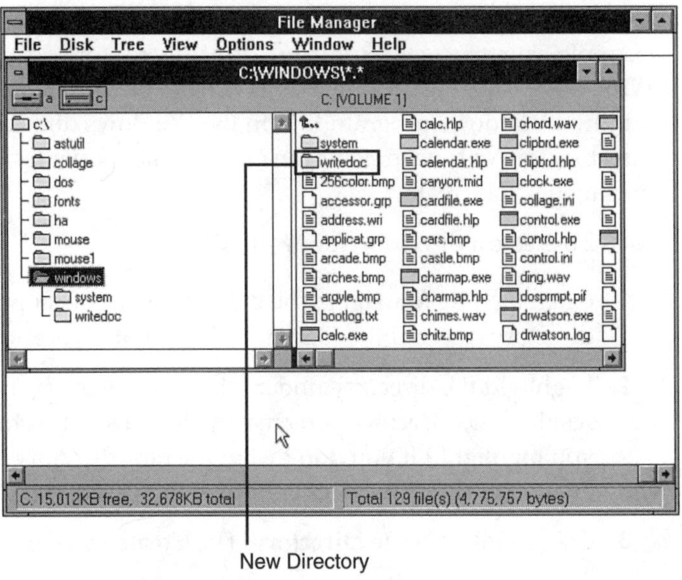

Figure 13.2 The WRITEDOC directory is added.

Delete a Directory

You may need to delete a directory. For example, you may create a directory in the wrong spot on the directory tree. Or, you may want to remove the directory for an application you no longer use. You can delete a directory with the File Manager.

To delete a directory, follow these steps:

1. Make sure you have the necessary copies of any files in the directory you are going to delete. (The files must be deleted before the directory can be deleted.)
2. From the File Manager directory tree, highlight the directory you want to delete.
3. Choose **File, Delete**. The Delete dialog box appears.
4. Make sure the directory shown is correct. Select **OK**.
5. A Confirm Directory Delete dialog box appears. Check the directory again, then select **OK**.
6. If files are in the directory, a Confirm File Delete dialog box appears for each file. You must select **OK** to delete each file before the directory can be deleted.

Do I have to Confirm Every File? The Delete Confirmation dialog box provides you a **Yes to All** command button to confirm the deletion of all files at once. Use this feature with caution.

I Hate When That Happens! Be very careful any time you delete a directory. Make doubly certain you are deleting the correct directory.

In this lesson, you learned how to create and delete directories. In the next lesson, you will learn how to find specific files within directories.

Find the File You Need with the File Manager

In this lesson, you will learn how to locate files quickly with the directory window and the Search command.

Opening and Closing a Directory Window

More than one directory window can be open at a time. This is useful when you are looking for files and even more useful when you want to copy or move files from one directory to another. (Copying and moving are covered in Lesson 15.)

To open a new directory window, choose **Window**, **New Window** from the File Manager. A window appears that is identical to the previous window except for the title on the window's title bar. Notice that each window's title now has a colon and a number following the name (see Figure 14.1). If you change the selected directory, the number disappears.

Shortcut to Creating a New Directory Window If you want the new window to display the contents of another disk drive, simply double-click on that drive's icon. Single-clicking the icon displays the drive's contents in the current window; double-clicking opens a new window to display the contents of the drive.

Arranging Windows Remember, you can arrange your windows using **Window**, **Cascade** or **Window**, **Tile**. The **Window** menu also lists the windows, placing a check mark in front of the active window.

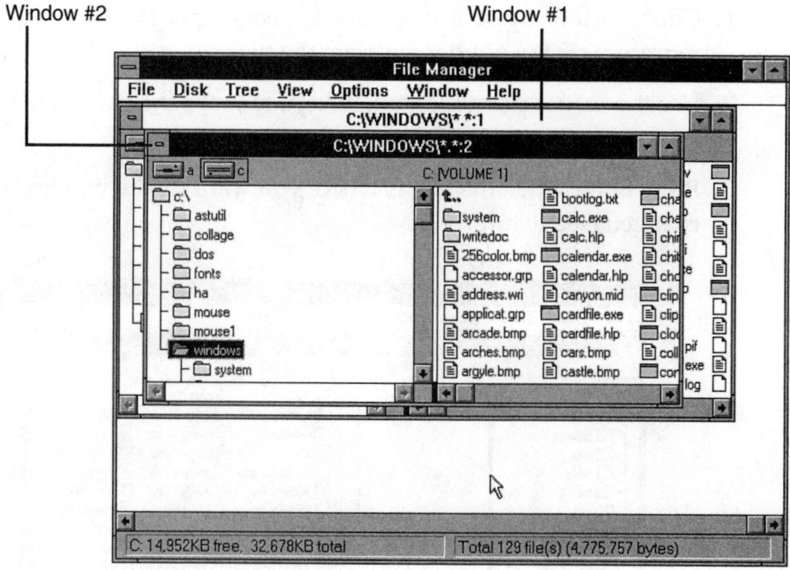

Figure 14.1 When a second window is opened, File Manager attaches a colon and a number (:1, :2) to each window title.

When you're finished with a directory window, close it by double-clicking on the **Control Menu** box or pressing **Ctrl+F4**.

Changing the Display

The File Manager's **View** menu controls how the directory window displays information.

In the examples you've seen, the directory tree and the list of files were both shown. You can choose to show only one or the other, and you can change the way each is shown.

To show only the tree, choose **View, Tree Only**; to show only the list of files (the *directory*), choose **View, Directory Only**. To show them both again, choose **View, Tree and Directory**.

If you elect to display both the tree and directory, you can change the amount of window space allotted to each. For example, you may want to see more files and less white space around the tree. Follow these steps to change the way the window space is divided between the panes.

1. Choose **View, Split**. A black line appears in the directory window, representing the divider between the two panes.
2. Use the mouse pointer or arrow keys to move the black line to the desired location (as shown in Figure 14.2).
3. Press **Enter** when the line is where you want it. The window display is changed (see Figure 14.3).

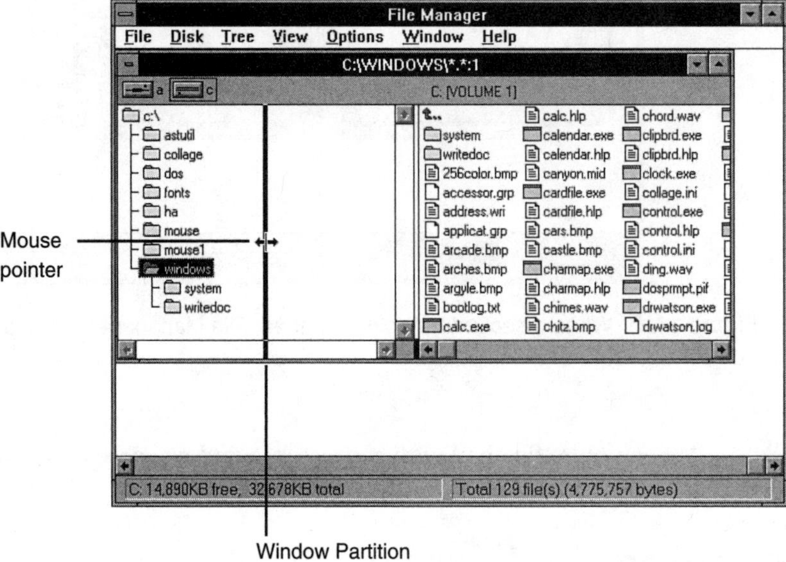

Figure 14.2 The line to select the split.

In Figure 14.3, only file names and icons are shown in the directory. The File Manager can display more information about each file if you desire. Choose **View, All File Details** to display the following information about each file:

- Size in bytes
- Last modification date
- Last modification time
- File attributes (to identify whether a file is hidden, system, archive, or read only)

Or, choose **View, Partial Details** to identify which of the above information you want displayed.

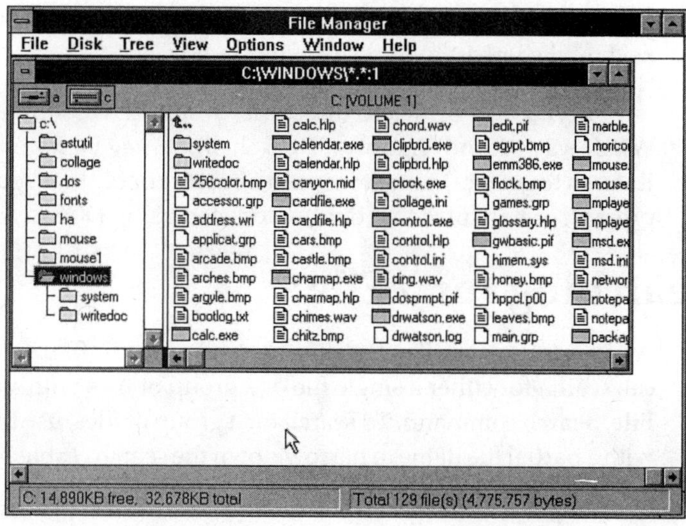

Figure 14.3 The completed split.

Controlling the Order of the Display

As shown in Figure 14.3, the files in the directory are in alphabetical order by file name. You may also sort the directory display by the following methods:

- **View, Sort by Type** arranges files alphabetically by extension. For example, *sample.doc* would come before *file.txt*, which would come before *budget.wri*.
- **View, Sort by Size** arranges files by size from largest to smallest.
- **View, Sort by Date** arranges files by date from newest to oldest.
- **View, By File Type** opens a dialog box that allows you to select certain types of files to include or exclude in the listing (program files, document files, directories, and so on).

After experimenting with these arrangements, you can restore the default setting by choosing **View, Sort by Name**.

Updating a Directory Window

Most often, when you create, change, or delete a file, the directory window is updated immediately. If it is not (as is the case with some networks), you can update the directory window yourself. Simply choose **Window, Refresh** (F5 is the keyboard shortcut to refresh a window).

If you add or delete directories from the DOS prompt (either outside of Windows or from Windows' DOS shell), it may be necessary to use **Windows, Refresh** to get File Manager to see a directory or file that you created from the DOS prompt, or to realize that one you deleted using DOS is gone.

Searching for a File

As you create more files, the ability to find a specific file becomes more critical. You can search for either a single file or a group of files with similar names using the **File, Search** command. To search for a group of files, use the wildcard * (asterisk) with a partial file name to narrow down the search. Table 14.1 shows some search examples and their potential results.

Table 14.1 Search Results Examples

Characters Entered for Search	*Sample Search Results*
rpt1.wri	rpt1.wri
rpt*.wri	rpt1.wri, rpt2.wri, rpt11.wri
c*.exe	calc.exe, calendar.exe
*.exe	calc.exe, calendar.exe, notepad.exe
c*.*	calc.exe, calendar.exe, class.wri

To search for a file, follow these steps:

1. From the File Manager, choose **File, Search**. The Search dialog box appears (see Figure 14.4).
2. In the **Search For** text area, enter the characters to search for. Use wildcards to identify unknown characters.
3. If you would like to search the entire drive, type **C:** in the **Start From** text box and make sure the **Search All Subdirectories** check box is active.

   If you would like to search only a certain directory and its subdirectories, type it in the **Start From** text box.

To search a single directory (no subdirectories), type it in the **Start From** text box and make sure the **Search All Subdirectories** check box is not active.

4. Select **OK** to begin the search. The Search Results window appears, showing the files that were found (see Figure 14.5).

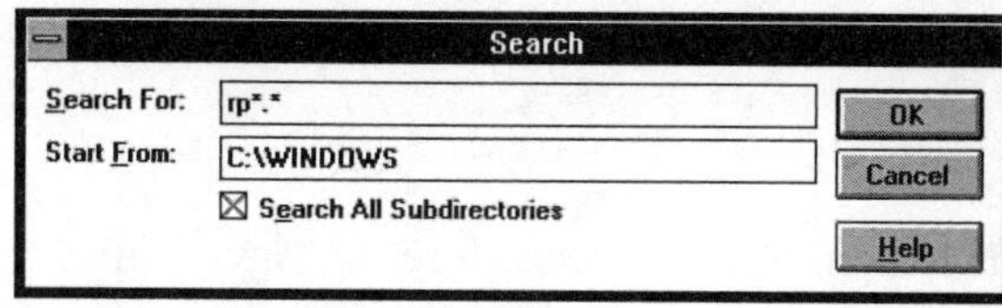

Figure 14.4 The completed Search dialog box.

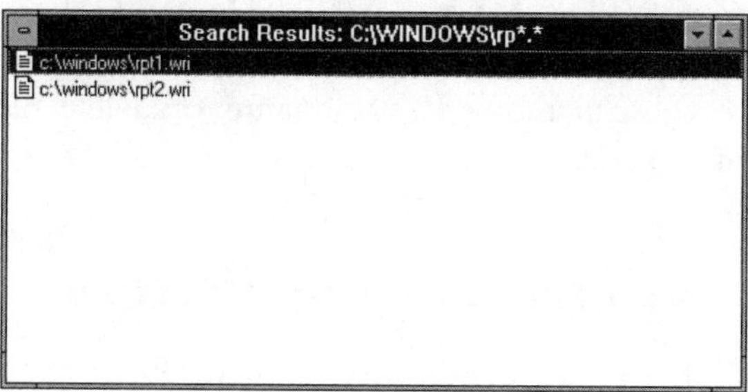

Figure 14.5 The search results.

In this lesson, you learned how to open and close directory windows, change the display and the order of the files shown, and update a directory window. You also learned how to search for a file through one or more directories. In the next lesson, you will learn how to move, copy, rename, and delete files and directories.

15 Managing Files and Directories with the File Manager

In this lesson, you will learn how to move, copy, rename, and delete files and directories.

Selecting and Deselecting Files or Directories

Before you can move, copy, rename, or delete files or directories, you must identify, or *select*, the ones you want. The following sections tell you how.

Select a Single File or Directory

To select a single file or directory from the File Manager's directory window, click on it. Or, press **Tab** to move the highlight bar from the directory tree to the directory window, and then use the keys shown in Table 15.1.

Selecting Multiple Contiguous Files or Directories

Selecting a single file is useful, but to really speed up operations, you will want to select multiple files and then execute commands that will affect the entire group. For example, you may want to select several files to be copied to a disk. Copying them all at once is much faster than copying each file individually.

Table 15.1 Keys to Select a File or Directory

Use This Key	*To Select*
↑	Previous file or directory
↓	Next file or directory
→	Subdirectory or file to the right
←	Higher level directory or file to the left

Use This Key	*To Select*
Home	First file or directory
End	Last file or directory
First letter of the name	Next file or directory starting with a given letter

It is easy to select multiple files or directories that are displayed contiguously in the File Manager directory window. Figure 15.1 illustrates a selection of contiguous files.

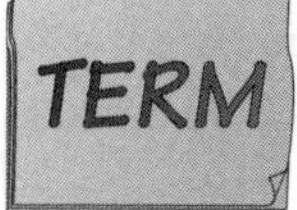

Contiguous Files When the files that you want to select are listed together in the File Manager, without any files that you *don't* want between them, they are *contiguous*.

To select contiguous files or directories with the mouse:

1. Click on the first file or directory that you want to select. When you click on it, it is highlighted.
2. Hold down the **Shift** key and click on the last file or directory that you want to select. All the items between the first and last selections are highlighted (including the first and last selections themselves).

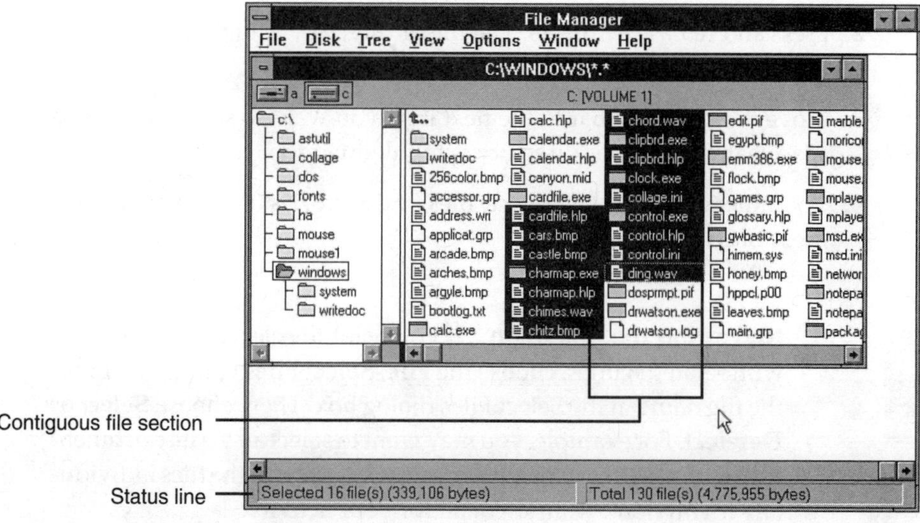

Figure 15.1 Selecting contiguous files.

To select contiguous files or directories with the keyboard:

1. Use the arrow keys to move the highlight to the first file or directory that you want to select. (Press **Tab** to move the highlight bar between the directory tree and the directory window.)
2. Hold down the **Shift** key and use the arrow keys to extend the highlight to the last file or directory you want to select.

To deselect a contiguous group of files or directories, select a file or directory outside the selected items.

Selecting Noncontiguous Files or Directories

Often, the files or directories you want to select are not contiguous but separated by several files that you do not want. However, this is not a problem. You can use the **Ctrl** key to select them.

To select or deselect an item with the mouse, hold down the **Ctrl** key while you click on the file or directory. The item you click on will be highlighted, and any other items you click on (while holding down the Ctrl key) will remain highlighted too.

With the keyboard it's a little more work, but still easy. Select or deselect individual items with the keyboard using the following steps:

1. Use the arrow keys to highlight the first file or directory that you want to select.
2. Press and release **Shift+F8**. The file or directory is highlighted, and the line around the selection blinks.
3. Move the highlight bar to the next item you want to select, and press the space bar. That file or directory is highlighted too.
4. Continue to select (or deselect) files or directories. When you are done, press **Shift+F8** again.

Narrowing the Selection If you want to select or deselect files with related names, choose the **File**, **Select Files** command. Enter the file name in the Select Files dialog box. Then, choose **Select** or **Deselect**. For example, you may want to select all Write document files with a .WRI extension, then deselect a few of the files individually if you don't want them all for your activity.

Figure 15.2 shows multiple noncontiguous files selected.

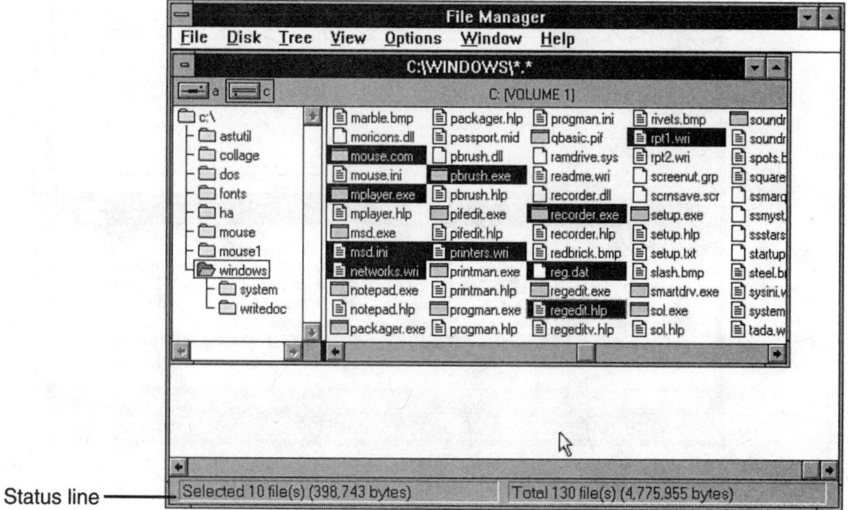

Figure 15.2 Selecting multiple noncontiguous files.

Moving or Copying Files or Directories

To move or copy files or directories through the File Manager, you *drag and drop*—that is, you select the items you want from your *source* directory, drag them to the *destination* directory, and then drop them there. You'll learn this technique in more detail in the steps that follow.

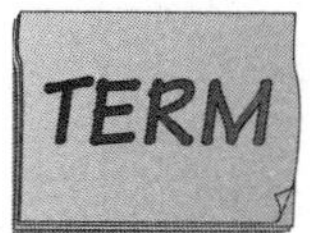

Move vs. Copy *Move* means the file or directory is no longer in the original spot but is in the new location. *Copy* means the original file or directory remains in the original spot, and a new copy of the file or directory is in a second location.

Before you move or copy, make sure the source directory window is visible, so you can highlight the file(s) that you're going to drag. Also, make sure that the destination drive or directory is visible, either as an open window or as an icon.

If you're copying between two directories, you can open both directory windows and then choose **Window, Tile**. Figure 15.3 shows a tiled display of the WINDOWS directory window (the *source* directory), and the empty WRITEDOC directory (the *destination* directory) ready for file copying.

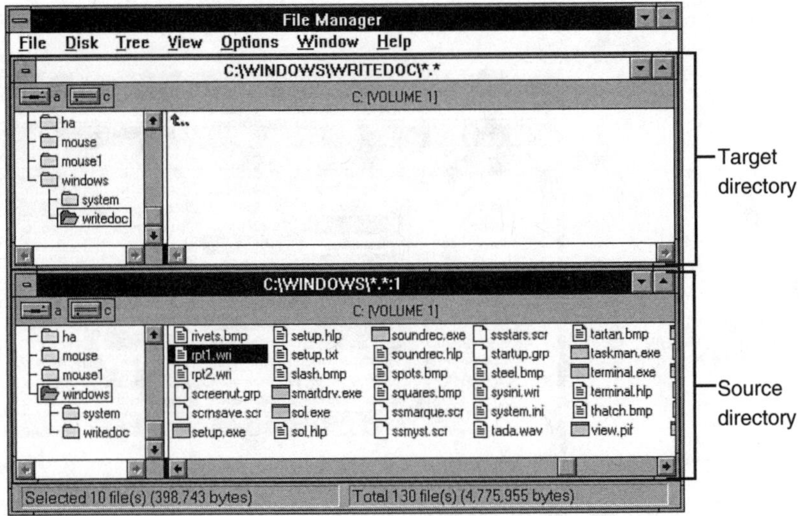

Figure 15.3 Two windows ready for moving or copying files.

Copying Files and Directories

With the mouse, use this procedure to copy:

1. Select the files or directories to copy.
2. Press the **Ctrl** key and drag the files or directories to the destination drive, window, or icon.
3. Release the mouse button and the **Ctrl** key.
4. A dialog box appears asking you to confirm the copy. Click on **OK**.

With the keyboard, use this procedure to copy:

1. Select the files or directories to copy.
2. Choose **File**, **Copy**. The Copy dialog box appears.
3. The selected files are listed in the From text box. Type the desired destination in the To text box, including the path to the destination drive and directory. Figure 15.4 shows a completed Copy dialog box.
4. Select OK by pressing the **Enter** key. Figure 15.5 illustrates the result of the copy. The Write document files have been copied into the WriteDoc directory.

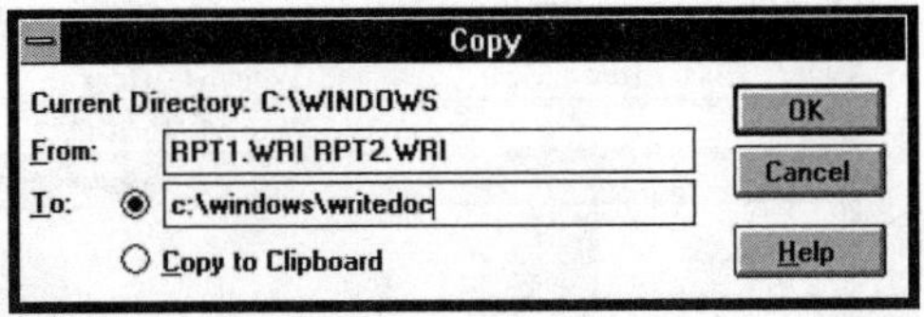

Figure 15.4 The Copy dialog box completed.

The File Is Already There If you attempt to copy a file or directory to a location where an identical file or directory exists, Windows lets you know with a message.

Moving Files and Directories

With the mouse, use these steps to complete a move:

1. Select the files or directories to move.
2. Drag the files or directories to the drive, window, or icon.
3. Release the mouse button.
4. A dialog box appears asking you to confirm the move. Click on **OK**.

With the keyboard, complete a move using these steps:

1. Select the files or directories to move.
2. Choose **File**, **Move**. The Move dialog box appears.
3. The selected files or directories are listed in the From text box. Type the desired destination in the To text box, including the path to the destination drive and directory.
4. Select OK by pressing the **Enter** key.

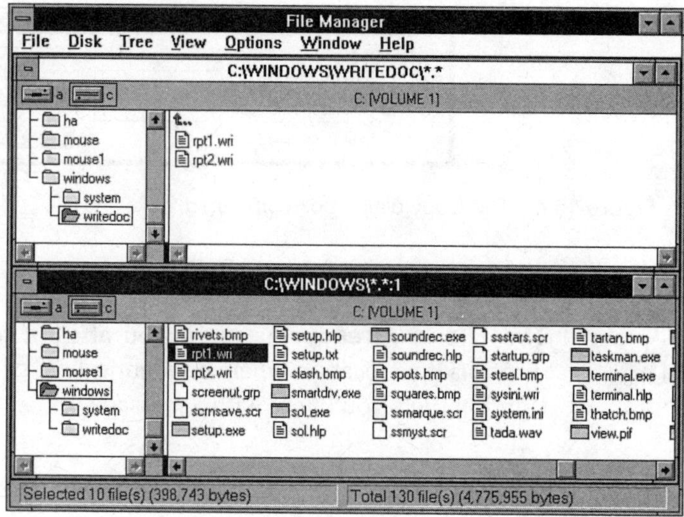

Figure 15.5 The completed copy operation.

Renaming Files or Directories

To rename your files, follow these steps:

1. Select the file or directory to rename.
2. Choose **File**, **Rename**. The Rename dialog box appears.
3. In the **T**o text box, type in the new name for the file or directory.
4. Select **OK**.

It Worked Yesterday Don't rename program files. Many applications will not work if their files have been renamed.

Deleting Files or Directories

You can delete files or directories, but be careful. Before you delete anything, it is a good idea to make a backup copy of any files or directories you might need later.

Better Safe Than Sorry A common use for the delete command is to delete the original after a file has been copied. Moving the file would accomplish the same result, but it's safer to copy, because you still have the original in case anything goes wrong.

To delete, follow these steps:

1. Select the file or directory to delete.
2. Choose **File**, **Delete**. The Delete dialog box appears, indicating what will be deleted.
3. Check the Delete dialog box carefully to make certain you are deleting what you intended to delete.
4. Select **OK**. You will be asked to confirm the deletion. If you are deleting a directory and there are files which must be deleted first, you will be asked to confirm each file deletion.

In this lesson, you learned how to copy, move, rename, and delete files and directories. In the next lesson, you will continue to enhance your skills with the File Manager by using it to format and copy floppy disks.

Formatting and Copying Floppy Disks with the File Manager

In this lesson, you will learn how to format and copy a floppy disk using the File Manager.

Formatting a Floppy Disk

When you buy a box of floppy disks, the floppy disks are usually unformatted. (You can buy formatted disks, but they're more expensive.) They're sold unformatted because some computers use operating systems other than DOS, and such systems need to format the floppy disks in their own format.

Therefore, before you can use a new floppy disk, you must format it to work with your computer's operating system (DOS). Formatting prepares the floppy disk by organizing its space into *sectors* and creating a *file allocation table* (*FAT*) to keep track of the data stored in each sector.

Recycled Disks You can format and reformat a floppy disk as often as you wish. When you format a previously used floppy disk, any files that were on the floppy disk are lost. Before formatting a used floppy disk, be certain the floppy disk does not contain files you want to keep.

Disks can be formatted from the DOS command line, but you may find it more convenient to format disks from within the File Manager. Follow these steps to format a floppy disk:

1. Insert the floppy disk into the drive.
2. From the File Manager, choose **Disk**, **Format Disk**. The Format Disk dialog box appears (see Figure 16.1).

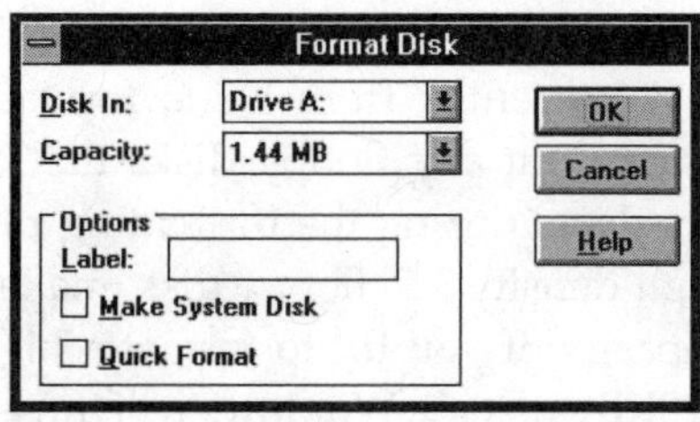

Figure 16.1 The Format Disk dialog box.

3. From the Format Disk dialog box, use the **Disk In**: drop-down list to select the drive the floppy disk is in.
4. Use the drop-down list to select the **Capacity**. Refer to Table 16.1 for a list of capacity choices.
5. Select **OK**.
6. A confirmation box appears. Carefully check the information.
7. Once you are certain the information for formatting is correct, select **OK**. The disk drive lights up during formatting and a message appears on your screen identifying how much of the formatting process is complete.
8. When the process is over, the Format Complete dialog box appears, listing the amount of space available on the newly formatted floppy disk and asking if you want to format another floppy disk. Select **Yes** to format another, or **No** to stop formatting.

Table 16.1 Floppy Disk Capacity to Specify when Formatting

Disk Diameter	*Disk Density*	*Capacities Available*
3.5"	Double	720KB
3.5"	High	1.44MB
5.25"	Double	360KB
5.25"	High	360KB or 1.2MB

High-density 5.25" floppy disks can be formatted at either 360KB or 1.2MB capacity, but high-density 3.5" floppy disks can be formatted at only one capacity: 1.44MB.

Your Floppy Disk Won't Format If the floppy disk has errors that prevent it from being formatted, Windows will tell you. Throw out any floppy disks that cannot be formatted or have problems during the formatting process. If the floppy disk is a high-density 3.5" floppy disk, make sure you format it at 1.44MB capacity; if you try to format a high-density 3.5" floppy disk at 720KB capacity, Windows will (falsely) report that the floppy disk has errors.

It is always a good idea to keep several formatted floppy disks available in case you need to move or copy files in a hurry.

Making System Disks

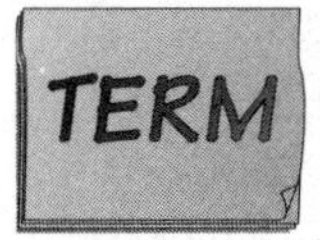

What Is a System Disk? A system disk contains operating system files you need to start your computer in the event your hard disk fails. With it, you can start your computer from the floppy disk drive.

You should always have at least one system disk on hand in case something goes wrong. A hard disk problem can lock you out of your system unless you have a system disk—so can an error in your CONFIG.SYS or AUTOEXEC.BAT file. With a system disk, you can boot from the floppy drive, bypassing the hard drive (*and* the error) until the problem can be found and corrected.

More Than One Drive If you have two floppy disk drives (A and B) of differing sizes (5.25" and 3.5"), your system disk must be the kind that fits on drive A (usually the 5.25" one). This is because when your computer boots, it checks drive A first for a disk, and if it finds none, it boots from the hard disk. It never checks drive B when booting, so you can't boot from there.

You can create a system disk when you format the floppy disk by checking the **Make System Disk** check box in the Format Disk dialog box. Or, to make a formatted floppy disk into a system disk, follow these steps:

1. From the File Manager directory window, select the icon for your hard disk. (This is where the operating system files reside.)
2. Insert a formatted floppy disk into drive A.
3. Choose **Disk, Make System Disk**. The Make System Disk dialog box appears for you to verify the drive.
4. Once you have verified the drive, select **Yes**. A message appears telling you that the system disk is being created. When the message disappears, the system disk is created.

Create a system disk for your computer and store it in a safe place. Someday you'll be glad that you took this precaution.

Copying a Floppy Disk

Disk Duplicating Made Easy Even if you are accustomed to doing your file and disk operations from the DOS prompt (moving, copying, formatting, deleting, and so forth), you might want to use the File Manager for copying disks, because unlike DOS, the File Manager does not require you to swap disks repeatedly when copying disks with higher capacities than 360KB.

If you want to copy *all* the files on one floppy disk to another, rather than each one individually, you can do it easily with the File Manager. The only condition is that both floppy disks must be of the same capacity. For example, if the source floppy disk is 1.44MB (high density), the destination floppy disk must also be 1.44MB.

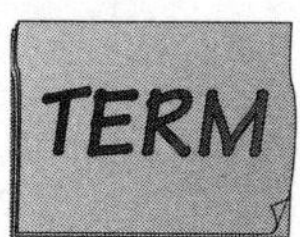

Which Is Which? The *source* floppy disk is the one you are copying from. The *destination* floppy disk is the one you are copying to.

Proceed with Caution When you copy a floppy disk, all files previously on the destination floppy disk are lost.

Follow these steps to copy a floppy disk:

1. Place the source floppy disk in the drive to copy *from.* If you have two drives of the same size and capacity, place the destination floppy disk in the drive to copy *to.*
2. From the File Manager, select the drive of the source floppy disk.
3. Choose **Disk, Copy Disk**.
4. A message appears reminding you that all the files on the destination floppy disk will be erased. Select **Yes** to go on.
5. The Copy Disk dialog box appears. If you are using two drives, the floppy disk will be copied without your having to swap floppy disks. If you are using one drive, Windows will instruct you when to swap the source and destination floppy disks. Follow the instructions.

In this lesson, you learned how to format disks and how to copy an entire floppy disk. You also learned how to create a system disk. The next lesson will conclude your work with the File Manager. You will learn how to start an application from the File Manager.

17 Starting an Application from the File Manager

In this lesson, you will learn how to start an application from within the File Manager.

Using the Run Command

In Lesson 7, you learned how to start an application using the application icon or the **F**ile, **R**un command from the Program Manager window. You can't select application icons from the File Manager, but you can still use the **F**ile, **R**un command.

There are several advantages to using the **R**un command from the File Manager:

- You can sort the files using **V**iew, Sort **b**y Type, which lets you see all the *executable* (.EXE) files grouped together. This allows you to quickly find the file that starts the program you want to use.
- No typing is required to start the application. You select the directory from the directory tree and the file from the directory window. Then, when you use the **F**ile, **R**un command, all the information is already entered in the appropriate blanks. Figure 17.1 shows the Run dialog box with the .EXE file for the Solitaire game ready to be run.
- You can specify start-up parameters for the application, just as you can from the DOS command line. (The manual for the application describes different start-up options.)

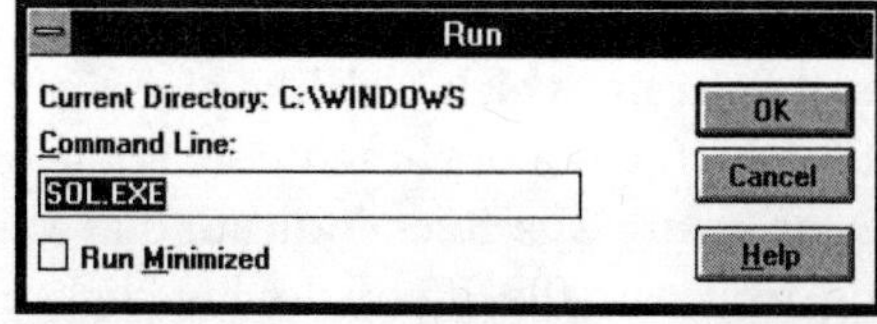

Figure 17.1 The Run dialog box with the Solitaire game .EXE file ready to run.

To use the **F**ile, **R**un command, follow these steps:

1. To reduce typing, select the appropriate directory and executable file from the File Manager directory tree and window.
2. From the File Manager window, choose **File**, **Run**. The Run dialog box appears.
3. When the command and any start-up options are entered, select **OK**.

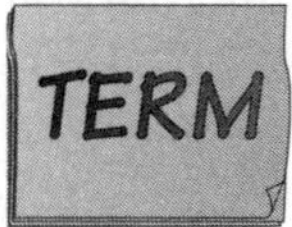

Executable Files Applications are started from executable files. These typically end in .EXE. Some applications are started from executable files that end in .COM, or from batch files (which end in .BAT), but this is less common.

Selecting the File to Run

There are other ways to start an application from the File Manager. You can locate the executable file and double-click on it. More importantly, Windows 3.1 allows you to open an application by double-clicking on a document created by the application.

Starting an Application from the Executable File

You can double-click on an executable file to start the application, rather than use the **F**ile, **R**un command. Note that you cannot add start-up parameters to the command. The advantage is that you can start an application from the directory window and bypass the Run command dialog box.

Starting an Application from an Associated File

There are three common types of file icons displayed by the File Manager. The one that looks like a miniature window indicates that this file is an executable file. This icon will appear next to all .EXE, .COM, and .BAT files.

The other icons (which look like pieces of paper with a corner turned down) indicate that the file is a document file. Some of these icons are blank and some have lines on them. The lines indicate that Windows knows what application created the document file. If you double-click on one of these icons, the *associated application* will open with the file you chose in a document window.

File association is a very powerful feature of Windows 3.1. It allows you to drag a document icon to different applications for processing. For instance, you can print an associated file simply by dragging its icon from the File Manager and dropping it into the Print Manager icon. This allows you to print a document (for example, a Write document) without having to open the application first.

Using Drag and Drop to Create Program-Item Icons

In Lesson 11, you learned how to add program-item icons to Program Manager groups. You can also add program-item icons to Program Manager groups using the File Manager. This procedure will likely test your ability to work with multiple open windows, but once you get the hang of it, you'll be on your way to becoming a Windows power user.

To create a new program-item icon using the File Manager, follow these steps:

1. Open the File Manager and locate the executable file that you want to appear as a program-item icon in a Program Manager group.

Give Yourself Room to Work You know that you will have to be able to see both the Program Manager window and the File Manager window to be able to complete this task. When you start the File Manager, resize the window to allow room on screen for the Program Manager window (see Figure 17.2).

2. Switch Tasks back to the Program Manager. Resize the Program Manager window so that you are able to see both the File Manager window and Program Manager window. You should also be able to see the group icon or window to which you wish to add the program-item icon.

To View All Your Groups in One Window The easiest way to see all your groups (especially in a small Program Manager window) is to iconize (minimize from a window to an icon) all the groups. Once all your groups are iconized, choose **Window, Arrange Icons** to bring all the group icons into view.

3. Drag the file in question from the File Manager to the Program Manager group to which you want to add the program-item icon.

4. When the mouse pointer is positioned over the appropriate Program Manager group window or icon, drop (release the mouse button) the file into the group. A new program-item icon appears in the group.

Notice that as you drag the file between the File Manager and the Program Manager, the mouse pointer appears as a circle with a line through it (like a no-smoking sign). This indicates that you cannot drop the file where the pointer is located (if you do, nothing will happen). When the mouse pointer is positioned over a Program Manager group window or icon, it turns into the familiar arrow pointer and a document icon with a plus sign in it (see Figure 17.2). This indicates that you can drop the file here.

As you can see, you can drag and drop executable files into a Program Manager group and they become program-item icons. Windows 3.1 allows you to do this with associated document files as well. For example, if you have a document that you work with regularly (for instance, Journal of Customer Service Calls), you can drag it to the Program Manager and drop it into a group. The new program-item will take the icon of the associated application. You can double-click the icon to open the application and the document at the same time.

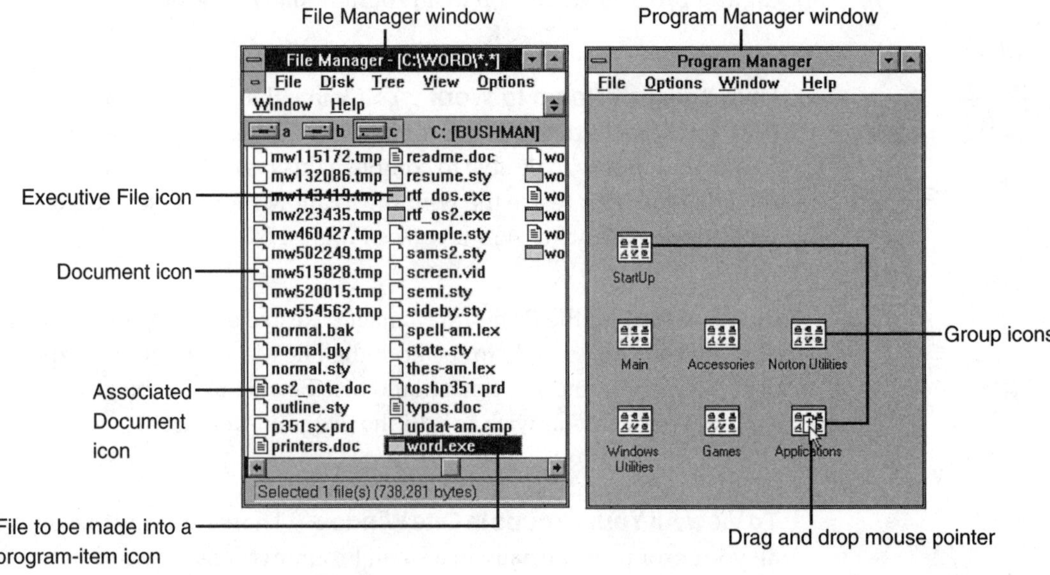

Figure 17.2 Dragging a file from the File Manager to a Program Manager group.

In this lesson, you learned how to start your applications in the File Manager. In the next lesson, you will learn how to get ready to print.

Getting Ready to Print

In this lesson, you will learn how to get ready to print, and how to set up any special typefaces.

Checking the Printer Installation

When you installed Windows, you configured the printer and the link to the printer. This is important because almost all Windows applications print using the Print Manager and the default printer defined through it. Before you attempt to print, you need to check Windows to make sure the settings are correct.

To check the print setup from Windows, go to the Printers dialog box using the following steps:

1. From the Program Manager, open the **Main** group icon.
2. Open the **Control Panel** program-item icon from the Main group window.
3. Open the **Printers** icon. The Printers dialog box appears (see Figure 18.1).

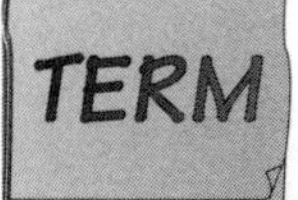

Default vs. Installed Printer The Printers dialog box identifies the Default Printer and the Installed Printers. The Default Printer is the one that the computer assumes is connected to your computer unless you select another printer. The Installed Printers are those for which special instructions (called *Printer Drivers*) are available on your computer. You can select an Installed Printer and then select the **Set As Default Printer** button to make it the Default Printer.

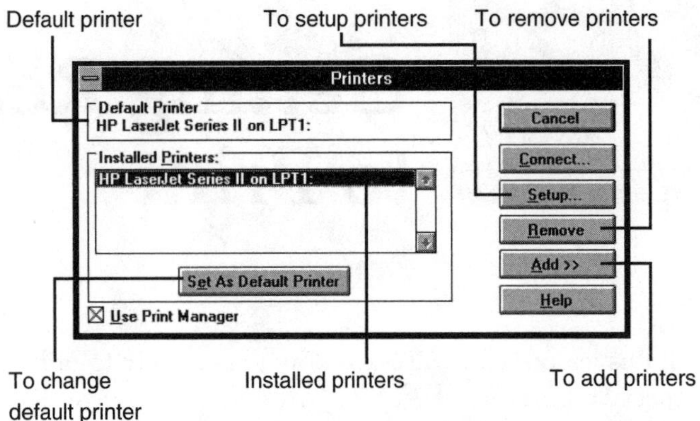

Figure 18.1 The Printers dialog box.

From the Printers dialog box, you can select the following buttons to check the settings.

- The **C**onnect button opens the Connect dialog box. On it, you can see the port (connection) to which your printer is attached. This port is usually LPT1 (for parallel printers) or COM1 (for serial printers).

  The Connect dialog box allows you to check or change the settings which control the timeout periods for the Print Manager. Timeouts define the length of time the Print Manager will wait to inform you of a printing problem.

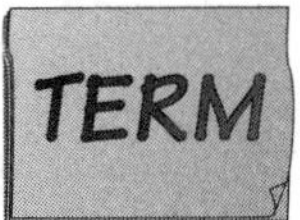

Printer Port The printer port is the connection on your computer to which the cable to your printer is attached. If the port description indicates Not Present, this means Windows does not detect that port on your computer. Check your printer manual to see whether your printer is parallel or serial and, therefore, will use the parallel or serial port.

- The **S**etup button allows you to enter information about your printer setup (see the dialog box in Figure 18.2). You can define the following:

  The **R**esolution in dots per inch (the more dots, the finer the resolution).

  The Paper Size, the Paper **S**ource.

The amount of **M**emory in your printer (check your printer manual if you are not sure).

The Orientation to either **P**ortrait (the short side of the paper is at the top) or **L**andscape (the long side of paper is at the top).

The number of **C**opies to print.

- The **A**dd button lets you add new printers to the Installed **P**rinters list. Just select the name of the printer, and then select the **I**nstall button.

What Disk? When you install new features to your Windows environment, have your installation diskettes close at hand. In the example above, Windows will probably ask you to insert one of the disks containing the printer drivers before it can carry out your instructions.

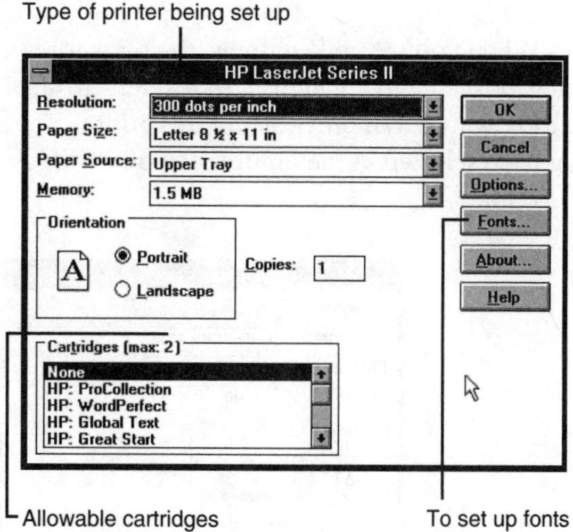

Figure 18.2 The dialog box for setting up your printer.

Once you have all the setup options in place, you may return to the Control Panel.

In addition to making sure Windows is ready for printing, you'll want to check your equipment. Things to double-check include:

- Is the cable between the computer and the printer securely attached on each end?

- Is the printer turned on?
- Is the printer ready for the computer's transmission with the ON LINE light on?
- Is paper loaded in the printer?

Working with Fonts

Many printers can print more than one character style or typeface (called a *font*). Check your printer manual to see if it is capable of printing multiple fonts. If it is, you will want to check the font setup in Windows before printing.

Where Are These Fonts? Fonts may be stored on disks or on cartridges which slide into the printer.

When you set up Windows, the fonts for your printer were identified. The dialog box shown in Figure 18.3 refers to an HP LaserJet Series II printer. Cartridges are commonly sold for this printer. The cartridge B:Times Proportional 1 has been selected. A maximum of two cartridges may be selected for this printer at one time.

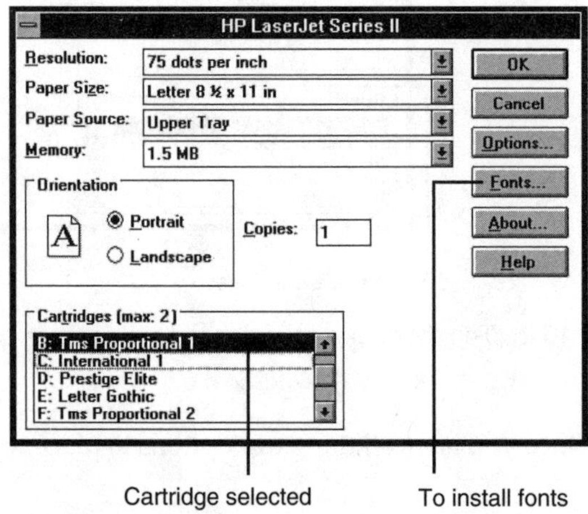

Figure 18.3 Font cartridge selected.

Use the **Fonts** button on the dialog box shown in Figure 18.3 to open the Font Installer dialog box. You can determine which fonts are installed from this dialog box.

To check the font setup:

1. From the Program Manager Main group window, open the **Control Panel**.
2. Open the **Printers** icon.
3. Select **Setup** on the Printers dialog box.
4. If your fonts are stored on cartridges, highlight the cartridge(s) you will use (based on the maximum number identified in the dialog box).
5. If your fonts are stored on floppy disk, select the **Fonts** button. The Font Installer dialog box appears. You may select the font you want from the list of available fonts.

Installing TrueType Fonts

Windows 3.1 comes with a number of TrueType fonts. These are fonts that appear in your printed document exactly as they do on your screen. The information your printer needs to print TrueType fonts is downloaded to your printer each time you print a document containing them.

Figure 18.4 shows the Fonts Installer dialog box with a number of TrueType fonts installed. To add fonts, follow these steps:

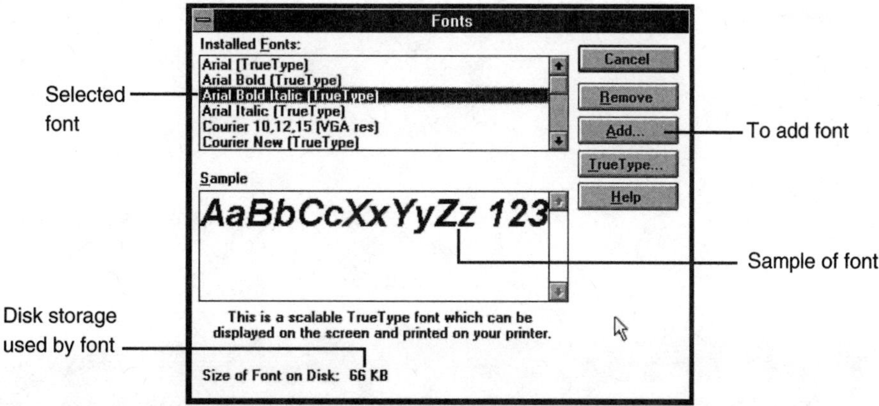

Figure 18.4 The Fonts dialog box.

1. From the Program Manager, open the **Control Panel**.
2. Open the **Fonts** icon. The Fonts dialog box, shown in Figure 18.4, appears.
3. Select **Add** from the Fonts dialog box.
4. From the Add Font File dialog box, select the directory where the font file is located, select the font to add, and select **OK**.
5. Once the font is added, you may add another font or close the dialog box.

Removing a Font from Memory or Disk

Fonts take up space in active memory as well as your hard disk. You may want to delete fonts you do not use to free memory or remove them entirely from your disk. To remove fonts, follow these steps:

1. From the Program Manager, open the **Control Panel**.
2. Open the **Fonts** icon. The Fonts dialog box appears.
3. Select the font to remove, and then select the **Remove** button.
4. A message appears for you to verify the removal. If you leave the **D**elete Font File from Disk box unchecked, the font is only removed from active memory. Check the box and the font file is removed from the hard disk as well.

In this lesson, you learned how to prepare to print. In the next lesson, you will learn how to print with the Print Manager.

Printing with the Print Manager

In this lesson, you will learn how to print through the Print Manager and check the status of your print jobs.

Purpose of the Print Manager

The Print Manager acts as the middleman between your printer and the application you are printing from. When you choose **File**, **Print** from most Windows applications, the font and file information is handed off to the Print Manager. The Print Manager then feeds the information to the printer. This allows you to continue working in your application while your job is printed.

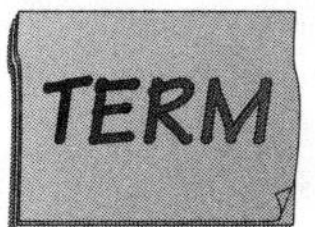

Print Jobs A *print job* (or simply *job*) is created when you choose the Print command from the application in which you are working.

Checking the Print Queue

When you print a document, the printer usually begins processing the job immediately. What happens if the printer is working on another job, sent by you or, in the case of a network printer, someone else? In this case, the Print Manager acts as a print queue and holds the job until the printer is ready for it.

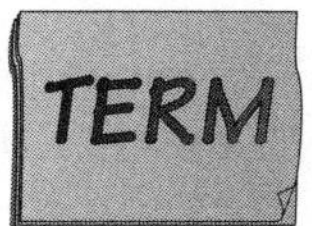

Print Queue The *print queue* is a holding area for jobs that have to be printed. If you were to list the contents of the queue, the jobs would appear in the order they were sent to the Print Manager.

Figure 19.1 illustrates the document NETWORKS.WRI in the print queue. As you can see, the percent of the document which has been printed is shown (34% of 63KB) along with the time and date the document was sent to print. Notice also that the printer is shown to be printing. This indicates the document was just sent to the queue and is beginning to print.

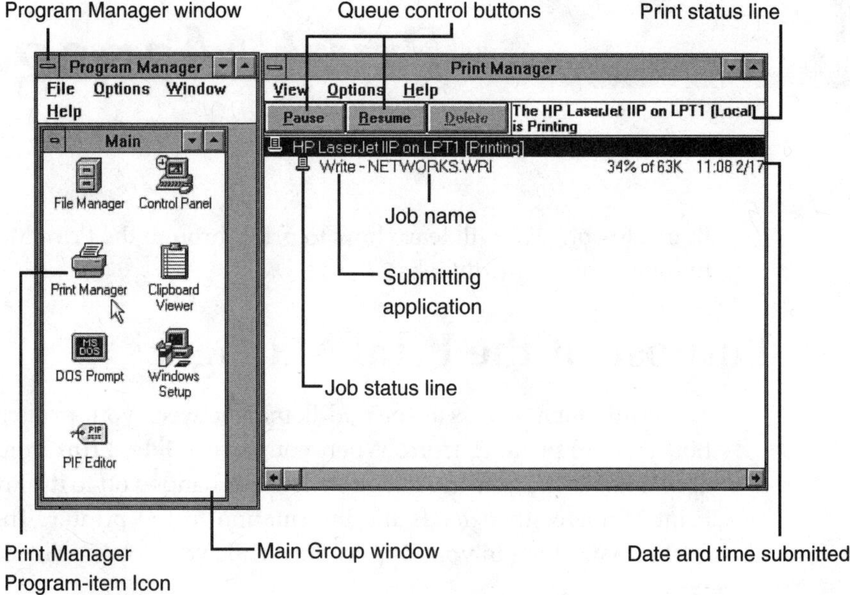

Figure 19.1 The Print Manager print queue window.

To display the print queue, follow these steps:

1. From the Program Manager, open the **Main** group icon.
2. Open the **Print Manager** icon (see Figure 19.1).
3. The Print Manager window appears with a list of *queued* documents. If no documents are waiting to print, a message tells you the printer is idle.

Controlling the Print Job

You can control print jobs once they are in the queue. This includes changing the order in which the jobs print, pausing and resuming the print job, or deleting a job before it prints.

Reordering Jobs in the Queue

To use the mouse to change the order of a job in the queue, drag the job entry to a new position in the list. To use the keyboard to reposition a job in the queue:

1. From the Print Manager window, use the arrow keys to highlight the document to be repositioned.
2. Hold down **Ctrl** and use the arrow keys to move the job to the new position in the queue.
3. Release the **Ctrl** key.

First Come, First Served You cannot reorder or place a job before the job that is currently printing.

Pausing and Resuming the Print Queue

You may want to pause the queue and then resume printing later. For example, the paper in the printer may be misaligned. Pausing the print queue will give you time to correct the problem.

To pause the print queue, select the **Pause** button or press **Alt+P** while in the Print Manager window. To resume printing, select the **Resume** button or press **Alt+R**.

Printer Stalled Your printer may stall while it is processing your print job. If it does, **stalled** will appear in the printer status line. Press **Alt+R** to start printing again. Chances are that a problem somewhere along the line caused the printer to stall, the queue will stall again, and you will have to solve the problem.

Delete a Print Job

Sometimes, you'll send a document to be printed and then change your mind. For example, you may think of other text to add to the document or realize you forgot to spell-check your work. In such a case, deleting the print job is easy. Follow these steps:

1. From the Print Manager window, select the job to delete.
2. Select the **Delete** button or press **Alt+D**.
3. A message appears for you to confirm the deletion.
4. Select **OK**.

Clear the Queue! To delete all the files in the print queue, choose **View, Exit** from the Print Manager menu bar or double-click the **Control Menu** box. Select **OK** from the Print Manager dialog box.

In this lesson, you learned how to print using the Print Manager and check the status of your print jobs. In the next lesson, you will learn how to use the Control Panel to control your windows.

Controlling Windows' Appearance with the Control Panel

In this lesson, you will learn how to change the look and performance of Windows by using the Control Panel.

The Control Panel is an application in the Main group that allows you to control many aspects of Windows. Those discussed in this lesson include:

- Colors displayed on-screen.
- What appears on your desktop.
- International language and display support.

Setting Colors

You can change the color of many components of Windows with the Control Panel. This can be important if you have a monochrome or LCD screen. These screens may not have the ability to display certain colors. This could cause a real problem if the color chosen to display command buttons cannot be displayed by your screen. Windows comes with several predefined color schemes for users with monochrome or LCD screens. The ability to control the color of certain Windows elements can also help you learn to use Windows faster. This is because you are able to look for a particular color and shape, instead of just a shape. Finally, you can adjust the colors displayed on your color monitor just for a change of pace.

Change colors with these steps:

1. From the Program Manager, open the **Main** group icon and then open the **Control Panel**.
2. Open the **Color** program-item. The Color dialog box appears.
3. Open the **S**chemes drop-down list box by clicking on the down arrow button or pressing **Alt+↓**. The predefined options appear (see Figure 20.1).

4. Use the arrow keys to scroll through the color scheme options. The display below Color Schemes illustrates the current selection.

5. Press **Enter** to select your choice.

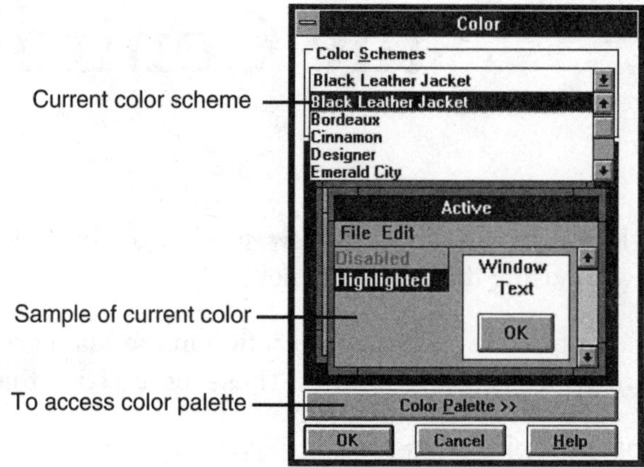

Figure 20.1 The Black Leather Jacket color scheme selected on the Color dialog box.

Test Your Artistic Aptitude After you become more comfortable with Windows, go into the Color dialog box and create your own color scheme. Select the **Show Palette** button. A new section of the Color dialog box appears. This will allow you to assign different colors to the various Windows components (title bar, buttons, menus, and so on). You can then save your creation as a Windows color scheme.

Changing the Desktop

Many visual and performance elements of your desktop can be changed through the Control Panel. The Desktop dialog box shown in Figure 20.2 has the following options.

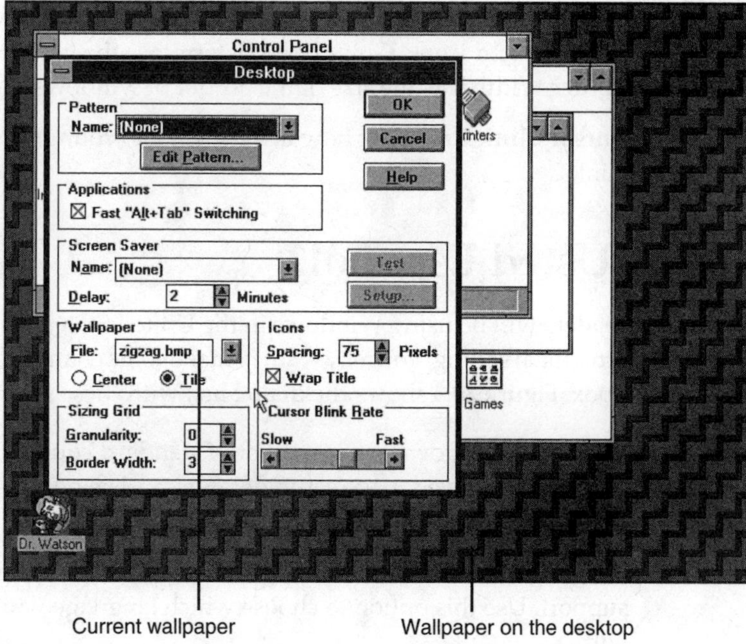

Figure 20.2 Desktop dialog box with Zigzag Wallpaper selected.

Pattern Name Select the pattern that is displayed on the desktop. This is a simple, two-color pattern (defined in the Color dialog box).

Applications Identify the speed at which windows cycle when you press Alt+Tab. This is the fast task-switching that Windows 3.1 offers.

Screen Saver If the same image remains on your screen for an extended period of time, you could damage your monitor. By selecting a screen saver, when your computer is inactive for the default time, Windows will automatically blank the screen and run a pattern across your screen. To continue working, press a key or move the mouse.

Wallpaper More elaborate than the Pattern selection, the Wallpaper option allows you to display .BMP files on your desktop. Windows comes with some very attractive wallpapers, or you can use Paintbrush to create your own.

Icons Determine icon **S**pacing and whether icon titles are wrapped to another line or cut off.

Sizing Grid Identify the setting of the magnetic grid which aligns windows and icons. Granularity determines the precision of the grid, and Border Width sets the size of the border of windows.

Cursor Blink Rate Set how fast the cursor (your marker in text boxes) blinks.

Habla Usted Español?

Most readers will be using Windows in the United States. But if you do work in an international setting, you may want to make some changes on the International dialog box. Figure 20.3 shows the dialog box with these settings:

- Country—Windows has a number of standard country settings on how units are displayed, page setup defaults, and so on. Use this option to choose the Country settings you wish to use.
- Language—Some Windows applications provide foreign language support. Use this option to choose which language you want to work with.
- Keyboard Layout—Windows supports a number of keyboard layouts. This controls the way keys are mapped to the special characters associated with the Language you have chosen to work with.
- Measurement—Use this drop-down list to choose which measurement system you want to work with, English or Metric.
- List Separator—In this text box, enter the character with which you want to separate elements of a list.
- Date Format—Use this command button to change the way long and short dates are displayed.
- Currency Format—Use this command button to change the way positive and negative currency values are displayed.
- Time Format—Use this command button to change the way time values are displayed.
- Number Format—Use this command button to change the way numbers are displayed.

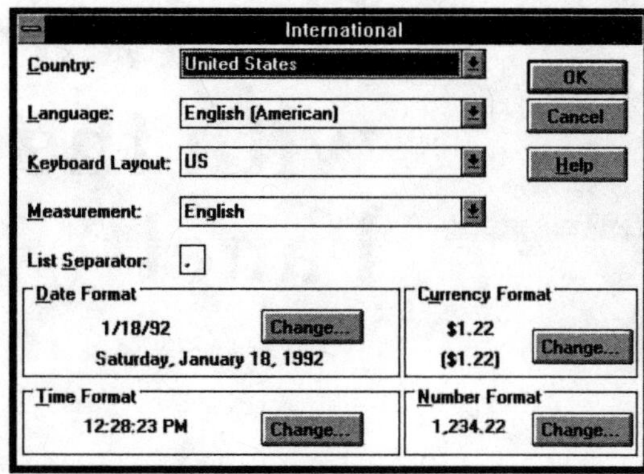

Figure 20.3 The International dialog box.

To control the international settings, follow these steps:

1. From the Control Panel window, open the **International** icon. The International dialog box appears.
2. Make the selections for the changes you desire.
3. Select **OK**. The changes take effect.

In this lesson, you learned how to set colors, change the desktop appearance, and give Windows an international flavor. In the next lesson, you will learn how to use the Control Panel to control hardware settings.

Controlling Hardware Settings with the Control Panel

In this lesson, you will learn to use the Control Panel to control hardware settings for ports, mouse, keyboard, date/time, drivers, and sound. Figure 21.1 displays the Control Panel and points out the icons you will be using in this lesson.

Altering the Date and Time

The system date and time is set in your computer. This is used to time-stamp files as they are created or modified. Also, many application programs allow you to automatically insert the date and time on-screen or when you print. Always make sure the date and time are correct.

To check or set the date and time, follow these steps:

1. From the Control Panel, open the **Date/Time** icon. The Date & Time dialog box appears (see Figure 21.2).
2. Use the **Tab** key or the mouse to move between digits in the date and time. Enter the appropriate date and time. To use the mouse, click on the portion of the date or time you want to change and click on the up or down arrow button to increment or decrement the value accordingly.
3. Select **OK** or press **Enter** to accept the changes you have made. Press **Esc** or select **Cancel** to close the dialog box without saving changes.

Modifying Mouse Settings

You can modify the settings for your mouse. The following settings can be changed:

- The speed of mouse tracking (how fast/far the pointer moves when you move the mouse).

- The speed of the double-click *(the time allowed between the first and second click so that your action is recognized as a double-click and not just two single-clicks).*
- The use of the left and right buttons can be swapped (for you lefties out there).
- A trail of mouse pointers that follow the pointer movement can be turned on or off. This will drive an unsuspecting user up the wall.

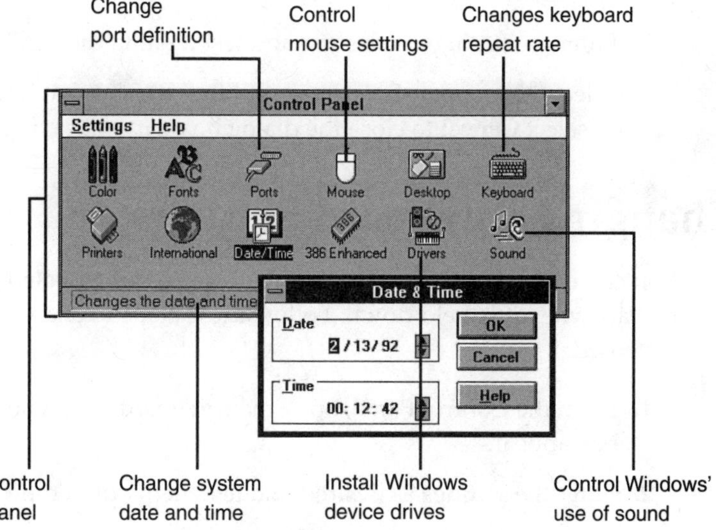

Figure 21.1 The Windows Control Panel.

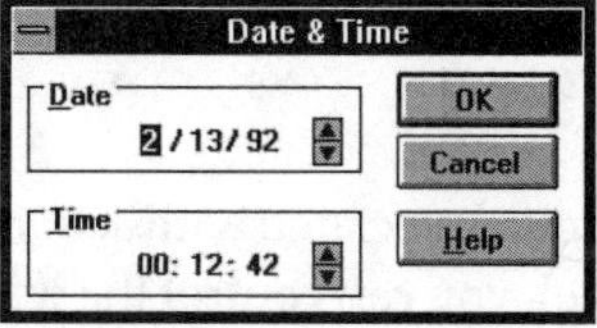

Figure 21.2 The Date & Time dialog box.

Try It, You'll Like It Always use the TEST area to try new settings before leaving the screen. For example, if you set the Double Click Speed all the way to Fast, you may not be able to double-click fast enough for it to register.

To modify these settings, follow these steps:

1. From the Control Panel, open the **Mouse** icon. The Mouse dialog box appears.
2. Enter the settings as desired and test them in the TEST area.
3. Select **OK** or press **Enter** to accept the changes you have made. Press **Esc** or select **Cancel** to close the dialog box without saving changes.

Changing Keyboard Settings

You can change how long it takes for a key to be repeated and how fast a key repeats when it is held down. Follow these steps to change the response of the keyboard:

1. From the Control Panel, open the **Keyboard** icon. The Keyboard dialog box appears.
2. Enter the settings as desired and test them out in the Test area.
3. Select **OK** or press **Enter** to accept the changes you have made. Press **Esc** or select **Cancel** to close the dialog box without saving changes.

Sound Control

Controlling sounds associated with actions or events can be simple or complex. At the simplest level, you can control the warning beep when you make an error or perform an action Windows does not recognize. If you have a sound card in your computer, you can set sounds for a variety of events in Windows.

To affect sound, follow these steps:

1. From the Control Panel, open the **Sound** icon. The Sound dialog box appears.
2. If you do not have a sound card in your computer, the Events and Files selections are grayed-out and unavailable. To turn off the warning beep,

leave the Enable System Sounds box blank. To enable the warning beep, make sure that box is checked.

3. If you have a sound card, you can select the different Events and, for each, assign a Files sound. Use Test to test out your sound selection. Also, make sure Enable System Sounds is checked.
4. Select **OK** or press **Enter** to accept the changes you have made. Press **Esc** or select **Cancel** to close the dialog box without saving changes.

Changing Ports

If you will be communicating with another computer or installing a new printer, you may need to change the settings for the port to which the modem or printer will be connected.

Through the Port icon, you can set the Baud Rate, Data Bits, Parity, Stop Bits, and Flow Control. Most manuals for communications software and hardware specify the settings that must be used. If you have trouble, contact the manufacturer or support line for the product(s) involved. To change port settings, follow these steps:

1. From the Control Panel, open the **Ports** icon.
2. Select the port designation (COM1 through COM4) assigned to the port you will use.
3. The dialog box appears containing the settings for that port.
4. Enter the settings as instructed by the manual or technical support person.
5. Select **OK** or press **Enter** to accept the changes you have made. Press **Esc** or select **Cancel** to close the dialog box without saving changes.

In this lesson, you learned how to change the time, hardware settings, mouse and keyboard, and sound. In the next lesson, you will learn how to create documents using Write.

22 Creating a Document with Write

In this lesson, you will create and print a letter using the Windows Write program.

Creating a Document

You may use Windows Write to create any document. This may include letters, memos, reports, lists, newsletters, and so on.

To create a document, follow these steps:

1. From the Program Manager window, open the **Accessories** group icon.
2. Open the **Write** program-item icon.
3. The Write window (shown in Figure 22.1) appears. As soon as you begin typing, you are creating a document.

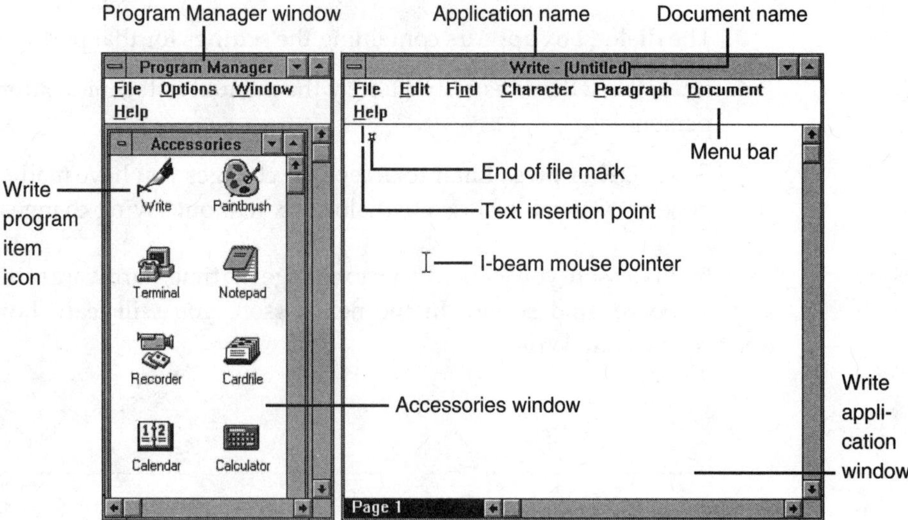

Figure 22.1 The Windows Write window.

Notice these portions of the Write screen in Figure 22.1:

- Application name (Write).
- Document name (untitled for now; a name is assigned when you save the document).
- The menu bar containing the Write menus.
- Scroll bars to move through the document.
- The text insertion point which marks the spot where text you enter will be placed.
- The I-beam mouse pointer that is used to move the text insertion point. Notice that as you point at the menu bar, the pointer changes back to the arrow pointer.

Entering Text

To enter text, begin typing. Do not press Enter at the end of each line (although you can if you like). Just allow the text to wrap around. Press **Enter** to mark the end of a paragraph.

Figure 22.2 shows a Write screen after entering text.

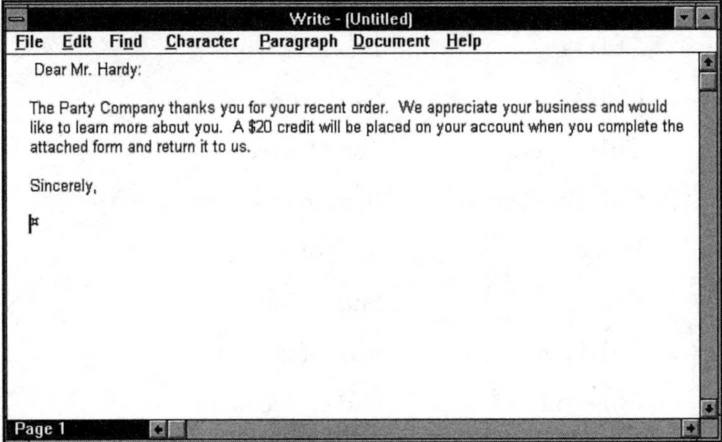

Figure 22.2 Text typed in the Write document.

Basic Editing

Everyone makes mistakes. Everyone changes his or her mind. When that happens, you can easily edit the document. Following are the specific techniques you'll use to edit your Write documents.

Moving the Text Insertion Point

To move the insertion point with the mouse, just point and click. To move the insertion point with the keyboard, see the options in Table 22.1. You can use these keys without disturbing existing text.

Table 22.1 Moving the Insertion Point with the Keyboard

Key	*Movement*
↓	Down a line
↑	Up a line
→	Right one character
←	Left one character
PageUp	Previous screen
PageDown	Next screen
Ctrl+→	Previous word
Ctrl+←	Next word
Ctrl+PageUp	Top of screen
Ctrl+PageDown	Bottom of screen
Home	Start of line
End	End of line
Ctrl+Home	Start of document
Ctrl+End	End of document

Inserting Text

To insert text among existing characters, simply place the insertion point (using the mouse or the keyboard) in the appropriate location and begin typing. The characters move to the right as you type.

Selecting Text

Before you edit a block of text, you first need to select it. For example, you need to select the text before you can copy it.

To use a mouse to select text:

1. Put the mouse pointer (I-beam) at the start of the text to select.
2. Press and hold down the mouse button.
3. Drag the mouse until the text selection is highlighted.
4. Release the mouse button.

Quickly Select an Entire Word To select a word, double-click on the word. If you double-click and hold down the last click, you can extend your selection by dragging the mouse pointer.

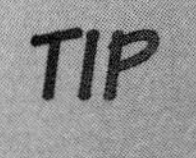

Select an Entire Paragraph When you move the mouse pointer to the left side of the Write window, it changes into an arrow that points to the right. Click the mouse button to select the entire line or double-click to select the entire paragraph.

To select text with the keyboard, follow these steps:

1. Place the insertion point before the first character of the text to be selected.
2. Press and hold down the **Shift** key.
3. Move the insertion point to the last character in the selection.
4. Release the **Shift** key.

Quickly Select an Entire Word To select an entire word using the keyboard, move the insertion point to the beginning of the word. Hold down the **Shift** key and the **Ctrl** key and use the arrow keys to highlight the words you want to edit.

Select the Entire Document Press **Ctrl+Home** to move the insertion point to the beginning of the document. Hold down the **Shift** and **Ctrl** keys and press the **End** key.

Deleting Text

To delete a single character, press the **Backspace** key to delete the character to the left. Press the **Delete** key to delete the character to the right. To delete larger amounts of text, select the text, then press the **Delete** key.

Copying and Moving Text

You may copy or move text from one location to another.

To copy or move text, follow these steps:

1. Select the text to copy or cut.
2. Choose **Edit, Copy**, or **Cut** from the menu bar.
3. Place your insertion point where you want to paste the text.
4. Choose **Edit, Paste**.

Basic Formatting

You can affect the appearance of your document on-screen and when printed by changing the formatting. Formatting refers to the appearance of a document, including character style and font, line spacing, and page layout.

Character Style

Write has five basic character styles (Bold, Italic, Underline, Superscript, and Subscript). To select (or deselect) the style of characters:

1. Select the Character menu, and then select the desired style. (The style will be used if a check mark appears before it. To cancel all styles, select Regular.)
2. Type your text. The text appears in the styles with the check mark.

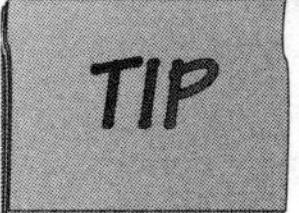

Changing Existing Text If you have already entered text and wish to change the character style, select the text and then set the character style.

You can also change the fonts that are used in your document. Select Character, Fonts... to access the Fonts dialog box, shown in Figure 22.3. You can choose a font before you enter the text, or you can select text you've entered and change the font.

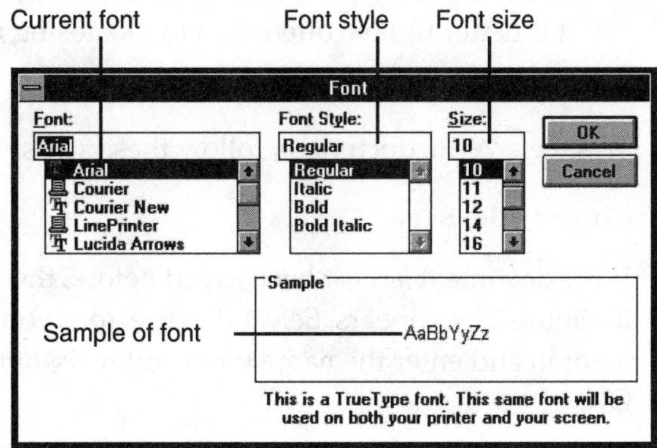

Figure 22.3 The Font dialog box.

Adjusting Margins

You may change the size of the margins from the default 1" top and bottom margin and 1.25" right and left margin. To change margins, follow these steps:

1. Select **Document, Page Layout**.
2. Type the margins you wish to use.
3. Select **OK**.

Line Spacing

Line spacing refers to the amount of space between lines. Follow these steps to change line spacing:

1. Put the insertion point in the paragraph to change.
2. Choose **Paragraph, Single Space, 1 1/2 Space**, or **Double Space**.
3. The line spacing for the paragraph changes.

Save the Write Document

Whether you are creating a Write document or another type of document file, *always* save your work often.

Better Saved Than Sorry When in doubt, save your document. It is better to save often than to risk losing hours of effort.

To save a Write document, follow these steps:

1. Choose **File, Save**.
2. If the document *has not* been saved before, the Save As dialog box shown in Figure 22.4 appears. Select the directory you want to save the document in and enter the name you want to assign to the document. Select OK.

   If the document *has* been saved before, Write will simply save the changes you made.
3. Once the document is saved, you are returned to the document window to continue work or to exit.

Notice that in Figure 22.4, the WRITEDOC directory is selected (the file folder symbol appears open and the files in the directory appear on the left). When OK is selected, the file LET1 will be saved to the WRITEDOC directory.

What About the File Extension? Write automatically assigns the .WRI extension to files created in Write. Notice that the file name is displayed in the title bar.

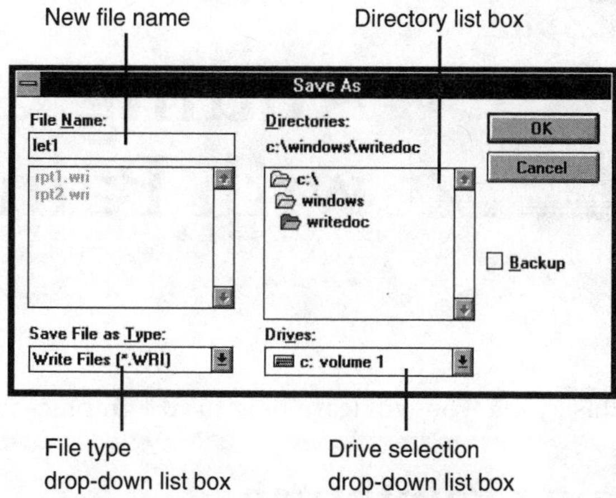

Figure 22.4 The dialog box for saving a new document.

Print the Document

Once your document is complete, you can print it. Follow these steps:

1. Choose **File**, **Print**.
2. The Print dialog box appears.
3. Identify the number of copies (if more than one) and the pages to print (if applicable) and select **OK**.
4. A dialog box appears to let you know the document is printing. To cancel the print job, press **Cancel**.

When What You See Is Not What You Get Sometimes the document doesn't print as planned. If there are formatting or document appearance problems, your problem is within the Write document.

In this lesson, you learned how to create and print a document in Write. In the next lesson, you will learn how to create graphics using Paintbrush.

Adding Graphics with Paintbrush

In this lesson, you will learn how to add graphics using Windows Paintbrush.

Opening Paintbrush

Paintbrush allows you to give your documents an artistic touch. To open a Paintbrush document, follow these steps:

1. From the Program Manager, open the **Accessories** group icon.
2. Open the **Paintbrush** program-item icon (see Figure 23.1).
3. The Paintbrush screen shown in Figure 23.1 appears.

In addition to familiar parts, the Paintbrush window shown in Figure 23.1 has a set of drawing tools (called the *toolbox*) on the left along with a *color palette* on the bottom of the window.

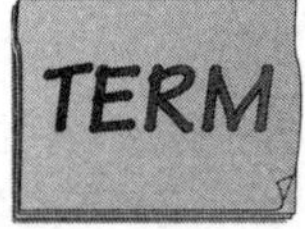

Background and Foreground Colors The box within a box to the left of the color palette shows the currently selected *foreground* and *background* colors. The foreground color is the color you'll use when you draw and the background color is the color of the backdrop.

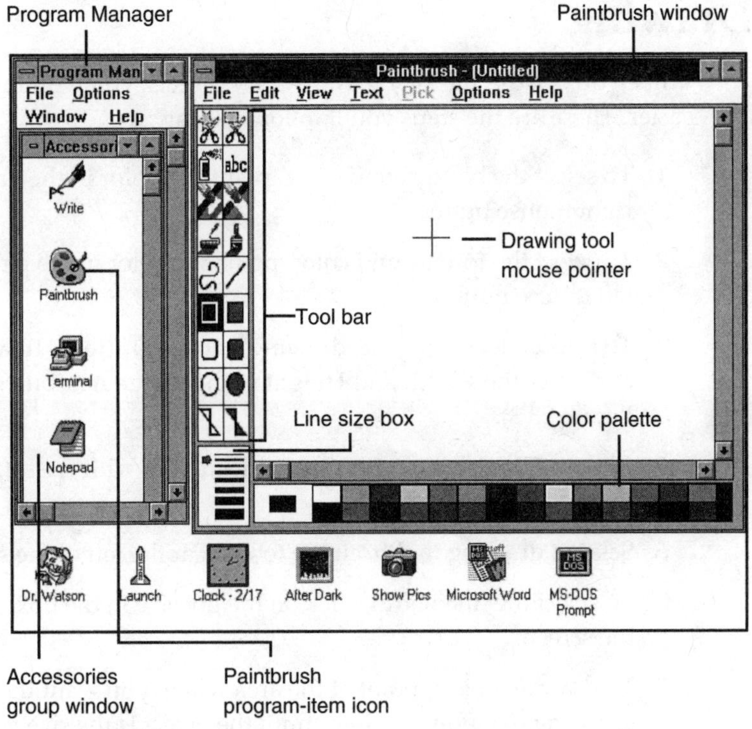

Figure 23.1 The Paintbrush screen.

The *linesize box* on the lower left of the window identifies the width of a line when you draw. Figure 23.2 shows each of the tools in the toolbox.

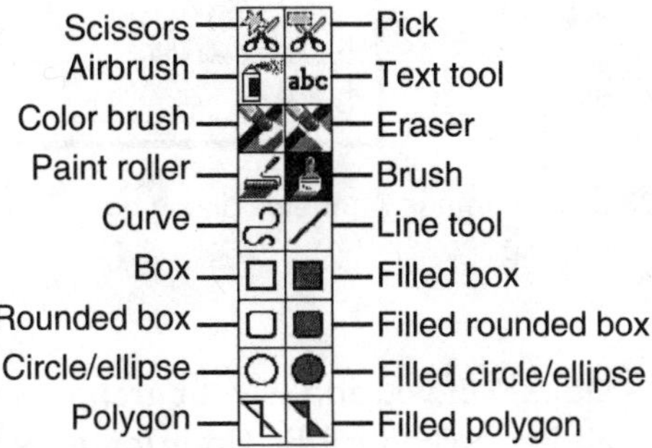

Figure 23.2 The tools in the toolbox.

Drawing

While you can use the keyboard to draw objects, you will find the mouse much easier. These are the steps you'll follow to draw:

1. To select the background color, point at a color in the palette and click the right mouse button.
2. To select the foreground color, point at a color in the palette and click the left mouse button.
3. To select the size of your drawing, choose **Options**, **Image Attributes**, and enter the **Width** and **Height** in the Image Attributes dialog box (see Figure 23.3).
4. Choose **File**, **New** to open a new document with the settings you entered in steps 1–3.
5. Select a drawing tool from the toolbox at the left of the screen.
6. To select the line width, click on the linesize in the box in the lower left of the screen.
7. To draw an object, point at the area where you want the object to appear and drag the mouse pointer until the object is the size you desire.

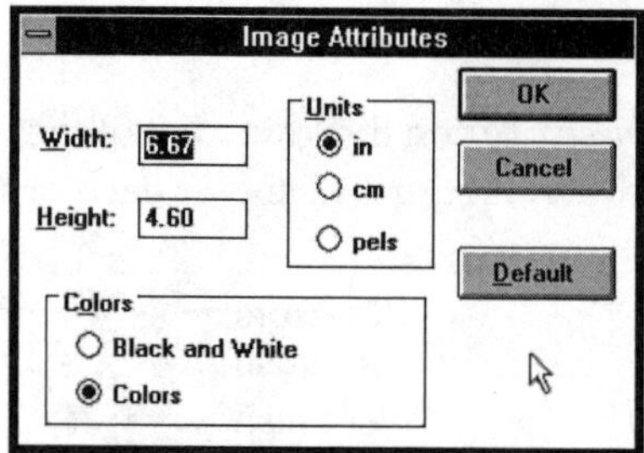

Figure 23.3 The Image Attributes dialog box.

Oops! If you add to your graphic and decide you don't like the addition, choose **Edit**, **Undo** (or press **Alt+Backspace**) to undo the change you made. Use this option carefully—all changes you have made since you last changed tools will be undone.

A Perfect Circle Every Time To draw a perfect circle, hold down the **Shift** key as you drag the mouse pointer. This technique can also be used to help you draw a perfect square and a perfectly straight line.

Adding Text

To add text to a graphic, follow these steps:

1. Select the **Text** tool.
2. Choose **Text, Font**.
3. From the Font dialog box, select the **Font, Font Style**, and **Size** and select **OK**.
4. Place the insertion point where you want to begin entering text.
5. Type the text.

Once You Leave, You Can Never Get Back You can't edit text once you have accepted it; you can only erase it. Because of this, be sure that what you've typed is correct before you move on.

Figure 23.4 displays a graphic with text created in Paintbrush. The selected Font is Arial (supplied by Windows). The Font Style is Bold. The **Size** is 20. As you can see, Paintbrush can create a company letterhead, cards, diagrams, charts, or any other graphic need.

Using the Keyboard

You can use the keyboard to draw (but you probably won't like it). The keys shown in Table 23.1 may be substituted for the mouse activities.

Table 23.1 Keys Used to Draw

Key	*Mouse Operation*
Insert	Press left mouse button
F9+Insert	Double-click on left mouse button

continues

Table 23.1 Continued

Key	*Mouse Operation*
Delete	Press right mouse button
F9+Delete	Double-click right mouse button
Insert+Arrow keys	Drag the mouse to draw

Figure 23.4 The balloon graphic with added text.

Saving the Drawing

Paintbrush allows you to save your work in a number of different formats. These include several bitmap formats (varying number of colors) and PCX, a common PC graphic file format. What format you choose depends on what you want to do with the file. If you plan to import the file into another program, make sure that you choose a format that the program can import. To save the drawing, follow these steps:

1. Choose **File, Save**.
2. If the file has not been saved before, choose a directory to save it in, name it, and select **OK**.

Printing the Drawing

To print the drawing:

1. Choose **File, Print**.
2. Complete the Print dialog box.
3. Select **OK**.

In this lesson, you learned how to create, save, and print a graphic. In the next lesson, you will learn how to use the many accessories that come with Windows.

24 Managing Time with the Accessories

In this lesson, you will learn how to use Windows' Calendar and Clock to manage your time more efficiently.

The Calendar

Windows' Calendar is handy to keep track of your daily or monthly schedule. Maintaining appointments, birthdays, holidays, and deadlines with the Calendar can help organize your life. And, if you tend to get engrossed with your work at the computer and forget the time, you can set an alarm to tell you when to quit.

Using the Calendar

To use the Calendar, follow these steps:

1. From the Program Manager, open the **Accessories** group icon.
2. Open the **Calendar** icon. A screen like the one shown in Figure 24.1 appears.
3. Choose **View**, **Month** or **Day** to view the current month or current day display. Figure 24.1 displays the Day View, Figure 24.2 displays the Month View.
4. To view a day from a month calendar view, select the day and press **Enter**.
5. From a day calendar, you may view or edit the information for the day. You may also set an alarm for the time line where your insertion point rests. Choose **Alarm**, **Set** to set an alarm for a particular time.
6. Select **Show**, and then select **Today**, **Previous**, **Next**, or **Date**... to change days.

7. When you are done using the Calendar, choose **File**, **Save**, enter a file name, and choose **OK**.

8. To leave the Calendar, choose **File**, **Exit**.

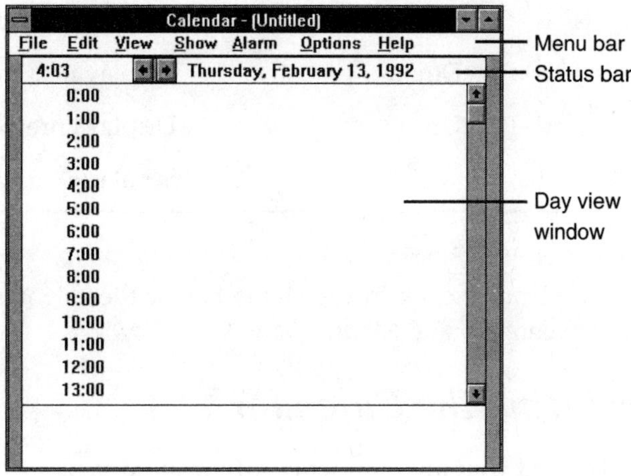

Figure 24.1 The Calendar screen—the Day View.

Table 24.1 lists shortcut keys you can use to move around in the Calendar.

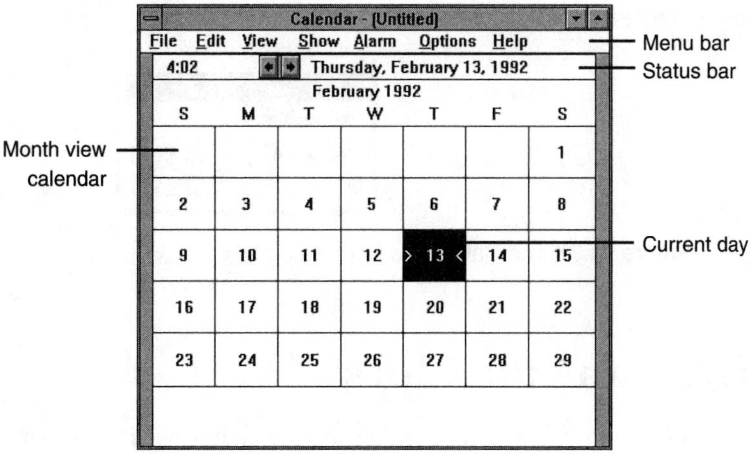

Figure 24.2 The Calendar screen—the Month View.

Table 24.1 Calendar's Shortcut Keys

Shortcut Key Sequence	*Description*
F8	Displays day view
F9	Displays month view
Ctrl+PageDown	Display next month/day
Ctrl+PageUp	Displays previous month/day
F5	Set alarm on day and time

Double-click in the status bar of the calendar (with the date) to switch between Day and Month View.

Printing the Calendar

To print your appointments, follow these steps:

1. From the Calendar, choose **File**, **Print**.
2. The Print dialog box, shown in Figure 24.3, appears.
3. Enter the date to print **From** and **To**.
4. Select **OK**.

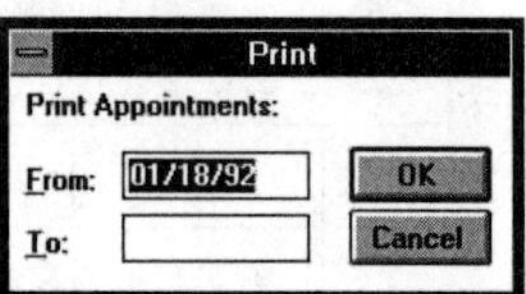

Figure 24.3 The Calendar's Print dialog box.

Handling the Clock

Windows' Clock can keep you on time. It may be displayed as an analog clock (see Figure 24.4) or a digital clock (see Figure 24.5).

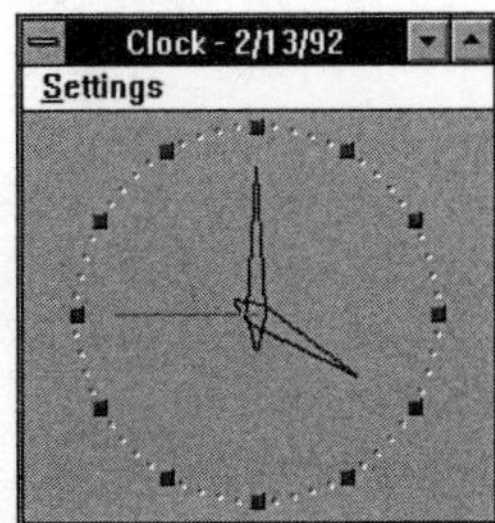

Figure 24.4 The analog clock.

To use the Clock, follow these steps:

1. From the Program Manager, open the **Accessories** group icon.
2. Open the **Clock** icon.
3. To switch between analog and digital display, choose **Settings**, **Analog** or **Digital**.
4. Close the clock using the **Control** menu.

Figure 24.5 The digital clock.

Time on My Hands, and My Windows The Clock has a nice feature that allows you to keep it in view at all times. First minimize the Clock. It still keeps time, even as an icon. Next, move it to a position where it will not be in the way and you will be able to see it. Finally, open the **Control** menu and choose **Always on Top**. When this option is active, a check mark appears next to it on the menu. This will keep the icon on top of all other windows, where you can always see it.

In this lesson, you learned how to manage time with the Calendar and Clock.

WORD FOR WINDOWS 2

Peter G. Aitken

Getting Started with Word

In this lesson, you'll learn what Word for Windows is, how to start Word, and how to quit the program. You'll also learn the parts of the Word for Windows screen.

What Is Word for Windows?

Microsoft Word has long been held to be the premier word processing program for the Window's operating environment. And now, with the release of version 2.0, the program is even better. In a single package, you have everything you need to create anything from a one-page memo to a polished 500-page report.

Any program with so much power is unavoidably somewhat complex. Learning all of its features can take some time—time that you don't have in your busy schedule. You need a fast method for learning the program's most important features. This book is just what you're looking for.

Starting Word for Windows

To start Word for Windows, it must be installed on your system. Follow the instructions provided in the Word for Windows package. After you install Word for Windows, your Windows Program Manager screen will include a Word for Windows 2.0 window, as shown in Figure 1.1.

Installation Before you can use Word for Windows, it must be installed on your system.

Finding the Program Manager If your Window's Program Manager screen is not visible, press **Alt+Esc** one or more times until it is displayed, or press **Ctrl+Esc** and select **Program Manager** from the Task List dialog box.

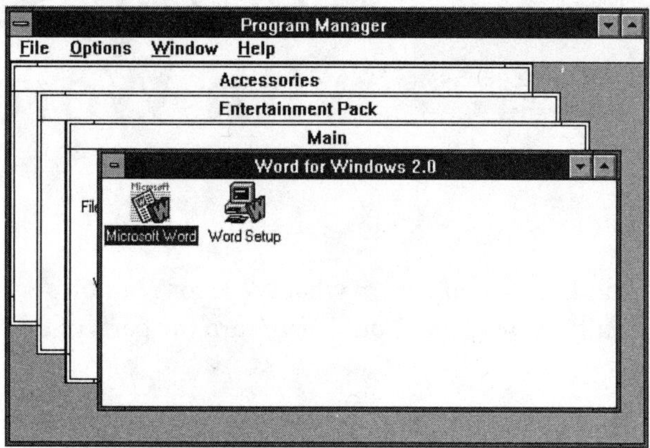

Figure 1.1 The Windows Program Manager screen.

Start Word for Windows by selecting the Microsoft Word icon, using either your mouse or the keyboard. Here are the steps to follow:

If you are using the mouse:

- Position the mouse pointer on the Microsoft Word icon. Then rapidly press and release the left mouse button twice.

If you are using the keyboard:

1. If necessary, press **Ctrl+F6** one or more times to make the Word for Windows 2.0 window the active window. This means to press and hold the **Ctrl** key, press the **F6** key, and then release both keys. (Notice that the color of the menu bar changes to indicate the active window.)

2. Use the arrow keys to move the highlight to the Microsoft Word icon, and press **Enter**.

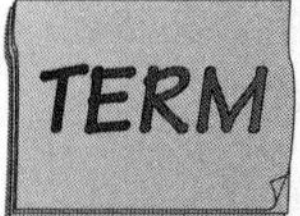

What's an Icon? An *icon* is a small graphic symbol that Windows uses to represent a program or screen window.

When Word for Windows starts, it first displays the opening screen with copyright notices and then displays its main screen.

Parts of the Screen

When you start Word for Windows, it displays its opening logo for a few seconds and then displays its main screen with a blank document, ready for your input. Take a moment to familiarize yourself with the Word for Windows screen. It contains a number of useful components. These are labeled in Figure 1.2.

- The *title bar* displays the program name and the name of the document being edited.
- The *menu bar* contains the main Word for Windows menu.
- The *Toolbar* displays buttons that you can select to perform commonly needed editing tasks. You must have a mouse to use the Toolbar.
- The *ribbon* is used to select character and paragraph formatting commands.
- The *ruler* controls margins, indents, and tab stops.
- The *work area* is where your document is displayed.
- The *scroll bars* are used to move around your document with the mouse.
- The *status line* displays information about your document.

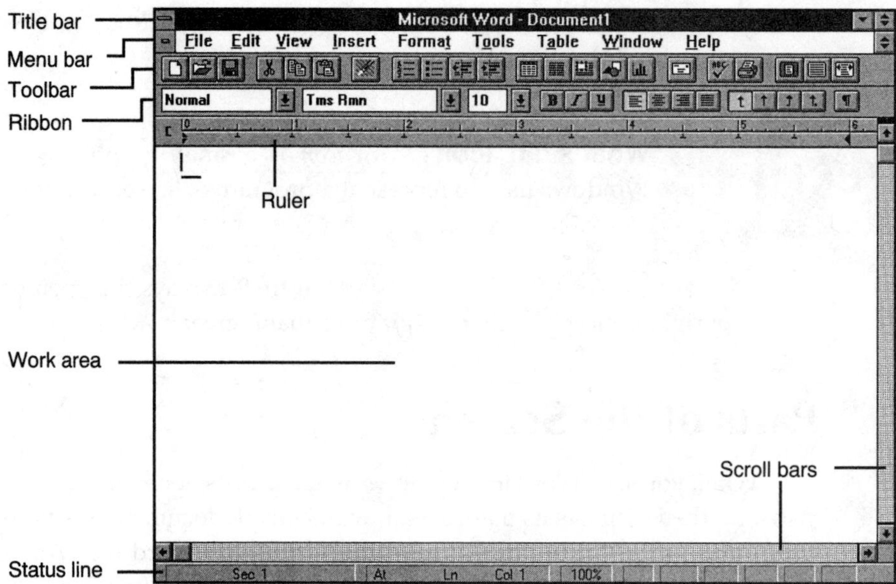

Figure 1.2 Components of the Word for Windows screen.

Quitting Word for Windows

When you're done using Word for Windows, quit the program by pressing **Alt+F4**. With the mouse, position the pointer on the box at the left of the title bar and double-click. If you have any unsaved documents, Word for Windows prompts you to save them. Then the program terminates, and you're returned to the Program Manager screen.

In this lesson, you learned what Word for Windows is and how to start and quit Word.

2 Using Menus and Giving Commands

In this lesson, you'll learn how to use Word for Windows menus and give commands using the mouse and the keyboard, and how to use the Toolbar.

Menu Structure

When you work with Word for Windows, you give it commands to instruct the program to carry out the desired tasks. Commands are usually entered by means of *menus*. Word for Windows has two types of menus:

- The *main menu* is displayed in the *menu bar*, on the second line of the screen.
- A *pull-down menu* is a list of commands associated with each choice on the main menu. When you choose a command on the main menu, its pull-down menu is displayed.

A pull-down menu is shown in Figure 2.1. When the menu system is active, the bottom line of the screen displays a brief description of the currently highlighted menu command. In Figure 2.1, for example, the Format Paragraph command is highlighted. The bottom of the screen tells you that this command "Changes the appearance and line numbering of the selected paragraphs."

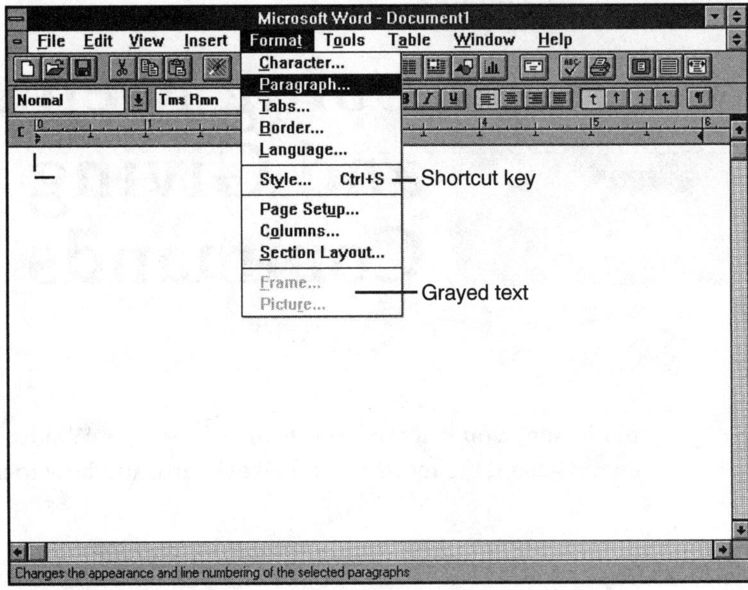

Figure 2.1 Word for Windows menus.

Selecting Menu Commands

You can select menu commands using the mouse, the keyboard, or a combination of the two.

To select a command from the main menu and display its pull-down menu:

- With the mouse, click on the desired command.
- With the keyboard, press **Alt** or **F10** to activate the main menu. Then press the letter corresponding to the desired command (the underlined letter), or move the menu pointer to the desired command using → or ← and press **Enter**.

To select a command from a pull-down menu:

- With the mouse, click on the desired command.
- With the keyboard, press the letter corresponding to the desired command (the underlined letter), or move the menu pointer to the desired command using ↑ or ↓ and press **Enter**.

When entering menu commands, you can cancel your most recent choice by pressing **Esc**. To cancel an entire command sequence, click anywhere outside the menu box.

Oops! If you enter the wrong command, cancel it by pressing **Esc** one or more times.

For the remainder of these lessons, menu command sequences will be condensed. For example, the instruction "select File New" means to select File from the main menu and then select New from the File pull-down menu. Whether you make the selection by manipulating the mouse or typing a key combination is up to you.

The Toolbar

The Toolbar contains buttons that you select with the mouse to perform frequently needed editing tasks. For example, the far left button represents the File New command, and the button next to it represents the File Open command. Clicking on a Toolbar button is quicker and more convenient than entering the entire command sequence.

In this lesson, you learned about Word for Windows menus and the Toolbar. In the next lesson, you'll learn how to use the Word for Windows help system.

3 The Help System

In this lesson, you'll learn how to use the Word for Windows on-line help system.

The Help Command

One way to access the help system is via the Help command on the main menu. As you can see in Figure 3.1, the Help pull-down menu has five commands.

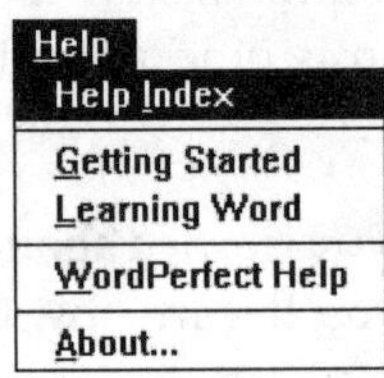

Figure 3.1 The Help menu.

- Help Index calls up the main help system index.
- Getting Started lists the lessons in the *Getting Started with Word* tutorial.
- Learning Word lists the lessons in the *Learning Word* tutorial.
- WordPerfect Help displays help for users of the WordPerfect word processing program.
- About... lists information about the Word for Windows program, such as the program version number and memory availability.

The major Help commands are explained below. Please refer to your program documentation if you would like detailed information on the Word for Windows tutorials and the WordPerfect Help command.

The Help Index

The Help Index is "command central" for the help system. Using the index, you can easily locate help information on any topic. To display the opening page of the index, select **Help Index** or press **F1** while working in your document (as opposed to while you're using the menus or a dialog box). The Help window is initially displayed as a smaller window overlapping part of your document screen, as shown in Figure 3.2.

Controlling the Help Window

Before learning how to use the index, you should know how to control the size and position of the Help window itself. The following material actually applies to all windows in Word for Windows and in Microsoft Windows as well. When a window is active, its title bar has a dark background. You can control the active window as follows:

If you are using the mouse:

- If you want the window to occupy the full screen, click on the *maximize button* (located at the far right end of the title bar, as shown in Figure 3.2). Once a window is maximized, this button changes to the *restore button,* with upward- and downward-pointing arrows, instead of just one upward-pointing arrow. Click on the restore button to return a maximized window to its original size.
- To move the window to a different screen location, position the cursor on the title bar and drag it to the desired location.
- To change the size or shape of the window, position the cursor on the window border so that the mouse pointer changes into a double-headed arrow. Drag the window outline to the desired size and shape, and then release the button.
- To close the Help window and return to your document, click anywhere outside the Help window. If the Help window is maximized, double-click on the control menu box to the immediate left of the title bar, as shown in Figure 3.2.

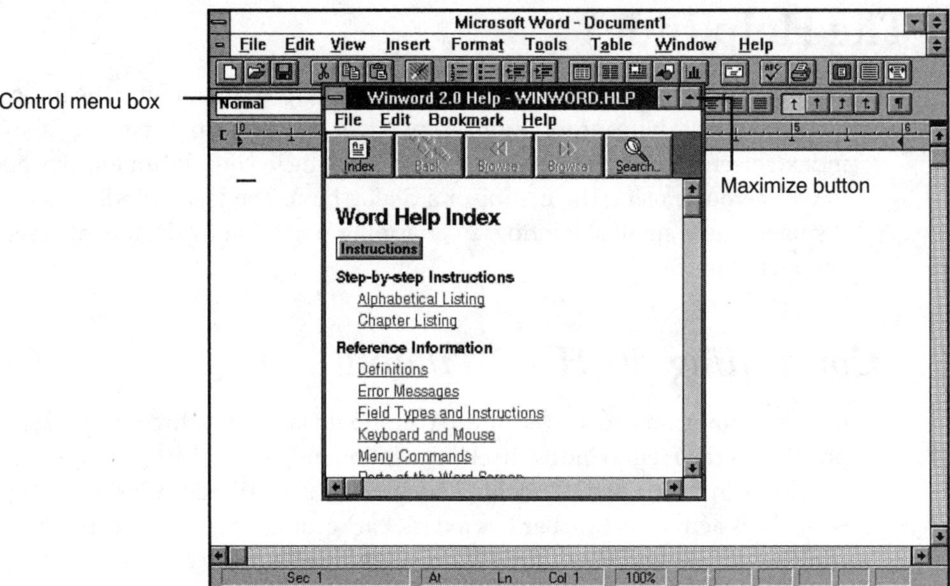

Figure 3.2 The Help window displaying the Help Index.

If you are using the keyboard:

Window control with the keyboard is accomplished using the Window Control menu, which is shown in Figure 3.3. Press **Alt+space bar** to display this menu.

See More! Maximize a window to view as much information as possible.

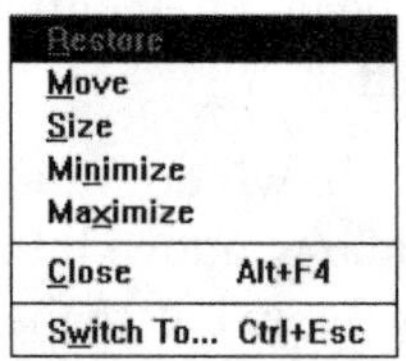

Figure 3.3 The Window Control menu.

- To maximize the window, select **Maximize** from the Window Control menu. To restore a maximized window, select **Restore**.
- To move the window, select **Move**, use the arrow keys to move the window outline to the desired position, and press **Enter**.
- To resize the window, select **Size**, use the arrow keys to change the window outline to the desired size or shape, and press **Enter**.
- To close the Help window and return to your document, press **Alt+F4**.

Using the Index

The Help window has five buttons at the top. Use these buttons to move around the help system. To select a button, click on it with the mouse or press **Alt+*n***, where *n* is the underlined letter in the button name. Remember that if a button is grayed, the corresponding option is not currently available.

- Index displays the Help Index.
- Back displays the last help topic you were viewing.
- Browse Forward and Browse Backward move you forward and backward between related help topics.
- Search displays a screen from which you can search for the topic of interest.

Where Is It? Use the Help Index to find the topic of interest.

Within the help system certain terms and phrases are underlined and displayed in a different color. A solid underline denotes a cross-reference. Selecting a cross-reference takes you directly to help information on that topic. A dotted underline denotes a term or phrase for which a definition is available. When you position the mouse on an underlined term, the mouse pointer changes to a pointing hand. You can use the keyboard to move a highlight bar between underlined terms by pressing **Tab** or **Shift+Tab**.

- To jump to a cross-reference, click on the term or highlight it and press **Enter**.
- To display a definition, point at it and press the left mouse button, or highlight it and press **Enter**. The definition will be displayed in a pop-up box while you hold down the mouse button or Enter key.

Context-Sensitive Help

The Word for Windows help system is *context sensitive*. This means that if you are selecting a menu command or entering information in a dialog box, pressing **F1** will automatically display help information on your current task. Once the Help window is displayed, you can use all of its features to access additional information. When you close the Help window, you are returned to your task right where you left off.

In this lesson, you learned how to use the Word for Windows help system. In the next lesson, you'll learn how to enter text into a document and move around the screen.

Creating a New Document

In this lesson, you'll learn how to create a new document.

Entering Text

When you start Word for Windows, you see a blank work area that contains only two items:

- The blinking vertical line marks the insertion point, the location where text you type will be inserted into the document and where certain editing actions will occur.
- The horizontal line is the end-of-document marker.

Since your new document is empty, these two markers are at the same location. To enter text, simply type it at the keyboard. As you type, the text is inserted and the insertion point moves to the right. If the line reaches the right edge of the screen, Word for Windows automatically moves to the start of the next line—this is called *wrapping*. Press **Enter** only when you want to start a new paragraph. As you enter more lines than will fit on the screen, Word for Windows automatically scrolls upward to keep the insertion point in view.

Leave It to Word Wrap Press **Enter** only when you want to start a new paragraph.

Moving Around the Screen

As you work on a document, you will often have to move the insertion point so that you can view or work on other regions of text.

To move the insertion point with the mouse:

- Up or down one line: Click on the up or down arrow on the vertical scroll bar.
- Up or down one screen: Click on the vertical scroll bar between the box and the up or down arrow.
- Up or down any amount: Drag the scroll bar box up or down.
- To any visible location: Click on the location.

To move the insertion point with the keyboard:

- Left or right one character: Press ← or →.
- Up or down one line: Press ↑ or ↓.
- Left or right one word: Press **Ctrl+** ← or **Ctrl +** →.
- Up or down one paragraph: Press **Ctrl+** ↑ or **Ctrl +** ↓.
- Start or end of a line: Press **Home** or **End**.
- Up or down one screen: Press **PgUp** or **PgDn**.
- Top or bottom of current screen: Press **Ctrl+PgUp** or **Ctrl+PgDn**.
- Start or end of the document: Press **Ctrl+Home** or **Ctrl+End**.

Selecting Text

Many Word for Windows operations require that you first select the text to be modified. For example, to change a word to italics, you must select the word first and then specify italics. Selected text is displayed on the screen in reverse video, as shown in Figure 4.1, which has the phrase "Dear Mr. Johnson" selected.

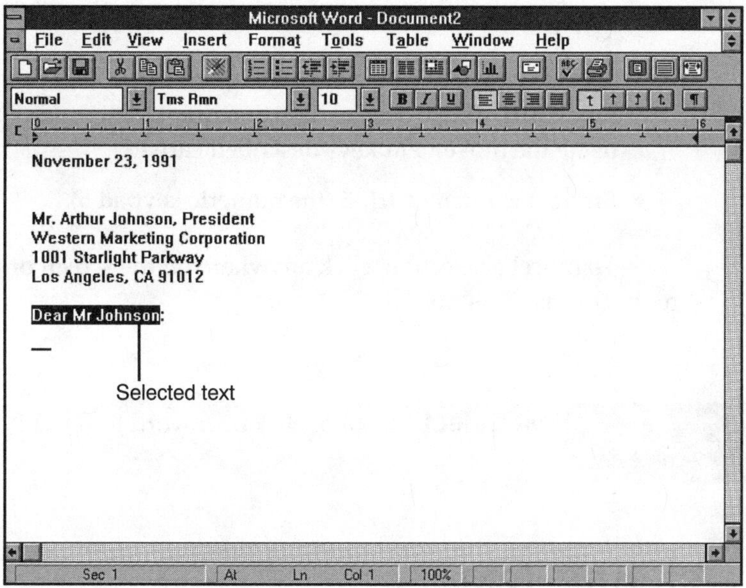

Figure 4.1 Selected text is displayed in reverse video.

You can select text with either the mouse or the keyboard. With the mouse, you can use the *selection bar,* an unmarked column in the left document margin. When the mouse pointer moves from the document to the selection bar, it changes from an I-beam to an arrow.

To select text with the mouse:

- Any amount: Point at the start of the text, and drag the highlight over the text.
- One word: Double-click anywhere on the word.
- One sentence: Press and hold **Ctrl** and click anywhere in the sentence.
- One line: Click on the selection bar next to the line.
- Multiple lines: Drag the selection bar next to the lines.
- One paragraph: Double-click on the selection bar next to the paragraph.
- Entire document: Press and hold **Ctrl** and click anywhere in the selection bar.

To select text with the keyboard:

- Any amount: Move the insertion point to the start of the text, press and hold **Shift**, and move the insertion point to the end of the desired text using the movement keys described earlier.
- Entire document: **Ctrl+5** (the numeric keypad 5).

To cancel a selection, click anywhere on the screen or use the keyboard to move the insertion point.

Fast Select Double-click on a word to select it.

Deleting Text

You can delete single characters or larger blocks of text.

- To delete the character to the right of the insertion point, press **Del**.
- To delete the character to the left of the insertion point, press **Backspace**.
- To delete a block of text, select the text and then press **Del** or **Backspace**.

If you make a mistake, you can recover deleted text with the **Edit Undo** command. Depending on how you deleted the text, this command appears on the Edit menu as either Undo Typing or Undo Edit Clear. In either case, the effect is the same: the deleted characters are replaced in their original position. You must select this command immediately after deleting and before performing any other action. You can also click on the **Undo** button on the Toolbar or press the shortcut key **Ctrl+Z**.

In this lesson, you learned how to enter, select, and delete text. In the next lesson, you'll learn how to save your document on disk.

Saving Documents

In this lesson, you'll learn how to name your document, save it to disk, and enter summary information.

Saving a Document for the First Time

When you create a new document in Word for Windows, it is stored temporarily in your computer's memory under the default name Document*n*, where *n* is a number that increases by 1 for each new unnamed document. The document is only saved until you quit the program or the power is turned off. To save a document permanently so you can retrieve it later, you must save it to disk. This is done with the **File Save** command, or by selecting the **File Save** button on the Toolbar.

When you save a document for the first time, you must assign it another name. When you select File Save for an unnamed document (or File Save As for any document), Word for Windows displays the Save As dialog box, as shown in Figure 5.1.

In the File Name text box, enter the name you want to assign to the document file. The name can be 1 to 8 characters long, and should be descriptive of the document contents. Then select **OK**. Word for Windows automatically adds the DOC extension when the file is saved.

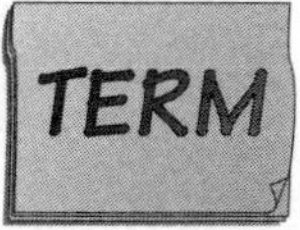

What's an Extension? The 1- to 3-letter part of a file name to the right of the period is the extension.

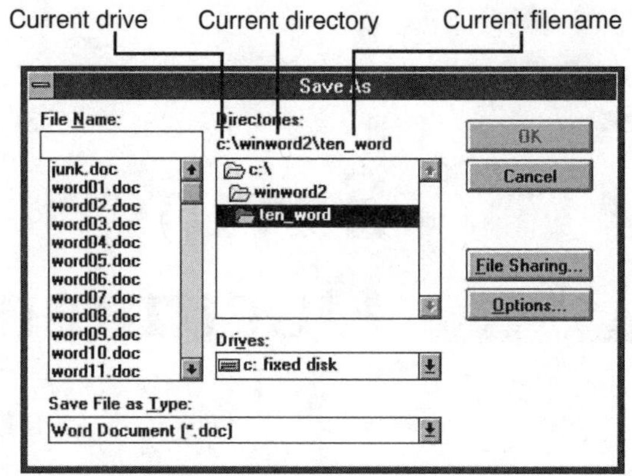

Figure 5.1 The Save As dialog box.

Next, Word for Windows displays the Summary Info dialog box, which is shown in Figure 5.2. This figure shows typical summary information that you might want to use. You can ignore this dialog box, or you can enter information here that will later be useful in keeping track of your documents.

- Title: Enter the title of the document. This is not the same as the document's file name.
- Subject: Enter a phrase describing the subject of the document.
- Author: Word automatically fills this field with the user name you entered when installing the program. You can change it if you like.
- Keywords: Enter one or more keywords related to the document contents.
- Comments: Enter any comments.
- Statistics: Click on the **Statistics** button to display information about the document, such as number of words, last date edited, and so on.

Viewing Statistics At any time, select **File Summary Info Statistics** to view a document's statistics.

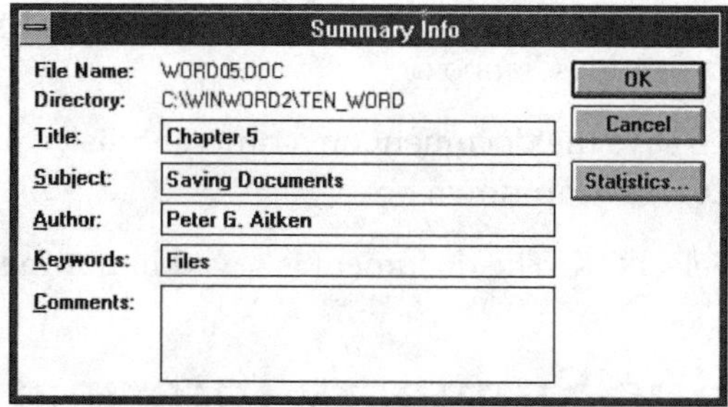

Figure 5.2 The Summary Info dialog box.

After entering any desired summary information, click on **OK**. Word for Windows saves the file, along with the summary information you entered, in a file with the name you specified. You are then returned to the document screen, with the newly assigned file name displayed in the title bar.

Saving a Named Document

As you work on a document, you should save it now and then to minimize possible data loss in the event of a power failure or other system problem. Once you have assigned a name to a document, the File Save command saves the current document version under its assigned name; no dialog boxes are displayed.

Don't Forget! Save your document regularly as you work on it.

Changing a Document Name

You may wish to save a named document under a new name. For example, you might want to keep the old version under the original name and the revised version under a new name. To change a document name, select **File Save As**. The File Save As dialog box is displayed with the current document name in the File Name text box.

1. Change the file name to the desired new name.

2. To save the document in a different directory, select the directory in the Directories list box.
3. To save the document on a different disk drive, select the drive from the Drives drop-down box.
4. Select **OK**. The document is saved under the new name.

Changing Summary Information

You can change the summary information associated with a document at any time. Select **File Summary Info**, and the Summary Info dialog box will be displayed. Make the desired changes; then select **OK**. The new information will be registered with the file the next time you save the file.

In this lesson, you learned how to save a document, change a document name, and enter document summary information. In the next lesson, you'll learn how to retrieve a document from disk.

6

Retrieving Documents

In this lesson, you'll learn how to retrieve a document from disk into Word for Windows, how to search for a specific file, and how to import documents that were created with other programs.

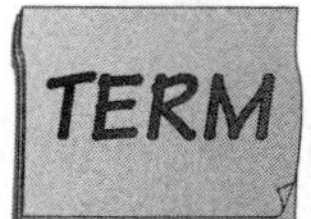

Retrieving a Document This means to reopen a document from your disk into Word for Windows so you can work on it.

Retrieving a Word for Windows Document

You can retrieve any document created with Word for Windows for further editing, printing, and so on. To do so, select **File Open** or click on the **File Open** button on the Toolbar. The File Open dialog box will be displayed, as shown in Figure 6.1.

Opening a Document Use **File Open** to work on a document that you saved earlier.

In the File Name text box, the current file template is listed. By default this is *.doc, meaning that the dialog box will list all files with the DOC extension (the default extension for Word for Windows files). The File Name list box lists all files in the current directory that match that description.

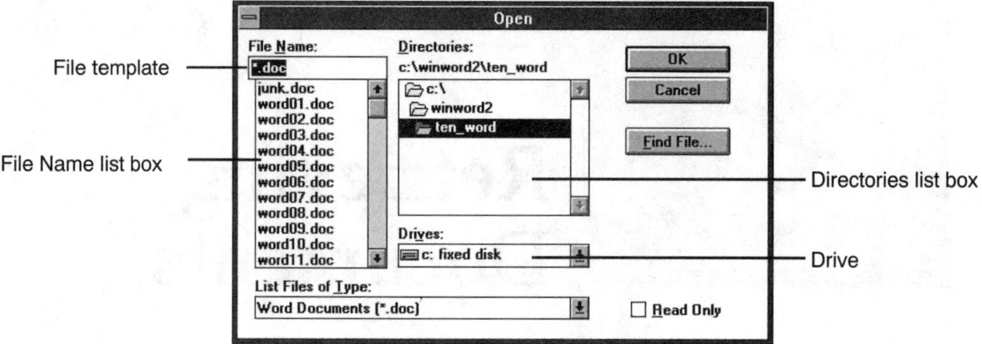

Figure 6.1 The File Open dialog box.

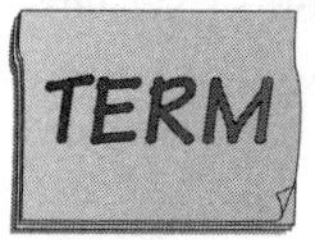

File Template A *file template* tells Word for Windows the types of file names to list.

- To retrieve a file, type its name in the File Name text box, and press **Enter**. You can also double-click on its name in the File Name list box. The file will be read from disk and displayed for editing.
- To retrieve a file from a different directory, select the desired directory from the Directories list box.
- To retrieve a file from a different disk, select the desired disk from the Drives drop-down box.
- To open a file in "read-only" mode, select the Read Only option before retrieving the file. If you modify a read-only file, you can save it only under a new name using the **File Save As** command—you cannot save modifications under the existing name.

Finding a File

If you cannot remember the name of the file you want to retrieve, use the **Find File** button in the File Open dialog box to find it by contents and/or summary information. When you select **Find File**, Word for Windows searches the disk/directory specified in the File Open dialog box for files that match the current file template. Then the dialog box shown in Figure 6.2 is displayed.

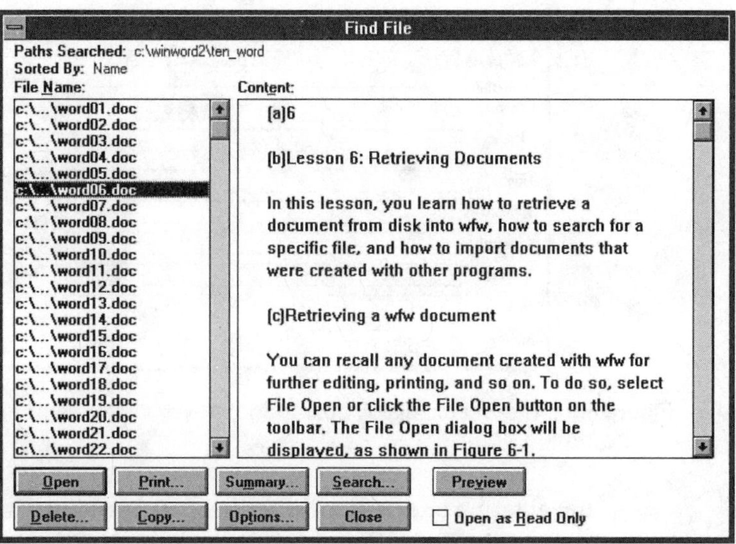

Figure 6.2 The Find File dialog box.

The items in this dialog box are as follows:

- The File Name list box lists all the files found. You can scroll through this list by using the keyboard or the mouse.
- The Contents box displays the contents of the highlighted file. When the Contents box is current, you can scroll using the keyboard or mouse to view more of the file's contents.
- Select **Open** to open the highlighted file.
- Select **Summary** to view the summary information for the highlighted file.

To locate one or more files based on certain criteria, select **Search**. The Search dialog box will be displayed, as shown in Figure 6.3.

In the fields in the Search dialog box, enter the criteria you want to find. For example, to find all files that include Sales in their titles, enter **Sales** in the Title text box. If you enter more than one criterion, Word for Windows will find files that match all of them.

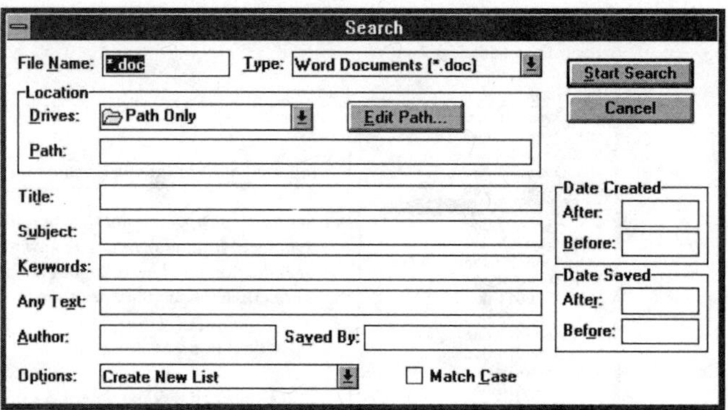

Figure 6.3 The Search dialog box.

After entering one or more criteria, select **Start Search**. Word for Windows again displays the Find File dialog box, but now the File Name list box lists only those files that meet the criteria you entered in the Search dialog box. You can use the File Find dialog box to view the file contents and open the desired file. To cancel the search and again list all files, you must return to the Search dialog box and erase the criteria you entered.

Memory Helper Use the Find File window to locate a file whose name you've forgotten.

Importing Documents

You can import documents that were created with other applications, converting them to Word for Windows format. For example, you could import a document that was created with WordPerfect 5.1, retaining all of its special formatting and fonts. Word for Windows can import from a wide variety of programs. To import a file, follow these steps:

1. Select **File Open** or click on the **File Open** button on the Toolbar. The File Open dialog box will be displayed.
2. Open the **List Files of Type** drop-down box. This list will include all of the conversion types that you specified during installation. Select the type of file you want to import.

3. The File Name list box will list all files of that type (with the indicated extension). Select the file to import.
4. Select **OK**. Word for Windows asks you to confirm the type of file being imported.
5. Select the type and then select **OK**. The file is imported and converted to Word for Windows format.

In this lesson, you learned how to retrieve Word documents. In the next lesson, you will learn how to change and control the screen display.

7

Controlling the Screen Display

In this lesson, you'll learn how to control the Word for Windows screen display to suit your working style.

Document Display Modes

Word for Windows offers four different modes in which you can display your document.

Normal Mode

Most often you'll probably want to work in Normal mode. This is Word for Window's, default display. Figure 7.1 shows a document in Normal mode. As you can see, all special formatting is visible on-screen. Different font sizes, italics, boldface, and other enhancements display on the screen very much as they will appear on the printed page. Certain aspects of the page layout, however, are simplified to speed editing. For example, headers and footers are not displayed. Normal mode is fine for most editing tasks.

Select **View Normal** to switch to Normal view. In the View menu, the currently selected mode has a dot displayed next to it.

Outline Mode

Use Outline mode to create outlines and to examine the structure of a document. Figure 7.2 shows the sample document in Outline mode. Here you can choose to view only your document headings, hiding all subordinate text. Document headings, along with subordinate text, can be quickly promoted, demoted, or moved to a new location. In order for this to be of much use, you need to assign heading styles to the document headings, a technique you'll learn more about in Lesson 15.

Select **View Outline** to switch to Outline view.

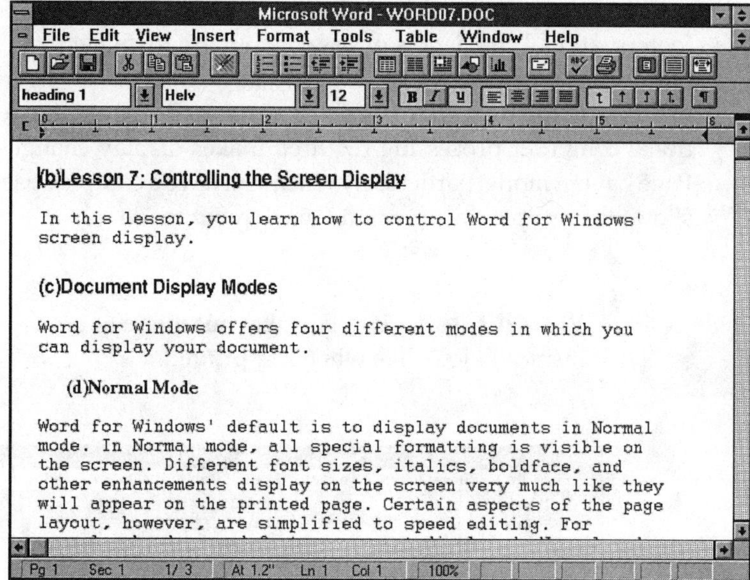

Figure 7.1 A sample document displayed in Normal mode.

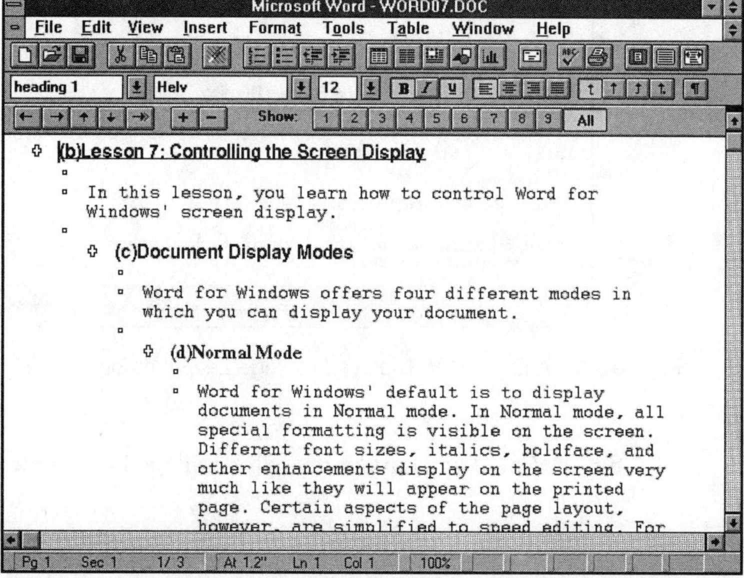

Figure 7.2 A document displayed in Outline mode.

Page Layout Mode

Page Layout mode displays your document exactly as it will be printed. Headers, footers, and all the details of page layout are displayed on the screen. You can perform editing in Page Layout mode, and in fact this mode is ideal when you are fine-tuning the details of page composition. Be aware, however, that the additional computer processing required makes display changes relatively slow in Page Layout mode, particularly when you have a complex page layout. Figure 7.3 shows the sample document in Page Layout mode.

View It First! Use Page Layout mode to see what your document will look like when it is printed.

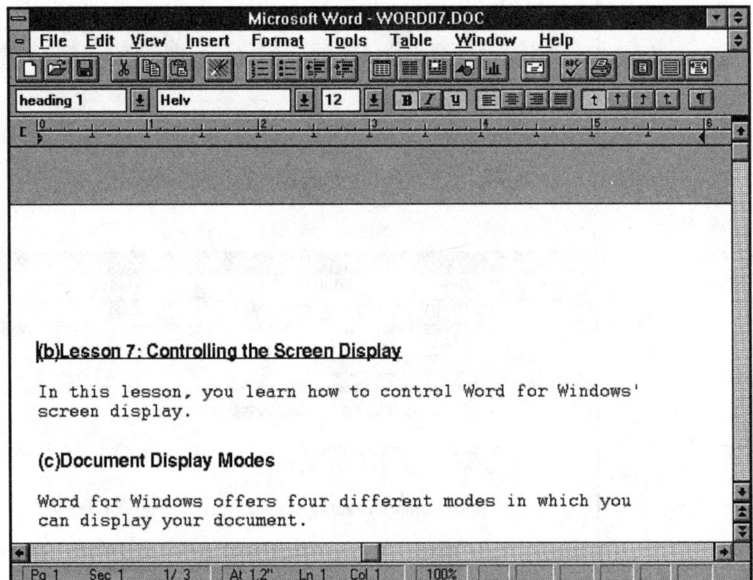

Figure 7.3 A document displayed in Page Layout mode.

Select **View Page Layout** to switch to Page Layout view.

Draft Mode

Draft mode is a display option that can be applied in both Normal and Outline views. As Figure 7.4 illustrates, a single generic font is used for screen display, and special formatting such as italics and boldface is indicated by underlining. Pictures are displayed as empty frames. Draft mode provides the fastest editing and screen display, and is ideal when you are concentrating on the contents of your document rather than its appearance.

To toggle Draft mode on or off, select **View Draft**. When Draft mode is active, a check mark is displayed next to the Draft command on the View menu.

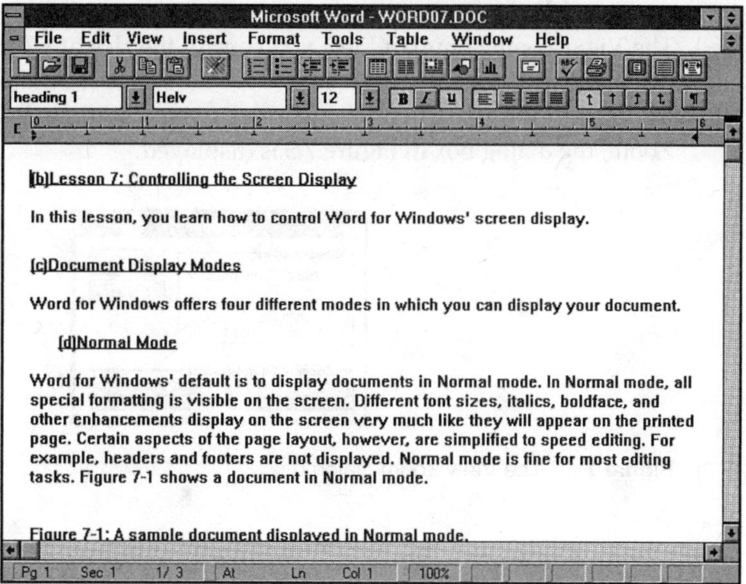

Figure 7.4 A document displayed in Draft mode.

Ruler, Ribbon, and Toolbar Display

Word for Windows' default is to display the ruler, ribbon, and Toolbar at the top of the editing screen. At times, however, you may want to hide one or more of these items to give yourself a larger work area and a less cluttered screen. Of course, you will not have access to the editing features of the item(s) you have hidden.

To control the screen display of the ruler, ribbon, and Toolbar, select **View** to display the View menu. Then select **Toolbar**, **Ribbon**, or **Ruler** to toggle the display of that item between on and off. On the View menu, items whose display is currently on are marked by a check mark.

The Whole Picture Hide the ribbon, ruler, and Toolbar when you need maximum text displayed.

Zooming the Screen

The View Zoom command lets you control the size at which your document is displayed on the screen. You can enlarge the size to facilitate reading small fonts, or decrease the size to view an entire page at one time. When you select View Zoom, the dialog box in Figure 7.5 is displayed.

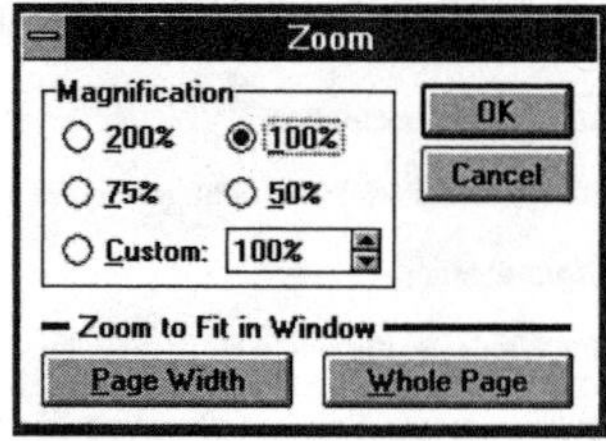

Figure 7.5 The View Zoom dialog box.

In this dialog box, you have the following options:

- Under Magnification, select the desired page magnification. 200% is twice normal size, 50% is half normal size, and so on. You can enter a custom magnification in the range 25–200%.
- Select **Page Width** to have Word for Windows automatically scale the display to fit the entire page width on the screen.
- Select **Whole Page** to have Word for Windows automatically scale the display to fit the entire page on the screen.

In this lesson, you learned how to control the Word for Windows screen display. In the next lesson, you'll learn about templates.

Using Templates

In this lesson, you'll learn how to use and create templates.

What Is a Template?

You may not be aware of it, but every Word for Windows document is based on a *template*. A template is a model, or pattern, that a document is based on. A template can contain boilerplate text, graphics, and formatting. It can also contain styles, glossary entries, and macros (all of which are covered in later lessons). Any document that is based upon a given template automatically contains all the elements of the template.

Recycle It! Word for Windows contains some templates for your use or modification, and you can create your own from scratch. Speed up your work by creating a specialized template for document types that you use frequently.

For example, let's say you write a lot of business letters. You could create a business letter template that contains your company's name and address, logo, and a closing salutation. Every time you need to write a business letter, you create a new document based on the template. Such a template is shown in Figure 8.1.

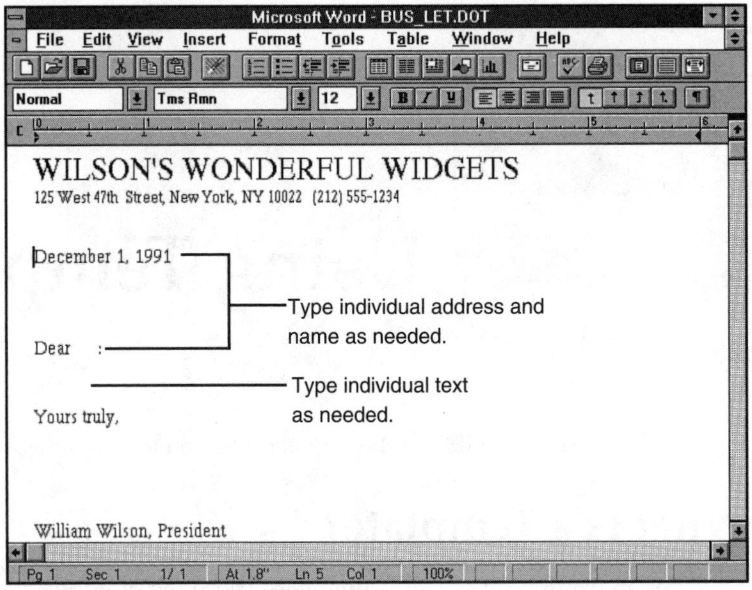

Figure 8.1 A business letter template.

By default, Word for Windows bases new documents on the NORMAL template, which is supplied with your Word for Windows package. This is a bare-bones template that contains only a few basic styles. Other Word templates are suitable for various business and personal uses. Templates are stored with a DOT extension in the Word directory.

Using a Template

When you create a new document, you must specify the template to base it on. To start a new document:

1. Select **File New**. The File New dialog box is displayed (Figure 8.2).
2. Under Use Template, select the name of the template you want to use.
3. Select **OK**. The new document is created based on the selected template.

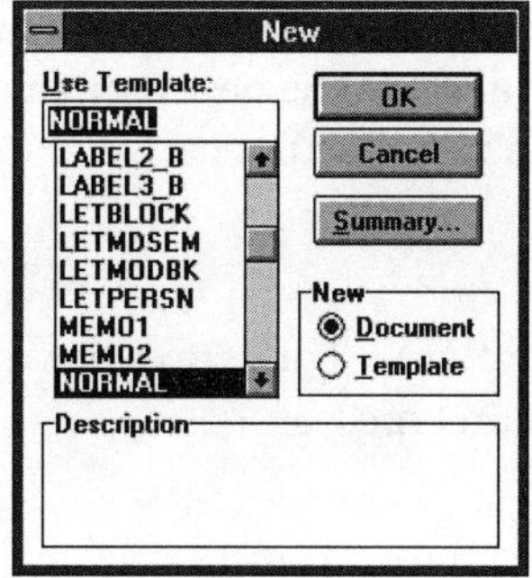

Figure 8.2 The File New dialog box lists available templates.

Template Confusion? If you're not sure which template to use, select NORMAL.

Once the document is created you can modify any aspect of it, including portions that originated in the template.

Creating a New Template

You can create new templates to suit your specific word processing needs. To create a new template:

1. Select **File New**. The File New dialog box is displayed.
2. Under New, select the **Template** option.
3. Under Use Template, be sure that **NORMAL** is selected.
4. Select **OK**. A blank document editing screen appears with a default name, such as TEMPLATE1.
5. Enter the boilerplate text and other items that you want to be part of the template.
6. Select **File Save As**. The File Save As dialog box is displayed.
7. In the File Name text box, enter a name of 1 to 8 characters for the template.

8. Select **OK**. The template is saved under the specified name, with the DOT extension added. The new template is now available for use each time you start a new document.

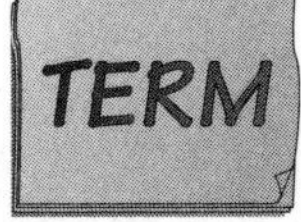

Boilerplate This is text that appears the same in all documents of a certain type.

Modifying an Existing Template

You can retrieve any existing template from disk and modify it. You can then save it under the original name or a new name. To modify a template:

1. Select **File Open**. The File Open dialog box is displayed.
2. Open the List Files of Type drop-down box and select **Document Templates**.
3. Under File Name, select the template that you want to modify.
4. Make the desired modifications and additions to the template.
5. To save the modified template under its original name, select **File Save**.
6. To save the modified template under a new name, select **File Save As** and enter a new template name.

If you modify the text in a template, those changes will not be reflected in documents based on the template before it was changed.

In this lesson, you learned about Word for Windows templates. In the next lesson, you'll learn how to move and copy text.

9 Moving and Copying Text

In this lesson, you'll learn how to move and copy text in your document.

Selecting Text

In Lesson 4, you learned how to select a block of text in order to delete it. You use the same procedure to select text you want to move or copy. Remember, selected text is displayed on the screen in reverse video.

Copying Text

When you copy text, you place a duplicate of the selected text in a new location. After you copy, the text exists in both the original and new locations. There are several methods available for copying text.

Save Your Fingers Copying text can save you typing. For example, copy a paragraph to a new location when you need to modify it slightly.

Using the Clipboard to Copy

The clipboard is a temporary storage location offered in Windows programs. You can copy text from one location in your document to the clipboard, and then paste it from the clipboard to the new location in your document.

1. Select the text to be copied. The selected text is highlighted, as shown in Figure 9.1.

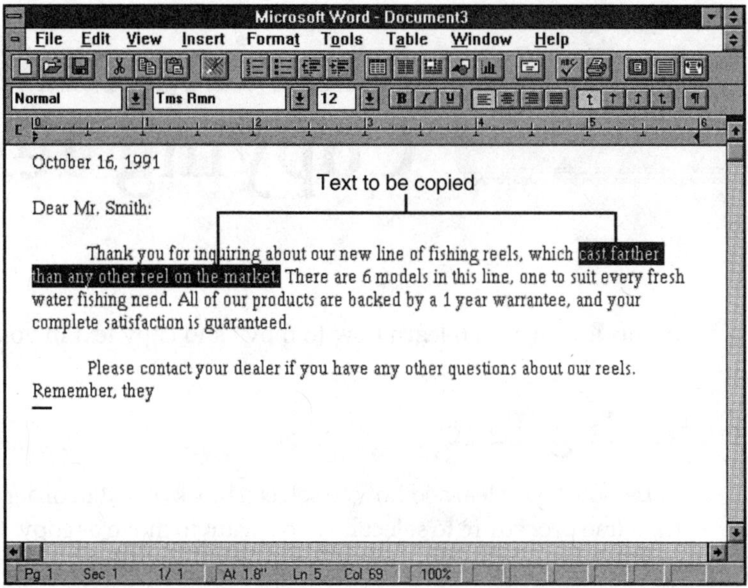

Figure 9.1 Highlighted text to be copied.

2. Select **Edit Copy**. You can also click on the **Copy** button on the Toolbar, or press **Ctrl+C**.
3. Move the insertion point to the new location for the text.
4. Select **Edit Paste**. You can also select the **Paste** button on the Toolbar or press **Ctrl+V**. The text is inserted at the new location, as shown in Figure 9.2.

Again and Again You can paste the same text from the clipboard more than once. The text remains there, throughout your work session, until it is replaced with new text.

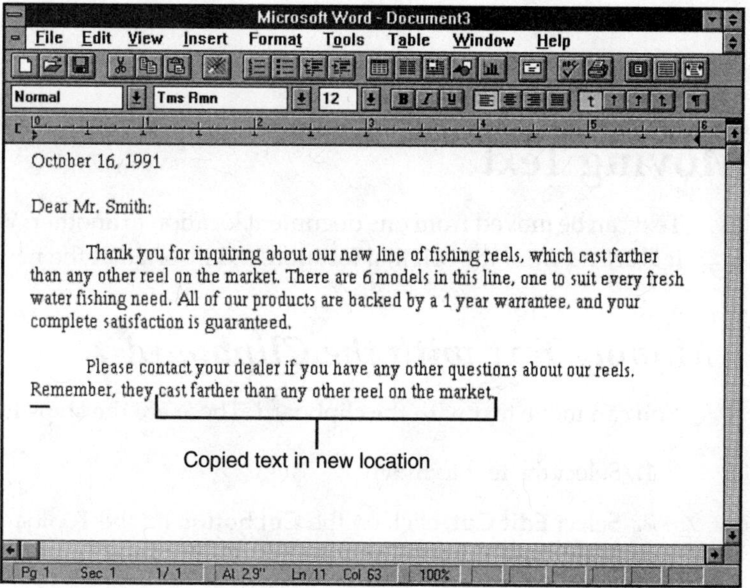

Figure 9.2 The copied text in the new location.

Using the Mouse to Copy

A shortcut for copying is available if you're using the mouse:

1. Select the text to copy.
2. Using the mouse, point at the insertion point for the text.
3. Press **Ctrl+Shift** and click the right mouse button.

Copying Text That You Just Typed

You can quickly insert a copy of text that you just typed at a different document location:

1. At one document location, type the text to be copied.

2. Move the insertion point to the second location for the text.
3. Select **Edit Repeat Typing**, or press **F4**.

Moving Text

Text can be moved from one document location to another. When you move text, it is *deleted* from the original location and inserted at the new location.

Moving Text with the Clipboard

You can move text with the clipboard. These are the steps to follow:

1. Select the text to move.
2. Select **Edit Cut**, click on the **Cut** button on the Toolbar, or press **Ctrl+X**. The selected text is deleted from the document and placed on the clipboard.
3. Move the insertion point to the new location.
4. Select **Edit Paste**, click on the **Paste** button on the Toolbar, or press **Ctrl+V**. The text is inserted into the document.

Moving Text with the Mouse

You can drag selected text to a new location using the mouse. This technique is particularly convenient for small blocks of text.

1. Select the text to be moved. (Figure 9.3 gives an example.)
2. Point at the selected text with the mouse, and press and hold the left mouse button.
3. Drag to the new location. As you drag, a dotted vertical line indicates where the text will be inserted.
4. Position the dotted line at the desired insertion point, and release the mouse button. The text is moved. (Figure 9.4 shows the new position of the selected text in Figure 9.3.)

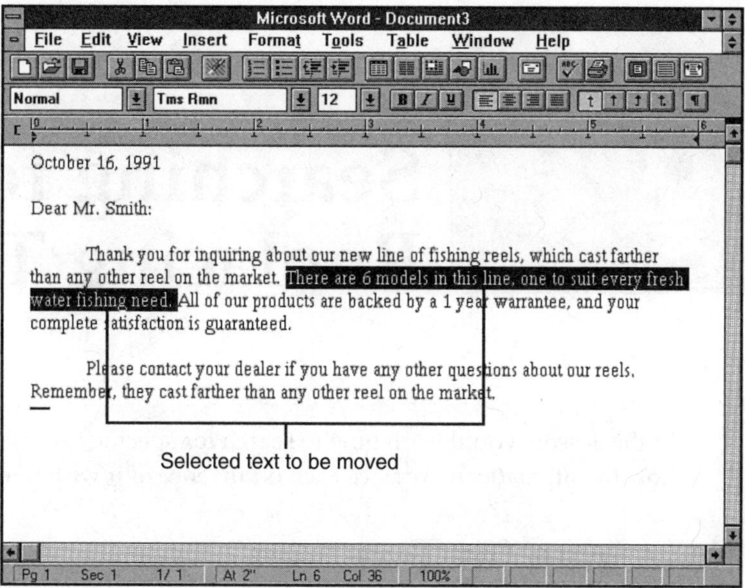

Figure 9.3 To move text, first highlight it.

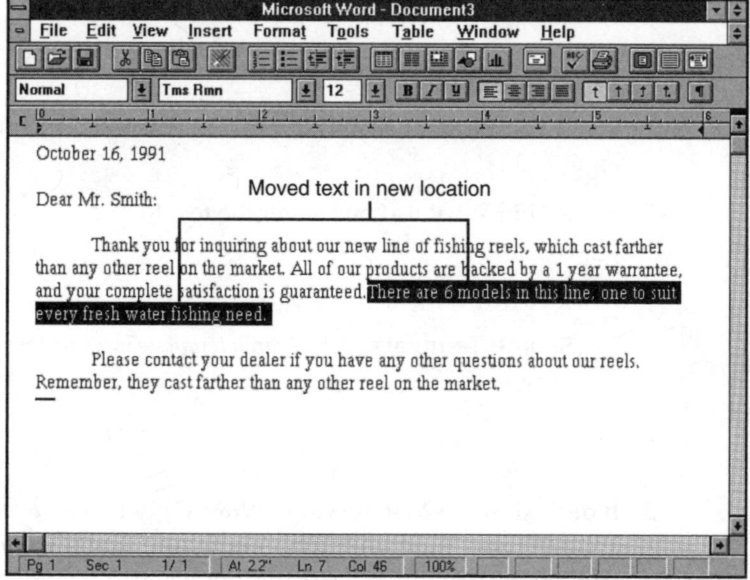

Figure 9.4 Cut the text and paste it in the new location, or drag it to the new location with the mouse.

In this lesson, you learned how to move and copy text. In the next lesson, you'll learn how to search and replace text in your document.

Searching for and Replacing Text

In this lesson, you'll learn how to search for specific text in your document, and how to automatically replace each occurrence of it with new text.

Searching for Text

You can have Word for Windows search through your document to find occurrences of specific text. The default is to search the entire document. If there is text selected, the search will be limited to the selection.

To search for text, follow these steps:

1. Select **Edit Find**. The Edit Find dialog box will be displayed, as shown in Figure 10.1.
2. In the Find What text box, enter the text to find. This is the search template.

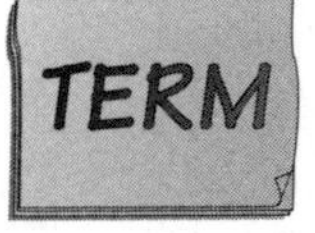

Search Template The *search template* is a model for the text you want to find.

3. If desired, select **Match Whole Word Only** to match whole words only. With this option off, a search template of "light" would match "light," "lightning," and so on. With this option on, it would match only "light."

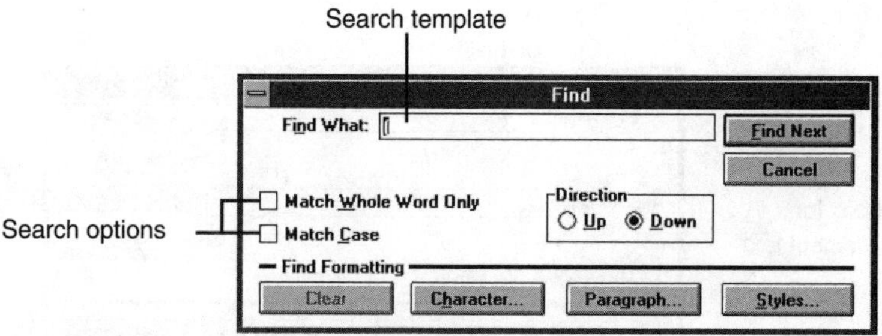

Figure 10.1 The Edit Find dialog box.

4. If desired, select **Match Case** to require an exact match for upper- and lowercase letters. If this option is not selected, Word searches for text of either case.
5. Under Direction, select **Down** to have Word for Windows search from the insertion point to the end of the document, or from the beginning of the selected text to the end. Select **Up** for the opposite direction of search.
6. Select **Find Next**. Word for Windows looks through the document for text that matches the search template. If it finds matching text, it highlights it in the text and stops, with the Edit Find dialog box still displayed.

   You now can do one of two things:

- Select **Find Next** to continue the search for another instance of the template.
- Press **Esc** to close the dialog box and return to the document. The found text remains selected.

If, after searching only part of the document, Word for Windows reaches the start of the document (for an upward search) or the end of the document (for a downward search), you are given the option of continuing the search from the other end of the document. Once the entire document has been searched, a message to that effect is displayed.

Finding and Replacing Text

The Edit Replace command is used to search for instances of text and replace them with new text. The Edit Replace dialog box is shown in Figure 10.2.

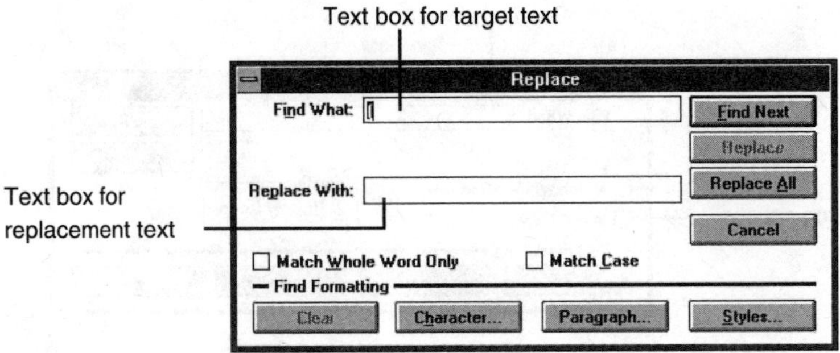

Figure 10.2 The Edit Replace dialog box.

Make entries in this dialog box as follows:

1. In the Find What text box, enter the target text that is to be replaced.
2. In the Replace With text box, enter the replacement text.
3. If desired, select the **Match Whole Words Only** and **Match Case** options, as explained earlier in this lesson.
4. Select **Replace All** to have Word for Windows go through the entire document, replacing all instances of the target text with the replacement text. You can also select **Find Next** to highlight the first instance of the target text.

Deleting Text To delete the target text, leave the Replace With box blank.

You now have three options:

- Select **Replace** to replace the highlighted text with the replacement text and then find the next instance of the target text.
- Select **Find Next** to leave the highlighted text unchanged and then find the next instance of the target text.
- Select **Replace All** to find and replace all remaining instances of the target text.

Saving Time To save typing, use abbreviations for long words and phrases, and then later use Replace to change them to final form.

Recovery! If you make a mistake replacing text, you can recover with the Edit Undo Replace command.

In this lesson, you learned how to search for and optionally replace text. In the next lesson, you'll learn how to add headers and footers to your documents.

Page Numbers, Headers, and Footers

In this lesson, you'll learn how to add page numbers, headers, and footers to your documents.

Adding Page Numbers

Many documents, particularly long ones, benefit from having numbered pages. Word for Windows offers complete flexibility in the placement and format of page numbers. To add page numbers to your document:

1. Select **Insert Page Numbers**. The Page Numbers dialog box is displayed, as shown in Figure 11.1.
2. Under Position, select the desired position on the page—**Top** or **Bottom**.
3. Under Alignment, select **Left**, **Center**, or **Right**.
4. The default number format is Arabic numerals (1, 2, 3). To select a different format (for example, i, ii, iii), click on the **Format** button and select the desired format.
5. Select **OK**.

When you add a page number using the above procedure, Word for Windows makes it part of the document's header or footer. Headers and footers are explained next.

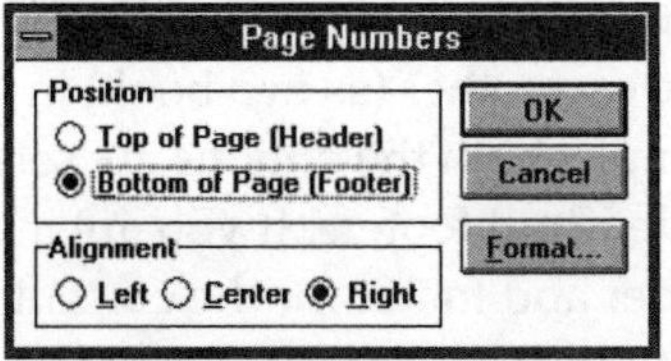

Figure 11.1 The Page Numbers dialog box.

What Are Headers and Footers?

A *header* or *footer* is text that is printed at the top (a header) or bottom (a footer) of every page of a document. A header or footer can be as simple as the page number, or it can contain chapter titles, authors' names, or any other information you desire. Word for Windows offers several header/footer options:

- The same header/footer on every page of the document.
- One header/footer on the first page of the document and a different header/footer on all other pages.
- One header/footer on odd-numbered pages and a different header/footer on even-numbered pages.

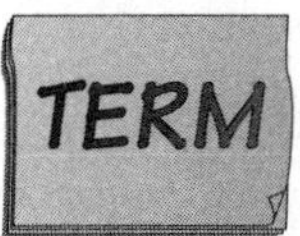

Headers and Footers The *header* is at the top of the page, and the *footer* is at the bottom.

Adding a Header or Footer

To add a header or footer to your document, follow these steps:

1. Select **View Header/Footer**. The Header/Footer dialog box is displayed, as shown in Figure 11.2.

   In this dialog box, the Header/Footer list box lists the headers and footers that are available. This list depends on whether none, one, or both of the Different First Page and Different Odd and Even Pages options are selected in the dialog box. The Different First Page option is useful if you want different header information to appear on page 1 than on all other pages. The Different Odd and Even Pages option is useful if the pages will face each other (as in a book) in your final document. In Figure 11.2, for example, both the options are selected, and therefore the list contains six headers and footers. If you are in Page Layout view, the list contains the header and footer for the current page.

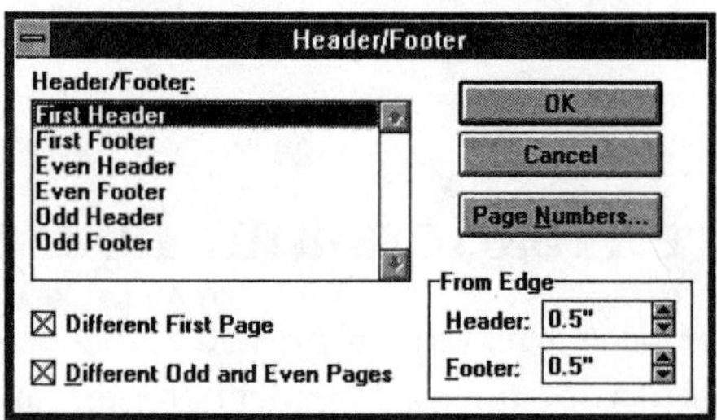

Figure 11.2 The Header/Footer dialog box.

2. Under From Edge, you can specify the distance between the header and the top of the page and between the footer and the bottom of the page. The default values of 0.5 inch are fine for most situations.
3. In the list box, highlight the name of the header or footer that you want to add. Then select **OK**. An editing window is opened at the bottom of the screen, as shown in Figure 11.3.

Different One Use the Different First Page option if you want a header or footer to appear on all pages except the first one.

4. Enter and edit your header/footer text in this window just as you would in the regular document screen.
5. You also may wish to insert any or all of the options shown in the special buttons at the upper left of the header/footer window.
   - The left button inserts the page number in the header/footer.
   - The middle button inserts the current date in the header/ footer.
   - The right button inserts the current time in the header/footer.
6. Once the header/footer is complete, click on the **Close** button. You are returned to your document.

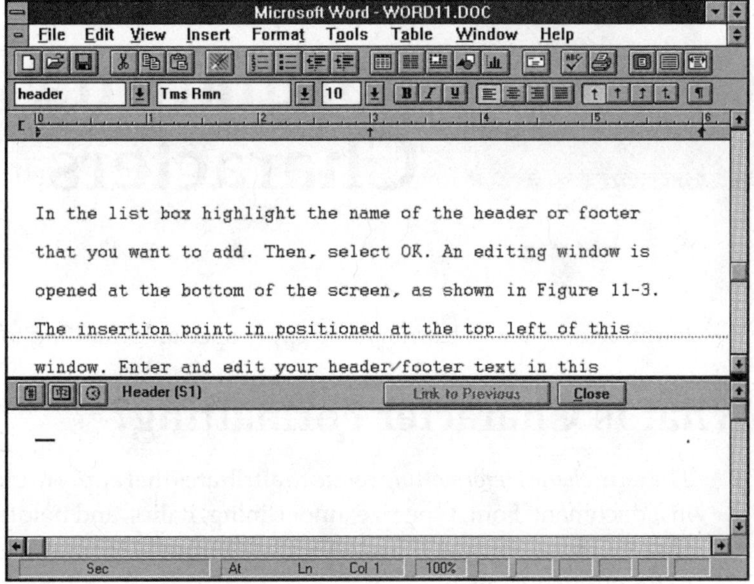

Figure 11.3 The header/footer editing window.

Editing a Header or Footer

To edit an existing header or footer, select **View Header/Footer**. Then in the dialog box, select the header/footer that you want to edit. The editing window opens, displaying the current header/footer text. Make the desired changes and select **Close**.

Deleting Headers and Footers To delete a header or footer, open it for editing and delete all of its text.

In this lesson, you learned how to add page numbers, headers, and footers to a document. The next lesson shows you how to format text.

12 Formatting Characters

In this lesson, you'll learn how to apply special formatting to characters.

What Is Character Formatting?

The term *character formatting* refers to attributes that apply to individual characters in a document. Font, type size, underlining, italics, and boldface are examples of character formatting. A character format can apply to anything from a single letter to the entire document.

Using Fonts

What Is a Font? A *font* is a particular style and size of letters and characters.

The style of a font is denoted by a name, such as Times Roman or Courier. The size of a font is specified in terms of points, with one point equal to 1/72 of an inch. As you enter text in a document, the ribbon displays the font name and point size currently in use. For example, in Figure 12.1, Courier 12 point is the current font.

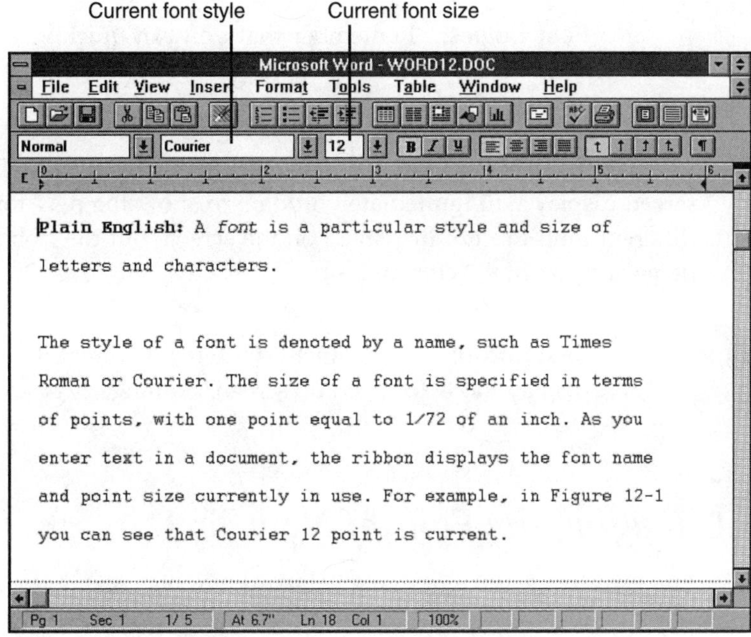

Figure 12.1 The ribbon displays the name and size of the current font.

Changing the Font of Existing Text

You can change the font style and/or size of any portion of your document, from a single character to the entire text. The exact fonts and sizes you have available will depend on your Windows installation and on the printer you are using. To change font and/or size, follow these steps:

1. Select the text to change. If the selection currently contains only a single font and size, they are displayed on the ribbon. If it contains more than one font or size, none are displayed.
2. To change the font, open the font drop-down box on the ribbon. With the mouse, click on the arrow next to the box. With the keyboard, press **Ctrl+F** and then press ↓.
3. Select the desired font. With the mouse, click on the font name. With the keyboard, use the arrow keys to highlight the name; then press **Enter**.
4. To change point size with the mouse, open the point size drop-down box on the ribbon and select the desired point size. With the keyboard, the procedure is the same except that you press **Ctrl+P** followed by ↓.

Fast Select! Remember that you can quickly select an entire document by pressing **Ctrl+5** (on the numeric keypad).

If you are in Page Layout view or in Normal view with Draft mode off, the screen display will immediately update to show the new font. In Draft mode, different fonts are not displayed on the screen, but the ribbon will display the name and size of the current font.

Fast Scroll! In documents with many different fonts, use Draft display mode to speed up screen scrolling.

Changing the Font of New Text

You can change the font that will be used for new text that you type as follows:

1. Move the insertion point to the location of the new text.
2. Follow the procedures for changing the font of existing text without first specifying a block of text.
3. Type the new text. It will appear in the newly specified font. Other text in your document will not be affected.

Bold, Underline, and Italics

The attributes boldface, italics, and/or underlining can be applied alone or in combination to any text in your document. These attributes are controlled by the toggle buttons marked **B**, *I*, and u on the ribbon.

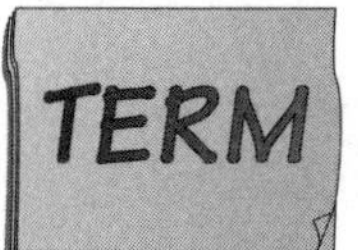

Toggle Buttons These are buttons that, when selected, turn the corresponding attribute on if it is off, and off if it is on.

To apply attributes to new text that you type:

1. Move the insertion point to the location of the new text.
2. Click on the ribbon button(s) for the desired formatting, or press **Ctrl+B** (bold), **Ctrl+I** (italics) or **Ctrl+U** (underlining). On the ribbon, the button for each attribute that is on appears depressed.

3. Type the text.
4. To turn off the attribute, click on the button again or press the corresponding key combination.

   To change existing text:

1. Select the text.
2. Click on the ribbon button(s) for the desired formatting, or press **Ctrl+B** (bold), **Ctrl+I** (italics) or **Ctrl+U** (underlining).

In Draft mode, the presence of any character formatting is indicated by underlining. In all other modes, the text appears on-screen with all formatting displayed.

In this lesson, you learned how to format characters. In the next lesson, you'll learn how to set page margins.

Setting Margins and Tabs

In this lesson, you'll learn how to set page margins. Word provides default margins for every template, but you can easily adjust them to suit your purposes.

Setting Left and Right Margins with the Ruler

The ruler displayed across the top of the Word for Windows work area makes setting margins easy. You can work visually rather than thinking in terms of inches or centimeters. The ruler is designed to be used with a mouse. It can also be controlled with the keyboard, but because it is a clumsy procedure, we will concentrate on using the mouse. See your Word for Windows documentation for keyboard details.

Displaying the Ruler If your ruler is not displayed, select **View Ruler** to display it.

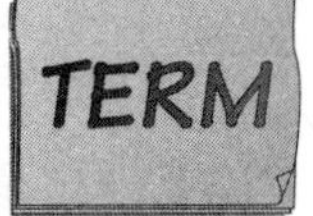

Margins The left and right margins are the distances, respectively, between the text and the left and right edges of the page.

Margin settings affect the entire document. To set margins, the ruler must be in margin scale; that is, the far left symbol is a small pair of triangles, as in Figure 13.1. If the far left symbol on the ruler is a left bracket, the ruler is in paragraph scale (which is covered in the next lesson). You must click on the bracket to switch the display to margin scale. When in margin scale, the left and right brackets on the ruler show the current margin settings. The numbers on the ruler show inches from the left edge of the paper.

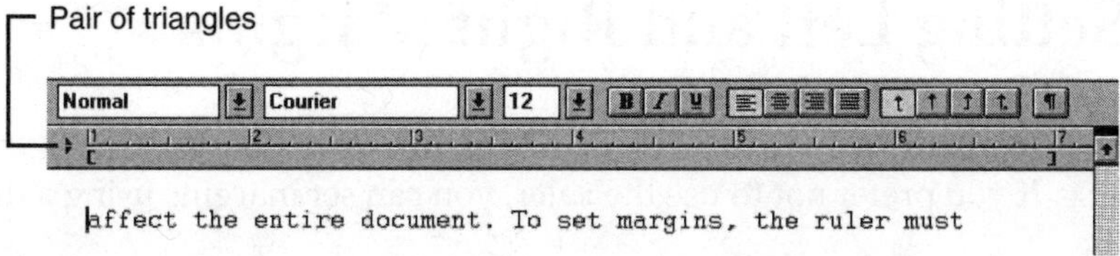

Figure 13.1 In margin scale, the ruler displays the margin settings.The two triangles at the far left indicate that the ruler is in margin scale.

To change either margin, simply point at its symbol and drag it to the new location. The screen changes immediately to reflect the new setting. Figure 13.2 shows a document with the right margin set at 4 inches. You cannot drag either margin to the left of the 0 mark on the ruler.

Changing Margins To change the margins for only a portion of a document, change the left and/or right indent (covered in the next lesson).

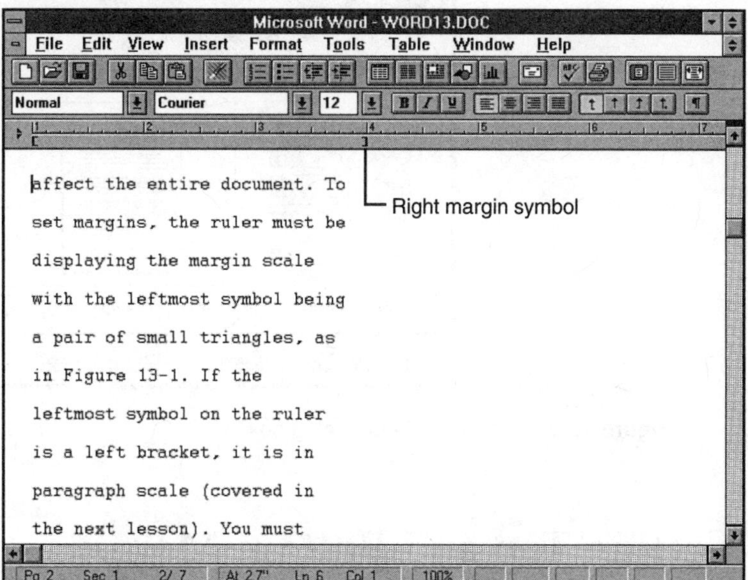

Figure 13.2 A document with the right margin set at 4 inches.

Setting Left and Right Margins with a Dialog Box

If you prefer not to use the ruler, you can set margins using a dialog box:

1. Select **Format Page Setup**. The Page Setup dialog box is displayed (see Figure 13.3).
2. Be sure that the **Margins** option at the top of the dialog box is selected.
3. In the Left box, click on the up or down arrows to increase or decrease the left margin. The numerical value is the distance between the left edge of the page and the left edge of text. The sample page in the dialog box shows what the settings will look like when printed.
4. In the Right box, click on the up or down arrows to increase or decrease the right margin. The value is the distance between the right edge of the page and the right edge of text.
5. Select **OK**.

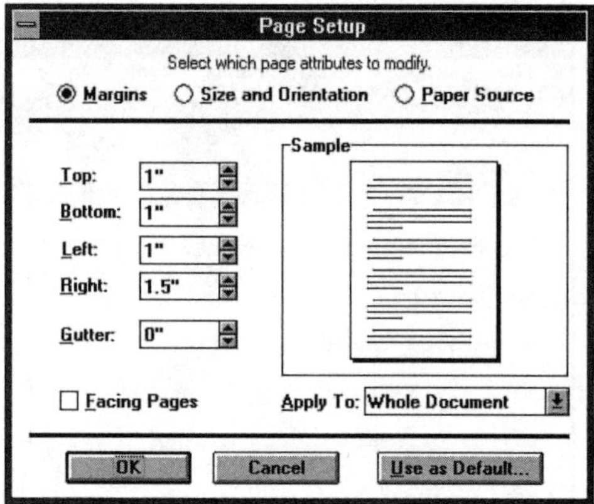

Figure 13.3 The Page Setup dialog box.

Setting Top and Bottom Margins

Use the Page Setup dialog box to change the top and bottom margins. These margins specify the distance between text and the top and bottom of the page.

1. Select **Format Page Setup** to display the Page Setup dialog box.

2. Be sure that the **Margins** option at the top of the dialog box is selected.
3. In the Top box, click on the up or down arrows to increase or decrease the top margin. In the Bottom box, click on the up or down arrows to increase or decrease the bottom margin. The sample page in the dialog box shows what the settings will look like when printed.
4. Select **OK**.

Header and Footer Margins Top and bottom margins do not affect the position of headers and footers. Use the View Headers/Footers command to specify the distance of headers and footers from the page edge.

In this lesson, you learned how to set page margins. The next lesson shows you how to use special indents and justification.

14 Setting Indents and Justification

In this lesson, you'll learn how to use indents and justification in your documents. These features help to further customize the overall flow and appearance of your text.

Indenting Paragraphs

Word for Windows allows you to set separately the indent for the left edge, the right edge, and the first line of a paragraph.

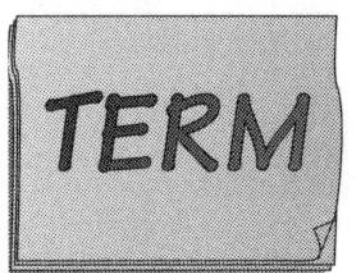

What Is Indentation? *Indentation* refers to the distance between the edges of a paragraph and the page margins.

Setting Indents with the Ruler

To set indents with the ruler, the ruler must be in paragraph scale, as indicated by the bracket displayed at the far left edge of the ruler (see Figure 14.1). If the ruler displays a pair of small triangles at the far left, it is in margin scale. Switch to paragraph scale by clicking on the triangles.

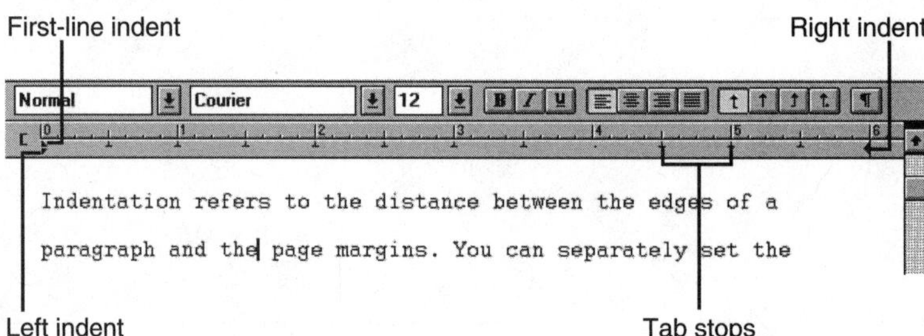

Figure 14.1 In paragraph scale, the ruler displays indents and tabs. The left bracket at the far left indicates that the ruler is in paragraph scale.

In paragraph scale, the ruler is calibrated in inches from the left margin. The symbols on the ruler are as follows:

- The upper of the two small black triangles (under the 0 in Figure 14.1) marks the current indent position of the first line of the paragraph.
- The lower small black triangle marks the current indent position of the left edge of the paragraph.
- The larger triangle (under the 6 in Figure 14.1) marks the current indent position of the right edge of the paragraph.
- The small inverted Ts mark tab stops.

To change indent positions, drag the indent symbols. If you select one or more paragraphs first, the new indents will apply only to the selected paragraphs. Otherwise, the new indents will apply only to new paragraphs that you type from the insertion point forward.

- Drag the upper small triangle to change the indent of the first line.
- Press and hold **Shift**, and drag the lower small triangle to change the indent of the left edge.
- Drag both small triangles to change the indents of the left edge and the first line at the same time.
- Drag the large triangle to change the right indent.

Setting Indents with a Dialog Box

If you prefer, you can set indents using a dialog box:

1. Select **Format Paragraph**. The Paragraph dialog box is displayed, as shown in Figure 14.2.
2. Under Indentation, click on the up and down arrows to increase or decrease the From Left, From Right, or First Line indentation settings. The sample page in the dialog box illustrates how the current settings will appear.
3. Select **OK**. The new settings are applied to any selected paragraphs or to new text.

Justifying Text

Word for Windows offers four justification options:

- Left justification aligns the left ends of lines.
- Right justification aligns the right ends of lines.
- Full justification aligns both the left and right ends of lines. (This book is printed with full justification.)
- Center justification centers lines between the left and right margins.

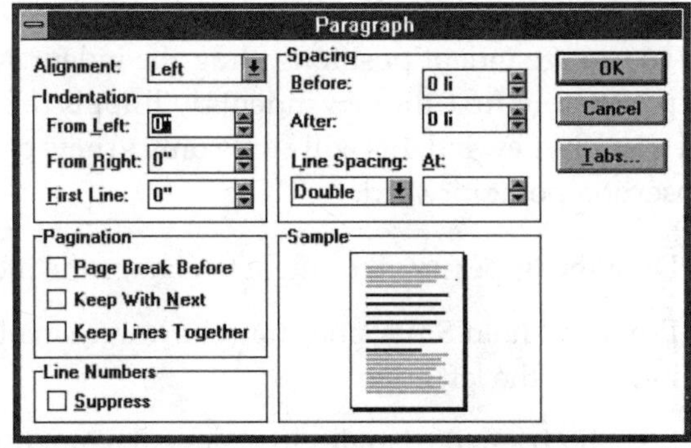

Figure 14.2 The Paragraph dialog box can be used to set indentation.

To change the justification for one or more paragraphs, first select the paragraphs to change; then click on one of the justification buttons on the ribbon.

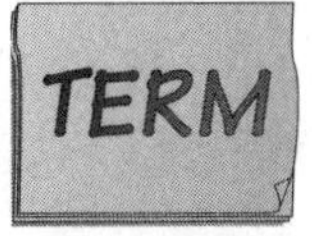

What Is Justification? *Justification* refers to the way in which lines on the page are aligned with the lines above and below them.

Displaying the Ribbon If the ribbon is not displayed, select **View Ribbon**.

If you would rather use a dialog box to change justification, select the paragraphs and then:

1. Select **Format Paragraph** to display the Paragraph dialog box.
2. Open the **Alignment** drop-down box.
3. Select the desired alignment.
4. Select **OK**.

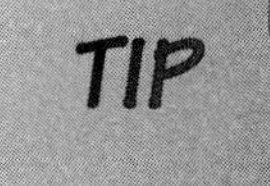

Changing Justification If you change justification without selecting any paragraphs, the new justification will apply to any new paragraphs that you type.

In this lesson, you learned how to set indentation and justification in your documents. In the next lesson, you'll learn how to use styles.

Using Styles

In this lesson, you'll learn how to use styles in your documents.

Understanding Styles

A style can be easily applied to any paragraph in any Word for Windows document. If you later modify and redefine a style, all paragraphs in the document to which that style has been assigned will automatically change to reflect the new definition.

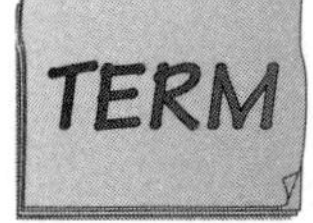

What Is a Style? A *style* is a named grouping of paragraph and character formatting that can be reused.

Styles apply only to paragraphs. In Word for Windows, one paragraph ends and another begins when you press Enter. You can display paragraph marks on your screen, showing the end of each paragraph, by clicking on the **Paragraph** button at the far right of the ribbon. Figure 15.1 shows a document with paragraph marks displayed. To turn them off again, click on the **Paragraph** button. Paragraph marks do not print.

Fast Select! To select an entire paragraph, double-click in the margin to the left of the paragraph.

Viewing Paragraph Names

When the insertion point is in a paragraph, the name of the style assigned to that paragraph is displayed in the Style box at the left end of the ribbon. Word for Windows can also display the name of the style assigned to each paragraph in your document. To open the style name area:

1. Select **Tools Options**. The Options dialog box is displayed.
2. Under Category, select **View** if it is not already selected.
3. Under Style Area Width, click on the up arrow to set a positive width for the style name area. A setting of 0.5" is good for most situations. To hide the style name area, enter a width of **0**.
4. Select **OK**. The screen now displays style names to the left of the text (see Figure 15.1).

You can see from Figure 15.1 that every paragraph has a style name. The style Normal is Word for Windows' default style. Note also that even a blank line is considered to be a paragraph because it begins and ends with a paragraph mark. The document templates supplied with Word for Windows contain a variety of predefined paragraph styles.

Assigning Existing Styles

To assign an existing style to one or more paragraphs:

1. Select the paragraph(s) to be formatted. To assign a style to a single paragraph, you need only place the insertion point anywhere in the paragraph.
2. Open the Style drop-down box on the ribbon. With the mouse, click on the arrow next to the box. With the keyboard, press **Ctrl+S** and then press ↓.
3. The box lists all defined styles. Select the desired style. With the mouse, click on the style name. With the keyboard, use the arrow keys to highlight the style name, and then press **Enter**.
4. The style is applied to the selected paragraphs.

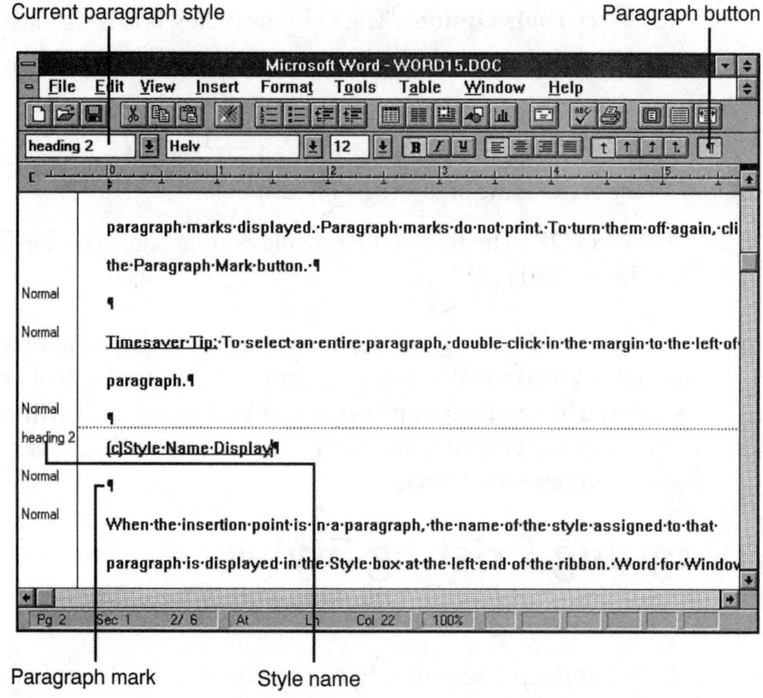

Figure 15.1 A screen with paragraph marks and style names displayed.

Defining New Styles

You can define new styles that meet your own personal needs. Once a style has been defined, you can apply it in other Word for Windows documents that you create from the same template. Here's how to define a style:

1. Create one paragraph with the desired formatting. Be sure the insertion point is in the paragraph.
2. Click on the Style box on the ribbon, or press **Ctrl+S**.
3. Type the new style name. It must be a name not already assigned to a style.
4. Click anywhere outside the Style box, or press **Enter**. The new style is created.

Modifying Existing Styles

You can change the formatting associated with an existing style. When you do so, all paragraphs in the document that have the style assigned will be modified. Here's how:

1. Select a paragraph with the style you want to modify. The style name will be displayed in the Style box on the ribbon.
2. Make the desired changes to the paragraph style.
3. Click on the Style box on the ribbon, and then click anywhere in the document window.
4. Word for Windows prompts you whether to redefine the style. Select **Yes**.
5. The style is redefined according to the new formatting.

Undoing Formatting To undo a style assignment, select **Edit Undo Formatting**.

Using the Standard Styles

Word for Windows comes supplied with a number of standard styles for commonly needed formatting, such as footnotes, index entries, and the like. To access these styles:

1. Select the paragraph(s) to format.
2. Select **Format Style**. The Style dialog box is displayed (see Figure 15.2).
3. Open the Style Name drop-down box and press **Ctrl+Y**. The standard style names are added to the style list.
4. Select the desired style by clicking with the mouse or highlighting it and pressing **Enter**.

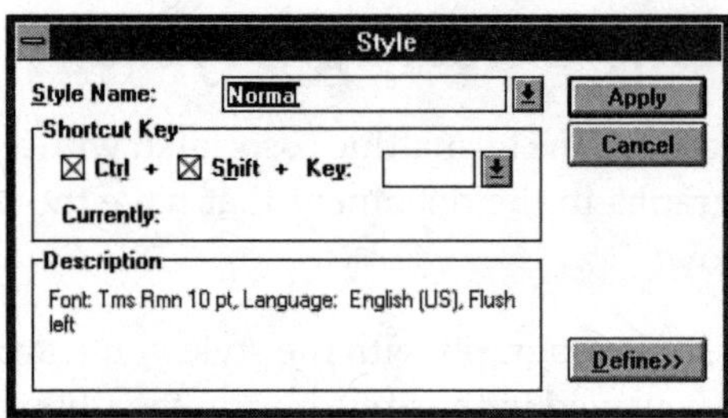

Figure 15.2 The Style dialog box.

In this lesson, you learned how to use styles to format your document. The next lesson shows you how to use glossaries.

Using Glossaries

In this lesson, you'll learn how to use glossaries.

What Is a Glossary?

A *glossary* is a collection of commonly used words, phrases, or sentences that are stored so they can be inserted into a document without having to type them each time. Typical uses for glossary entries are your company name, the closing sentence for a business letter, and your name and title. A glossary entry can contain just text or text along with special formatting.

Creating a Glossary Entry

To create a glossary entry, you must first type it into your document and add any special formatting that you want included. Then:

1. Select the text for the glossary entry. If you want its formatting included as well, be sure to include the ending paragraph mark in the selection.
2. Select **Edit Glossary**. The Glossary dialog box is displayed (Figure 16.1).

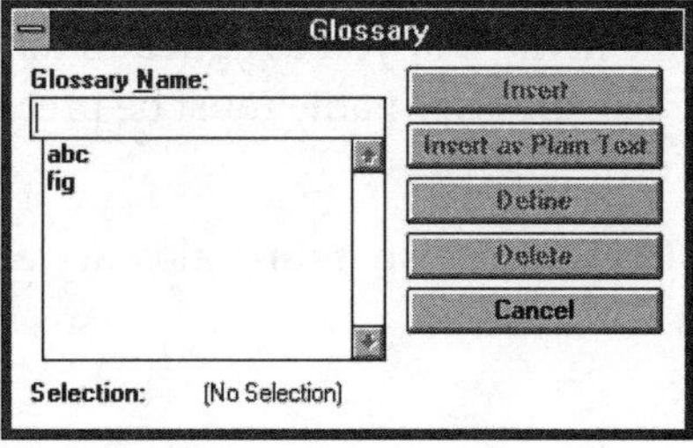

Figure 16.1 The Glossary dialog box.

3. In the Glossary Name text box, enter the name for the glossary entry. This should be a short name that is descriptive of the entry. You will later use this name when inserting the glossary entry into documents.

4. Select **Define**. What happens next depends on the template that your document is based upon:

   - If your document is based on any template besides NORMAL, Word for Windows offers you two choices as to where the glossary entry should be stored. Select **Global** to have the glossary entry available for all future documents. Select **Template** to have the entry available only for future documents created with the current template. Then select **OK**.

   - If your document is based on the NORMAL template, Word for Windows automatically stores the glossary entry so it will be available for all future documents.

Return Address Save time by creating a glossary entry that contains your name and address.

Inserting a Glossary Entry

You have two options for inserting a glossary entry into your document. The first method is fastest if you remember the name you assigned to the glossary entry:

1. Move the insertion point to the location where you want the glossary entry inserted.

2. Type the name that you assigned to the glossary entry, but do not press Enter. The glossary name must be preceded by a space or be the first item on a line.

3. Press **F3**. The corresponding glossary entry is inserted in place of its name.

Quick Access To insert a glossary entry, type the entry name and press **F3**.

If you are not sure of the glossary entry name, follow this procedure:

1. Move the insertion point to the location where you want the glossary entry inserted.
2. Select **Edit Glossary**. The Glossary dialog box is displayed with a list of defined glossary entries.
3. Type the name of the desired glossary entry, or select it from the list.
4. Select **Insert** to insert the glossary entry with its formatting. Select **Insert as Plain Text** to insert the glossary text without formatting.

Modifying a Glossary Entry

You can modify an existing glossary entry. Such modifications will not affect previous instances of the glossary entry in your documents.

1. Insert the glossary entry into a document as described earlier in this lesson.
2. Edit the text and/or formatting as desired.
3. Select the newly edited text, including the paragraph mark (if you want the formatting included in the glossary entry).
4. Select **Edit Glossary**. From the list of entries, select the name of the glossary you are modifying.
5. Select **Define**, and then select **Global** or **Template** storage.
6. When asked "Redefine Glossary Entry?," select **Yes**.

Deleting a Glossary Entry

You can delete an unneeded glossary entry from the glossary. Deleting a glossary entry has no effect on instances of the entry that were inserted previously.

1. Select **Edit Glossary**.
2. Type the glossary entry name, or select it from the list.
3. Select **Delete**. The entry is deleted.

In this lesson, you learned how to create, insert, modify, and delete glossary items. In the next lesson, you will learn how to create tables.

Tables

In this lesson, you'll learn how to add tables to your documents.

Uses for Tables

A *table* lets you organize information in a row and column format. Each entry in a table, called a *cell,* is independent of all other entries. You control the number of rows and columns in a table and the formatting of each cell. A table cell can contain anything except another table.

Why Tables? Use tables for columns of numbers, lists, and anything else that requires a row and column arrangement.

Inserting a Table

You can insert a new, empty table at any location within your document. Just follow these steps:

1. Move the insertion point to where you want the table.
2. Select **Table Insert Table**. The Insert Table dialog box, as shown in Figure 17.1, is displayed.

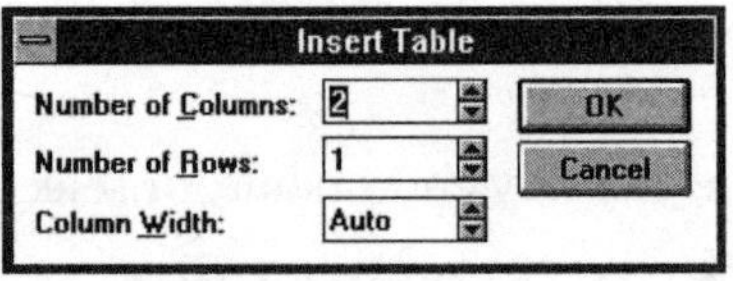

Figure 17.1 The Insert Table dialog box.

3. In the Number of Columns and Number of Rows boxes, enter the number of rows and columns the table should have. (You can adjust these numbers later if you wish.)
4. In the Column Width box, select the column width. Select **Auto** to have the page width evenly divided among the specified number of columns.
5. Select **OK**. A blank table is created with the insertion point in the first cell. Figure 17.2, for example, shows a blank table with 4 rows and 3 columns.

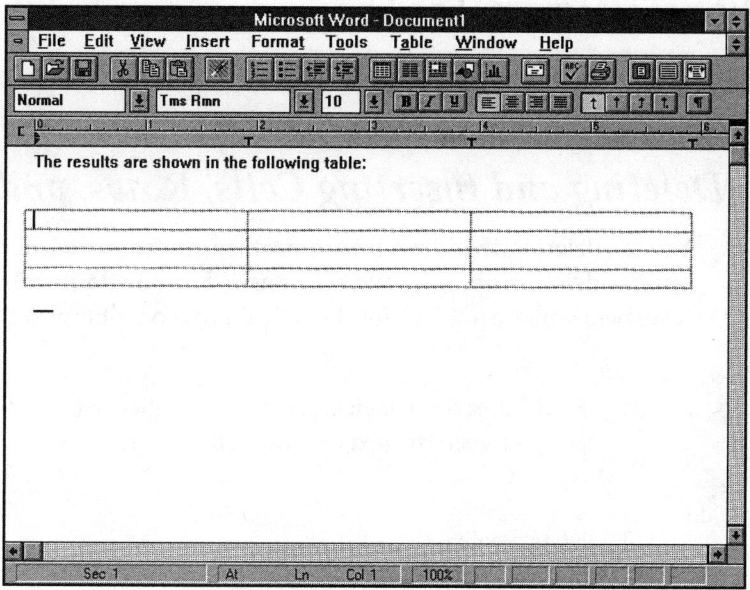

Figure 17.2 A blank table with 4 rows and 3 columns.

Working in a Table

When the insertion point is in a table cell, you can enter and edit text as you would in the rest of the document. Text entered in a cell automatically wraps to the next line within the column width. Navigate in a table using the special key combinations listed below:

Tab	Move to the next cell in a row.
Shift+Tab	Move to the previous cell in a row.

Alt+Home	Move to the first cell in the current row.
Alt+PgUp	Move to the top cell in the current column.
Alt+End	Move to the last cell in the current row.
Alt+PgDn	Move to the last cell in the current column.

If the insertion point is at the edge of a cell, you can also use the arrow keys to move between cells.

Formatting a Table

Once you've created a table and entered some information, you can format it to suit your needs.

Deleting and Inserting Cells, Rows, and Columns

You can delete individual cells, erasing their contents and leaving a blank cell. You can also delete entire rows and columns. When you do so, columns to the right or rows below move to fill in for the deleted row or column.

Fast Select! To select an entire cell, click in the left margin of the cell, between the text and the cell border.

To delete a cell:

1. Select the cell.
2. Press **Del**.

To delete an entire row or column:

1. Select any cell in the row or column to be deleted.
2. Select **Table Delete Cells**. A dialog box is displayed.
3. In the dialog box, select **Delete Entire Row** or **Delete Entire Column**.
4. Select **OK**. The row or column is deleted.

To insert a row or column:

1. Move the insertion point to a cell to the right of or below the location of the new column or row.
2. Select **Table Select Row** (if inserting a row) or **Table Select Column** (if inserting a column). The entire row or column becomes selected.
3. Select **Table Insert Columns** to insert a new, blank column to the left of the selected column. Select **Table Insert Rows** to insert a new, blank row above the selected row.

It Varies! The commands on the Table menu change according to circumstances. For example, if you have selected a column in a table, the Insert Columns command is displayed but the Insert Rows command is not.

To insert a new row at the bottom of the table:

1. Move the insertion point to the last cell in the last row of the table.
2. Press **Tab**. A new row is added at the bottom of the table.

Changing Column Width

You can quickly change the width of a column with the mouse:

1. Point at the right border of the column to change. The mouse pointer changes to double arrowheads.
2. Drag the column border to the desired width.

You can also use a dialog box to change column widths:

1. Select the column to change (as described earlier).
2. Select **Table Column Width**. A dialog box is displayed.
3. Under Width, type in the desired column width, or click on the up and down arrows to change the setting.
4. Click on **Next Column** or **Previous Column** to change the width of other columns in the table.
5. Select **OK**. The table changes to reflect the new column settings.

Adding Borders to a Table

On-screen, Word for Windows displays table cells separated by grid lines, but tables are normally printed without lines between cells. To add a border and grid lines, follow these steps:

1. Move the insertion point inside the table and select **Table Select Table.** The entire table will be selected.
2. Select **Format Border**. The Border Table dialog box is displayed, as shown in Figure 17.3.
3. Under Preset, make one of the following selections:

   Select **Box** to place a box around the outside of the table.

   Select **Grid** to place a box and also to place lines between cells in the table.

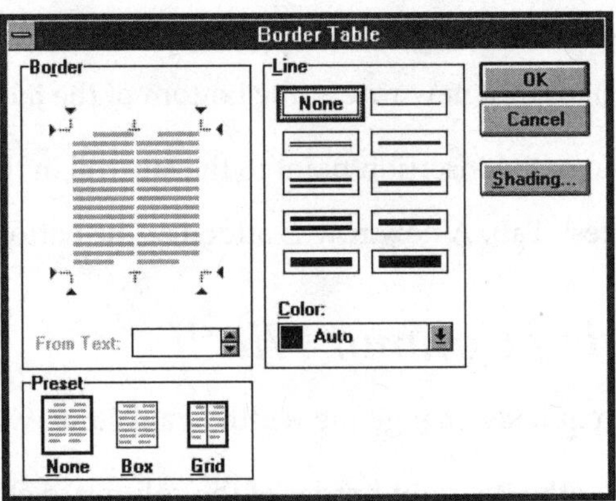

Figure 17.3 The Border Table dialog box.

   Select **None** to remove a box or grid that was added previously.

4. Under Line, select the type of line to be used for the box.
5. Select **OK**. The table is displayed and will be printed with the box and/or grid lines.

In this lesson, you learned how to add tables to your documents. In the next lesson, you'll learn about fields.

Fields

In this lesson, you'll learn how to use fields.

Uses for Fields

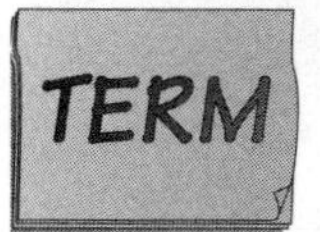

What's a Field? A *field* is a special code that retrieves information from another location and displays it in a document.

Word for Windows fields are very useful, making it unnecessary for you to manually update many types of information in your documents. Word for Windows has many field types available; here are some of the tasks most frequently performed with fields:

- Inserting the current date in a document.
- Sequentially numbering figures, tables, or other inserts with automatic update and renumbering.
- Inserting the document title or author in a document.
- Automatically maintaining page number references to specific document locations.

Your Word for Windows documentation and the help system have details on all of the field types.

When you're editing a document, field names appear enclosed in braces, like this: **{Date}**

At the time a document is printed, its fields are evaluated and the results printed in their places. The {Date} field, for example, would print the date set on the computer's clock.

Inserting a Field

You cannot insert a field simply by typing its name surrounded by braces. You must use the Insert Field command:

1. Move the insertion point to the location for the field.
2. Select **Insert Field**. The Field dialog box is displayed (see Figure 18.1).
3. In the Insert Field Type box, highlight the field to insert by clicking on it with the mouse or moving the highlight bar with the arrow keys.
4. To obtain information about a field, highlight its name and press **F1**.
5. If additional information is needed, the Instructions box will display choices for the highlighted field type. Select one of these.
6. Select **OK**. The field code is added to the document.

Document Title Insert the {title} field in a footer to print the document's title (from the Summary Information) on every page.

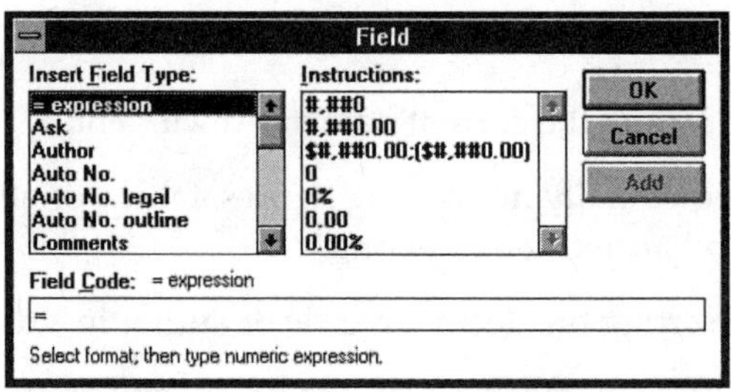

Figure 18.1 The Field dialog box.

Viewing Field Codes vs. Field Results

When editing a document, you have the option of viewing either the field codes or the field results. When field codes are displayed, the Field Codes command on the View menu has a check mark next to it. To toggle back and forth between viewing field codes and viewing field results, select **View Field Codes**.

Updating Fields

Some fields must be updated to ensure that they are accurate. You can update fields singly or in groups.

To update a single field:

1. Place the insertion point in the field (in either field code view or field result view).
2. Press **F9**.

To update multiple fields at one time:

1. Select the portion of the document containing the fields to update. To update all fields, select the entire document.
2. Press **F9**.

Locking a Field

At times you may want to "freeze" a field so it does not change, even if the entire document is updated. (For example, you might want to lock a {date} field so it will always reflect the document creation date.) This is done by *locking* a field. A locked field's display does not change on updating, even if the information the field retrieves has changed. To lock and unlock fields:

1. Position the insertion point in the field.
2. Press **Ctrl+F11** to lock the field. Press **Ctrl+Shift+F11** to unlock the field.

No F11 Key? If your keyboard has only 10 function keys, press **Alt+Ctrl+F1** to lock a field or **Alt+Ctrl+Shift+F1** to unlock a field.

In this lesson, you learned how to use fields in your documents. In the next lesson, you'll learn how to print your documents.

19

Printing Your Document

In this lesson, you'll learn how to print your document.

Quick Printing

To print a Word for Windows document, you must have installed and selected the printer you are going to use. The printer must be turned on and on-line. To print the entire document using the current settings:

1. Select **File Print**, or press **Ctrl+Shift+F12**. The Print dialog box is displayed (see Figure 19.1).
2. Select **OK** or press **Enter**. The document is printed.

Quick Printing To print one copy of the entire document, click on the **Printer** button on the Toolbar.

Printer Not Working? Refer to your Microsoft Windows and printer documentation for help.

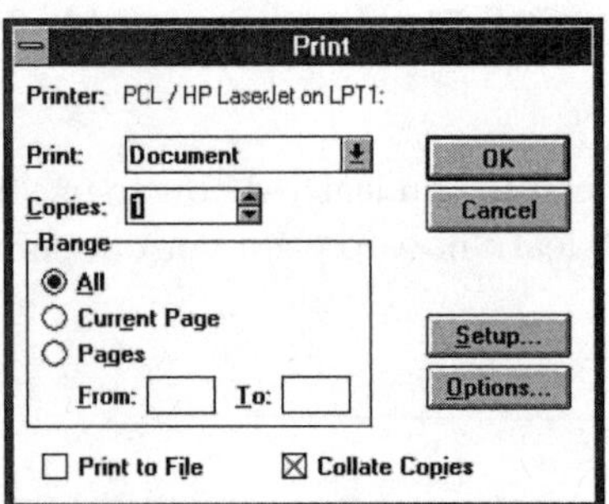

Figure 19.1 The Print dialog box.

Printing Part of a Document

You can print a single page of a document or a range of pages. This can be useful for checking the results of your formatting and other document components. Here's how:

1. If you're printing a single page, position the insertion point anywhere on the page to be printed.
2. Select **File Print** or press **Ctrl+Shift+F12**. The Print dialog box is displayed.
3. Under Range, select **Current Page** to print the page the insertion point is on. Select **Pages** to print a range of pages; then enter the beginning and ending page numbers in the From and To boxes.
4. Select **OK**. The selected page or pages is printed.

Setting Up the Page

By default, Word for Windows formats printer output for 8 1/2-by-11-inch paper in portrait mode. You can modify these settings if needed (if you want to print on 8 1/2-by-14-inch legal paper).

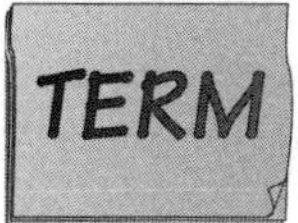

Portrait Orientation This is the default and prints lines parallel to the short edge of the paper. Landscape orientation prints lines parallel to the long edge of the paper.

To change the print orientation and the paper size:

1. Select **Format Page Setup**. The Page Setup dialog box is displayed.
2. Select the **Size and Orientation** option at the top of the dialog box.
3. Under Paper Size, open the drop-down box. Word for Windows lists several common paper sizes.
4. Select the desired paper size.
5. If you select **Custom**, use the Height and Width boxes to specify the actual paper size.
6. Under Orientation, select **Portrait** or **Landscape**.

7. Select **OK**. The new settings will be in effect for your document and will be used the next time it is printed.

Previewing the Print Job

You can view a screen display that previews exactly what your document will look like when printed. To do this:

1. Select **File Print Preview**. The current page is displayed in preview mode (see Figure 19.2).
2. Press **PgUp** or **PgDn** or use the scroll bar to view other pages.
3. Click on **Two Pages** to view two pages side-by-side. When two pages are displayed, click on **One Page** to return to single-page view.

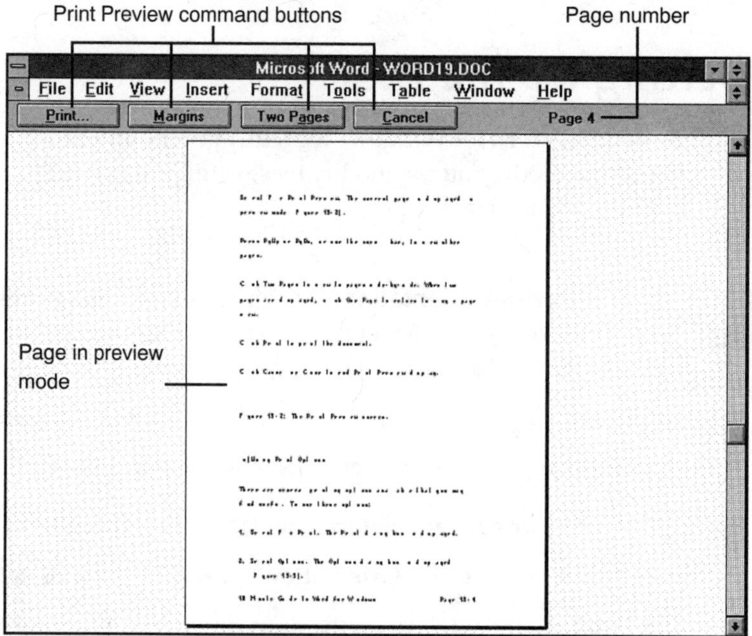

Figure 19.2 The Print Preview screen.

4. Click on **Print** to print the document.
5. Click on **Cancel** or **Close** to end Print Preview display (only one of these commands will be available at one time).

Using Print Options

There are several printing options available that you may find useful. To use these options:

1. Select **File Print**. The Print dialog box is displayed.
2. Select **Options**. The Options dialog box, as shown in Figure 19.3, is displayed.
3. Under Printing Options, select one or more of the following:
   - **Draft Output** produces draft output that prints faster but may lack some graphics and formatting (depending on your specific printer).
   - **Reverse Print Order** prints pages in last-to-first order. This setting produces collated output on printers with face-up output.
   - **Update Fields** automatically updates all document fields (except locked ones) before printing.
4. Select **OK**. You are returned to the Print dialog box.
5. Select **OK** to begin printing.

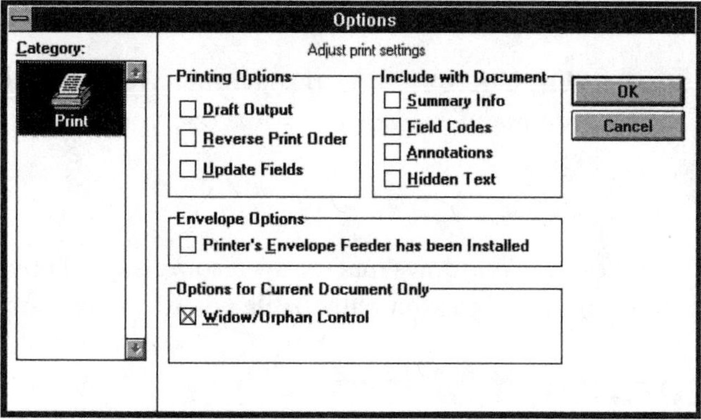

Figure 19.3 The Options dialog box.

In this lesson, you learned how to print your documents. In the next lesson, you'll learn how to use macros to save time.

Saving Time with Macros

In this lesson, you'll learn how to use macros to save time.

What Is a Macro?

A *macro* is a sequence of commands and keystrokes that has been recorded and saved by Word for Windows. You can easily play back a macro at any time, achieving the same result as if you had entered each command and keystroke individually. For example, you could create a macro that:

- Converts an entire document from single-spaced to double-spaced.
- Goes through a document and formats the first word of each paragraph in 18 point italics.
- Saves the document to disk and then prints it in draft mode.

Why Macros? Macros save time. By recording frequently needed command sequences as macros, you can save time and reduce errors.

Word for Windows macros are a complex and powerful feature. The basics you'll learn in this lesson will enable you to create many useful macros.

Recording a Macro

The simplest way to create a macro is to enter the keystrokes and commands yourself while Word for Windows records them. The only operations that Word for Windows cannot record are mouse editing actions. That is, a macro cannot record the mouse moving the insertion point or selecting text; you must use the keyboard for these actions while recording a macro. Other mouse actions, such as selecting menu commands or dialog box options, can be recorded in a macro.

To record a macro:

1. Plan the macro. It is often a good idea to try a macro out before recording to ensure that it works the way you want it to.
2. Select **Tools Record Macro**. The Record Macro dialog box is displayed (see Figure 20.1).
3. In the Record Macro Name box, enter a name for the macro. The name should be descriptive of the macro's function. Use any characters except spaces in the name.
4. Optionally, specify a shortcut key to associate with the macro. If you specify a shortcut key, you can run the macro by pressing that key. If you do not specify a shortcut key, you must select the macro name from a dialog box to run the macro. The available shortcut keys are the letter keys, number keys, function keys (except F1), and the Ins and Del keys, either alone or with Ctrl, Shift, or Shift+Ctrl.

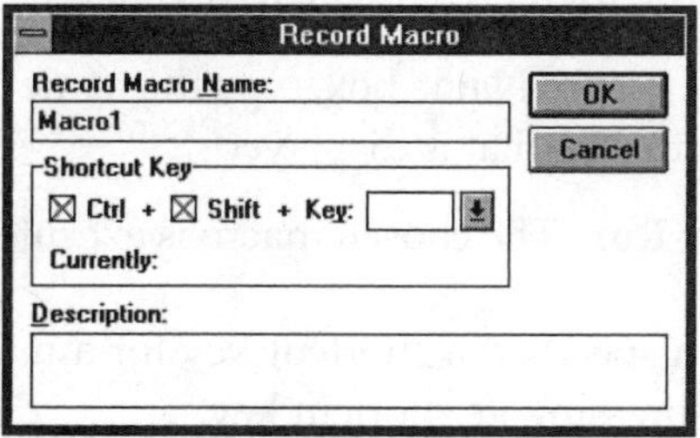

Figure 20.1 The Record Macro dialog box.

5. In the Description box, enter an optional, short description of the macro.
6. Select **OK**. What happens next depends on the template that your document is based upon:

   If your document is based on any template besides NORMAL, Word for Windows offers you two choices as to where the macro should be stored. Select **Global** to have the macro available for all future documents. Select **Template** to have the macro available only for future documents created with the current template. Then select **OK**.

   If your document is based on the NORMAL template, Word for Windows automatically stores the macro so it will be available for all future documents.

7. The word **REC** appears in the status line at the bottom of the screen, indicating that Word is recording keystrokes or commands. Execute the actions that you want in the macro. Use the keyboard, not the mouse, to select text and move the insertion point.

8. When finished, select **Tools Stop Recorder**. Macro recording is terminated and the macro is stored.

Playing Back a Macro

You can play back any macro at any time while you're working on a document, as follows:

1. Select **Tools Macro**. The Macro dialog box appears.

2. Under Show, select either **Global** or **Template** to determine which macros are displayed. If you select Global, all macros recorded with the Global option will be listed. If you select Template, only those macros stored with the Template option in the current template will be listed.

3. In the Macro Name box, type the name of the desired macro, or select it from the list that is displayed.

4. Select **Run**. The chosen macro is executed.

If you specified a shortcut key for a macro, you can play back the macro simply by pressing its shortcut key.

Shortcut Keys Specify a shortcut key for macros you will use frequently.

In this lesson, you learned how to record and play back a macro. In the next lesson, you will learn how to proof your documents using the spell checker and thesaurus.

21 Proofing Your Document

In this lesson, you'll learn to use Word for Windows' utilities to help proof your document.

Using the Spelling Checker

The spelling checker lets you verify and correct the spelling of words in your document. Word for Windows checks words against a standard dictionary and lets you know when it encounters an unknown word. You then can ignore it, change it, or add it to the dictionary.

To check spelling in a portion of a document, select the text to check. To check the entire document, first move the insertion point to the start of the document by pressing **Ctrl+Home**. Then:

1. Select **Tools Spelling**, or click on the **Spelling Check** button on the Toolbar. Word for Windows starts checking words beginning at the insertion point.
2. If a word is found in the document that is not in the dictionary, it is highlighted in the text and the Spelling dialog box is displayed (see Figure 21.1).
3. In the Spelling dialog box, the Not in Dictionary box displays the word that was not found in the dictionary.
    - If the spelling checker has found any likely replacements, they are listed in the Suggestions list box. In the dialog box, you have the following options:
    - To ignore the highlighted word and continue, select **Ignore**.
    - To ignore the highlighted word and any other instances of it in the document, select **Ignore All**.
    - To change the highlighted word, type the new spelling in the Change To box or highlight the desired replacement word in

the Suggestions list box. Then select **Change** (to change the current instance of the word) or **Change All** (to change all instances of the word in the document).

- To add the word to the dictionary, select **Add**.

4. The spelling checker proceeds to check the rest of the document. When it is finished checking, it displays a message to that effect. To cancel spell checking at any time, select **Cancel** in the Spelling dialog box.

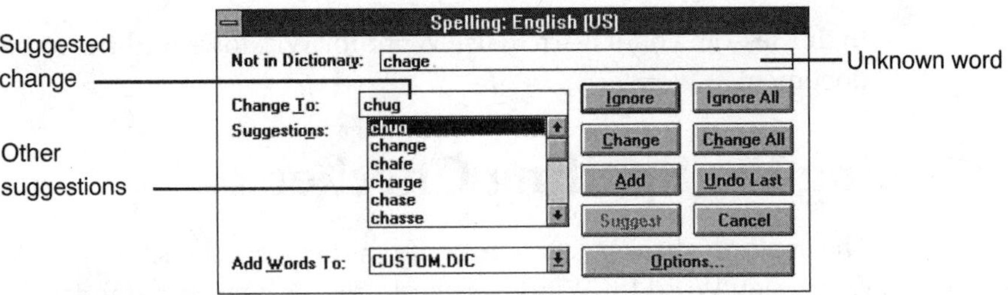

Figure 21.1 The Spelling dialog box.

Fast Check! To check the spelling of a single word, position the insertion point in or immediately to the right of the word, and press **F7**.

The Thesaurus

A thesaurus provides you with synonyms and antonyms for words in your document. Using the thesaurus can help you avoid repetition in your writing (and also improve your vocabulary). To use the thesaurus:

1. Place the insertion point on the word of interest in your document.
2. Press **Shift+F7**, or select **Tools Thesaurus**.
3. The Thesaurus dialog box opens (Figure 21.2). This dialog box has several components:
   - Synonyms For displays the word of interest.
   - The Meanings box lists alternative meanings for the word.
   - The Synonyms box lists synonyms for the currently highlighted meaning of the word.

- The Replace With box contains the highlighted meaning from the Meanings list.

4. While the Thesaurus dialog box is displayed, there are several actions you can take:
   - To find additional meanings and synonyms for the word in the Replace With box, select **Look Up**.
   - To find synonyms for a word in the Meanings or Synonyms list, select the word to display in the Replace With box, and then select **Look Up**.
   - To find synonyms for a word that is not listed, type the word into the Replace With box and select **Look Up**.
   - For some words, the thesaurus will display the term Antonyms in the Meanings list. To display antonyms for the selected word, highlight the term Antonyms and then select **Look Up**.
5. To replace the word in the document with the word in the Replace With box, select **Replace**.
6. To close the thesaurus without making any changes to the document, select **Cancel**.

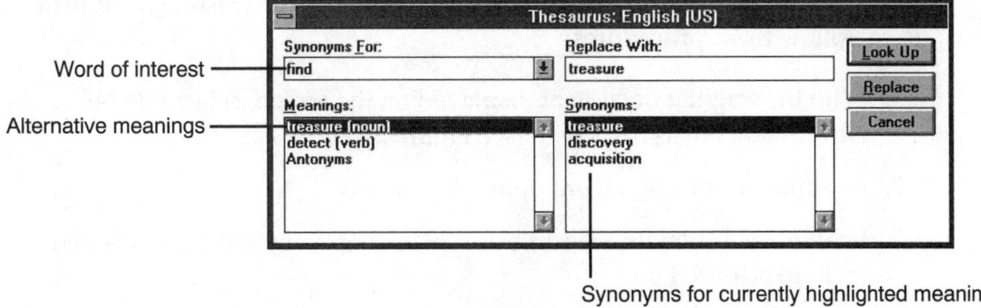

Figure 21.2 The Thesaurus dialog box.

Prevent Repetition Use the thesaurus to avoid repeating words in your document.

In this lesson, you learned how to use the spell checker and thesaurus. In the next lesson, you will learn how to work with multiple documents.

22 Working with Multiple Documents

In this lesson, you'll learn how to work with multiple documents in Word for Windows.

Why Use Multiple Documents?

You may feel that working on one document at a time is quite enough. In some situations, however, the ability to work on multiple documents at the same time can be very useful. You can refer to one document while working on another, and you can copy and move text from one document to another. Word for Windows can have as many as nine documents open simultaneously.

Starting a New Document

You can start a new document while you're working on an existing document. To do so, follow these procedures:

1. With the original document displayed on the screen, select **File New**. The New dialog box is displayed (see Figure 22.1).
2. Be sure that the **Document** option is selected.
3. Under Use Template, select the template that you want the new document to be based on.
4. If you want to enter summary information for the new document, select **Summary**. Enter the desired information in the Summary Info dialog box, and then select **OK**.

   Or

   If you do not want to enter summary information, select **OK** in the New dialog box.

5. A new, blank document window is opened over the existing document. The new document is assigned a default name by Word for Windows, such as DOCUMENT1, DOCUMENT2, and so on.
6. Enter text and edit the new document in the normal fashion. The original document remains in memory. If you close the new document, you will be returned to the original document.

Fast Open! To open a new document based on the NORMAL template, click on the **File New** button on the Toolbar.

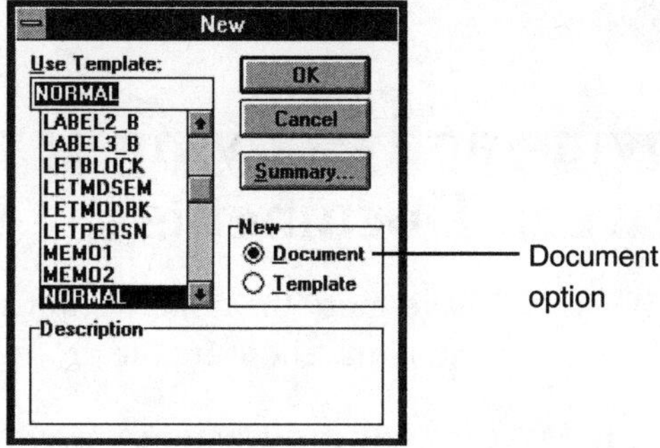

Figure 22.1 The New dialog box.

Opening an Existing Document

While working in one document, you can also open another existing document. Simply select **File Open**, or click on the **File Open** button on the Toolbar and select the name of the document file you want to open. A new window opens over the current document and displays the document. Both the newly opened and the original documents are in memory, and can be edited, printed, and so on.

Switching Between Documents

When you have multiple documents open at one time, only one of them can be active at a given moment. The active document is displayed on-screen and is the only one affected by editing commands. You can have as many as nine documents open at the same time, and you can switch between them at will.

To switch between open documents:

1. Select **Window**. The Window menu lists all open documents, with a check mark next to the name of the currently active document.
2. Select the document name to make active. You can either click on the document name with the mouse or press the key corresponding to the number listed next to the name on the menu.
3. The selected document becomes active and is displayed on the screen.

Next Please! To quickly cycle to the next open document, press **Ctrl+F6**.

Moving and Copying Text Between Documents

When you have more than one document open, you can move and copy text between documents. These are the procedures to follow:

1. Make the source document active, and select the text that is to be moved or copied.
2. Select **Edit Cut** (if moving the text) or **Edit Copy** (if copying the text). You can also click on the **Cut** and **Copy** buttons on the Toolbar.
3. Make the destination document active. Move the insertion point to the location for the new text.
4. Select **Edit Paste**, or click on the **Paste** button on the Toolbar.

Seeing Multiple Windows

At times you may want to have two or more open documents visible on the screen at the same time. To do so, select **Window Arrange All**. Word displays each open document in its own window in the work area. For example, Figure 22.2 shows three documents displayed in the work area. Note that each document window has its own title bar that displays the document name.

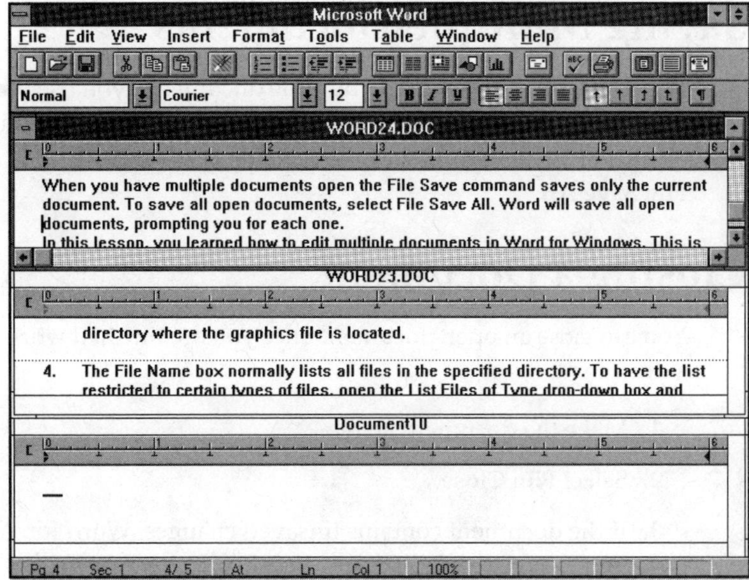

Figure 22.2 Multiple documents displayed with Window Arrange All.

Only one document can be current at any given time. The current document is indicated by a dark background in the title bar and a dark border. In Figure 22.2, WORD24.DOC is current. To make a different document window current, click anywhere in the window with the mouse. You can also press **Ctrl+F6** one or more times to cycle between windows, or use the Window command as described earlier in this chapter.

With multiple document windows displayed, you have control over the size and position of each window. You learned in Lesson 3 how to control Help windows. Use the same techniques to control document windows.

Redisplaying a Document at Full-Screen Size

To end multiple-document display and return to full-screen display of a single document:

1. Make current the document you want displayed full screen.
2. Maximize the window by pressing **Ctrl+F10** or by clicking on the **Maximize** box. The Maximize box is the upward pointing arrowhead immediately to the right of the window's title bar.

Saving Multiple Documents

When you are working with multiple documents, you use the **File Save** and **File Save As** commands that you learned in Lesson 5. These commands will save only the active document. You can save all open documents with a single command, **File Save All**.

Closing a Document

You can close an open document once you are finished working with it. To close a document:

1. Make the document active.
2. Select **File Close**.
3. If the document contains unsaved changes, Word for Windows prompts you to save the document.
4. The document is closed.

In this lesson, you learned how to work with multiple documents. In the next lesson, you'll learn how to add graphics to your document.

23 Adding Graphics to Your Documents

In this lesson, you'll learn how to add graphics to your documents.

Adding a Graphics File

A *graphics file* is a disk file that contains a graphic image created with another application. Word for Windows can utilize files created by a wide variety of applications, including Lotus 1-2-3, Windows Metafiles, Micrografx Designer, and AutoCAD. To add a graphics file to a Word for Windows document, follow these steps:

1. Move the insertion point to the location for the graphic.
2. Select **Insert Picture**. The Picture dialog box, shown in Figure 23.1, is displayed.
3. If necessary, use the Directories and Drives boxes to specify the drive and directory where the graphics file is located.
4. The File Name box normally lists all files in the specified directory. To have the list restricted to certain types of files, open the List Files of Type drop-down box and select the desired file type.
5. In the File Name box, type the name of the file to insert, or select the file name from the list.
6. To preview the picture in the Preview Picture box, select **Preview**.
7. Select **Link to File** if you want the graphic in your document updated when the graphics file changes.
8. Select **OK**. The graphic is inserted into your document.

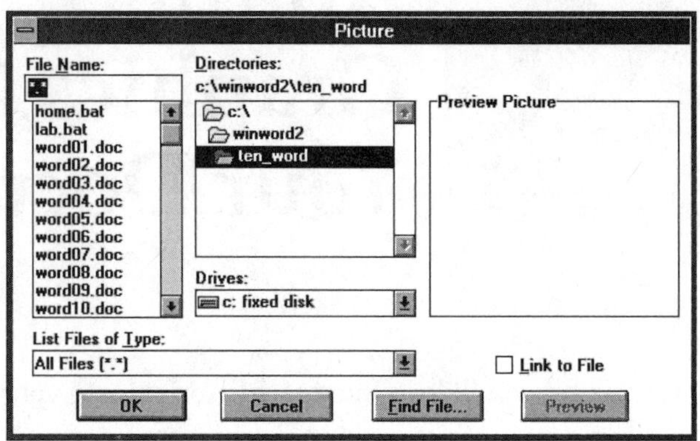

Figure 23.1 The Picture dialog box.

Displaying Graphics

In Draft display mode, the graphic is not displayed on-screen, but its position is marked by an outline. When Draft mode is off, the actual graphic is displayed, as shown in Figure 23.2. If you selected the Link to File option when inserting the file, Word for Windows inserts a field code. The screen will display this code when field codes are displayed.

Fast Takes When working on a document that contains graphics, you can speed up screen display and scrolling by using Draft mode.

Selecting a Graphic

Before you can work with a graphic in your document, you must select it:

- With the mouse, click on the graphic.
- With the keyboard, position the insertion point to the left of the graphic, and then press **Shift+→**.

When a graphic is selected, it is surrounded by eight small black squares called *sizing handles*.

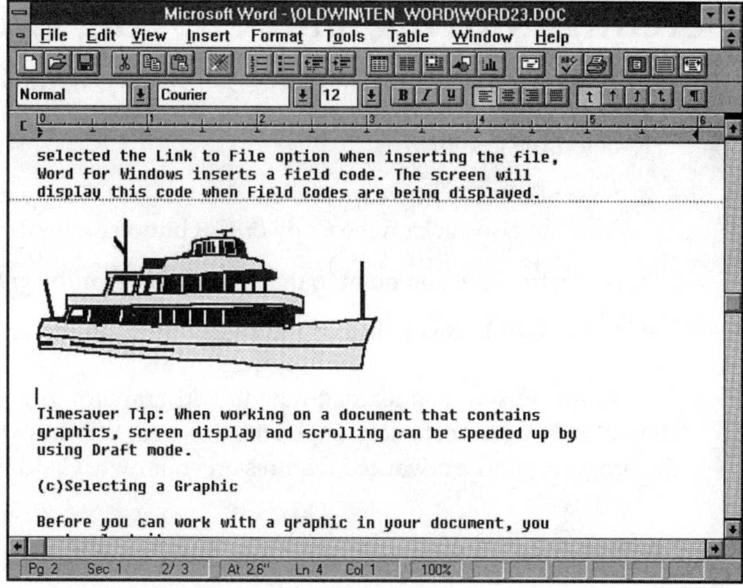

Figure 23.2 A document with a displayed graphic.

Cropping and Resizing a Graphic

You can resize a graphic in your document, displaying the entire picture at a different size. You can also crop a graphic, hiding portions of the picture that you don't want to display. To resize or crop a graphic:

1. Select the graphic.
2. Point at one of the resizing handles. The mouse pointer will change to a double-headed arrow.
3. To resize, press the left mouse button and drag the handle until the outline of the graphic is at the desired size. You can either enlarge or shrink the graphic.
4. To crop, press and hold **Shift**, and then press the left mouse button and drag a handle toward the center of the graphic.
5. Release the mouse button.

Deleting, Moving, and Copying Graphics

To delete a graphic, select it and press **Del**. To move or copy a graphic:

1. Select the graphic.
2. Select **Edit Copy** (to copy the graphic) or **Edit Cut** (to move the graphic). You can also click on the **Copy** or **Cut** button on the Toolbar.
3. Move the insertion point to the new location for the graphic.
4. Select **Edit Paste** or click on the **Paste** button on the Toolbar.

In this lesson, you learned how to add graphics to your documents. You should now be comfortable enough with Word for Windows to continue learning the program's more advanced features on your own. Good writing!

EXCEL 4 FOR WINDOWS

Michael Miller
Revised by Jennifer Flynn

1 Starting and Exiting Excel

In this lesson you will learn how to start and exit Excel. You will also learn the parts of an Excel worksheet window, and how to use the mouse.

Microsoft Excel 4.0

Perhaps you walked into work this morning to find that a new program has been installed on your computer. Your boss wants you to use this new program, Microsoft Excel 4.0, to create the monthly sales report. What do you do?

A few things are certain:

- You need a method of finding your way around Excel quickly and easily.
- You need to identify and learn the tasks necessary to accomplish your particular goals.
- You need a clear-cut, plain-English guide to the basic features of the program.

You need *Microsoft Office 6 in 1.*

Starting Excel

Starting Excel is like starting any other Windows program. To start Excel, Windows must be running. To start Windows:

1. Type **WIN** at the DOS prompt.
2. Press **Enter**.

Launch the Excel program from the Program Manager. The Program Manager is the main program within Windows. You use the Program Manager to run your other application programs and organize them into small groups. When you start Windows, the Program Manager is usually open and running. If the Program Manager window is not open:

- Double-click on the **Program Manager** icon, or press **Tab** until the Program Manager icon is selected and press **Enter**.

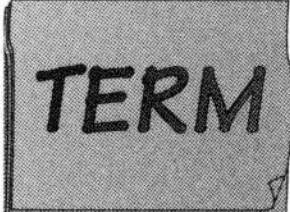

Double-click Double-clicking on a program icon will start the program. An icon is a small picture which represents something such as a program, a file, or a program group. To double-click, press the left mouse button two times in rapid succession.

With the Program Manager window open, start the Excel program:

1. To open the program group window which holds the Excel icon:
   - Press **Tab** to select the group icon and press **Enter**.

     Or

   - Double-click on the group icon (see Figure 1.1).
2. To select the Microsoft Excel icon:
   - Press **Tab** to highlight the icon and press **Enter**.

     Or

   - Double-click on the icon with the mouse.

The Excel opening screen appears with a blank worksheet titled Sheet1 (see Figure 1.2). The Excel program is now ready for you to use.

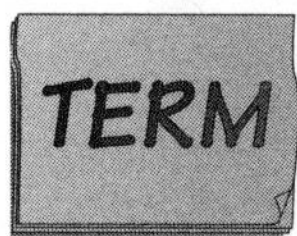

Worksheet A worksheet is a file which is divided into cells; each individual cell is the intersection of a horizontal row and a vertical column.

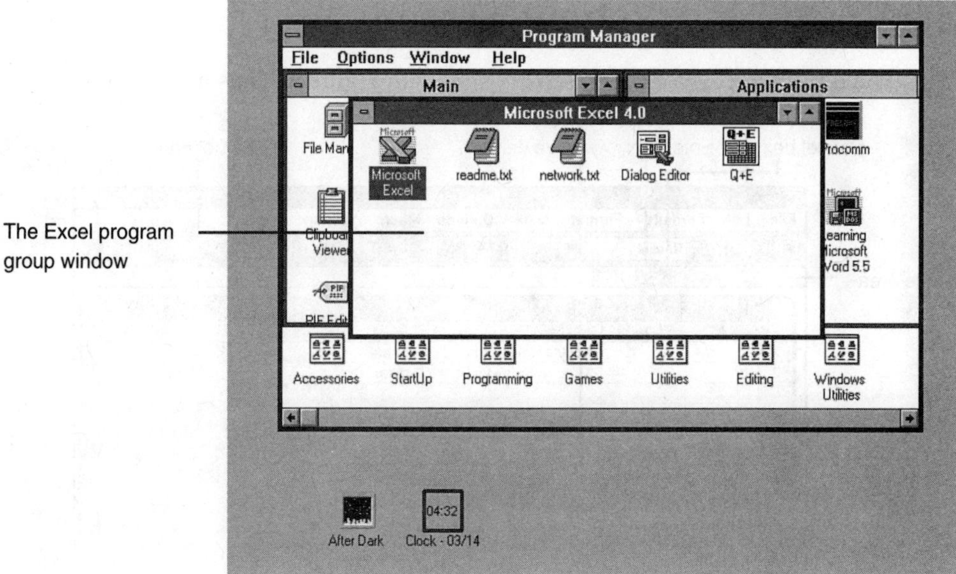

Figure 1.1 The Program Manager with the Excel group window open.

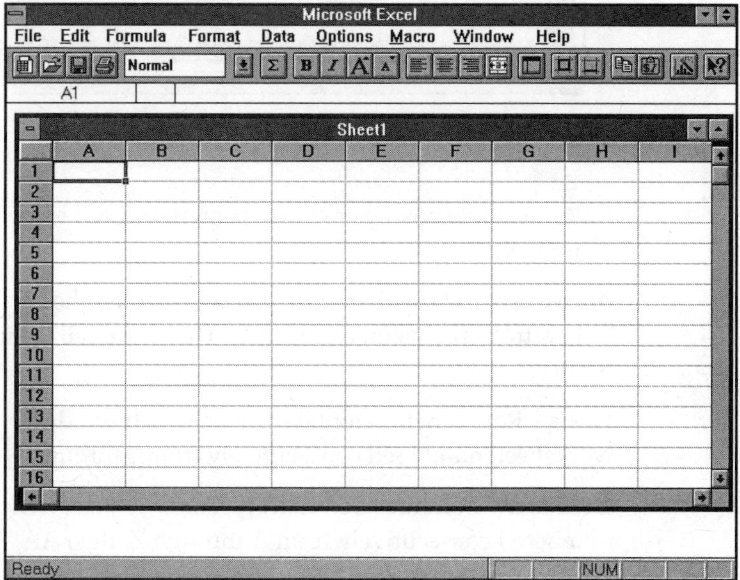

Figure 1.2 Excel's opening screen.

The Excel Worksheet Screen

The typical Excel worksheet screen, shown in Figure 1.3, has many parts.

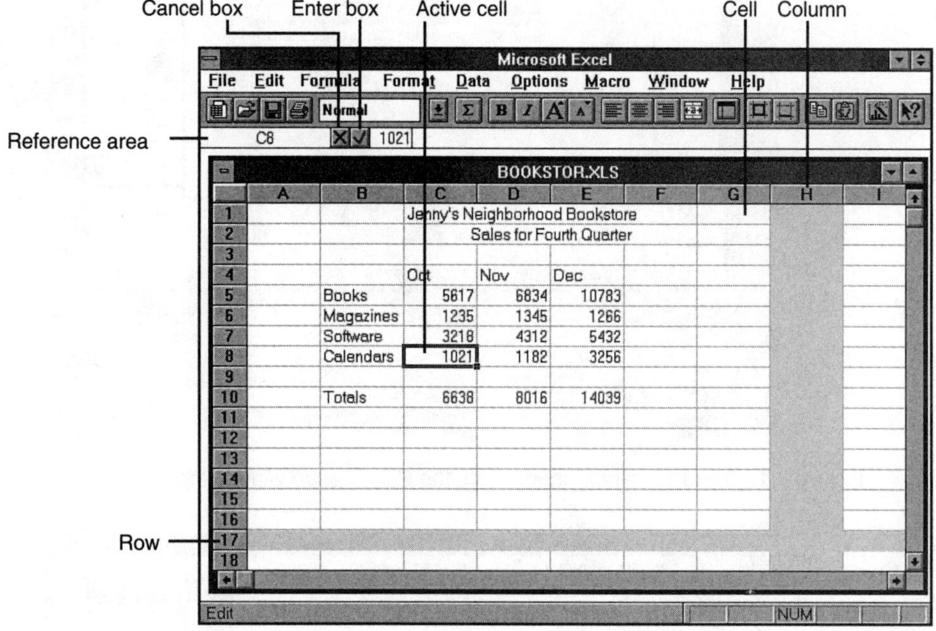

Figure 1.3 A typical Excel window.

Cell A single box where data is entered. A cell is the intersection of a column and a row.

Active cell The active cell will be affected by the current action—such as keystrokes or menu commands. The active cell is highlighted by a dark border.

Rows Rows are horizontal sections which run down the length of a worksheet, numbered consecutively from 1 through 16384.

Columns Columns are vertical sections which run across a worksheet, numbered consecutively from A through Z, then AA, AB, and on through IV.

Reference area Displays the name of the active cell. Cells are referenced first by column, and then by row—for example, cell A4 is the cell located in column A, row 4.

Formula bar Displays either the data or the formula for the contents of the active cell. You will be learning more about formulas in Lesson 10.

Cancel box Click here to cancel an entry to the active cell.

Enter box Click here to accept an entry to the active cell.

Toolbar Contains many icons (tools) you click on to perform various tasks (such as formatting and justification). The individual tools will be described in Lesson 2.

Exiting Excel

To exit Excel and return to Windows, follow these steps:

1. Pull down the **File** menu by pressing **Alt+F** or clicking on **File**.
2. Select the **Exit** command by clicking on it or pressing **X**. If you have unsaved files open, Excel will prompt you to save them. You will learn more about saving worksheet files in Lesson 3. Select the appropriate command button. Excel will then close and return you to Windows.

In this lesson, you learned how to start and exit Excel. You also learned about the main parts of the Excel window, and how to use a mouse. In the next lesson you will learn how to use the Toolbar.

2 Using the Toolbar

In this lesson, you will learn how to use Excel's Toolbars to save time when you work. You will also learn how to arrange them to suit your taste.

Selecting Standard Toolbar Tools

Excel displays the Standard Toolbar (see Figure 2.1) by default. To select a tool from a Toolbar, click on that tool with the mouse.

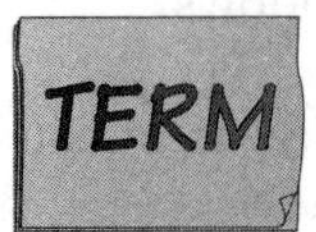

What Is a Toolbar? An Excel Toolbar is a collection of tools or shortcut icons displayed in a long bar which can be moved and reshaped to suit your needs.

Figure 2.1 The Excel Standard Toolbar.

The Standard Toolbar allows you to execute the most often used menu commands, as shown in Table 2.1.

Table 2.1 The Tools in the Standard Toolbar

Tool	*Description*
New Worksheet	Opens a new worksheet file
Open File	Opens an existing document
Save File	Saves an existing document

Tool	Description
Print File	Prints your current document
Style Box	Applies a style to the current cell
Autosum	Sums (totals) the cells above and to the left of the current cell
Bold	Makes the selected text bold
Italic	Makes the selected text italic
Increase Font Size	Increases the size of selected text to the next available size
Decrease Font Size	Decreases the size of selected text to the next available size
Left Align	Aligns the selected text on the left
Center Align	Centers the selected text
Right Align	Aligns the selected text on the right
Center Across Columns	Centers the selected text over the indicated columns
Auto Format	Automatically formats the various elements of a table
Outline Border	Places an outline around the selected cells
Bottom Border	Places a line under the selected cells
Copy Tool	Copies the selected cells or objects to the clipboard (same as Copy command)
Paste Formats	Pastes the formats of cells copied to the clipboard
ChartWizard	Starts the ChartWizard
Help	Use this tool to get help on any Excel menu or any part of an Excel worksheet.

Hiding and Displaying the Standard Toolbar

To hide a Toolbar, you can use the **Options** menu or the **Shortcut** menu.

To use the **Options** menu to hide or display a **Toolbar**:

1. Click on the **Options** menu or press **Alt+O**.
2. Click on **Toolbars**, or press **O**. The **Show Toolbars** dialog box appears.
3. Select the **Toolbar** you would like to hide or display.
4. To hide a Toolbar, choose **Hide** or press **Alt+I**. To display a **Toolbar**, choose **Show** or press **Alt+S**.

To use the **Shortcut** menu to hide or display a **Toolbar**:

1. Move the mouse pointer to an open space within the **Toolbar**.
2. Display the **Shortcut** menu by clicking with the right mouse button (see Figure 2.2).
3. Excel places a check mark next to the name of a displayed Toolbar. To remove a check mark (to hide a Toolbar), or to add a check mark (to display a Toolbar), select the name of the Toolbar from the Shortcut menu.

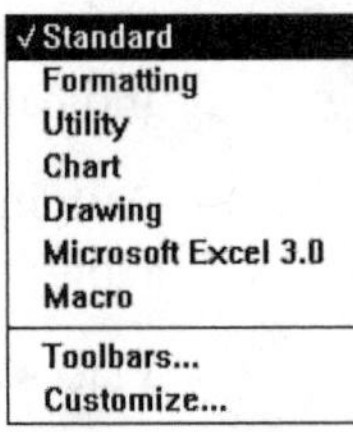

Figure 2.2 The Standard Toolbar Shortcut menu.

Using Other Toolbars

Excel has a total of nine Toolbars, including the Standard Toolbar shown in Figure 2.1. The additional Toolbars are listed below:

Formatting Shortcuts that include font selection, number formats, and shading.

Utility Common commands such as Copy, Repeat, and Undo.

Chart Commands used in customizing charts.

Drawing Tools used to draw simple figures.

Microsoft Excel 3.0 The standard **Toolbar** used in Excel Version 3.0.

Macro Used in creating macros, which are named series of commands that you program.

Macro Paused Used when a running macro is paused.

You may display any or all of the **Toolbars** in your work area. You can also move and resize the **Toolbars** to suit your taste.

Is It Getting Crowded in Here? Try to get in the habit of displaying only the **Toolbars** you need. Displaying a lot of unnecessary **Toolbars** will reduce your screen space and use memory.

Moving Toolbars

After you have displayed the Toolbars which you would like to use, you may position them in your work area where they are most convenient. Figure 2.3 shows a worksheet with three Toolbars in various areas.

When a Toolbar is initially displayed, it is placed at the top or bottom of the work area. To move a Toolbar:

1. Move the mouse pointer to an open space on the Toolbar.
2. Press and hold the left mouse button to drag the Toolbar to the new location. If you drag it close to an edge, the Toolbar will snap into the *Toolbar dock.*

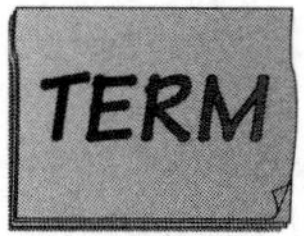

Toolbar Dock The Toolbar dock is located along each edge of the work area. When a Toolbar is moved close to the Toolbar dock, it will automatically snap into place along that edge. The **Drawing Toolbar** shown in Figure 2.3 is in the right Toolbar dock.

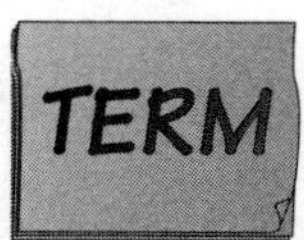

Floating Toolbars Any Toolbars that are not in a **Toolbar** dock are floating Toolbars. The **Utility** and **Chart Toolbars** shown in Figure 2.3 are floating Toolbars.

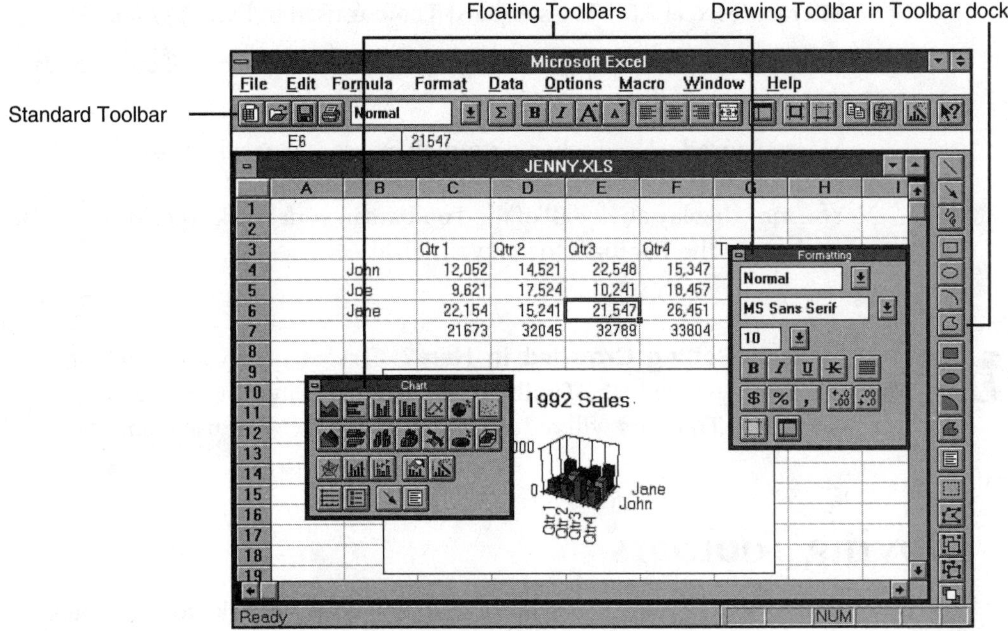

Figure 2.3 An Excel worksheet displaying three Toolbars.

Resizing Toolbars

To resize a Toolbar, grab it by the edge, like any window, and drag that edge to the new size. After a Toolbar has been resized, the tools within it will be rearranged to accommodate the new size. The Utility Toolbar shown in Figure 2.3 has been resized.

Using the Shift Command with Toolbar Tools

Some tools have twins that represent the opposite action. You can toggle between twin tools by using the **Shift** key. To switch between the actions of twin tools, hold down the **Shift** key as you click on the tool. For example, to draw a filled circle with the Circle tool, hold down the Shift key when you click on it. Likewise, to draw a circle with the Filled Circle Tool, hold down the **Shift** key as you click on it.

Put Away Those Tools! If you like using the **Shift** key with tools, save room on your **Toolbars** by removing one of each of the twin tools.

Tool	*Twin Tool*	*Toolbar*
Arc	Filled Arc	Drawing
Bring to Front	Send to Back	Drawing
Decrease Decimal	Increase Decimal	Formatting
Decrease Font Size	Increase Font Size	Standard
Delete	Insert	(can add to any Toolbar)
Delete Column	Insert Column	(can add to any Toolbar)
Delete Row	Insert Row	(can add to any Toolbar)
Filled Freehand Polygon	Freehand Polygon	Drawing
Filled Oval	Oval	Drawing
Filled Polygon	Polygon	Drawing
Filled Rectangle	Rectangle	Drawing
Group	Ungroup	Drawing
Paste Format	Paste Values	Standard
Print	Print Preview	Standard
Run Macro	Step Macro	Macro
Sort Ascending	Sort Descending	Utility
Zoom In	Zoom Out	Utility

In this lesson, you learned about the tools contained in the **Standard Toolbar** and about the eight other **Toolbars**. You learned how to customize your work area by repositioning and resizing the various **Toolbars**. In the next lesson, you will learn how to work with Excel's worksheets.

3 Working with Worksheets

In this lesson you will learn how to open and save existing Excel worksheets. You will also learn how to create new worksheets.

Saving a Worksheet

It is important to always save your data. Saving your worksheet before leaving Excel should become part of your working routine.

To save a worksheet:

1. Pull down the **File** menu.
2. Select the **Save** command; the dialog box shown in Figure 3.1 appears. (This dialog box only appears the first time you save a file.)
3. If this is a new worksheet, enter the name of the file in the **File Name** text box. You may use any combination of letters or numbers up to eight characters (no spaces), such as 1992BDGT. Excel automatically adds .XLS to the file name as an extension. The full file name is then 1992BDGT.XLS.
4. Click on **OK** or press **Enter**.

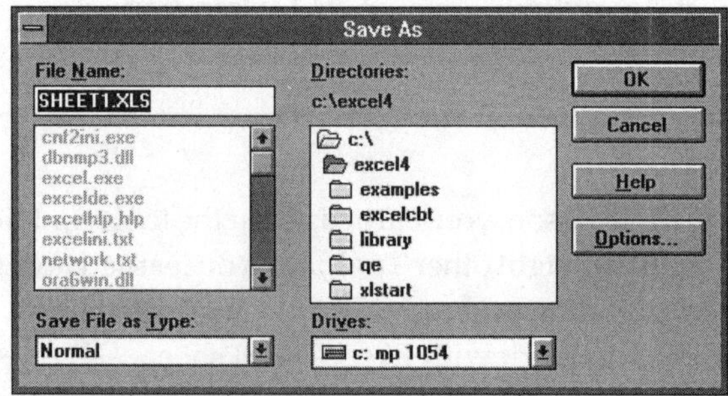

Figure 3.1 The File Save As dialog box.

Make a Mistake? Click on **Cancel** anytime before step 4 to cancel the File Save operation. If you've already saved the file, but you typed something wrong, save it again. Be sure to delete the unwanted copy after your work session.

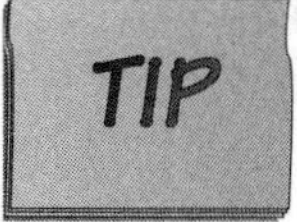

Save It Again If you saved the file previously, and you simply want to save the file and then continue working, use the keyboard shortcut for saving a file: **Shift+F12**. To do this, hold the **Shift** key down as you press **F12**, then release. Your file is now saved.

Saving a File with a New Name

You may want to save an existing worksheet with a different name, or in a different directory. You can do both of these things and more by using the Save **A**s command:

1. Pull down the **File** menu.
2. Select the **Save As** command. The dialog box shown in Figure 3.1 will appear.
3. If you wish to save the worksheet under a new name (you will then have two copies—the original, and this one), type the new file name over the existing name in the **File Name** text box.
4. To save the file to a different directory, double-click on that directory in the **Directories** list box. The directory shown below **Directories** will change.
5. To save the file on a different drive, activate the **Drives** drop-down list box by clicking on the arrow on the right of the list. A list of available drives will appear. Click on the drive you wish to save to.
6. To save the file in a different format, activate the **Save File as Type** drop-down list box by clicking on the arrow on the right of the list. A list of formats will appear. You can choose to save your file in Lotus, dBASE, and text format, among others.
7. Click on **OK** or press **Enter**.

Excel 4.0 offers you an even faster alternative for saving your document. Simply click on the **Save File** tool in the Standard Toolbar.

A Little Insurance Before making major changes to any document, it is always a good idea to save it first. That way, if something goes wrong with a new procedure, you can simply reopen the saved file.

Opening a New Worksheet

To open a new worksheet, follow these steps:

1. Pull down the **File** menu.
2. Select **New**; the dialog box shown in Figure 3.2 appears.
3. Choose **Worksheet**.
4. Click on **OK** or press **Enter**. A new worksheet opens on-screen with a default name in the title bar. Excel numbers the files sequentially. For example, if you already have Sheet1 open, your screen will read Sheet2.

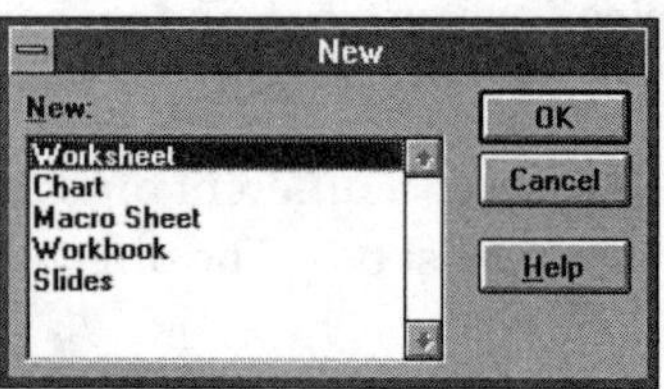

Figure 3.2 The New File dialog box.

Excel 4.0 provides you with a shortcut for opening a new file. Simply click on the **New Worksheet** tool on the Standard Toolbar.

Opening an Existing Worksheet

To open an existing worksheet, follow these steps:

1. Pull down the **File** menu.
2. Select **Open**; the dialog box shown in Figure 3.3 appears.
3. If the file is not in the current directory, select the **Directories** list box. Then select the directory you wish to change to.
4. If the file is not on the current drive, select the **Drives** list box. Then select the drive you wish to change to.
5. Choose the file you wish to open from the **File Name** box.
6. Click on **OK** or press **Enter**.

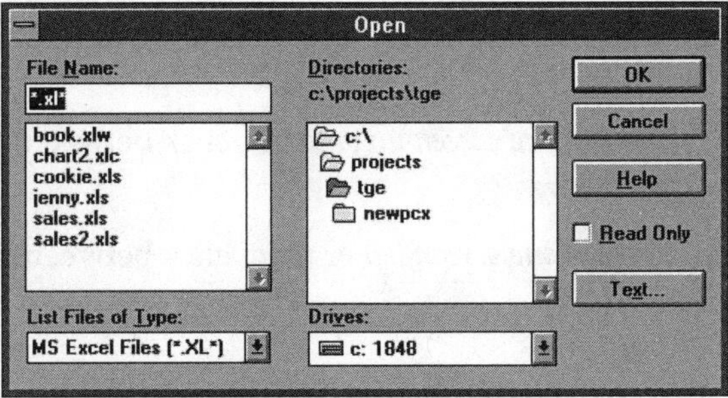

Figure 3.3 The Open dialog box.

Excel 4.0 provides you with a shortcut for opening a file. Simply click on the **Open File** tool on the Standard Toolbar.

Navigating a Worksheet

You can move around an Excel worksheet by using the mouse or the keyboard, whichever is more convenient.

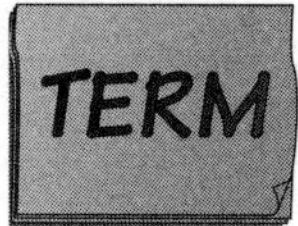

The Active Cell The cell which will receive input or be affected by any formatting commands is the active cell. The active cell or cells are surrounded by a dark line.

To move the active cell a short distance:

- Use any of the arrow keys. For example, to move down one row, press ↓.
- Click on any cell with the mouse.

Using the scroll bars located on the bottom and right sides of the worksheet is one of the easiest ways to move quickly around a large worksheet.

To scroll through one column, click on the right arrow located on the horizontal scroll bar.

To scroll through one row, click on the down arrow located on the vertical scroll bar.

To scroll one screen up or down, click between the arrows on the vertical scroll bar.

To scroll one screen left or right, click between the arrows on the horizontal scroll bar.

Going Somewhere? To scroll to a general location in the worksheet, drag the scroll box to the appropriate place within the scroll bar.

To use the keyboard to move around the worksheet, use one of the key combinations from Table 3.1.

Table 3.1 Worksheet Navigation Keys

Key	*Function*
↑	Move one cell up
↓	Move one cell down
← or Shift+Tab	Move one cell left

Key	*Function*
→ or Tab	Move one cell right
PgUp	Move one screen up
PgDn	Move one screen down
Ctrl+PgUp	Move one screen left
Ctrl+PgDn	Move one screen right
End+any arrow key	Move in the indicated direction, to the last cell with data
Ctrl+End	Move to the last cell in the worksheet
Ctrl+Home	Move to the first cell in the worksheet (A1)

When You Know Where You're Going You can move to a specific cell in the worksheet by selecting the **Goto** command on the **Formula** menu. In the **Reference box**, type the name of the cell you would like to move to (for example, type G12), and then click on **OK** or press **Enter**.

Moving Between Open Worksheets

Sometimes you may have more than one worksheet open at a time. There are many ways to move between open worksheets:

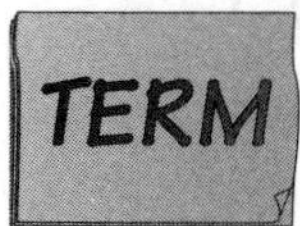

The Active Window If you have more than one worksheet open, only one of them is considered active—the worksheet where the cell selector is located. The title bar of the active worksheet will be darker than the title bars of other open worksheets.

If the worksheet you would like to move to is visible:

- Click on any part of that worksheet to make it active.

If the worksheet you would like to move to is not visible:

1. Pull down the **Window** menu. A list of open worksheets will appear at the bottom of the menu.
2. Select the worksheet you wish to move to.

Make Some Room You can temporarily move an open worksheet out of the way by reducing it to an icon at the bottom of the work area. Simply click on the **Minimize** button to minimize the worksheet. To restore the worksheet to its previous size, double-click on its icon.

Closing Worksheets

Closing a worksheet removes it from the screen. To close a worksheet:

1. Make the window you want to close active.
2. Pull down the **File** menu.
3. Choose **Close**.
4. If you have not yet saved the Worksheet, you will be prompted to do so.

In a Hurry? To quickly close a worksheet, double-click on the control button located in the upper left corner.

Save, Save, Save To avoid losing data, always save your worksheet files before closing them.

In this lesson, you learned how to open, close, and save worksheets. You also learned the basics for navigating a worksheet. The next lesson teaches you how to use Excel's workbooks.

Using Excel's Workbooks

This lesson teaches you how to use workbooks to organize your files.

Excel 4.0 offers you the ability to save multiple worksheets in a workbook.

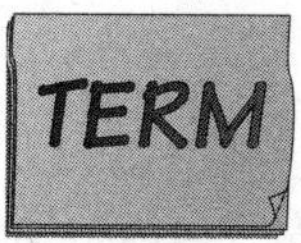

A Workbook A collection of worksheets, charts, and related information is called a workbook. Using workbooks is an easy way to keep all of the material for a related task together.

Building a Workbook

You start a workbook by first creating the workbook as if you were creating a file. You then add worksheet files to the workbook. To create a workbook:

1. Pull down the **File** menu.
2. Choose **New**.
3. In the **New** list box, choose **Workbook**.
4. Click on **OK** or press **Enter**. Your window should look similar to Figure 4.1.

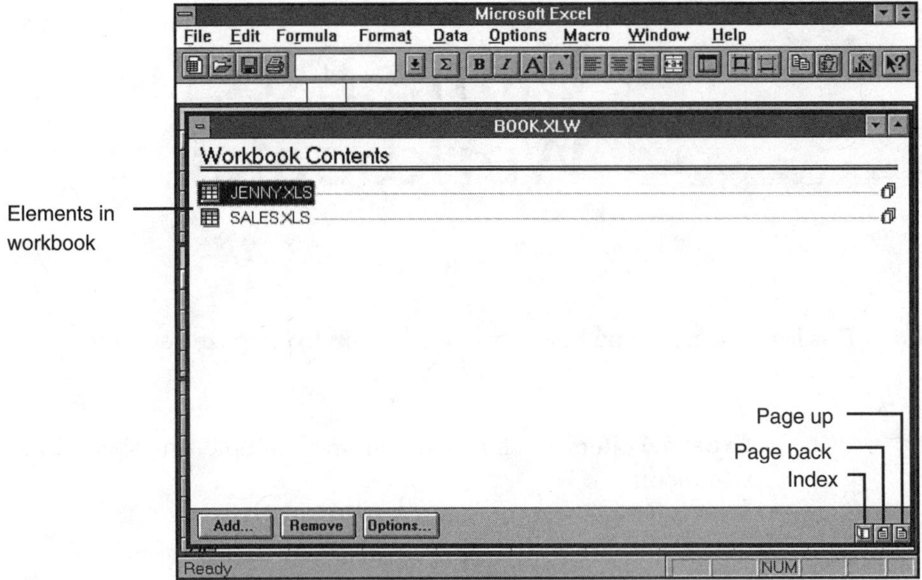

Figure 4.1 An Excel workbook.

You can add worksheets to a workbook, including new or unopened worksheets. To add worksheets to a workbook (when the workbook window is visible):

1. Click on **Add**.
2. From the Add to Workbook dialog box, select a worksheet to add from the list. (This step is necessary only when you're adding an existing, open workbook.)
3. Click on **Add**, **New**, or **Open**. (If you select **N**ew, the New dialog box appears so that you can specify what kind of document to add. Selecting **O**pen displays the Open dialog box so that you can select which worksheet to add.)
4. Repeat steps 1–3 until all the documents you want have been added to the workbook.
5. Click on **Close**.

Navigating Between Documents in a Workbook

There are many ways to navigate between documents in a workbook:

- From the workbook window, double-click on the documents you would like to switch to.
- At the bottom of a document or workbook window, activate the Shortcut menu by clicking on the **Contents** icon. Then select a document from the list.
- At the bottom of a document or workbook window, click on the **Left Paging** or **Right Paging** icon to move forward or backward one document in the workbook list.

Saving Documents in a Workbook

To save all the documents in a workbook:

1. Pull down the **File** menu.
2. Select **Save Workbook**.
3. If you wish to save the workbook under a new name (you will then have two copies—the original, and this one), simply type the new file name over the existing one in the File Name text box. Excel will automatically add the .XLS extension.
4. To save the workbook in a different directory, double-click on that directory in the **Directories** list box. The directory shown above Directories will change.
5. To save the workbook on a different drive, activate the **Drives** drop-down list box by clicking on the arrow on the right of the list. A list of available drives will appear. Click on the drive you wish to save to.
6. Click on **OK** or press **Enter**.

In this lesson, you learned how to use workbooks. The next lesson teaches you how to enter data in Excel.

5

Entering and Editing Data

In this lesson, you will learn how to enter different types of data in an Excel worksheet.

Types of Data

There are many types of data that you can enter into an Excel worksheet. These include:

- Text
- Numbers
- Dates
- Times
- Formulas

As you enter data into a cell, it appears in that cell and also in the formula bar, as shown in Figure 5.1.

Entering Text

Any combination of letters or numbers can be entered as text. Text is automatically left-aligned.

To enter text into a cell:

1. Select the cell into which you want to enter text.
2. Type the text.
3. Click on the **Enter** button on the formula bar or press **Enter**.

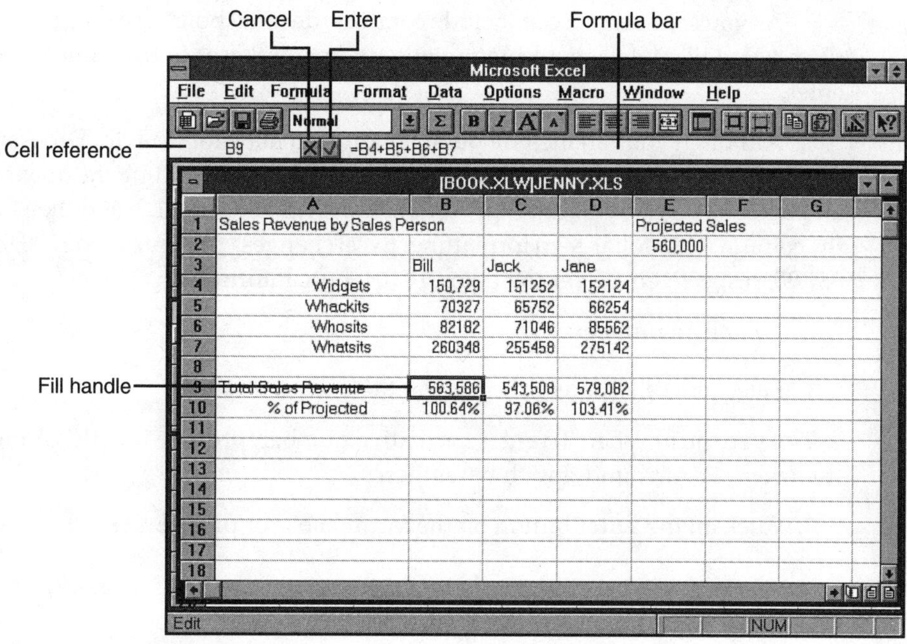

Figure 5.1 Data that you enter also appears in the formula bar.

Bail out! To cancel an entry before you are done, click on the **Cancel** button or press **Esc**.

Number Text You may want to enter a number as text (for example, a ZIP code). Precede your entry with a single quotation mark ('), as in '46220. The quotation mark is an alignment prefix that tells Excel to treat the following characters as text and left-align them in the cell.

Entering Numbers

Valid numbers can include the numeric characters 0–9 and any of these special characters: + – ( ) , $ % . E e. Numbers are automatically right-aligned.

As you can see, you can include commas, decimal points, scientific notation (E and e), dollar signs, percentage signs, and parentheses in the values that you enter.

Although you can include punctuation, you may not want to. For example, rather than type a column of a hundred dollar amounts including the dollar signs and decimal points, you can type numbers such as 700 and 81.2, and then format the column with dollar-sign formatting. Excel changes your entries to $700.00 and $81.20, respectively. Refer to Lesson 14 for more information.

To enter a number:

1. Select the cell into which you want to enter a number.
2. Type the number. To enter a negative number, precede it with a minus sign, or surround it with parentheses.
3. Click on the **Enter** button on the formula bar or press **Enter**.

Entering Dates and Times

Dates and times can be entered in a variety of formats. When you enter a date using a format shown in Table 5.1, Excel converts the date into a number which represents the number of days since January 1, 1900. This number is used whenever a calculation involves a date. Because a date is actually a number, when a date is entered correctly, it is right-aligned in the cell. You cannot perform calculations on a date that has not been entered correctly. If you enter a two-digit month, such as 04/08/58, it is truncated to one digit, 4/8/58.

Table 5.1 Valid Formats for Dates and Times

Format	*Example*
MM/DD/YY	4/8/58 or 04/08/58
MMM-YY	Jan-92
DD-MMM-YY	28-Oct-91
DD-MMM	6-Sep
HH:MM	16:50
HH:MM:SS	8:22:59

Format	*Example*
HH:MM AM/PM	7:45 PM
HH:MM:SS AM/PM	11:45:16 AM
MM/DD/YY HH:MM	11/8/80 4:20
HH:MM MM/DD/YY	4:20 11/18/80

To enter a date or time:

1. Select the cell into which you want to enter a date or time.
2. Type the date or time in the format in which you want it displayed.
3. Click on the **Enter** button on the formula bar or press **Enter**.

To Dash or to Slash You can use dashes (-) or slashes(/) when typing dates. Capitalization is not important, since it is ignored. For example, 21 FEB becomes 21-Feb. By the way, FEB 21 also becomes 21-Feb.

Day or Night? Unless you type AM or PM, Excel assumes that you are using a 24-hour military clock. Therefore, 8:20 is assumed to be AM, not PM, unless you type 8:20 PM.

Using Autofill

Excel 4.0 has a new tool that is designed to save you time in entering data in a series. A series is a collection of data with a logical progression, such as 1, 2, 3 or Qtr 1, Qtr 2, and Qtr 3.

Excel recognizes four types of series, shown in Table 5.2.

Table 5.2 Data Series

Series	*Initial Entry*	*Resulting Series*
Linear	1,2	3,4,5
	100,99	98,97,96
	1,3	5,7,9
Growth	10 (step 5)	15,20,25
	10 (step 10)	20,30,40
Date	Mon	Tue, Wed, Thur
	Feb	Mar, Apr, May
	Qtr1	Qtr2, Qtr3, Qtr4
	1992	1993, 1994, 1995
Autofill	Team 1	Team 2, Team 3, Team 4
	Qtr 4	Qtr 1, Qtr 2, Qtr 3
	1st Quarter	2nd Quarter, 3rd Quarter, 4th Quarter

To create a series using Autofill by dragging:

1. Enter the first two values in a series.
2. Select the two cells.
3. Drag the series to adjacent cells by dragging the fill handle located at the lower right corner of the selected cells (see Figure 5.1).
4. Release the mouse button, and Excel fills the cells with values based on the initial values.

To create a series using Autofill with the Series command:

1. Enter a value in one cell.
2. Select the cells into which you want to extend the series.
3. Pull down the **Data menu**.
4. Choose **Series**. The dialog box shown in Figure 5.2 appears.

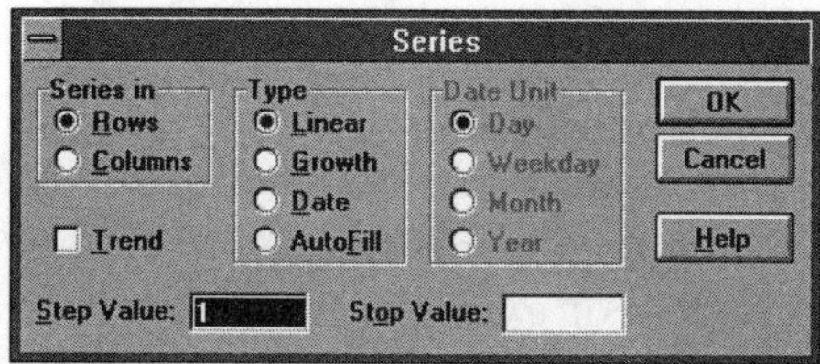

Figure 5.2 The Data Series dialog box.

5. Under **Series**, select **Rows** or **Columns**.
6. Under **Type**, choose a series type.
7. Adjust the **Step** value (amount between each series value), and **Stop** value (last value you want Excel to enter) if necessary.
8. Click on **OK** or press **Enter**, and the series is created.

Editing Data

After you have entered data into a cell, you may change it by editing.

To edit data in a cell:

1. Select the cell in which you want to edit data.
2. Position the cursor in the formula bar with the mouse, or press **F2** to enter **Edit** mode.
3. Use the **Backspace** key to delete characters to the left of the cursor, or the **Delete** key to delete characters to the right of the cursor. Type any additional characters. They will be added to the left of the cursor.
4. Click on the **Enter** button on the formula bar or press **Enter** to accept your changes.

Stop the Edit To cancel changes to a cell before you are done, click on the **Cancel** button or press **Esc**.

Using Undo

There is an easy way to undo the last change that you made to the worksheet. To undo a change:

1. Pull down the **Edit** menu.
2. Choose **Undo Typing**.

The actual command shown in step 2 will vary, depending on what you are trying to undo. For example, the **Edit** menu might display **Undo** Formatting, **Undo Sorting**, or **Undo Alignment**.

Act Fast to Undo a Change You will not be able to undo a change after you have changed something else. If you are not able to undo a change, **Can't Undo** will be displayed on the **Edit** menu.

To undo an **Undo** (reverse a change):

1. Pull down the **Edit** menu.
2. Choose **Redo**.

Like the **Undo** command, the **Redo** command will also vary, depending on what you are trying to redo. For example, the **Edit** menu might display **Redo Formatting**, **Redo Sorting**, or **Redo Alignment**.

Undo It Easier To quickly undo a change, press **Ctrl+Z**, or click on the **Undo** tool on the Utility Toolbar if you have that Toolbar displayed.

In this lesson you learned how to enter different types of data, and how to make changes and undo those changes.

6 Working with Ranges

In this lesson, you will learn how to select and name cell ranges.

What Is a Range?

A range is a rectangular group of connected cells. The cells in a range may all be in a column, or a row, or any combination of columns and rows, as long as the range forms a rectangle, as shown in Figure 6.1.

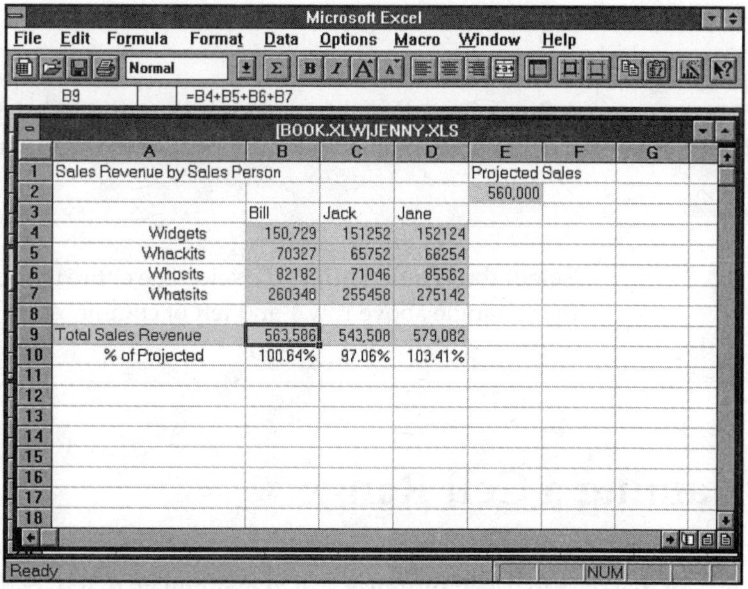

Microsoft Excel

File Edit Formula Format Data Options Macro Window Help

Normal

B9 =B4+B5+B6+B7

[BOOK.XLW]JENNY.XLS

	A	B	C	D	E	F	G
1	Sales Revenue by Sales Person				Projected Sales		
2					560,000		
3		Bill	Jack	Jane			
4	Widgets	150,729	151252	152124			
5	Whackits	70327	65752	66254			
6	Whosits	82182	71046	85562			
7	Whatsits	260348	255458	275142			
8							
9	Total Sales Revenue	563,586	543,508	579,082			
10	% of Projected	100.64%	97.06%	103.41%			
11							
12							
13							
14							
15							
16							
17							
18							

Ready NUM

Figure 6.1 A range is any combination of cells that forms a rectangle.

Learning how to use ranges can save you time. For example, you can select a range and use it to format a group of cells with one step. You can use a range to print only a selected group of cells. You can also use ranges in formulas.

Ranges are referred to by their anchor points (the top left corner and the lower right corner). For example, the ranges shown in Figure 6.1 are B4:D7, A9:D9, and F2.

Selecting a Range

To select a range, use the mouse:

1. Move the mouse pointer to the upper left corner of a range.
2. Click and hold the left mouse button.
3. Drag the mouse to the lower right corner of the range.
4. Release the mouse button. The selected range will be highlighted.

Sorry, Wrong Range If you accidentally select the wrong range, simply reselect it with the mouse.

A Quick Selection To quickly select a row or a column, click on the row or column name at the edge of the worksheet.

Select the Whole Thing To select the entire worksheet, click on the rectangle above row 1 and left of column A.

Naming a Cell Range

Sometimes, when working with a lot of data, it is more convenient to name parts of that data to use in formulas and to manipulate that data by sorting and such. Once a range is named, you can use that name (instead of the name of the cell locations) to refer to that data. For example, you could give a column which holds data for January the range name JAN.

To name a cell range:

1. Select the range of cells to be named.
2. Pull down the Formula menu.
3. Choose **Define Name**. The dialog box shown in Figure 6.2 appears.
4. You may accept the name that Excel provides (if any), or type in a new one in the **Name** text box. Valid names can include letters, numbers, - \ . or ?. Range names must begin with a letter, the minus sign, or the back slash (\).
5. Click on **OK** or press **Enter**.

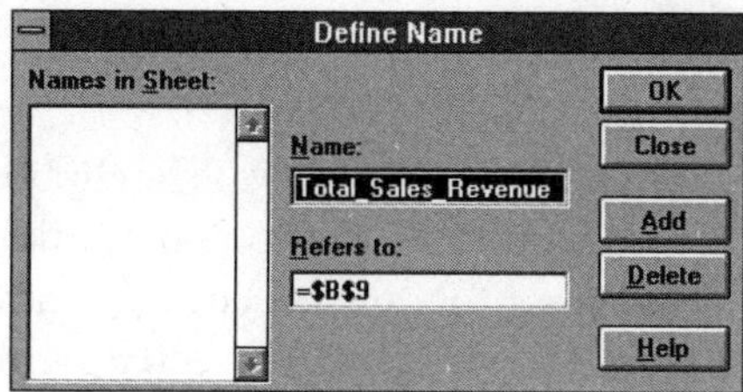

Figure 6.2 The Define Name dialog box.

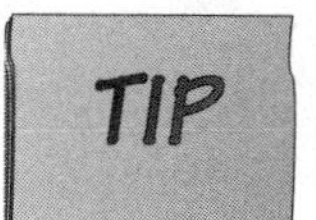

Name a Range Fast To quickly name a range, select the range to be named and press **Ctrl+F3**.

In this lesson, you learned how to select and name ranges. In the next lesson, you will learn how to copy, move, and erase data.

7 Copying, Moving, and Erasing Data

In this lesson, you will learn to organize your worksheet to meet your changing needs by copying, moving and erasing data.

When you copy or move data, a copy of that data is placed in a temporary storage area called the clipboard.

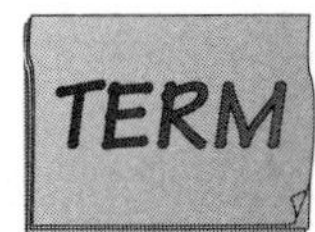

What Is the Clipboard? The clipboard is an area of memory that is accessible to all Windows programs. The clipboard is used by all Windows programs to copy or move data from place to place within a program, or between programs. The techniques that you learn here are the same ones used in all Windows programs.

Copying Data

You make copies of data to use in other sections of your worksheet. The data that you copy remains in place, and a copy of it is placed where you indicate.

To copy data:

1. Select the range or cell that you wish to copy.
2. Pull down the **Edit** menu.
3. Choose **Copy**.
4. Move the cursor to the first cell in the area where you would like to place the copy. To copy the data to another worksheet, change to that worksheet.
5. Pull down the **Edit** menu.
6. Choose **Paste**, and the data is copied.

Quick Copying To copy data quickly, select the data to be copied and press **Ctrl+Insert** or **Ctrl+C.** This copies the data to the clipboard. To paste, simply press **Enter**, or **Ctrl+V**.

Excel 4.0 offers you a fast way to copy—Drag and Drop. To use Drag and Drop, you use the fill handle, a small square located in the lower right corner of a selected cell. (If the fill handle doesn't appear, select **Options Workspace**, and then turn on the **Cell Drag and Drop** option.) Simply drag the fill handle to select the cells to which you wish to copy data. You can also copy by using tools. The **Copy** tool is located on the Utility Toolbar. You can also customize any Toolbar by adding the **Fill Right**, **Fill Down**, **Cut**, and **Paste** tools from the Customize dialog box.

Multiple Copies You can copy the same data to several places in the worksheet by repeating the **Edit Paste** command. Data copied to the clipboard remains there until it's replaced by something else.

Moving Data

Moving data is similar to copying, except that the data is cut from its original place and moved to the new location.

To move data:

1. Select the range or cell that you wish to move.
2. Pull down the **Edit** menu.
3. Choose **Cut**.
4. Move the cursor to the first cell in the area where you would like to place the data. To move the data to another worksheet, simply change to that worksheet.
5. Pull down the **Edit** menu.
6. Choose **Paste**, and the data is moved.

Move It! To move data quickly, select the data to be moved and press **Shift+Delete** or **Ctrl+X**. This moves the data to the clipboard. To paste, simply press **Enter** or **Ctrl+V**.

With Excel 4.0, you can use the Shortcut menu to save time when copying or moving data. Select the data to be copied or moved and click the right mouse button to open the Shortcut menu; then choose the appropriate command—**Cut**, **Copy**, or **Paste**. You can also move data to another location with **Drag and Drop**. Select the cells you want to move. Point to the border around them so that the mouse pointer changes from a plus to an arrow. Drag the border to a new location and release the mouse button.

Watch Out! When copying or moving data, be careful when you indicate the range where the data should be pasted. Excel will paste the data over any existing data in the indicated range.

Erasing Data

When erasing data from your worksheet, Excel gives you a lot of options. You can completely remove the data, or simply remove the cell's formatting, formulas, or attached notes.

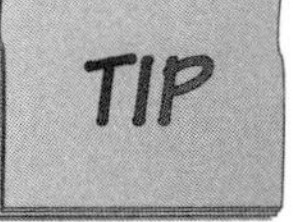

Remove All Data To completely remove data from a cell, use the **Edit Clear** command. The contents of the cell will be removed, but the surrounding cells will not be affected. When you use the **Delete** command, the cell is removed, and the data in surrounding cells is moved on top of it. You will learn more about the Delete command in the next lesson.

Using the Edit Clear Command

Use the **Edit Clear** command to remove all or part of the contents of a cell, without affecting the position of the surrounding cells. With the Clear command, you can remove the data from a cell, or just its formula, formatting, or attached notes.

To clear cells:

1. Select the range of cells you wish to clear.
2. Pull down the **Edit** menu.
3. Choose **Clear**. The Clear dialog box shown in Figure 7.1 appears.
4. Click on the option you would like to use: **Clear All**, **Clear Formats**, **Clear Formulas**, or **Clear Notes**.
5. Click on **OK** or press **Enter**.

A Clean Slate To clear data quickly, select the range of cells to be cleared and press the **Del** key. To clear formulas only, press **Ctrl+Del**.

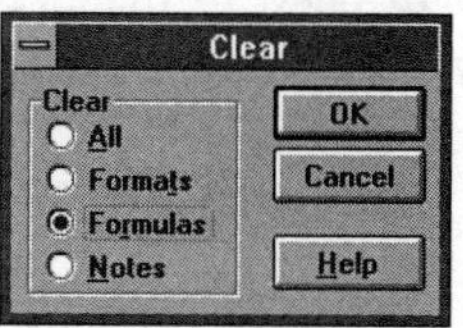

Figure 7.1 The Clear dialog box.

Excel 4.0 offers you another alternative to clear data—the Shortcut menu. Select the range of cells to be cleared and press the right mouse button to open the Shortcut menu. Choose **Clear** from the menu.

In this lesson, you learned how to copy and move data. You also learned how to clear data from cells. In the next lesson, you will learn how to delete and insert cells, rows, and columns.

Inserting and Deleting Cells, Rows, and Columns

In this lesson, you will learn how to rearrange your worksheet by adding and deleting cells, rows, and columns.

Inserting Individual Cells

Sometimes you will need to insert information into a worksheet, right in the middle of existing data. With the Insert command, you can insert a single cell, or whole rows and columns.

Confused? Inserting cells in the middle of existing data will cause those other cells to be shifted down a row or over a column. Exercise caution when inserting cells.

To insert a single cell or a group of cells:

1. Move your pointer to the place where you would like the new cell inserted or select the range where you want to insert new cells.
2. Pull down the **Edit** menu.
3. Choose **Insert**. The Insert dialog box shown in Figure 8.1 appears.

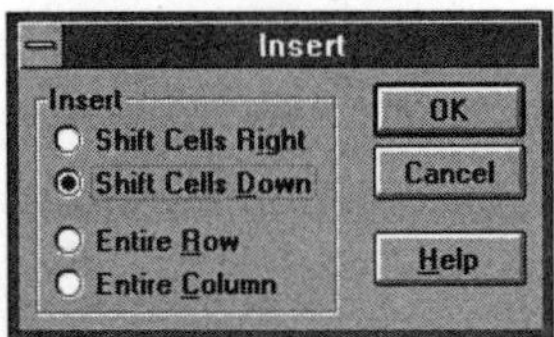

Figure 8.1 The Insert dialog box.

4. Select **Shift Cells Right** or **Shift Cells Down**.
5. Click on **OK** or press **Enter**. Excel inserts the cell and shifts the data in the other cells in the indicated direction.

Inserting entire rows and columns in your worksheet is similar to inserting a single cell.

To insert a row or column:

1. Move your pointer to the place where you would like the new row or column inserted.
2. Pull down the **Edit** menu.
3. Choose **Insert**. The Insert dialog box appears.
4. Select **Entire Row** or **Entire Column**.
5. Click on **OK** or press **Enter**. Excel inserts the row or column and shifts the data in the other cells in the appropriate direction. Figure 8.2 simulates a worksheet before and after a row is inserted.

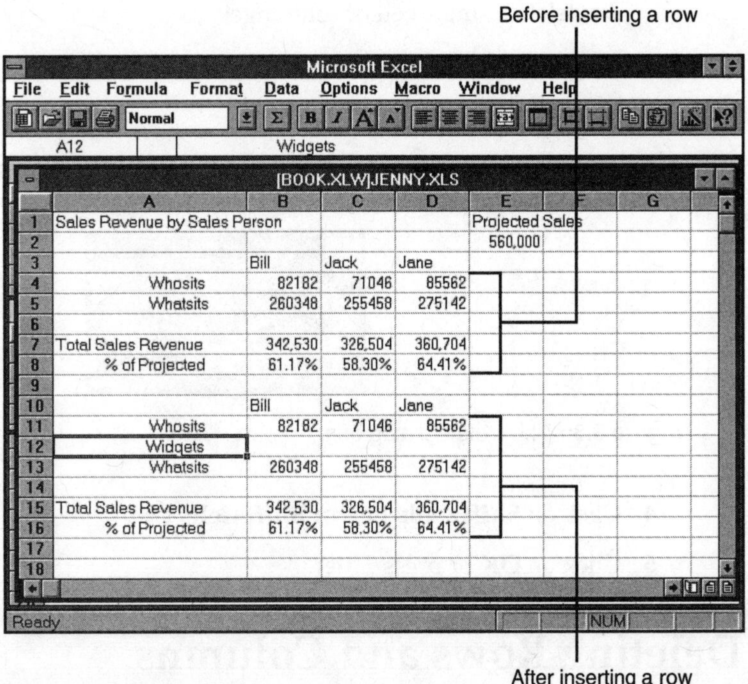

Figure 8.2 Inserting a row in a worksheet.

Insert Rows or Columns Quickly To insert rows or columns without displaying the dialog box, click on the letter or number, and then choose **Edit Insert**. You can also select multiple rows or columns to insert multiple rows or columns.

Excel 4.0 offers you several ways to insert data, and the Shortcut menu is one. Select the row or column where you would like to insert data, and press the right mouse button to open the Shortcut menu. Choose **Insert** from the menu. There are also three tools you can add to any Toolbar from the Customize dialog box—the Insert tool, Insert Column tool, and the Insert Row tool.

Deleting Individual Cells or Cell Ranges

Deleting cells is the opposite of inserting them. When you use the Delete command, the data in the surrounding cells moves up a row or over a column, covering the data in the cells you delete. So, you delete cells by moving data on top of the cells to delete.

To delete a single cell or cell range:

1. Select the cell or range of cells you wish to delete.
2. Pull down the **Edit** menu.
3. Choose **Delete**. The Delete dialog box shown in Figure 8.3 appears.

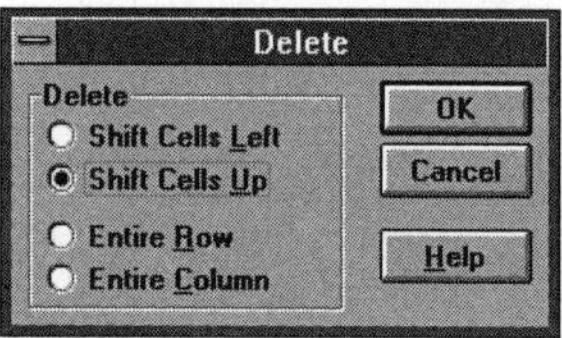

Figure 8.3 The Delete dialog box.

4. Click on **Shift Cells Left** or **Shift Cells Up**.
5. Click on **OK** or press **Enter**.

Deleting Rows and Columns

Deleting rows and columns is similar to deleting a single cell.

To delete a row or column:

1. Select the row or column you wish to delete.
2. Pull down the **Edit** menu.
3. Choose **Delete**. The Delete dialog box appears.
4. Click on **Entire Row** or **Entire Column**.
5. Click on **OK** or press **Enter**. Excel deletes the row or column and shifts the data in the other cells in the appropriate direction. Figure 8.4 simulates a worksheet before and after a row was deleted.

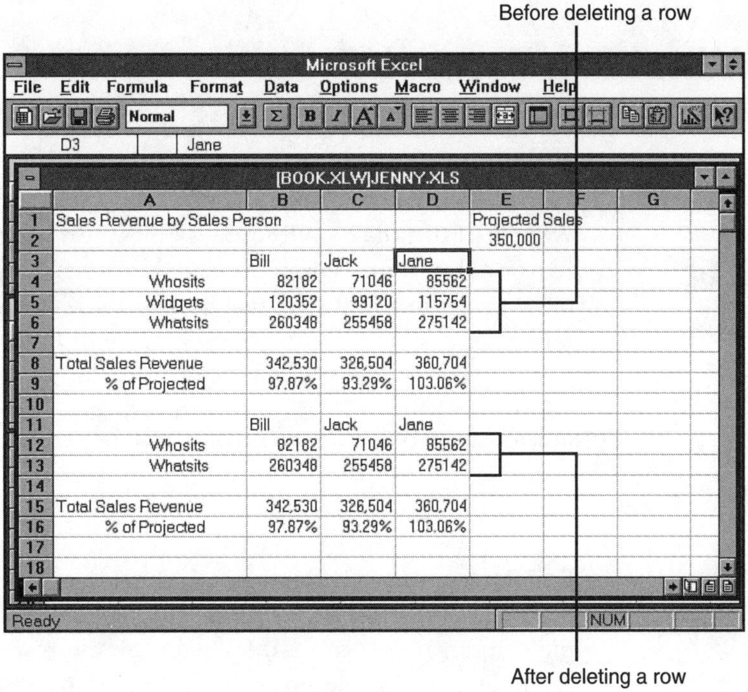

Before deleting a row

After deleting a row

Figure 8.4 Deleting a row in a worksheet.

Excel 4.0 offers you several ways to delete data, and one is to use the Shortcut menu. Select the range of cells to be deleted, and press the right mouse button to open the **Shortcut** menu. Choose **Delete** from the menu. There are also three tools that you can add to any Toolbar from the Customize dialog box—the Delete tool, the Delete Column tool, and the Delete Row tool.

In this lesson, you learned how to insert and delete rows and columns. In the next lesson, you will learn how to use formulas.

Writing Formulas

In this lesson, you will learn how to use formulas to calculate results in your worksheets.

What Is a Formula?

A formula is a mathematical expression which calculates a result.

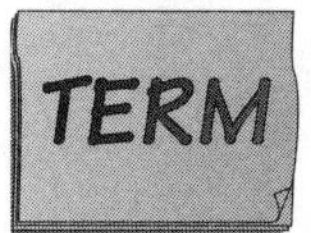

What is a Formula? A formula defines the relationship between two or more values. Formulas include references to the values in other cells, and formulas manipulate these values to produce results.

Formulas consist of numbers, mathematical operators, and references to other cells.

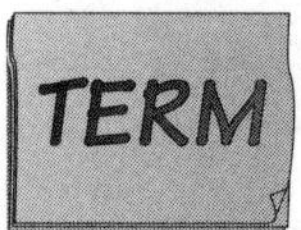

Cell References Expressions which reference the data stored in other cells are called *cell references*. A cell reference is written with the column reference first, followed by the row reference. For example, a cell in column E, row 4 is referred to as E4. When the pointer is in a particular cell, you see the cell reference in the reference area of the formula bar.

Entering Formulas

To enter a formula, you must include:

The equal sign (=) All formulas must begin with an equal sign. This is how Excel identifies the expression as a formula.

A cell reference You may, of course, include multiple cell references in order to manipulate the values of several cells.

You also may include:

Numbers For example, you could take the contents of cell B5 and divide it by the number 12 to get a monthly total.

Mathematical Operators A mathematical operator (such as + or –) is needed if your formula contains more than one cell reference or number.

Function A function performs a specific task, such as adding a group of numbers to compute a sum.

Range Reference When using functions, you may use range references, such as A2:E2, in order to write a formula which references the values of several adjoining cells.

Range Names You can use range names in place of range references in formulas.

You will learn more about functions and range references in the next lesson.

Writing a formula is like writing a mathematical expression. Formulas use the following mathematical operators, shown in Table 9.1.

Table 9.1 Mathematical Operators Used in Excel Formulas

Operator	*Meaning*	*Example*	*Result*
+	Addition	4+2	6
-	Subtraction	4-2	2
*	Multiplication	4*2	8
/	Division	4/2	2
^	Exponentiation	4^2	16

The following are example Excel formulas:

=J8	This will place the value of cell J8 in the cell containing the formula. When the value in J8 changes, this cell will change too.
=J8/12	Divides the value of cell J8 by 12.
=J8+A5	Adds the values of cells J8 and A5.
=(A5+J8)/4	Divides the total of cells A5 and J8 by 4
=J8*10%	Multiplies the value of cell J8 by 10%

To enter a formula:

1. Move the pointer to the cell where the formula will reside.
2. Type the equal sign (=).
3. Type the formula. The formula appears in the formula bar.
4. Press **Enter**, and the result is calculated.

Quick Cell References You can use the mouse when typing cell references. Just click on the cell that you want to reference in a formula, and the name of that cell appears in the formula at that point.

Error! Make sure that you did not commit one of these common errors: trying to divide by zero or a blank cell, referring to a blank cell, deleting a cell being used in a formula, or using a range name when a single cell name is expected.

Operator Precedence

When typing your formula in Excel, it is important to remember operator precedence.

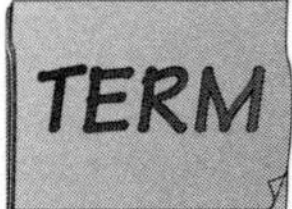

Operator Precedence The order in which a formula will be evaluated, based on the mathematical operators being used, is known as *operator precedence.*

Any formula which involves more than one mathematical operator will be calculated in steps. The order in which the steps are calculated is based on the mathematical operator involved. This is the order of precedence for mathematical operators in Excel:

%	Percentage
^	Exponentiation
* and /	Multiplication and Division
+ and –	Addition and Subtraction

For example, if you typed the following formulas, you would get these results:

Formula	*Result*	*Order of Calculation*
8-3*2	2	3 * 2 = 6, 8–6 = 2
(8-3)*2	10	8–3 = 5, 5 * 2 = 10

Displaying Formulas

Sometimes when you are working in a complex worksheet, it's nice to be able to verify the formulas involved. Moving from cell to cell in order to see the formula displayed in the formula bar can be time consuming. Excel offers you an alternative.

To display formulas (instead of their results):

1. Pull down the **Options** menu.
2. Choose **Display**. The Display Options dialog box shown in Figure 9.1 appears.

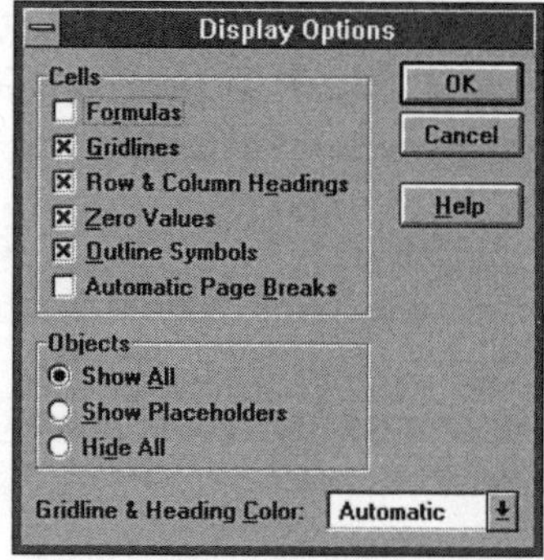

Figure 9.1 The Display Options dialog box.

3. Click on the **Formulas** check box. An X appears, indicating that the option has been turned on.
4. Click on **OK** or press **Enter**.

Display Formulas Quickly Use the keyboard shortcut, **Ctrl+'**, to display formulas. Hold down the **Ctrl** key, and press the apostrophe (').

Editing Formulas

Editing formulas is the same as editing any entry in Excel.

To edit a formula:

1. Select the formula you want to edit.
2. Position the cursor in the formula bar, or press **F2** to enter Edit mode.
3. Use the **Backspace** key to delete characters to the left of the cursor or the **Delete** key to delete characters to the right of the cursor. Type any additional characters. They will be added to the right of the cursor.
4. Click on the **Enter** button on the formula bar or press **Enter**.

Change Your Mind? To cancel changes to a cell before you are done, click on the **Cancel** button or press **Esc**.

Copying Formulas

Copying formulas is similar to copying other data in a worksheet. To copy formulas:

1. Select the formula that you wish to copy.
2. Pull down the **Edit** menu.
3. Choose **Copy**.
4. Move the cursor to the first cell in the area where you would like to place the copy. To copy data to another worksheet, change to that worksheet.
5. Pull down the **Edit** menu.
6. Choose **Paste**, and the data is copied.

To copy formulas quickly, try using the Drag and Drop fill handle. The fill handle is a small square that appears in the lower right corner when a cell is selected. Drag the fill handle to select the cells into which you wish to copy the formula. You may also use the Fill Down or Fill Right tools from the Customize dialog box. You can also copy with the Copy tool located on the Utility Toolbar. In addition, you can customize any Toolbar by adding the Cut and Paste tools from the Customize dialog box.

Keyboard Shortcuts If you prefer a more conventional method, try the keyboard shortcuts to copy formulas: select the formula to be copied, and press **Ctrl+Insert** or **Ctrl+C**. This copies the data to the clipboard. To paste, simply press **Enter**, or **Ctrl+V**.

Get an Error? If you get an error after copying a formula, verify the cell references in the copied formula. See "Using Relative and Absolute Cell Addressing" for more details.

Using Relative and Absolute Cell Addressing

When you copy a formula from one place in the worksheet to another, the cells that are referenced in the formula are adjusted to compensate for the movement.

Suppose you had a formula that added four cells together from column B to achieve a total. You want to use this same basic formula over and over in several columns. The formula would have to be adjusted to reference the four cells in the new column, C, not the original cells. Excel does this adjusting for you, as shown in Figure 9.2.

Cell references are adjusted for column C

Microsoft Excel

File Edit Formula Format Data Options Macro Window Help

Normal

C9 =C4+C5+C6+C7

[BOOK.XLW]JENNY.XLS

	A	B	C	D	E	F	G
1	Sales Revenue by Sales Person				Projected Sales		
2					560,000		
3		Bill	Jack	Jane			
4	Widgets	150,729	151252	152124			
5	Whackits	70327	65752	66254			
6	Whosits	82182	71046	85562			
7	Whatsits	260348	255458	275142			
8							
9	Total Sales Revenue	563,586	543,508	579,082			
10	% of Projected	100.64%	97.06%	103.41%			
11							
12							
13							
14							
15							
16							
17							
18							

Ready NUM

Figure 9.2 Excel adjusts cell references when copying formulas.

Sometimes, you do not want the cell references to be adjusted when formulas are copied. That's when absolute references become important.

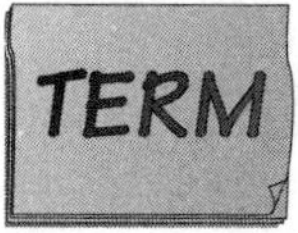

Absolute vs. Relative An *absolute reference* is a cell reference in a formula that does not change when copied to a new location. A *relative reference* is a cell reference in a formula which is adjusted when the formula is copied.

In Figure 9.2, the formula B4+B5+B6+B7 in cell B9 uses relative references. When the formula was copied from cell B9 to C9, its cell references were adjusted and the formula became C4+C5+C6+C7.

The formula in cells B10, C10, and D10 uses an absolute reference to cell E2, which holds the projected sales for this year. (B10, C10, and D10 divide the sums from row 9 of each column by the contents of cell E2.) If you didn't use an absolute reference, when you copied the formula from B10 to C10, the cell reference would be incorrect.

To create an absolute reference formula, you need only to put a $ in front of the cell address.

Some formulas use mixed references. For example, if you had the formula $A2/2 in cell C2, and you copied that formula to cell D10, the result would be the formula $A10/2. The row reference would be adjusted, but not the column. Using relative cell referencing as in the formula A2/2, when copied to cell D10, the result would be the formula B10/2.

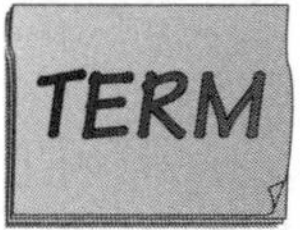

Mixed References A reference which is only partially absolute, such as A$2, or $A2 is called a *mixed reference*. When a formula which uses a mixed reference is copied to another cell, only part of the cell reference is adjusted.

In this lesson, you learned how to enter and edit formulas. You also learned when to use relative and absolute cell addressing. In the next lesson, you will learn how to use Excel's built-in functions in formulas.

Using Built-In Functions

In this lesson you will learn how to create complex formulas with Excel's built-in functions.

What are Built-In Functions?

Functions help to simplify complex formulas. They are built-in formulas provided by Excel. For example, instead of typing **=B1+B2+B3** to add three numbers, you can use a function (SUM) to total them. The SUM function is written **=SUM(B1:B3)**, which means you would have to write fewer numbers. Built-in functions can use range references such as B1:B3, or range names such as SALES.

There are many types of functions available—Mathematical functions, such as ROUND(); Statistical functions, such as AVERAGE(); Financial functions, such as FV(); and Date/Time functions, such as YEAR().

Using the AutoSum Tool

Since SUM is one of the most-used functions, Excel created a fast way to enter it. The AutoSum tool guesses what cells you want summed, based on where the cursor is when you activate AutoSum. If AutoSum selects an incorrect range of cells, you can edit the selection.

To use AutoSum:

1. Select a cell to hold the sum. You will have the best results if you choose a cell at the end of a row or column of data.
2. Click on the **AutoSum** tool on the Standard Toolbar.
3. If you need to adjust the range of cells that AutoSum has selected, edit the selection. You can also use the mouse or the cursor keys to adjust the range selection.

4. When the range is correct, click on the **Enter** box in the formula bar or press **Enter**. The total for the range selected is calculated.

Using Formula Paste Function

In order to enter formulas quickly and easily, use the Formula Paste Function command.

To enter a formula using the Paste command:

1. Move to the cell where you want to add a formula.
2. Pull down the **Formula** menu.
3. Choose **Paste Function**, and the dialog box shown in Figure 10.1 appears.

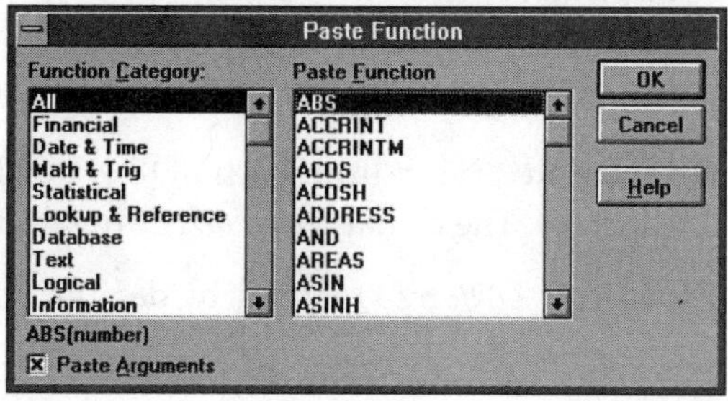

Figure 10.1 The Paste Function dialog box.

4. Select the function you want from the **Paste Function** list box. If you would like, you can narrow the display of functions by selecting a category from the **Function Category** list box. A sample of the function selected appears just below the **Function Category** list box.
5. If you do not want the arguments pasted into the formula bar along with the Function, deselect the **Paste Arguments** check box.

In this lesson, you learned about Excel's built-in functions. You learned how to enter functions quickly with the AutoSum tool and the **P**aste command.

11

Printing Your Worksheet

In this lesson, you will learn all you need to know to print your worksheet.

Changing the Print Setup

Before you print, you must choose how you want your worksheet printed. Use the **File Page Setup** command to display a dialog box offering options that affect the appearance of the printed worksheet. The options you can select from include:

Orientation Select from Portrait (8 1/2 by 11 inches) or Landscape (11 by 8 1/2 inches). The actual paper sizes are selected under Paper Size.

Paper Size 8 1/2 by 11 inches, by default. You can choose other sizes.

Margins You can adjust the size of the left, right, top, and bottom margins. You can also choose whether to center the data on the page horizontally or vertically.

Page Order You can indicate how data in the worksheet should be read and printed: in sections from top to bottom or in sections from left to right.

Scaling You can reduce and enlarge your worksheet or force it to fit within a specific page size.

Row or Column Heading You can specify that row and column headings are printed.

Cell Gridlines You can print the square lines around each cell.

Black and White Cells You can print the color in the worksheet as patterns, or choose plain black and white.

Start Page No.'s At You can set the starting page number to something other than 1.

Headers and Footers You can add headers (such as a title which repeats at the top of each page) or footers (such as page numbers, which repeat at the bottom of each page).

To change the page setup:

1. Pull down the **File** menu.
2. Choose **Page Setup**. The dialog box shown in Figure 11.1 appears.
3. Choose the options you would like to use.
4. Click on **OK** or press **Enter**.

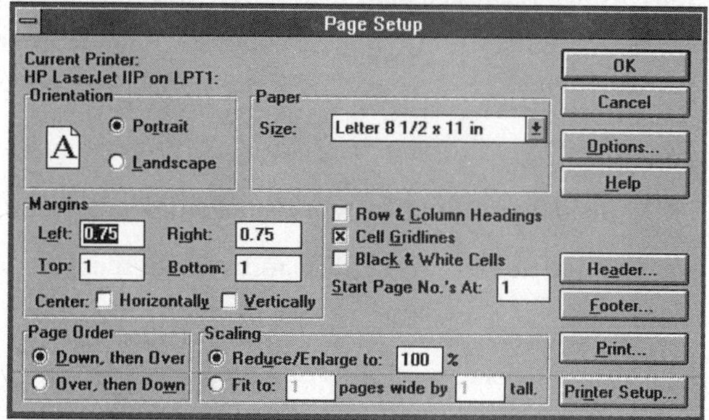

Figure 11.1 The Page Setup dialog box.

Choosing the Print Area

After selecting the options for the page setup, select the area of the worksheet that you wish to print. If you skip this step, Excel will print all the data in the worksheet.

To choose the print area:

1. Select the range of data you wish to print.
2. Pull down the **Options** menu.
3. Choose **Set Print Area**.

Printing Titles You can print a title at the top of each page from data in the worksheet. Select the **O**ptions Set Print **T**itles command. If you choose this option, do not include these cells in the print range.

Excel 4.0 has a quick way to set the print area—the Print Area tool, located on the Utility Toolbar.

Adjusting Page Breaks

When you print a worksheet, Excel will determine the page breaks based on the page setup and the selected print area. You may want to override the automatic page breaks with your own breaks. Before you add page breaks, you may want to try these things:

- Adjust the widths of individual columns to make the best use of space.
- Consider printing the worksheet sideways (using Landscape orientation).
- Change the left, right, top, and bottom margins to smaller values.

If after trying these, you still want to insert page breaks, first determine whether you need to limit the number of columns on a page or to limit the number of rows on a page.

If you want to limit the number of columns:

1. Move your cursor to the column to the right of the last column you want on the page. For example, if you want Excel to print only columns A through G on the first page, move your cursor to column H, one column to the right of G.
2. Move to row one of that column.
3. Pull down the **Options** menu.
4. Choose **Set Page Break**.
5. A page break (dashed line) appears.

If you want to limit the number of rows:

1. Move your cursor to the row just below the last row you want on the page. For example, if you want Excel to print only rows 1 through 12 on the first page, move your cursor to row 13, which is one row below row 12.
2. Move to column A of that row.
3. Pull down the **Options** menu.
4. Choose **Set Page Break**.
5. A page break (dashed line) appears.

One Step Page Breaks You can set the lower right corner of a worksheet in one step. Move to the cell located below and to the right of the last cell for the page, and then select the **O**ptions Set Page **B**reak command. For example, if you wanted cell G12 to be the last cell on that page, move to cell H13 and set the page break.

Make a Mistake? To remove a page break, move to the cell that you used to set the page break and select the **O**ptions **R**emove Page Break command. (To remove a vertical page break, place the cursor to the right of it. To remove a horizontal page break, place the cursor below it. The correct cell will be to the right and below the dotted lines which mark the page break.)

Previewing a Print Job

After you've determined your page setup, print area, and page breaks (if any), you can preview your print job before you print.

To preview a print job:

1. Pull down the **File** menu.
2. Choose **Print Preview**. Your worksheet appears as it will when printed, as shown in Figure 11.2.

A Close-Up View Zoom in on any area of the preview by clicking on it with the mouse. You can also use the **Zoom** button.

Printing

After setting the page setup and previewing your data, it is time to print.

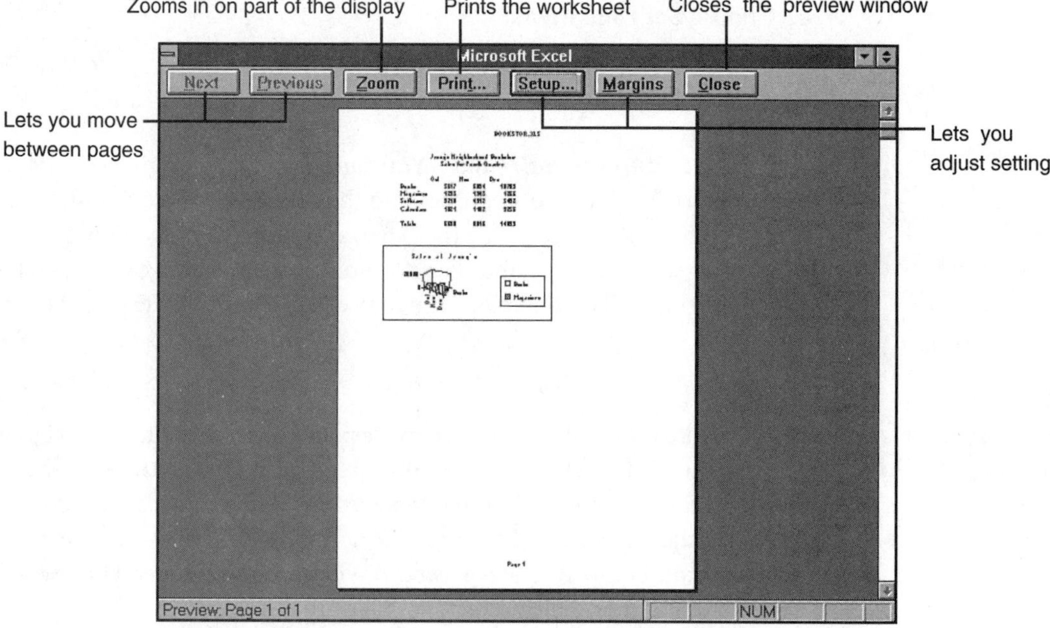

Figure 11.2 Your worksheet can be previewed before it is printed.

To print your worksheet:

1. Pull down the **File** menu.
2. Choose **Print**, and the dialog box shown in Figure 11.3 appears.
3. Select the options you would like to use.
4. Click on **OK** or press **Enter**.

Quick-Change Artist To reach the Print dialog box quickly, press the keyboard shortcut, **Ctrl+Shift+F12**.

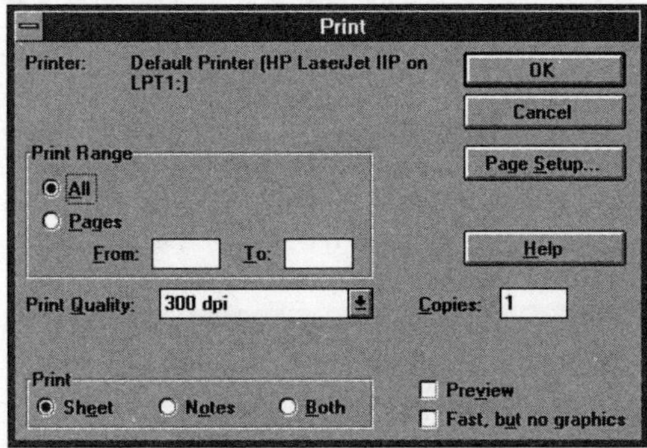

Figure 11.3 The Print dialog box.

Excel 4.0 offers you a quick method to print—the Print tool located on the Standard Toolbar.

In this lesson, you learned how to print your worksheet. In the next lesson, you will learn how to customize the formatting of numbers and text.

12 Adjusting Number Formats and Alignment

In this lesson, you will learn how to customize the appearance of numbers in your worksheet.

Numeric Display Formats

In Lesson 6, "Entering and Editing Data," you learned about the many formats for dates and times in Excel. Excel also offers you a variety of numeric formats from which to choose, as shown in Table 12.1.

Table 12.1 Excel's Numeric Formats

Number Format	*Display when you enter:*			
	2000	**2**	**-2**	**.2**
General	2000	2	-2	.2
0	2000	2	-2	0
0.00	2000.00	2.00	-2.00	.20
#,##0	2,000	2	-2	0
#,##0.00	2,000.00	2.00	-2.00	.20
$#,##0_);($#,##0)	$2,000	$2	($2)	$0
$#,##0.00_);($#,##0.00)	$2,000.00	$2.00	($2.00)	$0.20

Number Format	*Display when you enter:*			
0%	2000%	200%	-200%	
0.00%	2000.00%	200.00%	-200.00	
0.00E+00	2.00E+03	2.00E+00	-2.00E+	
#?/ ?	2000	2	-1	1/5

Changing the Display Format

After deciding on a suitable numeric format, follow these steps:

1. Select the cell or range you wish to format.
2. Pull down the **Format** menu.
3. Choose **Number**, and the dialog box shown in Figure 12.1 appears.

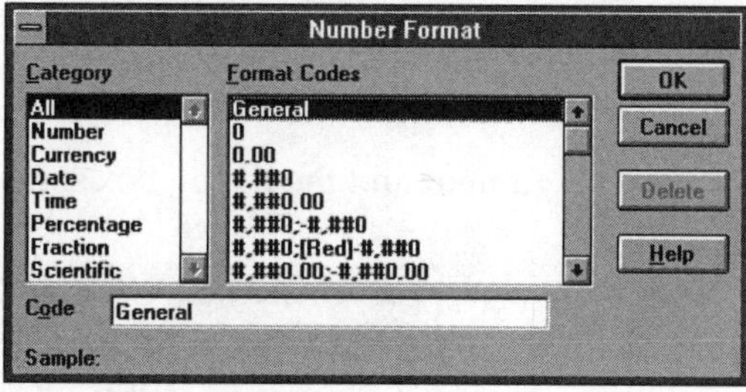

Figure 12.1 The Number Format dialog box.

4. Select the **Category** and **Format Code** you would like to use. A test result will display in the Sample box.
5. Click on **OK** or press **Enter**.

Pounding Headache? If a cell shows all pound signs (#######) after you apply a format, don't panic. Excel displays pound signs to let you know that the width of a cell is too small for a particular entry. See Lesson 15 to learn how to change column width.

The Formatting Toolbar There are many tools on the Formatting Toolbar you can use to quickly change number formats. Choose from the Currency, Percent, Comma, Increase Decimal Points, and Decrease Decimal Points tools. You can also change the Number format of a cell by using the Shortcut menu; press the right mouse button to display it.

Changing Alignments

When you enter data into an Excel worksheet, that data is aligned automatically. Text is aligned on the left, and numbers are aligned on the right.

Data can also be aligned vertically in a cell—at the top, at the bottom, or in the center of the cell. The default vertical alignment is bottom.

You can also rotate text (change its orientation) so that it reads sideways.

To change the alignment:

1. Select the cell or range you wish to align.
2. Pull down the **Format** menu.
3. Choose **Alignment** and the dialog box shown in Figure 12.2 appears.

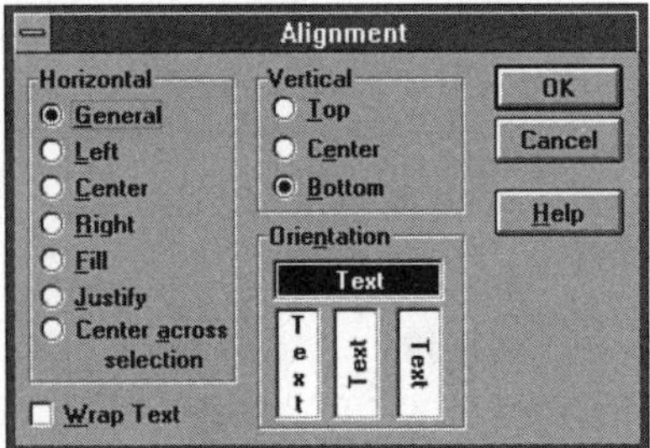

Figure 12.2 The Format Alignment dialog box.

4. Select the alignment you want.
5. Click on **OK** or press **Enter**.

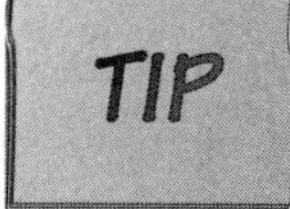

An Alignment Shortcut Use the Shortcut menu to change the alignment of a cell or range quickly. Highlight the cell or range you wish to align and press the right mouse button to activate the Shortcut menu.

With **Excel 4.0**, you can also use the Left Align, Center Align, and Right Align tools on the Standard Toolbar to change alignment.

A Lot to Align? To repeat the alignment format command in another cell, use the **R**epeat Alignment command from the **E**dit menu. (The command appears as **R**epeat Alignment only after you have adjusted the alignment in a cell or range.)

Centering Text over Multiple Columns

You may want to center your entry not within a cell, but over several cells. For example, you might want to center a title over a section of your worksheet. Excel 4.0 has an added feature which makes this easy to do.

To center text over multiple columns:

1. Select the range which contains the text you want to center.
2. Pull down the **Format** menu.
3. Choose **Alignment**.
4. Choose **Center** A**cross** **Selection**.
5. Click on **OK** or press **Enter**.

A Little Off-Center If your entry is not centered correctly, make sure that you select the entire range in which the text should be centered. For example, to center the words **1991 Sales** in cell C5 over three columns C, D, and E, select the range **C5:E5**.

Excel 4.0 offers you a fast way to center text—the Center Across Columns tool on the Standard Toolbar. You can also use the Shortcut menu to access the Alignment dialog box. Press the right mouse button to access the Shortcut menu.

Changing the Default Display Format and Alignment

When you enter the same type of data into a large worksheet, it is sometimes convenient to change the default format. You then can change the format for only those cells which are exceptions. Note that when you change the default, it affects all the cells in the worksheet.

You can change the default settings for number format, alignment, and others. To change the defaults:

1. Pull down the **Format** menu.
2. Choose **Style**. The Format Style dialog box appears.
3. In the Style Name list box, select **Normal**.
4. Click on the **Define** button, and the dialog box shown in Figure 12.3 appears.
5. Under Change, click on the **Number** check box to change the default format for numbers. Click on **Alignment** to change the default alignment for all cells. The appropriate dialog box appears.
6. Select the new default and click on **OK** or press **Enter**. You will be returned to the Format Style dialog box.

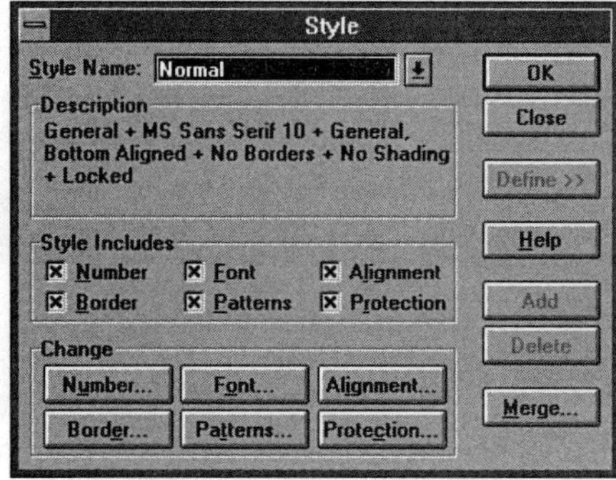

Figure 12.3 The Style dialog box.

7. Click on **OK** or press **Enter**.

In this lesson, you learned how to format numbers and align data to your preference. In the next lesson, you will learn how to format text.

13 Changing Text Attributes

In this lesson, you will learn how to change the appearance of text in your worksheet.

What Attributes Can You Change?

There are many textual attributes that you can change:

Style For example, Bold, Italic, Underline, and Strikeout.

Font For example, System, Roman, and MS Sans Serif.

Color For example, Red, Magenta, and Cyan.

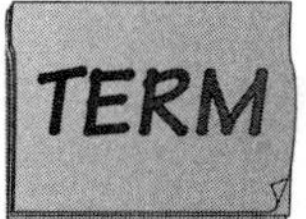

What Is a Font? *Font* refers to the combination of typeface, weight, and size. The size of a particular character is measured in *points*. (One point is equal to 1/72 of an inch.)

Figure 13.1 shows a worksheet after different attributes have been changed for selected text.

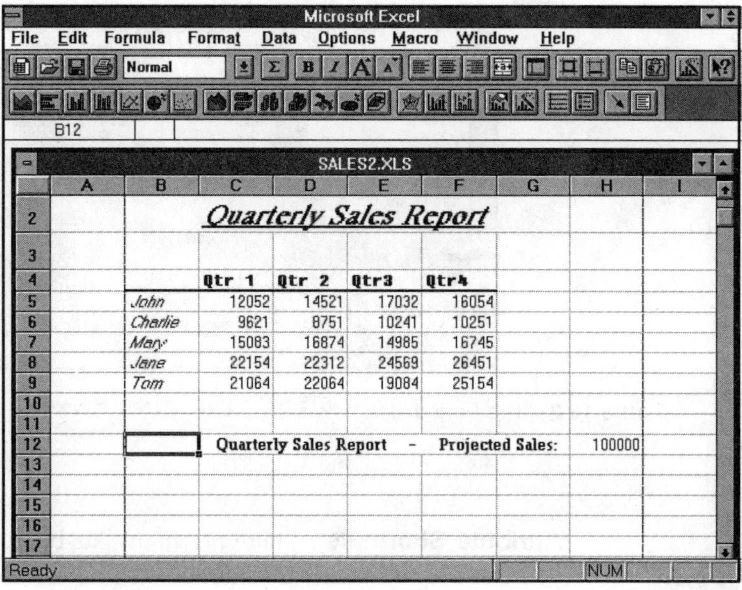

Figure 13.1 A sampling of several text attributes.

Using the Format Font Command

You use the **F**ormat **F**ont command to change the attributes of text in your worksheet.

To use the **F**ormat **F**ont command:

1. Select the cell or range which you want to format.
2. Pull down the **Format** menu.
3. Choose **Font.** The dialog box shown in Figure 13.2 appears.
4. Select the attributes you want to change.
5. Click on **OK** or press **Enter**.

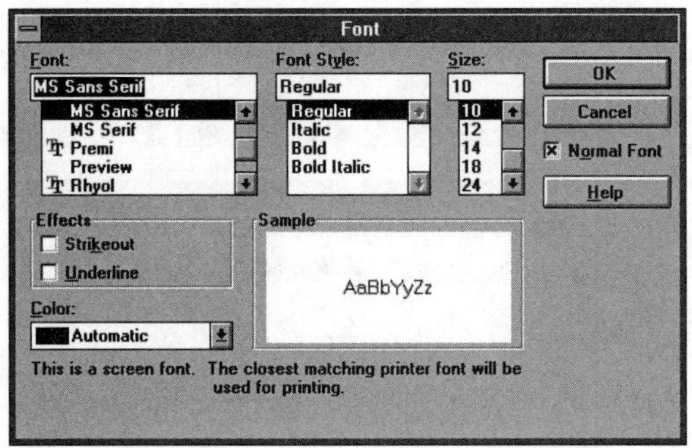

Figure 13.2 The Font dialog box.

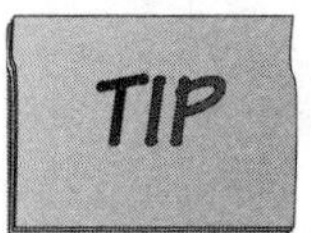

Attribute Shortcuts There are many keyboard shortcuts that you can use to quickly change text attributes. To change text to Normal, use Ctrl+1; for Bold, use Ctrl+B; for Italic, use Ctrl+I; for Underline, use Ctrl-U; and for Strikeout, use Ctrl-5.

Changing Text Attributes with Tools

Excel 4.0 offers many tools that you can use to quickly change text attributes. For example, the Standard Toolbar includes the Bold, Italic, Increase Font Size, and Decrease Font Size tools.

The Formatting Toolbar is also useful when changing text attributes. The Formatting Toolbar is shown in Figure 13.3.

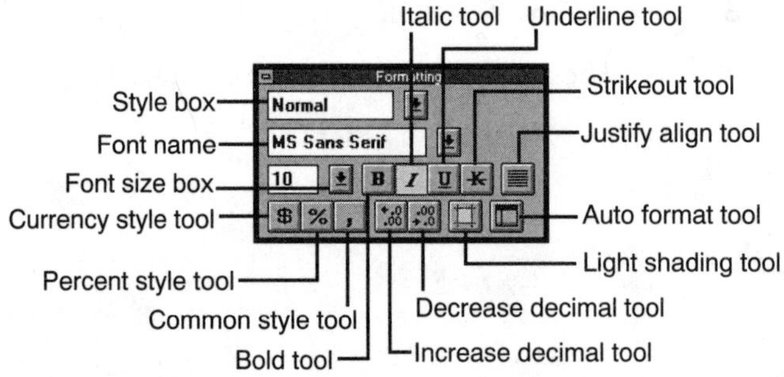

Figure 13.3 The Formatting Toolbar, moved and resized on the worksheet.

To use a tool to change text attributes:

1. Select the cell or range that you want to change.
2. Select the tool for the attribute you want to change, and the text changes.

Change Before You Type You can activate the attributes you want before you type text. For example, if you want a title in Bold, 12-point MS Sans Serif, set these attributes with the Format Font command, and then type the title.

In this lesson, you learned how to customize your text to achieve the look you want. In the next lesson, you will learn how to add borders and shading to your worksheet.

Formatting Cells

In this lesson, you will learn how to add pizzazz to your worksheets by adding borders and shading.

Using the Format Borders Command

You can use borders and shading to highlight important information such as totals, comparison values, and so on. Used sparingly, borders and shading can add emphasis to your worksheet data. You can place a dark line (border) on any cell in the following areas:

Left, Right Places the border on the left or right side of the cell or range.

Top, Bottom Places the border on the top or bottom side of the cell or range.

Outline Places the border around the edge of the cell or range.

A sample of several borders can be found in Figure 14.1.

To format the borders of a cell or range:

1. Select the cell or range to format.
2. Pull down the **Format** menu.
3. Choose **Border**. The dialog box shown in Figure 14.2 appears.
4. Select the border and style (thickness) you want.
5. Click on **OK** or press **Enter**.

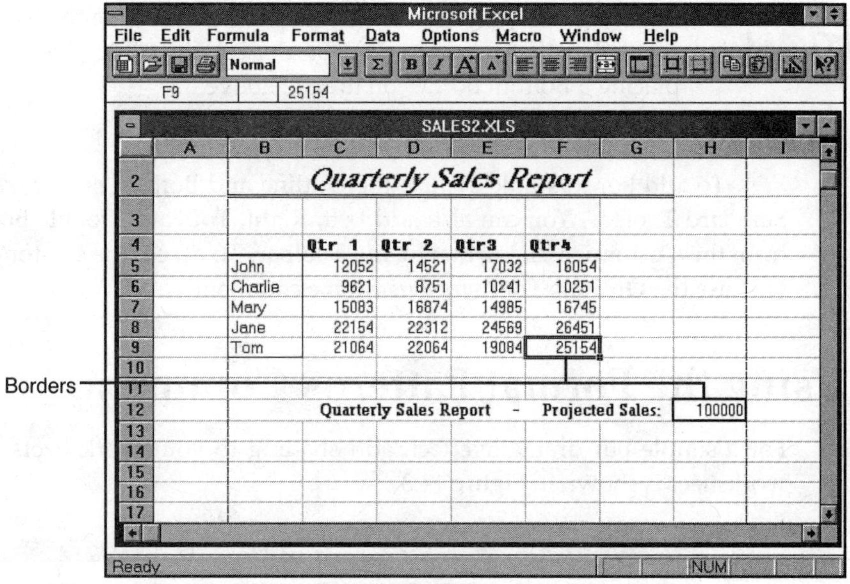

Figure 14.1 A sampling of borders.

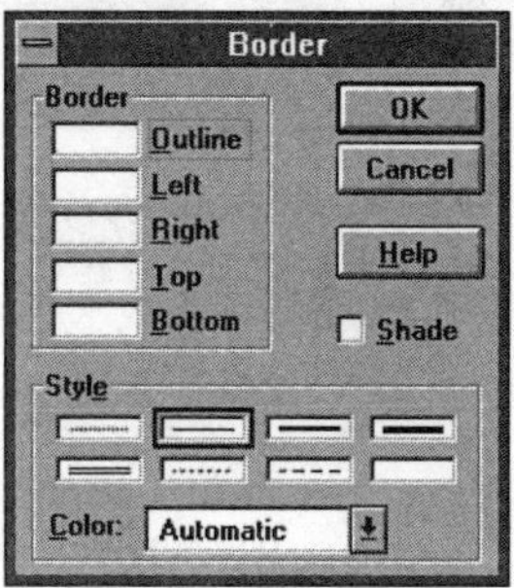

Figure 14.2 The Border dialog box.

Hiding Gridlines When adding borders to a worksheet, hide the gridlines for better effect. Select the **Options Display** command. Clear the X from the Cells Gridlines check box. To avoid printing gridlines with your worksheet, select the **File Page Setup** command and clear the X from the Cell Gridlines checkbox.

Borders Everywhere Borders are shared by adjoining cells, so remember that placing a Top border on one cell is the same as placing a Bottom border on the cell above it.

To add borders quickly, use the Outline and Bottom Border tools on the Standard Toolbar. You can also add Left, Right, Top, and Double Bottom tools from the Customize dialog box to any Toolbar. To access the Customize dialog box, use the **Options Toolbars Customize** command.

Using the Format Patterns Command

For a simple but dramatic effect, add shading to your worksheets. A sample worksheet is shown in Figure 14.3.

Microsoft Excel
File Edit Formula Format Data Options Macro Window Help
Normal
F8 26451
SALES2.XLS

Quarterly Sales Report

	Qtr 1	Qtr 2	Qtr3	Qtr4
John	12052	14521	17032	16054
Charlie	9621	8751	10241	10251
Mary	15083	16874	14985	16745
Jane	22154	22312	24569	26451
Tom	21064	22064	19084	25154

Quarterly Sales Report - Projected Sales: 100000

Ready NUM

Figure 14.3 A worksheet with added shading.

To add shading to cell or range:

1. Select the cell or range to which you want to add shading.
2. Pull down the **Format** menu.
3. Choose **Pattern**. The dialog box shown in Figure 14.4 appears.

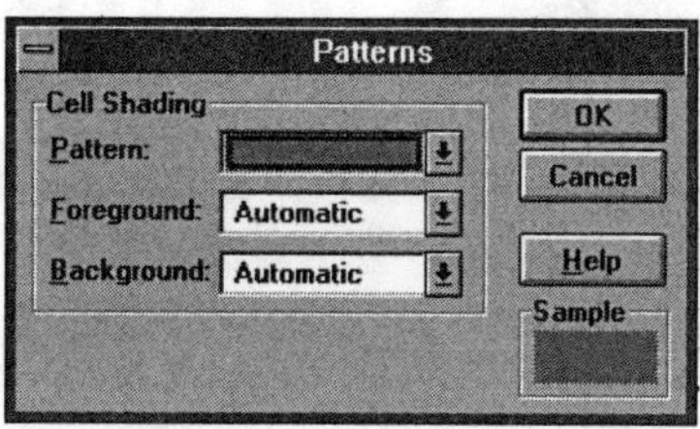

Figure 14.4 Selecting a shading pattern.

4. Select the shading pattern you would like to use. You can also select a **Foreground** or **Background** color. A preview of the result is displayed in the Sample box.
5. Click on **OK** or press **Enter**.

Keep It Light You can also apply light shading by selecting Format Border Shade.

Excel 4.0 offers two tools that you can use to shade cells. Choose from the **Drop Shadow** tool on the Drawing Toolbar or **Light Shading** tool on the Format Toolbar.

Other Formatting Tricks

Transfer Formatting You can quickly transfer formatting from one cell to another by selecting the **Paste Formats** tool on the Utility Toolbar.

A table, such as the Quarterly Sales Report shown in Figure 14.3, can be quickly formatted by using the AutoFormat tool on the Standard Toolbar. Excel recognizes the standard elements of a table, such as row and column headers, totals, and subtotals. When you use the AutoFormat tool, Excel adds lines, shading and number formatting (based on your preferences) to complete the table. You can change your table formatting preferences with the Format Autoformat command.

In this lesson, you learned some additional tricks to enhance the appearance of your worksheets. In the next lesson, you will learn how to change the sizes of rows and columns.

15 Changing Column Width and Row Height

In this lesson, you will learn how to adjust the column width and row height to make best use of the worksheet space. You can set these manually or let Excel make the adjustments for you.

Adjusting Width and Height with the Mouse

To use the mouse to change row height or column width:

1. Move the pointer to the heading for the row or column.
2. Move to the border, as shown in Figure 15.1.
3. Drag the border to its new location.
4. Release the mouse button, and the border is reset.

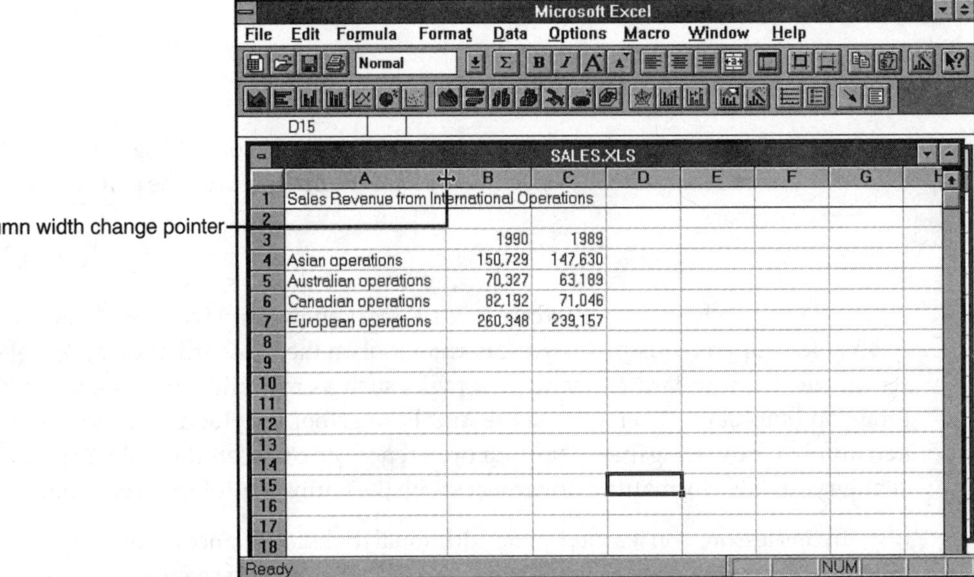

Figure 15.1 Your pointer changes when you move to the border of a row or column.

Custom-Fit Columns To reset the width for the best fit, double-click on the top right edge of the column. To change more than one column at a time, select as many columns as you like and then place the pointer on the top right edge of the selected columns and double-click.

Using the Keyboard

To use the keyboard to change the column width:

1. Pull down the **Format** menu.
2. Select **Column Width**, and the dialog box shown in Figure 15.2 appears.

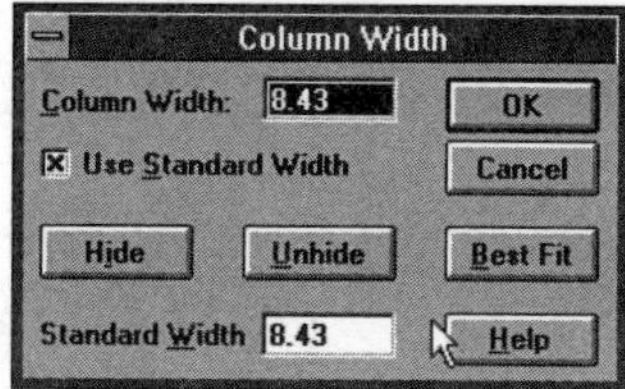

Figure 15.2 Changing the column width.

3. Type the number of characters you would like as the width. The standard width shown is based on the current default Font.
4. To use the Best Fit, click on the **Best Fit** button.
5. Click on **OK** or press **Enter**.

To use the keyboard to change the row height:

1. Pull down the **Format** menu.
2. Select **Row Height**, and the dialog box shown in Figure 15.3 appears.

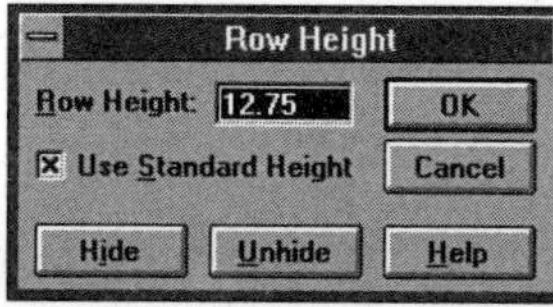

Figure 15.3 Changing the row height.

3. Type the number of characters you would like as the height. The standard height shown is based on the current default Font.

4. Click on **OK** or press **Enter**.

Set a New Standard To reset the standard width or height, type a new value in the dialog box.

In this lesson, you learned how to change the row height and column width. In the next lesson, you will learn how to use styles.

16 Formatting with Styles

In this lesson, you will learn how to use styles when formatting a worksheet.

What Is a Style?

The formats that you have learned to apply individually can be combined into a single step.

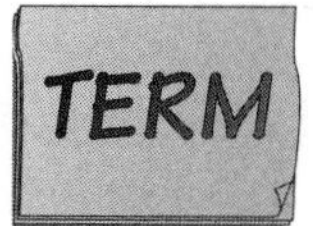

Show Your Style A *style* is a combination of certain formatting attributes.

When you apply a style to a cell or range, any existing attributes will be replaced. Each style can contain the following attributes:

- Number Format
- Font
- Alignment
- Border
- Pattern
- Protection

By now, you are familiar with all of these attributes but protection. Protection locks the contents of a cell or range to prevent a change (if the worksheet is also protected) or to hide the cell or range.

Excel has six default styles:

Normal The default style. Number is set to 0, Font to MS Sans Serif, Size to 10 point, Alignment of numbers is right, and Alignment of text is left, No Border, No Pattern, and Protection is set to locked.

Comma Number is set to #,##0.000

Comma (0) Number is set to #,##0.

Currency Number is set to $#,##0.00_); (Red) ($#,##0.00).

Currency (0) Number is set to $#,##0); (Red) ($#,##0).

Percent Number is set to 0%.

Applying Existing Styles

To apply an existing style to a cell or range using a mouse:

1. Select the cell or range.
2. Click on the down arrow to the right of the Style list box in the Standard Toolbar (see Figure 16.1).
3. Select the style you want from the list. The style is applied to the selected cell or range.

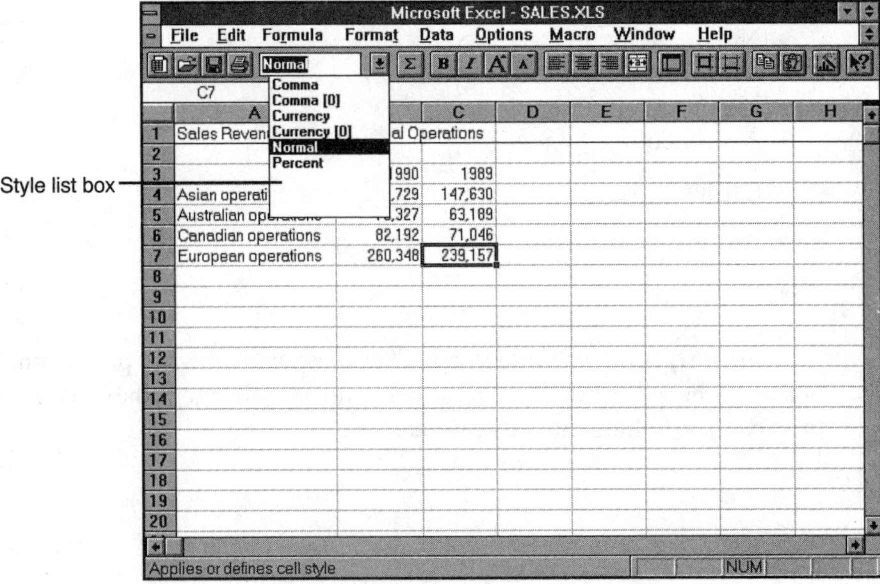

Figure 16.1 The Style list box.

To apply an existing style to a cell or range using the keyboard:

1. Select the cell or range.
2. Pull down the **Format** menu.
3. Use the arrow keys to select the style you want from the list. The style is applied to the selected cell or range.

Creating Styles

To save time, save your favorite formatting combinations as styles. You can create your own styles by definition, by example, or by copying.

To create a style by definition:

1. Pull down the **Format** menu.
2. Choose **Style**.
3. Type a name for the style in the **S**tyle Name list box.
4. Click on the **Define** button, and the dialog box shown in Figure 16.2 appears.

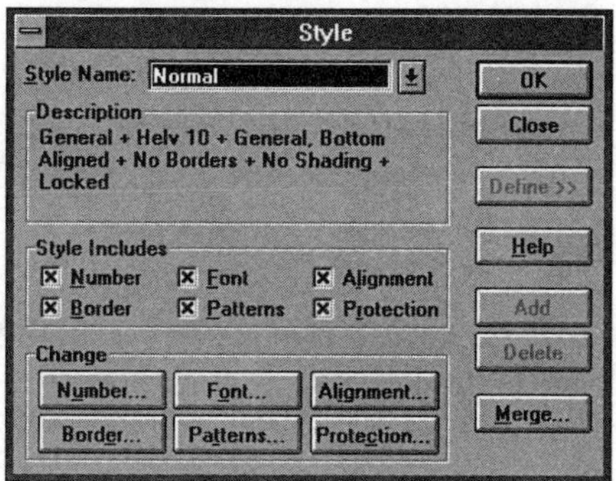

Figure 16.2 Defining a new style.

5. Remove the X from any check box whose attribute you do not want to include in the style.
6. If you want to change the definition of any attribute, click on the appropriate button. For example, to change the Number attribute in the style to $0.00, click on the **Number** button and change the format.
7. Click on **OK** or press **Enter**.

Change 'Em All If you change the attribute of a style, all cells in that style will also change.

To create a new style by example:

1. Select a cell whose format you want to save.
2. Click on the **Style** list box on the Standard Toolbar.
3. Type a name for the style.
4. Press **Enter**.

To copy existing styles from another worksheet:

1. Open both worksheets.
2. Switch to the worksheet to which you want to copy the styles.
3. Pull down the **Format** menu.
4. Choose **Style**.
5. Click on the **Define** button.
6. Click on the **Merge** button.
7. Select the name of the worksheet from which to copy.
8. Click on **OK** or press **Enter** to close the Merge dialog box.
9. Click on **OK** or press **Enter**.

In this lesson, you learned how to create and apply styles. In the next lesson, you will learn how to create charts.

17 Creating Charts

In this lesson, you will learn to create charts to represent your worksheet data graphically.

Charting with Excel

Excel offers you a variety of both two-dimensional and three-dimensional chart types from which to choose. A chart can be created as part of your worksheet or as a separate file.

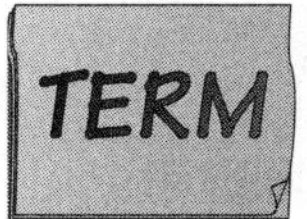

Embedded Charts A chart that is created as part of a worksheet is an embedded chart.

There are two ways to create an embedded chart:

- Use the ChartWizard tool, located on the Standard and Chart Toolbar.
- Use the tools found on the Chart Toolbar.

To create a chart as a separate document that appears in its own window, choose the **New** command on the **File** menu. Select the **Chart** option.

There are several terms that you will encounter when creating a chart:

Data Series A collection of related data, such as the monthly sales for a single division. A data series is usually a single row or column on the worksheet.

Axis One side of a chart. In a two-dimensional chart, there is an x-axis (horizontal) and a y-axis (vertical). In a three-dimensional chart, the z-axis represents the vertical plane, and the x-axis (distance) and y-axis (width) represent the two sides on the floor of the chart.

Legend Defines the separate elements of a chart. For example, the legend for a pie chart will show what each piece of the pie represents.

Choosing the Best Chart Type

Before you learn how to create a chart, take a moment to learn about the different types of charts and how to choose the best chart type for the data you want to graph. A sample of different charts is shown in Figure 17.1.

These are the major chart types and their purposes:

Pie Use this chart to show the relationship between parts of a whole.

Bar Use this chart to compare values at a given point in time.

Column Similar to the Bar chart; use this chart to emphasize the difference between items.

Line Use this chart to emphasize trends and the change of values over time.

Area Similar to the Line chart; use this chart to emphasize the amount of change in values.

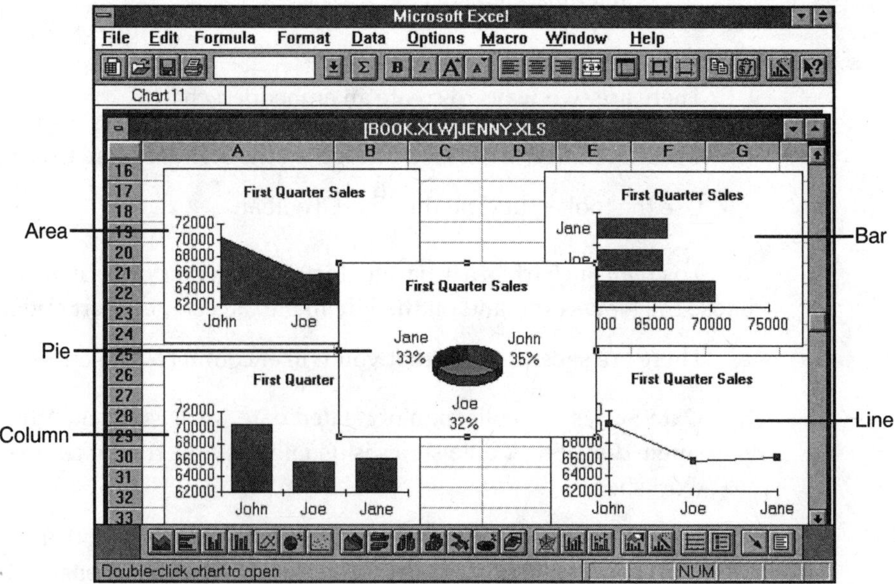

Figure 17.1 Different chart types.

Using the ChartWizard

ChartWizard leads you through the process of creating an embedded chart step-by-step. At each step, you can move back to previous steps and change your choices. ChartWizard will readjust the sample based on your current choices.

To create a chart using the ChartWizard:

1. Select the data you want to chart. Include row and column headings if you want to use them in the chart.
2. Click on the **ChartWizard** tool on the Standard or Chart Toolbar.
3. Point to the area on the worksheet where you would like to place the chart.
4. Click the left mouse button and hold to drag open the chart area. If you want a square area, hold down the **Shift** key as you drag. If you want your chart to exactly fit the borders of the cells it occupies, hold down the **Alt** key as you drag. When you have defined the chart area you want, release the mouse button.
5. A dialog box appears, asking you to make changes to the data area of the chart. When it is correct, click on **Next** or press **Enter**.
6. Select a chart type from the dialog box, shown in Figure 17.2.

Figure 17.2 ChartWizard asks you to choose the chart type you want.

7. ChartWizard will present you with additional selections, based on the chart type you choose. Complete those selections.

8. ChartWizard will display a sample chart, as shown in Figure 17.3. You may choose whether the data series is based on rows or columns, and choose the starting row and column. Click on **Next** or press **Enter**.

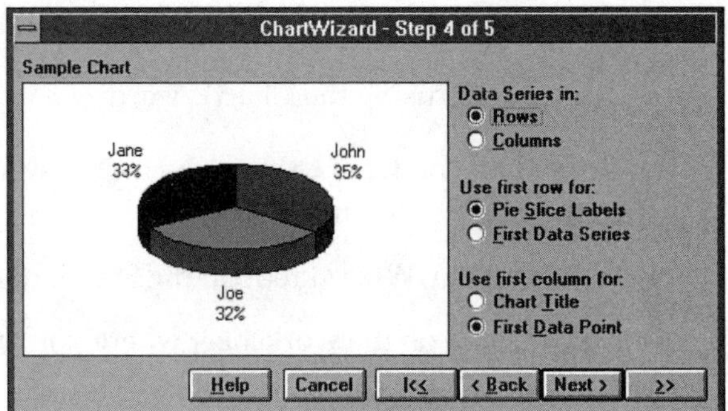

Figure 17.3 ChartWizard prepares a sample chart.

9. Add a legend, title, or axis labels. Click on **OK** or press **Enter**. Your completed chart appears on the worksheet.

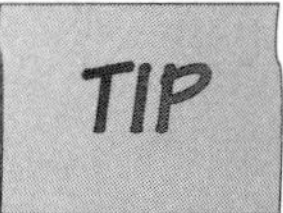

The Big Move To move an embedded chart, click anywhere in the chart area and drag it to the new location.

A Bit Cramped If you did not allow enough room for your chart, simply drag its borders to a new size.

Using the Chart Toolbar

After placing your finished chart on the worksheet, Excel opens the Chart Toolbar. You may use the Chart Toolbar to create a chart, or to change an existing chart. Figure 17.4 shows the Chart Toolbar.

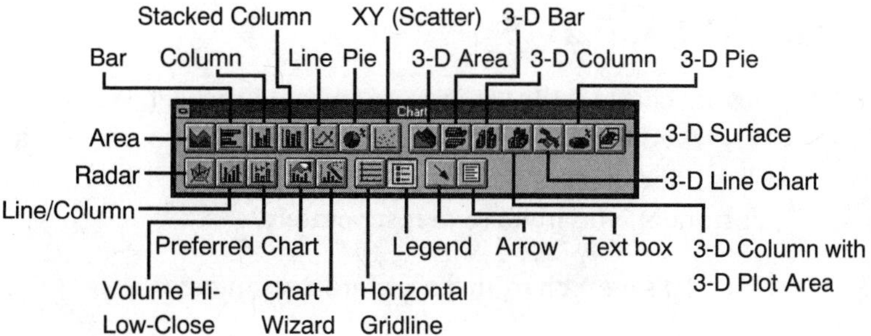

Figure 17.4 The Chart Toolbar.

To use the Chart Toolbar to create a chart:

1. Select the data you want to chart. Include row and column headings if you want to use them in the chart.
2. Click on the tool on the Chart Toolbar which represents the type of chart you want.
3. Point to the area on the worksheet where you would like to place the chart.
4. Click the left mouse button and hold to drag open the chart area. If you want a square area, hold down the **Shift** key as you drag. If you want your chart to exactly fit the borders of the cells it occupies, hold down the **Alt** key as you drag. When you have defined the chart area you want, release the mouse button. Excel creates your chart.

Presto! To quickly change the chart type, click on a different tool on the Chart Toolbar.

Still Not Satisfied? If you need to make changes to your chart, click on the **ChartWizard** tool to redefine the data area and make other changes.

Saving Charts

Saving charts is the same as saving a worksheet. If a chart is an embedded chart, it is saved when the worksheet is saved. You can also double-click on an existing chart, and then save that chart in a separate file. If the chart is in a separate document, you must save it separately.

To save a chart in a separate document:

1. Pull down the **File** menu.
2. Choose **Save**.
3. If this is a new chart, in the File **N**ame text box, enter the name of the file. You may use any combination of letters or numbers up to eight characters, such as 1992BDGT. Excel will automatically add .XLC to the filename as an extension for a chart. The full filename would then be 1992BDGT.XLC.
4. Click on **OK** or press **Enter**.

Printing a Chart

If a chart is an embedded chart, it will print when the worksheet is printed, but you can still print it separately if you want.

To print a chart:

1. If the chart is an embedded chart, open up a chart window by double-clicking on it. If the chart is in a separate file, open that file.
2. Pull down the **File** menu.
3. Choose **Print**.
4. Change any print options you would like.
5. Click on **OK** or press **Enter**.

Get It Down on Paper To print a chart quickly, select the Print tool on the Standard Toolbar.

In this lesson, you learned about the different chart types and how to create them. You also learned how to save and print charts. In the next lesson, you will learn how to enhance your charts.

Enhancing Charts

In this lesson, you will learn how to make your charts more appealing.

Resizing a Chart

If you are working on an embedded chart (a chart on a worksheet), prior to adding embellishments, you may want to resize it to allow for more room.

To resize a chart:

1. Select the chart that you want to resize.
2. Click on the border of the chart.
3. Drag the border of the chart to the desired size.

Adding a Title and a Legend

Adding text and a legend to an existing chart is easy.

To add a legend:

1. Select the chart to which you want to add a legend.
2. Click on the **Legend** tool on the Chart Toolbar.
3. If necessary, drag the borders of the legend box so that no information is hidden.

You can also add a legend by using the **C**hart menu, available through the Chart Window. To access the Chart Window, double-click on an embedded chart. Pull down the **Chart** menu and click on the **Add Legends** command.

To add a title or other text to a chart:

1. If the chart is an embedded chart, double-click on it to open the Chart Window.
2. Pull down the **Chart** menu.
3. Choose **Attach Text**. You can add a chart title, or a title for the x-axis (category), y-axis (series), or z-axis (values). You can also display the value for a data point. A data point is a part of a chart, such as a single column, bar, or plot point for a line. The Attach Text dialog box is shown in Figure 18.1.

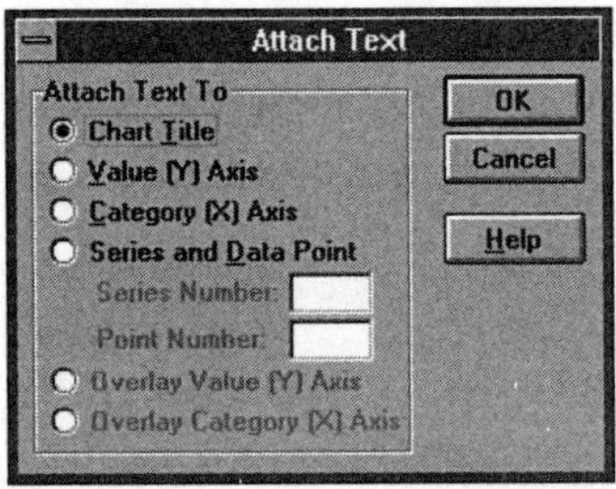

Figure 18.1 You can attach text to your chart in many ways.

4. Select the type of text you want to attach and click on **OK**.
5. Type your text in the formula bar.

If you want to change the font or the alignment or add a border, you must use the Format menu or the Shortcut menu.

You can also add text to the chart or to one of the axes by using the Text tool on the Chart Toolbar. A text box appears on the chart; type text into it. Move the text box and resize it to fit your needs.

Point It Out You can add arrows to a chart by selecting the **Arrow** tool on the Chart Toolbar or the **Add Arrow** option on the Chart menu.

Formatting Text on a Chart

To format text on a chart:

1. Select the text you want to format.
2. Click on the formatting tools on the Standard Toolbar (such as the Bold or Italics tools), or the Formatting Toolbar (such as Font Name or Size). The text changes based on the selections you make. Optionally, you can format text with the Format Text command.
3. If necessary, drag the borders of the text box so that its information shows.

Enhancing the Chart Frame

You can change the border and shading of the chart by using the Format Patterns command.

To change the border or shading of a chart:

1. Select the chart you want to change.
2. Pull down the **Format** menu.
3. Choose **Patterns**.
4. Select the border pattern and shading you want.
5. Click on **OK** or press **Enter**.

In this lesson, you learned how to improve the appearance of your chart. In the next lesson, you will learn about 3-D charts.

19 Working on 3-D Charts

In this lesson, you will learn how to choose an appropriate 3-D chart.

Choosing a 3-D Chart Type

There are 3-D versions for each of the major chart types: Pie, Bar, Column, Perspective Column, Line, Area, and Surface. Some of these 3-D charts are shown in Figure 19.1.

Use the following as a guide for choosing your 3-D chart:

3-D Pie Use this type to show the relationship between parts of a whole.

3-D Bar Use this type to compare values at a given point in time.

3-D Column Similar to 3-D Bar; use this type to emphasize the difference between items, while allowing easy viewing of data within a series.

3-D Line Use this type to emphasize trends and the change of values over time. 3-D lines are easier to identify.

3-D Area Similar to 3-D Line; use this type to emphasize the difference between different data series.

3-D Surface Similar to 3-D column; use this to determine the relationships between large amounts of data.

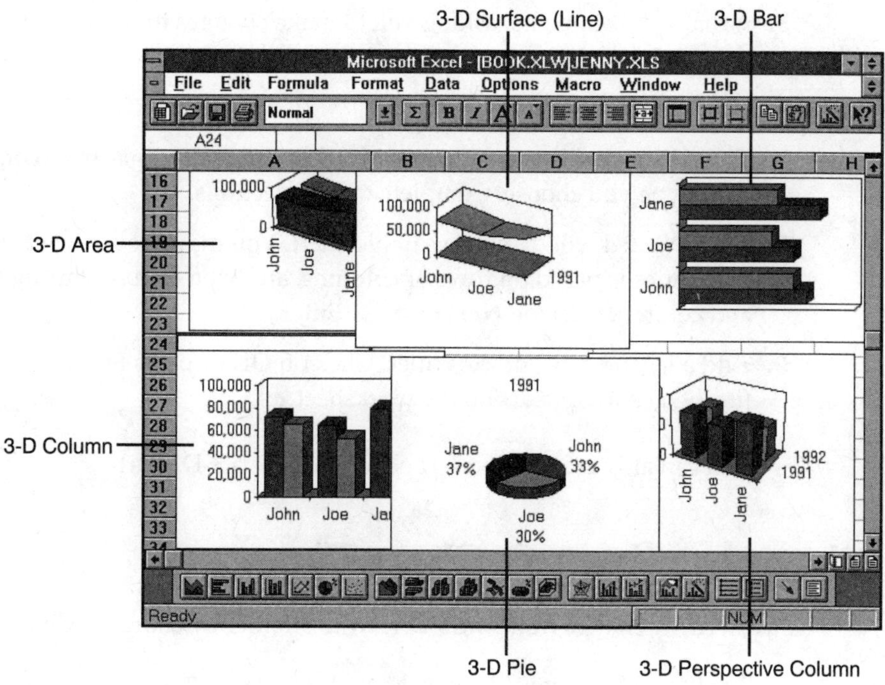

Figure 19.1 Examples of 3-D charts.

Creating a 3-D Chart

To create a 3-D chart, follow the same steps as you would in creating a 2-D chart.

To create a 3-D chart using the ChartWizard:

1. Select the data you want to chart. Include row and column headings if you want to use them in the chart.
2. Click on the **ChartWizard** tool on the Standard or Chart Toolbars.
3. Point to the area on the worksheet where you would like to place the chart.
4. Click the left mouse button and hold to drag open the chart area. If you want a square area, hold down the **Shift** key as you drag. If you want your chart to exactly fit the borders of the cells it occupies, hold down the **Alt** key as you drag. When you have defined the chart area you want, release the mouse button.

5. A dialog box appears, asking you to make changes to the data area of the chart. When it is correct, click on **Next** or press **Enter**.
6. Select a 3-D chart type.
7. ChartWizard will present you with additional selections, based on the chart type you choose. Complete those selections.
8. ChartWizard will display a sample chart. You may choose whether the data series is based on rows or columns, and then choose starting row and column. Click on **Next** or press **Enter**.
9. Add a legend, title, or axes titles. Click on **OK** or press **Enter**. Your finished chart appears on the worksheet.

You can also use the Chart Toolbar to create a 3-D chart.

Changing the 3-D Chart Type

You can easily change from one 3-D view to another by using the Chart Toolbar.

To change from one 3-D view to another:

1. Select the chart you want to change.
2. Using the Chart Toolbar, click on the 3-D chart tool you want to change to. Excel will change the chart type.

You can also browse through several variations of each chart type in the Chart Gallery.

To access the Chart Gallery:

1. Move to the chart window. If the chart is an embedded chart, then double-click on it to open the chart window.
2. Pull down the **Gallery** menu.
3. Choose any type of chart from the menu. The Chart Gallery dialog box shown in Figure 19.2 appears.

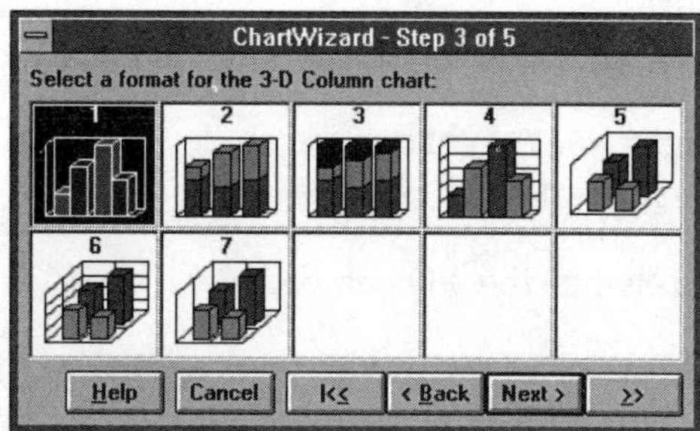

Figure 19.2 Browse among various chart types by using the Chart Gallery dialog box.

Using Multicategory 3-D Charts

When your worksheet has many interrelated values, using a 3-D chart will help you sort the data visually. Suppose you had a worksheet which showed the sales figures for each quarter, for each salesperson. Using a 3-D chart will help you pick out the top salesperson for each quarter easily. Such a chart is shown in Figure 19.3.

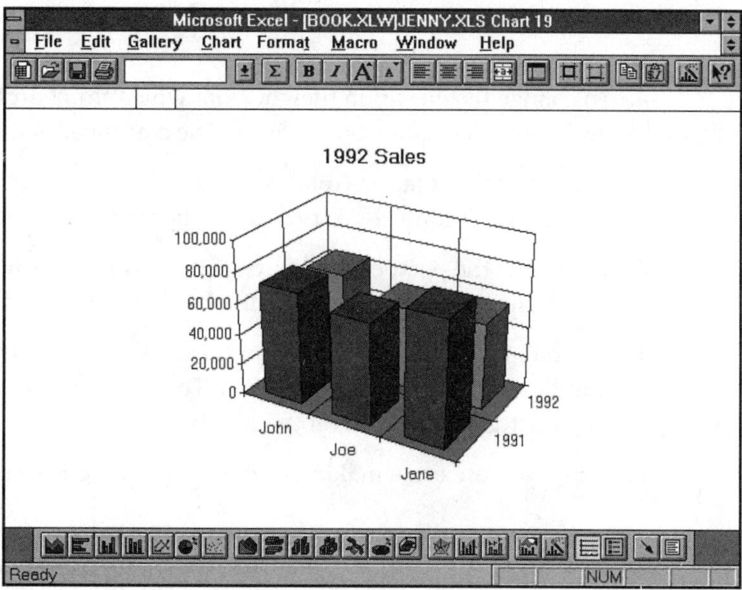

Figure 19.3 A 3-D chart helps you sort out relationships in a complex set of data.

Changing the 3-D Perspective

You might want to change the angle, elevation, or perspective of a 3-D chart in order to make it more pleasing.

To change the 3-D perspective:

1. Select the 3-D chart you want to change. If it is an embedded chart, double-click on it to open the chart window.
2. Pull down the Format menu.
3. Choose **3-D View**. The dialog box shown in Figure 19.4 appears.

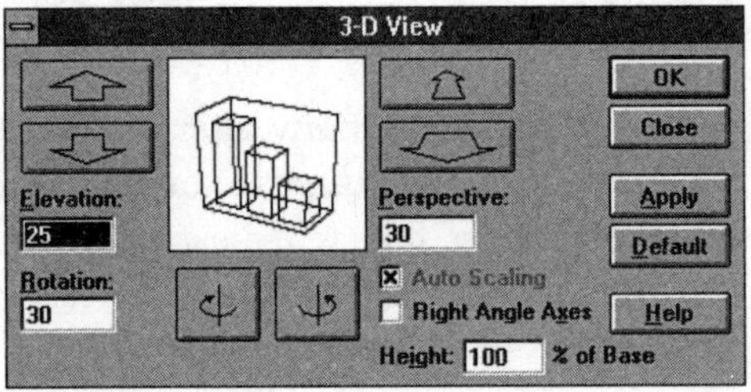

Figure 19.4 Changing the 3-D view.

4. To change the elevation (height from which the chart is seen), click on the up or down elevation controls, or type a number in the Elevation box.
5. To change the rotation (rotation around the z-axis), click on the left or right rotation controls, or type a number in the Rotation box.
6. To change the perspective (perceived depth), click on the up or down perspective controls, or type a number in the Perspective box.
7. As you make changes, they are reflected in the wire-frame picture in the middle of the 3-D View dialog box. To see the proposed changes applied to the actual chart, click on the **Apply** button.
8. When you are done making changes, click on **OK** or press **Enter**.

In this lesson, you learned how to create a 3-D chart and how to change it to meet your needs. In the next lesson, you will learn how to create a database.

20 Creating a Database

In this lesson, you will learn how to create your own database.

Planning a Database

A database is a collection of interrelated records—for example, a checkbook or an address book. Figure 20.1 shows a sample database.

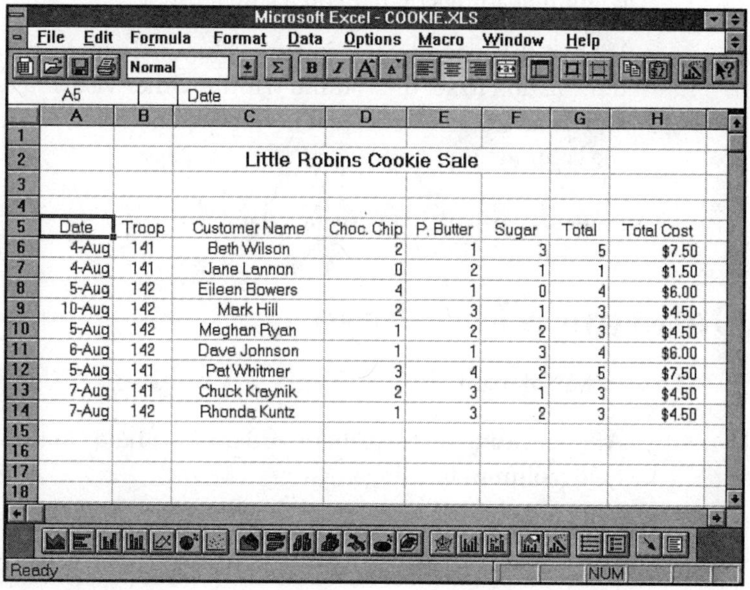
Microsoft Excel - COOKIE.XLS
File Edit Formula Format Data Options Macro Window Help
Normal
A5 Date
Little Robins Cookie Sale
Date Troop Customer Name Choc. Chip P. Butter Sugar Total Total Cost
4-Aug 141 Beth Wilson 2 1 3 5 $7.50
4-Aug 141 Jane Lannon 0 2 1 1 $1.50
5-Aug 142 Eileen Bowers 4 1 0 4 $6.00
10-Aug 142 Mark Hill 2 3 1 3 $4.50
5-Aug 142 Meghan Ryan 1 2 2 3 $4.50
6-Aug 142 Dave Johnson 1 1 3 4 $6.00
5-Aug 141 Pat Whitmer 3 4 2 5 $7.50
7-Aug 141 Chuck Kraynik 2 3 1 3 $4.50
7-Aug 142 Rhonda Kuntz 1 3 2 3 $4.50
Ready
NUM

Figure 20.1 Sample database.

Here are some database terms you should be familiar with:

Database Range The collection of cells that make up the database, including the row and column titles.

Record The collection of cells (fields) that make up a single item (row) in the database.

Field Part of a record with a specific type of information. A single column in the row.

Field Name The name of a field (column heading).

Before you create a database, you should ask yourself a few questions:

- What fields make up an individual record? (Enter the records in rows.) Familiar examples of field information for a database with records about people are name, address, phone number, social security number, and so on.
- What is the most often referenced field in the database? (This field should be placed in the first column.)
- What should the column headings be? (The database works best with column headings that are on a single row.)
- What is the longest value in each column, if you know it? (Use this information to set the column widths. Otherwise you can make your entries and then use Best Fit in the Column Width dialog box to adjust the columns.)

Now you are ready to create a database.

Defining a Database

To create a database:

1. After deciding on the general order of the fields in the database, enter the field (column) headings.
2. Type the individual records (in rows).
3. Select the database area, including the column headings.
4. Pull down the Data menu.
5. Choose **Set Database**. Excel automatically names the range Database.

Forget Someone? To add records to a defined database, either add the rows above the last row in the database, or use the Data Form dialog box.

Using Data Forms to Add, Edit, or Delete Records

Data forms are like index cards; there is one data form for each record in the database. It's easier to flip through these data form cards than to move among the actual records in your database, so you should use data forms to add, edit, or delete database records.

To access the Data Form dialog box:

1. Pull down the **D**ata menu.
2. Choose **Form**, and the dialog box shown in Figure 20.2 appears.

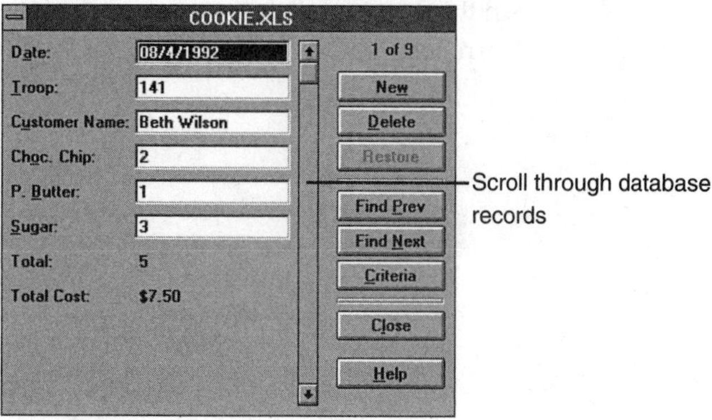

Figure 20.2 The Data Form dialog box.

To add a record to the database:

1. Select the **New** button.
2. Type data in each of the fields.
3. Click on **OK** or press **Enter**.

To change data in a record:

1. Select the record you want to change by selecting the **Find Prev** or **Find Next** buttons, or by using the scroll bars to move through the database.
2. Change the data you want, and click on **OK** or press **Enter**.

Come Back! To restore data changed in a field before you press Enter, select the **Restore** button.

To delete a record:

1. Select the record you want to change by selecting the **Find Prev** or **Find Next** buttons, or by using the scroll bars to move through the database.
2. Select **Delete**.
3. Click on **OK** or press **Enter**.

In this lesson, you learned how to create a database. In the next lesson, you will learn how to sort the database and find individual records.

21 Finding and Sorting Data in a Database

In this lesson, you will learn how to sort a database and how to find individual records.

Finding Data with a Data Form

To find records in a database, you must specify the individual criteria (qualifiers). You could type something specific like **Red** under the Color field of the form, or something that must be evaluated, like **<1000** (less than 1000) in the Sales field.

Table 21.1 Excel's Comparison Operators

Operator	*Meaning*
=	Equal to
>	Greater than
<	Less than
>=	Greater than or equal to
<=	Less than or equal to
<>	Not equal to

You can also use the following wildcards when specifying criteria:

? Represents a single character

* Represents multiple characters

For example, in the Name field, type **M*** to find everyone whose name begins with an *M*. To find everyone whose three-digit department code has *10* as the last two digits, type **?10**.

To find individual records in a database:

1. Pull down the **Data** menu.
2. Choose **Form**.
3. Select the **Criteria** button; the dialog box shown in Figure 21.1 appears.

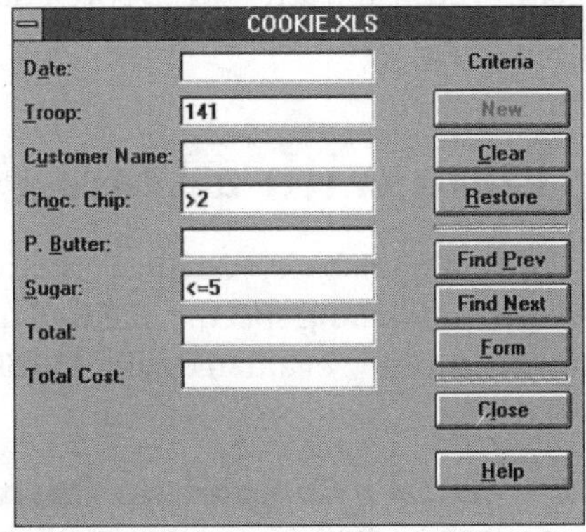

Figure 21.1 Selecting search criteria.

4. Type the criteria you would like to use in the appropriate fields. Use only the fields you want to search.
5. Click on **Form** or press **Enter**.
6. Select **Find Next** or **Find Prev** to locate certain matching records.
7. When you are done reviewing records, select **Close**.

Sorting Data in a Database

To sort a database, first decide which field to sort on. For example, an address database could be sorted by Name or by City—or it could be sorted by Name within City within State. Each of these sort fields is considered a *key*.

You can use up to three keys when sorting your database. The first key in the above example would be Name, then City, and then State. You can sort your database in ascending or descending order.

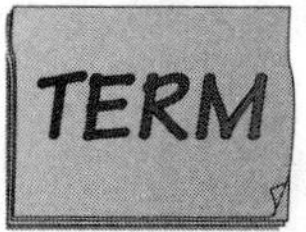

Sort Orders Ascending order is alphabetical (A-Z), and descending order is reverse (Z-A).

For the Record When you select the database range to sort, include all of the records but not the column headings.

To sort your database:

1. Select the area to be sorted. Make sure to include all of the data in the database but do not include the column headings.
2. Pull down the Data menu.
3. Choose **Sort**, and the dialog box shown in Figure 21.2 appears.

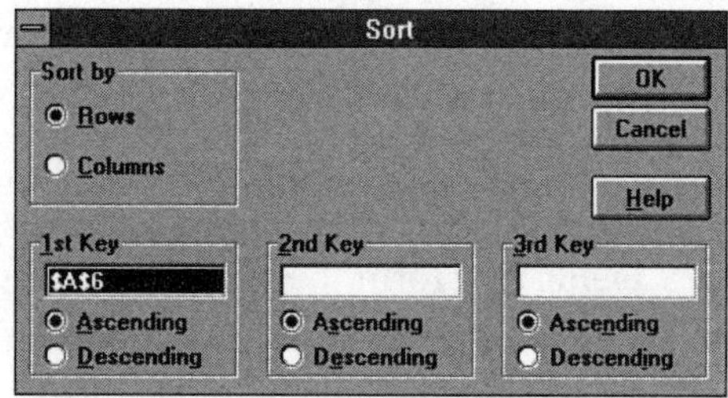

Figure 21.2 Selecting the sort criteria.

4. Make sure you are sorting by rows, since your database contains its records in rows.
5. Type at least one sort key, and select **Ascending** or **Descending** order.
6. Click on **OK** or press **Enter**.

Save First Before sorting, save your database file. Then if the sort does not work out, you still have your original file. If you make a mistake, you can undo the sort by selecting the **Undo Sort** command on the Edit menu (or press **Ctrl+Z**).

22 Summarizing and Comparing Data in a Database

In this lesson, you will learn how to summarize data in complex databases.

Using the Crosstab ReportWizard

Excel 4 has the ability to create crosstab reports with the Crosstab ReportWizard. It can be used to assemble data from complex databases for analysis. Suppose you had a database which kept track of your sales each day, by product, salesperson, and store. You can create a report which summarizes the amount of each product sold at each store by each salesperson.

When you create a crosstab report, you must specify three elements:

Row Fields that form the rows for the report. You can have up to eight rows. For example, these could be *stores*.

Column Fields that form the column headings for the report. You can have up to eight columns. For example, this could be *salespeople.*

Value These are the values you want added for each intersection of a column or row. For example, in a crosstab report displaying stores in rows and salespeople in columns, the value added at each intersection could be the amount of CD or record sales (or both) by each salesperson at each store. If you want the number of records that match row and column categories, leave this blank. In our example, this could be *products* or left blank.

A sample database is shown in Figure 22.1.

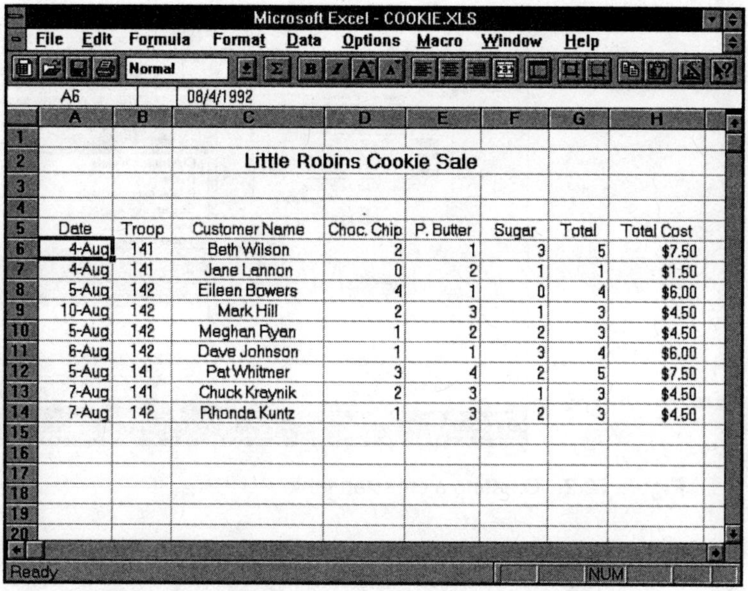
Microsoft Excel - COOKIE.XLS
File Edit Formula Format Data Options Macro Window Help
Normal
A6
08/4/1992
Little Robins Cookie Sale
Date Troop Customer Name Choc. Chip P. Butter Sugar Total Total Cost
4-Aug 141 Beth Wilson 2 1 3 5 $7.50
4-Aug 141 Jane Lennon 0 2 1 1 $1.50
5-Aug 142 Eileen Bowers 4 1 0 4 $6.00
10-Aug 142 Mark Hill 2 3 1 3 $4.50
5-Aug 142 Meghan Ryan 1 2 2 3 $4.50
6-Aug 142 Dave Johnson 1 1 3 4 $6.00
5-Aug 141 Pat Whitmer 3 4 2 5 $7.50
7-Aug 141 Chuck Kraynik 2 3 1 3 $4.50
7-Aug 142 Rhonda Kuntz 1 3 2 3 $4.50
Ready
NUM

Figure 22.1 A sample database.

Creating a Crosstab Table

To create a crosstab table:

1. Pull down the **Data** menu.
2. Choose **Crosstab**.
3. Select the **Create a New Crosstab** button, and the dialog box shown in Figure 22.2 appears.
4. Select the **Row**, **Column**, and **Value** categories.
5. Answer any additional requests for information.
6. Click on the **Create It** button. Figure 22.3 shows a sample crosstab table.

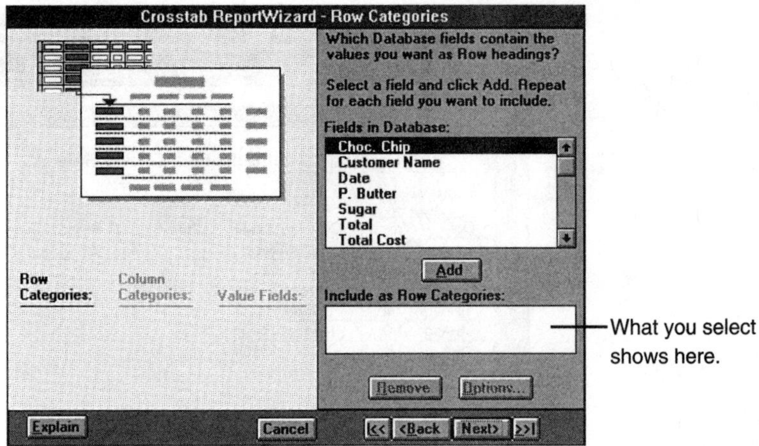

Figure 22.2 Creating a crosstab table.

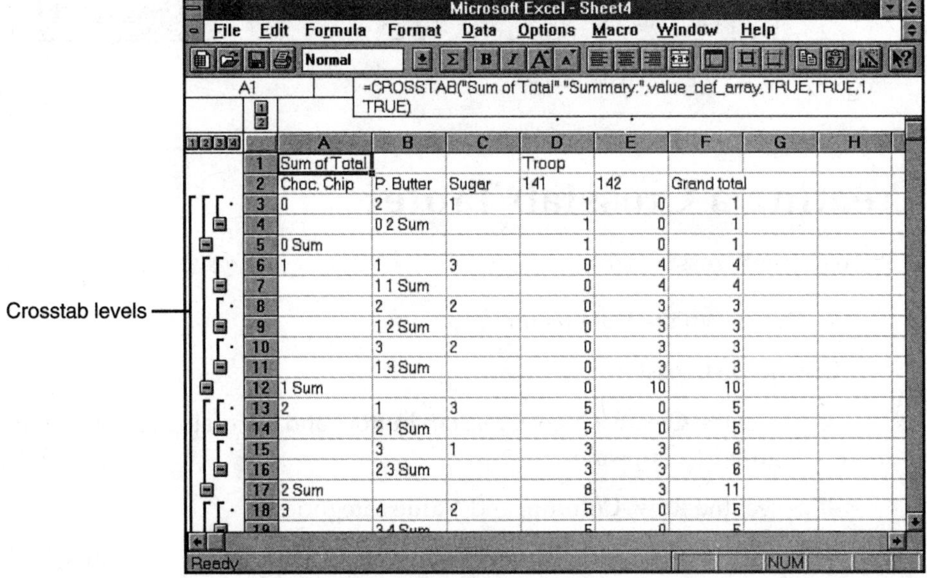

	A	B	C	D	E	F	G	H
1	Sum of Total			Troop				
2	Choc. Chip	P. Butter	Sugar	141	142	Grand total		
3	0	2	1	1	0	1		
4		0 2 Sum		1	0	1		
5	0 Sum			1	0	1		
6	1	1	3	0	4	4		
7		1 1 Sum		0	4	4		
8		2	2	0	3	3		
9		1 2 Sum		0	3	3		
10		3	2	0	3	3		
11		1 3 Sum		0	3	3		
12	1 Sum			0	10	10		
13	2	1	3	5	0	5		
14		2 1 Sum		5	0	5		
15		3	1	3	3	6		
16		2 3 Sum		3	3	6		
17	2 Sum			8	3	11		
18	3	4	2	5	0	5		

Figure 22.3 A sample crosstab table.

Recalculating a Crosstab Table

If you add or change data in a database, you will want to recalculate your crosstab table.

To recalculate a crosstab table:

1. Pull down the **Data** menu.
2. Choose **Crosstab**.
3. Choose the **Recalculate An Existing Table** button.

In this lesson, you learned how to create crosstab reports.

POWERPOINT

Joe Kraynak and Seta Frantz

1 Starting and Exiting PowerPoint

In this lesson, you will learn what PowerPoint is and how to start and exit PowerPoint. You will also learn about the parts of the PowerPoint presentation screen.

What is PowerPoint?

PowerPoint is a *presentation graphics program*. That is, it allows you to place text, art, and graphs on *slides* to create a slide show. The slide show can then be printed, displayed on-screen, or transformed into 35mm slides or overhead transparencies. A sample slide is shown in Figure 1.1.

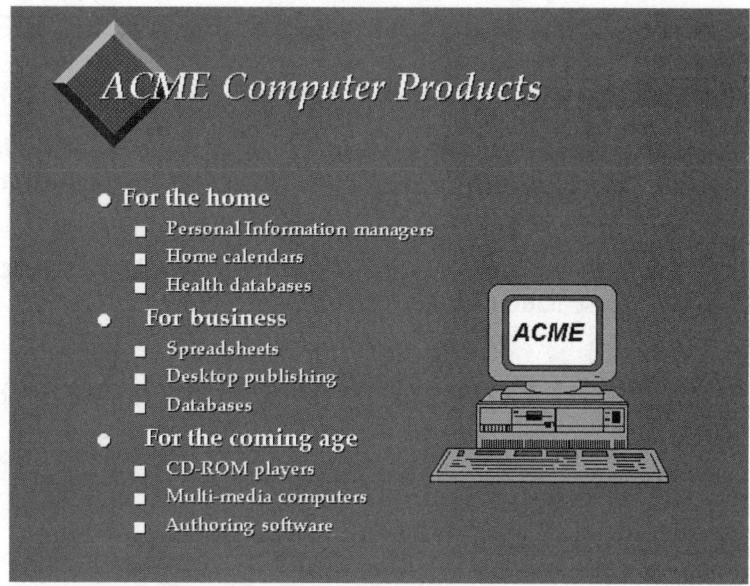

Figure 1.1 A sample slide created with PowerPoint.

Understanding Presentations

A *presentation* is a collection of slides designed to present an idea, prove a point, or convince an audience to take some action. With PowerPoint you can create the slides you want to include in the presentation in any order. PowerPoint provides the tools you need to rearrange the slides later.

Speaker Notes and Audience Handouts

In addition to creating slides, you can use PowerPoint to create speaker notes pages and audience handouts. Each speaker notes page can include a copy of one of the slides in the presentation plus any details the speaker wants to point out.

Audience handouts contain copies of all the slides including any text that the presenter wants to add. Handouts provide the audience with a way of reviewing the material later.

Starting PowerPoint

Before you start PowerPoint, you should have a basic understanding of how to get around in Microsoft Windows. If you have not already done so, please read the section in this book on Windows 3.1. To start PowerPoint, perform the following steps:

1. Start Windows and display the **Program Manager**.
2. If the Microsoft PowerPoint program group is not displayed, click on **Window** in the menu bar and select **Microsoft PowerPoint**.
3. Double-click on the **Microsoft PowerPoint** icon, or use the arrow keys to highlight the icon, and press **Enter**. PowerPoint starts, and a blank Presentation window appears (see Figure 1.2).

A Look at PowerPoint's Application Window

The PowerPoint window (shown in Figure 1.2) contains the same elements you will find in most Windows programs: a Control menu icon, a title bar, Minimize and Restore buttons, and so on.

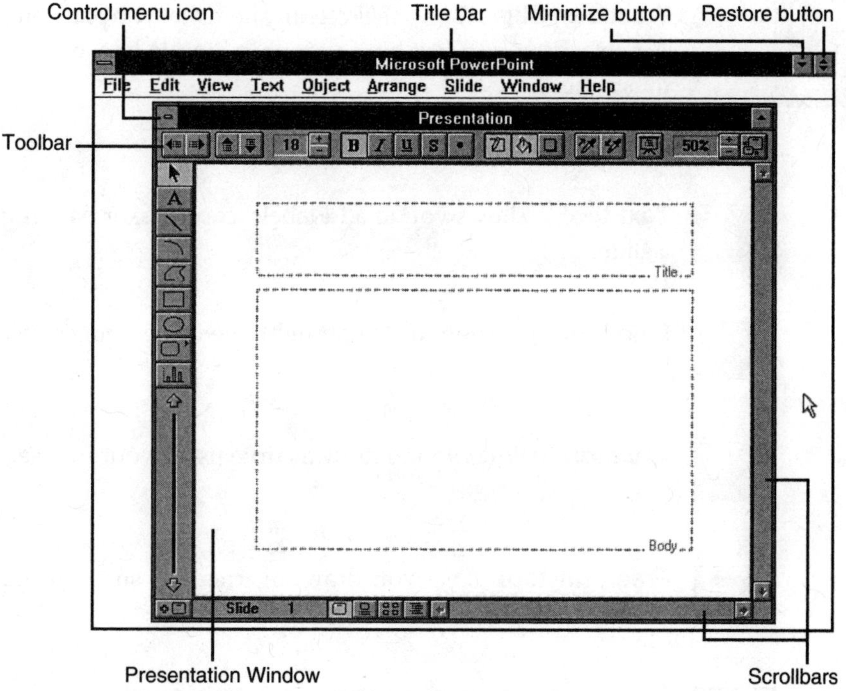

Figure 1.2 The Microsoft PowerPoint application window.

In the center of the PowerPoint window is a *Presentation window*. You will use this window to create your slides and arrange the slides in a presentation. This window contains a Tool Palette, a Toolbar, and additional tools, which are described in the following sections.

The Tool Palette

The Tool Palette contains the following tools that allow you to add objects, captions, and graphs to your slides:

Selection tool If you select this tool, the mouse pointer turns into an arrow. You can then use the pointer to select, move, and resize objects on a slide.

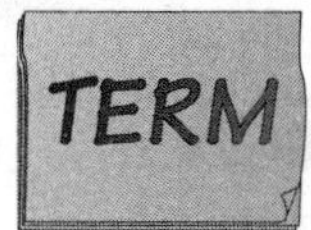

What's an Object? An *object* is any item that you place on a slide. An object can be a text box, a graph, a simple line, or a complex illustration.

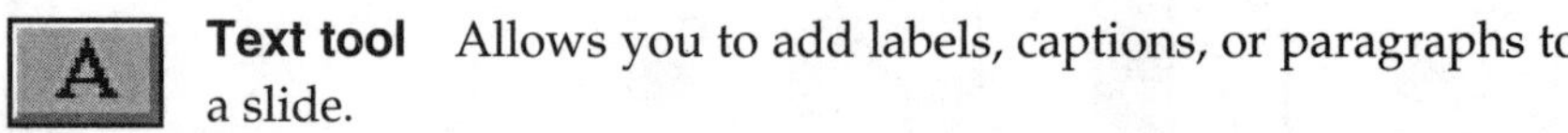

Text tool Allows you to add labels, captions, or paragraphs to a slide.

Line tool Lets you draw a straight line using your mouse.

Arc tool Allows you to draw a curve using your mouse.

Freeform tool Lets you draw an irregular shape using your mouse.

Rectangle tool Lets you draw a rectangle with square corners.

Ellipse tool Lets you use the mouse to draw a circle or oval.

Shape tool When you select this tool (by clicking and holding the left mouse button), a menu of shapes appears. You can select the shape you want to draw, and then use your mouse to draw it.

Graph tool Lets you create or import a graph into a slide.

To select a tool in the Presentation window, move the mouse pointer over the tool and click the left mouse button.

The Toolbar

The Toolbar, located just below the Presentation window title bar, places the following commonly used commands and formatting tools at your fingertips:

Outline buttons If you are creating an outline, use these buttons to move a paragraph in the outline left or right to change its level in the outline and up or down to change its place in the outline.

Text Formatting buttons Use these buttons to change the size of the text; to make the text bold, italic, or underlined; to add a shadow to the text; or to add a bullet symbol.

Object Attribute buttons These buttons allow you to change the appearance of a graphic object. You can draw a line (border) around the object, fill the object with a color, or add a shadow to the object.

Apply Style buttons These buttons allow you to pick up styles from existing text or objects and apply the styles to other text or objects.

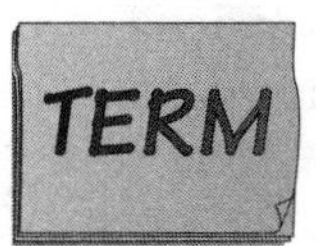

What's a Style? A style is a collection of formats applied to an object. For example, if you use 24-point bold, italic text, the style consists of three formats: 24-point, bold, and italic.

Slide Show button This button displays an on-screen slide show using the slides you created. This allows you to preview the slide you create.

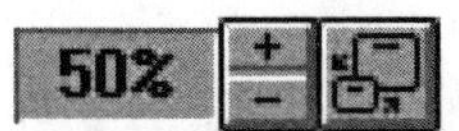

Scale buttons These buttons allow you to zoom in on a slide to see more detail, or zoom out to see the entire slide. The Home View button switches back and forth between the fit-in-window size and the previous view you chose.

The Slide Buttons

In addition to the buttons in the Toolbar and the Tool Palette, PowerPoint provides several tools for working with the slides in a presentation. These tools are located in the lower left corner of the Presentation window:

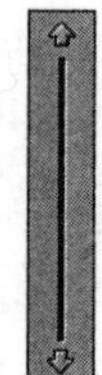

Slide Changer The Slide Changer allows you to change from one slide to the next. Drag the lever on the Slide Changer down to display the next slide, or up to display the previous slide.

Slide Counter As you move from one slide to the next in a presentation, the slide counter displays the number of the currently displayed slide.

New Slide Button The New Slide button creates a new, blank slide in the presentation.

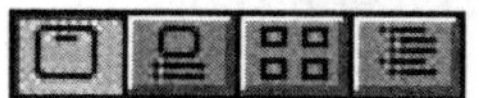

View Buttons The View buttons switch the display to show different elements of the presentation. Initially, the Slide View button is pressed so only one slide appears on-screen at a time. In Note view, you can see the notes added to each slide. Slide Sorter view allows you to rearrange the slides by moving small versions of the slides on-screen. Outline view allows you to create and work with a presentation as an outline.

Getting Help

If you need help performing a task in PowerPoint, you can use PowerPoint's on-line help. To get help, pull down the **Help** menu and select **Contents** or press **F1**. A list of Help topics appears, as shown in Figure 1.3.

Context-sensitive Help If a dialog box is displayed on-screen, you can view information about that dialog box by pressing the **F1** key.

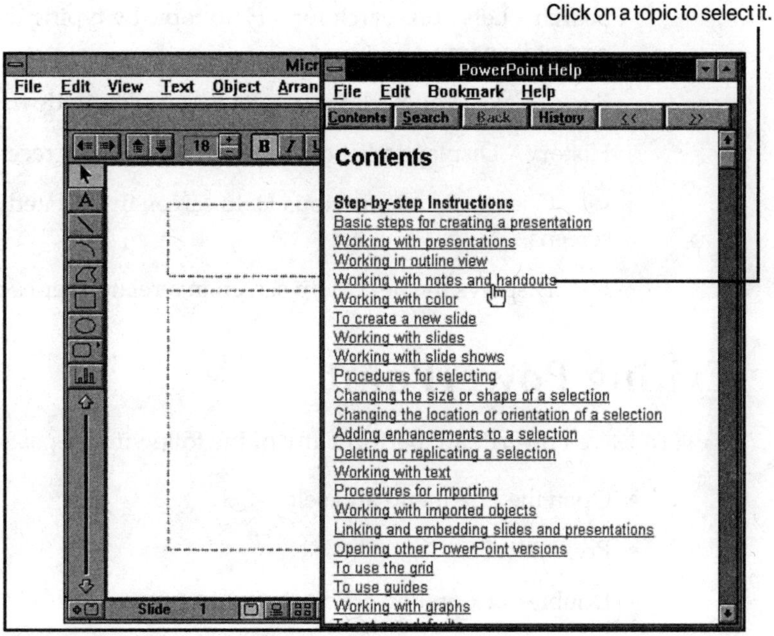

Click on a topic to select it.

Figure 1.3 The Help table of contents displays a list of topics.

Navigating the Help System

To view information about one of the topics listed, click on the topic or tab to it and press **Enter**. Another Help window will appear, with information about the selected topic. This window may also contain two types of *hypertext links* (solid- and dotted-underlined) that let you get more information about related topics.

If you select a topic that is solid-underlined, PowerPoint will open a Help window for that topic. If you select a term that is dotted-underlined, PowerPoint displays a definition for that term. To select a topic or term, click on it or tab to it and press **Enter**.

Using the Help Buttons

At the top of the Help window is the following series of buttons, designed to help you move around the Help system. To use one of the buttons, click on it, or press the key that corresponds to the highlighted letter in the buttons name.

Contents Displays a list of Help topics from which you can choose.

Search Lets you search for a Help topic by typing the topic's name or part of its name.

Back Takes you back to the previous Help window.

His**t**ory Displays a list of Help topics you most recently looked at.

<< Goes back to a previous Help screen in a related series of Help screens.

>> Displays the next Help screen in a related series of Help screens.

Exiting PowerPoint

To leave PowerPoint, perform any of the following steps:

- Open the **File** menu and select **Exit**.
- Press **Alt+F4**.
- Double-click on PowerPoint's **Control menu** icon.

In this lesson, you learned how to start and exit PowerPoint, you learned about the parts of the Presentation window, and you learned how to get on-line help. In the next lesson, you will learn how to prepare for a presentation.

Preparing for a Presentation

In this lesson, you will learn how to prepare for a new presentation by selecting a printer and choosing a slide setup.

Choosing a Target Printer

Before you start creating slides, speaker's notes, and audience handouts, you should select the printer(s) you want to use. By selecting a printer, you are telling PowerPoint which typestyles and type sizes are available on that printer, and for your presentations.

If you have only one printer, and you already use it for all your Windows applications, you do not have to select a printer (just use the printer you set up in Windows). However, if you use two printers (say, a color printer and a black-and-white printer), you should specify which printer you want to use for slides (usually a color printer), and which one for speaker's notes and audience handouts (usually a black-and-white printer). To select a printer, perform the following steps:

1. Open the File menu and select Print Setup. The Print Setup dialog box appears, as shown in Figure 2.1.
2. In the Slides option group, select the printer you want to use for printing your slides. Either choose Default Printer (to choose the currently active Windows printer), or choose Specific Printer and select a printer from the drop-down list.
3. To enter any specific details about the selected printer, click on the Setup button to the right of the Slides option group, and enter the desired information. (For more information about setting up a printer in Windows, refer to your Windows documentation.)
4. In the **Notes, Handouts and Outline** option group, select the printer you want to use for printing speaker's notes, audience handouts, and outlines. Either choose Default Printer, or choose Specific Printer and select a printer from the drop-down list.

5. To enter any specific details about the selected printer, click on the **Setup** button to the right of the Slides option group, and enter the desired information.

6. Click on the **OK** button, or tab to it and press **Enter**.

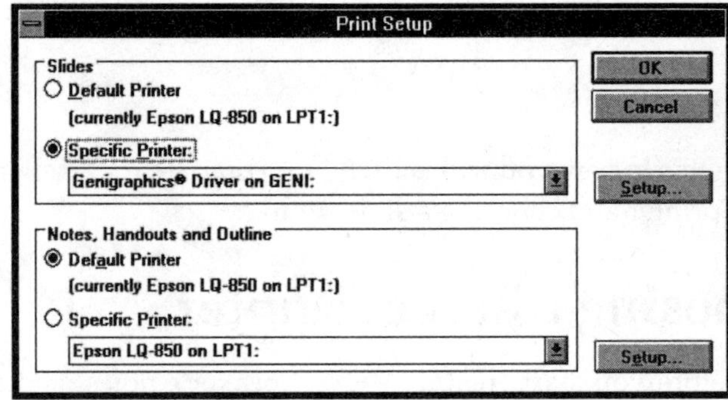

Figure 2.1 Use the Print Setup dialog box to select the printer(s) you want to use.

Changing Printers Later If you select a different printer later, the new printer may not offer fonts that match the fonts of the original printer. PowerPoint will attempt to find the closest available font, but you should still go back through the slides and make sure the font substitutions are to your liking.

Choosing a Slide Setup

A *slide setup* tells PowerPoint the dimensions of the paper, slides, or transparencies on which to print. By specifying the dimensions before you start creating your slides, you will have a more accurate picture of how the slides will look as you are creating them. To choose a slide setup, perform the following steps:

1. Open the **File** menu and select **Slide Setup**. The Slide Setup dialog box appears, as shown in Figure 2.2.

2. Open the **Slides Sized** for drop-down list, and select one of the following options:

   On-screen Show This option sets the width and height of the slides specifically for an electronic presentation.

   Letter Paper (8.5 x 11 in) This is the default setting. It prints the slides sideways on 8.5-by-11-inch paper.

   A4 Paper (210 x 297 mm) Select this option to print on international-size paper.

   35mm Slides This option creates slides that can be transformed into actual 35mm slides for a slide projector. You can send your presentation file to an outside vendor to have it transformed into slides.

   Custom Select this option to specify dimensions that are not listed. Use the **Width** and **Height** boxes below the drop-down list to enter the dimensions in inches.

3. Select one of the following options in the Orientation group to specify the direction you want the slides printed:

   Portrait This option prints the slide as you would print a business letter. The slide is taller than it is wide.

   Landscape This option prints the slide along the wide edge of the page, making the slide wider than it is tall.

4. To start numbering the slides with a number other than 1, enter a number in the Number Slides From box. (You may want to start with a different number, for example, if this presentation picks up where another left off.)
5. Click on the **OK** button. A warning box may appear, telling you that you may have to edit all existing slides if you changed the dimensions.
6. Because you have no existing slides, click on the **Change** button. This puts the dimension changes into effect.

Existing Slides If you change the dimensions after creating one or more slides, PowerPoint automatically scales the slides according to the new dimensions. You should review the slides to make sure they still look the way you want them to look.

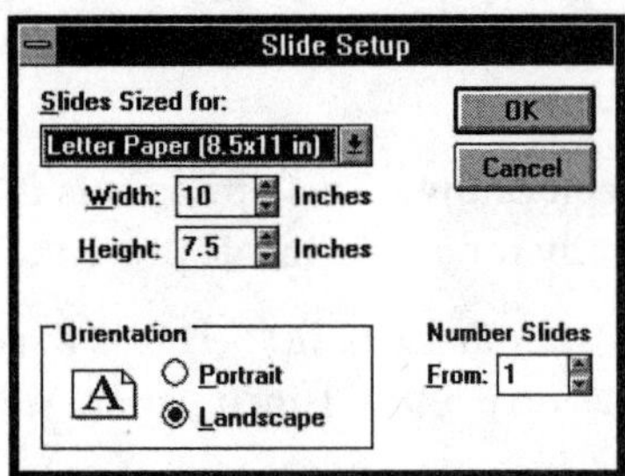

Figure 2.2 Use the Slide Setup dialog box to specify the dimensions, orientation, and numbering of the slides.

In this lesson, you learned how to choose a printer and a slide setup to tell PowerPoint how you intend to reproduce your slides, notes, and audience handouts. In the next lesson, you will learn how to save, close, and open a presentation.

Saving, Closing, and Opening Presentations

In this lesson, you will learn how to save a presentation to disk, close a presentation, and open a new or existing presentation.

Saving a Presentation

Although you have not yet created a slide, it is a good idea to save your presentation and give it a name. Once you have saved the file for the first time, you can quickly save any additional work you do on the presentation later.

To save a presentation for the first time, perform the following steps:

1. Open the **File** menu and select **Save**, or press **Ctrl+S**. The Save As dialog box appears, as shown in Figure 3.1.
2. In the **File Name** text box, type the name you want to assign to the presentation (up to eight characters). (Do not type a filename extension; PowerPoint will automatically add the extension .PPT.)
3. To save the file to a different disk drive, pull down the Drives drop-down list and select the letter of the drive.
4. To save the file in a different directory, select the directory from the **Directory** list.
5. Click on the **OK** button. The file is saved to disk.

Quick Saves Now that you have named the file and saved it to disk, you can save any changes you make to the presentation simply by pressing **Ctrl+S**.

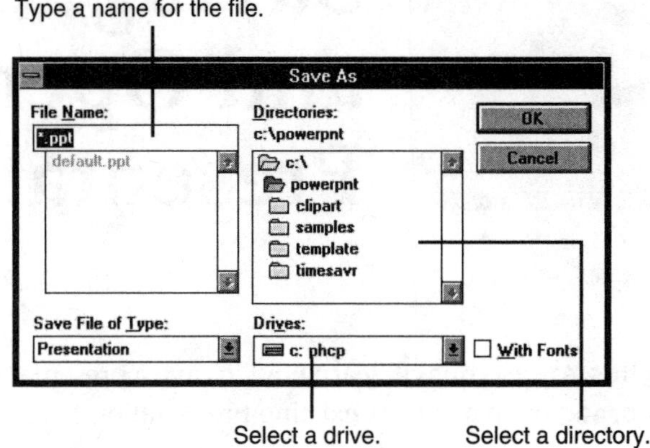

Figure 3.1 The Save As dialog box.

To create a copy of a presentation under a different name, open the **File** menu and select the Save **A**s command. Use the Save As dialog box to enter a different name for the copy. You can then modify the copy without affecting the original.

Closing a Presentation

You can close a presentation at any time. This closes the Presentation window, and allows you to use the space on-screen for a different presentation. To close a presentation, perform the following steps:

1. If more than one Presentation window is displayed, click on any portion of the window you want to close. This activates the window.
2. Open the **File** menu and select **Close**, or press **Ctrl+F4**. If you have not saved the presentation, or if you haven't saved your most recent changes, a dialog box appears, as shown in Figure 3.2, asking if you want to save your changes.
3. To save your changes, click on the **Yes** button. If this is a new presentation, the Save As dialog box appears, as in Figure 3.1. If you have saved the file previously, your changes are saved in the file, and the Presentation window closes.
4. If the Save As dialog box appears, enter a name for the file and any other information as explained earlier. Then, click on the **OK** button.

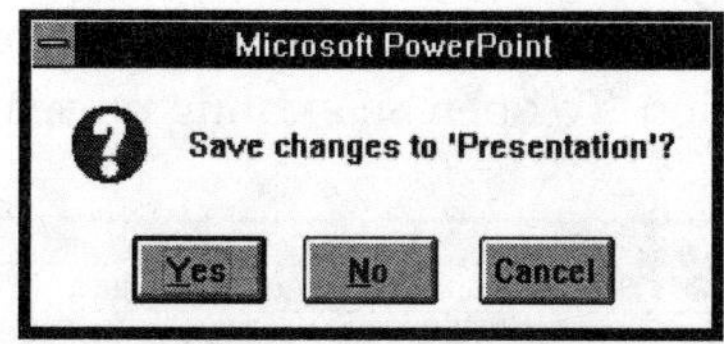

Figure 3.2 If you try to close a presentation without saving your work, PowerPoint warns you.

Opening a Presentation

You can open a new or previously created presentation at any time, and you can have more than one presentation displayed on-screen. The following sections explain how to open a new or existing presentation.

Opening a New Presentation

Whenever you want to start creating a new presentation from scratch, you can open a new Presentation window. To open a new presentation, perform the following steps:

1. Open the **File** menu and select **New**. If no presentation is currently open, a new Presentation window appears. If a presentation is open, PowerPoint displays the New dialog box, shown in Figure 3.3.
2. Choose one of the following options to specify the format you want to use for the new presentation:

   Use format of **a**ctive presentation Choose this option if you want to use the format of an existing presentation that is currently displayed on-screen.

   Use **d**efault format Choose this option if you want to use PowerPoint's default format.
3. Click on the **OK** button. PowerPoint opens a new Presentation window.

Opening an Existing Presentation

Once you have saved a presentation to disk, you can open the presentation and continue working on it at any time. You can also open a sample PowerPoint presentation to get some ideas for your own presentation or to use the format from the presentation. To open an existing presentation, perform the following steps:

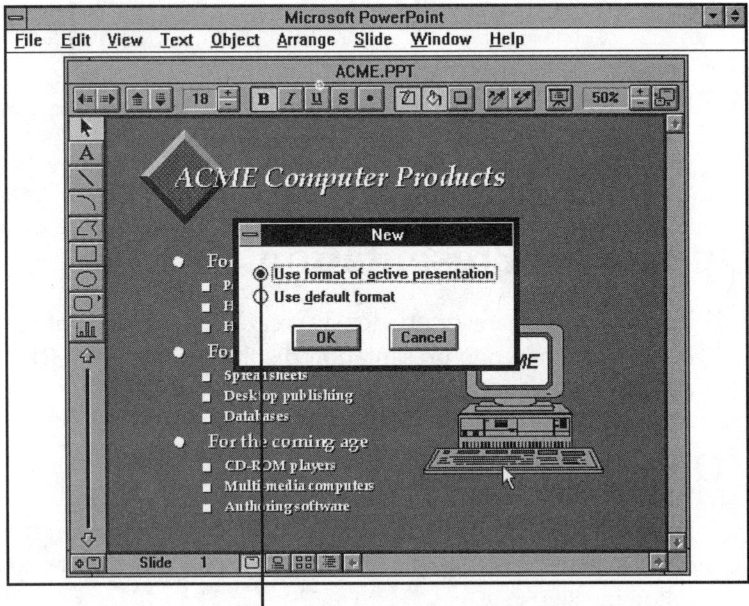

Figure 3.3 The New dialog box asks you to specify the format you want to use for the presentation.

1. Open the **File** menu and select **Open**, or press **Ctrl+O**. The Open dialog box appears.
2. Pull down the **Drives** drop-down list, and select the letter of the drive on which the file is stored.
3. In the **Directories** list, select the directory in which the presentation file is stored. The list below the **File Name** text box displays the names of all the presentation files (files that end in .PPT) in the selected directory.
4. In the list below the **File Name** text box, click on the file you think you want to open. The first slide in the presentation appears in the preview area (see Figure 3.4).
5. To open a copy of the file instead of the original, choose **Open Untitled Copy**. By opening an untitled copy, you can change the presentation without affecting the original.

6. To open the presentation file, double-click on its filename, or highlight the filename and click on the **OK** button. PowerPoint opens the presentation.

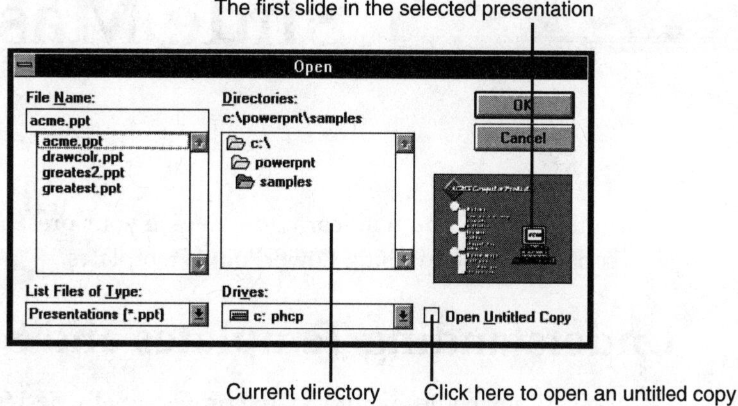

Figure 3.4 The Open dialog box lets you select and preview the presentation.

View a Sample Presentation PowerPoint comes with several sample presentations, which are stored in the \POWERPT\SAMPLES directory. To get a general idea of how a slide show works, open one of these samples, and use the slide changer to flip through the slides. Or open a sample as an untitled copy, and modify it to suit your needs.

In this lesson, you learned how to save, close, and open presentations. In the next lesson, you will learn how to apply a template to your presentation to give your slides a professional and consistent look.

Using PowerPoint's Templates and Slide Master

In this lesson, you will learn how to give your presentation a professional and consistent look by using PowerPoint's templates.

Understanding Templates and Slide Masters

PowerPoint comes with over 160 professionally designed slides you can use as *templates* for your own presentations. That is, you can apply one of these pre-designed slides to your own presentation, to give the slides in your presentation the same look as the professional slides.

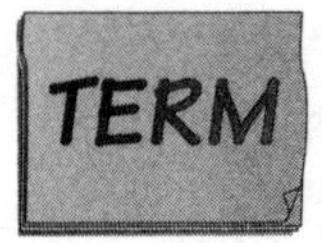

What Is a Template? A template is a predesigned slide that comes with PowerPoint. It contains a color scheme and a general layout for each slide in the presentation. The template makes it easy for you to create a presentation; you simply fill in the blanks on each slide.

Each template has a *Slide Master* that works in the background to control the background color, layout, and style of each slide in the presentation. This provides all the slides in your presentation with a consistent look. In the following sections, you will learn how to select a template for your presentation and modify the Slide Master.

Selecting a Template

Any PowerPoint presentation file can act as a template. Initially, you will want to use one of PowerPoint's sample files as a template for your presentation.

However, once you have created a presentation of your own, you can use it as a template, as well. To apply a template to your presentation, perform the following steps:

1. Open the **File** menu and select **Apply Template**. The Apply Template dialog box appears.
2. In the **Directories** list, change to the C:\POWERPNT \TEMPLATE directory. The template subdirectories appear. Each subdirectory contains a set of templates for a particular type of presentation: 35mm slides, black-and-white overheads, color overheads, and on-screen video presentations.
3. Select the template subdirectory for the type of presentation you want to create. A list of templates appears in the **File Name** list.
4. Click on a file name in the list, or tab to the list and use the ↓ key to highlight a name. When you highlight the name of a template, a slide appears in the preview area, showing what the template looks like. (See Figure 4.1.)
5. Press **Enter** or double-click on the name of the template you want to use. You are returned to your presentation, and the template is now in control of your presentation.

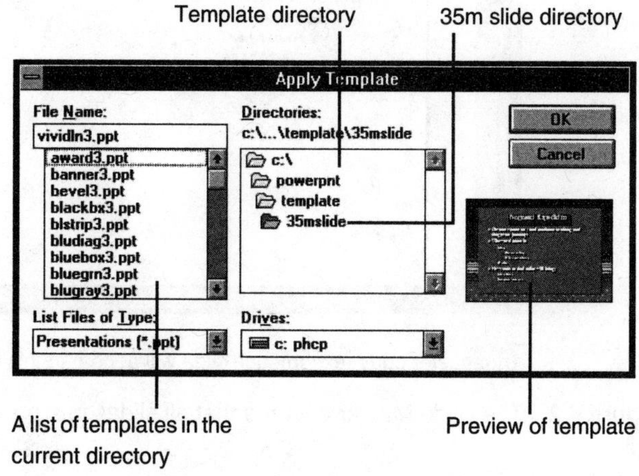

Figure 4.1 The Apply Template dialog box lets you preview a template before you apply it.

Apply Templates at Anytime You do not have to apply a template before you begin creating your presentation. You can change the template at anytime, and your entire presentation will take on the look of the new template. Note that a template will replace any background information you have added in Slide Master with its own. For more information on background information, see Lesson 16.

Editing the Slide Master

Every presentation has a Slide Master that controls the overall appearance and layout of each slide. A sample Slide Master is shown in Figure 4.2.

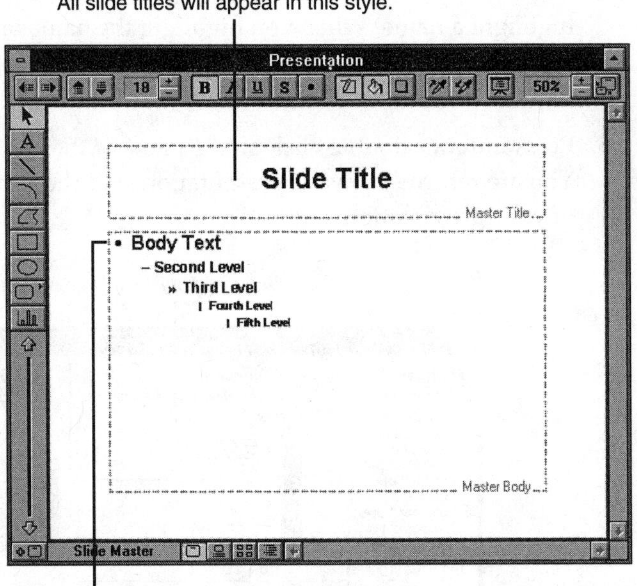

Figure 4.2 The Slide Master ensures that all slides in a presentation have a consistent look.

The two most important elements on the Slide Master are the *Master Title* and *Master Body* objects. The Master Title object contains the formatting specifications for each slide's title; that is, it tells PowerPoint the type size, style, and color to use for the text in the title of each slide. The Master Body object contains the formatting specifications for all remaining text on the slide. For most of PowerPoint's templates, the Master Body object sets up specifications for a bulleted list: these include the type of bullet, as well as the type styles, sizes, and indents for each item in the list.

In addition to the Master Title and Body, the Slide Master can contain the background color, a border, a code that inserts page numbers, your company logo, a clip art object, and any other elements you want to appear on *every* slide in the presentation.

To view the Slide Master for a presentation, perform the following steps:

1. Open the **V**iew menu and select **Slide Master**. The Slide Master appears, as shown in Figure 4.2.
2. To return to Slide view, open the **V**iew menu and select **S**lides, or click on the **Slide view** button as shown here:

Missing the View? To return to Slide view, you must have a slide or an active presentation on-screen.

The Slide Master is like any slide. In the following lessons, when you learn how to add text, graphics, borders, and other objects to a slide, keep in mind that you can add these objects on individual slides or on the Slide Master. When you add the objects to the Slide Master, the objects will appear on *every* slide in the presentation.

In this lesson, you learned how to give your presentation a consistent look by applying a template to it. You also learned how to display the Slide Master. In the next lesson, you will learn how to create a basic slide.

Creating a Slide

In this lesson, you will learn how to create a basic slide, add a slide to a presentation, and move from slide to slide.

Creating Your First Slide

In the previous lesson, you learned that the Slide Master contains two objects: a Master Title and a Master Body. When you switch to Slide view, you will see a slide that contains two similar objects: the *Title object* and the *Body object* (see Figure 5.1). In the following sections, you will learn how to type text into these objects to create a slide.

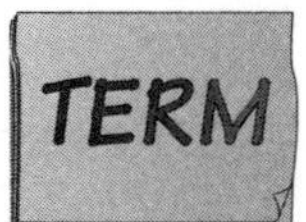

The Slide Master Is in Control When typing a title and bulleted list, keep in mind that the Slide Master is controlling the appearance of the title and bulleted list on each slide.

Creating a Slide in Slide View

In Slide view, one slide is displayed on-screen at a time. You can type text for the existing objects (Title and Body) and add objects on this slide to create the look you want. To add a title and bulleted list in Slide view, perform the following steps:

1. Type a title in the **Title object**. When you start typing, the Title object gets smaller to show the actual size of the text, and the insertion point appears:

ACME Computer Products

2. Click on the **Body object**. The selection rectangle appears around the Body object, showing the object is active.

3. Type the first entry that you want to appear in the bulleted list. As you type, the Body object gets smaller, and a bullet appears to the left of your text.

4. Press **Enter**. Another bullet appears, showing that you can type another entry for the list.

5. Continue typing entries until you have completed the list.

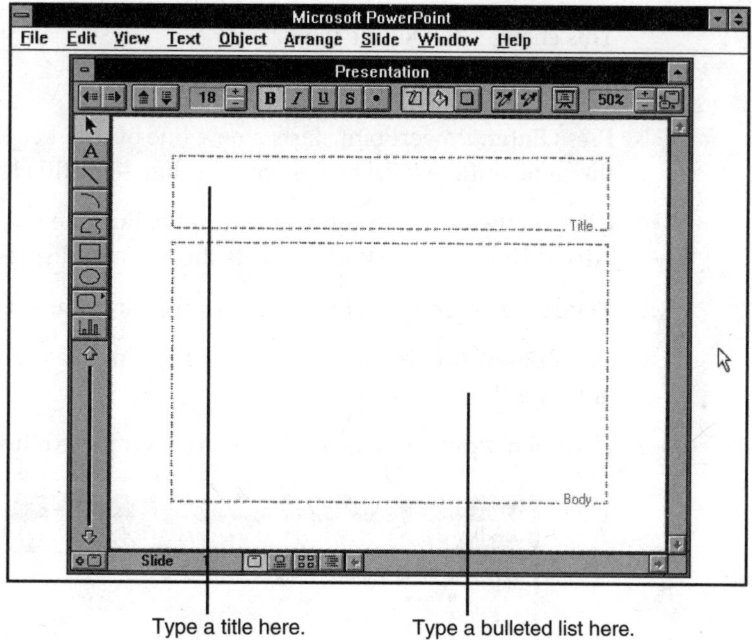

Figure 5.1 You can create a slide by typing a title and a bulleted list.

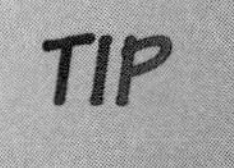

Too Looong If your text is too long for the slide, consider continuing onto another slide, creating two columns, or changing the font and size of the text (see Lesson 8).

Creating a Slide in Outline View

In Slide view, slides are not displayed as actual slides. Instead, PowerPoint displays the title and bulleted list that appears on each slide. In other words, the presentation appears as an outline. To create a slide in Outline view, perform the following steps:

1. Open the **View** menu and select **Outline**, or click on the **Outline** button as shown:

   This changes to Outline view.
2. Type a title for the first slide you want to create.
3. Press **Enter**. PowerPoint starts a new line of text, keeping the new line at the same outline level as the previous line—the title level.
4. Click on the Demote button to indent the line one level, or press **Alt+Shift+→**. PowerPoint indents the line and displays a bullet.
5. Type the first entry that you want to appear in the bulleted list.
6. Press **Enter**. Another bullet appears, showing that you can type another entry for the list. (See Figure 5.2.)
7. Continue typing entries until you have completed the list.

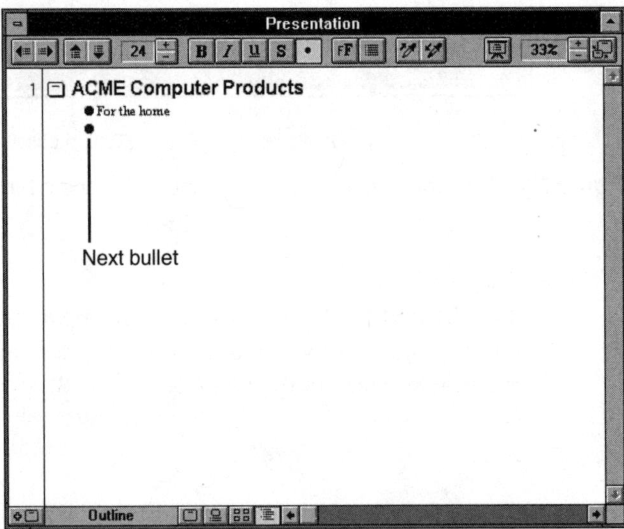

Figure 5.2 Each time you press Enter, a bullet appears, allowing you to type an entry.

Not Every Slide Needs a Title and Bulleted List The title and bulleted list are convenient for creating a presentation. However, they are not essential. If you want to create a slide that does not contain a title or bulleted list, select the **Title text** or **Body text** box and press **Del**. You can then add any other objects you want to the slide as explained in later lessons.

Working with a Bulleted List

The bulleted list is a powerful tool for helping you organize and present ideas and supporting data for your presentation. As you type entries, keep in mind that you can change an entry's level and position in the list. To change the position or level of an entry, use the arrow keys or mouse to move the insertion point anywhere inside the entry, and then perform one of the following actions:

Click on this button to move the entry up in the list.

Click on this button to move the entry down in the list.

Click on this button to indent the entry to the next lower level in the list. The item will be indented, the bullet will change, and the text will usually appear smaller.

Click on this button to remove the indent and move the entry to the next higher level in the list. The item will be moved to the left, the bullet will change, and the text will appear larger.

Dragging Paragraphs You can quickly change the position or level of a paragraph by dragging it up, down, left, or right. To drag a paragraph, move the mouse pointer to the left side of the paragraph until it turns into a four-headed arrow. Then, hold down the mouse button and drag the paragraph to the desired position.

In later lessons, you will learn how to change the appearance of the bullet, the style and size of text for each entry, and the amount the text is indented for each level.

Adding a Slide to Your Presentation

When you are finished creating your first slide, you may want to add another slide to your presentation. To add a slide, perform any of the following steps:

- Click on the **New Slide** button, as shown:

- Press **Ctrl+N**.
- Open the **Slide** menu and select **New Slide**.
- In Outline view, press **Enter** after the last bulleted item, and then click on the **Promote** button, as shown below, or press **Alt+Shift+←** until you are at the Title level in the outline:

Moving from Slide to Slide

When you have more than one slide in your presentation, you will need to move from one slide to the next in order to work with a specific slide. The procedure for moving to a slide depends on whether you are working in Slide view or Outline view:

- In Outline view, use your mouse or the cursor-movement keys to move to the slide you want to work with.
- In Slide view, drag the Slide Changer (see Figure 5.3) until the slide you want to work with is displayed. Then release the mouse button.

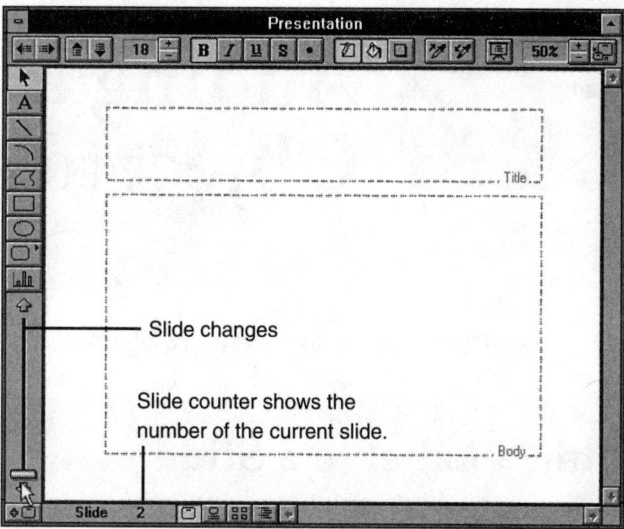

Figure 5.3 Drag the Slide Changer to change to the next slide.

In this lesson, you learned how to create a basic slide, add a slide to your presentation, and move from slide to slide. In the next lesson, you will learn how to create additional text objects.

6 Adding a Text Object to a Slide

In this lesson, you will learn how to add a label and text box to a slide and how to align the text.

Adding a Label to a Slide

Labels are small amounts of text that allow you to call attention to important elements on the slide. For example, if you are creating a training presentation, labels might point to important parts of a machine. To add a label to a slide, perform the following steps:

1. Click on the **Text** tool as shown here:

2. Move the mouse pointer to where you want the label to start (anywhere off the Title and Body objects), and click the left mouse button. A blinking *insertion point* appears, showing where the text will be inserted.
3. Type the label.
4. Click anywhere outside the label.

If you go back and click on the label, a *selection box* will appear around the label, as shown in Figure 6.1. You can drag the box to move it, or drag a corner of the box (as shown) to resize it. PowerPoint will wrap the text automatically as needed to fit inside the box.

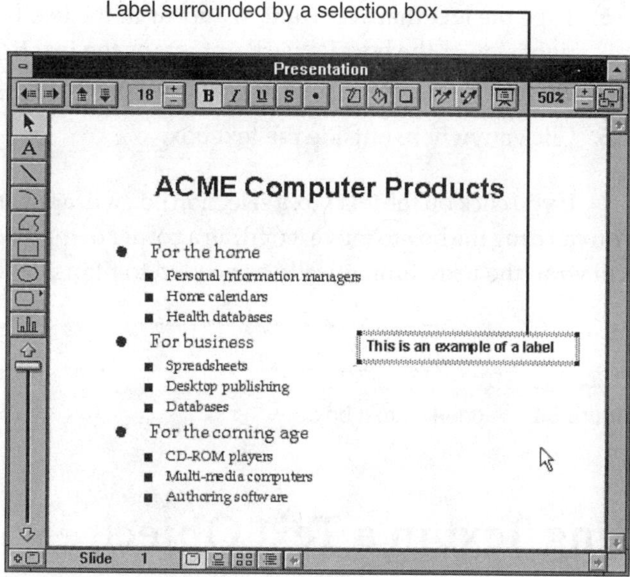

Figure 6.1 Click on your label after creating it to display the selection box.

Adding a Text Box to a Slide

A *text box* is similar to a label but is generally used for holding more text (for example, an entire paragraph or a bulleted list). To create a text box, perform the following steps:

1. Click on the **Text** tool as shown here:

2. Move the mouse pointer to where you want the upper left corner of the text box to appear (anywhere off the Title and Body objects).
3. Hold down the mouse button, and drag the mouse pointer to the right until the box is the desired width.
4. Release the mouse button. A one-line text box appears. (See Figure 6.2.)

5. Type the text that you want to appear in the text box. When you reach the right side of the box, PowerPoint wraps the text to the next line and makes the box one line longer. To start a new paragraph, press **Enter**.
6. Click anywhere outside the text box.

If you click on the text box a selection box will appear, as shown in Figure 6.1. You can drag the box to move it or drag a corner of the box to resize it. PowerPoint will wrap the text automatically as needed to fit inside the box.

Figure 6.2 A one-line text box.

Editing Text in a Text Object

To edit text in a text object, first click on the text object to select it, then click on the **Text** tool. Then, perform any of the following steps:

- *To select text,* drag the **I-beam pointer** (see Figure 6.3) over the text you want to select. (To select a single word, double-click on it.)
- *To delete text,* select the text and press the **Del** key.
- *To insert text,* click the mouse pointer where you want the text inserted, and then type the text.
- *To replace text,* select the text you want to replace, and then type the new text. When you start typing, the selected text is deleted.
- *To copy and paste text,* select the text you want to copy, and choose the **Copy** command from the **Edit** menu, or press **Ctrl+C**. Move the insertion point to where you want the text pasted (it can be in a different text box), and choose **Paste** from the **Edit** menu, or press **Ctrl+V**.
- *To cut and paste (move) text,* select the text you want to cut, and choose the **Cut** command from the **Edit** menu, or press **Ctrl+X**. Move the insertion point to where you want the text pasted (it can be in a different text box), and choose **Paste** from the **Edit** menu, or press **Ctrl+V**.

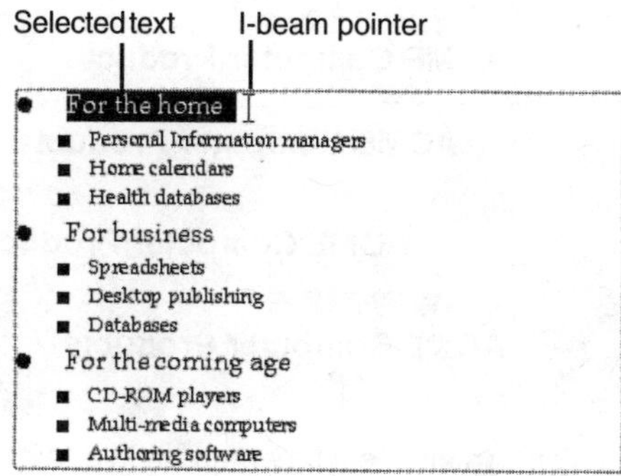

Figure 6.3 To select text, drag the I-beam pointer over the text.

Changing the Text Alignment and Line Spacing

When you first type text, it is set against the left edge of the text box and is single-spaced. In this section, you will learn how to change a paragraph's alignment and line spacing.

You can change the alignment for any paragraph in a text box by performing the following steps:

1. Click anywhere inside the paragraph whose alignment you want to change.
2. Open the **Text** menu and select **Alignment**. The Alignment submenu appears.
3. Select **Left, Center, Right**, or **Justify** to align the paragraph as desired. (See Figure 6.4 for examples.)

Quick Key Alignment To quickly set the alignment for a paragraph, click inside the paragraph and press one of the following key combinations: **Ctrl+[** for left alignment, **Ctrl+]** for right alignment, or **Ctrl+** to center the text.

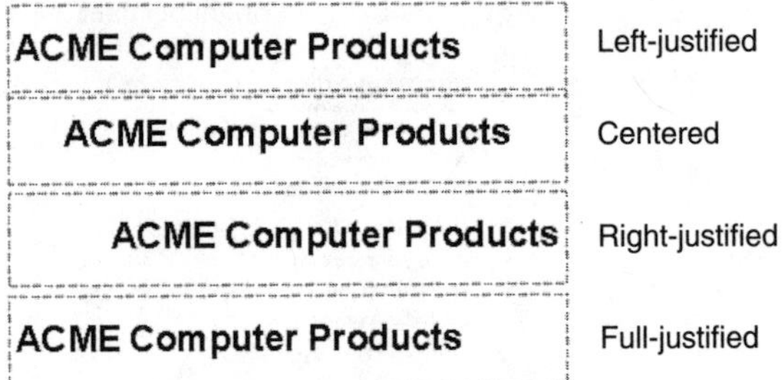

Figure 6.4 You can align each paragraph in a text box.

To change the line spacing in a paragraph, perform these steps:

1. Click inside the paragraph whose line spacing you want to change, or select all the paragraphs whose line spacing you want to change.
2. Open the **Text** menu and select **Line Spacing**. The Line Spacing dialog box appears, as shown in Figure 6.5.
3. Click on the arrow buttons to the right of any of the following text boxes to change the line spacing:

   Line Spacing This setting controls the space between the lines in a paragraph.

   Before Paragraph This setting controls the space between this paragraph and the paragraph that comes before it.

   After Paragraph This setting controls the space between this paragraph and the paragraph that comes after it.

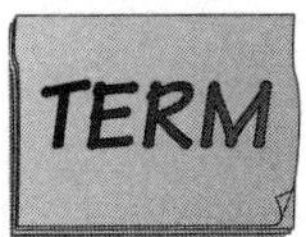

Lines or Points? The drop-down list box that appears to the right of each setting allows you to set the line spacing in *lines* or *points*. A line is the current line height. A point is a unit commonly used to measure text. A point is approximately 1/72 of an inch.

4. Click on the **OK** button. Your line spacing changes are put into effect.

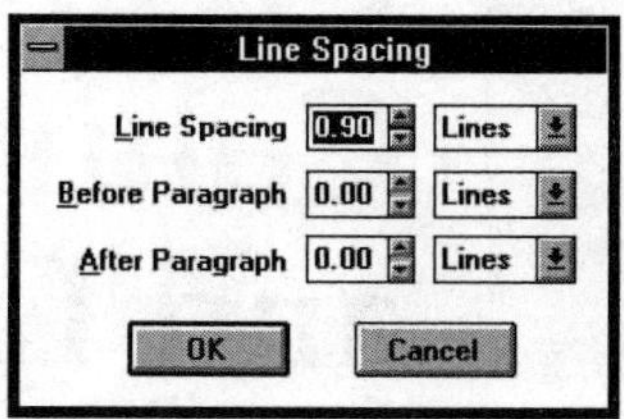

Figure 6.5 The Line Spacing dialog box.

In this lesson, you learned how to add labels and basic text objects to a slide, as well as how to change the text alignment and line spacing. In the next lesson, you will learn how to use tabs and indents to create columns and lists.

7 Creating Columns and Lists

In this lesson, you will learn how to use tabs to create columns of text, and indents to create bulleted lists, numbered lists, and other types of lists.

Using Tabs to Create Columns

A presentation often uses tabbed columns to display information. For example, you may use tabs to create a three-column list like the one shown in Figure 7.1.

In addition to hardware products, we carry a varied line of software:

Business	**Home**	**Education**
WordPerfect	Quicken	Reader Rabbit 2
Microsoft Word	The New Print Shop	Oregon Trail
PowerPoint	Microsoft Works	BodyWorks
Excel	TurboTax	Where in the World is Carmen Sandiego?

Figure 7.1 You can use tabs to create a multicolumn list.

To set the tabs for such a list, perform the following steps:

1. Select the text object for which you want to set the tabs.
2. Click inside the paragraph whose tabs you want to set, or select two or more paragraphs.
3. Open the **Text** menu and select **Show Ruler**. The ruler appears above the text box.
4. Move the mouse pointer over the icon for the type of tab you want to set:

Aligns the left end of the line against the tab stop.

Centers the text on the tab stop.

Aligns the right end of the line against the tab stop.

Aligns the tab stop on a period. This is useful for aligning a column of numbers that use decimal points.

5. Hold down the mouse button and drag the icon below the ruler to where you want to set the tab stop (see Figure 7.2).
6. Repeat steps 4 and 5 for each tab stop you want to set.
7. To change the position of an existing tab stop setting, drag it on the ruler to the desired position. To delete an existing tab stop setting, drag it off the ruler.
8. Open the **Text** menu and select **Hide Ruler**.

TIP

Turning the Ruler On and Off To turn the ruler on or off quickly, press **Ctrl+R**.

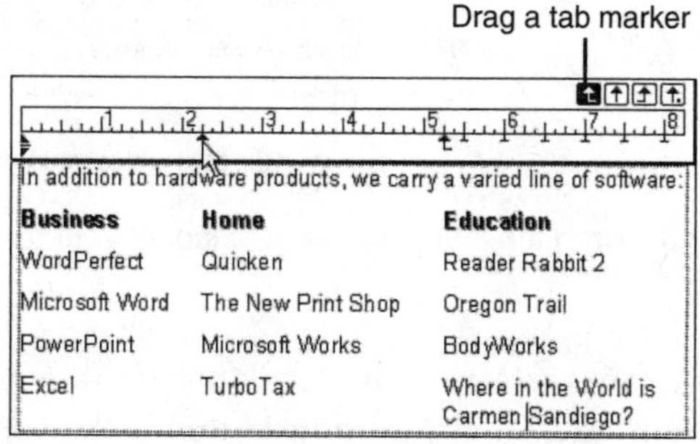

Figure 7.2 The ruler lets you enter and change tab stop settings.

Using Indents to Create Lists

Indents allow you to indent one or more lines of a paragraph from the left margin. You have already seen indents used in the Master Body to create a bulleted list.

You can use indents in any text object to create a similar list or your own custom list.

To indent existing text, perform the following steps:

1. Select the text object that contains the text you want to indent.
2. Click inside the paragraph whose indents you want to set, or select two or more paragraphs.
3. Open the **Text** menu and select **Show Ruler**. The ruler appears above the text box.
4. Drag one of the indent markers (as shown in Figure 7.3) to set the indents for the paragraph:

   Drag the **top marker** to indent the first line.

   Drag the **bottom marker** to indent all subsequent lines.

   Drag the line between the top and bottom markers to indent all the text.
5. Open the **Text** menu and select **Hide Ruler**.

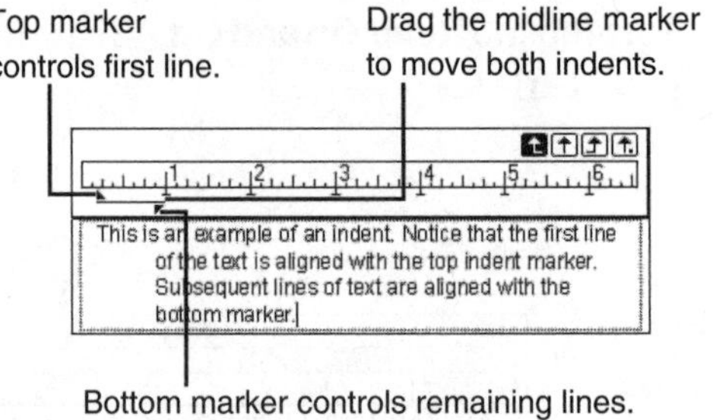

Figure 7.3 Drag the indent markers to indent your text.

You can create up to five levels of indents within a single text box. To add an indent level, click on the **Demote** button in the Toolbox or press **Alt+Shift+→**. A new set of indent markers appears, showing the next level of indents. You can change these new indent settings as explained above.

Once you have set your indents, you can create a numbered or bulleted list by performing the following steps:

1. Type a number and a period, or type the character you want to use for the bullet.

2. Press the **Tab** key to move to the second indent mark.

3. Type the text you want to use for this item. As you type, the text is wrapped to the second indent mark, as shown in Figure 7.4.

Quick Bullets To enter a bullet quickly, click on the **Bullet** button in the Toolbox. This inserts a dot and a tab, so all you have to do is type the text.

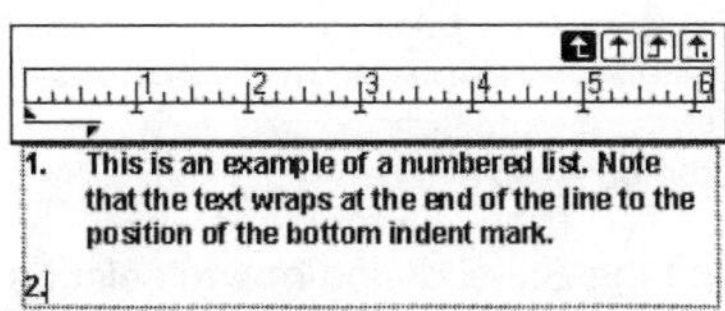

Figure 7.4 PowerPoint automatically wraps the text for you.

Changing the Bullet Character

By default, whenever you click on the **Bullet** button in the Toolbox to insert a bullet, PowerPoint inserts a large dot for the bullet. However, you can change the appearance of the bullet at any time by performing the following steps:

1. Select the paragraph(s) in which you want to change the bullet character.
2. Open the **Text** menu and select **Bullet**. The Bullet dialog box appears, as shown in Figure 7.5.
3. Pull down the **Bullets From** list, and select the character set from which you want to choose a bullet. The dialog box displays the characters in the selected set.
4. Click on the character you want to use for the bullet.
5. To set the size of the bullet, use the up and down arrows to the right of the **Size** text box.
6. To select a color for the bullet, pull down the **Special Color** drop-down list and select the desired color.
7. Select the **OK** button. The bullet character is changed for all selected paragraphs.

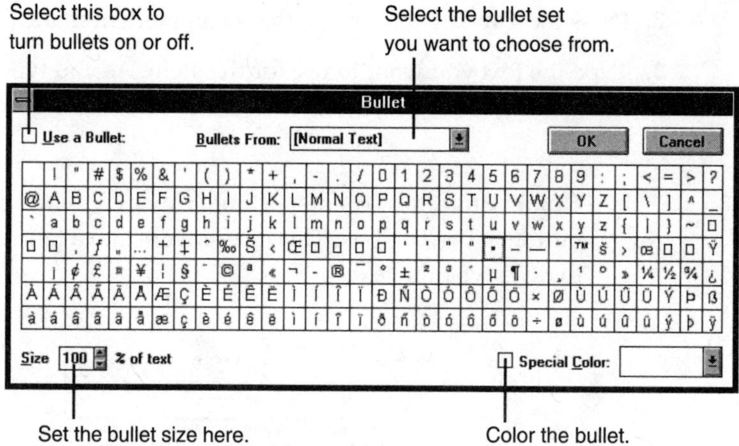

Figure 7.5 Use the Bullet dialog box to select a bullet character.

Changing the Indents and Bullets on the Slide Master

The Master Body on the Slide Master contains a template for creating a bulleted list on each slide. You can change the indents and bullet characters used in this template to change them for all subsequent slides. To do this, perform the following steps:

1. Open the **View** menu and select **Slide Master**. The Slide Master appears.
2. Click on the **Master Body** object to select it, and then press **F2** to select all the paragraphs.
3. Open the **Text** menu and select **Show Ruler**. The ruler appears at the top of the Master Body object, as shown in Figure 7.6.
4. Change any of the indents as described earlier in this lesson.
5. Click inside the paragraph whose bullet character you want to change, and then change the character as explained earlier in this lesson.
6. Click on the **Slide view** button to return to Slide view.

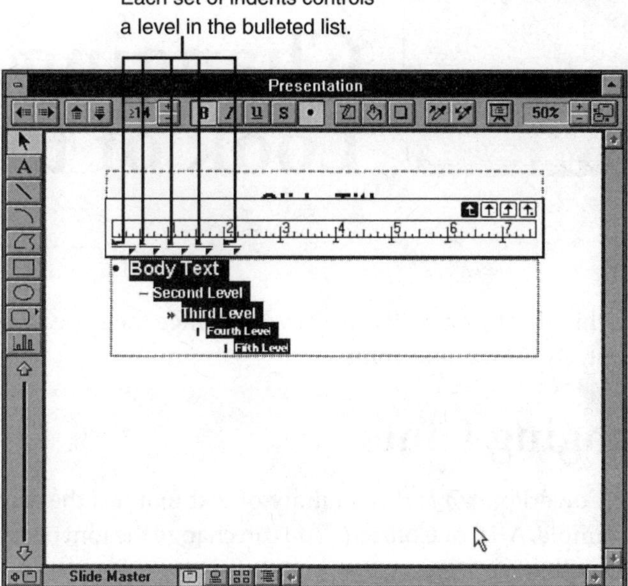

Figure 7.6 Change the indents in the Master Body to change the indents for the Body text in all slides.

The changes you made to the Master Body will now affect the bulleted lists you create in the Body text object on every slide.

In this lesson, you learned how to create columns with tabs, create lists with indents, and change the bullet character for bulleted lists. In the next lesson, you will learn how to change the style, size, and color of text.

Changing the Look of the Text

In this lesson, you will learn how to change the appearance of text by changing its font, style, size, and color.

Changing Fonts

In PowerPoint, a *font* is a family of text that has the same design or *typeface* (for example, Arial or Courier). You can change the font of existing text by performing the following steps:

1. To change the font for existing text, select the text. (If you change fonts without selecting text, the selected font becomes the default font for any text you type in the presentation.)
2. Open the **Text** menu and select **Font**. The Font submenu appears, as shown in Figure 8.1.
3. Select the font you want to use. If you selected text, the selected text appears in the new font. If you did not select text, when you type the text it will appear in the selected font.

Title and Body Text Do not change fonts for Title or Body text on individual slides. If you do this, you override the font selections in the Slide Master, and risk making the slides in your presentation inconsistent. Later in this lesson, you will learn how to change the appearance of text on the Slide Master.

Changing the Size of Text

PowerPoint allows you to keep the design of the text the same while changing its size. Text size is measured in points; there are approximately 72 points in an inch.

To change the size of text, perform the following steps:

1. To change the size of existing text, select the text.
2. Open the **Text** menu and select **Size**. The Size submenu appears.
3. Select the size you want to use. To specify a size not on the submenu, select **Other**, type the size you want to use, and press **Enter**. The selected text appears in the specified size.

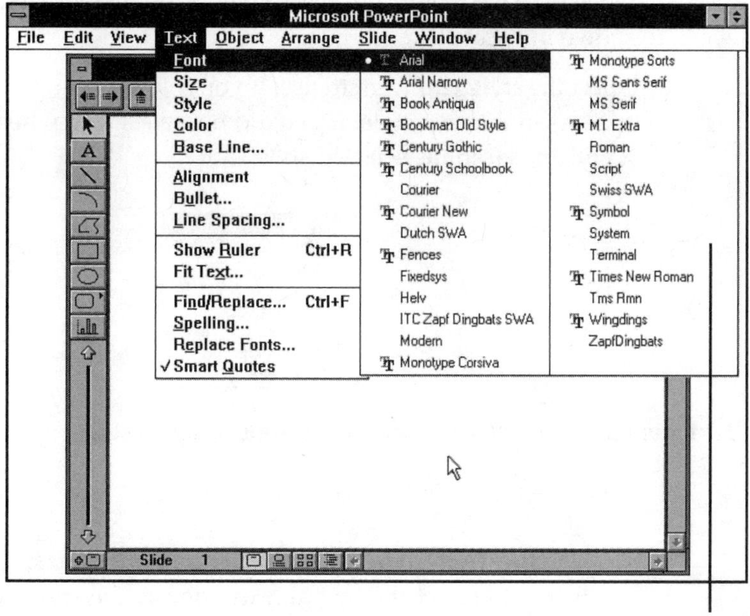

Figure 8.1 The Font submenu displays the fonts you can use.

Use the Text Size Buttons A quick way to change the size of text is to select the text and use the text size buttons in the Toolbox:

Click on the + button to increase the text size or click on the - button to decrease it.

Styling Your Text

In addition to fonts and sizes, you can add *styles* (including bold and italics) to your text in order to emphasize it. When you add a style to the text, its font and size remain the same, but the appearance of the text is changed. To add a style, perform the following steps:

1. To change the style of existing text, select the text.
2. Open the **Text** menu and select **Style**. The Style submenu appears, as shown in Figure 8.2.
3. Select the style you want to use. If you selected text, the selected text appears in the new style. If you did not select text, when you type the text it will appear in the selected style.

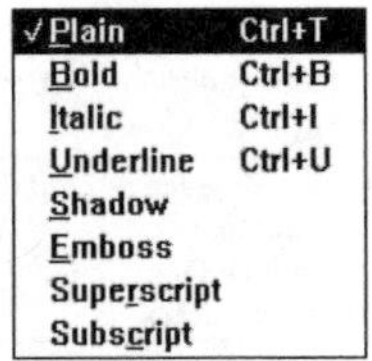

Figure 8.2 The Style submenu displays the available styles.

Use the Text Style Buttons A quick way to change the style of text is to select the text and use one of the style buttons in the Toolbox:

Click on a button to turn the style on or off.

Changing the Text Color

The procedure for changing text color is very similar to the procedure for selecting a font, size, or style. Perform the following steps:

1. To change the color of existing text, select the text.
2. Open the **Text** menu and select **Color**. The Color submenu appears.
3. Select a color from the submenu or select **Other Color**. If you select a color from the list, the text appears in the specified color. If you select Other Color, the Other Color dialog box appears, as shown in Figure 8.3.
4. If you chose **Other Color**, select a color from the dialog box, and then click on the **OK** button.

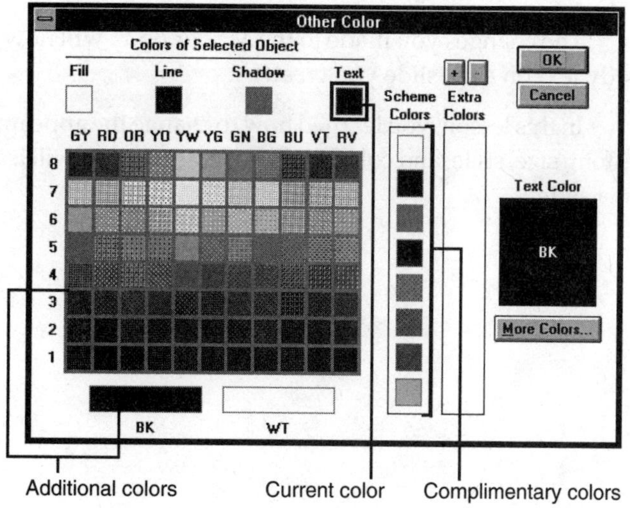

Figure 8.3 Use the Other Color dialog box to select a color that is not in the current color scheme.

Watch Those Color Schemes The colors listed on the Color submenu complement the background colors in the template. If you choose an "other" color, you risk using one that will clash with the background colors and make your slides look inconsistent.

Formatting Text on the Slide Master

The Master Title and Master Body on the Slide Master contain the font, size, style, and color settings for the title and body text on each slide. You can change the settings on the Slide Master to change them for all subsequent slides. To do this, perform the following steps:

1. Open the **View** menu and select **Slide Master**. The Slide Master appears.
2. Select the text in the **Master Title** or **Master Body** object whose font, size, style, or color you want to change.
3. Change any of the text attributes as desired.
4. Click on the **Slide view** button to return to Slide view.

The changes you made to the Master Body will now affect the Title text and Body text on each slide you create.

In this lesson, you learned how to change the appearance of text by changing its font, size, style, and color. In the next lesson, you will learn how to draw objects on a slide.

Drawing Objects on a Slide

In this lesson, you will learn how to use PowerPoint's drawing tools to draw graphic objects on a slide.

PowerPoint's Drawing Tools

PowerPoint's drawing tools are displayed along the left side of the Presentation window. The general procedure for drawing an object is to click on a tool, and then use the mouse to drag the shape to the desired size and dimensions. The following sections provide instructions for using each tool.

Drawing a Line

The *Line tool* lets you draw a straight line. To draw a line, perform the following steps:

1. Click on the **Line** tool.

2. Move the mouse pointer to where you want the end or center of the line to start.
3. (Optional) While drawing the line, hold down one or both of the following keys:

   Ctrl to draw the line out from a center point.

   Shift to make sure the line is horizontal, vertical, or at a 90-degree angle.

4. Hold down the mouse button and drag the mouse to draw your line.
5. Release the mouse button.
6. To add an arrow tip to the line, open the **Object** menu, select **Arrow-heads**, and select the desired arrow tip.

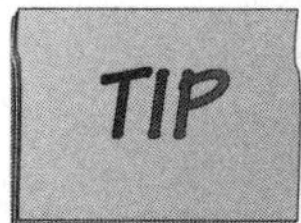

Changing the Line Thickness To change the thickness of a line, select the line, open the **Object menu**, select **Line Style**, and select the desired line thickness.

Drawing an Arc

The *Arc tool* lets you draw a curved line. To draw an arc, perform the following steps:

1. Click on the **Arc** tool.

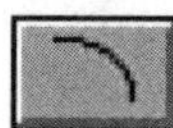

2. Move the mouse pointer to where you want the end or center of the arc to start.
3. (Optional) While drawing the arc, hold down one or both of the following keys:

   Ctrl to draw the arc out from a center point.

   Shift to make sure the arc is circular rather than oval.
4. Hold down the mouse button and drag the mouse to draw the arc.
5. Release the mouse button.

To change the angle of the arc, double-click on the arc, or select it and choose **Edit Arc** from the **Edit** menu. A handle appears at each end of the arc, as shown in Figure 9.1. Drag a handle to change the arc's angle.

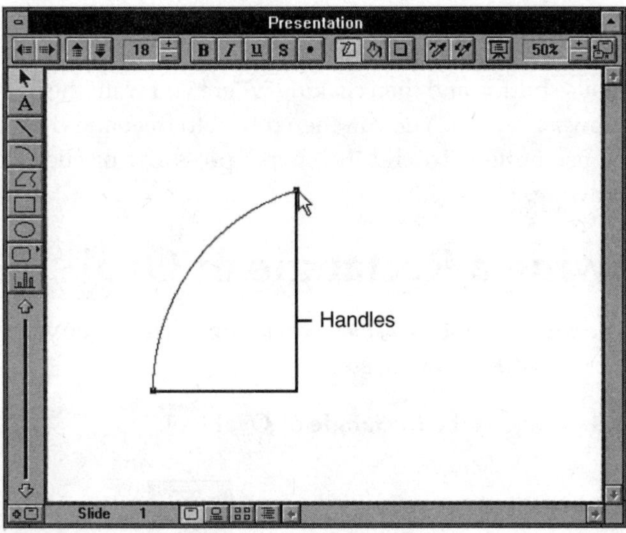

Figure 9.1 Drag a handle to change the arc's angle.

Drawing a Freeform Object

The *Freeform tool* lets you draw just as if you were using an on-screen pencil. You can draw an object made up of several straight lines (a polygon) or a freehand object.

To draw a polygon, perform the following steps:

1. Click on the **Freeform** tool.
2. Move the mouse pointer to where you want the object to start, and click the mouse button. This anchors the first line.
3. Move the mouse pointer (do not drag) to the place where you want the first line segment to end, and click the mouse button.
4. Continue moving the mouse pointer and clicking to add line segments to the figure.
5. To complete the polygon, perform one of the following steps:

   To create a closed shape: Click near the beginning of the first line. The end of the last line is connected to the beginning of the first line.

   To create an open shape: Press the **Esc** key or click outside the drawing area.

To draw a freehand object, select the **Freeform** tool and then drag the mouse around on-screen to draw your lines. You can draw straight lines by releasing the mouse button and then clicking where you want the line to end, just as you did to draw a polygon. You can then return to freehand drawing by holding down the mouse button. To end the shape, press **Esc** or click near the beginning of the drawing.

Drawing a Rectangle or Oval

The *Rectangle* and *Oval tools* work in much the same way. To use one of these tools, perform the following steps:

1. Click on the **Rectangle** or **Oval** tool.

2. Move the mouse pointer to where you want an end (or the center) of the object to be.
3. (Optional) While drawing the object, hold down one or both of the following keys:

   Ctrl to draw the rectangle or oval out from a center point.

   Shift to draw a square or a circle.
4. Hold down the mouse button and drag the mouse to draw the object.
5. Release the mouse button.

Drawing a PowerPoint Shape

PowerPoint comes with several predrawn objects that you can add to your slides. To add one of these objects, perform the following steps:

1. Move the mouse pointer to the Shape tool and hold down the mouse button. The Shape menu appears, as shown in Figure 9.2.
2. Click on the shape you want to draw.
3. Move the mouse pointer to where you want an end or the center of the shape to be.
4. (Optional) While drawing the object, hold down one or both of the following keys:

Ctrl to draw the shape out from a center point.

Shift to draw a shape that retains the dimensions shown on the Shape menu.

5. Hold down the mouse button and drag the mouse to draw the object.
6. Release the mouse button.

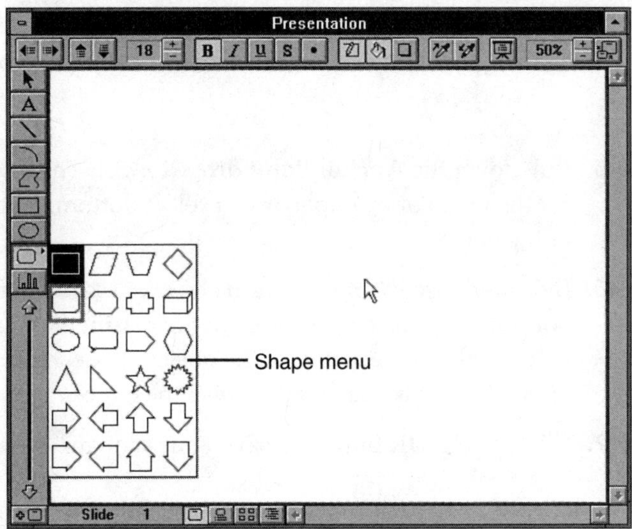

Figure 9.2 Select the desired shape from the Shape menu.

Changing an Existing Shape You can change an existing shape into a different shape. Select the shape you want to change, open the **Object** menu, select **Change Shape**, and select the shape you want to use.

Adding Text to an Object

You can add text to a rectangle, oval, or shape, by performing the following steps:

1. Click on the object in which you want the text to appear.
2. Type the text. As you type, the text appears in a single line across the object.
3. Open the **Text** menu and select **Fit Text**. The Fit Text dialog box appears, as shown in Figure 9.3.

4. Select one of the following options to have the text included in the object:

   Adjust Object Size to Fit Text changes the size of the object to fit around the existing text.

   Word-wrap Text in Object wraps the text so it fits inside the object.

Viewing the Effects of Your Changes You can drag the title bar of the dialog box to move the dialog box away from the object. That way, you will be able to view the effects of your changes as you work.

5. Pull down the **Anchor Point** drop-down list and select an anchor point for the text. For example, if you select Bottom, text will sit on the bottom of the object.
6. If desired, use the **Box Margins** boxes to set the left, right, top, and bottom margins for your text. By increasing the margins, you force the text in toward the center of the object. By decreasing the margins, you allow the text to reach out toward the edges.
7. Click on the **OK** button to save your changes.

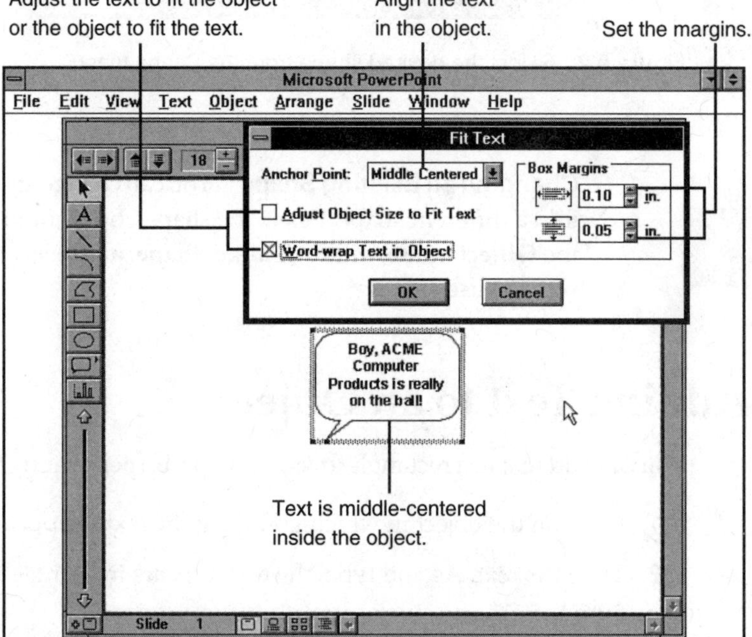

Figure 9.3 Use the Fit Text dialog box to position your text inside the object.

Adding Clip Art to a Slide

In this lesson, you will learn how to add PowerPoint clip art images and other pictures to a slide, and how to recolor and crop pictures.

Opening a Clip Art Library

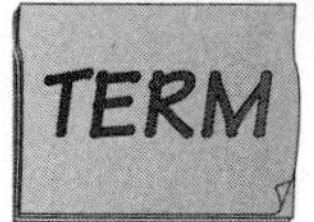

Clip Art Clip art is a collection of previously created images or pictures that can be incorporated into a slide presentation.

PowerPoint contains several Clip Art libraries that are stored on disk as presentation files. To use a piece of clip art from one of these libraries, you must first open the desired Clip Art library by performing the following steps:

1. Open the **File** menu and select **Open Clip Art**. The Open Clip Art dialog box appears.
2. In the **D**irectories list, make sure the C:\POWERPNT \CLIPART directory is selected. A list of clip art libraries appears in the **File Name** list.
3. Click on a file name in the list, or tab to the list and use the ↓ key to highlight a name. When you highlight the name of a Clip Art library, a slide appears in the preview area, showing a sample piece of clip art.
4. Press **Enter** or double-click on the name of the Clip Art library you want to use. PowerPoint opens a presentation window for the selected Clip Art library, and displays a list of slides in **Outline** view. (See Figure 10.1.)
5. Display the slide you want to use by performing either of the following steps:

   Double-click on the number to the left of the desired slide.

   Click on the **Slide view** button, and use the Slide Changer to display the slide.

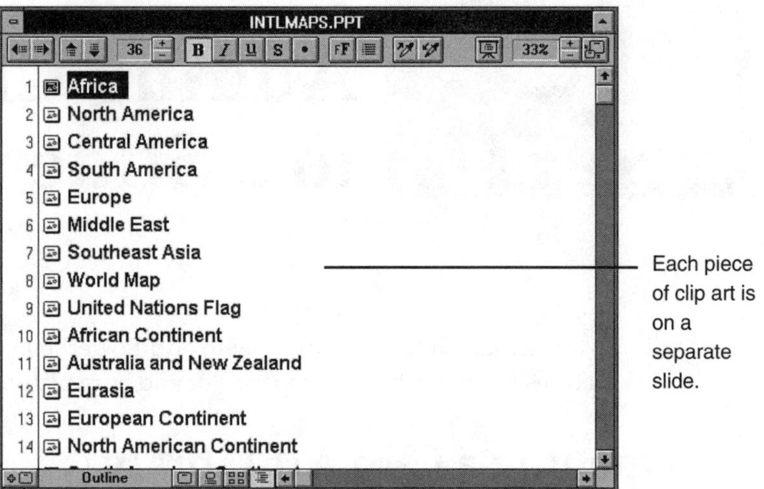

Figure 10.1 The Clip Art library is opened as a presentation in Outline view.

Copying and Pasting a Clip Art Object

Once you have displayed the slide that contains the clip art object you want to use, you can copy the object from its slide and paste it into your slide. Perform the following steps:

1. Click on the object you want to copy. A selection box appears around the object. (See Figure 10.2.)
2. Open the **Edit** menu and select **Copy**, or press **Ctrl+C**. The selected object is copied to the Windows Clipboard.
3. Change to the Presentation window that contains the slide on which you want to paste the object.
4. Open the **Edit** menu and select **Paste**, or press **Ctrl+V**. The object is pasted from the Clipboard onto the slide.
5. Move the mouse pointer over the clip art object, hold down the mouse button, and drag the object to the desired position.

Picture Too Big? If the picture is too big or too small, drag a corner of the picture to resize it. To retain the proportions of the picture as you resize it, hold down the **Shift** key while dragging.

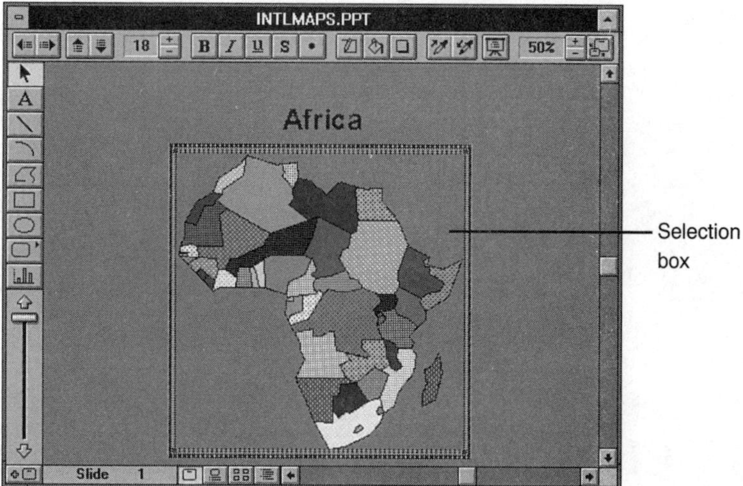

Figure 10.2 When you select the clip art object, a selection box appears around it.

Inserting Pictures Created in Other Programs

In addition to inserting clip art objects, PowerPoint allows you to insert pictures created in other graphics programs. To insert a picture, perform the following steps:

1. Open the **Edit** menu and select **Insert**. The Insert submenu appears.
2. Select **Picture**. The Insert Picture dialog box appears, as shown in Figure 10.3.
3. Use the **Drives** drop-down list to select the drive that contains the picture file.
4. Use the **Directories** list to change to the directory that contains the file. A list of graphics files appears in the File Name list.
5. Click on a file name in the list, or tab to the list and use the ↓ key to highlight a name.
6. To link the graphics file to this slide, select **Link to File**. If you make this selection, then whenever you change the file using the program you used to create it, the same changes will appear on your PowerPoint slide.
7. Click on the **OK** button. The picture is inserted on the slide.
8. Move the mouse pointer over the clip art object, hold down the mouse button, and drag the object to the desired position.

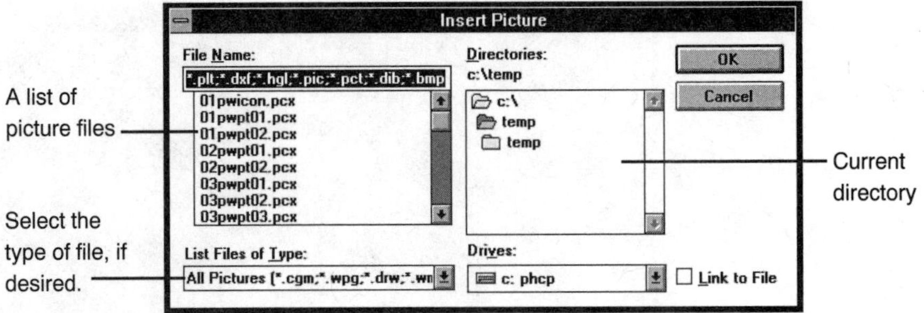

Figure 10.3 Use the Insert Picture dialog box to insert a picture created in another program.

Changing the Colors of a Picture

When you paste a clip art image or insert a picture on a slide, the picture appears in its original colors. These colors may clash with the colors in your presentation. To change the colors in a picture, perform the following steps:

1. Click on the picture whose colors you want to change. A selection box appears around the picture.
2. Open the **Object** menu and select **Recolor Picture**. The Recolor Picture dialog box appears, as shown in Figure 10.4.
3. Select a color you want to change in the **Change From** list. An X appears in the check box next to the color.
4. Use the drop-down menu to the right of the selected color to choose the color you want to change to.

Using the Other Option At the bottom of each color's drop-down menu is the **Other** option. Select this option if you want to use a color that is not listed on the menu.

5. Click on the **Preview** button to view the effects of your change.
6. Repeat steps 3 through 5 for each color you want to change.
7. Click on the **OK** button to put your changes into effect.

Cropping a Picture

If you do not want to use an entire picture on your slide, you can crop the picture to use only a portion of it. To crop a picture, perform the following steps:

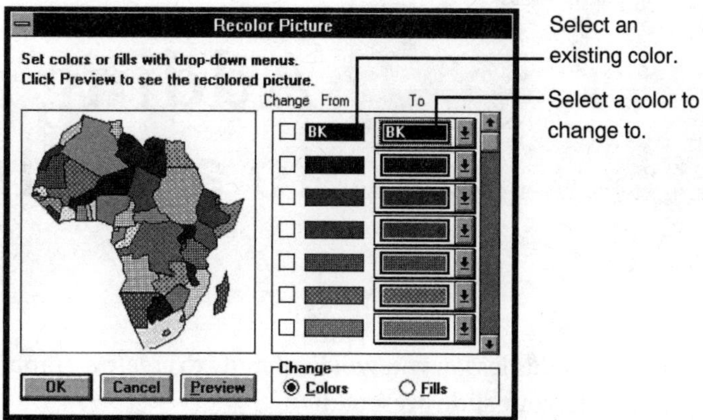

Figure 10.4 Use the Recolor Picture dialog box to change the colors in a picture.

1. Click on the picture you want to crop. A selection box appears around the picture.
2. Open the **Object** menu and select **Crop Picture**. The mouse pointer changes into a cropping tool, as shown here:

3. Move the cropping tool over one of the picture's handles (the corner of the picture), hold down the mouse button, and drag the mouse to cut off the desired portion of the picture.
4. You can crop from other corners until only the desired portion of the picture is shown.
5. When you are done, click anywhere outside the object.

Uncropping Saves the Day If you cut off part of a picture by mistake, you can uncrop it to reveal the part you cut off.

In this lesson, you learned how to add clip art objects and other pictures to your slides. In the next lesson, you will learn how to add a graph to a slide.

Adding a Graph to a Slide

In this lesson you will learn how to create a graph, enter and edit data, and add it to your slide presentation.

Starting the Graph Program

To create graphs, you can use the embedded graphics program called Microsoft Graph which comes with PowerPoint. The great thing about using Microsoft Graph is that you can create a variety of graphs without ever leaving PowerPoint.

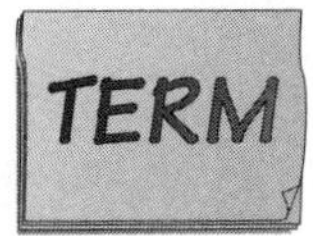

What's an Embedded Program? Embedded programs are those you can run without having to leave PowerPoint. You can create and edit objects in an embedded program like Graph, and then put those objects in PowerPoint; the objects become embedded in your presentation.

To create a graph on a slide for your presentation, perform the following steps:

1. Go to the slide to which you would like to add the graph.
2. Click on the **Graphing** tool.

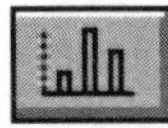

3. Drag a box onto the slide that is the approximate size of the graph you want to create.
4. When you release the mouse button, the Microsoft Graph window will appear (as shown in Figure 11.1).

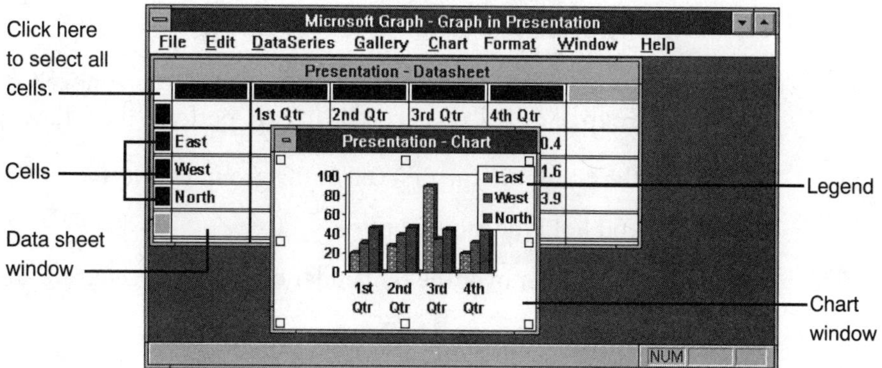

Figure 11.1 The Microsoft Graph Window.

Adding Data to the Datasheet

The *Datasheet* is set up very much like a spreadsheet with rows, columns, and cells. Each rectangle in the Datasheet is a cell which can hold text or numbers. When you enter data into the Datasheet, Graph will convert the data into a graph which is displayed in the Chart window. To enter data into the Datasheet, follow these steps:

1. Make the **Datasheet** window active by clicking anywhere on the window.
2. Click on the cell you want to change (or to which you want to add data), and enter the new cell information.
3. Click on the next cell to change, or use your arrow keys to move from one cell to another.
4. Repeat steps 2 and 3 until all your data is entered.
5. Activate the Chart window by clicking anywhere on the window to display the effects your data has created on the chart.

Editing the Data in the Datasheet

You may need to edit and move the data around in the Datasheet to meet your graphing needs.

Cut, Copy, Paste, and Clear Cells

You can cut, copy, paste, and clear cells in the Datasheet—one cell at a time, or as a selected group of cells. To select cells to edit, perform the following steps:

1. Place the pointer in the first cell of the group to select.
2. Click and hold the mouse button.
3. Drag the pointer over the remainder of cells to be selected, and release the button.

Quick Select Select an entire row or column by clicking on the black rectangle above the column (or to the left of the row).

4. Open the **Edit** menu and select either **Cut**, **Copy**, **Paste**, or **Clear**.

Select All To select every cell in the Datasheet, open the **Edit** menu and select **Select All** or click on the upper-leftmost square in the Datasheet (see Figure 11.1).

Deleting Rows and Columns

You can delete any unwanted rows and columns in the Datasheet. To delete, perform the following steps:

1. Click on any cell in the row or column you want to delete.
2. Open the **Edit** menu and select **Delete Row/Col**.
3. In the Delete Row/Col dialog box, select **Delete Rows** or **Delete Columns**.
4. Click on **OK** to delete the row or column.

Inserting Rows and Columns

You can insert a blank row or column into the Datasheet pushing aside the rows and columns. To insert, perform the following steps:

1. Click on the row or column you want to push over one column or down one row.

2. Open the **Edit** menu and select **Insert Row/Col.**
3. In the Insert Row/Col dialog box, select **Insert Rows** or **Insert Columns.**
4. Click on **OK** to insert the row or column.

Changing Column Width

There may be times when the data entry you make in a Datasheet cell is too long and you will need to adjust the width of the column. To change the column width, perform the following steps:

1. Select the columns or cells you want to adjust.
2. Open the **Format** menu and select **Column Width.**
3. In the Column Width dialog box, type a number from 1 to 255 (as shown in Figure 11.2).

Standard Width The standard width is 9. Click on the **Standard Width** box to revert to the standard column width.

4. Click on **OK** to save your changes.

Quick Width Adjustment Place the pointer between the black rectangles above the columns. Hold down the mouse button and drag the line to adjust the column width.

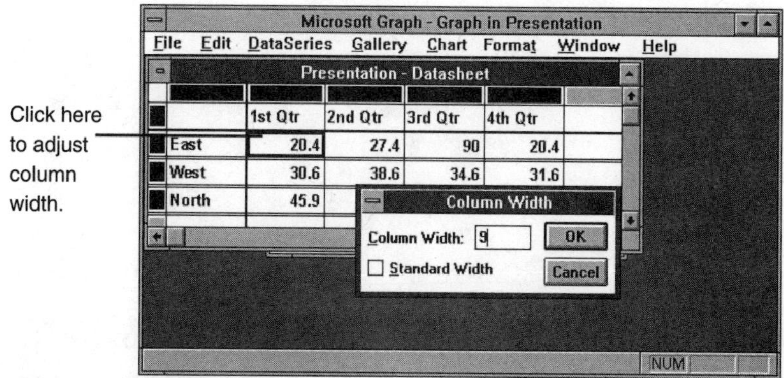

Figure 11.2 The Column Width dialog box.

Adding the Graph to the Slide

To add the graph to the slide, perform the following steps:

1. Open the **File** menu and select **Exit and Return to Presentation** (see Figure 11.3).
2. Click on the **OK** button. The graph is added to the slide.

Return to Graph To edit a graph once it has been added to a slide, double-click on the graph to return to Microsoft Graph window.

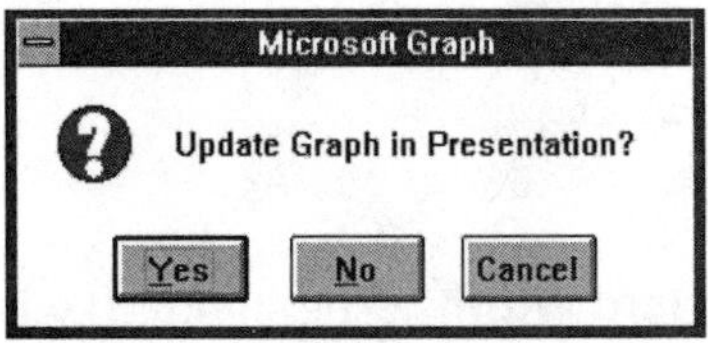

Figure 11.3 Click on Yes to add the graph to the slide.

In this lesson, you learned how to create a graph, enter and edit data, and add the graph to a slide. In the next lesson, you will learn how to modify and edit the graph.

12 Editing Your Graph

In this lesson, you will learn how to edit and enhance your graphs for the slide presentation.

Editing a Graph from PowerPoint

After you have added a graph to your PowerPoint slide presentation, you can edit that graph as many times as you like. You can move, copy and paste, and display your Datasheet data in many different types of graphs and colors.

Moving the Graph on the Slide

You can move the position of the graph on the slide by performing the following steps:

1. Click anywhere on the graph.
2. Drag the graph to a different position on the slide.

Copy and Paste a Graph

You can copy a graph from one slide to another in the same presentation, or to another presentation.

1. Click anywhere on the graph.
2. Open the **Edit** menu and select **Copy**.
3. Click on the **Slide Changer** to select the slide to copy the graph to.
4. Open the **Edit** menu and select **Paste**. A duplicate graph is pasted into the slide.

Changing Graph Types

You can change the way your Datasheet data is displayed by changing the graph type. To select a different graph type, perform the following steps:

1. Double-click on the graph in the slide.
2. Open the **Gallery** menu and select one of the twelve graph types of your choice. For example, click on **3-D Pie** and the dialog box shown in Figure 12.1 appears.
3. Click on one of the graph types.
4. Click on **OK** to apply the graph types to your data.

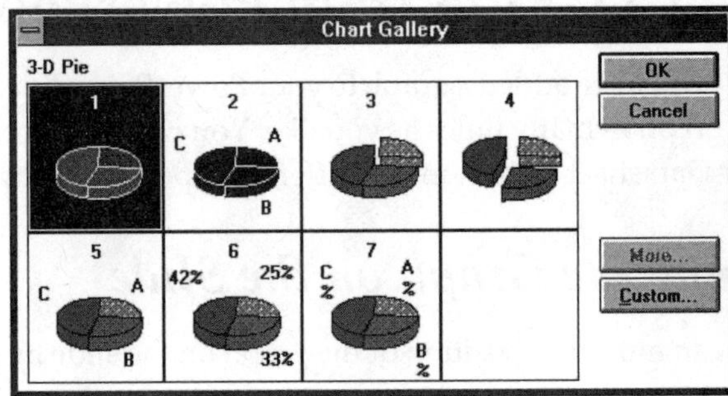

Figure 12.1 The 3-D Pie Chart Gallery dialog box.

Changing Graph Colors

You can apply different colors and patterns to the elements of a graph by performing the following steps:

1. Double-click on the graph in the slide.
2. Open the **Format** menu and select **Color Palette**.
3. The Color Palette dialog box appears, as shown in Figure 12.2.
4. The current default colors are listed. To alter any of these colors, click on the color you want to change.
5. Click on the **Edit** button.
6. To adjust the amount of color, hue, saturation, and luminosity, click on the up or down arrows in the color control boxes. (These are labeled **Color/Solid, Hue, Sat, Lum**; see the right half of Figure 12.2.)

7. When you have the color you want, click on the **OK** button.
8. Repeat steps 5 through 7 to change any other colors in the palette.

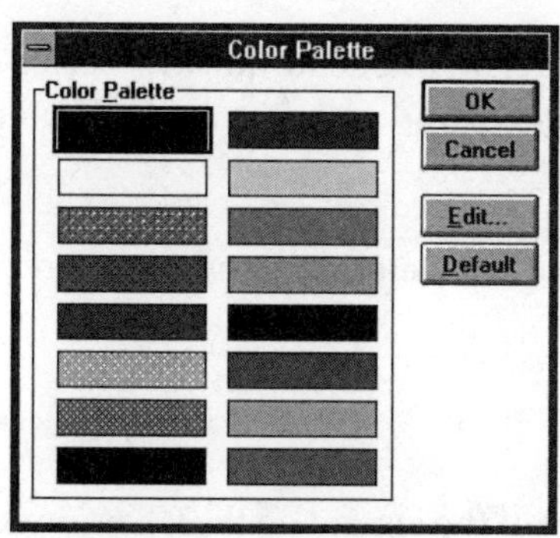

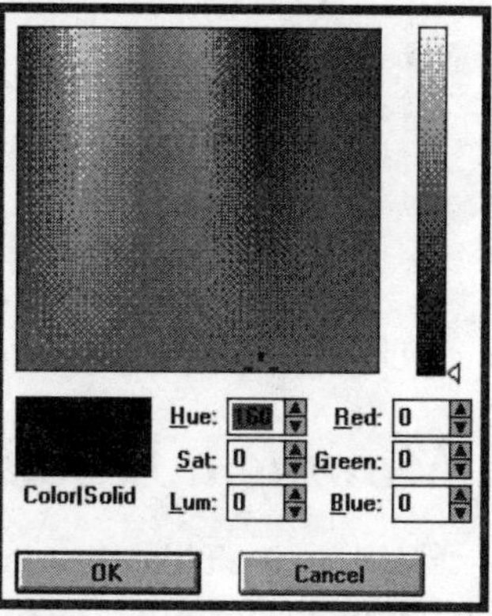

Figure 12.2 Changing the colors of the graph.

Editing Legends

The *legend* provides a guide to each color, pattern, or symbol represented on the graph. You can add, delete, or move the legend, and format its font, color, style and borders.

Adding a Legend

You can add a legend to the graph by performing the following steps:

1. Double-click on the graph in the slide.
2. Open the **Chart** menu and select **Add Legend**.

There Is No Add Legend If you already have a legend on the graph, the Chart menu will not have the Add Legend menu option available.

Deleting a Legend

To delete a legend, perform the following steps:

1. Double-click on the graph in the slide.
2. Open the **Chart** menu and select **Delete Legend**.

Quick Delete To delete a legend quickly, select it by clicking anywhere on the legend, and pressing the **Delete** key.

Once you delete a legend, the **Delete Legend** command on the Chart menu changes to **Add Legend**.

Moving a Legend

If you don't like the placement of the legend on the Chart window, you can move it by performing the following steps:

1. Double-click on the graph in the slide.
2. Click on the legend in the Chart window.
3. Drag the box to the new position in the Chart Window.

Formatting a Legend

You can change the appearance of the information in the legend by performing the following steps.

1. Double-click on the graph in the slide.
2. Click on the legend in the Chart Window.
3. Open the **Format** menu and select **Patterns**. The Area Patterns dialog box will appear (as shown in Figure 12.3).
4. To adjust the border style, color, and line weight, choose an option from the drop-down lists.
5. To adjust the pattern, foreground color, and background color, choose an option from the drop-down lists.
6. To format the legend text font, click on the **Font** button and select an option.
7. To reposition the legend, click on the **Legend** button and select an option.
8. Click on **OK** to save changes.

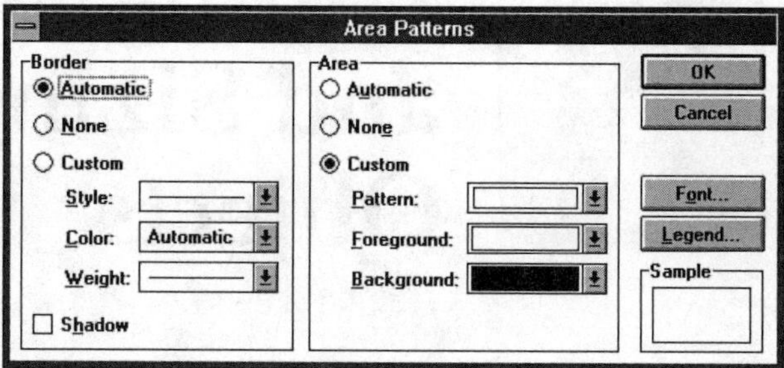

Figure 12.3 The Area Patterns dialog box.

In this lesson, you learned how to move and copy graphs, select different graph types, adjust colors, and work with legends. In the next lesson, you will learn how to position and size objects on a slide.

Editing, Moving, and Sizing Objects

In this lesson, you will learn how to edit, move, and resize objects on the slide presentation.

As you may have already discovered, objects are the building blocks with which you create slide presentations in PowerPoint. Objects are the shapes you draw, the graphs you create, the pictures you import, and the text you type. In this and the next lesson, you will learn how to manipulate objects on your slides for impressive presentations.

Selecting Objects

You must first select an object before you can edit, copy, move, and resize an object. To select an object, perform the following steps:

1. Click on the **Selection** tool, as shown here:

2. Click on any part of an object. A *selection box* will surround the object selected.

Selecting with a Box Another selection option is to drag a selection box around the object. This is accomplished by clicking and dragging the mouse pointer around the object to create a rectangle.

Editing Objects

There may be times when you need to edit an object. You can cut, copy, paste, and delete any object in the slide presentation.

Cutting Objects

Cutting an object from a slide deletes it and places it in the Windows Clipboard to be pasted by you elsewhere. Cut an object by performing the following steps:

1. Select an object to cut.
2. Open the **Edit** menu and select **Cut**. The object will be placed in the Clipboard.

Copying Objects

Copying an object on a slide makes a copy and places it in the Windows Clipboard; then you can paste it elsewhere. Figure 13.1 shows an object copied using the Copy and Paste commands (described in the next section). To copy an object, perform the following steps:

1. Select an object to copy.
2. Open the **Edit** menu and select **Cut** (or press **Ctrl+C**). The object will be placed in the Clipboard.

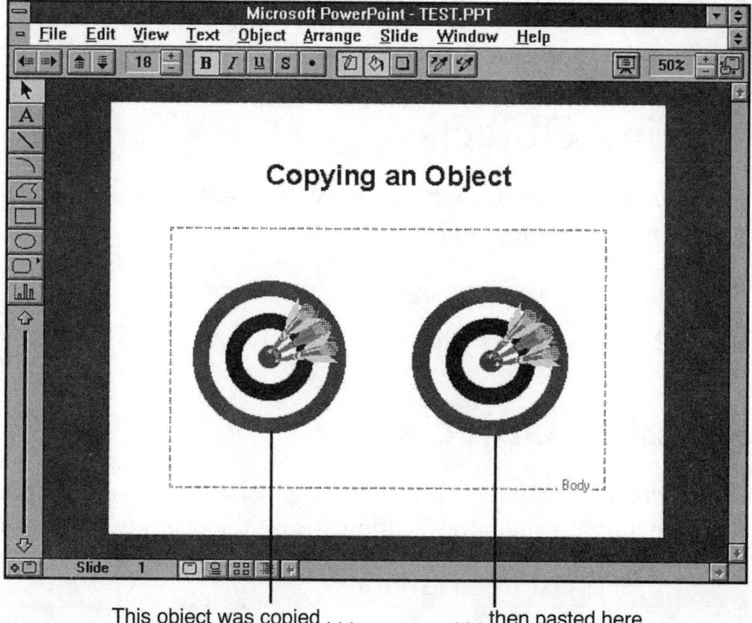

Figure 13.1 A copied object.

Pasting Objects

Once you have placed an object in the Windows Clipboard by cutting or copying, *pasting* will put that object back into the slide. To paste an object, follow these steps:

1. Position the pointer on your slide at the place where you want the object to appear.
2. Open the **Edit** menu and select **Paste** (or press **Ctrl+V**). The object will be copied from the Clipboard.

Deleting Objects

Deleting an object will remove it from the slide without placing it in the Windows Clipboard. To delete an object, perform these steps:

1. Select the object to delete.
2. Open the Edit menu and select Clear. The object will be deleted.

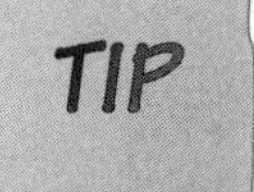

Quick Delete You can also delete an object from a slide by selecting it, and then pressing the **Del** key.

Moving Objects

If an object is not in the correct position on a slide, you can move it to a new location by following these steps:

1. Place the pointer over the object to move.
2. Click and drag the object to a new location.

Resizing Objects

There may be times when an object you have created or imported is not the right size for your slide presentation. Resize the object by performing these steps:

1. Select the object to resize.

2. Drag one of the *resize handles* (see Figure 13.2) until the object is the desired size.
3. Release the mouse button and the object will be resized (see Figure 13.2).

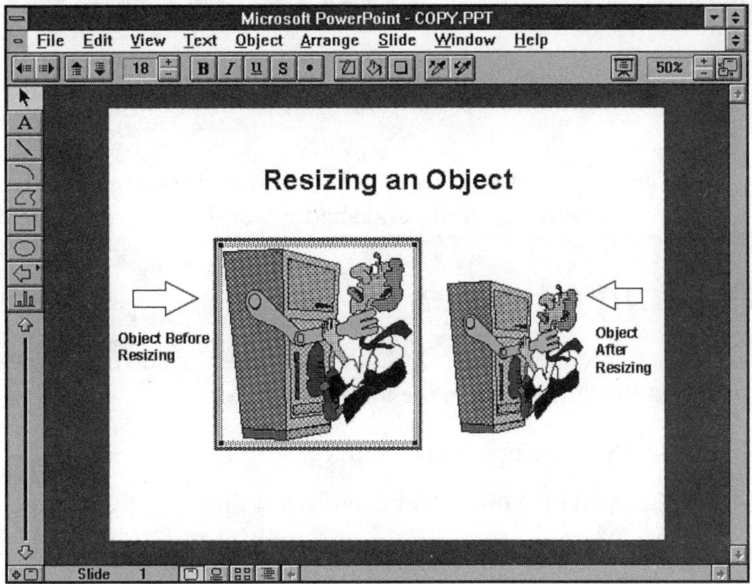

Figure 13.2 Before and after resizing an object.

In this lesson, you learned how to select, edit, move, and resize an object in a slide. In the next lesson, you will learn how to change the look of an object.

Changing the Look of Objects

In this lesson, you will learn how to edit the look of an object on a slide by adding borders, colors, patterns, and shadows and how to group and ungroup objects.

Adding a Frame

You can frame an object by adding a line which surrounds the shape of the object. To add a line, perform the following steps:

1. Select the object to be framed.
2. Open the **Object** menu and select **Line**.
3. Click on a line color, and a frame with the selected color will surround the selected object (as shown in Figure 14.1).

You can also click on the **Line** tool (see Figure 14.1) to turn a frame on or off quickly after selecting the object.

Thicken It Up You can change the thickness of the line that frames an object by selecting **Line Style** from the **Objects** menu.

Adding a Fill

Filling an object can add emphasis and texture, and make it stand out in a slide presentation (see Figure 14.2). An object can be filled with one or two colored patterns, shaded colors, or with one color and shading as the background. To fill an object, perform these steps:

1. Select an object to fill.
2. Open the **Object** menu and select **Fill**.

3. Select one of the following options:

None	Removes a fill.
Background	Fills with the same color as the background and shading.
Shading	Sets the solid color fill to be shaded.
Patterned	Fills objects with a pattern, background, and foreground colors that you select.
Color Scheme	Fills an object with a solid color you select.

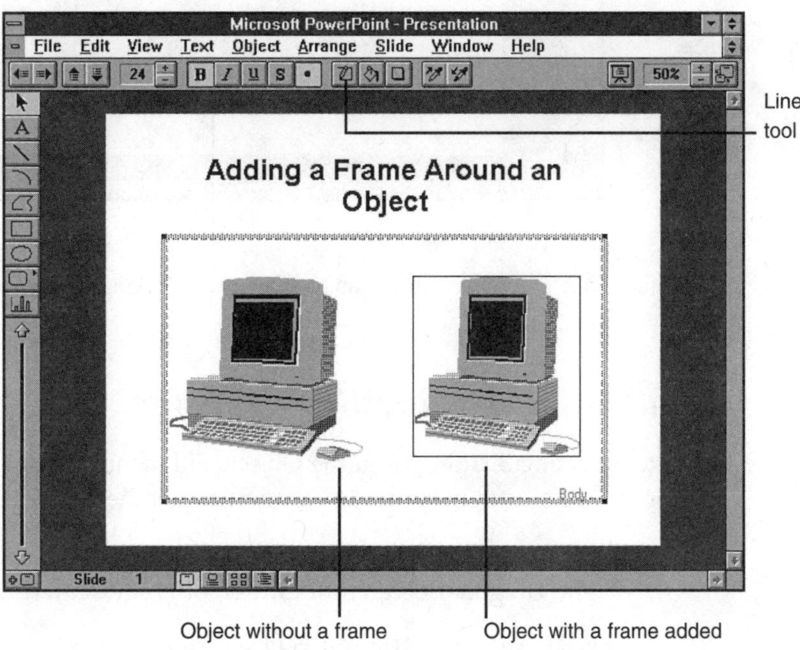

Figure 14.1 A frame around an object.

Make It Empty To turn off the fill quickly, click on the **Fill** tool (see Figure 14.2).

The Shading and Patterned options in the list have dialog boxes that appear after you select them. For more information on these dialog box options, refer to the sections that follow.

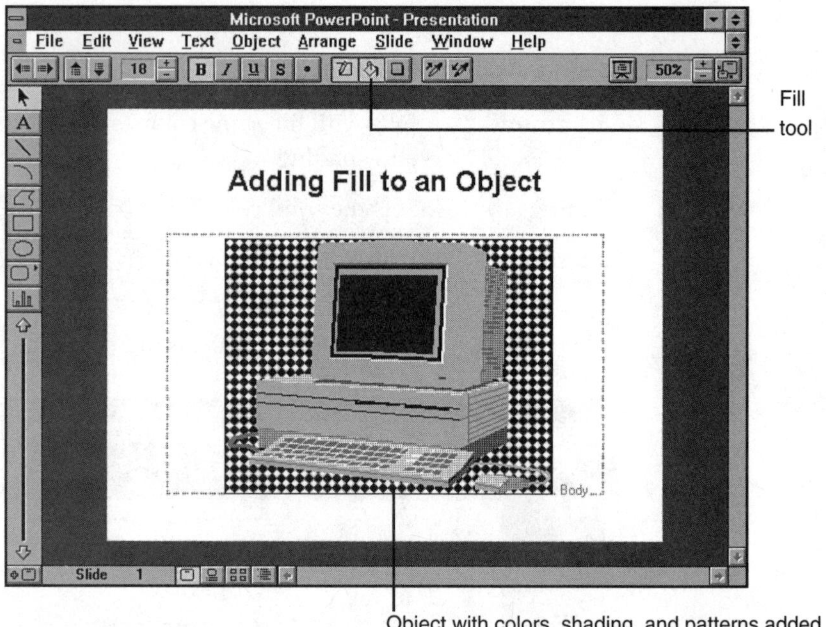

Figure 14.2 An object which has been filled with colors and patterns.

Shaded Fill Dialog Box Options

After selecting Shading from the Objects Fill menu, the Shaded Fill dialog box appears (as shown in Figure 14.3). Select any of the following options:

1. Select one of the following Shade Styles: **Vertical**, **Horizontal**, **Diagonal Right**, **Diagonal Left**, **From Corner**, or **From Center**.
2. Select one of the **Variants** displayed.
3. Select a color by clicking on the **From**: list box.
4. Move the slide from **Dark** to **Light** for the color selected.
5. Click on **OK** to save the settings.

Patterned Fill Dialog Box Options

After selecting **P**atterned from the **O**bjects **F**ill menu, the Patterned Fill dialog box appears as shown in Figure 14.4. Select any of the following options:

1. Select one of the patterns displayed in the **Pattern** box.

2. Select a **Foreground** color for the pattern from the drop-down list.
3. Select a **Background** color for the pattern from the drop-down list.
4. Click **OK** to save your settings.

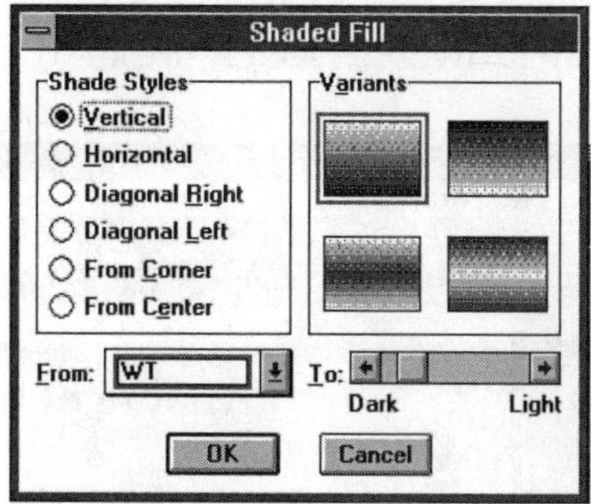

Figure 14.3 The Shaded Fill dialog box.

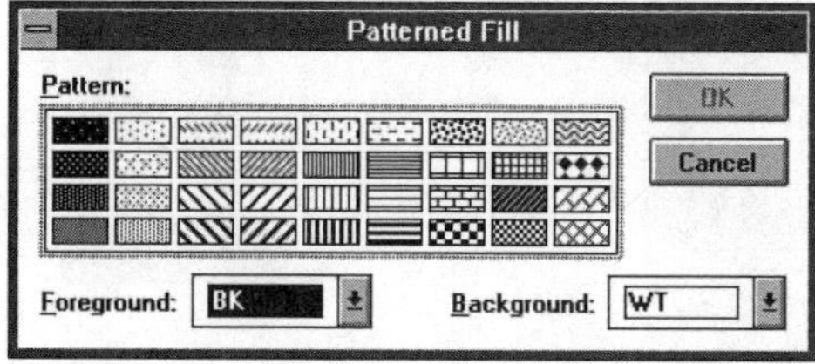

Figure 14.4 The Patterned Fill dialog box.

Adding a Shadow

Adding a shadow gives a 3-D effect to an object, as shown in Figure 14.5. To add a shadow, perform these steps:

1. Select the object to which you want to add a shadow.
2. Open the **Object** menu and select **Shadow**.
3. Select a color for the shadow.

I Don't Want a Shadow Anymore If an object already has a shadow, repeating these steps and selecting None will remove it.

Emboss It! To emboss an object, click on Embossed from the Objects Shadow submenu, and select a color.

After selecting the object, you can also turn a shadow on or off quickly—just click on the **Shadow** tool (see Figure 14.5).

Figure 14.5 The Statue of Liberty with a shadow added.

Group and Ungroup Objects

Grouping objects combines them so you can work with them together. *Ungrouping* objects allows you to work on separate pieces of an object, to change their color, font, or size.

Grouping Objects

1. Click and drag a selection box around the objects you want to group.
2. Open the **Arrange** menu and select Group (or press **Ctrl+G**).

Ungrouping Objects

1. Select the grouped object.
2. Open the **Arrange** menu and select **Ungroup** (or press **Ctrl+H**).

Regrouping Objects

1. Select one of the objects that was previously grouped.
2. Open the **Arrange** menu and select **Regroup**.

In this lesson, you learned how to edit an object by adding a frame, colors, patterns, shadows, grouping, and ungrouping. In the next lesson, you will learn about adding colors to your slide presentation.

15 Working with Colors

In this lesson, you will learn how to choose a color scheme, change and switch its colors, copy it, and apply it to other presentations.

Choosing a Color Scheme

Color schemes in PowerPoint are sets of professionally balanced colors (eight in each one), designed to be used as the primary colors in a slide presentation. Each color scheme consists of Background, Lines and Text, Shadows, Title Text, Fills, and Other Colors. Using and changing colors in your slide presentations will make them look appealing and professional.

1. Open the **Slide** menu and select **Color Scheme**. The Color Scheme dialog box appears (as shown in Figure 15.1).
2. Choose the **Choose** a **Scheme** button. The Choose a Scheme dialog box appears (as shown in Figure 15.2).
3. Select a **Background** color.
4. Select a **Text** color.
5. Select the **Remaining Colors**.
6. Click on **OK** when finished selecting colors. The Color Scheme dialog box reappears. (See Figure 15.1.)
7. Choose one of the options in the **Apply To** box. One will apply the selected colors only to the current slide on-screen; the other applies them to all slides in the presentation.
8. Click on **OK** to save the color scheme.

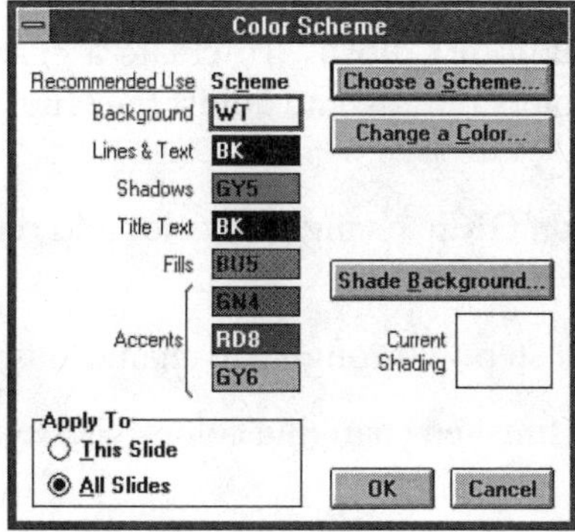

Figure 15.1 The Color Scheme dialog box.

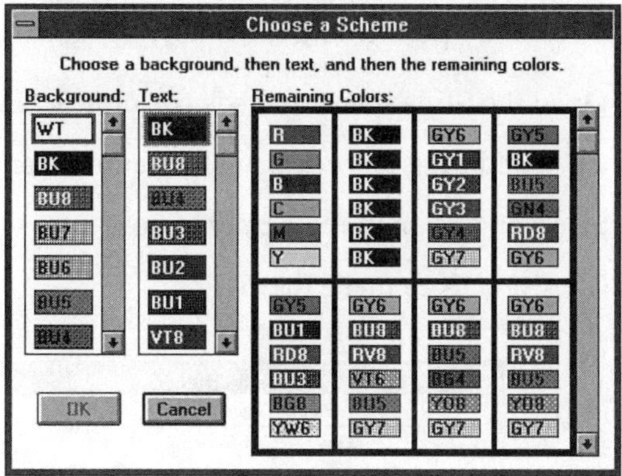

Figure 15.2 The Choose a Scheme dialog box.

Changing a Color Scheme

You can change any color in a color scheme to create your custom color combinations. For example, you can create your own color combinations that match your company colors or logo. To change a color scheme, perform the following steps:

1. Open the **Slide** menu and select **Color Scheme**.
2. Click on a color in the scheme to be changed.
3. Choose the **Change a Color** button. The Change a Color dialog box appears, as shown in Figure 15.3.
4. Select a color.

Custom Colors To create a custom color, click on the **More** Colors button, and adjust the **Hue**, **Saturation**, and **Luminance**.

5. Click on **OK** to change the color and return to the Color Scheme dialog box.
6. Repeat steps 2 through 5 to change any other colors.
7. When finished changing colors, click on **OK**.

Switching Colors in the Scheme

If you don't like the location of a color in the color scheme, you can switch it with another color by performing the following steps:

1. Open the **Slide** menu and select **Color Scheme**.
2. Click and drag to switch a color in the scheme to a new location.
3. Select an option in the **Apply to** box.
4. Click on **OK** to make the switch.

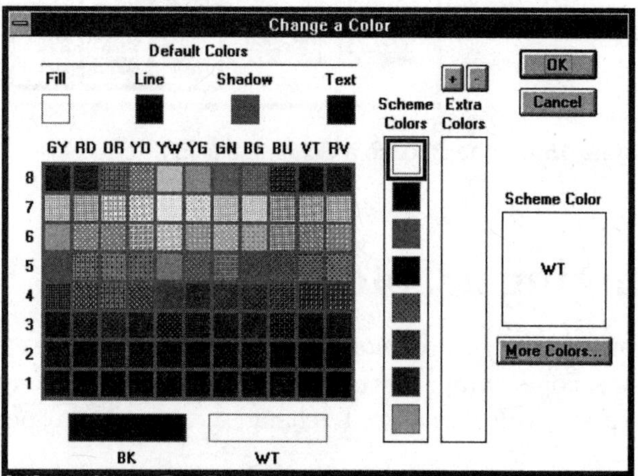

Figure 15.3 The Change a Color dialog box.

Copying and Applying a Color Scheme to Other Presentations

You can reuse a color scheme you have created in one presentation by copying it and applying it to another presentation. This is particularly useful if you have created a custom color scheme. To copy a color scheme from one presentation to another, perform these steps:

1. To open the presentation that contains the color scheme you want to copy, open the **File** menu and select **Open**.
2. Open the **View** menu and select **Slide Sorter**, or click on the **Slide Sorter** button as shown here:

3. Select the slide which contains the color scheme you want to copy.
4. Open the **Edit** menu and select **Pick Up Scheme**, or click on the **Pick Up Scheme** tool as shown here:

5. Change to the presentation to which you want to copy your chosen color scheme by opening the **File** menu and selecting **Open**.
6. Select the slide(s) to which you want to apply the color scheme.

Selecting Multiple Slides You can select more than one slide by holding down the **Shift** key as you select a slide.

7. Open the **Edit** menu and select **Apply Scheme**, or click on the **Apply Scheme** tool as shown here:

In this lesson, you learned how to choose, change, switch, and copy a color scheme to other presentations. In the next lesson, you will learn how to add final touches to the Slide Master.

16

Adding Final Touches to the Slide Master

In this lesson, you will learn how to add background items such as art, text, date, time, and page numbers to the Slide Master.

Background Items

Background items you add to the Slide Master appear on every slide and printed page, to add consistency to your slide presentation. You can add background items such as shapes, text, date, time, page numbers, and pictures.

Adding Pictures

You can add pictures, graphics, and art to the background so they appear on each slide. For example, you can have your company logo (or graphics representing your company, department, or project) displayed on each slide. (See Figure 16.1.) To add pictures to the background of the Slide Master, follow these steps:

1. Open the **View** menu and select **Slide Master**.
2. Create (draw), paste, or insert a picture or graphics into the Slide Master.
3. Move the picture to where you want it to appear on every slide.

Adding Text

You can add text that you want to appear on every slide to the Slide Master. For example, you can add the presentation's title, the company or project name, or the author's name (see Figure 16.1). To add text to the background of the Slide Master, perform these steps:

1. Open the **View** menu and select **Slide Master**.
2. Click the **Text** tool as shown here:

3. Click where you want the text to appear on the slide.
4. Type the text.
5. (Optional) Change the font, size, or color of the text.

Adding Date, Time, or Page Number

PowerPoint can stamp the date, time, and page number on your slides and pages automatically, to provide a record of when you print or run a slide show. PowerPoint will substitute the date with / / (slashes), the time with :: (colons), or page number with ##(pound signs).

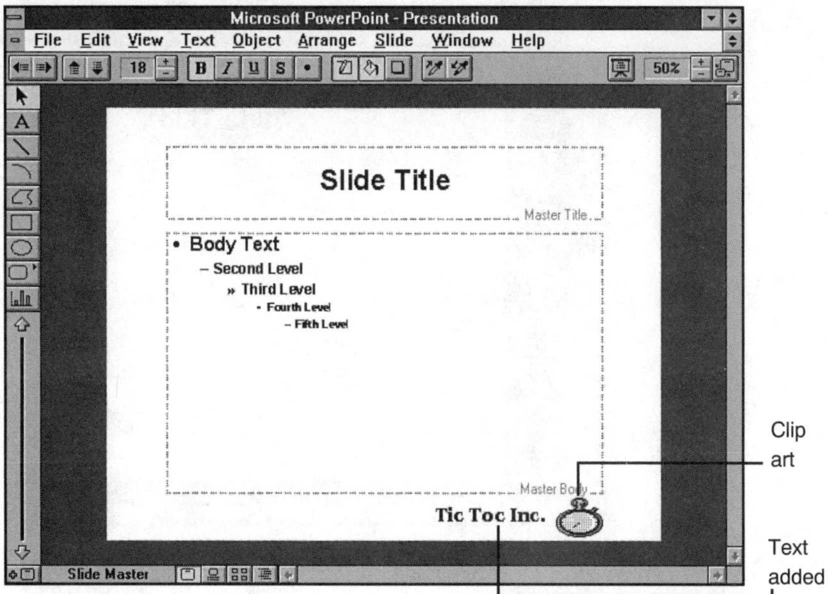

Figure 16.1 Slide Master with clip art and text added as background items.

There are two ways to add the date, time, or page number to the Slide Master. You can use the menu or type them yourself. To add the date, time, or page number, perform the following steps:

Menu Method

1. Click on the **Text** tool.
2. Click where you want the information to begin on the slide.

Date, Time, Page You may want to add text to precede the date, time, and page number symbols (for example, **Page Number** or **Date Printed**).

3. Open the **Edit** menu and select **Insert**.
4. Select the date/time/page number to add to the Slide Master. The placeholding characters will be placed where you specified, as shown in Figure 16.2.

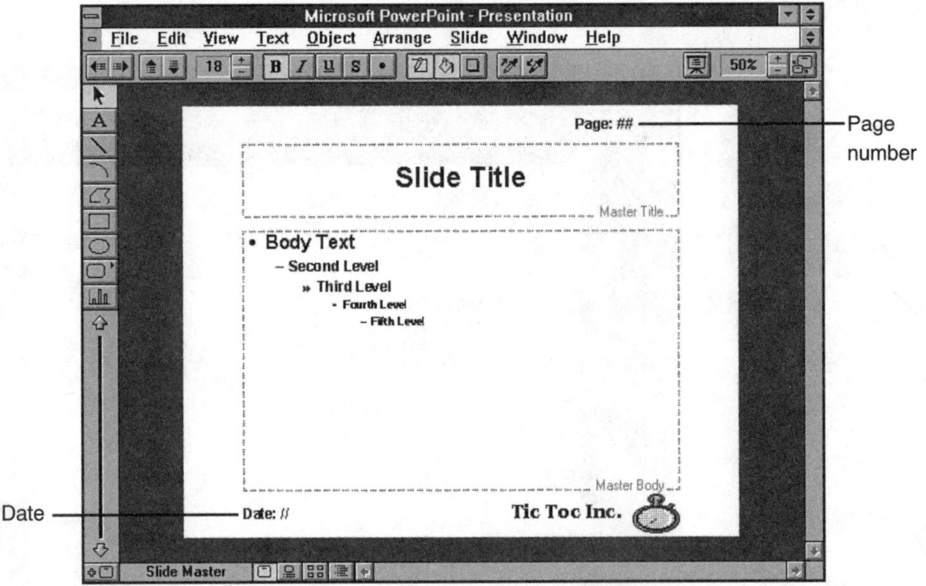

Figure 16.2 The date and page number added to the Slide Master.

Input Method

1. Click on the **Text** tool.
2. Click where you want the information to begin on the slide.
3. Type // for the date, :: for the time, or ## for the page number.

In this lesson, you learned how to add pictures, text, date, time, or page numbers to the Slide Master so they will appear automatically on every slide in the presentation. In the next lesson, you will learn how to rearrange slides in the presentation.

Rearranging the Order of Slides

In this lesson, you will learn how to rearrange the order of your slides in the presentation.

There may be times when you will need to rearrange the sequence of slides you have created in the presentation. In PowerPoint, you are given the ability to reorder the slides in either Slide Sorter view or Outline view.

Rearranging in Slide Sorter

Slide Sorter view shows miniature versions of the slides in your presentation. This allows you to view many of your slides at one time. To rearrange the slides in Slide Sorter view, perform the following steps:

1. Click on the **Slide Sorter view** button, as shown here:

2. Click and drag the slide you want to move to a new location.

Get a Bigger Picture To enlarge the slides so you can see more detail on the slide, click on the **Zoom In (+)** button. Note, however, that you cannot move to a slide while you are zoomed.

Rearranging in Outline View

The Outline view arranges your slides with title and body text displayed, allowing an overview of the slides in your presentation. To change the order of the slides in Outline view, follow these steps:

1. Click on the **Outline View** button, as shown here:

2. Select the slide you want to move by clicking either on the slide number or the slide icon.

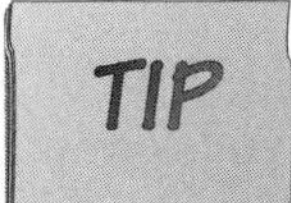

One at a Time You don't necessarily have to move an entire slide in the presentation. You can move only the slide's data—from one slide to another—by selecting only what you want to move, and dragging it to its new location.

3. Click on the **Move Up** or **Move Down** arrows, as shown here:

or drag the slide to its new position.

In this lesson, you learned how to rearrange the slides in a presentation, in either the Slide Sorter or Outline view. In the next lesson, you will learn how to delete, copy, and add slides to a presentation.

Deleting, Copying, and Adding Slides

In this lesson, you will learn how to delete, copy, or add a slide to your presentation.

Most people don't create a perfect slide presentation on the first try. PowerPoint gives you the capability of making changes—such as adding, copying, pasting, and deleting slides—after you have created the slide presentation.

Deleting Slides

To delete a slide you no longer need, you can use the Slide view, Notes view, Outline view, or Slide Sorter view. Perform the following steps, from any of these views, to delete a slide:

1. Select the slide to delete.
2. Open the **Slide** menu and select **Delete Slide**. The selected slide will be deleted.

More Than One In the Outline and Slide Sorter views, you can select more than one slide by pressing the **Shift** key as you select slides.

Oops! If you delete a slide accidentally—*before you do anything else*—open the **Edit** menu and select **Undo**.

Cutting, Copying and Pasting Slides

There are times when you see changes that need to be made to better organize your slide presentation. To cut, copy, and paste a slide, perform the following steps:

1. Depending on the view you are in, select the slide you want to cut or copy.
2. Open the **Edit** menu and select **Cut** or **Copy**.
3. Click in front of the slide that occupies the place where you want to insert the cut or copied slide.
4. Open the **Slide** menu and select **Paste**. PowerPoint will paste the slide into its new location (see Figure 18.1).

Adding Slides

You can insert a new slide into an existing presentation. To add a new slide, perform these steps:

1. Open the **Slide** menu and select **New Slide** or click on the **New Slide** button.
2. A new slide will appear (see Figure 18.2).

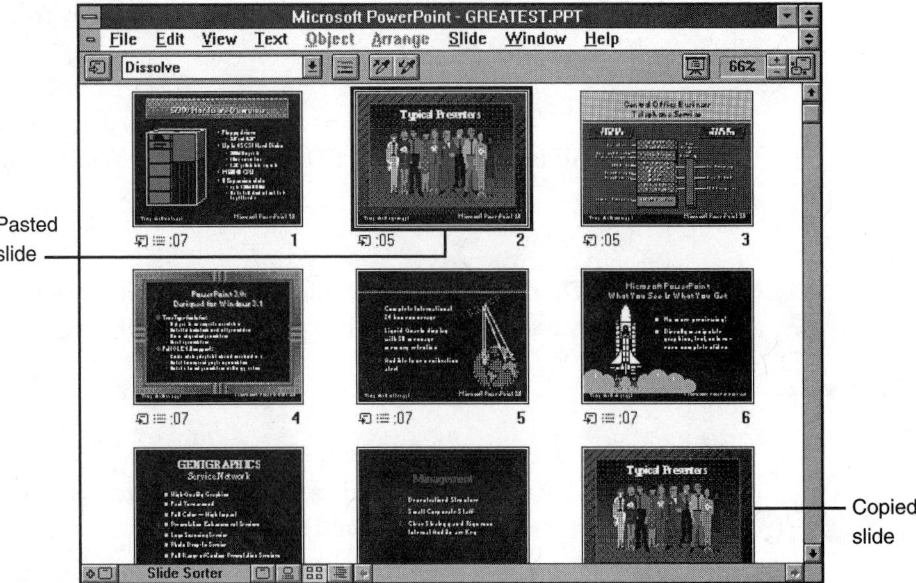

Figure 18.1 A slide copied and pasted in Slide Sorter view.

New Slide Quick The shortcut key combination for a new slide is **Ctrl+N**. A new slide will appear in all views. In Slide view and Slide Sorter, the new slide will become the selected slide.

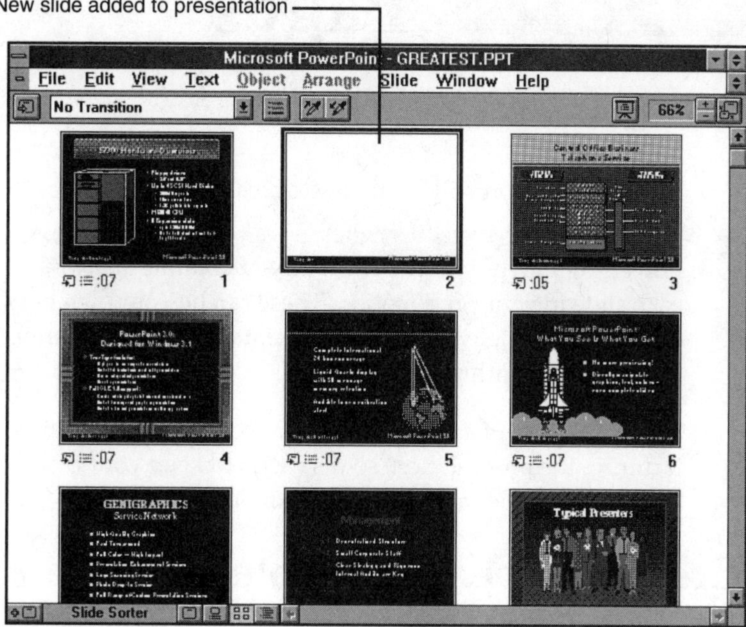

Figure 18.2 A new slide added in Slide Sorter view.

In this lesson, you learned how to delete, copy, and add slides to a presentation. In the next lesson, you will learn how to add speaker's notes to your presentation.

Creating Speaker's Notes Pages

In this lesson, you will learn how to create speaker's notes to help you during the delivery of your presentation.

PowerPoint gives you the capability of creating *speaker's notes* to correspond to each slide in your presentation. These can be your own personal notes, and they can help in the delivery of your presentation. They can enhance the effectiveness of your slides with greater emphasis and more efficient communication.

At the top of each *notes page* is a reduced image of the slide. You can refer to it during the presentation, so it's easier to keep your place. Your personal notes appear below the image, as shown in Figure 19.1.

Creating Speaker's Notes

To create a speaker's notes, you must change to Notes view, select the Body object, and enter your notes. To create the speaker's notes, perform the following steps:

1. Click on the **Slide Changer** to move to the slide you want to add a note to.
2. Open the **View** menu and select **Notes** or click on the **Notes View** button, as shown here:

3. The Notes window will look similar to Figure 19.1. Check to make sure you have the right slide.
4. Click on the **Notes Page Body** object to select it.
5. Type your notes that correspond to the slide into the slide image area.

Printing Notes To print out your speaker's notes, see Lesson 23 for instructions.

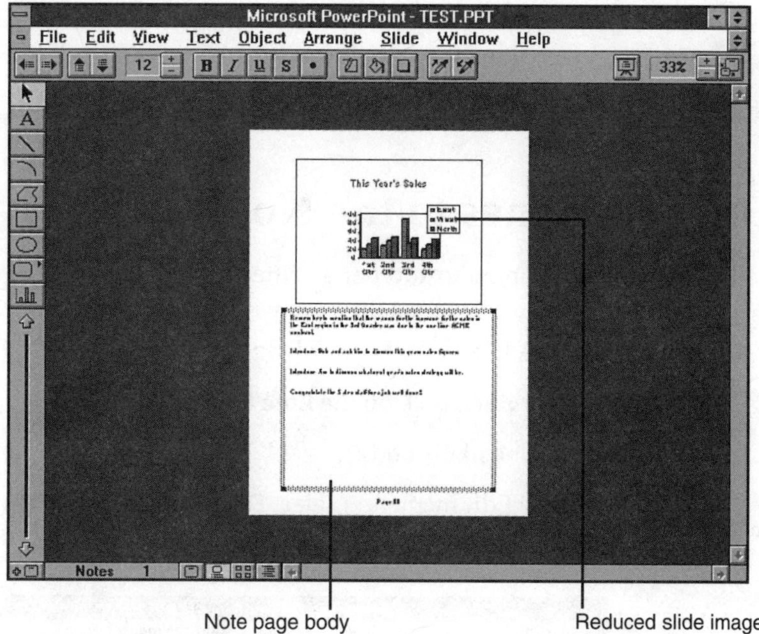

Figure 19.1 Example of a speaker's notes page.

Changing the Size of the Slide

When you are in Notes view, the slide image at the top of the screen will appear at 33% of view. If you want to reduce or enlarge the view on the notes page, perform the following steps:

Why So Small? 33% of view means that the slide has been reduced down to 33% of its original (100%) size to fit on the notes page during a presentation.

1. In **Notes** view, click on the **Slide Changer** to move to the slide for which you want to enlarge or reduce the view.
2. Click on the **View Scale + button** to enlarge the size of the slide, or the – button to reduce the size, as shown here:

33%

Keep Clicking Click on the **View Scale buttons** as many times as needed to enlarge or reduce the size of the slide. See Figure 19.2 for a notes page which has been enlarged to 66%.

Adding Lines to the Notes Page

If you are planning to add handwritten notes later—or want to give your notes pages to your audience so they can write down ideas or further notes—you can add lines to the page (as shown in Figure 19.3). To add lines, perform these steps:

1. In **Notes** view, click on the **Line** tool.
2. Draw a line in the body.
3. Open the **Edit** menu and select **Duplicate** (or press **Ctrl+D**) to add more lines to the page.

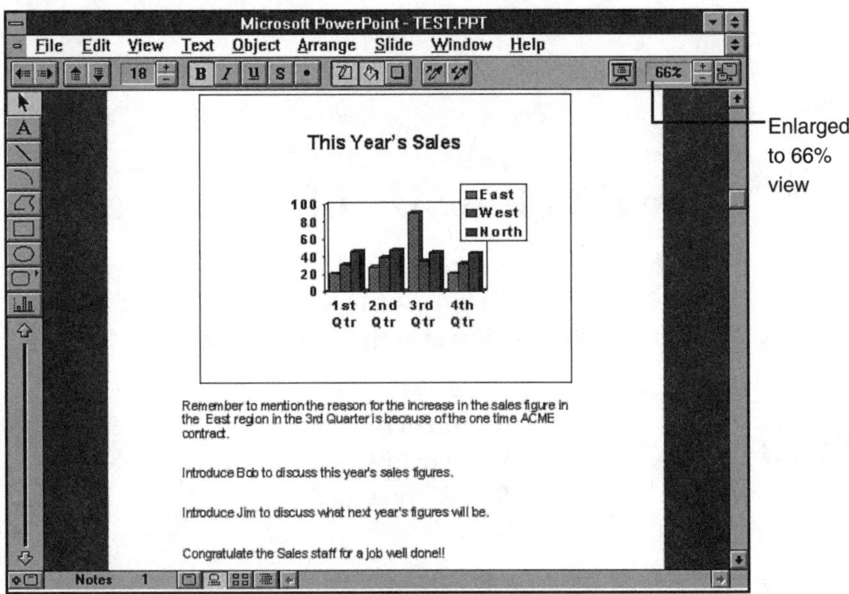

Figure 19.2 A notes page enlarged to 66% view.

My Lines Don't Add Up! When you add lines to the notes page, they are indented. To line them up any way you want, simply drag them to a new location.

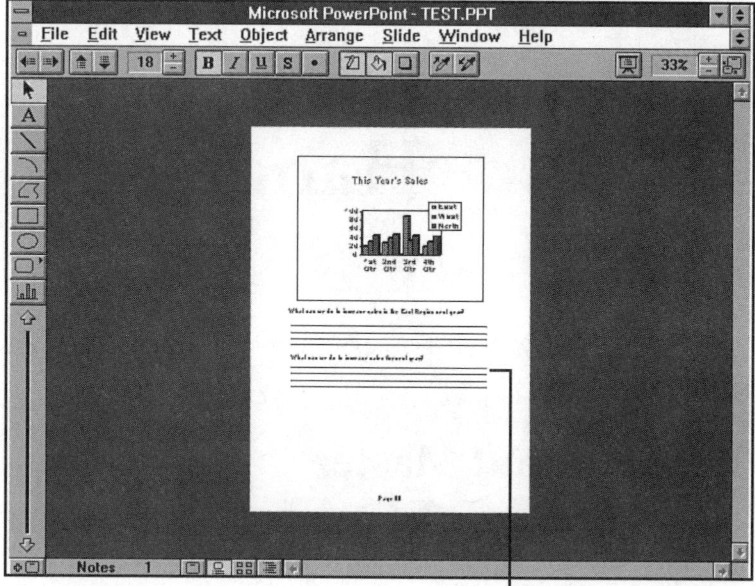

Figure 19.3 A notes page with lines added for handwritten text.

Changing the Appearance of the Notes Page

You can change the way the notes page looks by using the Notes Master. Working in the Notes Master is similar to working with the Slide Master. You can:

- Add background information (such as the date, time, or page numbers).
- Move or resize the notes page objects.
- Choose a color scheme.
- Set up the Master Body.

To change the notes page, follow these steps:

1. Open the **View** menu and select **Notes Master**, or click on the **Notes View** button. (This button toggles between the Notes Master and the notes page.)
2. Change any of the elements of the notes page as you would a Slide Master. See Lesson 16 for instructions.

In this lesson, you learned how to create a speaker's notes page to help in the delivery of a presentation. In the next lesson, you will learn how to create audience hand-outs.

Creating Audience Handouts

In this lesson, you will learn how to create audience handouts to pass out during your slide presentation.

The Handout Master

PowerPoint gives you the capability of creating handouts of the slides on your presentation. Passing these out to your audience is helpful when you have a lot of informative slides. The audience can take the slide images with them to digest in detail later.

The Handout Master has *slide image placeholders* so you can see where a slide image will be placed on a handout (see Figure 20.1). You have the choice of having two, three, or six slide images on a handout page, depending on your printer. To use the Handout Master, open the **View** menu and select **Handout Master**, or click on the **Slide Sorter View** button (which toggles between Slide Sorter view and Handout Master) as shown here:

Printing Handouts To print your audience handouts, see Lesson 23 for instructions.

Changing the Appearance of Handouts

By using the Handout Master, you can change the way the audience handouts look. You can:

- Add background information (such as the date, time, or page numbers).
- Choose a color scheme.

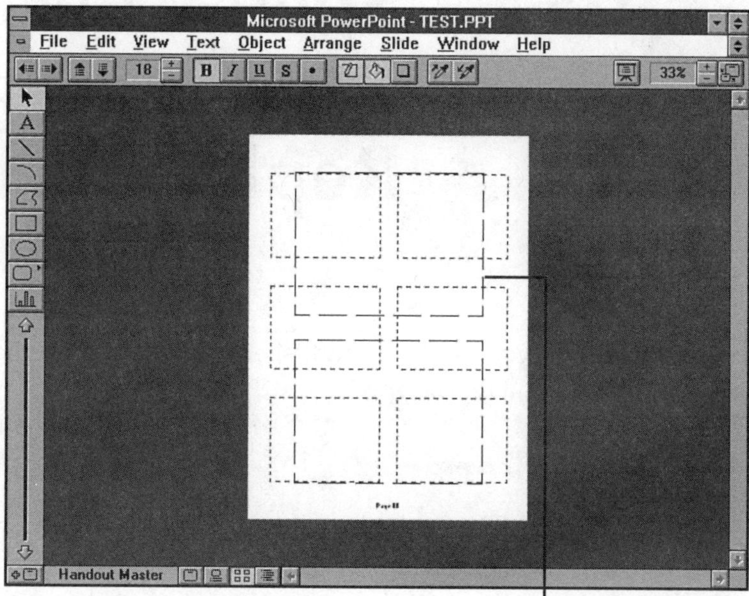

Figure 20.1 The Handout Master screen.

To change the appearance of your handouts, follow these steps:

1. Open the **View** menu and select **Handout Master**, or click on the **Slide Sorter** button. (This button toggles between the Slide Sorter view and the Handout Master.)
2. Change any of the elements of the handout page as you would a Slide Master. (See Lesson 16 for instructions.)

In this lesson, you learned how to create audience handouts to accompany your slide presentation. In the next lesson, you will learn how to spell-check your slide presentation.

Spell-Checking and Finding and Replacing Text

In this lesson, you will learn how to spell-check text in your slide presentation, and how to find and replace specific text.

Spell-checker

PowerPoint uses a built-in dictionary to spell-check your entire presentation—including all slides, outlines, note and handout pages, and all four master views. If a word is not recognized, you can add that word to a *custom dictionary*, or use a custom dictionary from other Microsoft applications. To check your spelling, perform these steps:

1. Open the **Text** menu and select **Spelling**. The Spelling dialog box appears (as shown in Figure 21.1).
2. Click on the **Check Spelling** button. The first misspelled word will appear, as shown in Figure 21.2.
3. Click on the **Suggest** button to have PowerPoint list possible correct spellings for the misspelled word.

Don't Want to Change the Spelling? If a word appears that you know is spelled correctly (like your name), and you do not want to replace it, click on the **Ignore** button. To add this word into your custom dictionary so PowerPoint will recognize it in the future, refer to the next section.

4. Click on the correct word in the list. Use the scroll bar to see more of the list.
5. Click the **Change** button to replace the misspelled word with the selected word in the slide.

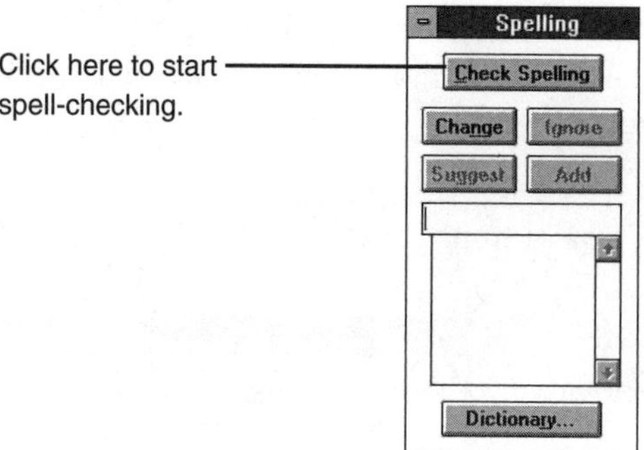

Figure 21.1 The Spelling dialog box.

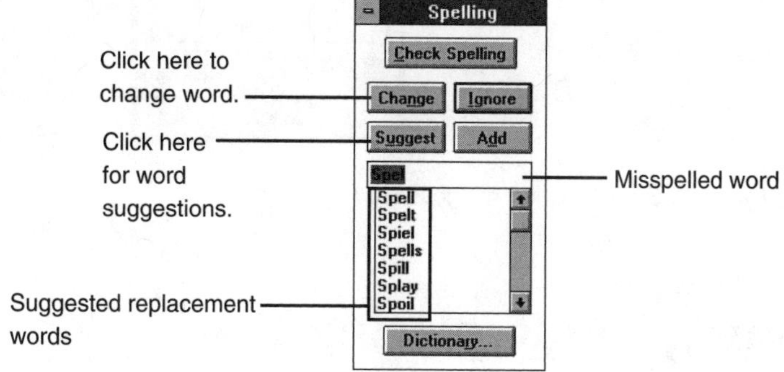

Figure 21.2 Suggestions for a misspelled word.

Adding a Word to the Custom Dictionary

There may be times when the spell-checker does not recognize a word, and assumes it is a misspelled word. A good example of this is your name (or those of other people), company names, technical jargon, and so on. To add these words to the custom dictionary, follow these steps:

1. Open the **Text** menu and select **Spelling**. The Spelling dialog box appears.
2. Click the **Check Spelling** button. The first misspelled word will appear.
3. When a misspelled word appears that you want to add to the custom dictionary, click on the **Dictionary** button. The Custom Dictionary dialog box will appear (as shown in Figure 21.3).
4. Click on the + button. The word will be added to the custom dictionary.

Delete from Dictionary To delete a previously added word from the custom dictionary, select the word in the list, and click on the – button.

5. Click on the **Close** button.

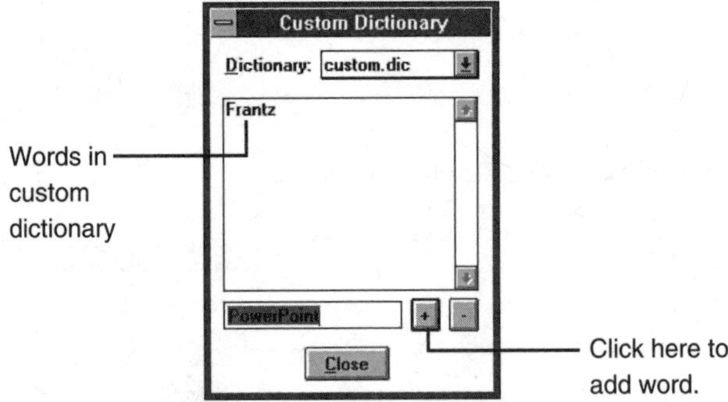

Figure 21.3 The Custom Dictionary dialog box.

Finding and Replacing Text

You can search for text and replace it in PowerPoint by performing the following steps:

1. Open the Text menu and select **Find/Replace**. The Find/Replace text box will appear, as shown in Figure 21.4.
2. Type the word you want to search for in the Find Text box.
3. (Optional) In the Replace With box, type a word to replace the searched word.
4. Click the **Find** button. PowerPoint finds the word in the Find Text box.
5. (Optional) Click on the **Replace** button.
6. Click on the **Find** button to find the next occurrence of the word.

Quick Replace To replace a word automatically and then find the next word, click on the **Replace**, then **Find** button. To replace all occurrences of the searched word automatically, and insert the replacement word without being prompted, click on the **Replace All** button.

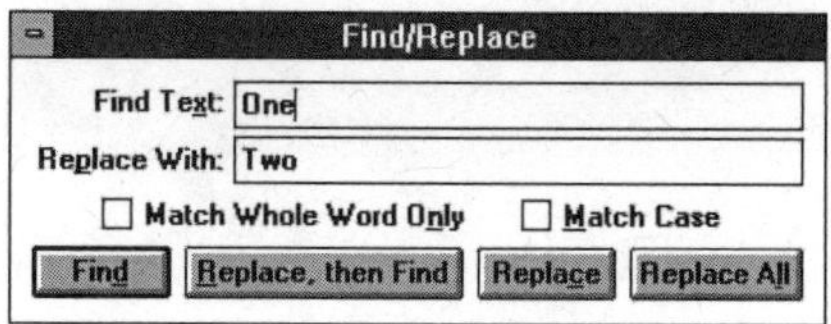

Figure 21.4 The Find/Replace dialog box.

In this lesson, you learned how to check your presentation for misspelled words, and how to find and replace words. In the next lesson, you will learn how to view a slide show.

Viewing a Slide Show

In this lesson, you will learn how to set up and run a slide show in PowerPoint.

An electronic slide show is a lot like using a slide projector, except you can add impressive and professional visual effects (*transitions*) that move on and off the screen during the show. Slide transitions include Blinds Horizontal, Checkerboard across, Cut, and Cover Up; there are a total of 46 transitions you can choose.

Adding a Slide Transition

To apply a slide transition to a slide, perform the following steps:

1. Click on the **Slide Sorter** button.
2. Select the slide to which you want to add a transition effect.
3. Click on the down arrow of the **Transition Effect** box on the Toolbox, as shown in Figure 22.1.

More Than One To select more than one slide, hold down the **Shift** key while you click on slides.

4. Click on an effect. Use the scroll bars to see more of the list.

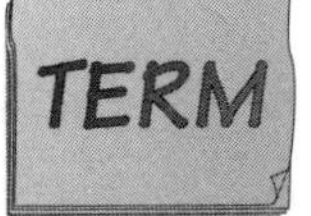

Transition Icons PowerPoint places a *transition icon* below the lower left corner of the slide, to indicate that an effect has been applied.

5. To display the slide show with the effect(s) you added, click on the **Slide Show** tool, as shown here:

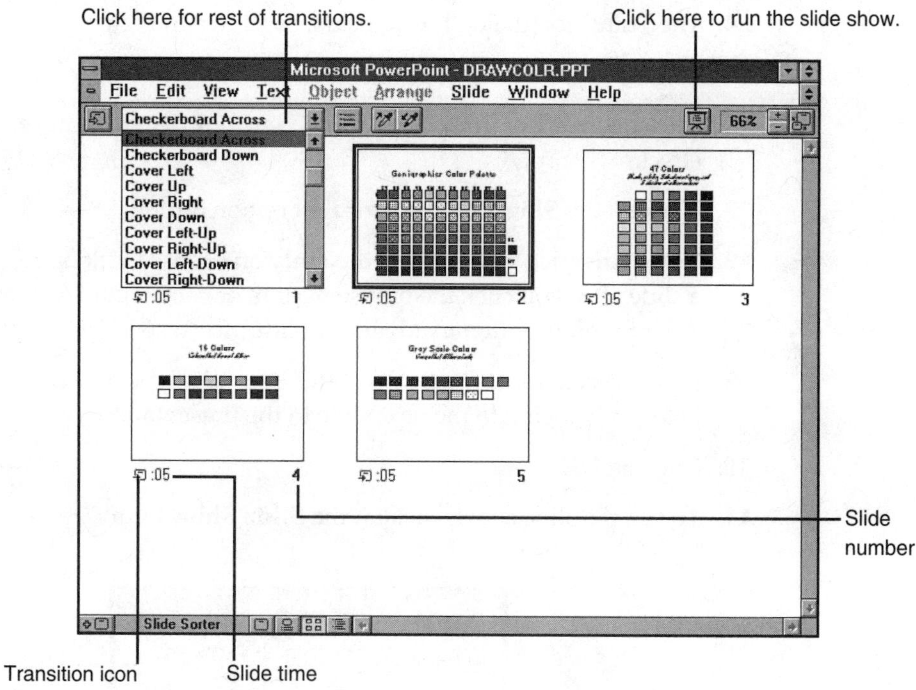

Figure 22.1 Adding transition effects to selected slides.

6. Click on the mouse button or press the **Spacebar** to move through the slides. Press **Esc** to stop the slide show at any time.

Adding Timing

You can add transition effects to all the slides in your presentations, and add timing for them to move on and off the screen during the slide show. To add transitions and timing, perform the following steps:

1. Click on the **Slide Sorter** button.
2. Open the **Edit** menu and select **Select All**.
3. Open the **Slide** menu and select **Transition**, or click on the **Transition** button (on the Toolbox) as shown here:

4. The Transition dialog box appears, as shown in Figure 22.2.
5. Click the **down arrow** in the **Effect** list box.
6. Click on an effect from the list. The view box demonstrates the transition effect.
7. Click on the **Slow**, **Medium**, or **Fast** option button.
8. In the **Advance** box, click on the **Only** on Mouse Click option to advance a slide after you click the mouse button, or click on the Automatically After Seconds option to advance a slide after a specified amount of time.
9. If you selected **Automatically After Seconds**, type the seconds to wait before advancing to the next slide in the presentation.
10. Click on **OK.**
11. To run the slide show, click on the **Slide Show** button.

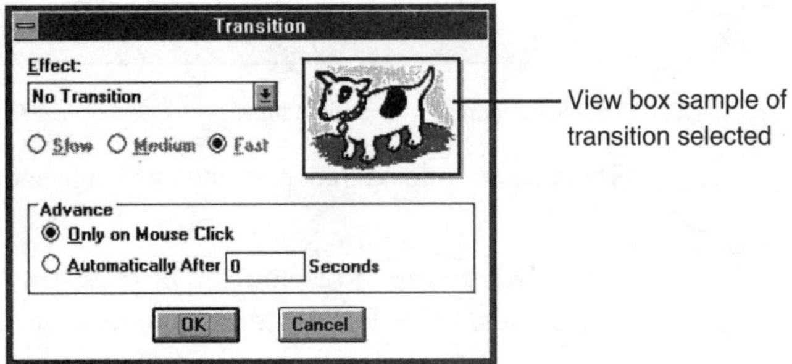

Figure 22.2 The Transition dialog box.

In this lesson, you learned how to create and run a slide show presentation. In the next lesson, you will learn how to print your slides, notes, and audience handouts.

Printing Slides, Outlines, Notes, and Handouts

In this lesson, you will learn how to print your slides, outlines, speaker's notes, and audience handouts.

You can use the File Print command to print your slides, outlines, speaker's notes, and audience handouts. The Print dialog box allows you to specify what to print, the print range, number of copies, black and white, and scale to fit paper.

Printing Slides

PowerPoint will scale your slides automatically to the printer you have selected. To print out your slides, follow these steps:

1. Open the **File** menu and select **Print**. The Print dialog box will appear, as shown in Figure 23.1.

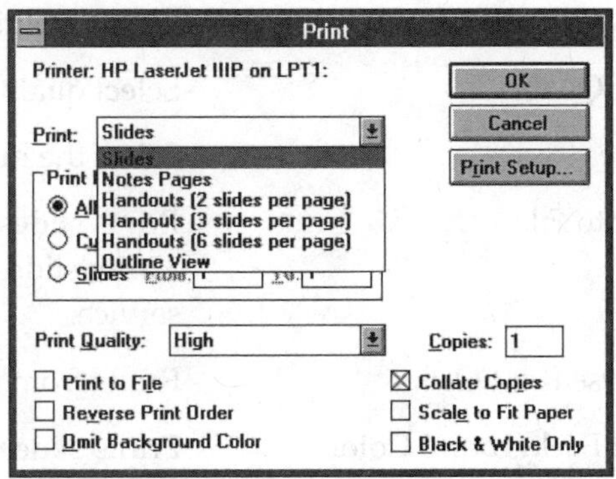

Figure 23.1 The Print dialog box.

2. Click on the **Print** drop-down list box.
3. Click on one of the **Print Format** options listed in Table 23.1.

4. Select any of the print options listed in the Print dialog box. (These are listed in Table 23.2.)

5. Click on **OK** to print.

Table 23.1 Print Format Options

Option	*Description*
Slides	Prints slides, one per page.
Notes Pages	Prints speaker's notes pages.
Handouts (2 slides per page)	Prints 2 slides per page.
Handouts (3 slides per page)	Prints 3 slides per page.
Handouts (6 slides per page)	Prints 6 slides per page.
Outline View	Prints outline according to view scale setting.

Table 23.2 Print Dialog Box Options

Option	*Description*
Print Range	Select a range of slides to print **A**ll, Curr**e**nt Slide, or **S**lides **F**rom: and **T**o:
Print **Q**uality	Select quality from drop-down list.
Copies	Select the number of copies to print.
Print to **F**ile	Prints slides to a presentation file to create 35mm slides, or to send to Genigraphics service.
Reverse Print Order	Prints from last to first page.
Omit Background Color	Prints slides, handouts, notes, and outlines without the background color.
Collate Copies	Prints multiple copies in reverse order so they are organized numerically while being printed.
Scal**e** to Fit Paper	Scales slides automatically to fit paper size.

Option	*Description*
Black & White Only	Turns fill colors to white and text and borders to black.
P**r**int Setup...	Click this button to select or set up a new printer.

In this lesson, you learned how to print your slides, outlines, speaker's notes, and audience handouts. Have fun creating PowerPoint slide presentations.

MAIL FOR WINDOWS

Jennifer Flynn

1 Starting and Quitting Microsoft Mail

In this lesson, you will learn how to start and exit Microsoft Mail.

Microsoft Mail

You've just installed Microsoft Mail, and now you are anxious to use it. You have some familiarity with computers, so you don't relish having to wade through several manuals before you can send a simple message.

With your busy schedule, what you want is a simple, straightforward guide that teaches what you need to know without teaching you every nuance of this new program.

A few things are certain:

- You need a way to move around Microsoft Mail quickly and easily.
- You need to identify and learn the tasks necessary to accomplish your particular goals.
- You need a clear-cut, plain-English guide to learn about the basic features of the program. You need *Microsoft Office 6 in 1*.

Logging In to Microsoft Mail

Microsoft Mail is found in the Applications group within Program Manager. To start Microsoft Mail:

1. Open the **Applications** group. (Windows for Work-groups users will find Microsoft Mail in the Main group.)
2. Double-click on the **Microsoft Mail** icon.

First Time Only The very first time you use Microsoft Mail, you will need to connect to the postoffice. (In later sessions, the postoffice you belong to is remembered, and you are automatically connected to it by Mail.) Choose **Connect to an existing postoffice**.

3. To log in, type your mailbox name, press **Tab**, and type your password. The password will not be displayed. (See Figure 1.1.)

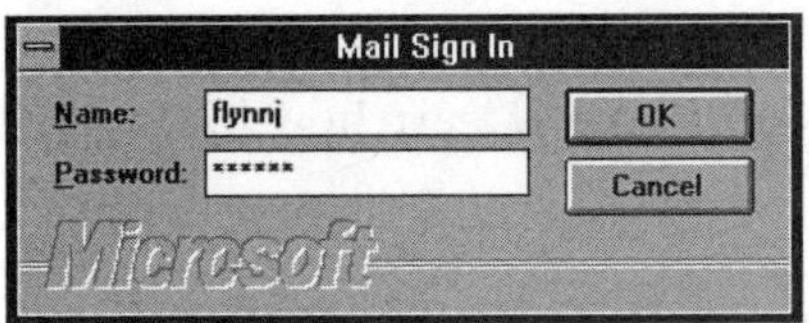

Figure 1.1 Logging in to Microsoft Mail.

Forgot Your Password? See your system administrator.

After you log in, you will see the screen displayed in Figure 1.2.

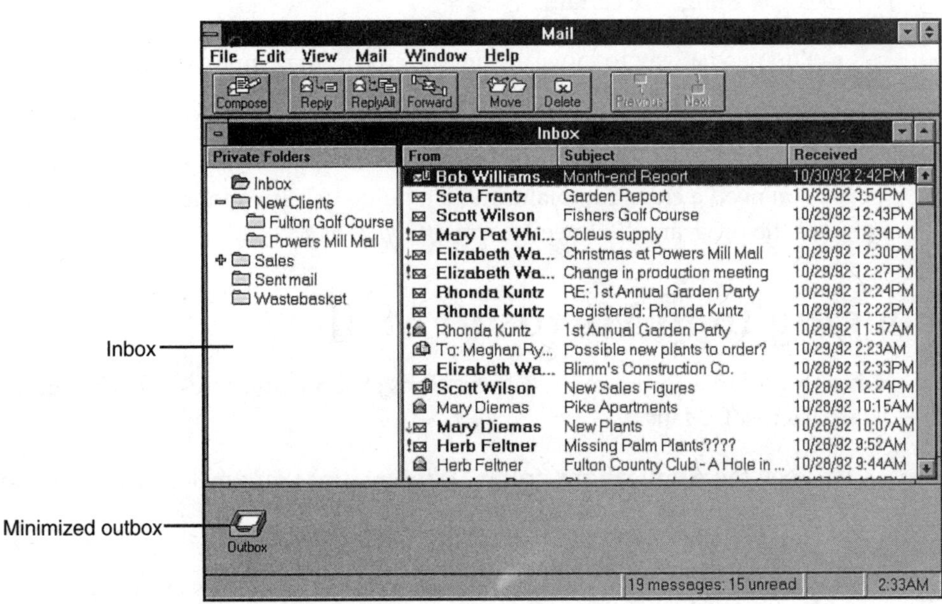

Figure 1.2 The Microsoft Mail for Windows screen.

Quitting Microsoft Mail

Microsoft Mail offers two ways to quit. If you choose **Exit**, you will quit Mail, but you will still be able to access the postoffice with other applications such as Schedule+. If you choose **Exit and Sign Out**, you will be disconnected from the postoffice and will need to log back in to use Mail.

Not the Final Exit Even if you choose **Exit and Sign Out**, you will still be able to receive mail as long as you are connected to the network.

Wait a Minute, Mr. Postman! If you sign out of Mail, you will not be notified when you receive mail. Mail must be active before you will be notified. Therefore, I recommend that you don't exit Mail until the end of the day.

1. Open the **File** menu.
2. Select either **Exit** or **Exit and Sign Out**.

Quick Exit You can double-click on the **Control-menu** button to exit and sign out of Mail quickly.

In this lesson, you learned how to start and quit Microsoft Mail. In the next lesson, you will learn about the Microsoft Mail screen.

2 What Is Microsoft Mail?

In this lesson, you will learn how Microsoft Mail works. You will also be introduced to the Microsoft Mail screen and its component parts.

A Look at the Microsoft Mail System

A *network* is a system that connects different computers so that programs, data files, and printers can be shared. Through this system of interconnecting cables, Microsoft Mail can send and receive messages.

Working Offline If your network is *down* (not functional), you can still work in Microsoft Mail. Working when you are not connected to a network is called working offline. Simply create your messages and send them later when you are connected to the network, as described in Lesson 10.

Your network has a *system administrator*, a person who is in charge of setting up new users and maintaining the system. Microsoft Mail requires an administrator to maintain the *postoffice*, a central directory where messages are stored. Your network may have several postoffices if your company is large.

Each user has a *mailbox* at the postoffice where individual messages are stored. Users are added or deleted from the system by the system administrator.

Your network may be connected to other networks through a *gateway*. A gateway is a program which provides a path to another mail system. Through a gateway, you can send messages to users on a mail system different from Microsoft Mail. The gateway program translates the message for the other mail system. Your system administrator can provide you with additional information about gateways that are connected to your network.

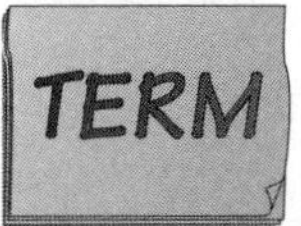

Gateway A program which provides a link through the network to another mail system.

Windows for Workgroups Users Windows for Workgroups Mail does not offer the ability to connect to gateways.

The Process of Sending a Message

To send a message with Microsoft Mail, you select users from an address list which was created by the system administrator. Alternatively, you can select users from a personal address book which you establish.

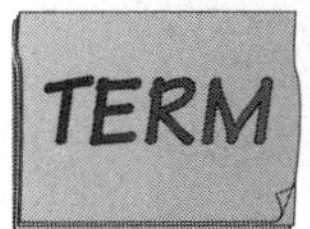

Personal Address Book A personal address book contains the names of users to whom you frequently send messages. You copy users from the central address list to create a personal address book.

After selecting a user (or users) to send a message to, you can select the name or names of users to receive a Cc (courtesy copy) of the message.

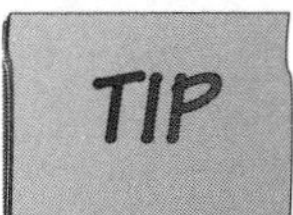

Groupies You can connect several users together in a *personal group* for faster message addressing. For example, you could create a group called Sales which contains all of the sales people.

After the message is addressed, you enter the message text and send the message. You can also attach files to be sent with the message. Now that you understand a little about the Mail system, let's take a closer look.

The Microsoft Mail Screen

After starting Microsoft Mail and logging in, you will see the screen shown in Figure 2.1.

The Mail screen contains several components:

Menu Use the menu to select commands.

Tool bar If you have a mouse, you can use the tool bar instead of the menu to work with messages.

Inbox This window contains all of your incoming messages.

Outbox This window (shown in Figure 2.1, reduced to an icon) contains all of your outgoing messages.

Status bar Shows the current time. If the Inbox is open, you will also see the number of messages and the total unread messages displayed. You will also see mailbox icons from time to time as messages are sent or received.

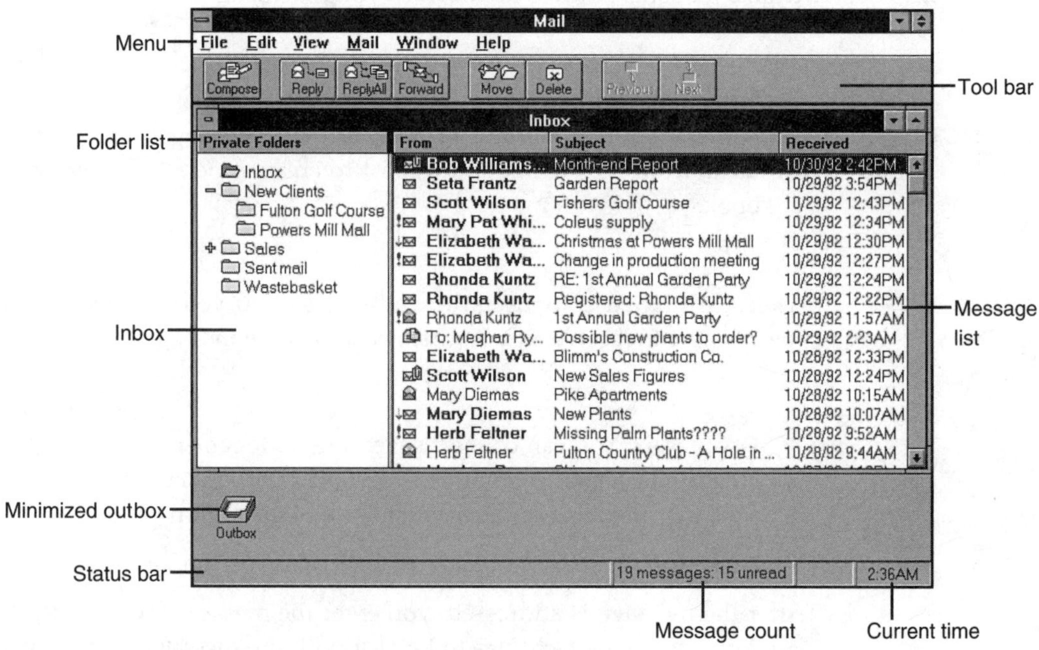

Figure 2.1 The Microsoft Mail screen.

Using the Tool Bar

Mail provides a tool bar for issuing common commands with the mouse. The tool bar is located under the menu bar, as shown in Figure 2.1.

The tool bar includes the Compose, Reply, ReplyAll, Forward, Move, Delete, Previous, and Next commands. You will learn how to use each of these commands in upcoming lessons.

To issue a command from the tool bar, simply click on the appropriate command button. For example, to delete a message, select the message you want to delete and click on the **Delete** button.

Looking at the Inbox

When you log in to Mail, it displays the contents of the Inbox. The *Inbox* contains all of the messages that have been sent to you which have not yet been deleted or moved.

You can place your Inbox messages in folders (and subfolders) for better organization, as shown in Figure 2.2. For example, the folder New Clients contains two subfolders, Fulton Golf Course and Powers Mill Mall. A plus sign (+) next to a folder (such as Sales) indicates subfolders that are not displayed. A minus sign indicates that all subfolders are displayed. You will learn to create folders in Lesson 19.

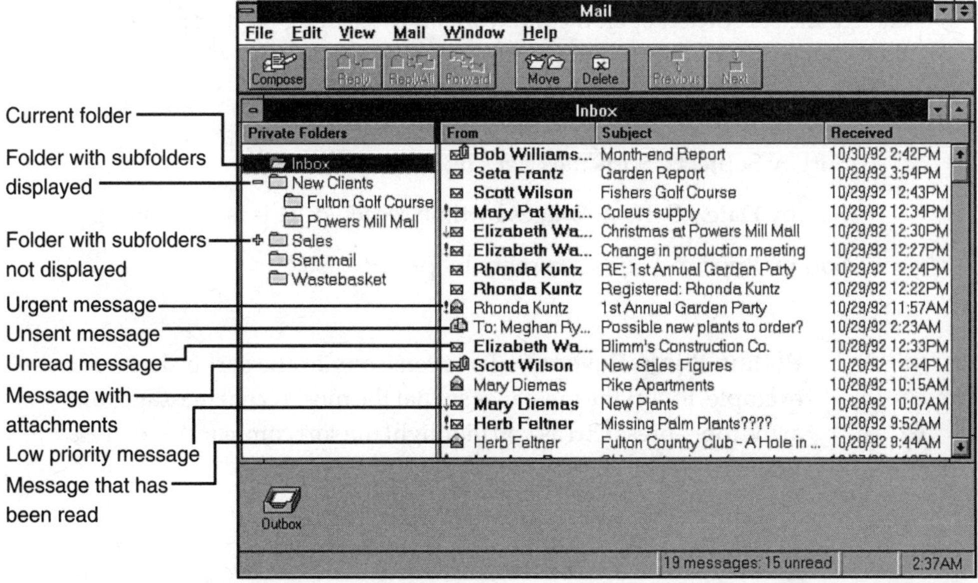

Figure 2.2 The Inbox displays important information about your messages.

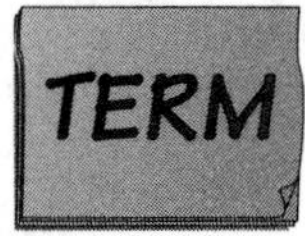

Could You Throw This Away for Me? When Mail is first installed, three folders are set up in the Inbox: Inbox (incoming messages), Sent Mail (copies of outgoing messages), and Wastebasket (messages to delete).

Message headers are displayed on the right side of the Inbox window. The *message list* displays the sender's name, the subject, and the date and time the message was received. One of the following icons appears next to each message:

Closed envelope An unread message. Unread messages also appear in bold, with larger letters so that they are easily identified.

Open envelope A message that has been read.

Exclamation point A message with an urgent priority.

Paperclip A message with attachments.

Down arrow A message with a low priority.

Open envelope with letter A message which has not yet been sent.

Messages are initially displayed in the order in which they are received. To change the sort order, open the **View** menu by clicking on it or pressing **Alt+V**, then choose one of these commands:

Sort by **S**ender Sorts messages by who sent them.

Sort by Sub**j**ect Sorts messages by subject matter.

Sort by **D**ate Sorts messages by time received. This is the default.

Sort by Priorit**y** Sorts messages by priority.

Putting It into Reverse To reverse any of the sort orders—for example, to sort the messages so that the most recent messages are at the top—press **Ctrl** as you highlight the sort command and press **Enter**.

Sort It Out! Quickly change the sort order of messages by clicking on the appropriate button in the Message window. For example, to sort by subject, click on the **Subject** button at the top of the window.

In this lesson, you learned about the Mail system and how it works. You also learned about the Microsoft Mail screen. In the next lesson, you will learn how to use the Mail help system.

3 Using Mail's Help System

In this lesson, you will learn how to use Mail's help system.

Accessing Help

Microsoft Mail has an extensive help system with a complete index and animated demonstrations. Mail's help system is context-sensitive, so that when you access help, you are automatically provided with information that's pertinent to whatever you're working on.

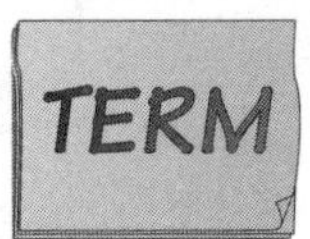

Context-Sensitive Help Help that is pertinent to the context in which you are working.

To access help, you can either:

- Press **F1**.

  OR

- Open the **Help** menu by pressing **Alt+H**, and select a command: **Contents**, **Index**, or **Demos**.

Using the Table of Contents

When you select the Help Contents command, you see a screen like the one shown in Figure 3.1.

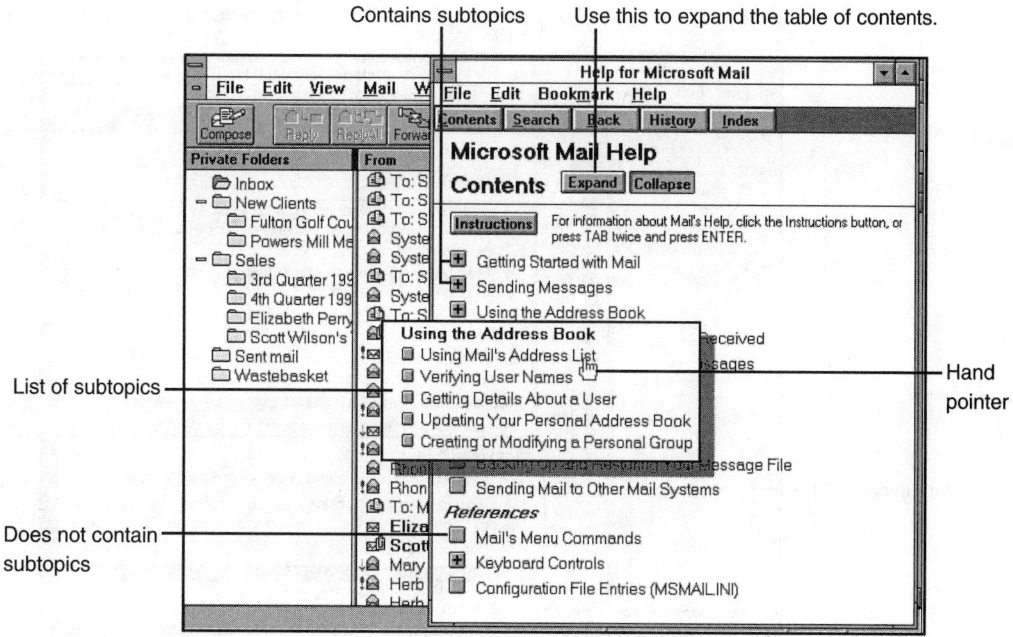

Figure 3.1 Help's Table of Contents.

The Table of Contents lists the major topics contained in the help system. Some topics contain several subtopics, indicated by a plus sign. To expand the Table of Contents so each topic is displayed, select the **Expand** button. To collapse the Table of Contents to major headings, select the **Collapse** button.

To activate a topic with the keyboard, press **Tab** until it is highlighted and press **Enter**. To activate a topic with the mouse, click on it. (When the mouse pointer is over a topic, definition, or pop-up screen, it changes into a hand pointer.)

When you activate a heading which contains subtopics, a second listing will be displayed, as shown in Figure 3.1.

Using Topic Information

When you select a topic from one of the listings in the Table of Contents, you jump to another screen which contains information on that topic, as shown in Figure 3.2.

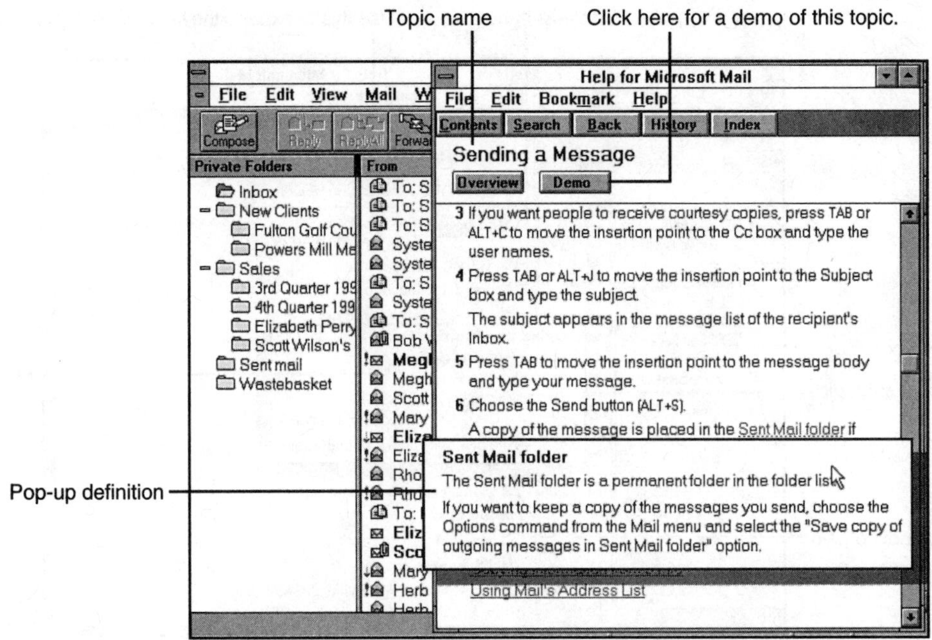

Figure 3.2 Selecting a topic from the Table of Contents provides detailed information.

Several commands are found on each topic screen:

Contents Returns you to the Table of Contents.

Search Allows you to search for a specific topic.

Back Returns you to the previous help screen.

History Displays a listing of all the help screens you've accessed so far.

Index Displays the help index.

Overview Provides a quick overview of this topic.

Demo Displays an animated demo on this topic.

Depending on the topic, you may see up to two different kinds of colored text:

Solid underline colored text Selecting this text will jump you to a related topic.

Dotted underline colored text Selecting this text will display a definition of the term found in this text on a pop-up screen. To remove a pop-up screen, press **Esc**.

Searching for a Specific Topic

When you use the Search button, the Search dialog box is displayed (see Figure 3.3).

To use the Search dialog box, follow these steps:

1. Enter a subject in the text box.
2. If necessary, select a subject from those listed.
3. Select **Show Topics**. A list of available topics is displayed.
4. Select a topic, then select **Go To**.

To close the search window at any time, press **Esc**.

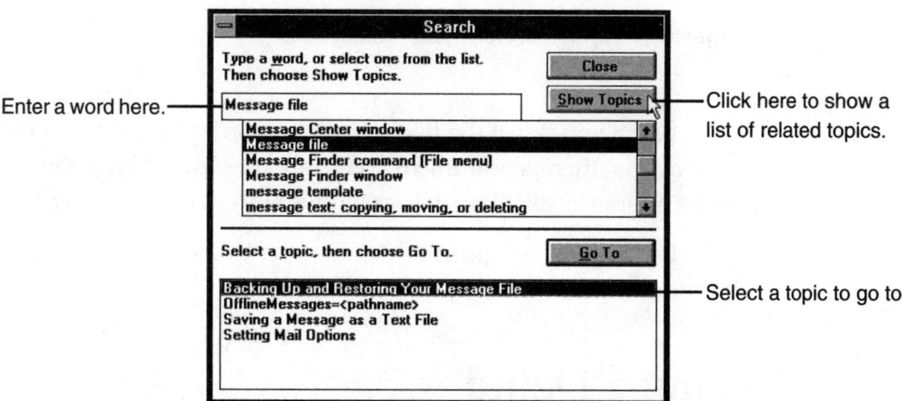

Figure 3.3 The Search dialog box helps you to find a specific topic.

Using the Help Index

Selecting the Help Index command will display the Index dialog box, as shown in Figure 3.4.

To find a word, either:

- Click on the first letter of the word.

OR

- Press **Tab** until the first letter of the word is selected, and press **Enter**.

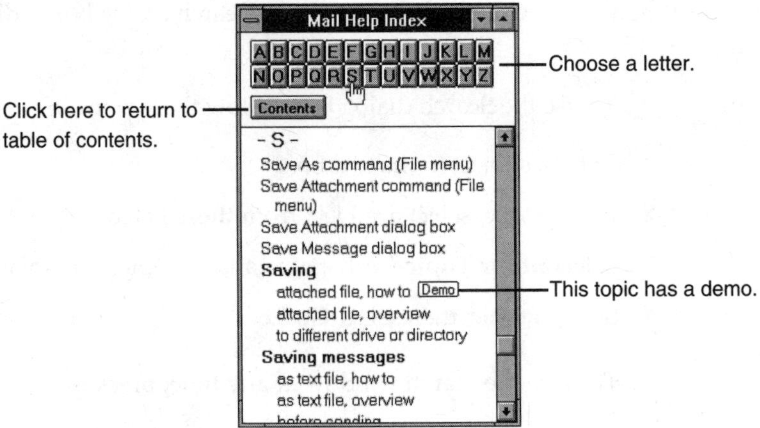

Figure 3.4 The Mail Help Index dialog box.

When you select the first letter of a word, you are taken to that part of the index. From there, use the scroll bars or **Page Up** and **Page Down** to find a topic. Select a topic by clicking on it or highlighting it and pressing **Enter**.

If you want to return to the Table of Contents screen, select the **Contents** button.

Playing a Demo

Microsoft Mail comes with several animated demos which visually explain how to use specific features. There are several ways to access a demo:

- Select the **Help Demos** command.
- Select the **Demo** button displayed at the top of some topic windows.
- Select a topic in the index which indicates that a demo is available.

If you use the **H**elp **D**emos command, a list of available topics will appear, as shown in Figure 3.5. Mail keeps track of the number of demos you have completed, as shown by the figure. Review the navigational instructions first by pressing **T**.

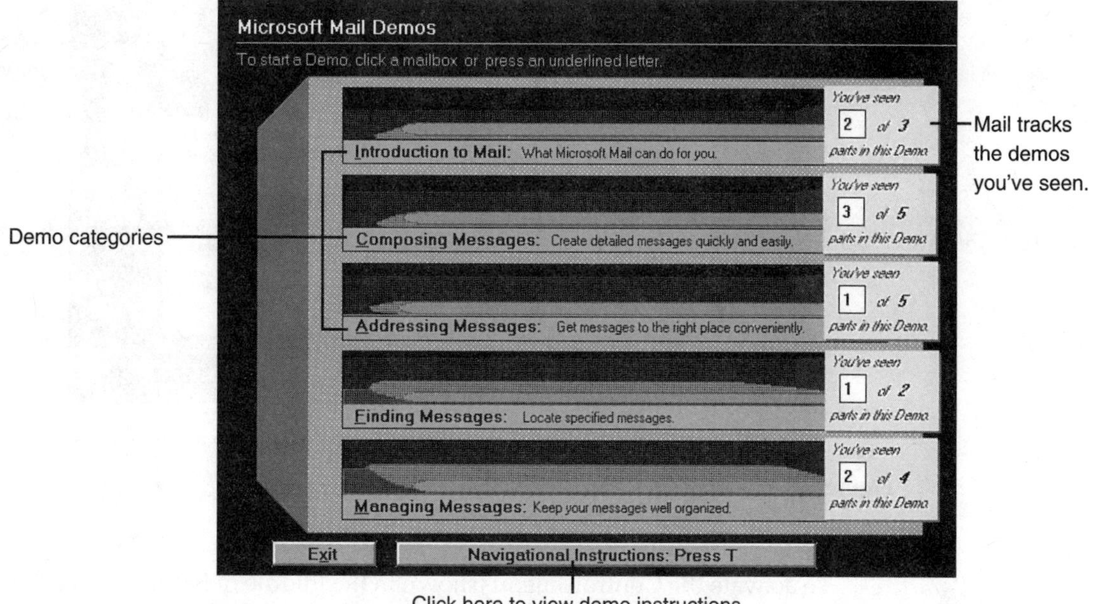

Figure 3.5 You can select from several different demo topics.

Select a topic (by pressing the underlined letter or by clicking on it), and a list of demos will appear (see Figure 3.6). Completed demos are indicated by a postmark on the envelope. Each demo takes only a few minutes to complete. During the demo, you can use the **B**ack and **N**ext buttons to move back and forth between screens.

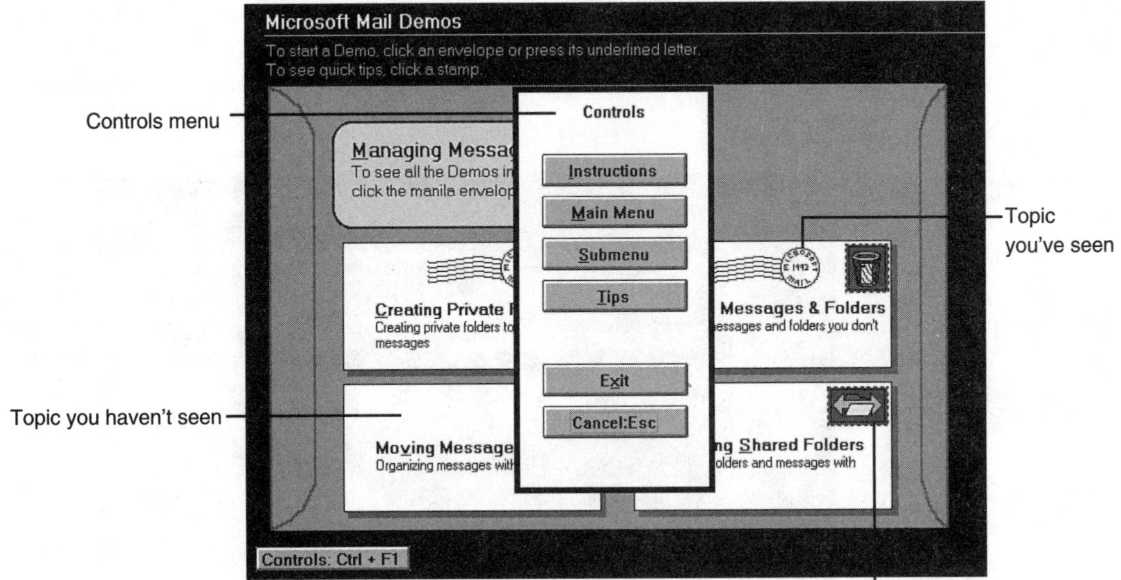

Figure 3.6 Select a specific demo to play.

To activate the Controls menu (shown in the middle of Figure 3.6), click on the **Controls** menu button or press **Ctrl+F1**. From the Controls menu, you can navigate back to the Main Menu, to a submenu, or to an Instructions screen.

In this lesson, you learned how to use Mail's help system. In the next lesson, you will learn how to use Mail's address lists.

Addressing Messages

In this lesson, you will learn how to access the Address Book when composing messages.

Sending a Message to a Selected User

When you want to send a message, you first issue the Compose command by one of two methods:

- Click on the **Compose** button on the tool bar.

  OR

- Open the **Mail** menu (press **Alt+M**) and select the **Compose Note** command (press **N**).

  A window opens, like the one shown in Figure 4.1.

Keep Your Composure You can quickly compose a new message by pressing **Ctrl+N**.

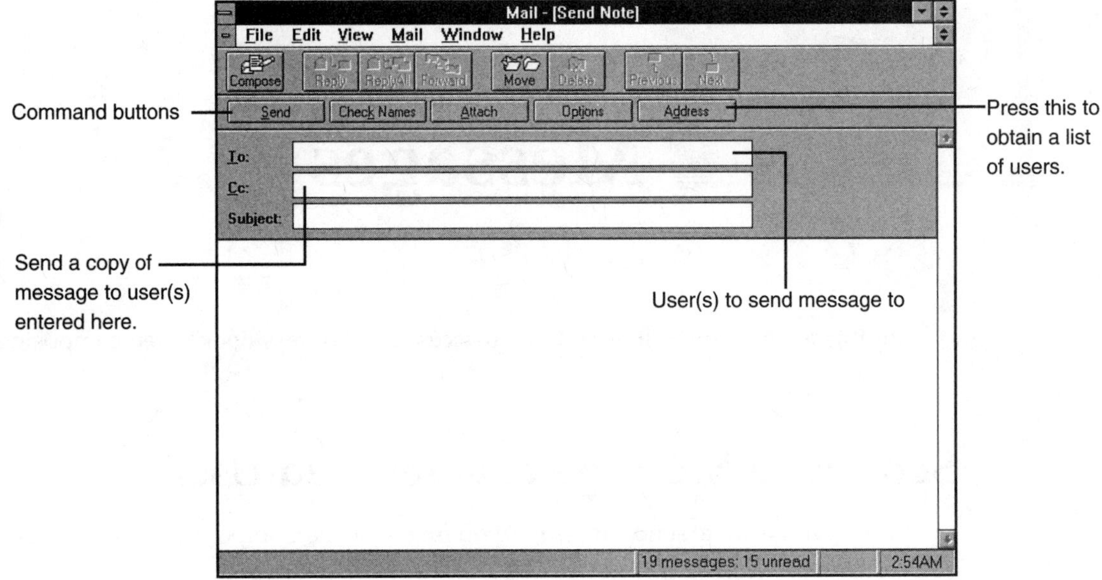

Figure 4.1 The Send Note window.

With the Compose Note window open, follow these steps to select an addressee:

1. Click on the **Address** button or press **Alt+D**. The Address window appears (see Figure 4.2).

Selecting a User from a Different Postoffice To access the global list of users, click on the **Directory** button or press **Ctrl+L**. Select **Global Address List** and press **Enter**.

2. Use the **arrow** keys, **Page Up**, **Page Down**, **Home** (to move to the first person in the list), or **End** to highlight a user. If you have a mouse, you can use the scroll bars to scroll through the list.
3. Press **Enter** to send a message to the selected user, or click the **To** button.
4. If you want, select another user and press **Alt+C** or click the **Cc** button to send a courtesy copy to a user.
5. When you are finished selecting users, press **Enter** or click **OK** to return to the Send Note window. You are now ready to compose a message, which you will learn to do in Lesson 5.

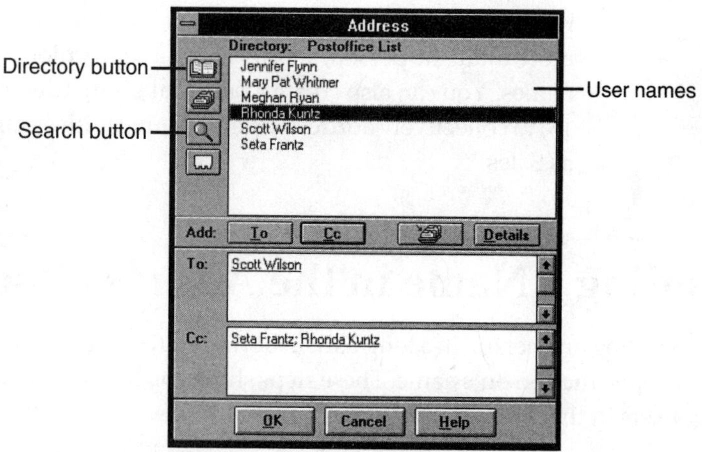

Figure 4.2 The Address window.

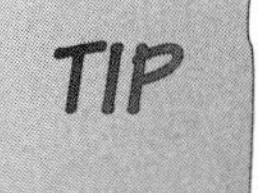

Lost and Found Find a user quickly by pressing the first few characters of the user's name. For example, to find Jane Doe, type J or Ja, and Mail will scroll you to the first user whose name matches those letters.

In the Send Note window, you can enter a user's name instead of selecting it from the Address list, but it must match exactly. Prior to sending any message, Mail verifies each name against the Address list. If the name is correctly entered, it is underlined to indicate that it has been verified. Use the **Check names** button (or press **Alt+K**) to verify any name that you enter manually.

Now I Cc! There is no difference between using the To and Cc fields of the Send Note window, in terms of results; anyone listed in either field will receive your message. Treat the Cc field in the same manner as the cc notation often used at the end of a typewritten memo—the use of cc generally means that the recipient is not directly involved, but is receiving a courtesy copy of the message as an FYI.

He's Making a List... If you want to address your message to more than one person, simply insert a semi-colon (;) between user names. You can also create a personal group (described in Lesson 13) to collectively address several people with a single name, such as Sales.

Finding a Name in the Address Book

Finding one person in a long list can be difficult, especially if you are not sure how to spell the person's name. These steps show you how to use Name Finder to locate users in the Address Book:

1. From the Address window, click on the **Search** button (a small magnifying glass) or press **Ctrl+F**. The Name Finder dialog box appears.
2. Type a few letters from the person's name. If you want to search for a specific last name, type a space and a few characters from the last name. Here are some examples (assuming that the address list is sorted by first name):

   Ja Will find users with first names Jane and Janet, but not Joe.

   P Ja Will find Peggy James, Paul Jansen, and Peter Jantz, but not Paulina Jenkins.

   Pe Ja Will find Peggy James and Peter Jantz, but not Paul Jansen.

   (space)Jo Will find the last names Jones and Johnson.

Getting Details About a User

When your system administrator adds a new user, she can include additional information such as the person's phone number, department, office location, mail stop number, and so on. To view any of this information, select a user in the Address window and click the **Details** button or press **Alt+D**. The Details window, shown in Figure 4.3, will appear. To return to the Address window, press **Esc** when you are done.

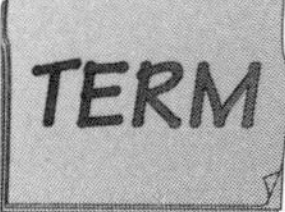

Mail Stop A mail stop number is often used in large corporations to sort mail. The mail stop number acts like a ZIP code, indicating the location (mail drop) nearest to an individual where internal mail is delivered. By adding a mail stop number to a letter or other internal document, mail can be quickly sorted and delivered to an individual within the corporation.

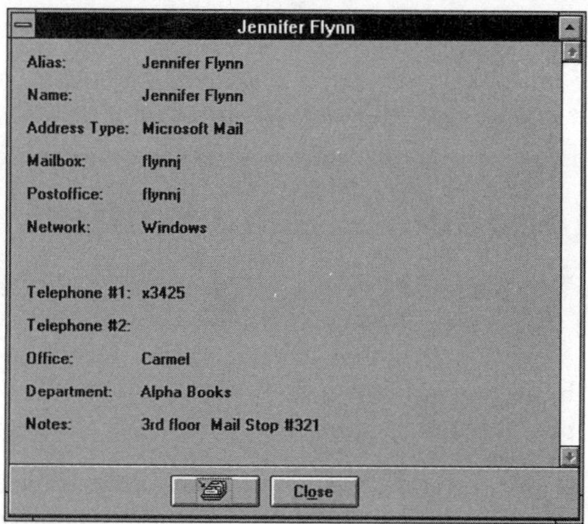

Figure 4.3 The Details window provides additional information about a user.

In this lesson, you learned how to access the Address Book while composing a message. In the next lesson, you will learn how to enter the message text and send a message.

5 Sending Messages

In this lesson, you will learn how to enter and send messages.

Entering the Message Subject

Enter a message subject so your users can easily identify what your message is about. To do so, follow these steps:

1. In the Send Note window, press **Tab** or **Alt+J** to move to the Subject text box, shown in Figure 5.1.
2. Enter a brief description of the message. This description will be displayed (along with your name and the time that the message was received) in the user's Inbox.

Entering Your Message

After entering the description of your message, you are ready to enter the message itself:

1. Press **Tab** to move to the message area.
2. Enter the message. If you make a mistake, press **Backspace** and retype. You can use the keys listed in Table 5.1 to edit your message.

Wrap It Up! You should not press Enter at the end of each line; Mail will automatically *wrap* words to the next line when they bump into the right-hand margin.

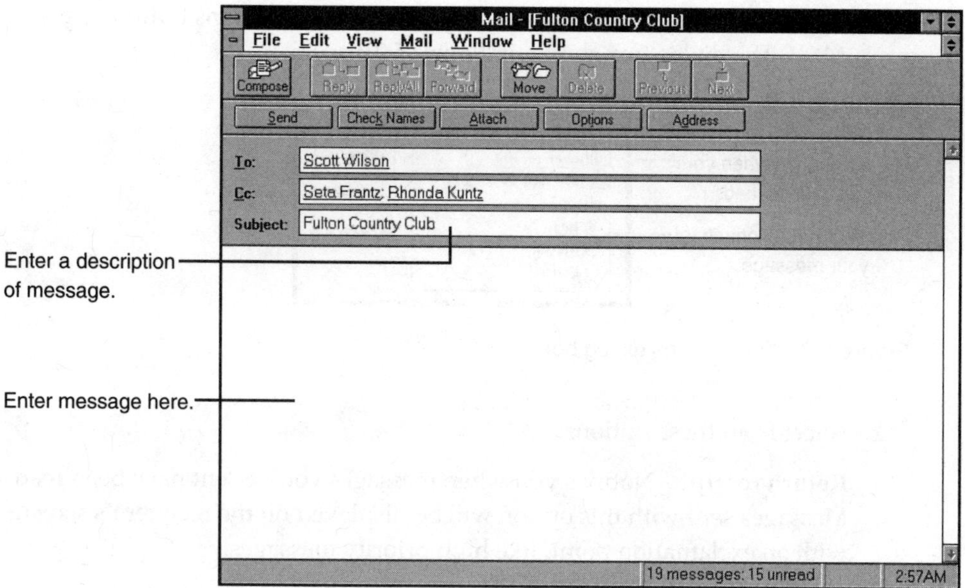

Figure 5.1 Enter a description of your message in the Subject text box.

Table 5.1 Quick Keys for Editing Messages

Press this...	*...to do this.*
Backspace	Delete the previous character.
Enter	Start a new paragraph.
Page Up	Move up one screen.
Page Down	Move down one screen.
Home	Move to the beginning of the line.
End	Move to the end of the line.

Setting Message Options

Prior to sending your message, you may want to change the default message options. To change a message option:

1. From within the Send Note window, click on the **Options** button or press **Alt+I**. The dialog box shown in Figure 5.2 appears.

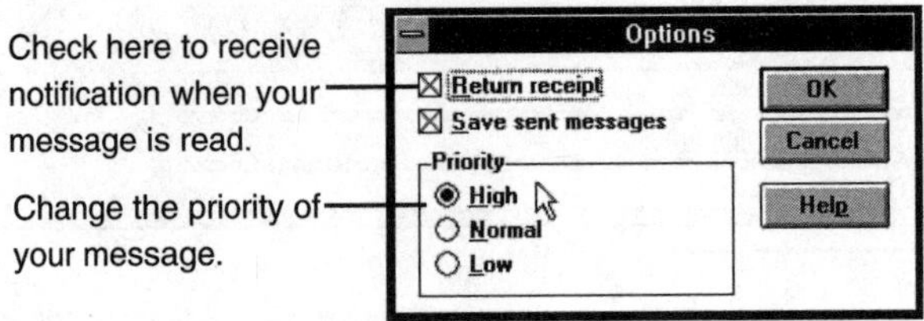

Figure 5.2 The Options dialog box.

2. Select from these options:

   Return receipt Notifies you when messages you've sent have been read. Messages sent with this option will be displayed on the recipient's screen with an exclamation point, like high priority messages.

   Save sent messages Saves a copy of messages you send in the Sent Mail folder.

   Priority Makes an exclamation point (**H**igh priority messages) or a down arrow (**L**ow priority messages) appear on the recipient's screen in front of your message.

3. When you are done, press **Enter** or click **OK** to return to the Send Note window.

Return to Sender After the recipient reads a message that you've marked with the **R**eturn receipt option, you will receive a message with the word **Registered** shown in the Subject column of the message list. You can read your receipt to learn when the message was read (see Figure 5.3).

Sending Your Message

Once your message is addressed and composed, you are ready to send it. To send your message, click on the **Send** button or press **Alt+S**.

Unless you have changed the default options, a copy of the message you sent will be saved in the Sent Mail folder. You will learn more about reading messages (including those you've sent) in Lesson 6.

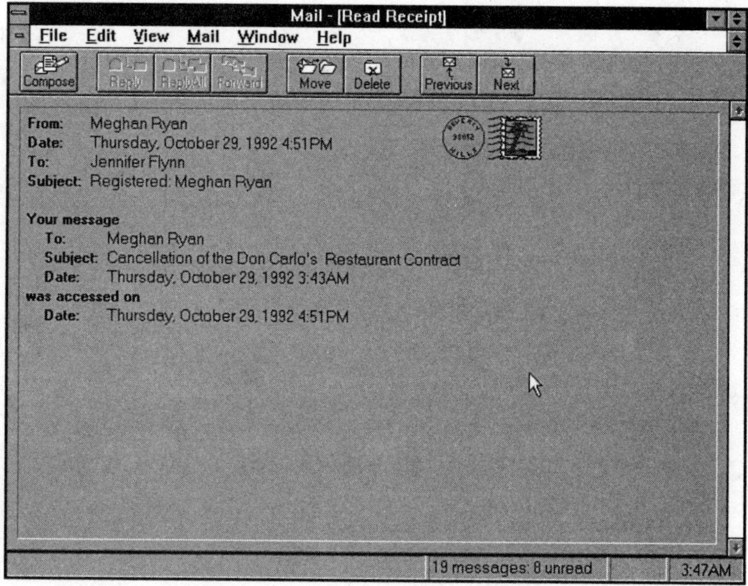

Figure 5.3 When a registered message is sent, you get a receipt.

Deliver da Letter.... If for some reason your message could not be delivered, you will be notified. Open the notification and you will see your original message, along with the reason for the non-delivery. Use the **Send Again** button to resend the message after the problem has been resolved.

In this lesson you learned how to enter a message and send it. In the next lesson, you will learn how to read messages you receive.

6 Reading Messages

In this lesson, you will learn how to read messages that have been sent to you or that you have sent and saved in your Sent Mail folder.

Selecting a Message to Read

Messages that have been sent to you are stored in the Inbox folder. If you have not yet read a message, it is displayed with a closed envelope, as shown in Figure 6.1. When a message has been read, it is displayed with an open envelope.

To read a message:

1. If the Inbox folder is not open, use the arrow keys to highlight it and press **Enter**, or double-click on the **Inbox** folder.
2. Press **Tab** to move to the right side of the window and use the arrow keys to highlight a message.
3. Press **Enter** or double-click on a message to open it.

To review messages you've sent, follow these same instructions, but open the **Sent Mail** folder instead.

You can scroll through the message with the mouse or with the arrow keys. Use the **Page Up** and **Page Down** keys to scroll through a message quickly.

Next, Please After you've opened a message, you can easily read the next message in the list by either clicking on the **Next** button, or pressing **Alt+V** to open the **View** menu and selecting **Next** by pressing **N**. To view the previous message, click on **Previous**, or press **Alt+V** and then **P**. Press **Esc** when you are done viewing messages.

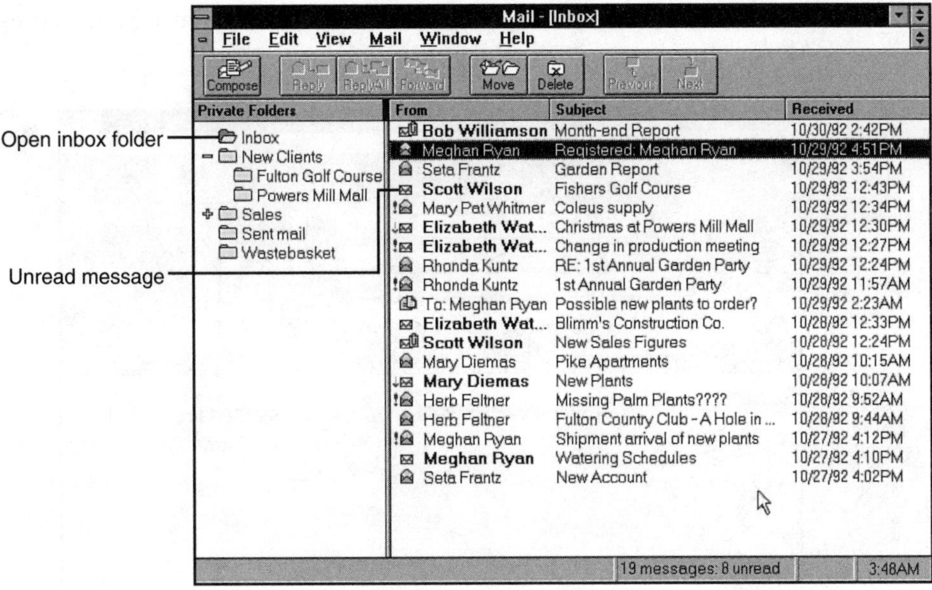

Figure 6.1 Unread messages are displayed with a closed envelope.

Locating a Specific Message to Read

If you want to find a message from a specific person, or about something in particular, follow these steps:

1. Open the **File** menu by clicking on it or pressing **Alt+F**.
2. Select the **Message Finder** command by clicking on it or pressing **G**. The Message Finder dialog box appears, as shown in Figure 6.2.
3. Enter the information to search for by filling in as many of the text boxes as needed:

   From Searches for messages from a specific person.

   Subject Searches for a particular message based on its description.

   Recipients Searches the courtesy copy field for a match.

   Message Text Searches the text of a message for a match.

   Where to Look Select this button to open an additional dialog box which can be used to identify the folders to search. You may select a single folder or all folders.

4. When you have entered the information to search for, click **Start** or press **Alt+S**.

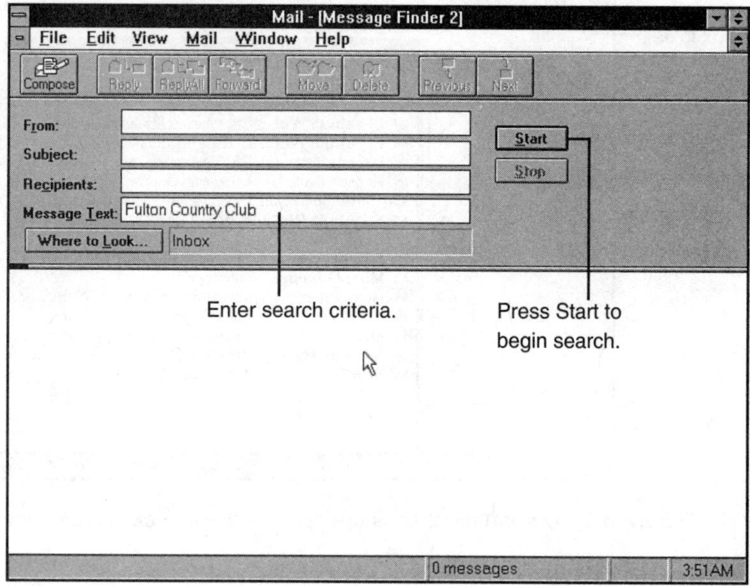

Figure 6.2 You can find messages easily with message Finder.

Hide and Seek? If the search seems to be taking too long and you wish to quit, click **Stop** or press **Alt+S** again.

When the search is complete, the messages are listed below the search box, as shown in Figure 6.3. You can open, delete, move, or perform any other task on the listed messages.

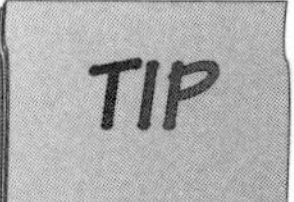

Multiple Personalities To search for messages sent to you by more than one person, enter both names separated by a semi-colon (;). Use this same technique in any of the Message Finder boxes. For example, enter **sales; success** to find messages that discuss successful sales months.

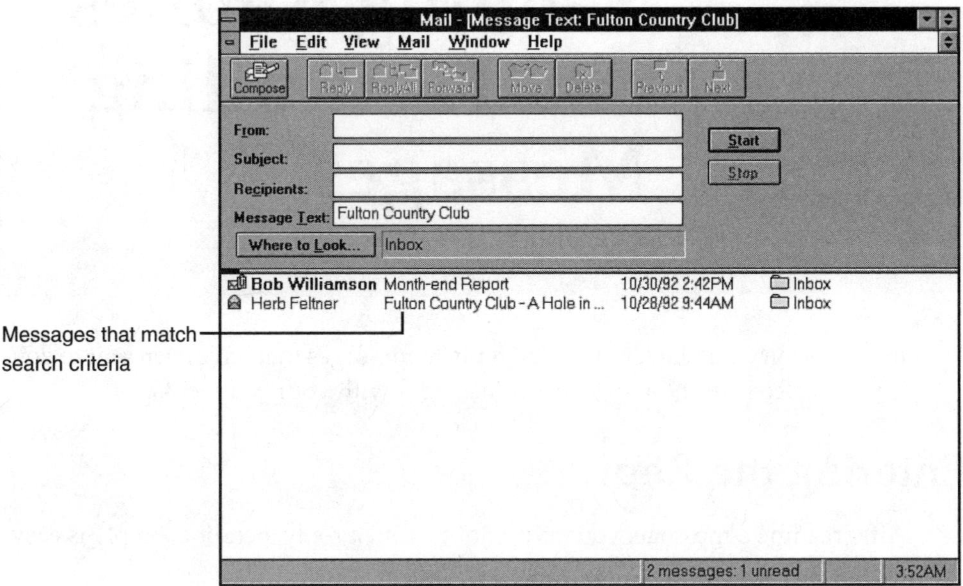

Figure 6.3 The search is on!

In this lesson, you learned how to find a message and read it. In the next lesson, you will learn how to reply to a message.

7 Sending Replies and Forwarding Messages

In this lesson, you will learn how to reply to messages that have been sent to you. You will also learn how to forward messages with your comments.

Entering the Reply

After reading a message, you may want to send a reply. Sending a reply is easy:

1. Select the message you want to reply to.
2. Click the **Reply** button or press **Ctrl+R**. To send a reply to everyone listed in the To and Cc boxes, click **Reply All** or press **Ctrl+A**. The reply window appears, as shown in Figure 7.1.
3. Enter your message. The original message appears below the line. You can perform any normal message task (such as include attachments or change the priority) and delete all or part of the original message if you want.
4. When you are ready to send the message, click the **Send** button, or press **Alt+S**.

Replies to messages are displayed on the recipient's computer with an RE: in front of the subject, as shown in Figure 7.2.

Forwarding a Message

Forward a copy of a message along with your comments to a colleague. To forward a message:

1. Select the message you wish to forward.
2. Click the **Forward** button or press **Ctrl+F**. The forward window appears, as shown in Figure 7.3.
3. Enter the name of the person to whom you would like to forward the message in the **To** box, and that of any courtesy copy recipients in the **Cc** box.

4. Enter your comments. The original message appears below the line. You can perform any normal message task (such as include attachments or change the priority) and delete all or part of the original message if you want.

5. When you are ready to send the message, click the **Send** button, or press **Alt+S**.

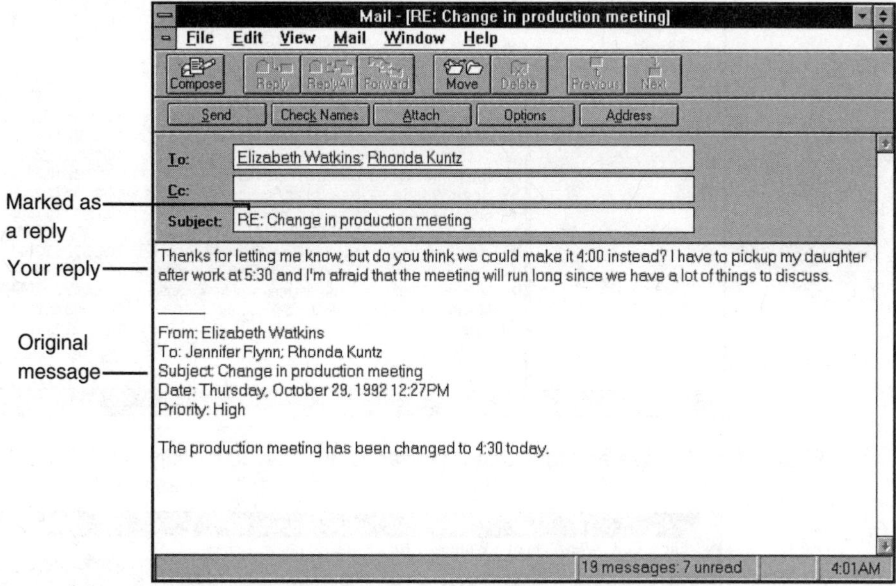

Figure 7.1 You can address your reply to the sender or to everyone involved.

Forwarded messages are displayed on the recipient's computer with an FW: in front of the subject, as shown in Figure 7.2.

Fast Forward You can also drag a message to the Outbox to forward it.

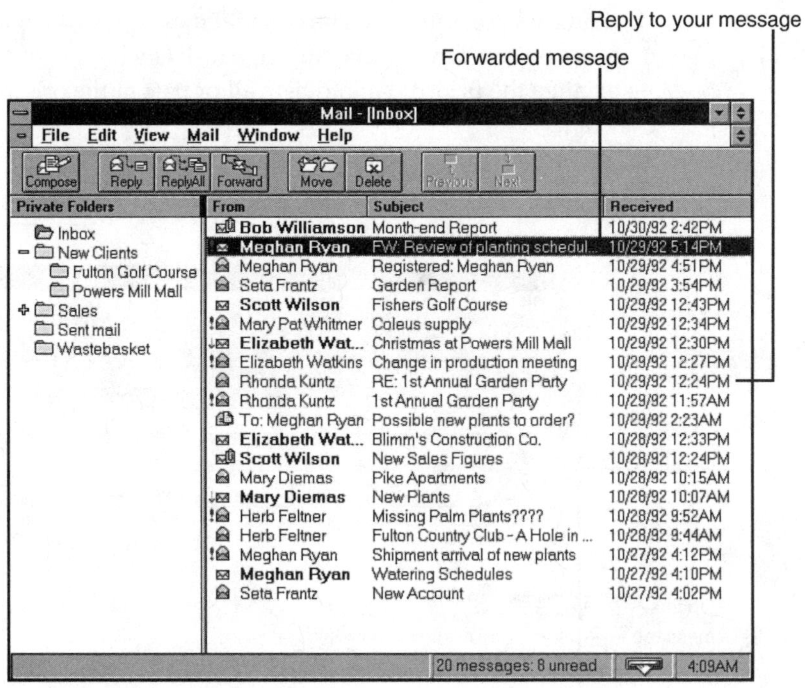

Figure 7.2 Replies and forwarded messages are easy to identify.

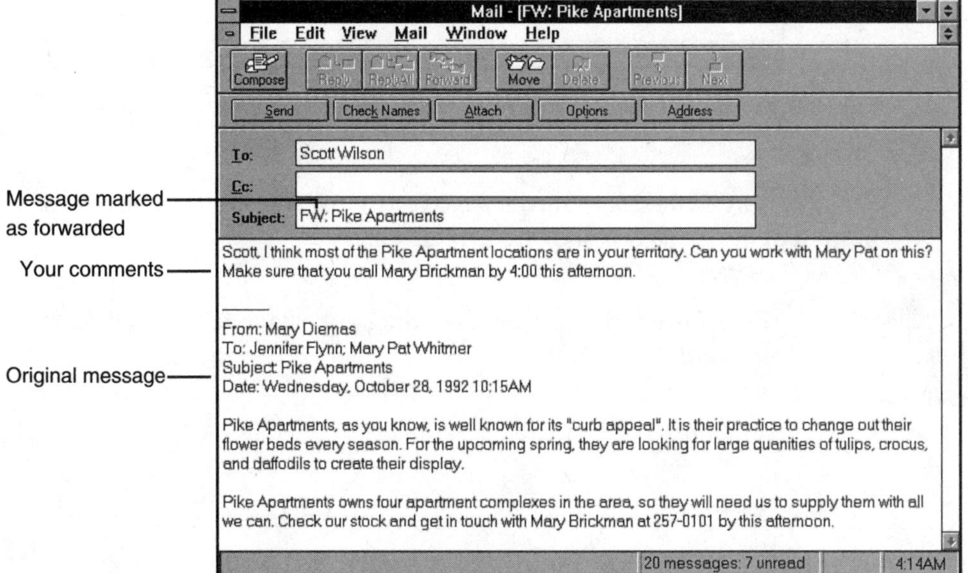

Figure 7.3 You can forward a message along with your comments.

8 Deleting Messages

In this lesson, you will learn how to delete unwanted messages.

Before You Delete a Message

After reading a message, you may want to save it in a folder (described in Lesson 19), or you may want to simply delete it.

See It in Print! Before deleting a message, you can print it out and file the hard copy. See Lesson 22 for a detailed explanation.

Selecting Messages

You can delete one message at a time, or several. To select a single message, simply click on it with the mouse, or use the arrow keys to highlight it. To select several messages, use one of the following techniques.

Selecting Contiguous Messages

Messages that are together in a list are *contiguous*.

To select contiguous messages with the mouse:

1. Click in the area in front of the message icon (see Figure 8.1) on the first message you want to select.
2. Drag the mouse down the list until all of the messages you want are selected. The contiguous messages are now highlighted, as shown in Figure 8.1.

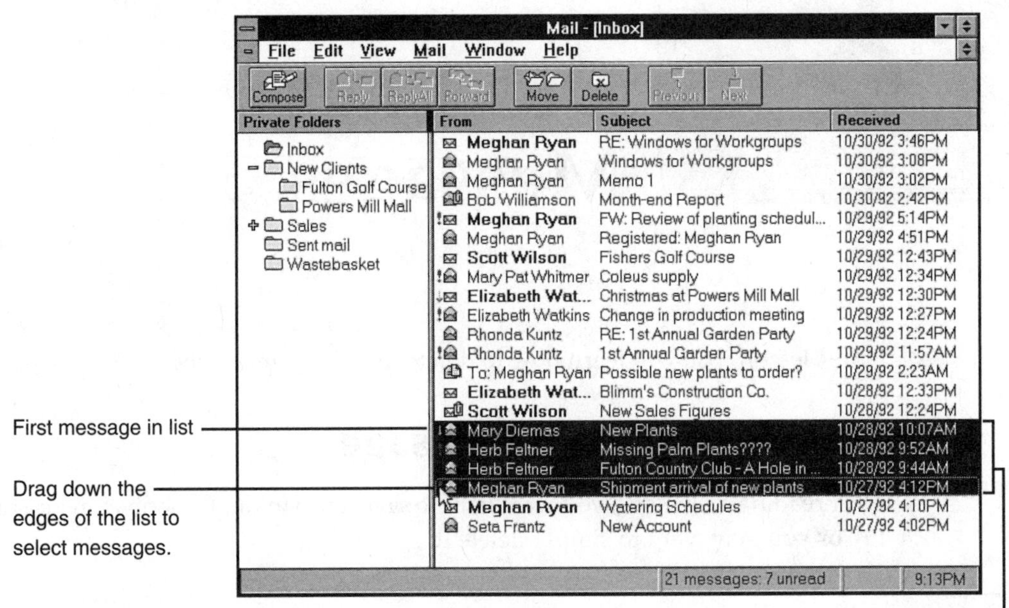

Figure 8.1 Selecting contiguous messages.

To select contiguous messages with the keyboard:

1. If necessary, press **Tab** to move to the message list.
2. Use the arrow keys to move to the first message you want to select.
3. Press and hold the **Shift** key.
4. Use the arrow keys to move down the list until all of the messages you want are selected. The messages are highlighted.

Selecting Non-Contiguous Messages

Messages that are not together in a list are *non-contiguous*.

To select non-contiguous messages with the mouse:

1. Click on the first message you want to select.
2. Press and hold the **Ctrl** key.
3. Click on the additional messages you want to select. The non-contiguous messages are now highlighted, as shown in Figure 8.2.

To select non-contiguous messages with the keyboard:

1. If necessary, press **Tab** to move to the message list.
2. Use the arrow keys to move to the first message you want to select.
3. Press and hold the **Ctrl** key.
4. Use the arrow keys to move down the list to an additional message you want to select.
5. Press the **Spacebar** to select the additional message.
6. Repeat steps 4 and 5 until all the messages are highlighted.

Deleting Unwanted Messages

After you have selected the message(s) you want to delete, follow these steps to delete the unwanted message(s) with the mouse:

1. Select the message(s) you want to delete.
2. Drag the selected messages to the Wastebasket folder.

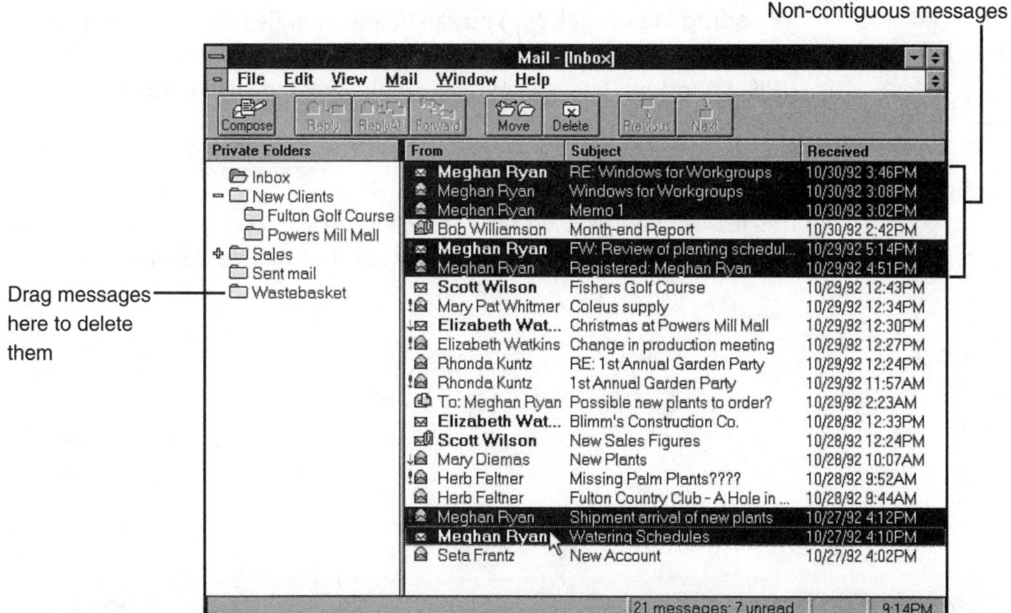

Figure 8.2 Selecting non-contiguous messages.

To delete unwanted message(s) with the keyboard:

1. Select the message(s) you want to delete.
2. Open the **File** menu by pressing **Alt+F**.
3. Select the **Delete** command by pressing **D**.

Fast Delete You can quickly delete selected messages by pressing the **Del** key.

The messages you delete are placed in the Wastebasket folder. Those messages will not be deleted permanently until you log out of Mail.

Windows for Workgroups Users The folder that holds your deleted mail is called Deleted Mail instead of Wastebasket.

Reading Messages? You can delete a single message after you read it by clicking on the **Delete** key or pressing **Ctrl+D** from the Read window. The next message in the message list will automatically be displayed.

In this lesson, you learned how to delete unwanted messages. In the next lesson, you will learn how to retrieve messages that you've deleted by mistake.

Retrieving Deleted Messages

In this lesson, you will learn how to retrieve messages that are currently marked for deletion.

Retrieving a Deleted Message

Because messages are not deleted until you log out of Mail, you can retrieve them if you change your mind. When you retrieve a message, it is moved from the Wastebasket folder to a folder that you select. Because the retrieved message will not be in the Wastebasket folder when you log out of Mail, it will not be deleted.

Act Now for Extra Savings You must retrieve a deleted message *before* you log out of Mail, or it will be permanently deleted.

Windows for Workgroups Users The folder which holds your deleted mail is called Deleted Mail instead of Wastebasket.

To retrieve a deleted message with the mouse:

1. Open the **Wastebasket** folder by double-clicking on it.
2. Select the message(s) you want to retrieve.
3. Drag the selected message(s) to any folder you wish.

Selection Process For a review on how to select multiple files, go to Lesson 8.

To retrieve a deleted message with the keyboard:

1. If necessary, press **Tab** to move to the Folder list.
2. Open the **Wastebasket** folder by highlighting it and pressing **Enter**.
3. Press **Tab** to move to the Message list. Select the message(s) you want to retrieve.
4. Open the **File** menu by pressing **Alt+F**.

Fast Moves You can move selected messages in one step by pressing **Ctrl+M**.

5. Select the **Move** command by pressing **M**. A dialog box, like the one shown in Figure 9.1, will appear.
6. Indicate where you want the message moved to by selecting a folder from the displayed list and pressing **Enter**. If a folder contains subfolders that are not displayed, press the **+** key to display them.

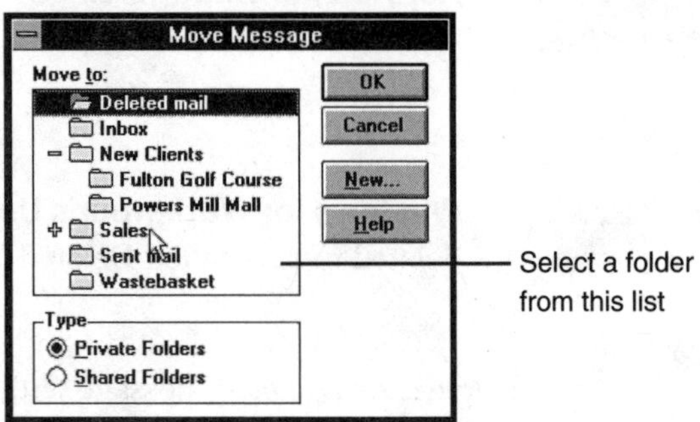

Figure 9.1 Move the deleted message to a folder you select.

In this lesson, you learned how to retrieve messages that had been marked for deletion. In the next lesson, you will learn how to create a message that you will send at a later time.

10 Preparing a Message to Send Later

In this lesson, you will learn how to prepare messages in advance to send at a later time.

Saving a Message So You Can Send It Later

You can create a message to send at a later time. Create the message in the regular way following the instructions in Lessons 4 and 5—*but don't send the message.*

To save your message to send at a later time:

1. After entering your message (as described in Lesson 5), press **Ctrl+F4** or double-click the **Control-menu** box.
2. The dialog box shown in Figure 10.1 will appear. Answer yes by clicking on the **Yes** button, or pressing **Y**.

Your message is saved in the Inbox. You can open it and make additional changes later if you wish. Unsent messages are displayed with an open envelope and letters icon, as shown in Figure 10.2.

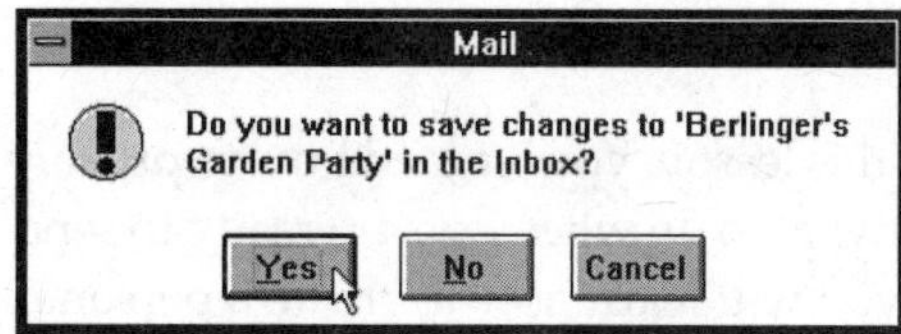

Figure 10.1 Answer yes to save your unsent message.

Do You Send the Same Type of Message Often? Create a message template with the instructions found in Lesson 24.

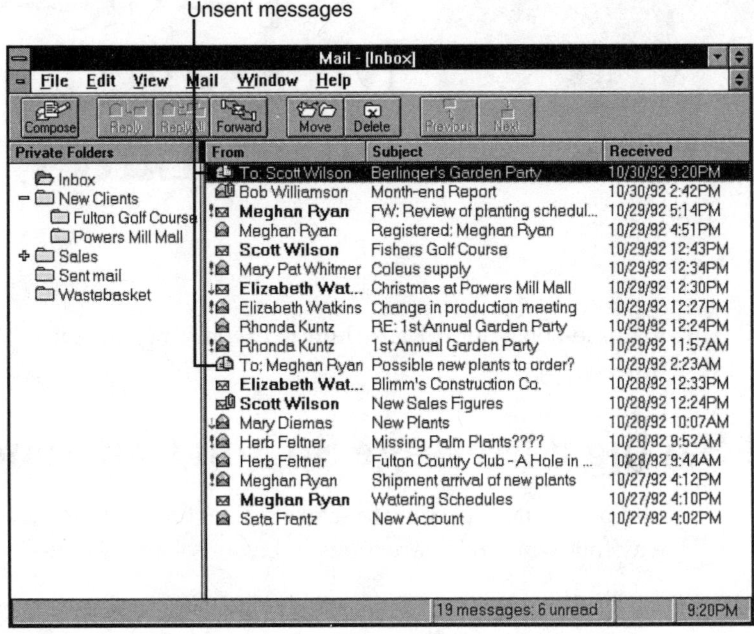

Figure 10.2 It's easy to identify an unsent message.

Sending Your Unsent Message

Later, when you're finished composing your message, you can send it. To send a previously unsent message:

1. Open the unsent message by selecting it and pressing **Enter**.
2. Click the **Send** button or press **Alt+S**.

In this lesson, you learned how to prepare a message to send later. You also learned what to do when you are ready to send your unsent message. In the next lesson, you will learn how to create a personal address book.

11 Creating a Personal Address Book

In this lesson, you will learn how to create your own address book.

Adding a User to Your Personal Address Book

You can create your own address book with names selected from the postoffice address book. Having your own address book will make it easier to send messages to those people with whom you converse frequently.

To create a personal address book, you simply select the users you want to add. To add a user to your personal address book:

1. Open the **Mail** menu by clicking on it or pressing **Alt+M.**
2. Select the **Address book** command by clicking on it or pressing **D**. The Address Book dialog box opens, as shown in Figure 11.1.

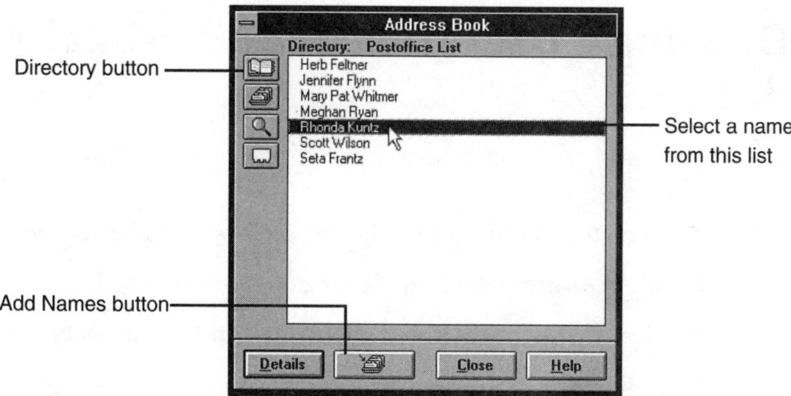

Figure 11.1 The Address Book window.

3. Select a name to add to your personal address book by clicking on it or moving the arrow keys to highlight it.

Different Postoffice? If you need to add a user from a different postoffice, click on the **Directory** button or press **Ctrl+L**. Select the postoffice you want to access and press **Enter**.

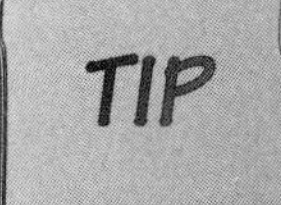

Lots of Friends? Add multiple names to your Address book by selecting several names before issuing the Add names command.

4. Add the name to your personal address book by clicking the **Add Names** button or pressing **Ctrl+A**.
5. Repeat steps 3 and 4 for additional names.
6. When you are done, press **Esc** to close the Address Book window.

Forgot Someone? You can add names to your personal address book as you're composing a message. Simply click on the **Add Names** button or press **Ctrl+A** in the Address dialog box.

Deleting a User from Your Personal Address Book

If you need to delete a user from your personal address book, follow these instructions:

1. Open the **Mail** menu by clicking on it or pressing **Alt+M**.
2. Select **Address Book** by clicking on it or pressing **D**.
3. Press **Ctrl+P** or click on the **Personal Address Book** button. This will display your personal address book.
4. Select the name you want to remove.

5. Click on the **Remove** button as shown in Figure 11.2, or press **Alt+R**. A dialog box will appear, asking you to confirm the deletion. Press **Enter** or click **Yes**, and the user is removed from your personal address book as well as any personal groups you may have created. (Personal groups are described in Lesson 13.)

Make Your Selection You can delete more than one user at a time by selecting multiple users before issuing the **R**emove command. Use the same techniques described in Lesson 8 for selecting multiple users.

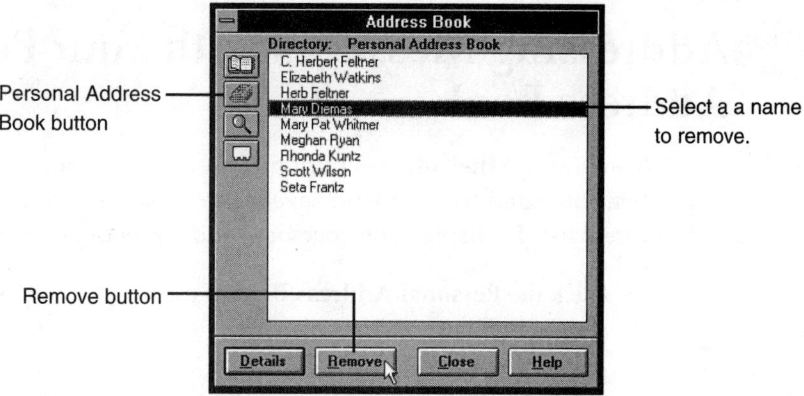

Figure 11.2 Keep your personal address book updated by deleting users you no longer need.

In this lesson, you learned how to create a personal address book. In the next lesson, you will learn how to use this personal address book when addressing messages.

12 Using a Personal Address Book

In this lesson, you will learn how to use your personal address book when sending messages.

Addressing Messages with Your Personal Address Book

When you use the Address button from the Send Note window (for example, when you are addressing a message to send to someone), it displays the postoffice address list. To display your personal address book, you must either:

- Click the **Personal Address Book** button in the Address window, as shown in Figure 12.1.

  OR

- Press **Ctrl+P**.

Once your personal address book is displayed, you can select users (or personal groups, which are explained in Lesson 13) to place in the **To** and **Cc** fields of your message. Simply follow the same techniques described in Lesson 4:

1. Use the **arrow** keys, **Page Up**, **Page Down**, **Home** (to move to the first person in the list), or **End** to highlight a user. If you have a mouse, you can use the scroll bars to scroll through the list.
2. Press **Enter** to send a message to the selected user, or click the **To** button.
3. If you want, select another user and press **Alt+C** or click the **Cc** button to send a courtesy copy to a user.

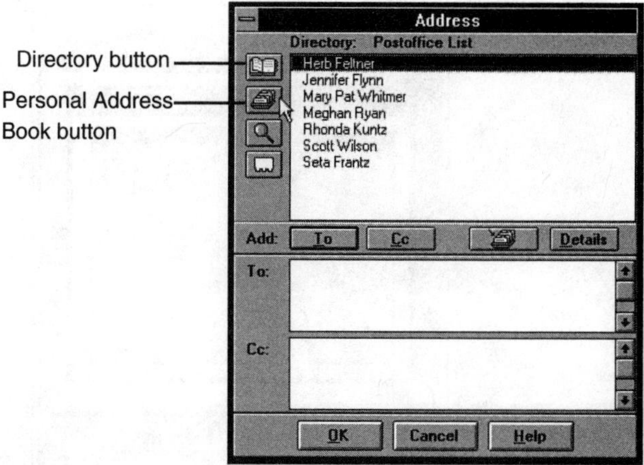

Figure 12.1 Use the Personal Address Book button to access your personal address book.

Lost Someone? By pressing the first few characters of the user's name, you can locate him or her quickly in the user list. For example, to find Jane Doe, type **J** or **Ja**, and Mail will scroll you to the first user whose name matches those letters.

Switching Back to the Postoffice Address Book

After you've opened your personal address book, you may need to return to the postoffice address list. To switch between address books, follow these steps:

1. Click on the **Directory** button, or press **Ctrl+L** and press **Enter**. The Open Directory dialog box appears, as shown in Figure 12.2.
2. Select the address book to display by highlighting it with the arrow keys or clicking on it.
3. Press **Enter** or click **OK**, and the selected address book will be displayed in the Address Book window.

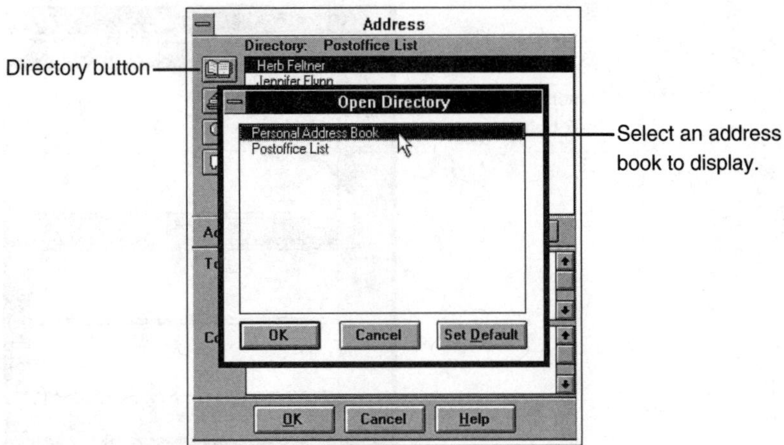

Figure 12.2 Switch between address books with the Directory button.

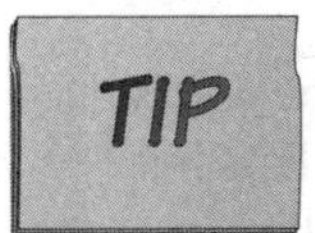

Where's My List? Make your personal address book appear every time you open the Address Book window by selecting **Personal Address Book** in the Open Directory dialog box and clicking on the **Set Default** button or pressing **Alt+D**.

In this lesson, you learned how to access your personal address book and use it to address your messages. In the next lesson, you will learn how to create personal groups.

13 Creating a Personal Group

In this lesson, you will learn how to create personal groups.

Creating Your Personal Groups

If you often send messages to whole departments or other groups of people, create your own personal groups. For example, you could create a group called Sales for all of the sales staff in your organization. When addressing a message to all salespeople, you could select the **Sales** group from your personal address book, as shown in Figure 13.1, and your message would be sent to all of the salespeople in the group.

You can create as many personal groups as needed. The same users can be included in multiple groups. For example, as the head of Marketing, Meghan Ryan could be included in the Marketing group and also in the Sales group.

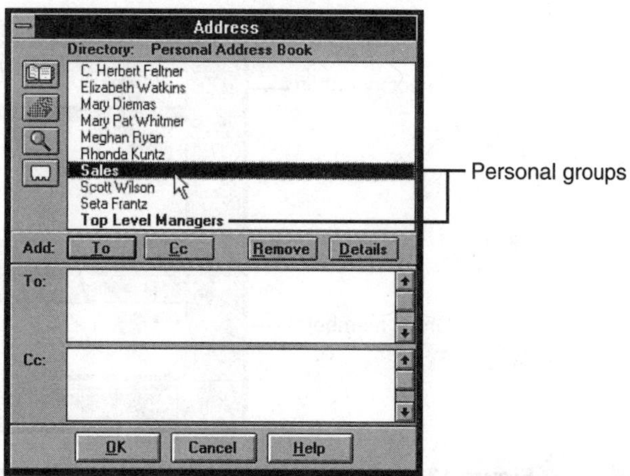

Figure 13.1 Addressing a message to a group is as easy as addressing a message to a single user.

To create a personal group:

1. Open the **Mail** menu by clicking on it or pressing **Alt+M**.
2. Select the **Personal Groups** command by clicking on it or pressing **G**. The dialog box shown in Figure 13.2 will appear.

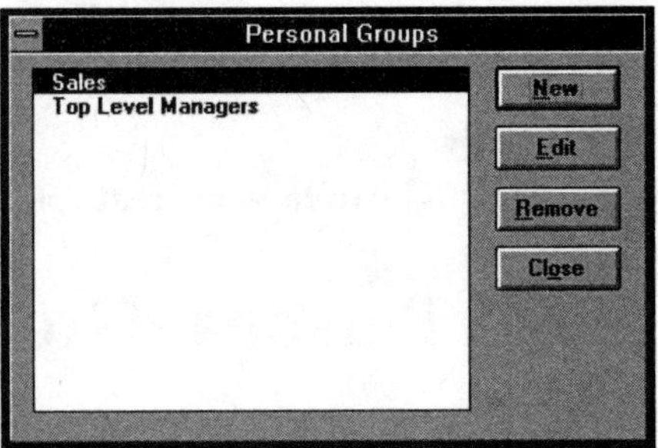

Figure 13.2 Add new groups with the Personal Groups dialog box.

3. Click on **New** or press **Alt+N**.
4. Enter the new group name. The name can be up to 19 characters long, including spaces.
5. Click **Create** or press **Enter**. A list of user names will appear, as shown in Figure 13.3.

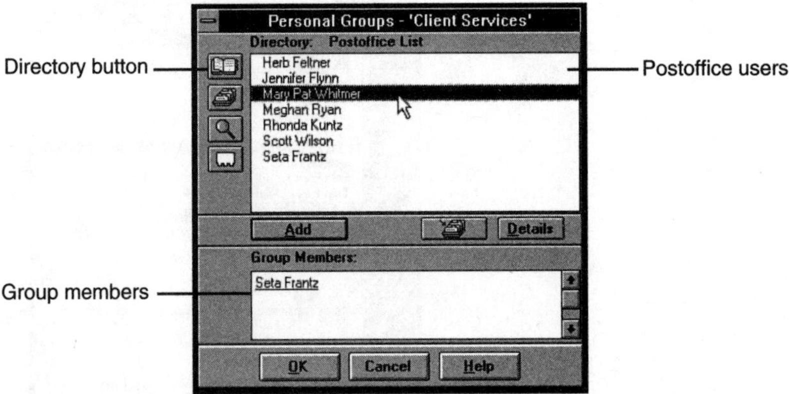

Figure 13.3 Select the users for your new group with this dialog box.

Need to Switch to a Different Postoffice? If you need to add a user from a different postoffice, click on the **Directory** button or press **Ctrl+L**. Select the postoffice you want to access and press **Enter**.

6. Select users for your group by double-clicking on them, or highlighting them with the arrow keys and pressing **Enter**. Selected users will appear in the Group Members section of the dialog box, as shown in Figure 13.3.
7. After selecting the last user for the group, press **Enter** or click **OK**, and you will be returned to the Personal Groups dialog box.
8. Repeat steps 3 through 7 to create additional groups. Press **Esc** or click on the **Control-menu** button when you are done.

Adding and Deleting Users from a Personal Group

From time to time, you may need to add or delete members from your personal groups. Follow these steps to add a new member to a personal group:

1. Open the **Mail** menu by clicking on it or pressing **Alt+M**.
2. Select the **Personal Groups** command by clicking on it or pressing **G**. The Personal Groups dialog box shown in Figure 13.2 will appear.
3. Select a group to edit by clicking on it or highlighting it with the arrow keys and pressing **Enter**.
4. Click on **Edit** or press **Alt+E**. The selected address book will appear, as shown in Figure 13.3.
5. Select a user by clicking on the user's name or highlighting it with the arrow keys.
6. To add the selected user, press **Enter**.
7. Repeat steps 5 and 6 to add additional users to the group.
8. When you are done, press **Ctrl+O** or click **OK**, and you will be returned to the Personal Groups dialog box.
9. Repeat steps 3 through 8 to edit a different personal group. Press **Esc** when you are done.

Follow these steps to delete users from a personal group:

1. Open the **Mail** menu by clicking on it or pressing **Alt+M**.
2. Select the **Personal Groups** command by clicking on it or pressing **G**. The Personal Groups dialog box shown in Figure 13.2 will appear.
3. Select a group to edit by clicking on it or highlighting it with the arrow keys and pressing **Enter**.
4. Click on **Edit** or press **Alt+E**. The selected address book will appear, as shown in Figure 13.3.
5. Press **Tab** to move to the Group Members area.
6. Select a user by clicking on the user's name or moving to the first letter of the user's name with the arrow keys.
7. To delete the selected user, press **Delete**. If necessary, delete any leftover semicolons.
8. Repeat steps 5 and 6 to delete additional users from the group.
9. When you are done, press **Ctrl+O** or click **OK**, and you will be returned to the Personal Groups dialog box.
10. Repeat steps 3 through 9 to edit a different personal group. Press **Esc** when you are done.

In this lesson, you learned how to create a personal group and how to add and delete group members. In the next lesson, you will learn how to use a personal group to address a message.

Using a Personal Group

In this lesson, you will learn how to use your personal groups when addressing messages.

Sending Messages to a Personal Group

Sending messages to a personal group is as easy as sending messages to a single user:

1. Click the **Compose** button on the tool bar or press **Ctrl+N**, or open the **Mail** menu (press **Alt+M**) and select the **Compose Note** command (press N).
2. Click on the **Address** button or press **Alt+D**. The Address window appears.
3. If necessary, press **Ctrl+P** or click on the **Personal Address Book** button to change to your personal address book as shown in Figure 14.1.

Personal Address Book button

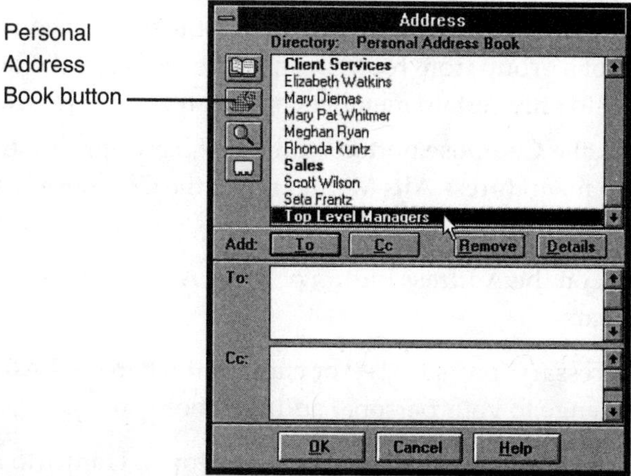

Figure 14.1 The Address window.

4. Use the **arrow** keys, **Page Up**, **Page Down**, **Home**, or **End** to highlight a personal group.
5. Press **Enter** or click the **To** button to send a message to the selected group.
6. If you want, select another group or a single user and press **Alt+C** or click the **Cc** button to courtesy copy the message to them.
7. When you are done addressing your message, press **Enter** or click **OK** to return to the Send Note window. Complete the message and send it in the normal manner, as described in Lesson 5.

The message will be sent to all members in the group, plus any additional users you may have selected.

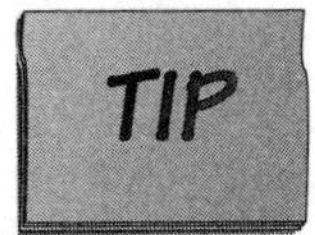

Direct Mail You can simply type in a group's name in the **To** or **Cc** boxes of the Send Note window, instead of selecting it from the Address dialog box. Make sure, however, that you spell the name correctly so it will match the group name found in your personal address book.

Sending Mail to Selected Members of a Group

Having personal groups set up can make it easy to send messages to large numbers of people. However, there may be times when you need to exclude some members of a group from receiving a single message. Follow these steps to send a message to only certain members of a group:

1. Click the **Compose** button on the tool bar or press **Ctrl+N**, or open the **Mail** menu (press **Alt+M**) and select the **Compose Note** command (press **N**).
2. Click on the **Address** button or press **Alt+D**. The Address window appears.
3. If necessary, press **Ctrl+P** or click on the **Personal Address Book** button to change to your personal address book.
4. Use the **arrow** keys, **Page Up**, **Page Down**, **Home** (to move to the first name in the list), or **End** to highlight a personal group.

5. Click on **Details** or press **Alt+D**. The Group Detail window opens, as shown in Figure 14.2.

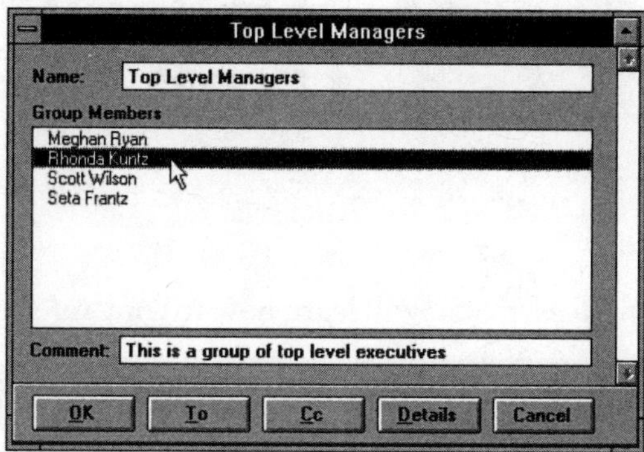

Figure 14.2 You can view the members of a group from the Group Detail window.

6. To send a message to only certain members of a group, select them from the list:

   With the mouse: Press and hold the **Ctrl** key as you click on the names of the users you want to select. To select a contiguous range of users, click on the first user in the range, press and hold the **Shift** key, and click on the last user in the range.

   With the keyboard: Press and hold the **Ctrl** key as you highlight individual names by using the arrow keys to move up or down the list. When you have the user's name highlighted, press the **Spacebar** to select it from the list.

7. When you have selected the users you want to send a message to, click the **To** button or press **Alt+T**.

8. Repeat steps 3 through 5 to send courtesy copies to another group or to selected users. Select the users you want and press **Alt+C** or click the **Cc** button to send a courtesy copy of the message to them.

9. When you are finished addressing your message, send it in the normal manner, as described in Lesson 5. The message will be sent to only those group members listed in the **To** or **Cc** boxes of the Send Note window.

In this lesson, you learned how to send messages to all the members of a group or to only selected members. In the next lesson, you will learn how to include files with your messages.

15 Copying Information from a File

In this lesson, you will learn how to copy information from a file into a message.

Copying Information into a Message

With Mail, you can copy information from a file into a message, instead of retyping it. For example, you could copy text into a Mail message from a report that was originally created in Word for Windows. Or you could copy spreadsheet data instead of re-entering it. (Beware: there are some special problems that occur when copying data that has to retain some type of format, such as data that appears in columns. You'll learn how to cope with this problem later in this lesson.) Follow these instructions to copy information:

1. Start Mail and create a new message or open an existing one.
2. Start the original application and open the file which contains the information you want to include in your message.

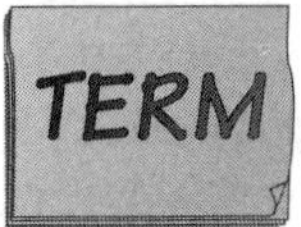

Original Application The program (such as Word for Windows) that was used to create the file whose information you now want to include in your Mail message.

3. Select the information you want to copy.
4. Open the **Edit** menu by clicking on it or pressing **Alt+E**.
5. Select the **Copy** command by clicking on it or pressing **C**. This will copy the selected information to the Clipboard.

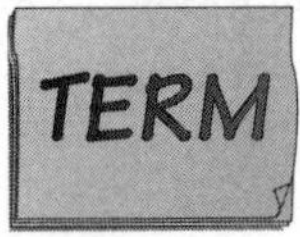

Clipboard A special area in memory that Windows uses to hold information as it is copied or moved from one document to another.

6. Move to the place in the Mail message where you want the information copied.
7. In the **Send Note** window, open the **Edit** menu by clicking on it or pressing **Alt+E**.
8. Select the **Paste** command by clicking on it or pressing **P**. The information on the Clipboard will be copied to your current location in the open message, as shown in Figure 15.1.

Didn't Copy? Most DOS applications do not access the Clipboard correctly, so you may not be able to copy information from their files. You can insert an entire file by following the instructions for inserting text files later in this lesson.

Original information in spreadsheet

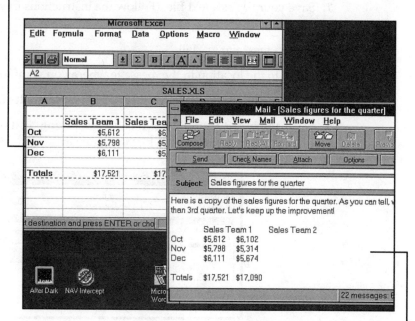

Information copied into mail messages

Figure 15.1 You can copy information from a pre-existing file into a message.

Line Up, Please! Information copied in this manner will lose the formatting created in the host application. For example, the spreadsheet information shown in Figure 15.1 has lost its column alignment and the bold formatting that had been applied to the headings. Follow the instructions in Lesson 18 to learn how to copy information from a file and retain its formatting.

Copying an Entire Text File into a Message

If you have a file created in a DOS application, chances are you will not be able to simply copy text from that file into a Mail message. Because most DOS applications cannot access the Windows Clipboard, the copy instructions given in the previous section will not work. You can, however, copy the entire contents of a text file into a message by following these instructions:

1. Save your file as a text file. (Follow the instructions in your application's manual.)
2. Open a message in Mail.
3. Move to the location in the message where you want to insert the text file.
4. Open the **Edit** menu by clicking on it or pressing **Alt+E**.
5. Select the **Insert from File** command by clicking on it or pressing **F**. The dialog box shown in Figure 15.2 will appear.

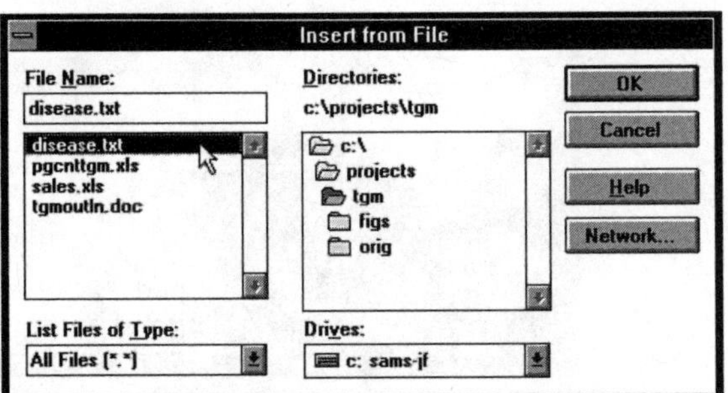

Figure 15.2 You can insert a complete text file into a message using this dialog box.

6. Select the text file you want to insert into your message and press **Enter**. The entire contents of the text file is inserted at your current location in the message. You can delete any part of the text file once it is inserted.

Including Files and Messages

In this lesson, you will learn how to include files with messages.

Attaching a File to a Message

You can send a complete file with a message if you want. Using this method, you can send any file with your message, such as a document file (even one created with a DOS application), a program, or a batch file. A copy of the file or files is attached to the message and sent as a big package to the recipient.

If the recipient has the same application that the file was created in, she can open the file from the Read Message window and edit it. For example, if you created a document using Microsoft Word or even Lotus 1-2-3, you could send that file with a message to one of your co-workers. If your co-worker has the Microsoft Word or Lotus 1-2-3 program, she can open your file and make changes, print it, or do anything else that's necessary. (In this lesson, you'll learn how to send messages with attached files. In the next lesson, you'll learn how to open messages that you receive which have attached files.)

Give Me a Hint Help your recipient identify the original application (the source of the attached file) by mentioning it in your Mail message. Mail will take its best guess and assign an icon to the attached file, but if the proper file associations are not set up, the assigned icon might not be clear.

Follow these instructions to attach a file to a message:

1. Open a new message by clicking on the **Compose** button or pressing **Alt+M**, and then pressing **N**.
2. Enter any message you would like. When you are at the point in the message where you want to attach a file, click on the **Attach** button or press **Alt+A**. The Attach dialog box will appear, as shown in Figure 16.1.

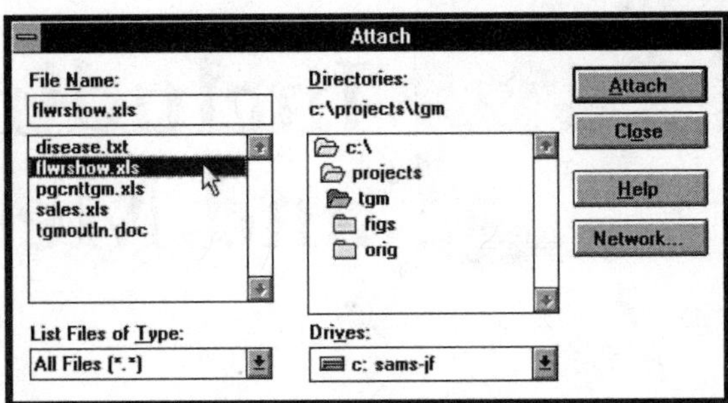

Figure 16.1 You can attach any file you want to a message.

3. Select the file you want to attach and press **Enter**. An icon which represents the file is inserted at the current location within the message, as shown in Figure 16.2.
4. Repeat step 3 for any additional file(s) you want to attach. When you are done, click on the **Close** button or press **Alt+O**.

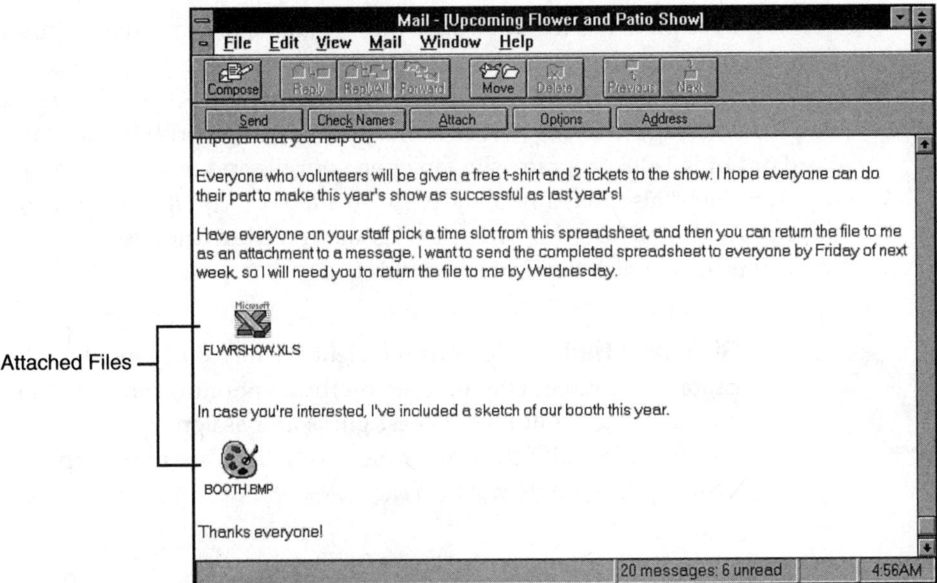

Figure 16.2 A file attached to a message is represented by an icon.

5. Click on the **Send** button or press **Alt+S** to send the message with the attached file(s).

Do You Have Windows 3.1? If so, you can attach a file to a message by dragging that file from the File Manager window onto the message. You can also drag a file onto the Outbox and a message will be created with the file attached.

In this lesson, you learned how to send a file with a message. In the next lesson, you will learn how to work with messages you receive that have files attached.

Working with Attachments to Messages

In this lesson, you will learn how to work with files that are attached to messages.

Opening an Attachment

If you receive a message with a file attached, you can use either the mouse or the keyboard to open the file. Messages with files attached are displayed with a paper clip icon in the Message window.

Do You Have the Right Program? You must have your own copy of the program which was used to create the file in order to open that file in Mail. The icon used to represent the file will give you an idea of the program you need to open that file.

To open an attached file with the mouse:

1. Open the message that contains the attached file.
2. Double-click on the icon which represents the file. The program which created the file is started, with the file open and ready to edit, as shown in Figure 17.1.

To open an attached file with the keyboard:

1. Open the message and move to the icon which represents the file you want to open.
2. Select the icon by pressing the **Shift** key and using the **arrow** keys.
3. Open the **File** menu by pressing **Alt+F**.
4. Select the **Open** command by pressing **O**. The program which created the file is started, with the file open and ready to edit, as shown in Figure 17.1.

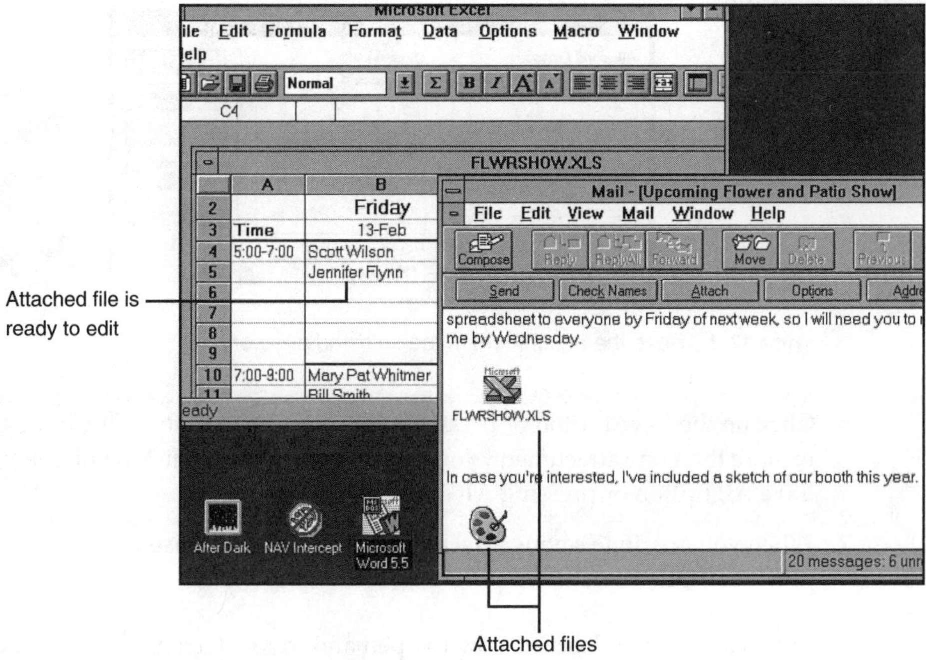

Figure 17.1 You can edit attached files.

Saving an Attached File

When a file is attached to a message and sent, it arrives on your system incorporated into the message. If the message is deleted, so are the attached files. While a file is attached, you can work on it and even save changes, but those changes are still part of the original message package; if the message is deleted, you will lose the file and your changes. It's best to separate the attached file from the original message by using the **Save Attachment** command. You can save an attached file in whatever directory you would like:

1. Open the **File** menu by clicking on it or pressing **Alt+F**.
2. Select the **Save Attachment** command by clicking on it or pressing **A**. The Save Attachment dialog box will appear (see Figure 17.2).
3. Select an attachment from the **Attached Files** list box.
4. Select the drive and directory to use when saving the file.
5. If you want, type a new name for the file in the **File Name** text box.

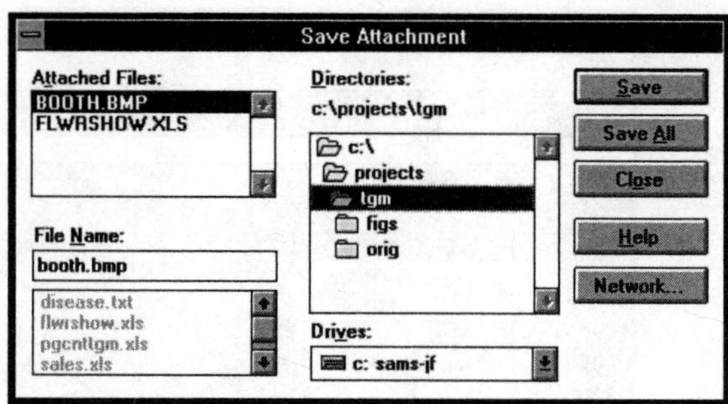

Figure 17.2 Save the attachment in the selected directory.

6. Click on the **Save** button or press **Alt+S** to save the attached file. If there is more than one attachment, you can save them all by clicking on the **Save All** button or pressing **Alt+A**.

7. When you are done saving attachments, click on the **Close** button or press **Alt+O**.

In this lesson, you learned how to open and save attachments. In the next lesson, you will learn how to embed an object in a message.

18 Embedding an Object in a Message

In this lesson, you will learn how to embed an object in a message.

What Is an Object?

Objects can be createdby most Windows applications. Objects are parts of files that retain a relationship with the application which created them. For example, a part of an Ami Pro file that is copied into a message remembers that it is an Ami Pro document. Because of this, objects can be edited by the recipient of your message. Therefore, the recipient of a message with an Ami Pro object embedded in it can open Ami Pro from Mail and edit the object.

Making a Change You can still embed objects in messages, even if the recipient does not have a copy of the originating program. However, without the program, the recipient will not be able to change the embedded object.

Unlike information that is simply copied from a file, embedded objects retain their formatting. For example, in Figure 18.1, the information copied from an Excel spreadsheet has retained its columnar format. (For a comparison, turn back to Figure 15.1, and look at the same data that was simply copied into a message.) An object embedded into a message from a Word for Windows or other word processing document will likewise retain its text formatting (bold, underline, italics, and so on).

So why would you want to simply copy information from a file (as explained in Lesson 15)? Embedding an object (as explained in this lesson) has obvious advantages:

- The data retains its formatting (so it looks better).
- The recipient can work with the data in the original application and make changes.

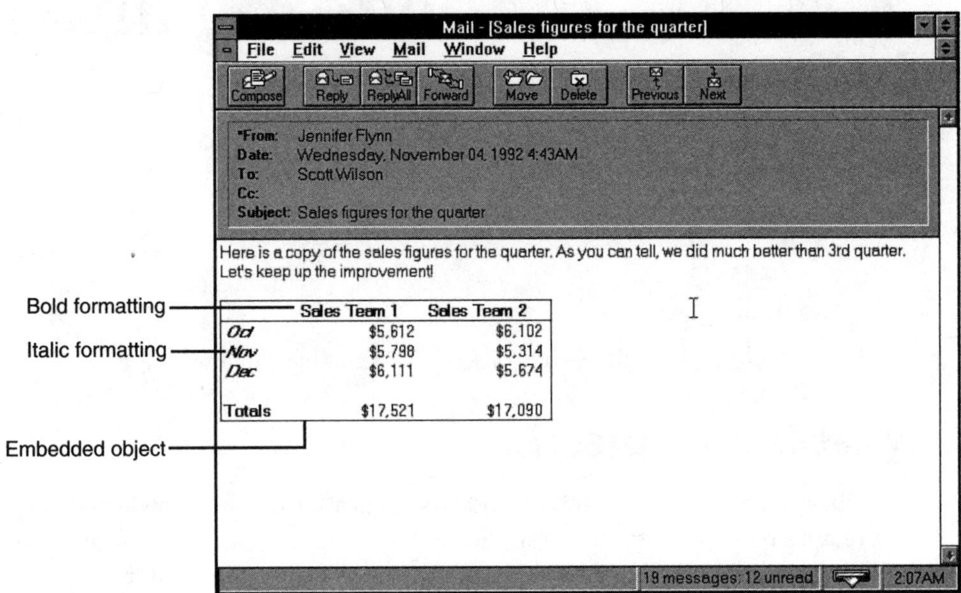

Figure 18.1 An object retains its original formatting.

So when would you copy information, and not embed it? When you have no other choice (the application does not support OLE—object linking and embedding), or the information you're copying does not contain any special formatting, so it doesn't deserve the special treatment.

Embedding an Object in a Message

Follow these steps to embed an object in a message:

1. Start Mail and create a new message or open an existing one.
2. Start the original application and open the file which contains the information you want to embed in your message.
3. Select the information you want to copy.
4. Open the **Edit** menu by clicking on it or pressing **Alt+E**.
5. Select the **Copy** command by clicking on it or pressing **C**. This will copy the selected information to the Clipboard.
6. Move to the place in the Mail message where you want the object embedded.

7. In the Send Note window, open the **Edit** menu by clicking on it or pressing **Alt+E**.
8. Select the **Paste Special** command by clicking on it or pressing **S**. The Paste Special dialog box appears asking you to identify the Data Type.
9. Select the appropriate data type and click on the **Paste** button or press **Alt+P**. The object on the Clipboard will be embedded into your open message in the current location, as shown in Figure 18.2.

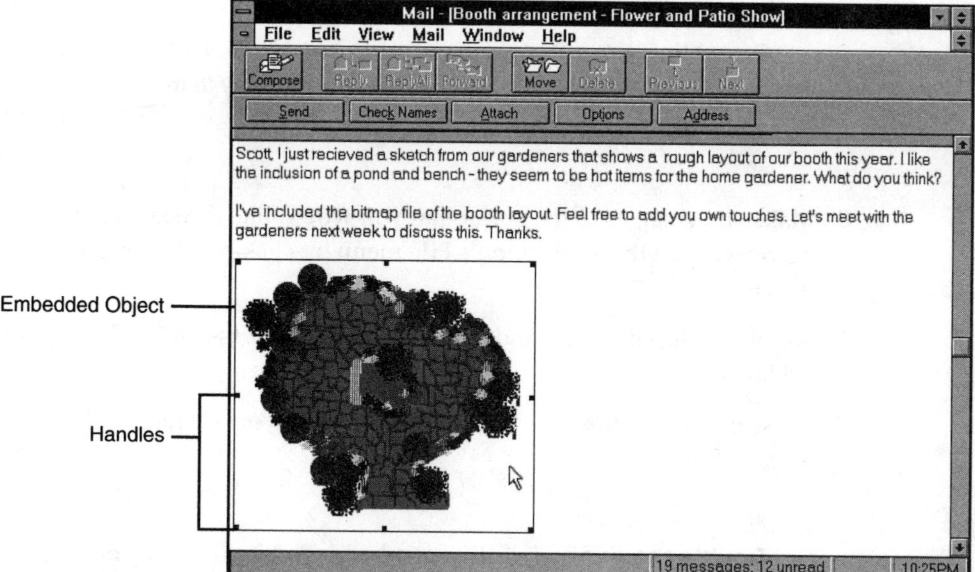

Figure 18.2 You can copy information from a pre-existing file and embed it into a message.

Editing an Embedded Object

You can edit an embedded object in a message you receive or that you're composing. Follow these steps:

1. Open the message that contains the embedded object.
2. Click on the object. If you are using the keyboard, hold the **Shift** key and select the object by using the arrow keys. The object will be surrounded by a box with *handles*.

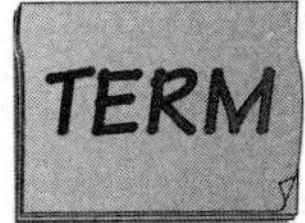

Handles Small boxes that surround an object. You can use these boxes to move and resize the object by dragging them with the mouse.

3. Open the **Edit** menu by clicking on it or pressing **Alt+E**.
4. Select the **Object** command by clicking on it or pressing **O**. The application that was used to create the object opens, with the object ready to edit.

Protecting Your Sources In order to edit an object, you must have a copy of the source application on your system.

5. Make any changes to the object that you would like. To save your changes, open the application's **File** menu by clicking on it or pressing **Alt+F**.
6. Select the **Update** command by clicking on it or pressing **U**. The object is updated.
7. Close the application in the usual manner, and you are returned to Microsoft Mail.

Double the Fun! To edit an embedded object quickly, double-click on it. The application that created the object will open immediately.

In this lesson, you learned how to create and edit embedded objects in a Mail message. In the next lesson, you will learn how to use folders to organize your Mail system.

Using Folders to Organize Mail

In this lesson, you will learn how to use folders to organize your messages.

Creating a Folder

Folders are used to organize the messages you receive. For example, if you are in charge of the Sales department, you might want a folder called Sales.

You can create subfolders if you wish. For example, you could create a subfolder under Sales for each of your salespeople. The Sales folder could hold general sales information and messages, and each subfolder could hold messages sent or received from each salesperson.

Microsoft Mail comes with three folders already set up: Inbox, Sent Mail, and Wastebasket (called Deleted Mail in Workgroups for Windows). These folders each serve a specific purpose; you cannot delete or rename them. To create a folder of your own:

1. Open the **File** menu by clicking on it or pressing **Alt+F**.
2. Select the **New Folder** command by clicking on it or pressing **N**. The New Folder dialog box opens.
3. Enter the name of the folder in the **N**ame text box.
4. If you would like other users to have access to this folder, select **Shared**.
5. To determine where the new folder should be placed, click on the **Options** button or press **Alt+O**. The dialog box expands, as shown in Figure 19.1.
6. Under **Level**, select either **Top Level Folder**, or **Subfolder Of:**. If you select **Subfolder Of:**, select the parent folder from the list box.
7. If this is a shared folder, select the rights you want other users to have: **R**ead, **W**rite, and **D**elete.

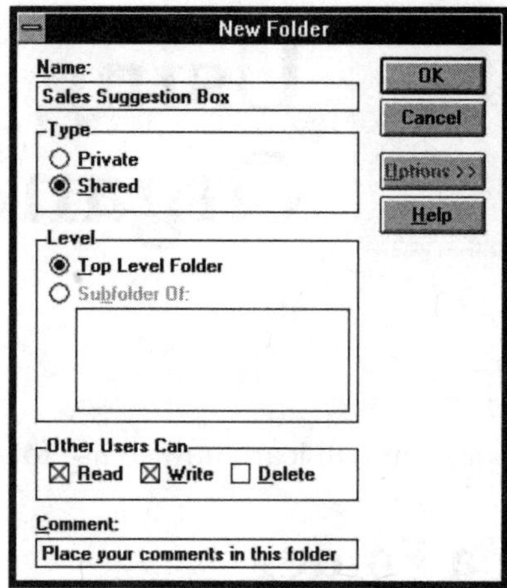

Figure 19.1 The expanded version of the New Folder dialog box.

8. When you are done making selections, click the **OK** button or press **Enter**. The folder is added to the Folder List.

Deleting Folders

When you delete a folder, all of the messages in that folder will also be deleted. To delete a folder:

1. Select the folder from the Folder List by clicking on it or using the arrow keys to highlight it.
2. Press **Delete**. A message box will appear, asking for confirmation.
3. Click the **Yes** button or press **Y** to delete the folder.

Expanding and Collapsing Folders

In the Folder List, folders that contain subfolders *which are currently displayed* (expanded) are marked with a minus sign, as shown in Figure 19.2. Folders that contain subfolders *which are not currently displayed* (collapsed) are marked with a plus sign. You can expand and collapse the Folder List to customize the display.

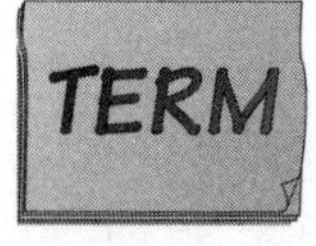

Collapsed and Expanded Folders Collapsed folders are those which do not currently display their subfolders (marked with a plus). Expanded folders are those which currently display their subfolders (marked with a minus).

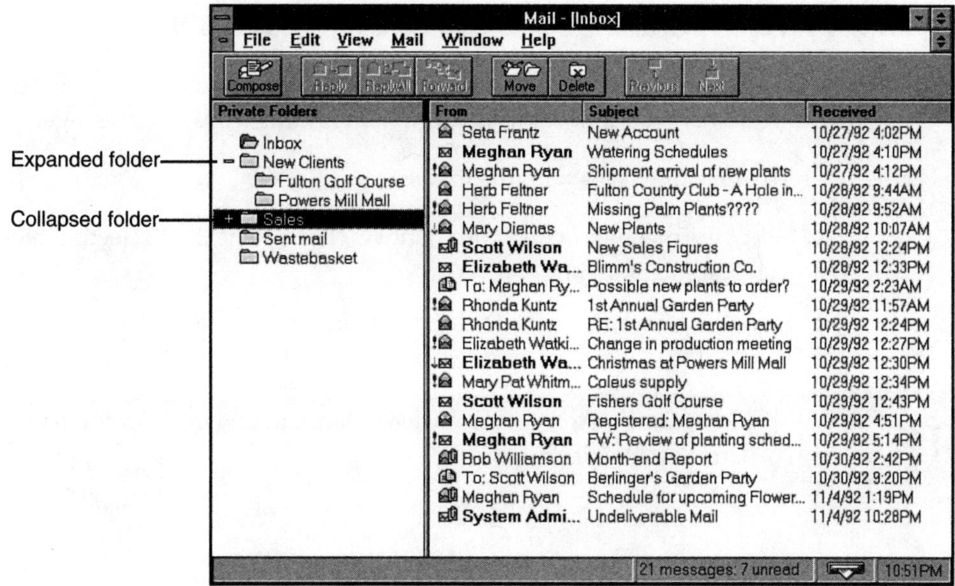

Figure 19.2 Folders that contain subfolders are marked with a plus or a minus.

To collapse a folder:

1. Select the folder by clicking on it or highlighting it with the arrow keys.
2. Press the - key.

To expand a folder:

1. Select the folder by clicking on it or highlighting it with the arrow keys.
2. Press the + key.

Which Key to Press? It's easy to remember which key to press when customizing your Folder List. A collapsed folder is displayed with a + sign. To expand it, use the + key! The same holds true with expanded folders, which are displayed with a - sign, and can be collapsed by pressing -.

Moving Messages Between Folders

To stay organized, move your messages into the appropriate folder after reading them. This way, you'll never have a problem finding a specific message.

To move messages with the mouse:

1. Select the messages you want to move. (For a review on selecting messages, see Lesson 8.)
2. Drag the messages to the folder you want them to reside in.

Copy Cat! To copy files instead of moving them, hold down the **Ctrl** key as you drag the files.

To move messages with the keyboard:

1. Select the messages you want to move. (For a review on selecting messages, see Lesson 8.)
2. Open the **File** menu by pressing **Alt+F**.
3. Select the **Move** command by pressing **M**. The Move Messages dialog box shown in Figure 19.3 will appear.

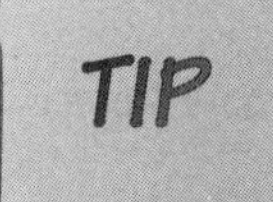

Fast Moves To move messages quickly, select them and press **Ctrl+M**.

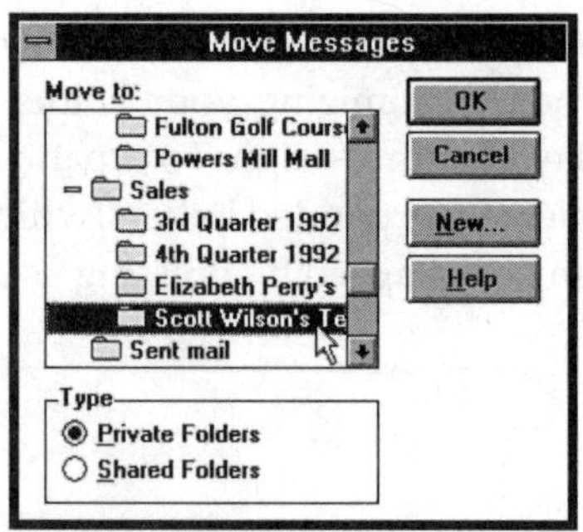

Figure 19.3 The Move Messages dialog box.

4. Select the folder you want the messages moved to by highlighting it with the arrow keys.
5. If you need to create a new folder to move the messages to, press **Alt+N** and enter the name of the new folder.
6. When you have selected a folder, press **Enter** and the messages are moved.

Copy Right! To copy messages instead of moving them, choose the **File Copy** command in step 3.

In this lesson, you learned how to create folders and move messages into them. In the next lesson, you will learn how to find a misplaced message.

Editing Messages

In this lesson, you will learn how to make changes to your messages.

Selecting Text in a Message

Before you can copy, move, or delete text, you must first select it. You can select text with the keyboard or a mouse. To select with the keyboard, follow these steps:

1. Use the arrow keys to move to the first character you want to select.
2. Press and hold the **Shift** key.
3. Using the **arrow** keys, move to the last letter you want to select. Selected text is highlighted, as shown in Figure 20.1.

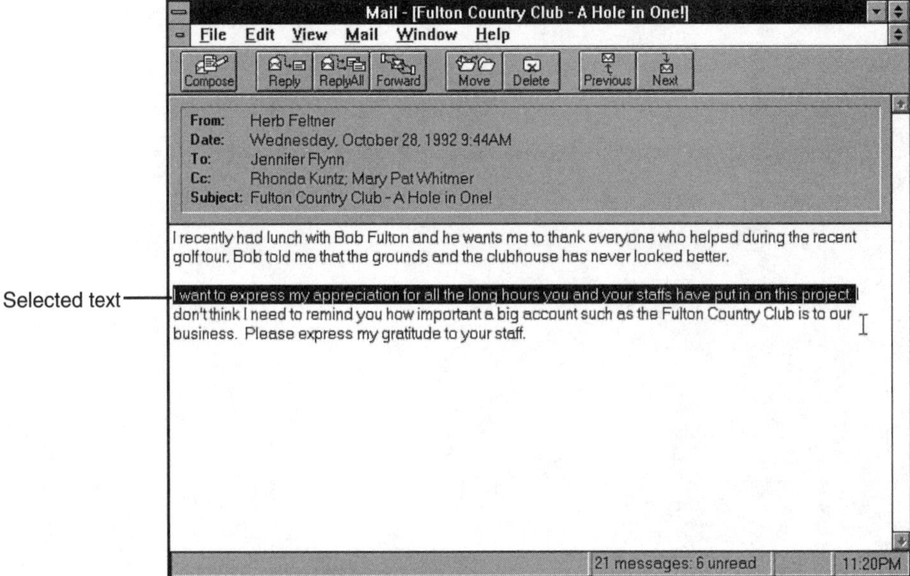

Figure 20.1 Text you select is highlighted.

To select text with a mouse, follow these steps:

1. Click on the first character you want to select. Continue to hold the mouse button down.
2. Drag the mouse pointer to the last character you want to select, and release the mouse button. The selected text is highlighted, as shown in Figure 20.1.

Copying Message Text

When you copy text, the original text is left in its current location, and a copy is placed wherever you like. Once text has been selected, it can be copied to another message or to an additional place in the same message. Follow these steps:

1. Select the text you want to copy.
2. Open the **Edit** menu by clicking on it or pressing **Alt+E**.
3. Select the **Copy** command by clicking on it or pressing **C**. The selected text is copied to the Windows Clipboard.
4. If you want to copy the text to another message, open that message now.
5. Move the cursor to the location in the message where you would like to place the selected text.
6. Open the **Edit** menu by clicking on it or pressing **Alt+E**.
7. Select the **Paste** command by clicking on it or pressing **P**. The selected text is copied to the current location.

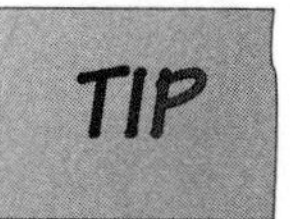

Fast Copy Instead of using the Edit Copy command, you can select the text to be copied and press **Ctrl+C**. To paste the text into its new location, press **Ctrl+V**.

Moving Message Text

When you move text, the original text is deleted from its current location and placed wherever you indicate. Once text has been selected, it can be moved to another message, or to an additional place in the same message. Follow these steps:

1. Select the text you want to move.
2. Open the **Edit** menu by clicking on it or pressing **Alt+E**.
3. Select the **Cut** command by clicking on it or pressing **T**. The selected text is moved to the Windows Clipboard.
4. If you want to move the text to another message, open that message now.
5. Move the cursor to the location in the message where you would like to place the selected text.
6. Open the **Edit** menu by clicking on it or pressing **Alt+E**.
7. Select the **Paste** command by clicking on it or pressing **P**. The selected text is moved to the current location.

Fast Moves Instead of using the Edit Cut command, you can select the text to be moved and press **Ctrl+X**. To paste the text into its new location, press **Ctrl+V**.

Deleting Message Text

You can easily delete selected text. Follow these steps:

1. Select the text you want to delete.
2. Press the **Delete** key.

In this lesson, you learned how to copy, move, and delete text within a message. In the next lesson, you will learn how to spell check your messages.

Using the Spelling Checker

In this lesson, you will learn how to use the spelling checker to proofread your messages.

Spell Checking a Message

Nothing is more embarrassing than a misspelled word—especially if the message was sent to your boss. You can save yourself potential embarrassment by checking your messages before you send them.

Windows for Workgroups Users The Spelling option is not included with your Mail program. If you need to spell check a message, copy the text into your word processor and spell check it there.

Horrible Speller? You can have every message automatically spell checked before it is sent. See Lesson 23 for more details.

You can use the spelling checker to check the spelling of a single word, a paragraph, or an entire message. Follow these instructions to spell check a message:

1. If you want to spell check only part of a message, select the text you want to check. Do not select any text at all if you want to spell check the entire message.
2. Open the **Edit** menu by clicking on it or pressing **Alt+E**.

3. Select the **Spelling** command by clicking on it or pressing **L**.
4. When the spelling checker encounters a misspelled word, the Spelling dialog box will appear, as shown in Figure 21.1.

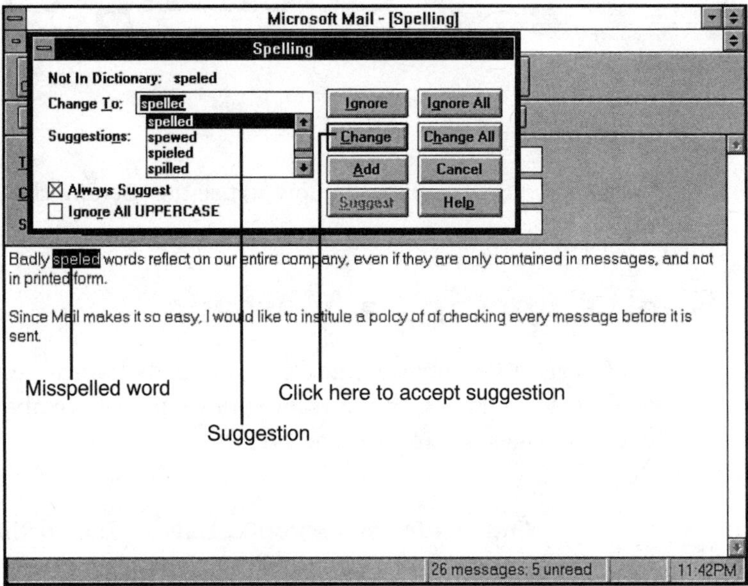

Figure 21.1 Select an option to correct your misspelled word.

5. To correct the misspelled word, either:
   - Enter the correct spelling in the Change **T**o: text box.

     OR

   - Ask the spelling checker to provide suggestions by clicking the **Suggest** button or pressing **Alt+S**. Select a suggested word from the Suggestio**n**s list box by clicking on it or highlighting it with the arrow keys.

May I Make a Suggestion? The spelling checker will provide suggestions automatically if you select the Always Suggest check box.

The spelling checker provides additional options for dealing with misspelled words. Press **Alt** plus the bold letter to select the option with the keyboard, or click on the button with your mouse:

Ignore—Ignore the word and continue spell checking the message.

Ignore All—Ignore all occurrences of this word in the message and do not flag them as misspelled.

Change All—Change all occurrences of the misspelled word automatically.

Add—Add this word to your personal dictionary.

Suggest—Suggest a correct spelling for the word.

Ignore All UPPERCASE—Ignore any word that is in uppercase.

Quick Spell You can quickly spell check a document by pressing **F7**.

Correcting Duplicate Words

If you type the same word twice in a row, as in the sentence below:

This sentence contains a duplicate word word.

the spelling checker will display a Spelling dialog box with two additional buttons, as shown in Figure 21.2.

To correct the sentence, select one of these options:

- Select **Delete** to delete the first occurrence of the word.
- Select **Delete All** to delete all duplicate occurrences of the same word.

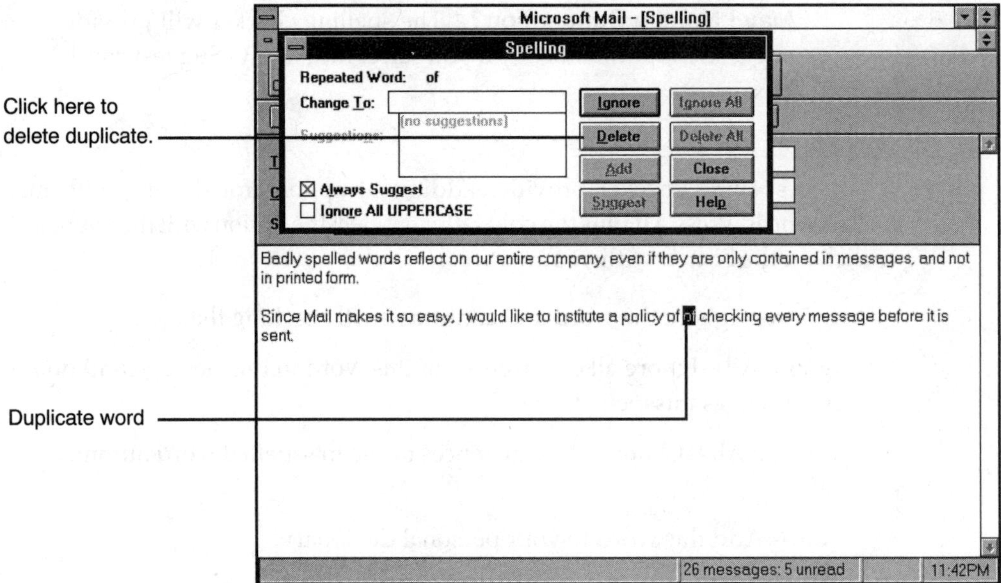

Figure 21.2 The spelling checker also looks for duplicate words.

In this lesson, you learned how to spell check your messages. In the next lesson, you will learn how to print a message.

Printing a Copy of Your Messages

In this lesson, you will learn how to print your messages.

Printing a Message

Before you delete a message, you can print a copy of it for your files. To print message(s), follow these steps:

1. Select the messages you want to print from the message list. (See Lesson 8 for instructions on selecting more than one message.)
2. Open the **File** menu by clicking on it or pressing **Alt+F**.
3. Select the **Print** command by clicking on it or pressing **P**. The Print dialog box will appear, as shown in Figure 22.1.
4. You can choose to have each message printed on a separate page by deselecting the **Print Multiple Notes** on a Page check box.

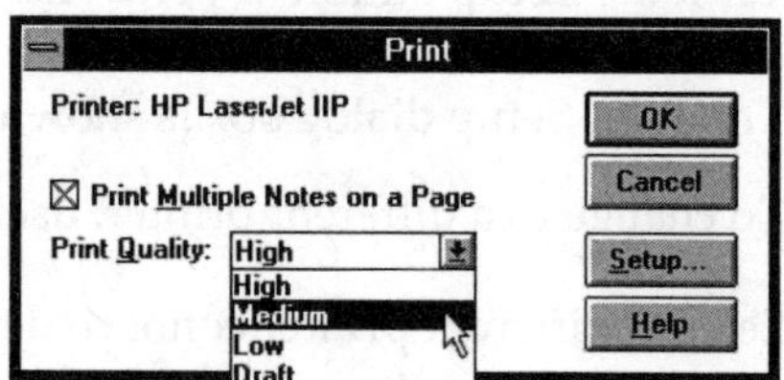

Figure 22.1 The Print dialog box.

5. You can lower the level of print quality (and reduce the amount of time it takes to print the messages) by using the Print **Q**uality drop-down list box.
6. You can change your print setup (described in the next section) by clicking on the **Setup** button or pressing **Alt+S**.
7. When you are ready to print, press **Enter** or click **OK**.

Singles You can print a single message after reading it by using these same instructions. Simply access the **File** menu from the Read Note window.

Quick Print To print selected messages quickly, simply press **Ctrl+P**.

Printing Attached Files When you print a message, embedded objects will also print, but not attached files. To print attached files, print from the application that created the file.

Changing Your Print Setup

You can change the printer you use to print your messages by using the Print Setup dialog box. You can access the Print Setup dialog box in one of two ways:

- Open the **File** menu (press **Alt+F**) and select the **Print Setup** command (press **R**).

  OR

- Click the **Setup** button or press **Alt+S** from the Print dialog box.

  The Print Setup dialog box is shown in Figure 22.2.

  To change to a different printer, use one of the following methods:

- Select a different printer connected to your computer by using the **Specific Printer** drop-down list box.

  OR

- Select a network printer with the **Network...** button. Connecting to a network printer is covered in more detail in a later section of this lesson.

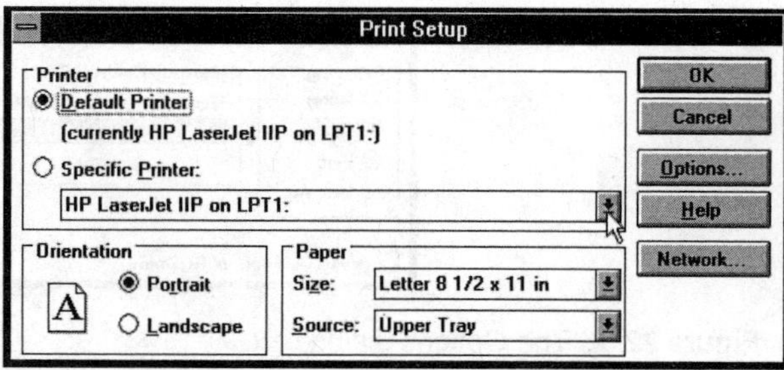

Figure 22.2 The Print Setup dialog box.

You can change the orientation of the printed message between Portrait (the default) and Landscape. Simply click on the appropriate option button or press **Alt+R** for Portrait or **Alt+L** for Landscape.

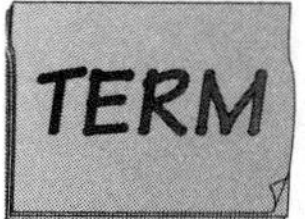

Portrait vs. Landscape Landscape orientation means that the message is printed along the paper's widest edge, as in 11" x 8 ½". Portrait orientation for the same size paper prints the message as 8 ½" x 11".

You can change the paper size or source by using the appropriate drop-down list box. Press **Alt+Z** to change the paper size and **Alt+S** to change the source.

Changing Printer Options

You can adjust the quality of your printed messages through the Options dialog box. To access the Options dialog box, click on the **Options** button in the Print dialog box or press **Alt+O**. The Options dialog box is shown in Figure 22.3.

If you have a laser printer, you can choose from these dithering options: None, Course, Fine, Line Art. Additional time may be required to print messages of different dithering. Use this option to improve the quality of graphics included in your messages. If you have a dot matrix printer, use the Gray scale option to improve the quality of your graphic images.

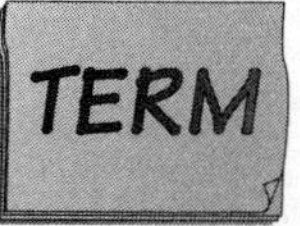

Dithering Adjusts the quality (detail) of printed graphics.

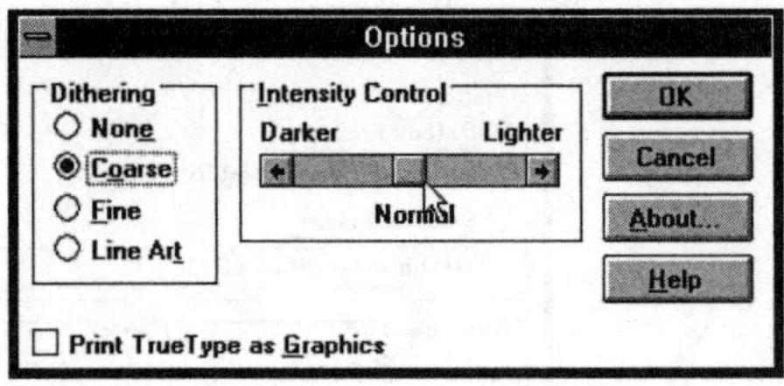

Figure 22.3 The Options dialog box.

You can darken the text of your messages (like a copier) by changing the intensity. With a laser printer, drag the scroll box to the left or right, or press **Alt+I** and use the arrow keys to move the scroll box. With a dot matrix printer, use the **Duplex** option to darken the text.

If you use Windows' Truetype fonts, you can have them printed as graphics by selecting the **Print Truetype as Graphics** option. Using this option will require less printer memory and less time. This option works best when you have a lot of graphics in a message and only one or two Truetype fonts.

Keep Your Options Open Additional options may appear in the Options dialog box, depending on the type of printer you have.

Printing Your Messages on a Network Printer

Often the printer which is connected to your network server is of a better quality than the printer connected to your computer. To use a network printer to print your messages, use the Connect Network Printer dialog box, shown in Figure 22.4. To access the Connect Network Printer dialog box, use the **Network...** button from the Print Setup dialog box.

Use the Device Name drop-down list box to select the device to connect to from among the available printer ports on your computer. LPT1 is typically assigned to your local printer, so you may want to select a different printer port to retain access to both the network printer and your local printer.

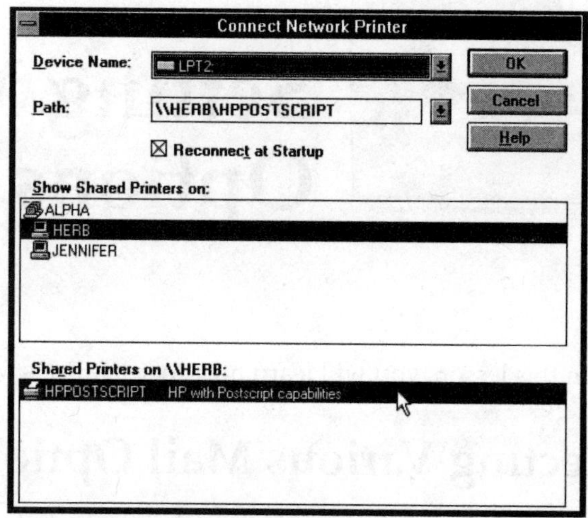

Figure 22.4 The Connect Network Printer dialog box.

To display a list of available network printers, either select the network path to the printer in the **P**ath drop-down list box, or select a computer from those listed under the **S**how Shared Printers on: area. For example, by selecting the computer marked HERB, any shared printer that is connected to HERB will be displayed in the Shared Printers area. Once a path has been identified, a list of available printers will appear in the Shared Printers area. Select one of the listed printers, and press **Enter** or click **OK**. Your messages will print on the selected network printer. Check the Reconnec**t** at Startup option if you would like to automatically connect to the network printer each time you start Windows.

In this lesson, you learned how to print your messages. In the next lesson, you will learn how to set various Mail options.

23 Setting Mail Options

In this lesson, you will learn how to set various Mail options.

Selecting Various Mail Options

You can change various Mail options through the Options dialog box. To access the Options dialog box:

1. Open the **Mail** menu by clicking on it or pressing **Alt+M**.
2. Select the **Options** command by clicking on it or pressing **O**. The Options dialog box will appear, as shown in Figure 23.1.

Through this dialog box, you can change what happens when Mail sends, receives, or discards messages.

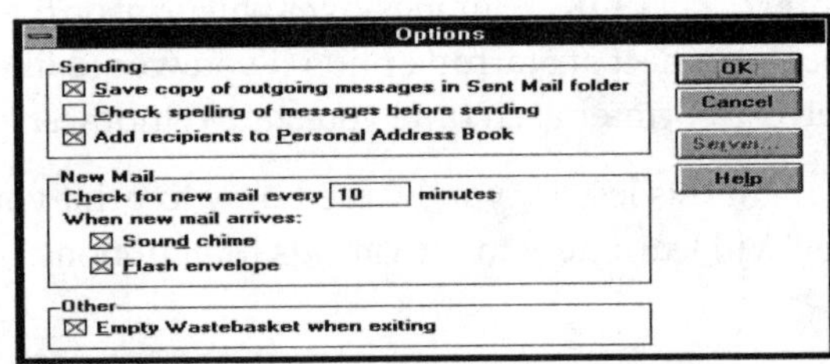

Figure 23.1 The Options dialog box.

Changing the Options for Mail You Send

There are three options you can change which affect mail that you send:

- Save copy of outgoing messages in Sent Mail folder—This option is on by default. If you turn this option off, Mail will not save copies of the messages you send.

- Check spelling of messages before sending—When this option is on, Mail will check the spelling of all messages before they are sent. This option increases the amount of time it takes to send a message. To spell check an individual message, see Lesson 21.
- Add recipients to Personal Address Book—This option is on by default. When this option is on, your message recipients will be added to your personal address book.

Changing Options for Mail You Receive

There are three options you can change which affect mail that you receive:

- Check for new mail every XXXX minutes—Change how often Mail checks the network for messages. You can enter any number of minutes from 1 to 9999.
- Sound chime—This option is on by default. If this option is on, a chime will sound whenever you receive a message.
- Flash envelope—This option is on by default. If this option is on, an envelope will flash on the cursor whenever a message is received.

Changing Other Mail Options

There are a few additional Mail options you can select:

- Empty Wastebasket when exiting—This option is on by default. If you recall from Lesson 8, when you delete a message, it is not actually deleted, but moved to the Wastebasket folder. If this option is on, the messages that you've indicated for deletion will be permanently deleted when you log out of Mail. If this option is not on, messages marked for deletion will accumulate in the Wastebasket folder until you delete them yourself.

Windows for Workgroups Users Your delete folder is called Deleted Mail, not Wastebasket.

- Server—Use this command button to access additional server related options, such as the location of your message file. Options vary by system.

In this lesson, you learned how to change various Mail options. In the next lesson, you will learn how to create a message template for messages you send often.

Creating a Message Template

In this lesson, you will learn how to create a message template for messages that you send often.

Saving the Message Template

You can create a message template (a message that contains information that can be reused) for messages that you send often. A sample template is shown in Figure 24.1.

Creating a message template is similar to saving an unsent message. To create the template, follow these steps:

1. Compose a new message. Enter only the information (such as recipient names, etc.) that doesn't change.
2. After entering your template information, press **Ctrl+F4** or double-click the **Close** box.
3. A dialog box will appear. Answer yes by clicking on the **Yes** button, or pressing **Y**.

Organize Your Templates Store your template in a special folder called Templates so you can locate them easily. See Lesson 19 for details on creating folders.

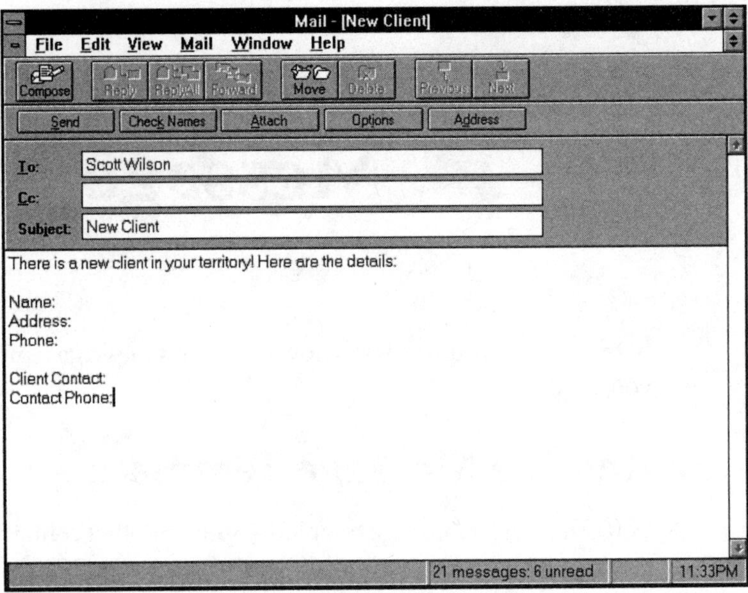

Figure 24.1 Create a message template for basic messages that you send often.

Using Your Message Template

When you are ready to use your message template, follow these steps:

1. Select the message from the message list and click the **Forward** button or press **Ctrl+F**. Your message template will appear.
2. Add or change any information you need. Click the **Send** button or press **Alt+S** to send your message. Your original template remains in your message file.

Drag and Drop You can drag the message template to the **Outbox** instead of clicking the **Forward** button.

In this lesson, you learned how to create and use message templates. In the next lesson, you will learn how to back up your messages.

Maintaining Your Mail System

In this lesson, you will learn how to archive (back up) your messages.

Archiving Your Messages

You should perform regular backups of your system, including your message file.

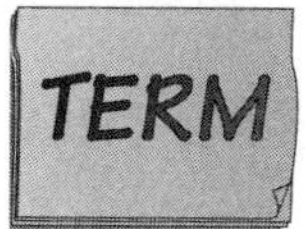

Message File The file MSMAIL.MMF is where all of your messages are stored. This file can be kept either on your computer or on the server.

Even if you perform regular backups on your own system, if your message file is on the server of your network, it may not be backed up. If your message file is damaged or deleted, you will lose all of your messages if you don't have a backup of your message file. For this reason, you should back up your message file often.

To perform a backup of your message file:

1. Open the **Mail** menu by clicking on it or pressing **Alt+M**.
2. Select the **Backup** command by clicking on it or pressing **B**. The Backup dialog box will appear, as shown in Figure 25.1.
3. Enter the name of your backup file. You can call it anything you like using up to eight characters. The filename extension should be .MMF, as in BACKUP.MMF.
4. If you want, you can change the drive and directory that will be used to store the file.
5. When you are ready to backup your message file, press **Enter** or click **OK**. A copy of your message file is saved under the name you indicated.

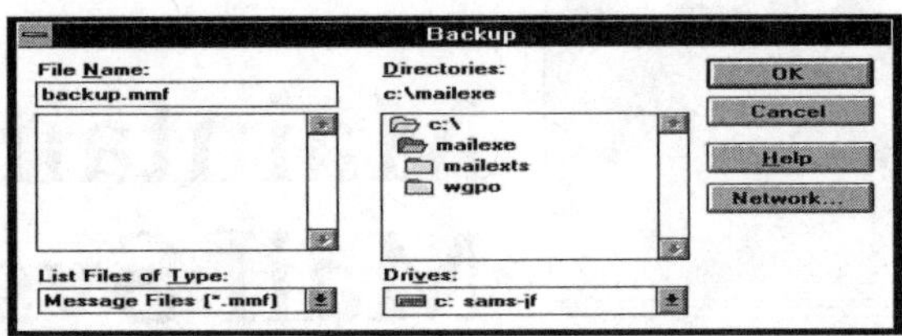

Figure 25.1 The Backup dialog box.

Back Up What You Say You should perform a backup of your message file at least once a week, or more often if you receive a lot of important messages. As added protection, you can copy your message file onto a diskette (in case something happens to your hard drive).

What To Do If Your Message File Is Damaged

If your message file is damaged or deleted, you will receive a warning when you log into Mail. Press **Enter**, and the Open Message File dialog box will appear, as shown in Figure 25.2.

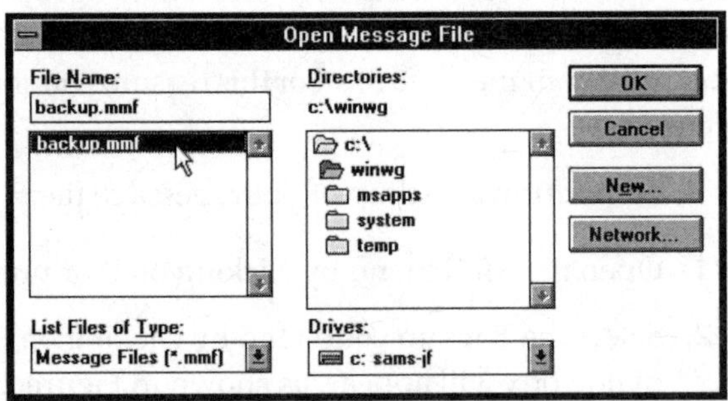

Figure 25.2 The Open Message File dialog box.

Follow these steps to restore your message file:

1. Select your backup file from the file list. If necessary, change drives and directories until you locate your backup file.

2. If you want to create a new message file (because you don't have a backup), click on **New** or press **Alt+E**.
3. After you've selected your backup file, press **Enter** or click **OK**.
4. You will see the message: **This message file is a backup file. Would you like to make it your primary message file?** Click on **Yes** or press **Alt+Y**. Your backup file will be converted for use as your regular message file.

If You Don't Convert Your Backup File If you answer **No** to the message in step 4, your backup file will not be converted, but it will be opened. You will then be able to move, copy, and delete the messages in the file. New messages you receive will not be saved in this file. When you log back into Mail at a later time, you will receive the same error message as before: **Your message file could not be found.** For this reason, you should always answer **Yes** to convert your backup file.

In this lesson, you learned how to back up your message file and how to restore it if the message file becomes damaged. In the next lesson, you will learn how to send messages through Schedule+.

26 Scheduling Meetings with Schedule+

In this lesson, you will learn how to send messages through Schedule+.

What Is Schedule+ ?

Schedule+ is an appointment and task scheduler by Microsoft which is available separate from Microsoft Mail. (Schedule+ comes free with Windows for Workgroups.)

Schedule+ is an electronic day planner which you can use to schedule your appointments, meetings, and daily tasks. You can respond to requests for meetings sent by Schedule+ from within Microsoft Mail. Likewise, you can read replies to your own meeting requests as you would any other Mail message.

Sending a Request for a Meeting

Schedule+ contains several windows:

Appointment Book This window displays today's appointments.

Message window Similar in function to the Message window in Mail. Use this window to read and send replies to meeting requests.

Planner This window displays your appointment schedule for several weeks. Meeting requests originate from the Planner window.

One at a Time, Please! You can display only the Appointment Book or the Planner at any one time.

To send a request for a meeting:

1. Change to the Planner window, shown in Figure 26.1.
2. Select a time for the meeting.
3. If necessary, change the names of the attendees by clicking on the **Change** button or pressing **Alt+C**. The Select Attendees dialog box will appear. The Select Attendees dialog box looks and acts just like the Address window explained in Lesson 4.
4. From the Planner window, click on **Request Meeting...** or press **Alt+R**. The Send Request dialog box, shown in Figure 26.2, appears.
5. Enter the purpose of the meeting in the Subject text box.
6. Enter your meeting request.
7. If you'd like to receive a written response, check the **Ask for Responses** check box.
8. When you are ready to send the request, click **Send** or press **Alt+S**.

Schedule+ sends the request for a meeting.

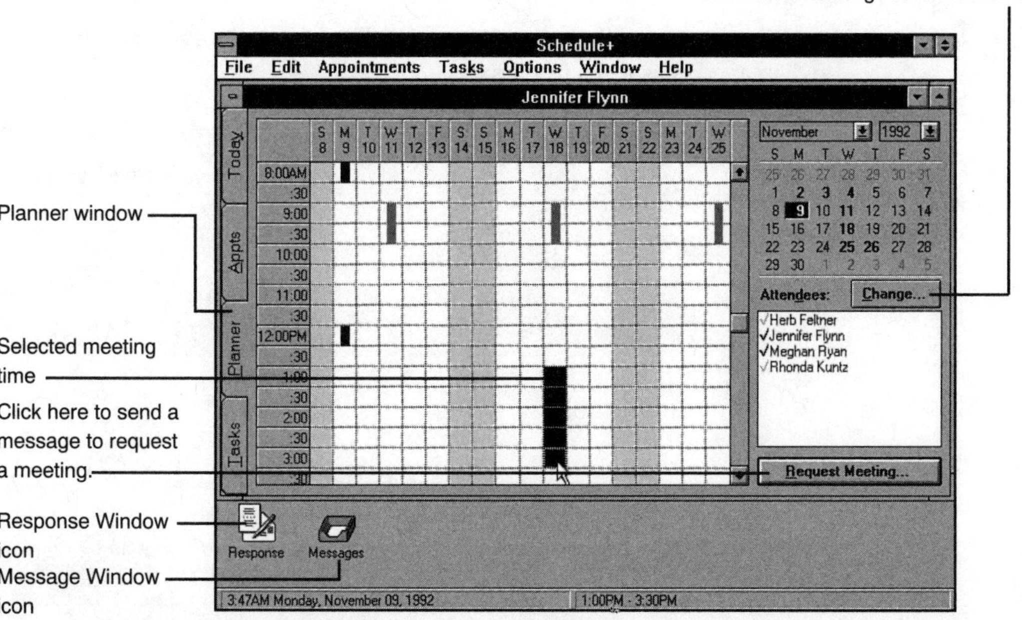

Figure 26.1 Send meeting requests from the Planner window.

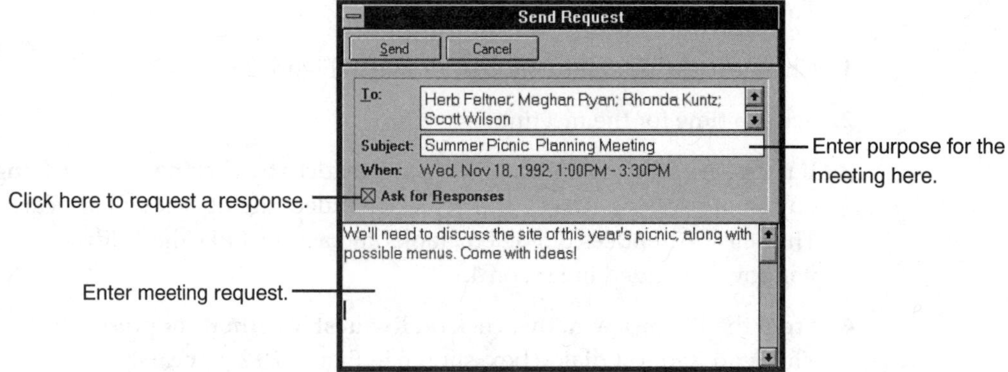

Figure 26.2 Type your request for a meeting into this dialog box.

Responding to a Request for a Meeting

Once a request for a meeting is received, it can be read either in Mail or in Schedule+. Reading the request is similar in both Mail and Schedule+:

1. Select the message from the **Message** window in either Mail or Schedule+. (In Mail, meeting requests look just like any other message.)
2. Press **Enter** to open the meeting request. The Meeting Request dialog will be displayed, as shown in Figure 26.3.

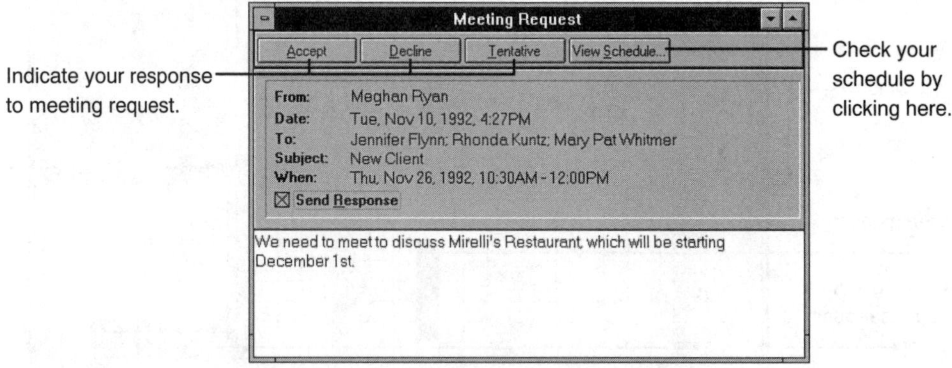

Figure 26.3 We request your presence . . .

To reply to a request for a meeting:

1. If necessary, you can access your schedule (even from within Mail) by clicking **View Schedule** or pressing **Alt+S**.
2. Select your response from the following option buttons:

   Accept—Displays a check mark in front of the message in the Schedule+ Message window, or the word Yes in front of the message in Mail's Message window.

   Decline—Displays an X in front of the message in the Schedule+ Message window, or the word No in front of the message in Mail's Message window.

   Tentative—Displays a question mark in front of the message in the Schedule+ Message window, or the word Tentative in front of the message in Mail's Message window.
3. If a response was requested, a Response dialog box will be displayed. Enter your response to the meeting request, and click **Send**.

Reading a Response to a Meeting Request

Reading a response is similar in Mail and Schedule+:

1. Select the response from the **Message** window in either Mail or Schedule+. (In Mail, meeting responses look just like any other message.)
2. Press **Enter** to open the meeting response. The **Response** window will display, as shown in Figure 26.4.

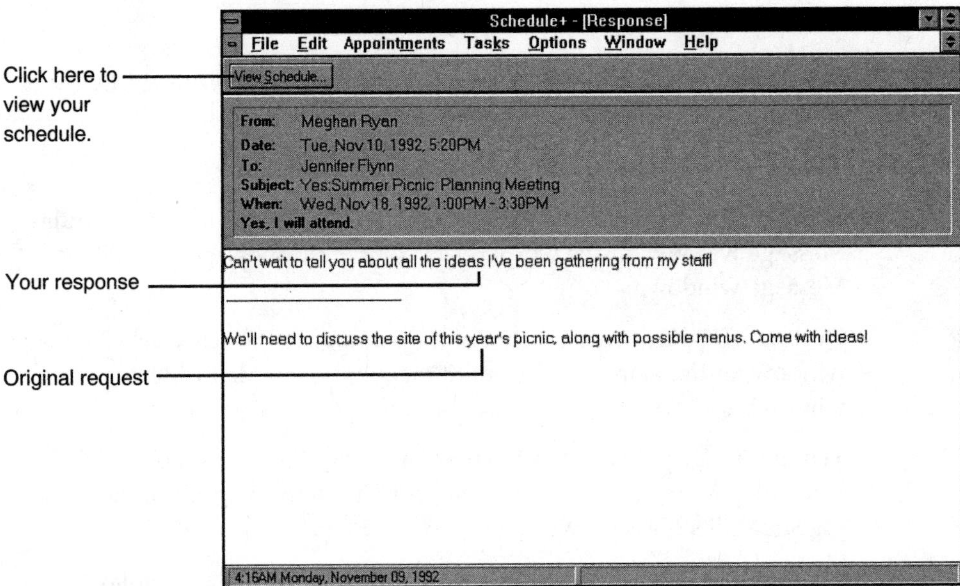

Figure 26.4 You can read the responses to your meeting request in both Mail and Schedule+.

In this lesson, you learned how Schedule+ can be used with Mail to schedule meetings with your co-workers. You should now feel comfortable using Microsoft Mail.

ACCESS

Carl Townsend

1 Getting Started with Microsoft Access

In this lesson, you'll learn what Access is and some basic database concepts, as well as how to start Microsoft Access, examine the basic startup screen, and quit.

What Is Microsoft Access?

Microsoft Access is a popular *database management system* (DBMS). You might think that a database program would be hard to use, but you are in for a nice surprise.

Microsoft took the anxiety out of learning and doing database management, by creating an easy-to-use system called Microsoft Access. This program is so easy to use that you can be doing productive work in a few minutes—using your computer to organize, store, retrieve, manipulate, and print information.

With Microsoft Access, you can:

- Enter and update your data.
- Quickly find the data you need.
- Organize the data in meaningful ways.
- Create reports, forms, and mailing labels quickly from your data.
- Share data with other programs on your system.

The lessons in this book will show you how to use these Access features.

Database Concepts

If you are new at working with databases, here are some basic concepts:

- *Database* A collection of objects for managing facts and figures. A database could be used for keeping track of a videotape library, an inventory, a customer list, or a Christmas card list. A database contains one or more tables, as well as other objects (such as reports). An Access database is stored as a single file.

- *Table* An object in a database that stores facts and figures in two-dimensional form, in rows and columns.
- *Field* A category of information in a table, such as an address, tape title, or customer ID. Fields correspond to the columns of a table.
- *Record* A collection of all facts and figures relating to an item in a table. Records correspond to the rows.
- *Object* An identifiable unit in a database, such as a table, query, report, or form.

More concepts will be introduced in later chapters.

You can think of a database management system as a filing cabinet. Each database is like a hanging folder in the cabinet; the various objects (including the tables) are like manila folders in the hanging folder.

Starting Microsoft Access

Before using Microsoft Access, you must install it on your computer. Once Microsoft Access is installed, you should be able to start it from Windows.

Start Windows by typing **WIN** at the DOS prompt. Program Manager will start automatically under Windows. Make the Microsoft Access group active by clicking on its *group icon* (see Figure 1.1), or by highlighting the group with the arrow keys and pressing **Enter**. If the group is not visible, select it from Program Manager's Window menu. Then start Microsoft Access in either of two ways:

- Double-click on the **Microsoft Access** icon.
- Highlight the icon with the arrow keys, and press **Enter**.

Microsoft Access will start, displaying a Microsoft Access *startup window*. Its menu bar will contain two options: **File** and **Help** (see Figure 1.2). Its tool bar contains a single button, a question mark. From this startup window, you can create or open a database, or perform basic database management.

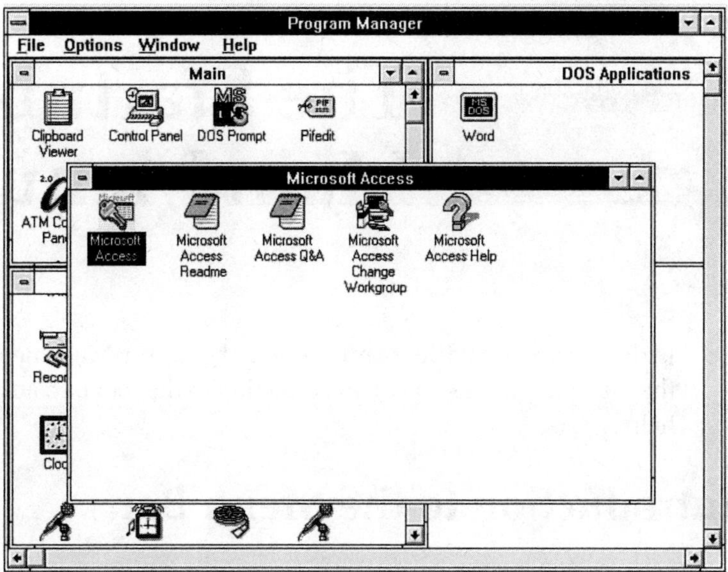

Figure 1.1 The Microsoft Access program group.

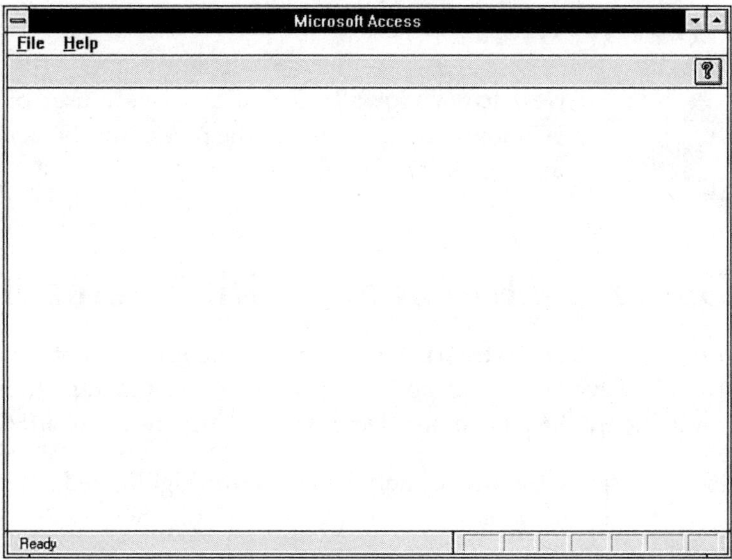

Figure 1.2 The Microsoft Access startup window.

Quitting Microsoft Access

To quit Microsoft Access, double-click on the **Control menu** box or press **Alt+F4**.

2 The Startup Main Menu

In this lesson, you will get a brief look at the startup Main menu options, learn how the menu bar works, get an introduction to the tool bar, and find out how to get help.

Introduction to the Menu Bar

Microsoft Access uses *dynamic menus*; the options on the menu bar change, depending on how you are using the program. When you first start the program, there are only two options: **F**ile and **H**elp. Once you open a database, you will see the menu bar change, and there will be more options.

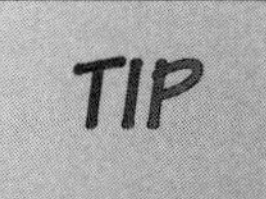

New to Windows? If you are a new user of Windows and Windows applications, see the part of this book on Windows 3.1 for more information.

Using the Keyboard with Microsoft Access

The keyboard is used to type text into a dialog box or database table. You may find the keyboard useful for activating menu commands, though it might be less efficient than the mouse. Here is how to use the keyboard to initiate commands:

1. Press the **Alt** key and then press the highlighted letter of the desired menu name.
2. When the drop-down menu is displayed, press the highlighted letter of the desired option.

During the rest of the book, I will give instructions on only the mouse method.

Using Special Keys

A number of keys function as shortcuts for certain operations in Microsoft Access. For example, there are shortcut keys to cancel an operation, cut or copy text, and close the program.

Table 2.1 The Microsoft Access Shortcut Keys

Key	*Function*
Alt+F4	Close Microsoft Access
Alt+–	Select the Control menu of the document window
Alt	Set the Menu mode (for keyboard menu operations)
Enter	Initiate the selected command
Esc	Cancel menu
F1	Initiate the Help system
Shift+F1	Initiate context-sensitive Help
Ctrl+F10	Maximize the document window
Ctrl+X	Cut to the Clipboard
Ctrl+C	Copy to the Clipboard
Ctrl+V	Paste from the Clipboard
Del	Clear
Shift+F2	Zoom in
F5	Move to the record number box
F6	Open a property sheet from a table design
Ctrl+F6	Cycle between open windows
F7	Open the Find dialog box
F9	Recalculate the window fields
Shift+F9	Re-query the underlying table
F11	Return to the database window
Shift+F12	Save a database object
Ctrl+Break	Cancel a query, filter, or find operation

continues

Table 2.1 Continued

Key	*Function*
Ctrl+'	Insert the same value as in the previous record
Ctrl+;	Insert the current date
Ctrl++	Add a new record
Ctrl+Enter	Add a new line to memo field

Introduction to the Tool Bar

Just under the menu bar is a *tool bar* with various *buttons* that can simplify tasks. Like the menu options, these change depending on the operations you are performing. We will introduce these buttons throughout the book as you need them. For now, note the single Help button (see Figure 2.1) which appears in the startup window.

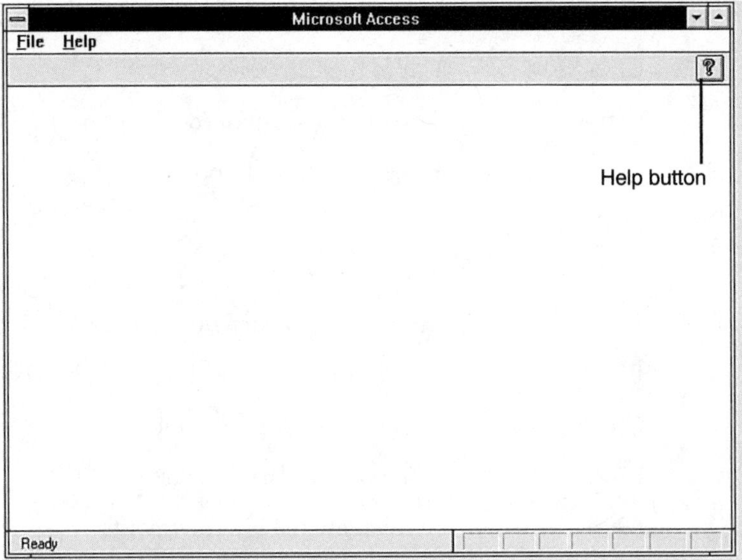

Figure 2.1 The Help button.

Getting Help

You can get help at any time by pressing the **F1** key, choosing **Help** on the menu bar, or clicking on the **Help** button on the tool bar. Choosing **Contents** from the **Help** menu will open a Help Table of Contents (see Figure 2.2), enabling you to get help on any topic. Double-clicking the upper-left Control menu box of this window (or selecting **Exit** from the **File** menu) will close the Help window.

If you want help about a specific command, it is often easier to use the *context-sensitive Help*. To use this mode, select the command with the keyboard, but don't activate it with the Enter key as you normally would. Instead, press **Shift+F1**.

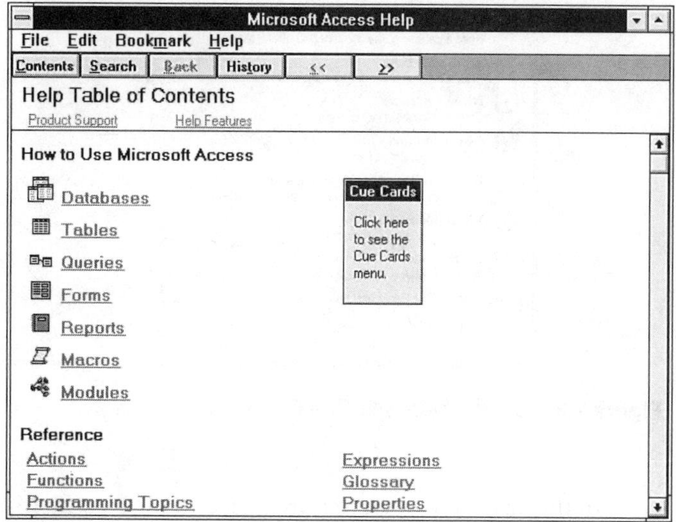

Figure 2.2 The Help window.

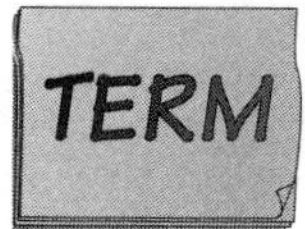

Need Help on a Command? *Context-sensitive help* is a feature that gives you more information on-screen about how to use the current command.

Another method of getting help is to use the Cue Cards that are part of Microsoft Access. These electronic tutorials guide you through various processes, such as creating a database. To use the Cue Cards:

1. Choose **Help** from the **Main** menu.

2. Select **Cue Cards** from the **Help** menu.
3. Now you can select options such as help on creating a database (see Figure 2.3).

The Cue Cards lie on top of the normal Microsoft Access windows. While you continue working with the program, the Cue Cards guide you.

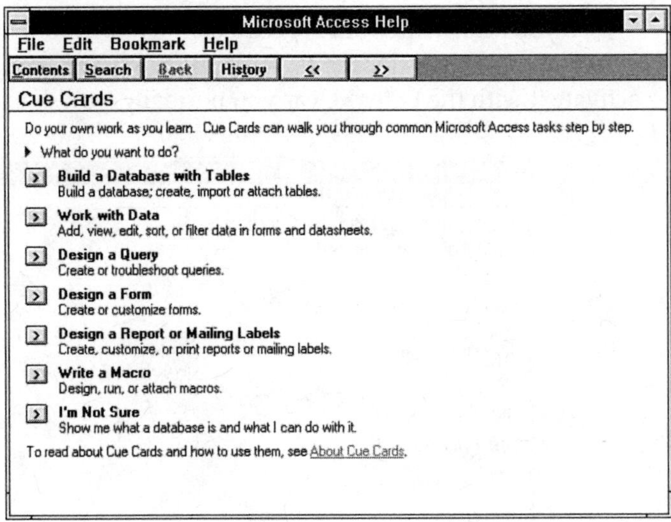

Figure 2.3 Getting help with Cue Cards.

In this lesson, you were introduced to the startup Main menu options; you also learned how the menu bar works and how to get help. Now let's create a database.

3

Creating a Database

In this lesson, you will learn how to create a database for tables, reports, and other objects.

Plan Your Database

Suppose you've just been given the task of tracking an important mailing list for your organization: a prospect list for the salespeople. Microsoft Access is a good choice for managing this prospect list. It's easy to use, the salespeople can learn it quickly, and it has all the features we need. Let's see how it's done!

Your first step is to define a database. Once that is done, you can decide what tables, reports, forms, and queries are needed. This example is a very simple database; a single table and a few reports will manage the prospects.

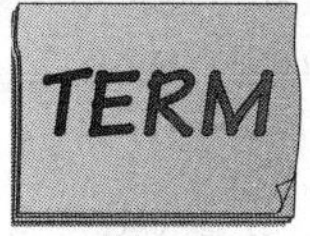

Tables in Databases In the preceding example, the prospects' addresses can be put in a *table*, a Microsoft Access object that stores the information in rows and columns. Then the table can be stored in the database (which is, as you'll recall, a single file). You can add reports and forms to this same *database file*.

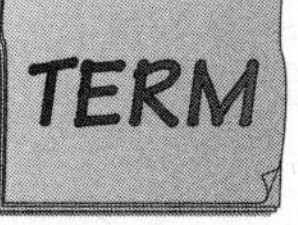

Records and Fields in Tables In a Microsoft Access table, the rows are called *records* and the columns are called *fields*.

The more complex the environment, the better your database design will be if you follow these general rules:

- Look at how the information is currently managed.
- Define the new objectives, and build from them.
- Avoid putting too much information in a single table.

If you are building a system for tracking orders (for example), you could put customers' addresses in a separate table; that way the order table need not duplicate them in every order. You might put an order's line items in another table, so that every line-item record does not duplicate the entire order. Microsoft Access will then permit you to link the three tables together, so they appear to act as one.

Creating Your Own Database

Now that you've learned how the menu works, let's create a database as a first step in managing your data for reports and labels. Each database file will store tables, queries, reports, and forms associated with the database.

To create a new database, follow these steps:

1. Choose **New Database** from the **File** menu. The New Database dialog box is displayed (see Figure 3.1).
2. In the File **N**ame text box, type the name for your new database. The name is limited to eight characters. (The default name is **db1.mdb**. You need not type the extension.)
3. (Optional) If you want to save the database in a different directory, click on (or **Tab** to) the **D**irectories list box, and select the desired directory. To select a directory, click on it, or scroll to it using the arrow keys.
4. (Optional) If you want to save the database on a different drive, **Tab** to (or click on) the Drives list box. To display the drives, press **Alt+↓**, or click on the down arrow. Click on the drive you want, or use the arrow keys to select it.
5. Press **Enter** or click on **OK**.

Once the database is created, a Database window appears on-screen (see Figure 3.2). The new database is open; you can use the displayed window to add tables, reports, and other objects to the database, and use any objects already created. Notice the list box in the dialog box is empty. You have not yet created any tables, forms, or reports. Also notice that you now have more menu options on the menu bar, and buttons on the tool bar.

Enter name of new database here.

Figure 3.1 Entering the name of the new database.

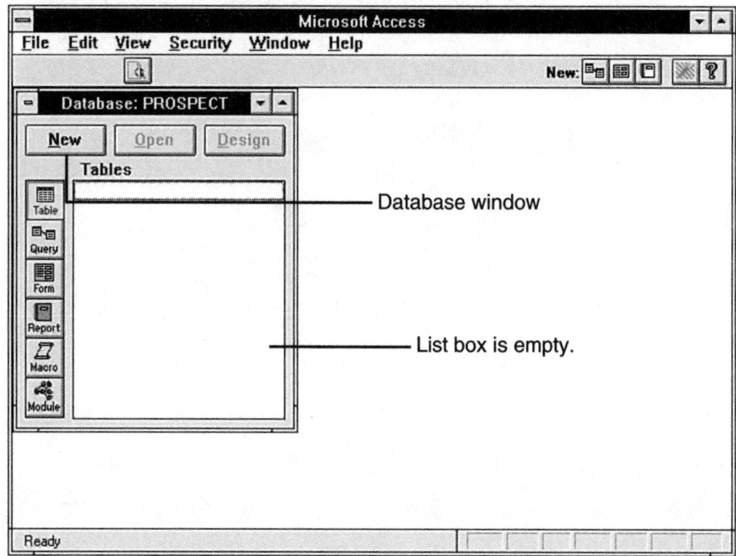

Figure 3.2 The Database window.

What Happened to Those Buttons? The Design and Open buttons are dim at this time because no objects have been created in the database yet.

Closing the Database

Closing the database ensures all objects are properly stored in the database, and returns you to the startup window. To close the database, choose **Close Database** on the File menu. The startup window appears again; if you wish, you can open another database or create a new one.

Some Cautions About Closing Closing the database makes sure everything is stored on the disk properly. Only one database can be open at a time in the program. If your database is damaged, see Lesson 21.

In this lesson, you learned how to create and close a database. In the next lesson, you will learn how to create a simple table to hold data.

Creating a Simple Table

In this lesson, you'll learn how to create a simple table to hold your data.

Designing a Table

First you need to define what information you want to put in the table. For now, let's look at a database for managing sales prospects. The database will have a single table with the prospects' addresses. All we really need to store now is the name, full address, phone number, a tickle date, a region code, and sales totals for the last six months.

Review: What a Table Is As you'll recall, a *table* is an object you create in your Access database. You use it to organize information into rows and columns. The rows are called *records* and the columns are called *fields*.

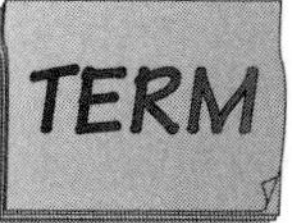

Tickle Date The *tickle date* is the date when the salesperson should call that person again.

Keep It Simple Keep the database simple. Don't try to put everything you know about the prospect in the file. Decide what data you need to accomplish your purpose, and in what form it should be. Once you have started entering data, you can redefine the database structure as needed for additional data. It's still a good rule, however, to plan ahead as much as possible. It's easier to enter all data for a record at one time than try to add something to each record later.

When you design your table, identify a type of item that will be unique for each record in the table, such as a Social Security number, membership number, or model number for an inventory. Make this unique item the first field in the record; it will be used later as the *primary key*. Access uses the primary key field to *index* your database (see Setting the Primary Key later in this lesson). For our example, we'll use the first field to give each person an identification number. The first field will be our primary key field.

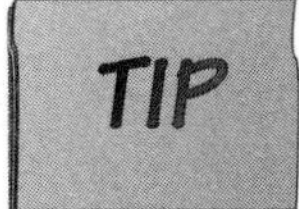

What's in a Name? Don't use a person's name for your primary key field. There could be two people in your database with the same name, and Access won't allow two primary key fields to have exactly the same information.

Creating a Table

Now let's create a table for our prospects. If you have already created a database using the steps in the last chapter, use the following steps to open that database:

1. Choose **Open Database** from the **File** menu.
2. Choose your database from the **File Name** list.
3. Click on **OK** or press **Enter**. The empty database will appear in the window (see Figure 4.1).

Creating a Database If you have not yet created a database, create one (and name it PROSPECT) by choosing **New Database** from the **File** menu, typing **PROSPECT** in the File **N**ame text box, and choosing **OK**.

Be sure the word **Tables** is displayed over the list window in the dialog box. If it is not displayed, click on the Table button on the left side of the dialog box (see Figure 4.1). To create a new table, choose the **New** button by clicking on it or pressing **Alt+N**. Microsoft Access opens a Table window in Design view (see Figure 4.2). You can use this window to create the structure of your table.

Click here to create a new table.

Microsoft Access

File Edit View Security Window Help

New:

Database: PROSPECT

New Open Design

Tables

Table Query Form Report Macro Module

If "Tables" is not displayed, click on this button.

Ready

Figure 4.1 The Database window.

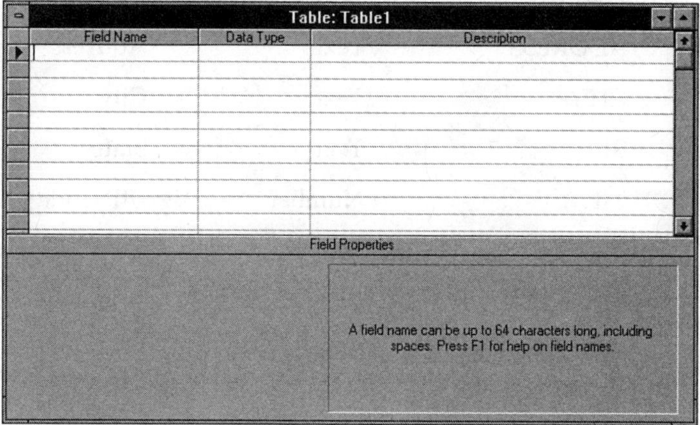

Figure 4.2 Design view for a new window.

You define a table by telling Access what the structure of the table will be. The structure of a table is made up of *fields*. Each field must have a field name, as in **PHONE#** or **LNAME**. You must also specify a certain type of data for each field, such as **Text** or **Number**. You can also enter a simple description if you want. Access supports these data types:

- *Text* text and numbers that aren't used in calculations.
- *Memo* long text strings (multiple sentences).
- *Date/Time* dates and times.
- *Number* numbers used in calculations.
- *Currency* currency values.
- *Counter* an integer which is incremented automatically.
- *Yes/no* logical values that can be true or false.

For our mailing list, use the following fields:

Field Name	*Type*	*Description*
ID	Number	Identification Number
LNAME	Text	Last Name
FNAME	Text	First Name
ADDRESS	Text	Address
CITY	Text	City
ST	Text	State
ZIP	Number	ZIP Code
TICKLE	Date	Call-back date
PHONE	Text	Telephone number
REGION	Number	Region
SALES	Number	Sales for last six months

To create the database structure, follow these instructions:

1. If necessary, move the cursor to the first field's text box, and enter a field name (for example, **ID**).
2. Press **Enter** or **Tab** to move to the **Data Type** column.
3. A default value of **Text** will be entered. If you want to use Text as the data type, simply press **Enter**, or **Tab** to the next column. If you want a

different data type, click on the down arrow, or press **Alt+↓** to open the Data Type list box. (For this example, choose **Number** from the list box.)

4. If necessary, press **Enter** (or **Tab** to the last column) and type in a description for the field. For the example, type in **Identification number**.
5. Press **Enter** (or **Tab** to the next row), and type in the information for the second field. Continue until all the fields you need have been defined.

Setting Field Properties

Each field has certain *properties* you must set. You have already named each field; for now, the only properties you need to set are the format properties of the ID, ZIP, TICKLE, REGION, and SALES fields. The text fields do not need to be set. To set the properties, follow these steps:

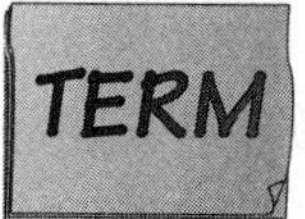

Property A property of a field is a particular characteristic such as size, color, or name.

1. To set the ID field's size, click on any box in the row that defines the ID field. The Field Properties box at the bottom of the screen will display the current field's properties (see Figure 4.3).
2. Click on the **Field Size** box; you'll see an arrow pop up. Click on it (or press **Alt+↓**) to display your options.
3. Choose **Long Integer** to use whole numbers only.

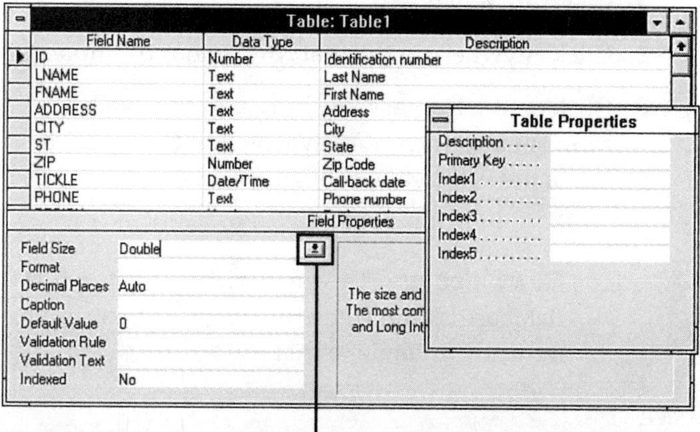

Click here to display list of property options.

Figure 4.3 The Properties list.

4. Click on any box in the **ZIP** row, and change the field size to **Long Integer** by repeating steps 2 and 3.
5. Click on any box in the **REGION** row, and change the field size to **Integer**.
6. To set the TICKLE field's format, click on any box in the **TICKLE** row, and click on the **Format** property box.
7. To open the list box, click on the arrow (or press **Alt+↓**); choose **Medium Date**.
8. To set the SALES format, click on any box in the SALES row, and click on the **Format** property box.
9. Open the list box, and select **Currency**.

Setting the Primary Key

For the next step, you should set the primary key. The value in this field will be unique for each record, which permits faster access to the table. Microsoft Access does this by creating an index on the primary key field. To set the primary key, follow these steps:

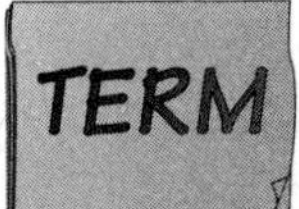

Indexing Organizing or sorting a database's records according to the content of one or more fields is called *indexing* the database.

1. Select **Table Properties** from the **View** menu to view the current indexes (there are none).
2. Click anywhere in the first row (in our example, this is the **ID** row).
3. Click on the **Primary key** button in the tool bar, or select **Set Primary Key** from the Edit menu. A key icon will appear in the row selector area to the left of the first field (see Figure 4.4).

Row Selector The small triangle to the left of the first field of the database is called the *row selector*. Clicking on any field in a row will move the triangle to that row.

Selecting Multiple Fields You can select multiple fields for the primary key. Hold down the **Ctrl** key while clicking on the row selector for each field you want to include. After each row is highlighted, click on the **Primary Key** button. A key icon will appear in each highlighted row.

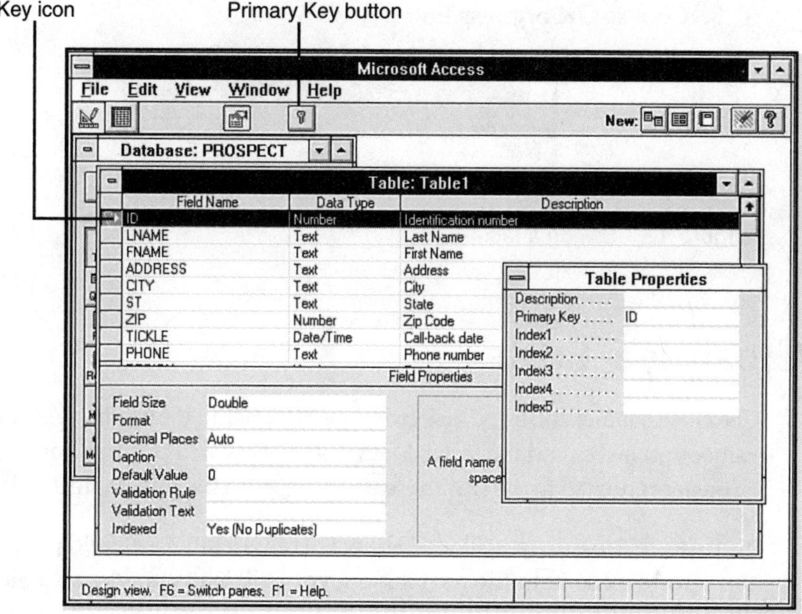

Figure 4.4 Setting the primary key.

If you have not selected a primary key when you save the table, Access will ask you if you want to create one before it saves the table. If you answer Yes, a new **Counter type** field will be created, and it will be used as the primary key field. If you already have a field for counter type, it will be chosen as the primary key field.

Now each time you redisplay the table (as you would do when switching from Design to Database view), it will be reordered by primary key fields (in our example, by ID number).

Saving the Table

Once the table is finished, save it by following these steps.

1. Choose the **Save As** command from the **File** menu.
2. Enter the name for the table (see Figure 4.5).
3. Choose **OK** or press **Enter**.

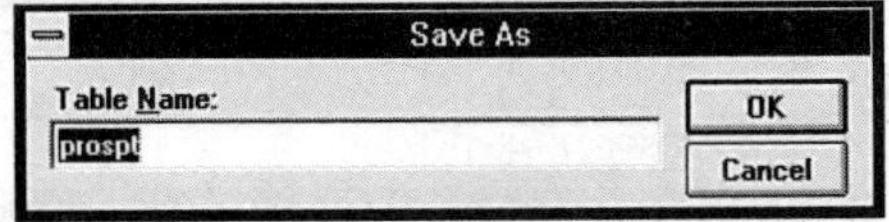

Figure 4.5 Saving a table.

Closing a Table

To close a table, choose **Close** from the **File** menu. If any changes have been made since you last saved the table, Microsoft Access will prompt you to save the table. You are returned to the Database window, with the new table displayed in the list.

In this lesson, you learned how to create a table, set field properties, save the table, and close it. In the next lesson, you will learn how to add data to the table.

Adding Data to a Table

In this lesson, you will learn how to add records to a table, edit them, and print them.

Opening the Table

In the last two lessons you created your database and added a table. Now it's time to place your facts and figures into their appropriate fields of the table. Every time you enter a complete row of fields, you have entered one complete record into the database.

Before you can add records to a table, you must open the database (if it is not already open) and the table. To open a database, choose **Open** Database from the **File** menu. Select the desired database and choose **OK**.

Quick Return to the Window If a database is open, a Database window will be displayed. A title bar will show the name of the database, though the window may be hidden under another window. Press the **F11** key to return quickly to any open Database window.

Once you have opened a database (such as the one you created in earlier lessons), examine the Database window. Be sure the word Tables is displayed at the top of the list box. If not, click on the **Tables** button to the left of the list box. The list now displays the current tables in the database. Select the desired table (such as PROSPT), and then select **Open** or double-click on the table name. The table will open, showing empty rows and columns like a spreadsheet (see Figure 5.1). This is called the Datasheet view.

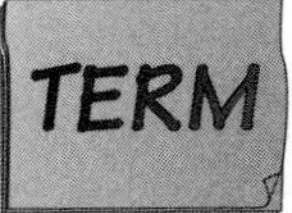

Datasheet View A *datasheet* is a view of a table that displays the data with the records in rows and the fields in columns.

When viewing tables, you can use either **Table Design** view or **Datasheet** view. You can use the two far-left icons on the **View** menu to switch between these choices.

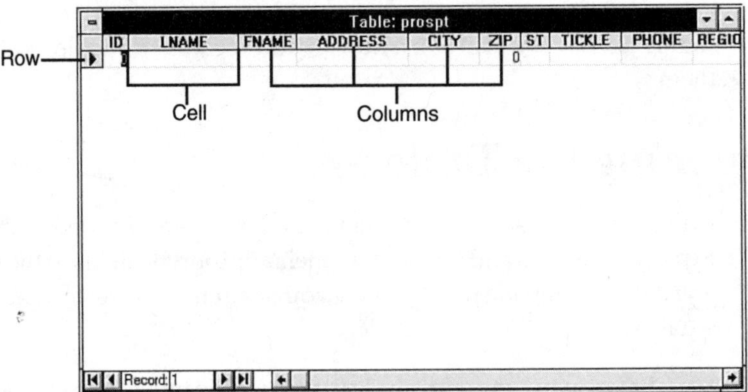

Figure 5.1 An empty datasheet for adding records.

Adding Records

If you have just created a table, there will be no records in the table. To add a record to the datasheet, fill in the cells for the first row. Use the **Tab** key, the **Enter** key, or the arrow keys to move the cursor between the columns as you fill in the data. Pressing **Shift+Tab** will move you backward through the columns. After completing the entry of a record, use the **Tab** key to move to the first field of the next row, and enter that record. Continue until you have added all the records you want to add (see Figure 5.2).

Adding Records to Existing Records in a Table

If a table already contains records, any records you add will be placed at the end of the datasheet. For example, open the **PROSPT** table (if it isn't already open). At the end of the datasheet, you will see an asterisk marking a blank or empty record. To add a record, you would fill out this record, which in turn opens another record.

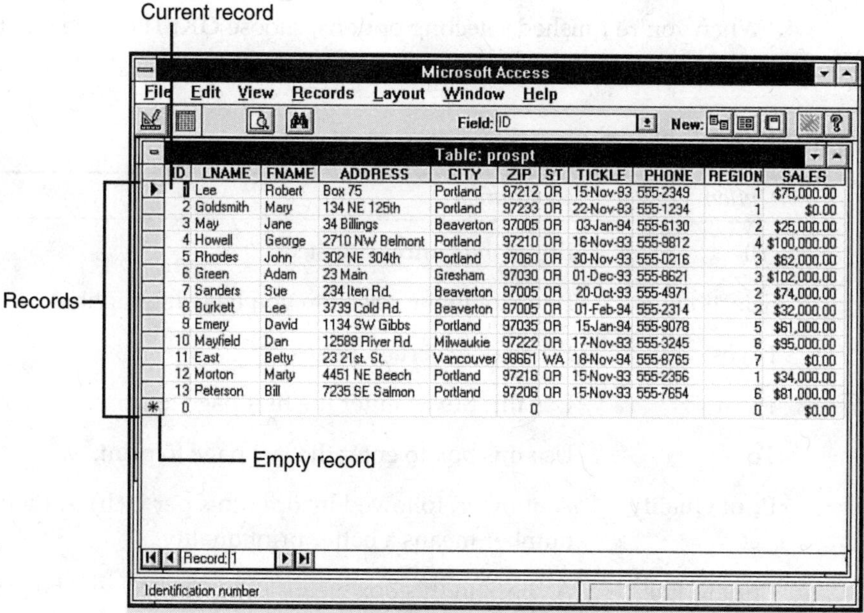

ID	LNAME	FNAME	ADDRESS	CITY	ZIP	ST	TICKLE	PHONE	REGION	SALES
1	Lee	Robert	Box 75	Portland	97212	OR	15-Nov-93	555-2349	1	$75,000.00
2	Goldsmith	Mary	134 NE 125th	Portland	97233	OR	22-Nov-93	555-1234	1	$0.00
3	May	Jane	34 Billings	Beaverton	97005	OR	03-Jan-94	555-6130	2	$25,000.00
4	Howell	George	2710 NW Belmont	Portland	97210	OR	16-Nov-93	555-9812	4	$100,000.00
5	Rhodes	John	302 NE 304th	Portland	97060	OR	30-Nov-93	555-0216	3	$62,000.00
6	Green	Adam	23 Main	Gresham	97030	OR	01-Dec-93	555-8621	3	$102,000.00
7	Sanders	Sue	234 Iten Rd.	Beaverton	97005	OR	20-Oct-93	555-4971	2	$74,000.00
8	Burkett	Lee	3739 Cold Rd.	Beaverton	97005	OR	01-Feb-94	555-2314	2	$32,000.00
9	Emery	David	1134 SW Gibbs	Portland	97035	OR	15-Jan-94	555-9078	5	$61,000.00
10	Mayfield	Dan	12589 River Rd.	Milwaukie	97222	OR	17-Nov-93	555-3245	6	$95,000.00
11	East	Betty	23 21st. St.	Vancouver	98661	WA	18-Nov-94	555-8765	7	$0.00
12	Morton	Marty	4451 NE Beech	Portland	97216	OR	15-Nov-93	555-2356	1	$34,000.00
13	Peterson	Bill	7235 SE Salmon	Portland	97206	OR	15-Nov-93	555-7654	6	$81,000.00
0					0				0	$0.00

Figure 5.2 The datasheet after entering a few records.

In the record selection area to the left of the first field, a right triangle marks the current record. If a blank record is entered accidentally here, delete it by selecting it and then choosing **Undo Current Record** from the **Edit** menu. Close the table and database when you are through adding records.

Saving Records

Microsoft Access saves your records to disk as you enter them. Each time you move the cursor to the next record, the program saves the record you just entered (or changed), automatically.

Printing a Datasheet

Sometimes it's easier to look at your datasheet on paper, rather than scrolling through it screen by screen on your monitor. You can print your datasheet by following these steps:

1. Make sure your datasheet is in the active window.
2. Select **Print** from the **File** menu.
3. A dialog box will appear, showing the options listed in Table 5.1.

4. When you're finished selecting options, choose **OK**. The table will be printed.

Table 5.1 The Print Dialog Box Options

Option	*Description*
All	Prints the entire datasheet.
S**e**lection	Prints only the selection you have highlighted.
Pages	Prints only certain pages.
From	Use this box to enter the first page to print.
To	Use this box to enter the last page to print.
Print **Q**uality	A number, followed by dpi (dots per inch). A higher number means a better print quality.
Print to Fi**l**e	A check in this box means the datasheet will be printed to a file, not to paper.
Copies	Type the number of copies you want.
Collate Cop**i**es	Collates pages if you select more than one copy.

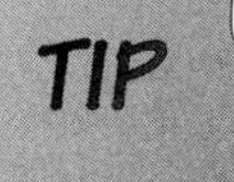

Print Preview If you want to see what your datasheet will look like before it's printed, select **Print Preview** from the **File** menu, or click on the **Print Preview** button on the tool bar. You can view different pages by clicking on the arrows at the bottom left of the window. To exit, press **Esc**.

You can use the Print Setup dialog box to change other options. This dialog box will be displayed if you select **Setup** from the Print dialog box or **Print Setup** from the **File** menu.

Using this dialog box, you can change any of the options shown in Table 5.2.

Table 5.2 The Print Setup Dialog Box Options

Option	*Description*
Default Printer	When selected, Access prints to the default printer.
Specific Printer	When selected, Access prints to the printer of your choice.
Portrait	Prints the datasheet across the narrow width of the paper.
Landscape	Prints the datasheet across the wide width of the paper.
Size	Select the size of paper to use.
Source	Specify whether you want to print from the paper tray or from your own paper (manual feed).
Margins	Specify Left, Right, Top, or Bottom margins.
Data Only	A check in this box will tell Access to print only the data on the datasheet (no embedded objects).

Can't Print? Access will display the **Print** command in the **File** menu only if you are in Datasheet view. To change to Datasheet view, select **Datasheet** from the **View** menu, or click on the **Datasheet View** button on the tool bar.

Closing a Table

When you have finished entering data, you should close the table and database. This will ensure that everything is saved to the disk properly and no data is lost. To close the table, follow these steps:

1. Choose **Close** from the **File** menu. The table will be saved to the disk and will no longer be displayed.

2. When you are through with the database itself, close it by choosing **Close Database** from the **File** menu.

A Word to the Wise Although Microsoft Access saves the records as you enter them, a wise computer user will not trust this feature to ensure complete safety. You have no assurance that all your data is on the disk until the database is closed. If you plan to take a break from the computer, close the database; open it again when you return.

In this lesson you learned how to add records to a table, save the records, and print them. In the next lesson you will learn how to edit your records.

Editing Records

In this lesson you will learn how to move around in a datasheet, edit existing records, and move and copy data.

Moving Around in the Datasheet

Once your records are entered, you might discover a few errors that need to be fixed. Fortunately, moving around the datasheet is easy. You can use the shortcut keys in Table 6.1 to move the cursor position.

Table 6.1 Moving around with the keyboard

Press	*To*
Tab	Move the cursor from left to right across a record.
Shift+Tab	Move the cursor from right to left.
Arrow keys	Move up, down, right, or left.
PageUp	Scroll up through the datasheet one screen at a time.
PageDown	Scroll down through the datasheet one screen at a time.
Home	Move the cursor to the beginning of a record.
End	Move the cursor to the end of a record.
Ctrl+Home	Put the cursor in the far-left field of the first record.
Ctrl+End	Put the cursor in the far-right field on the last record.

You can also use the mouse to click on any field you want to edit. You can click on the arrows in the scroll bars to scroll up, down, left, or right, one row or column at a time. You can also click inside the bar to move one screenful at a time, or drag the scroll box to a new location (see Figure 6.1). When you move the scroll box, the screen moves proportionately.

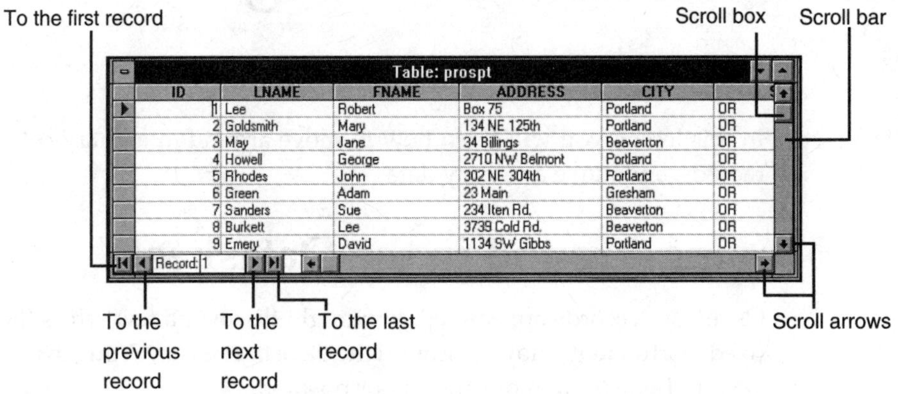

Figure 6.1 Use the scroll boxes to move around the datasheet.

Editing Existing Records

To edit a record in a datasheet, first select the field in the record you want to edit. Using the mouse, you can position the cursor anywhere in the field. Or you could use the keyboard to move to the field, and do one of two things:

- If the data in the field is highlighted, you can start typing. The highlighted data will be deleted and the new data will replace it.
- If the data in the field is highlighted, but you don't want to delete everything, press **F2**; this lets you move around in the field with the arrow keys. When you're finished, press **F2** again.

Deleting Entire Records

If you want to delete an entire record, click on the **row selection box** to the far left of the record. An arrow will appear in the box, and the whole record will be highlighted. Select **Delete** from the **Edit** menu or press the **Delete** key. A dialog box will appear asking you to confirm your action. Select **OK**.

Inserting a Record

Since Access sorts the datasheet by the primary key field, your records are inserted in the proper sequence automatically. If you are using sequential numbers as your primary key fields, you will have to renumber your records to allow for the new record. If you have ten records, for example, and you need to insert a new record as number eight, you would change the primary key fields in records eight, nine, and ten. Then you could simply type in the new record in the bottom row, using the number **8** in the primary key field. When Access saves the datasheet, the records will be in numerical order.

Copying and Moving Data in the Datasheet

You can use the **E**dit menu to simplify your editing by cutting or copying selected material and pasting it. *Cutting* a selection will move the data from the datasheet to the Clipboard. *Copying* a selection will keep the data in its original place, and keep a copy in the Clipboard. To copy the data from the Clipboard, paste it to your datasheet.

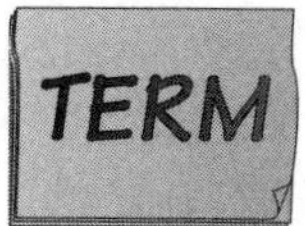

The Clipboard The data you cut or copy is temporarily stored in an area called the *Clipboard* until you paste it into your datasheet. The Clipboard keeps the same information ready for you to paste until you cut or copy something new. This allows you to use the **P**aste command repeatedly without having to cut or copy the same data.

Cutting Versus Deleting Cutting a selection is different from deleting it. When you *cut* data, it is deleted from the original location, but a copy of it is saved in the Clipboard for later retrieval. If you *delete* data, it is gone for good.

Moving Records

For example, pretend you have a database exactly like the one in Figure 6.2. After typing the records, you realize that Marty Morton's ID number is actually 13, and

Bill Peterson's is number 12. You would move Marty Morton's record by using the Cut command. Here's how:

1. Highlight the data you want to move. In this case, click on the **row selection box** to the left of the row to highlight Marty Morton's entire record.
2. Open the **Edit** menu and select **Cut** (see Figure 6.2).
3. A dialog box will appear, asking you to confirm your changes. Select **OK**.
4. To paste the selection to a new location, first you position the cursor in the correct row. In this case, move the cursor to the row beneath Bill Peterson's record.
5. Highlight an area that is exactly the same size as your selection. For this example, you would click on the **row selection box** to select the entire row.
6. Select **Paste** from the **Edit** menu.

To make your sample datasheet correct, all you would have to do now is change the ID numbers for Marty Morton and Bill Peterson.

Copying Records

Copying selected data is similar to cutting it. The only difference is that the data is not deleted from the original location. For example, seven of the people listed on the datasheet in Figure 6.2 live in Portland; instead of typing the city's name time after time, you can paste copies in each City field. You would:

1. Highlight the data you want to copy. In this case, you would highlight **Portland** after the first time you type it.
2. Select **Copy** from the **Edit** menu. Access copies **Portland** to the Clipboard (see Figure 6.3).
3. Position the cursor in the correct location. For our example, your cursor would be in the **City** field.
4. Be sure that the area you have selected to paste the data to is the same size as the area of the data you copied to the Clipboard.
5. Select **Paste** from the **Edit** menu.

For our example, you could just select **Paste** every time you have to enter "Portland," as long as you don't cut or copy anything else to the Clipboard.

Select Cu**t** from the **E**dit menu.

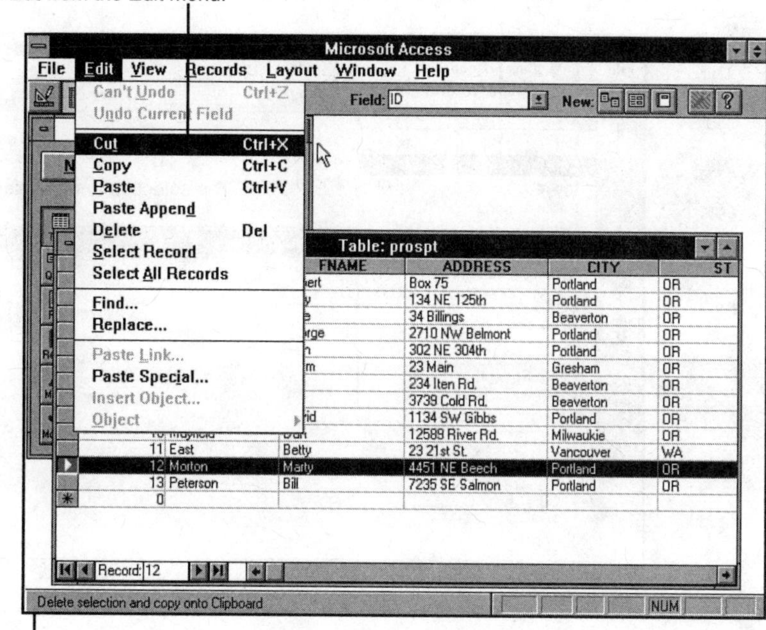

Click on the Row Selector to highlight the entire row.

Figure 6.2 Cutting a selection to the Clipboard.

Duplicate Records? If you are copying an entire record to a new location, be sure to change the data in the primary key field. You must have different information in each primary key field so Access can distinguish between records.

Appending Your Selection If you want to paste your cut or copied data to the end of your datasheet, select **Paste Append** from the **Edit** menu. This command will paste your selection to the last empty record in your datasheet, automatically.

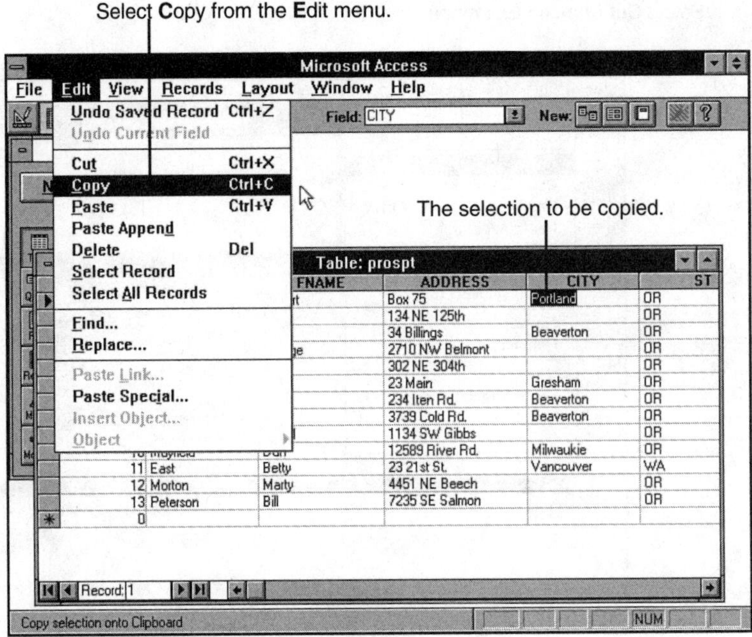

Figure 6.3 Copying a selection to the Clipboard.

In this lesson, you learned how to move around in the datasheet and edit existing records. In the next lesson, you will learn how to edit and rearrange fields in the table structure.

Changing the Structure or the View of a Table

In this lesson, you'll learn how to modify a table's structure by deleting, inserting, and rearranging fields.

Changing the Structure of a Table

Changing the structure of a table does not cause any data loss unless you delete a field, or change the field properties to a format that doesn't support the existing data.

If you want to change a table's structure, first click on the **Design View** button on the tool bar to put the table in Design view.

Deleting a Field

You may decide you don't need a particular field anymore, and want to delete it from the table. This will save disk space and simplify future data entry.

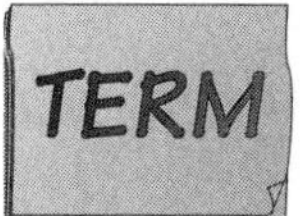

Fields Versus Records Don't confuse the terms *field* and *record*. Fields are pieces of information about each item in your database; they are stored as columns in the table. Records identify all the information about a particular item, and are stored as rows. All the information for Dan Mayfield, for example, might be stored as a single record (row). His address, city, state, Zip, and telephone number are all fields in that record.

To delete a field, follow these steps:

1. If necessary, open the database by choosing **Open Database** on the **File** menu.
2. If necessary, switch the display to **Design** view by clicking on the **Design View** button on the tool bar, or by choosing **Table Design** from the **View** menu (see Figure 7.1).

3. Click on the row selector for the row that defines the field to delete (or use the arrow keys, and press **Shift+Spacebar** to highlight the row selector).
4. Choose **Delete Row** from the **Edit** menu or press the **Del** key.
5. Choose **OK**.

The field and all data in it will be deleted.

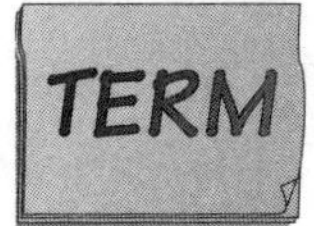

Row Selector The *row selector* is the triangle pointer in the space just to the left of the first column in the table.

Be Sure Be sure you have selected the correct field. Once you have deleted the field, all data in that field will be lost, and will not be recoverable. Data in other fields will not be affected.

Inserting a Field

After you have created a table, you may want to add a new field. For example, after creating a database of a club membership, you may decide to add a field later that defines when the member first joined the club. Microsoft Access permits you to add new fields at any time, without losing data in existing fields.

To add a new field:

1. If necessary, switch the display to **Design** view by clicking on the **Design View** button on the tool bar, or by choosing **Table Design** from the **View** menu (see Figure 7.1).
2. Click on the row selector for the row just below where you want to add the new field (or use the **arrow** keys and move to the row, then press **Shift+Spacebar**).
3. Choose **Insert Row** from the **Edit** menu or press the **Insert** key.
4. Define the new field by entering the field name, data type, and description (see Lesson 4).

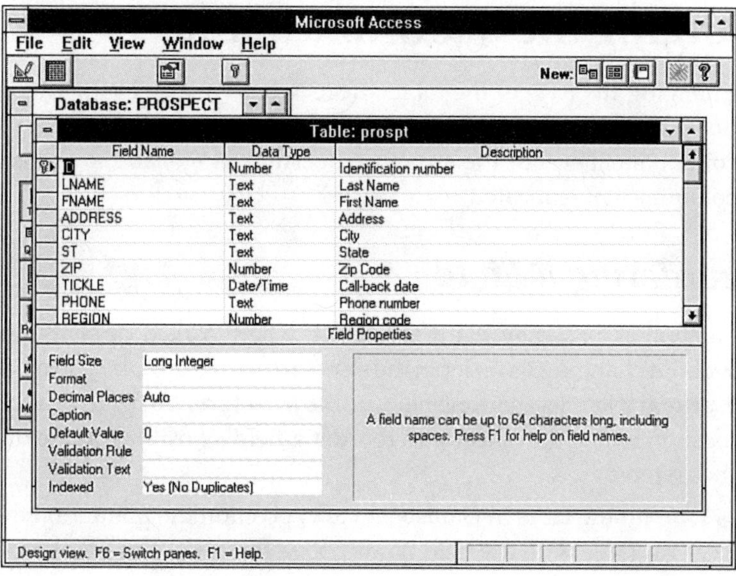

Figure 7.1 Table Design View.

Rearranging the Fields

There may be times when you want to rearrange the fields in a table. You may want to move a primary field (used for an index) so that you may also use it as the first field, or (in our example database) move the phone number field so it comes before the Tickle field.

1. If necessary, switch the display to **Design** view by clicking on the **Design View** button on the tool bar, or by choosing **Table Design** from the **View** menu.
2. Select the entire row for the field you want to move.
3. Click and hold the left mouse button on the **row selector**, and drag the row. When the row is where you want it to be, release the mouse button.

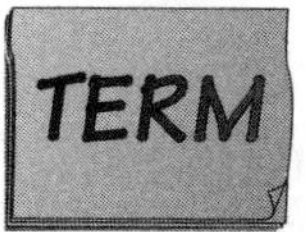

Drag Move the mouse pointer by holding down the left mouse button and moving the mouse.

Changing the View of a Table

Changing the *view* of the table affects what you see in the Datasheet view, but doesn't change the basic underlying structure. For example, you can make a column smaller, but the structure doesn't change, and any data in the smaller column is not truncated.

Reordering a Field

Sometimes you may want to change where a field appears on the datasheet without changing its order in the structure. (For example, you might want to keep a primary key as the first field in the structure, but give it a more convenient location on the datasheet.) To reorder a field's position on the datasheet, follow these steps:

1. With the table in Datasheet view, position the pointer on the **field selector** (area with the field name above the row). The pointer changes to a downward arrow.
2. Click on the **field selector** to select the entire field.
3. Click and hold the left mouse button on the **field selector** and drag the column to the new position.
4. To deselect the field, click anywhere else in the datasheet.

Resizing a Field or Column

Resizing a field's column width permits you to tighten up the view, which in turn lets you display more data at a time. To resize the column width for a field, follow these steps:

1. Position the pointer to the right of the column you want to resize, on the line between the field titles. The pointer changes to indicate the border can be moved.
2. Drag the line until the column is the desired size.

Resizing a Row You can resize a row in the same way by dragging the line that separates the rows. Note, however, that resizing one row affects all the rows; they all resize at once.

Save Your Changes

You can use **Save Layout** on the **File** menu to save the new layout. Once you have modified the database's structure, choose **Close Database** from the **File** menu to save your changes.

In this lesson, you learned how to open a table, and how to delete, insert, rearrange, resize, and reorder fields in the table's structure. In the next lesson, you will learn how to create a form.

8 Displaying Tables with Forms

In this lesson, you will learn how to create forms and arrange records in forms.

Introduction to Form Creation

Forms permit you to enter, edit, and display data, one record at a time. If you use a Datasheet view to enter records, usually not all the fields will be visible at once. You will have to scroll constantly as you add, edit, and view records. Using forms, on the other hand, lets you see all the fields of a single record at once. This simplifies data entry.

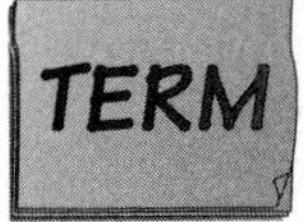

Form An object you can use to enter, edit, view, or print data records.

Microsoft Access includes a FormWizard button to help you put together forms. This lesson shows you how to use it.

Creating a Form

To create a form, start with the **Database** window open; click on the **Form** button (see Figure 8.1) to select the Forms option (the button will turn red). The Database window will then list all the forms in the database (if it's new, none will be listed). Click on the **New** button in the **Database** window, and you will get a New Form window (see Figure 8.2).

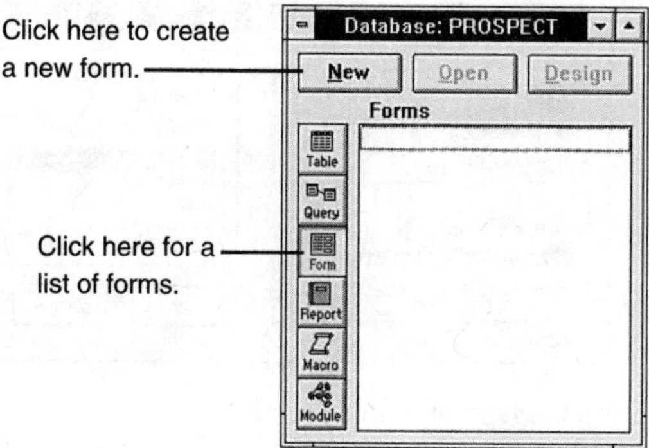

Figure 8.1 The Database window.

Figure 8.2 The New Form window.

1. In the Select A Table/Query: text box, click on the **down arrow** at the right (or press **Alt+↓**). A list box will open, displaying the tables for which you can build forms. (In this example, the only available table is PROSPT.)
2. Click on the name of the table for which you want to build a form.
3. Choose the **FormWizards** button (or press **Alt+W**).
4. On the first FormWizard screen, you are asked to select an AccessWizard. Choose **Single-column** and then click on **OK** or press **Alt+O** (see Figure 8.3).
5. On the next screen, you will be asked to select the fields to display in the form (see Figure 8.4). Select >> to move all your fields to the **Field order on form:** box on the right. Click on **Next**.

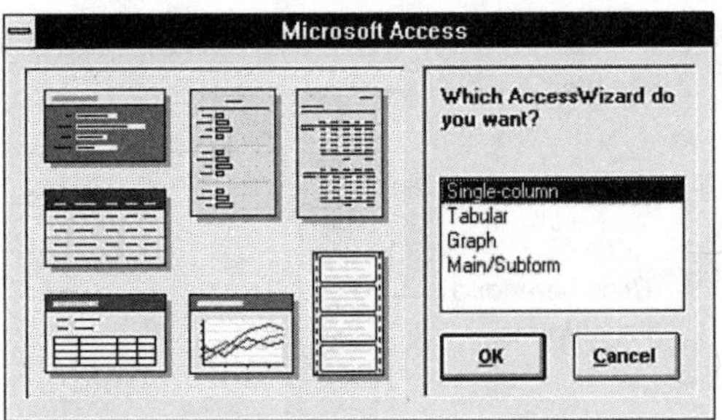

Figure 8.3 Choosing the type of form.

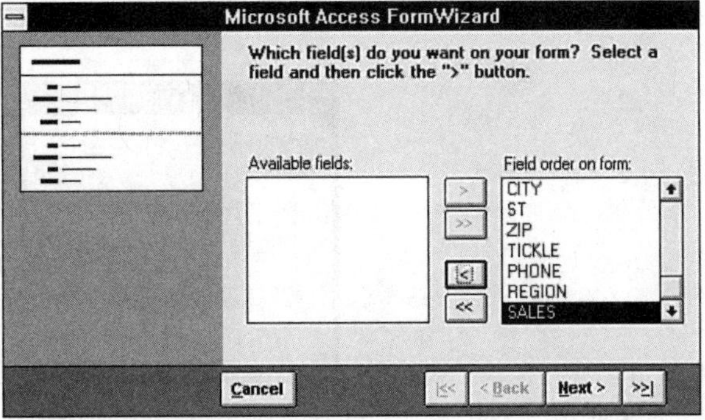

Figure 8.4 Choosing the fields for the form.

6. Select a look for the form by choosing **Standard**, and then click on **Next** (see Figure 8.5).

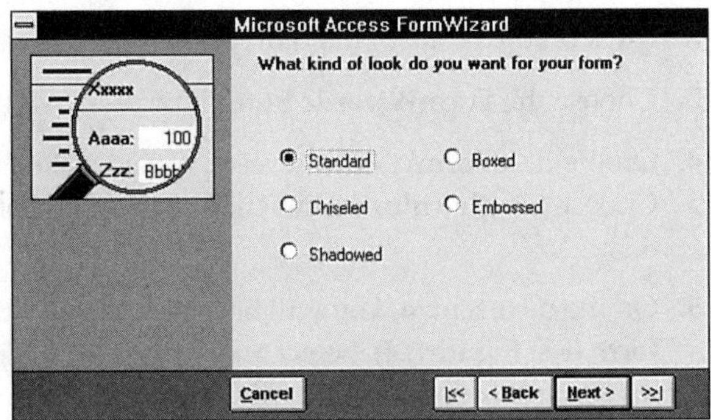

Figure 8.5 Choosing the type of format.

7. On the next screen, enter a title for the form (see Figure 8.6), and click on **Open**. FormWizard creates the form, and displays the database's first record in it (see Figure 8.7).

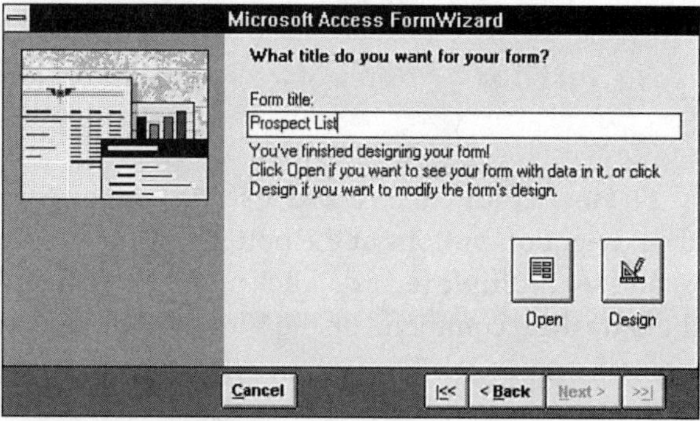

Figure 8.6 Entering the form's title.

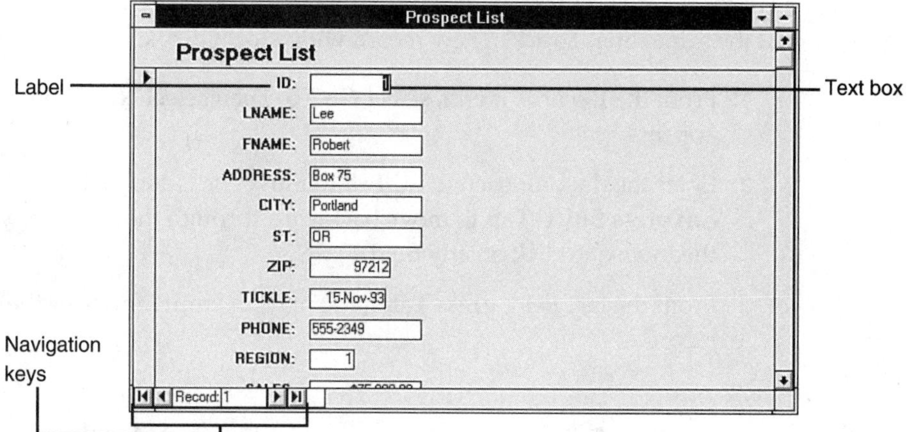

Figure 8.7 The final form.

Viewing Records with a Form

The form you have created can be used to display (view), add, change, delete, or print records. The various objects on the form are known as controls.

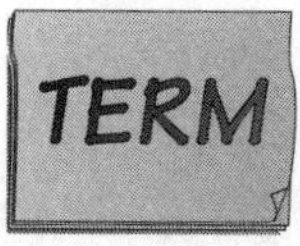

Control On a form or report, a *control* is an object that displays data from a field, the result of a calculation, a label, graph, picture, or another object.

Areas of the form that are used for input (for text or numbers) are called *text boxes*. Labels identify each text box, as well as a title for the form. There may also be a *check box* on some forms for entering logical values. (The next lesson shows you other types of controls.)

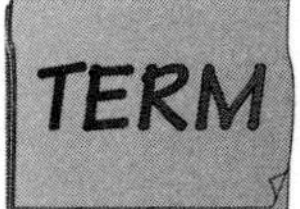

Text box An area of a form used to enter data.

To view a particular record, use the Go To command on the Records menu, or the navigation buttons at the bottom of the window. To return to a Datasheet view and see multiple records, click on the **Datasheet View** button on the tool bar, or the **Datasheet** command on the View menu. You can use the **Form View** button (or select **Form** on the View menu) to return to Form view.

Adding Records with a Form

Forms simplify adding records, because the new records' fields are all displayed at the same time. To add a new record with a form displayed, follow these steps:

1. From the Records menu, select **Go To**. Then select **New** from the list that appears.
2. Enter the data for each field; **Tab** to move the cursor between fields. You can press **Shift+Tab** to move backward through the fields, or you can use the mouse to click on any field.
3. From the last field, press **Tab** to display an empty form for the next record.

Oops! Use the Undo Current Field command of the Edit menu if you need to restore a field. To restore a previously typed value, use the Undo Typing command from the Edit menu.

Automatic Saving As you enter or edit records, the previous record you entered or edited is saved automatically. You don't need to do anything else to save records as you enter them.

Saving the Form

Once the form design is completed, you should save the form if you intend to use it in the future. To save an open form, follow these steps:

1. Choose **Save Form As** from the File menu.
2. Enter the name of the form you want to save. (Avoid using the name of any existing table, query, report, or other form.)
3. Choose **OK** or press **Enter**.

Printing Data with a Form

To print data using an open form, follow these steps:

1. Choose **Print** from the **File** menu.
2. Click on **OK** or press **Enter**. The data will be printed using the form.

Print Preview If you want to see what your form will look like before you print it, select **Print Preview** from the **File** menu or click on the **Print Preview** button in the tool bar. To exit the Print Preview window, press **Esc**.

Closing a Form

Once you are through using a form, close it to remove it from the screen. To close a form, choose **Close** from the **File** menu. The new form's name will be on the list in the Database window.

In this lesson, you learned how to create a form using FormWizard, and how to view a record in the form. In the next lesson, you will learn how to customize a form for your specific needs.

9 Creative Form Design

In this lesson, you will learn how to customize forms to meet your specific needs. You will learn how to add, resize, and move the labels and text boxes on the form, customize the text, and add fields to controls.

Modifying a Form Design

Once you have created a form with FormWizard, you may want to change the design. Microsoft Access makes this easy: you simply use the mouse to drag and resize.

To start redesigning a form, open your database and click on the **Form** button in the Database window. The list of the current forms will be displayed. Highlight the form you want to modify, and choose the **Design** button (see Figure 9.1). The form will open in Design view (see Figure 9.2).

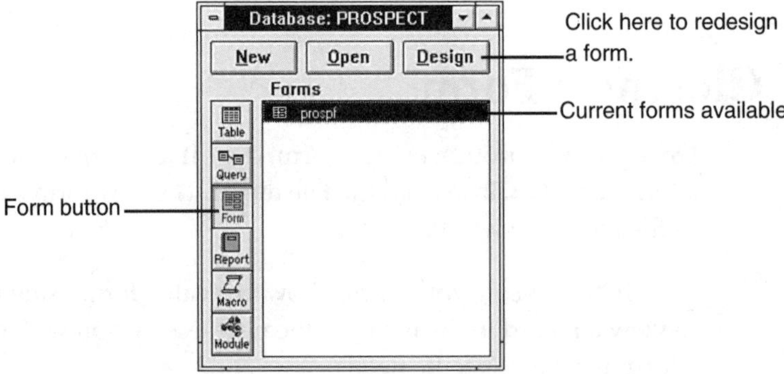

Figure 9.1 The Form window.

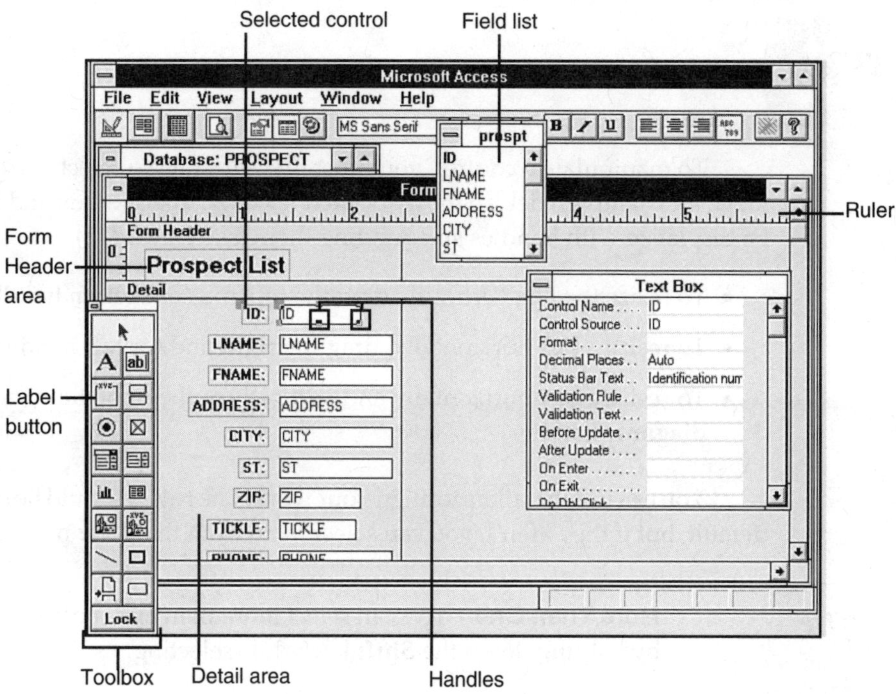

Figure 9.2 Starting to modify a form.

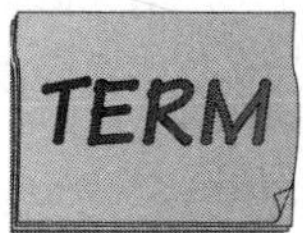

Toolbox Versus Tool Bar Notice that in Design view a new window called a *toolbox* is displayed. It is a special set of buttons that doesn't appear on the regular tool bar. You can use these buttons to design forms. You can move the toolbox by dragging its top title bar, and turn it on or off from the **V**iew menu.

Notice the differences between this view and a normal form display. The title is now in a separate Form Header area, and an empty Form Footer area has been added. The labels and text boxes are in a Detail area. The tool bar is displayed by default, but you can change your options on the **V**iew menu so the Field **L**ist or the Propert**i**es List is displayed.

Resizing Controls

As you'll recall, each object on the displayed form is called a control. In the Design view, you can move and resize these controls, and add new ones.

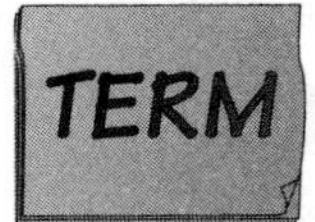

Control An object on a form or report.

To manipulate a control, you must first select it. To select a text box with a label, for example, click on the associated text box. The text box and its label will be displayed with handles surrounding them (see Figure 9.2).

- To resize the box vertically, drag the **top** and/or **bottom** handles.
- To resize a box horizontally, drag the **right** and/or **left** handles.
- To resize a box horizontally and vertically at the same time, drag the **diagonal** handles.

You can use the rulers to align your work. The rulers should be displayed by default, but if they aren't, you can select them from the **View** menu.

More Than One You can select more than one control at a time by holding down the **Shift** key while selecting.

Moving Controls

Microsoft Access permits you to move a text box and its associated label, together or separately. To move them separately, select the control, then drag the large handle in the upper left corner (this is known as the *move handle*). When you move the text box or label separately, the mouse pointer will look like a pointing hand.

To move the text box and label together, click on the control until the pointer looks like a hand with the palm showing. Now drag the text box and its label to the new position.

Use Multiple Selections to Align To maintain the current alignment while you are moving multiple controls, select them together, and then move them.

Adding a Label

A *label* is simply text added to the form to display information. The *title* already on the form is one type of label. You can add additional labels (such as your company name) to the form.

To add a label, use the special toolbox that appears the first time you open a form in Design view. If it is not already displayed, you can get it by choosing Toolbox from the View menu. Click on the **Label** button in the first row of the toolbox. Move the mouse pointer to the form, click on the appropriate place, and enter the text for the label.

Customizing Text

You can modify any text by changing the font, size, color, alignment, and attributes (normal, bold, and italic). To change the appearance of text in a control, follow these steps:

1. Select the control you want to modify. If it contains text, the tool bar will display additional buttons for modifying the text (see Figure 9.3).
2. To change the attributes, click on the **Bold**, **Underline**, or **Italic** buttons in the tool bar.
3. To change the alignment, click on the **Left**, **Center**, or **Right** buttons in the tool bar.
4. If you want to change the font and font size, set them from the tool bar.

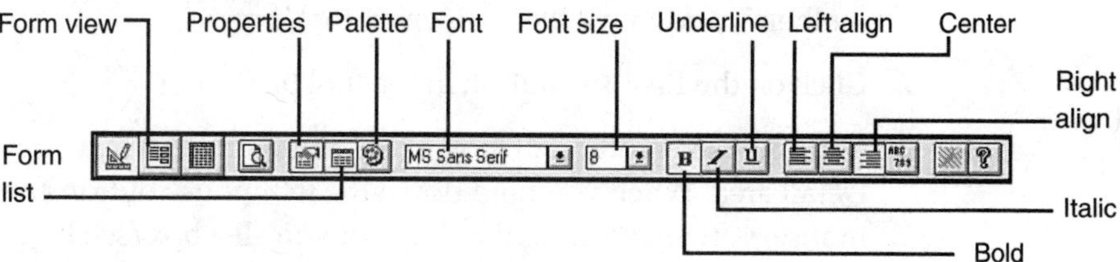

Figure 9.3 Modifying text using the tool bar.

After you have completed your work, resize the label to the new text by choosing **Size to Fit** from the Layout menu. Now you can modify the color of the text as needed.

To set the color of the text, follow these steps:

1. Click on the **Palette** button, or select **Palette** from the View menu.
2. From the Palette window (see Figure 9.4), you can set the color of the text, or you can set separate colors for fill and outline (simply click on the color of your choice). You can also set the appearance of the text and the border width (normal, raised, or sunken).

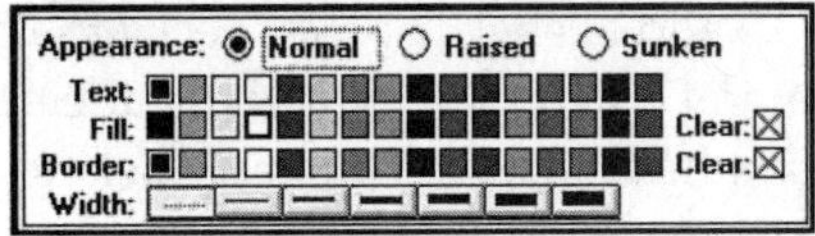

Figure 9.4 The Palette window.

Using a List Box with a Form

Sometimes it's faster and easier to select a preset choice from a list box than to type in text. For example, in our sample database, all customers live in one of five different cities. For the sake of this example, let's assume that all of your future prospects will also live in one of those cities. If you want to be able to choose the name of the city quickly, and be sure it's spelled right, it's a good idea to select it from a list box.

To create a list box for your city field, follow these steps:

1. Clear an area with sufficient room for the list box. In our example, you would delete the city field (select the text box and the label and press the **Delete** key), select the fields beneath it (press the **Shift** key as you click on them), and move them down an inch or so.
2. Click on the **List Box** button in the tool bar.
3. Your mouse pointer will look like a plus sign (+) when you move it to the Detail area. When you hold down the left mouse button and drag the mouse, you are creating the shape of your list box (see Figure 9.5).
4. If the controls are the wrong size (or in the wrong place), fix them using what you learned earlier in this lesson.
5. If the Properties box is not displayed, click on the **Properties** button or select **Properties** from the View menu.
6. Click on the **list box** so that its properties are displayed.
7. Change the appropriate properties (see Figure 9.6). For our example, change:

- the Control Name to **CITY**.
- the Row Source Type to **Value List**.
- the Row Source to **Portland;Beaverton;Gresham;Vancouver;Milwaukee**.

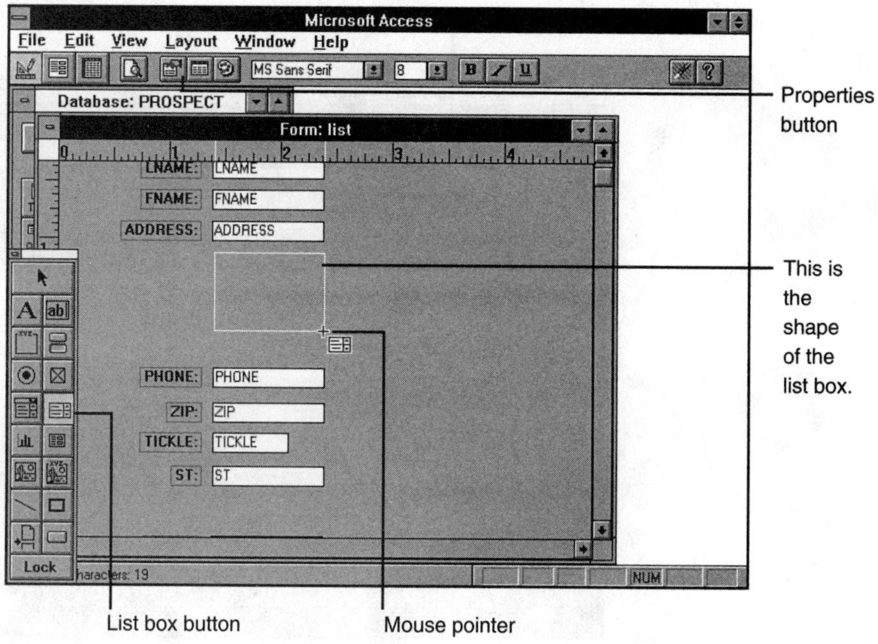

Figure 9.5 Creating the shape of the list box.

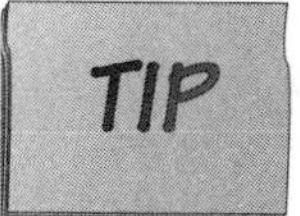

What Goes in the List Box? You can't simply type your choices into the list box. You have to enter them in the **Properties** box under **Row Source**. When entering your choices, use semicolons (without spaces) to separate them.

8. Your label might be wrong, but you can edit it. For our example, change the label to **CITY**.

To see how your new list box looks in the form, click on the **Form View** button or select **Form** from the View menu (see Figure 9.7). If the form doesn't look right, you can go back to Design view and change it. If you have scroll bars in your list box and you don't want them, you can make your list box longer by resizing it in Design view.

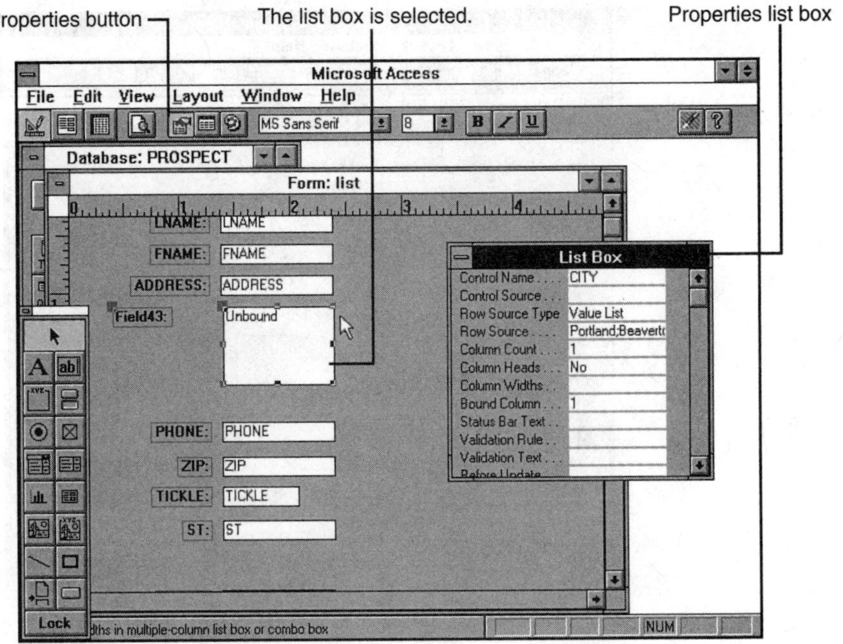

Figure 9.6 Changing the properties of a list box.

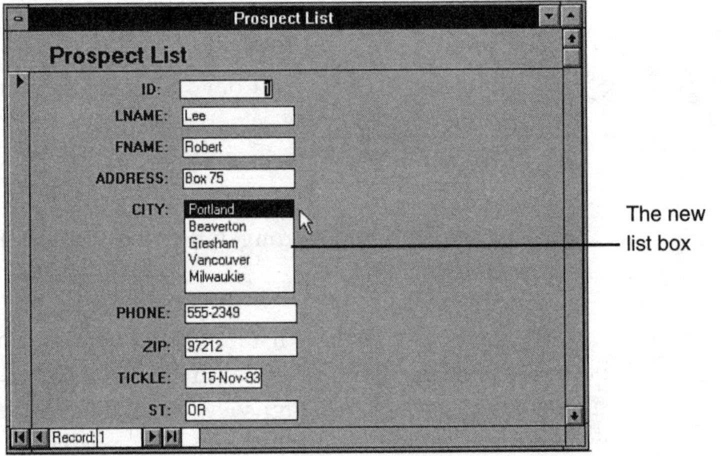

Figure 9.7 The completed list box.

List Versus Combo Instead of making a list box, you might want to make a *combo box*, so you are not restricted to preset choices. A combo box lets you type a value or choose from the list. To make one, select the **Combo Box** icon from the tool bar, and follow the steps for making a list box. When you use a combo box, your choices aren't displayed automatically; you have to select the **down arrow** button to see them.

Save It! Be sure to save the form if you want to keep it; use **Save** from the **File** menu. Close the form when you are through using it, using **Close** on the **File** menu.

In this lesson, you have learned how to customize a form to meet your specific needs. In the next lesson, you will learn how to query your database for information.

10 Querying a Database

In this lesson, you'll learn how to query a database.

Introduction to Queries

Most of the time you will want specific information when using a database. You won't want to look at the entire database when making a decision. The PROSPECT database for sales (for example) might contain hundreds of names, each with its own tickle date entered from the previous call. Suppose, as a salesperson, you want only the names that have today's tickle date. To get them, you must build a query to access the database and retrieve only the names that meet this criterion. Then you can print a report from the query, containing only names and phone numbers.

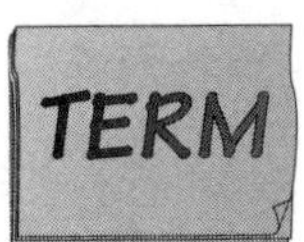

What's a Query? A *query* works much like a question directed at a database. In effect, it asks (for example), "Which prospects have today's tickle date?" The query also has a *condition* included, such as "What records have a tickle date *equal to* today's date?"

Creating a Query

Now let's create a simple query for getting today's prospects from the PROSPECT database, using the tickle date.

1. If the database is not open already, open it so that the Database window is displayed.

2. Choose the **Query** icon. The list window (see Figure 10.1) will display any current queries on the database. (In this example, there are none.)
3. To create a new query, choose the **New** button on the **Database** window. An Add Table dialog box is displayed (see Figure 10.2).
4. Select the table(s) you want to use for the query (in this example, the PROSPT table). If you want more than one, choose **Add** after each one. After the last table is selected, choose **Close**.
5. The fields of the table are displayed in a list box in the Query window. Any field that is used for a primary key is in boldface. Using the mouse, drag the fields you want to see in the query to the **Field** row of the **Query** window (see Figure 10.3). In this example you would drag **TICKLE, LNAME, FNAME, PHONE,** and **REGION** one at a time to the **Field** row. Place the fields in the columns, in the same order you want them to follow in the query.

Add Fields Fast You can also use the drop-down list in each Field cell to add a field.

6. Click on the **Datasheet View** button to see the results of the query. (You can see the button in Figure 10.3.)

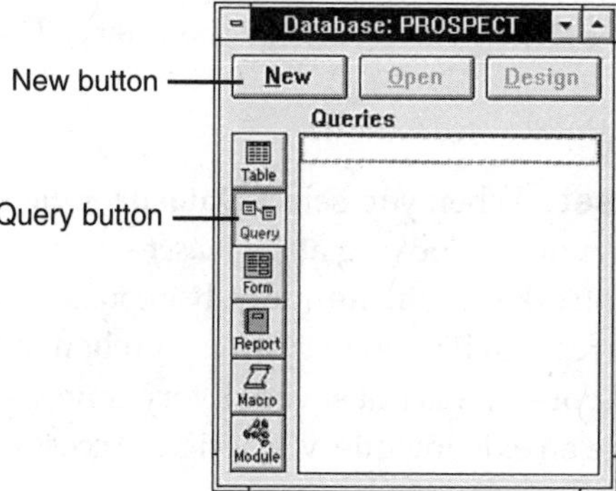

Figure 10.1 The Database window.

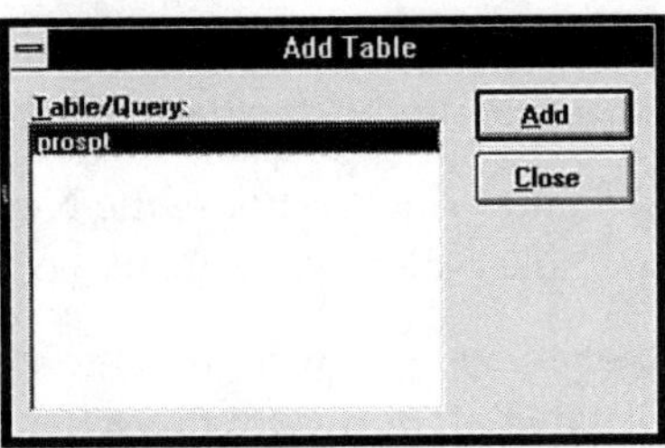

Figure 10.2 Adding tables for the query.

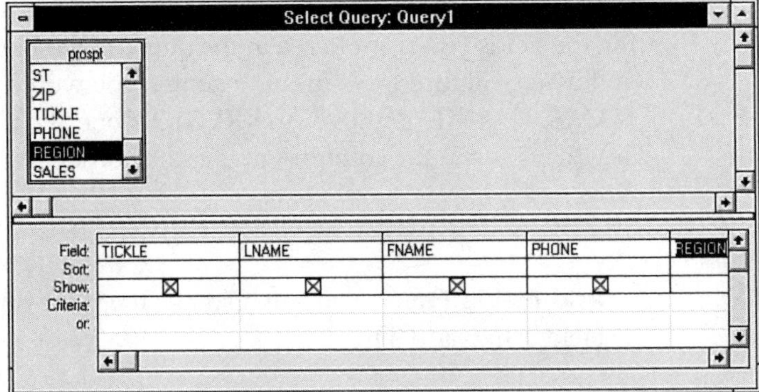

Figure 10.3 The fields of the table that are available for selection.

Figure 10.4 shows the results of the query. These results are known as a *dynaset*.

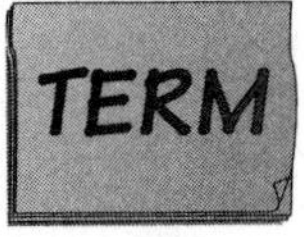

Dynaset When you select **Datasheet** view after you design the query, you are looking at a *dynaset*—a dynamic set of the records that you asked for in the query. It is considered *dynamic* because the query results change every time you change the data. Each dynaset is temporary; it is not saved. Every time you query a database or change an existing query's design, Access creates a new dynaset.

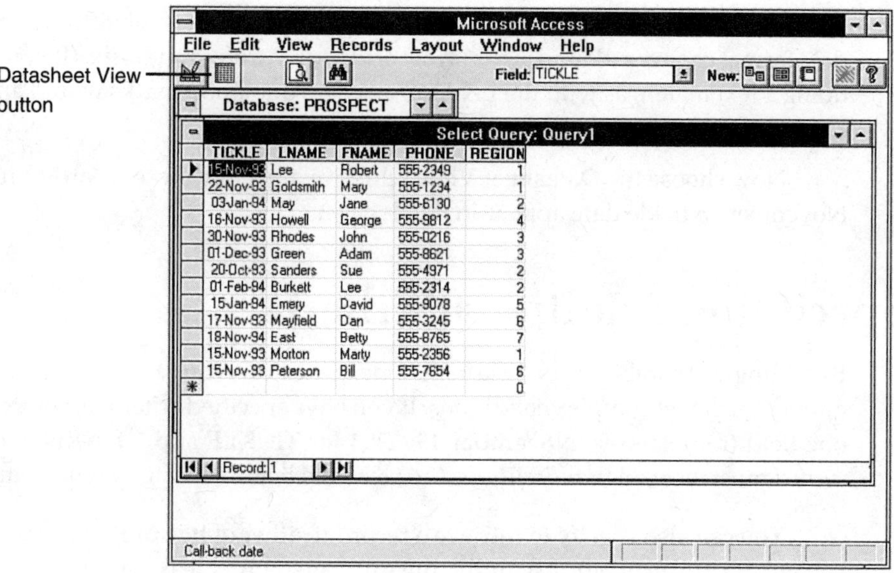

Figure 10.4 The results of the query.

Now click on the **Design View** button to return to Design view, or choose **Query Design** from the View menu.

Selecting Specific Records

Now suppose you want only specific records from the table, such as those with today's tickle date. To do this, you must specify *criteria.*

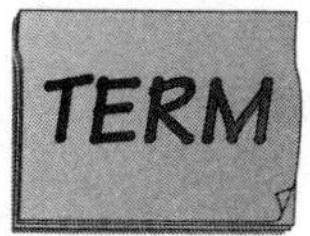

Criteria Criteria are conditions that a record must meet. If a record doesn't meet the criteria, it is left out of the dynaset. As Access creates a dynaset, it will include only the records that meet the criteria you set. In our example, there is just one criterion: the tickle date.

You can use the **Criteria** row in the **Query** window to specify the conditions for record selection. If today's date is November 15, 1993, and you want records for only this date, you could enter **15-Nov-93** as the criterion in the column with the field name TICKLE. Notice that after you press **Enter** to complete the entry, the date format changes. Pound signs (#) are added as a prefix and suffix. (If you were doing a text match, as with the LNAME column, quotation marks would appear around the text.)

Now choose the **Datasheet View** button again. Only those records with the November 15 tickle date appear in the dynaset.

Specifying Additional Criteria

By adding and combining criteria in the Query window, you can do very powerful queries that meet complex conditions. If you have specified criteria for more than one field (for example, **November 15, 1993** for TICKLE and **1** for REGION), a record must meet all the conditions for each field before the query will include it.

You can also specify to retrieve a record if either of two or more conditions is met (an *OR condition*). Assuming the salesperson was leaving town for a few days, you could specify as a condition of **>=15-Nov-93 OR<=17-Nov-93**. You could also specify a criterion as a list of values using the IN function, such as **IN(CA,WA)** for the ST field.

Saving the Query

When you have finished designing your query, save it by using the Save **A**s command from the **F**ile menu.

Beware of Table Names When you save your query, *do not use the name of any table in your database*. Otherwise, the save will overwrite the table, and you will lose all your table data. You will get a warning message, but it's too easy to ignore the message if you're in a hurry.

In this lesson, you learned how to query a database. In the next lesson, you will learn how to modify and print the queried data.

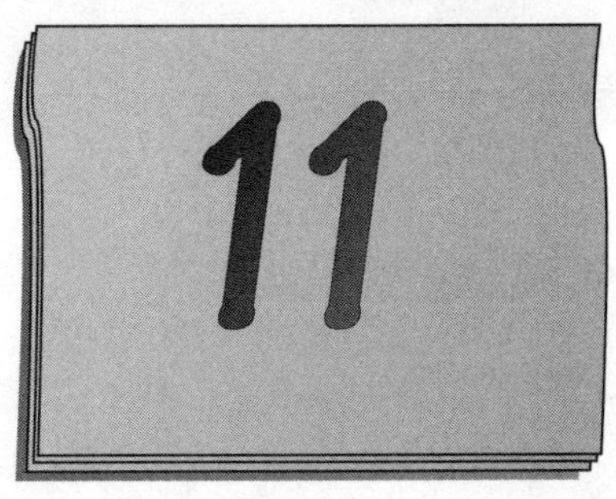

Modifying and Printing Queries

In this lesson, you will learn how to edit tables from a query, modify a query, calculate totals, and print the results of a query.

Editing Tables from a Query

When you use a query on a single table, you can edit the table directly from the displayed query. Display the query in Datasheet view, and edit it as you would the original table. To see your changes in the table, close the Query window and open the table.

Can't Edit a Query? If two or more tables are linked in a query, there may be ambiguity regarding which table contains the data. In that case, Microsoft Access may not let you edit the data in the query. (See Lesson 20.)

Modifying a Query

Queries can be modified to include new fields, new criteria, or reordered columns. Modify queries in Query Design view (see Figure 11.1).

Selecting Columns

To add, delete, or insert columns, first you must select a column. This specifies where the action is to occur. To select a column, click on the ***field selector*** (which highlights the entire column).

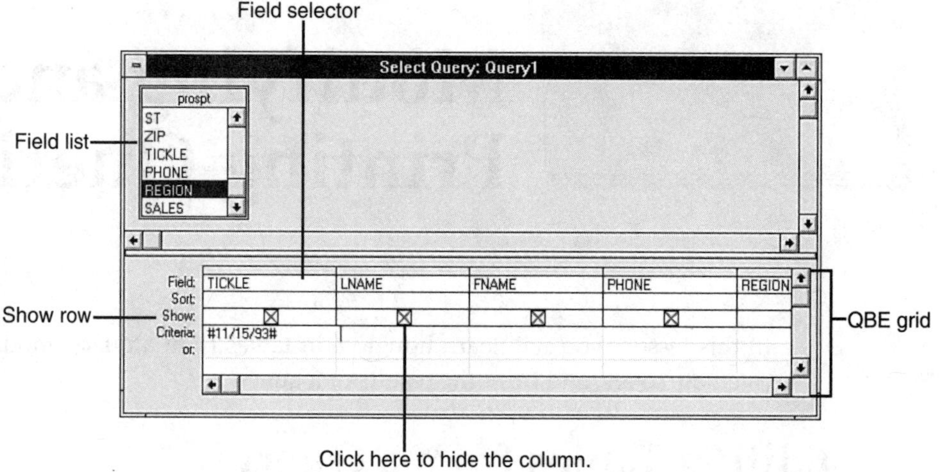

Figure 11.1 The Query Design window.

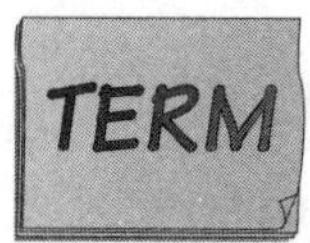

Field Selector The little box over the top cell of each column. When you click on this box, the entire column becomes highlighted.

Modifying the Criteria

You can modify the criteria at any time by editing the Criteria row in the QBE grid.

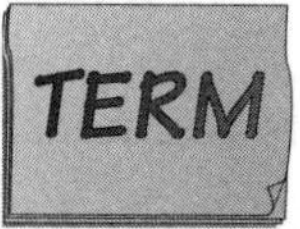

QBE Grid As you create a query, you use a table called a *QBE grid* to define grouping, sort order, and criteria.

Moving a Column

To move a column in a query, follow these steps:

1. Be sure you are in **Query Design** view.
2. Select the entire column you want to move.
3. Drag the column to the new location.

Deleting a Column

To delete a column in a query, follow these steps:

1. Be sure you are in **Query Design** view.
2. Select the entire column you want to delete.
3. Choose **Delete** from the Edit menu, or press the **Delete** key.

Inserting a Column

To insert a blank column into a query, follow these steps:

1. Select the column to the right of where you want to insert the new column.
2. Choose **Insert Column** from the Edit menu.
3. Choose a field name from the drop-down list box in the top cell.

Resizing a Column

To resize a column in a dynaset, drag the border of the field selector.

Hiding a Column

There may be times you want to hide a column in a query. For example, you may want to specify criteria for a field, but prefer not to display that field in the Datasheet view. To hide a column, go to that column in the QBE grid (in **Design** view), and click on the box in the row titled **Show**. The **X** will disappear from the box to show that the column will not be displayed in the dynaset.

Calculating Totals

You can also use a query to show totals. For example, assume the sales to each customer are added to the query, but you only want to see the total sales for each region. You would follow these steps:

1. Design your query grid so Access will use only the appropriate fields to do the calculations. For our example, you would delete all the columns except the **REGION** and **SALES** columns.

2. Click on the **Totals** button in the tool bar, or select **Totals** from the **View** menu. A new row called **Total** will appear just below the **Field** row (see Figure 11.2).
3. Click on the **Total** row, in the column you want to calculate. For our example, you'd click on the **SALES** column.
4. Use the drop-down list box to select the type of calculation you want. In our example, you want the total sales, so you'd select **Sum**.
5. To see the results of your query, click on the **Datasheet View** button, or select **Datasheet** from the **View** menu. In our example's dynaset, the **SALES** column will show the total sales for each region.

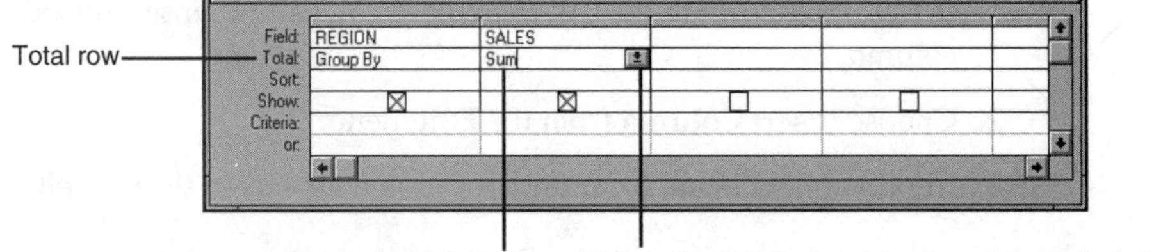

Figure 11.2 Using a query to calculate totals.

Printing the Dynaset

If your query results are important, it's a good idea to have a printout of your dynaset, since Access won't save it. To print the dynaset, be sure the Query is in Datasheet view, then follow these steps:

1. Select **Print** from the **File** menu.
2. Select any option from the **Print** dialog box.
3. When you're finished selecting options, choose **OK**.

Print Preview If you want to see what your dynaset will look like before it's printed, select **Print Preview** from the **File** menu, or click on the **Print Preview** button on the tool bar. You can view different pages by clicking on the arrows at the bottom left of the window. To exit, press **Esc**.

In this lesson, you learned how to modify a query, calculate totals of columns, and print a dynaset. In the next lesson, you will learn how to find data using a form.

12 Finding Data by Using Forms

In this lesson, you will learn how to use forms to find specific data in tables, and how to use forms with filters to create subsets of data.

Tables, Forms, or Queries?

Using tables to find data has limitations. With a table, you can usually see only a few fields at a time. However, forms and queries allow you to get around the size limitations of a table. With a form you can find specific data, create subsets of data, sort data in a specific order, and locate data that meets specified criteria.

Using an Existing Form The instructions in this lesson require that you use a form that has been created previously. If you haven't created a form yet, please refer to Lesson 8 to learn how.

Finding Data Using a Form

If you need to find data quickly, and you don't want to take the time to build a query, use a form. You can do a simple search, and locate the record you need. For example, suppose you need a telephone number for a certain prospect quickly. Let's see how to find it!

To find a value quickly, follow these steps:

1. Open the form from the Database window if it is not already open. (Select the form from the list, and either double-click on it or press **Alt+O**.)
2. Select the field to search by clicking on the title of the field, or by pressing the **Tab** key until the field is selected. For our example, you would select the **PHONE** field.

3. Click on the **Find** button on the tool bar, or choose **Find** from the **Edit** menu.
4. When the **Find in field:** dialog box appears, enter the data you wish to find in the Find What text box (see Figure 12.1).

Figure 12.1 Finding data with a form.

5. Choose any of the options listed in Table 12.1.
6. Choose **Find First**.
7. Access finds the first occurrence of the data you specified. If this is not the record you want, choose the **Find Next** button to move to the next occurrence.
8. When the search is complete, a dialog box will appear asking you if you want to start the search from the top again. Choose **No**, then close the **Find in field:** dialog box.

Can't See Your Form? If you can't see your form because the dialog box is in the way, move the dialog box by clicking on its title bar and dragging the box to a new location.

Table 12.1 Options for the Find in field: dialog box.

Option	*Description*
Where	Lets you choose from three options:
Any Part of Field	Matches the data you specified at every occurrence.
Match Whole Field	Matches only the text you specify.

Option	*Description*
Start of Field	Finds only the matches that occur at the beginning of a field.
Current Field	Searches only the highlighted field.
All Fields	Searches every field.
Up	Searches toward the beginning of the table.
Down	Searches toward the end of the table.
Match Case	Finds only the matches that are in the same case as the data you specified.
Search Fields as Formatted	Finds matches based on how they appear on screen, not the format they were stored in.

Creating a Filter

You might want to display all the records that contain certain information instead of viewing them one by one with the Find command. Or you might want to specify criteria in more than one field. To accomplish either one, use a filter to create a subset of specific data.

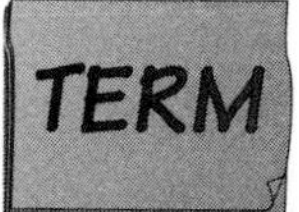

Filter A *filter* uses the data you specify to create a temporary datasheet of certain records (called a subset). A filter can be created only when you are using a form, never from a table or a query.

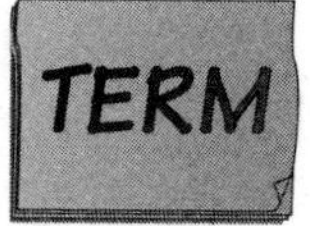

Subset A *subset* is a group of records that contain the data you specified in the filter. The subset is similar to a query's dynaset.

For example, suppose you had to create a subset of the prospects in Region 1 from the PROSPECT database. Follow these steps to create a filter:

1. Open the form from the **Database** window if it is not already open.
2. Click on the **Edit Filter/Sort** button on the tool bar, or choose **Edit Filter/Sort** from the **Records** menu.

3. The Filter window opens (see Figure 12.2). Notice that you can define criteria and select a sort order, but you can't perform calculations (as you can in a query).

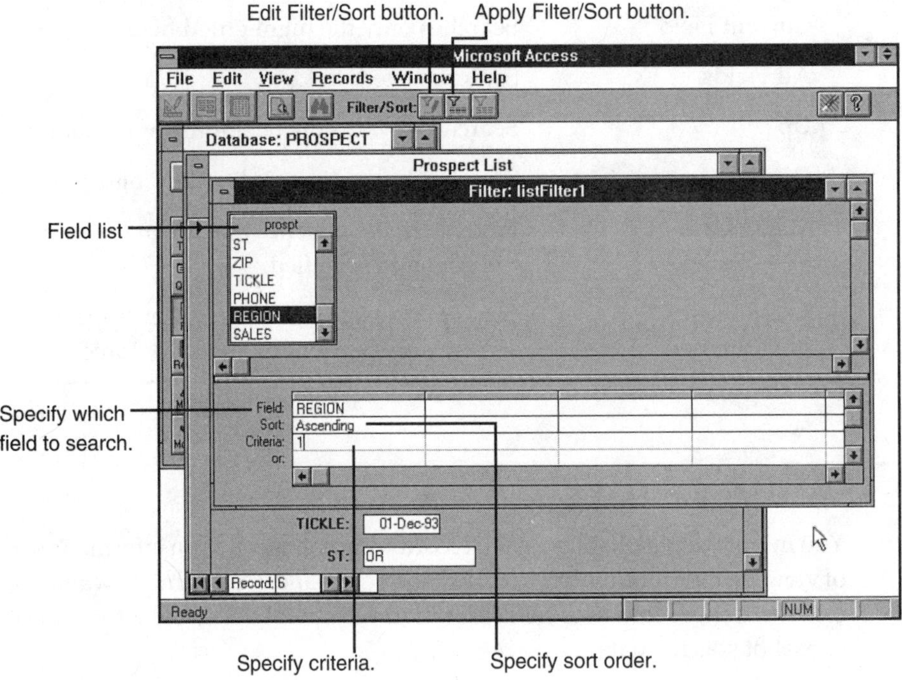

Figure 12.2 The Filter window.

4. From the **field list**, drag the desired field to the **Field** row. For our example, drag the **REGION** field to the first cell in the first column.

5. Enter the data you want Access to search for in the Criteria row. For our example, you would type the number **1** in the **Criteria** row to tell Access to search for all of the REGION fields that contain the number 1 (see Figure 12.2).

6. Specify the sort order in the **Sort** row. In our example, you would choose **Ascending** so the prospects would be in alphabetical order.

7. To see the results in a subset, click on the **Apply Filter/Sort** button on the tool bar, or choose **Apply Filter/Sort** from the **Records** menu (see Figure 12.3).

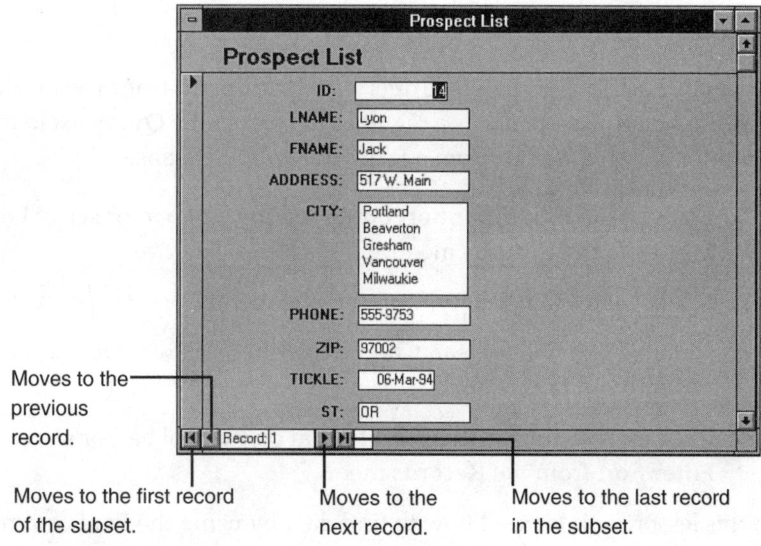

Figure 12.3 The result of using a filter.

Don't Panic! Subsets, much like dynasets, are only temporary datasheets. When you create a filter, you are not changing your data in any way. Access is simply extracting the information you want from your table, and making it easier for you to view.

Saving a Filter

Because subsets are temporary, they cannot be saved. However, the filters that create the subsets can be saved as queries. To save a filter, select **Save As Query** from the **File** menu when you are in the **Filter** window. Name your filter, and then press **Enter** or click on **OK**.

Naming Filters When saving the filter as a query, don't use the name of any existing table, or the table and its data will be overwritten.

Using a Filter Saved as a Query

After you have saved a filter as a query, you can open it from a form whenever you want. You can also open it as a regular query from the **Query** list in the Database window. To open a filter from a form, follow these steps:

1. Click on the **Edit Filter/Sort** button on the tool bar, or select **Edit Filter/ Sort** from the **Records** menu.
2. Select **Load From Query** from the **File** menu.
3. A dialog box will appear. Choose the filter you want to use, and click on **OK** or press **Enter**.
4. Click on the **Apply Filter/Sort** button on the tool bar, or select **Apply Filter/Sort** from the **Records** menu.

In this lesson, you learned how to find data by using the Find command and by using a filter. In the next lesson, you will learn how to create and use indexes.

Using Indexes

In this lesson, you will learn how to create single-field and multiple-field indexes.

Creating Indexes

Indexes are used to access a specific record in a table quickly. If you have large tables, you will find that using an index speeds up the process of locating records. When you index a field, you are telling Access where to find the data, (as with an index in a book). Unlike subsets and dynasets, you cannot see an index. It is not a tool for viewing data, it is simply a way for Access to find your data more quickly.

Indexes are saved along with the table, and are changed automatically whenever you make changes in your fields. For this reason, it is probably not a good idea to use an index if you update your data often. When you change a lot of information, it can take Access quite a while to update the indexes. They are handy, however, if you search for data a lot—especially when you specify one or two particular fields in the search.

For example, say that you have a large table that stores records of clients. You search this table often for the last names of certain people, using the LNAME field. In this situation, using an index would allow you to find the data you need, quickly. To create an index, follow these steps:

1. Make sure you are in **Table Design** view.
2. Click on the field you want to index. Its properties will be shown in the window at the bottom of the screen. For our example, you would click on the **LNAME** field.
3. Click on the **Indexed** field in the **Field Properties** box.
4. Use the drop-down list box to select the conditions for your index. You can tell Access not to accept any duplicate values in the field, or you can specify that duplicates are okay (see Figure 13.1). In our example, you would choose **Yes (Duplicates OK)** because there might be more than one customer with the same last name.

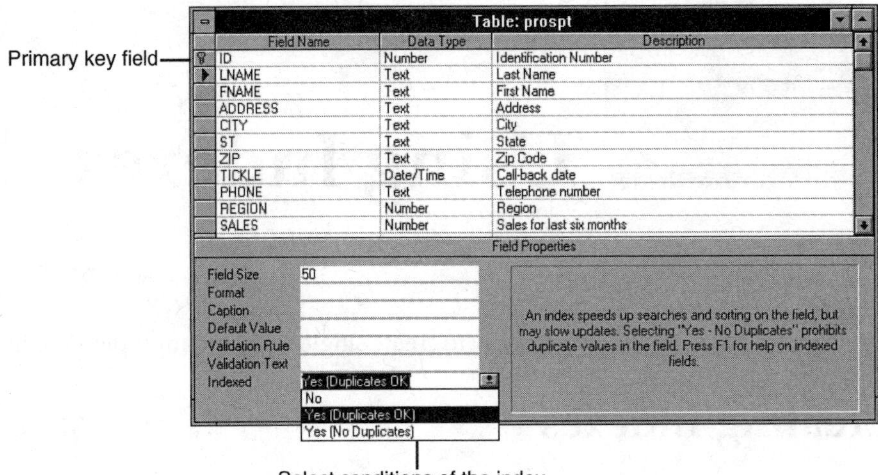

Figure 13.1 Creating an index for a field.

Primary Key Fields When you create a primary key field (see Lesson 4), Access automatically creates an index for that field. The index property will be set for Yes (No Duplicates) so that Access can use the primary key field to distinguish between the records in the table.

Multiple-Field Indexes

If you have a large table, you might search for records by using criteria in two different fields. In that case, you should consider creating indexes for the two (or more) fields you search most often.

For example, our sample table from the last section contains the names of our clients. If we have hundreds of records, chances are good that there are several people who have the same last name. If you are searching for a client named Susan Jones, it's easier for Access to filter through all the Joneses if you create an index for the FNAME field too.

To create a multiple-field index, follow these steps:

1. Make sure you are in **Table Design** view.
2. Click on the **Properties** button on the tool bar, or select **Properties** from the **View** menu.

3. The Properties box should show your primary key field and a list of fields labeled Index 1–5. Select **Index1** if this is the only index you have.
4. In the Index1 field, type in the names of the fields to index separated by semicolons. For our example, you would type **LNAME;FNAME** (see Figure 13.2).
5. To create the index, save the table by selecting **Save** from the File menu.

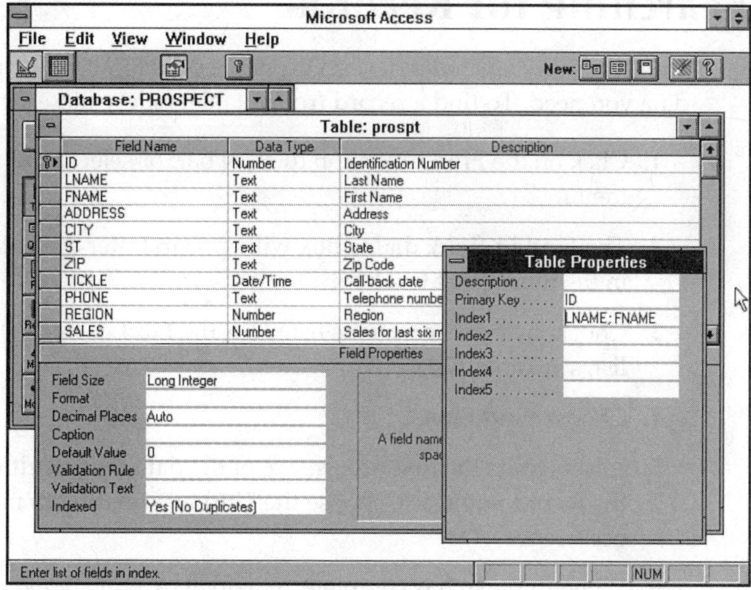

Figure 13.2 Creating a multiple-field index.

Deleting Indexes

You can create as many indexes as you need, but remember that using them will slow down the process of updating your records. You should index only those fields you search often. If you want to delete an index for a field that you don't search often, change the **Indexed** property to **No** by using the drop-down list in the **Field Properties** box.

To delete a multiple-field index, select the index you want to delete in the **Table Properties** box, and press the **Delete** key.

What Am I Deleting? When you delete an index, you aren't actually deleting anything. Your fields (and the data in them) remain exactly the same. You are simply telling Access that it doesn't have to remember where your records are for that field any more.

Searching for Records

Once you have created indexes, you can use the **Find** command to search for the data you need. To find a record from a table, follow these steps:

1. Click on the **Find** button on the tool bar, or select **Find** from the **Edit** menu.
2. The **Find in field:** dialog box will appear. Enter the data you wish to find in the Find What text box.
3. Choose any of the options listed for the **Find in field:** dialog box (for a list, see Table 12.1).
4. Choose **Find First**.
5. Access finds the first occurrence of the data you specified. If this is not the record you want, choose the **Find Next** button to move to the next occurrence.
6. When the search is complete, a dialog box will appear asking you if you want to start the search from the top again. Choose **No**, then close the Find in field: dialog box.

In this lesson, you learned how to use indexes. In the next lesson, you will learn how to create reports.

Creating and Using Reports

In this lesson, you will learn how to create a simple report from a table.

Using Reports

Reports are useful for communicating to people in an organized way. With Microsoft Access, one of the best ways to communicate your message is with a form or report. Lesson 8 showed you how to use forms to communicate your message. In this lesson, we'll look at using reports. Which should you use? Forms are useful for doing simple reports as well as viewing and editing your data. They are limited, however, in that you can't group data to show group and grand totals, you have less control over the layout, and you can't insert a report into a form. Reports can't be used to view or edit data, but you have more layout control, can group data for totals, and you can insert a report or graph into a report (see Lesson 17).

Creating a Report

Microsoft Access includes a ReportWizard feature which makes it simple to create reports from tables or queries. You will use it in this lesson to create a report from a table.

To create a report, open the database, if it is not already open, using **Open Database** on the **File** menu. When the Database window is displayed, choose the **Report** button at the left, then select **New**. A New Report window is displayed (see Figure 14.1).

Figure 14.1 Starting to create a new report.

In the **Select A Table/Query** text box, click on the **down arrow** at the right or press **Alt+↓**. A list box will open, displaying available tables from which you can build reports. Click on the name of the desired table for the report. Now choose the **ReportWizards** button by clicking on it, or by pressing **Alt+W**. The following steps will help walk you through the ReportWizards:

1. On the first screen, select the **AccessWizard** you want to use. Choose **Single-column**, and then **OK** (see Figure 14.2).
2. Choose the fields for the report or select **>>** to move all the fields to the list box (see Figure 14.3). Then choose **Next**.
3. Choose the sort order from the fields (see Figure 14.4), and choose **Next**.
4. Choose the look for the report. For our example, choose **Executive** (see Figure 14.5) and click on **Next**.
5. Enter a title for the report (see Figure 14.6), and choose **Print Preview**.

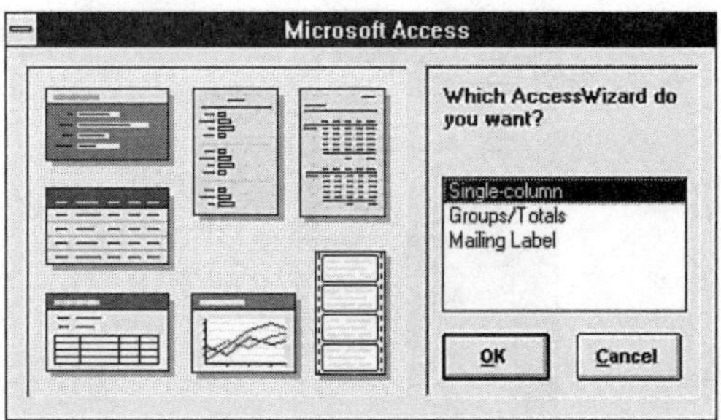

Figure 14.2 Choosing the layout for the report.

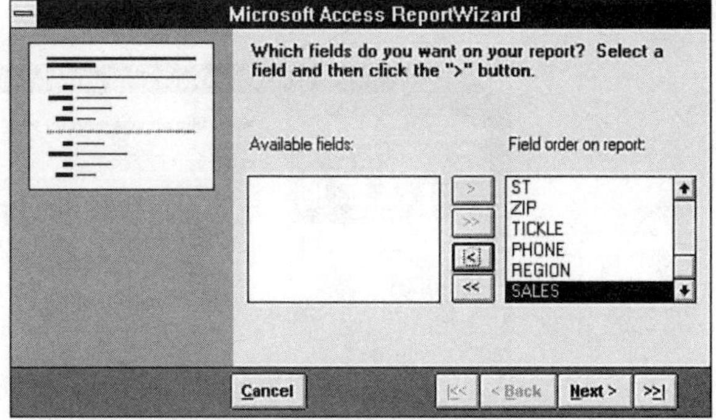

Figure 14.3 Choosing the fields to report.

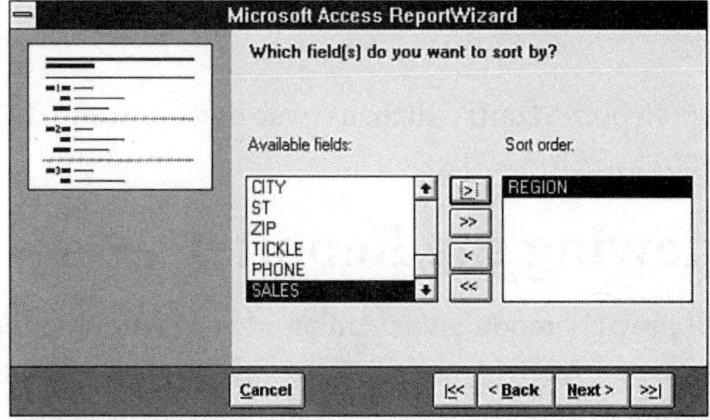

Figure 14.4 Choosing the sort order for the report.

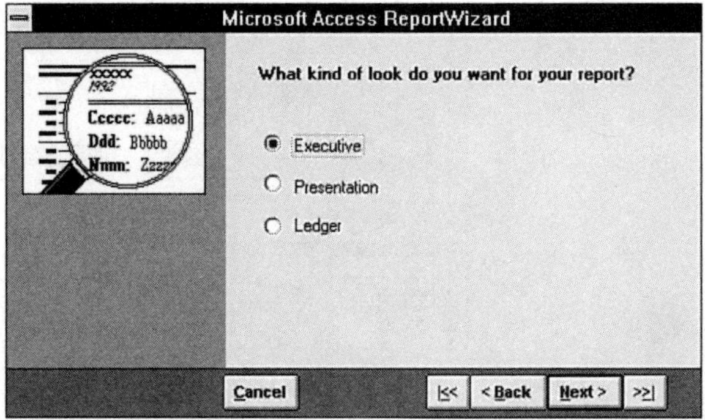

Figure 14.5 Choosing the style of the report.

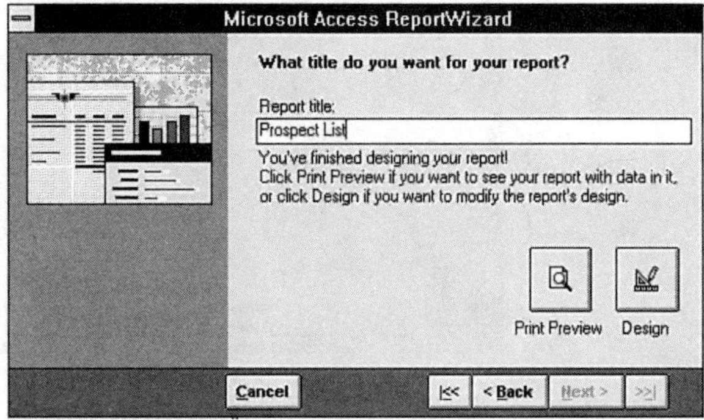

Figure 14.6 Entering the report title.

ReportWizard will then create the report and display a preview of what will print.

Previewing the Report

The preview mode gives you an idea of what the report will look like and the number of pages that will print before actually printing it. The pages will be magnified, and you can scroll through them using the horizontal and vertical scroll bars. You can use the Page buttons at the bottom of the window to scroll through the pages. The inside arrows move you a page at a time. The outside arrows move you quickly to the first or last page.

To see the entire page, move the cursor to the page (it becomes a small magnifying glass), and click. You can return to the magnified view again by clicking where you want to view.

Preview You can always return to the Preview mode of a given report by choosing **Print Preview** from the **File** menu.

Printing the Report

You can print the report by choosing the **Print** button on the **Print Preview** window or by choosing **Print** from the **File** menu. A Print dialog box will be displayed. Set the options you wish, and then choose **OK**.

Saving the Report

After you have created the report, you should save it. To save the report, choose **Save As** from the **File** menu. Enter the name you wish to use for saving the report, and choose **OK**. Do not use the name of any existing table, query, or form.

In this lesson, you learned how to create a report. In the next lesson, you will learn how to create custom reports.

Creating Custom Reports

In this lesson, you will learn how to customize a report form.

Modifying a Report Form

You can modify your report in various ways—moving items to other locations, resizing them, adding labels, and setting text attributes. To modify a report form, follow these steps:

1. Open the database, and choose the **Report** button in the Database window. Existing reports in the database are shown in the list.
2. Highlight the report you want to modify, and choose the **Design** button in the Database window. The report is displayed (see Figure 15.1) and can be modified, much like a form. The Toolbox is displayed by default, and you can turn on the **Report Properties** box by selecting **Properties** from the **View** menu.

Resizing Controls

Each object on the displayed report is a control. In the report's Design view, you can move and resize the controls, as well as add new controls.

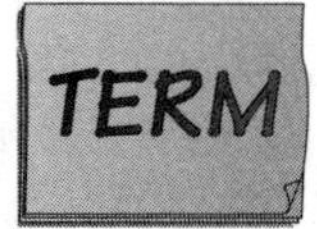

Control An object on a report or form that displays the data in a field, a calculation result, specific text, a graph, a picture, or another object.

To manipulate a control, you must first select it. To select a text box with a label, click on the associated text box. The text box and its associated label will be displayed with handles (see Figure 15.1). The handles show as small black squares. Moving the mouse pointer to a handle will change the pointer to an arrow (when you are resizing the box) or a hand (when you are moving the box).

- To resize the box vertically, drag the **top** and **bottom** handles.
- To resize a box horizontally, drag the **right** and **left** handles.
- To resize a box horizontally and vertically at the same time, drag the **diagonal** handles.

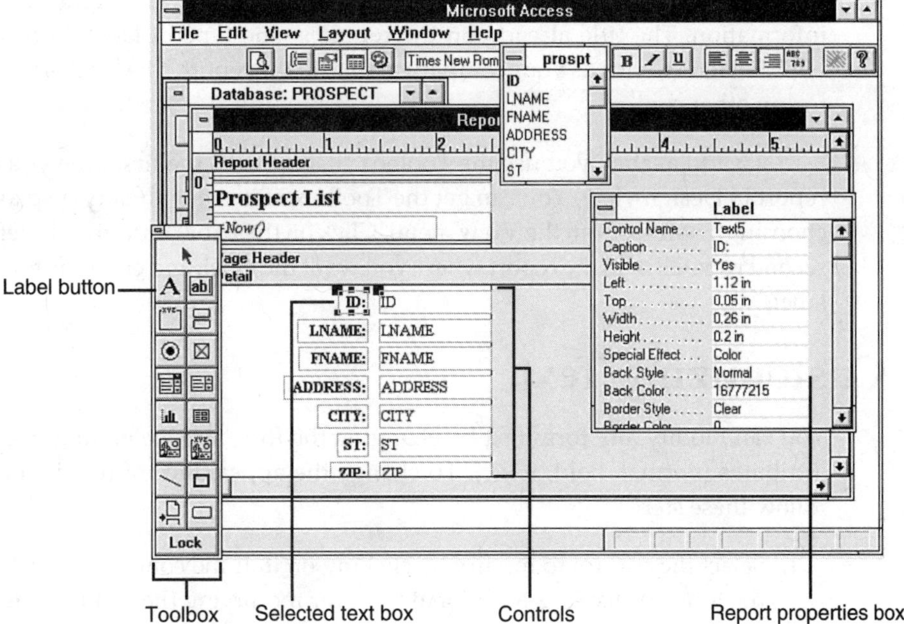

Figure 15.1 The Report Design view.

Use the displayed rulers to align your work. You can select more than one control at a time by holding down the **Shift** key while clicking on them.

Moving Controls

Microsoft Access permits you to move a text box and its associated label together, or you can move each separately. To move a text box or label separately, select the control, and then drag the large handle in the upper left. This handle is known as the *move handle*. The cursor will be a pointing hand.

To move the text box and label together, click on a control until the pointer is a flat-palm hand, and drag the text box and its label to the new position.

Use the Rulers The rulers can help with alignment when moving and resizing controls.

Adding a Label

A *label* is simply text that is added to the report at a later time to display information. The title already on the report is one type of label. You can add additional text, such as your company name, to the report. The label is not bound to any other control.

To add a label, you use the Toolbox that appears the first time you open a report in Design view. You can get the Toolbox, if it is not already displayed, by choosing **Toolbox** from the **View** menu. Click on the **Label** button at the left in the second row. Click in the report where you want the label, and enter the text for the label.

Customizing Text

You can modify any form text by changing the font, size, color, alignment, and attributes (normal, bold, italic). To change the appearance of text in a control, follow these steps:

1. Select the control to modify by clicking on it. If the control contains text, the tool bar displays additional tools for modifying the text (see Figure 15.2).
2. Click on any of the following buttons to customize.

Button	*Function*
Bold	Toggles boldface on or off.
Italic	Toggles italics on or off.
Underline	Toggles underlining on or off.
Left align	Sets the text to left alignment.
Center align	Centers the text in the margins.

Button	*Function*
Right align	Sets the text to right alignment.
Font	Selects the desired font.
Size	Sets the font size.

Figure 15.2 The tool bar for modifying text features.

3. To set the color of the text, click on the **Palette** button, or select **Palette** from the **View** menu. From the Palette window (see Figure 15.3), you can set the color of the text or you can set separate fill and outline colors. You can also set the appearance (normal, raised, sunken) of the text and the border width. To close the Palette window double-click on the small bar in the upper left of the window.

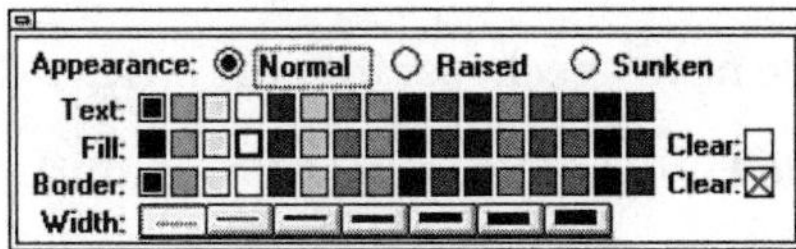

Figure 15.3 The Palette window.

4. After you have completed your work, choose **Size to Fit** from the **Layout** menu to resize the label to the new text.

Adding a Field to a Report

You can add fields to a report after it is created. Open the report in Design view and then open the field list. You can then drag fields to the appropriate place on the report.

Creating a Report with Grouped Data

You can use Microsoft Access to create reports with grouped data, showing subtotals and totals. For example, suppose you want to create a report showing sales by region with the grand sales total. You would use ReportWizard to create the report from the same table. Use this procedure:

1. Select **Report** from the Database window.
2. Choose **New** on the Database window.
3. On the New Report window, choose the **PROSPT** table from the list box, and then choose **ReportWizard**.
4. On the screen that selects the AccessWizard, select **Groups/Totals**. Choose **OK**.
5. On the new screen, select the fields to print and their order. Select **ID**, **LNAME**, **FNAME**, **REGION**, and **SALES**. Choose **Next**.
6. On the new screen, select to group by **REGION**. Choose **Next**.
7. On the new screen, select how to group as **Normal**. Choose **Next**.
8. On the next screen, set the sort order to **SALES**. Click on **Next**.
9. Set the **Look** to **Executive** (the default), and choose **Next**.
10. Enter the title, and choose **Print Preview** to see the report.

This procedure will create a report with the sales totaled by region, including a grand total.

In this lesson, you learned how to customize reports. In the next lesson, you will learn how to create mailing labels.

16 Creating Mailing Labels

In this lesson, you'll learn how to print simple mailing labels from your data in the database.

Introduction to Using Mailing Labels

The ability to create mailing labels is important for using address lists effectively. For example, you could print labels from the PROSPT prospect list created in Lesson 5, and use them to mail brochures or letters to the prospects.

Mailing labels come in many sizes and types. Some labels are designed for sprocket-feed printers that pull the labels through. Other labels come in sheets, and are designed for laser printers. Labels can also come in single-, two-, or three-column sizes. A two-up label, for example, means the labels are in two columns. Microsoft Access has the ability to print addresses with a wide variety of label types, and will support most of the common label sizes.

Use the Proper Labels for Your Printer! The adhesive gum used with standard peel-off labels does not work properly with the high temperatures of a laser printer. The labels can come off inside the printer and jam. Instead, use peel-off labels designed for laser printers.

Creating a Mailing Label Report

Using the Microsoft Access ReportWizard, you can create a special type of report that prints mailing labels. You can then save the report and use it again later.

This procedure will use examples from the table created in Lesson 5, or you can use any sample database with an address table (such as the Customer table in the NWIND database provided with Access). To create a report:

1. If the database is not already open, use **Open Database** on the **File** menu to open it.
2. When the Database window is displayed, choose the **Report** button at the left, then select **New**. A New Report window is displayed (see Figure 16.1).

Figure 16.1 The New Report window.

3. In the New Report window's **Select Table/Query** text box, click on the **down arrow** at the right, or press **Alt+↓**. A list box will open, displaying available tables and queries.
4. Click on the name of the desired table for the mailing labels. Now choose the **ReportWizards** button by clicking on it, or by pressing **Alt+W**. (Steps 5–9 walk you through the ReportWizard.)
5. On the first ReportWizard screen, choose **Mailing Label** and then click on **OK** (see Figure 16.2).
6. From the Available fields list, choose the fields you want on the mailing label; using the **right arrow**, place them in the **Label appearance** box in the order you would like them printed.

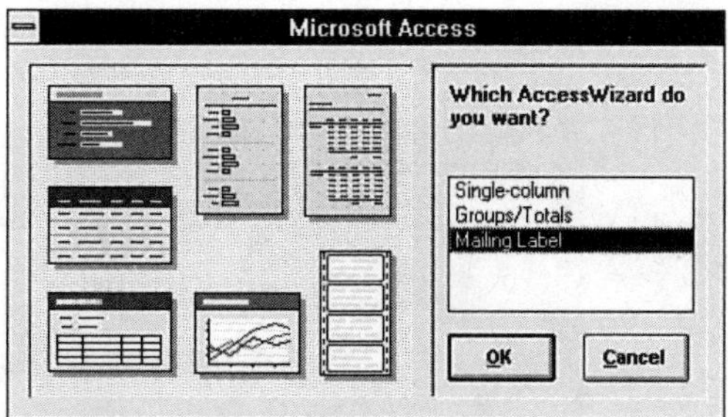

Figure 16.2 Choosing the mailing label report type.

7. Use the **Punctuation** buttons to enter the punctuation on the label. Here FNAME and LNAME are placed on the first line, ADDRESS on the next line, and CITY, ST, and ZIP on the third line. Punctuation is added as appropriate. Press the **Return** button between lines (see Figure 16.3). Choose **Next**.

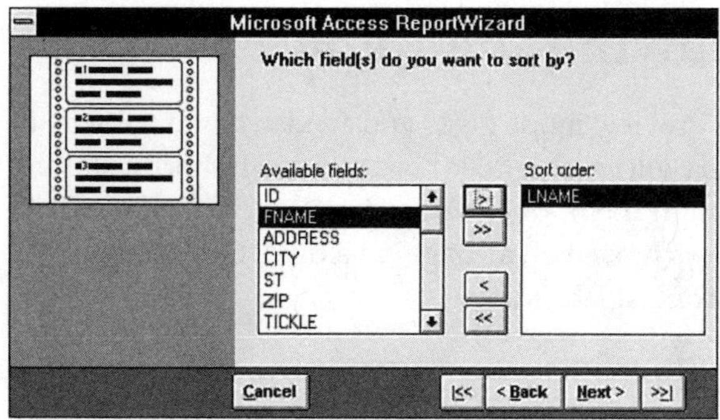

Figure 16.3 Entering punctuation on the mailing label.

8. Choose the sort order of the labels to print by placing the field names in the Sort order box, using the **right arrow**. Here the sort is by LNAME. Choose **Next**.

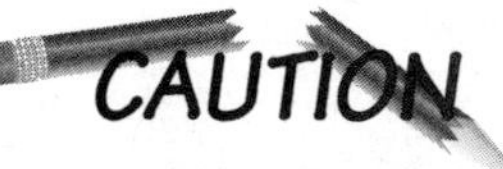

What If I Make a Mistake? If you make a mistake, use the backward arrow to clear the last change.

9. To choose the size of your mailing label, scroll to the correct size (see Figure 16.4), and select **Next**.

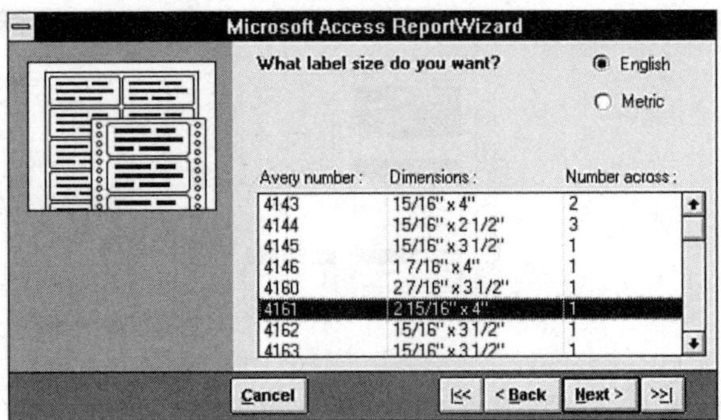

Figure 16.4 Choosing the mailing label size.

10. Select **Print Preview** from the last screen.

ReportWizard will then create the mailing label report, and display a preview of what will print.

Previewing the Report

The Preview mode gives you an idea of what the mailing labels will look like; the labels will be magnified. You can use the horizontal and vertical scroll bars to scroll through them, or the page buttons (at the bottom of the window). The inside arrows move you a "page" at a time; the outside arrows move you quickly to the first or last labels.

To see the entire "page," move the cursor (it becomes a small magnifying glass) to the page and click. You can return to the magnified view again by clicking where you want to view.

You can always return to the Preview mode of the mailing label report by choosing **Print Preview** from the **File** menu.

Printing the Mailing Labels

You can print the labels by following these steps:

1. Choose the **Print** button on the **Print Preview** window, or choose **Print** from the **File** menu. A Print dialog box will be displayed.
2. Set the options you want.
3. Choose **OK**.

Saving the Report

After you have created the label report, you should save it for future use. To save the report, follow these steps:

1. Choose **Save As** from the **File** menu.
2. Enter the name you want to use for saving the mailing label report. Do not use the name of any existing table, query, or form.
3. Choose **OK**.

In this lesson, you learned how to create and print mailing labels. In the next lesson, you will learn how to create graphs.

17

Creating Graphs

In this lesson, you will learn how to add a graph to a report.

Introduction to Graphing

Graphs show information in visual relationships, and are especially useful for people who don't have time to read an entire report. A busy manager, for example, may find it quicker to look at a graph of sales by region than to decipher a statistical report.

Lesson 5's prospect database shows sales by region, so this lesson will refer to it. (You can use any database to try the procedure, including the Access samples; in that case, the database, table, and field names will be different.) First we will create a query on which the report will be based. Then we will create the report without the graph, using ReportWizard. Finally, we will use the Report Design view, and add the graph with a GraphWizard utility.

Creating the Query

First, let's create the query that shows sales by region. Open the database (if necessary); choose **Query** and **New** in the Database window.

1. In the Add Table window, choose **PROSPT** and click on the **Add** button.
2. Choose the **Close** button to close the Add Table window.
3. Scroll to find **REGION** in the list box. Drag **REGION** from the list to the first cell of the Field row of the grid.
4. Move **SALES** from the list to the next cell of the Field row of the grid.
5. Click on the **Total** button in the tool bar (or select **Totals** from the **View** menu) to add a Total row to the grid.

6. In the Total row, the cell under the Field row's **SALES** cell has the words **Group By**. Click on this **Group By** cell to open the drop-down list box, and choose **Sum**.
7. Click on the **Datasheet View** button to verify the totals in a dynaset.
8. Save the query (as **SALESQ** for this example), using the Save Query **A**s command on the **F**ile menu.
9. Press **F11** (or close the Query window) to return to the Database window.

Creating the Report

Now that this query has shown us sales by region, use ReportWizard to create a report based on the query.

1. Click on **Report** and then **New** in the Database window.
2. In the **T**able/Query text box, select the query you just created and saved (**SALESQ**).
3. Choose **ReportWizards**.
4. Select **Single Column** and **OK**.
5. On the next screen, choose the fields for the report. Select **>>** to move both the fields to the list box. Then choose **Next**.
6. On the next screen, choose the sort order (**REGION**) from the fields, and then select **Next**.
7. On the next screen, choose **Executive** and then **Next**.
8. On the next screen, enter a title and choose **Print Preview**. Verify that the report totals are correct.

Adding the Graph

Now add the graph to the report by following these steps:

1. Set the report to Design view by clicking on **Cancel** (if necessary) in the Print Preview window.

Get Back to Design You can always get to a report's Design view from a preview by clicking on **Cancel**.

2. Scroll down the Report window so that you have 23 inches of space under the footer section.
3. Click on the **Graph** button in the Toolbox (see Figure 17.1). If the Toolbox isn't showing, select it from the **View** menu.

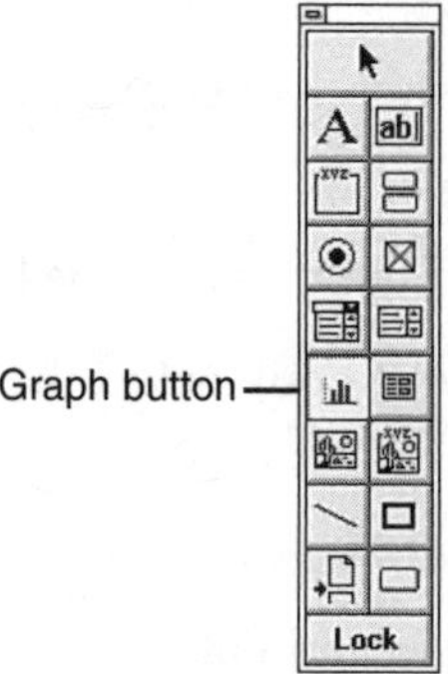

Figure 17.1 The Graph button in the Toolbox.

4. Using the mouse, drag to draw a control in the area below the report footer section for the graph. Make it about two inches high and six inches wide; use the rulers as necessary. (This will be the size not only of the control, but of the eventual graph.) When you complete the drag, a dialog box will be displayed (see Figure 17.2).

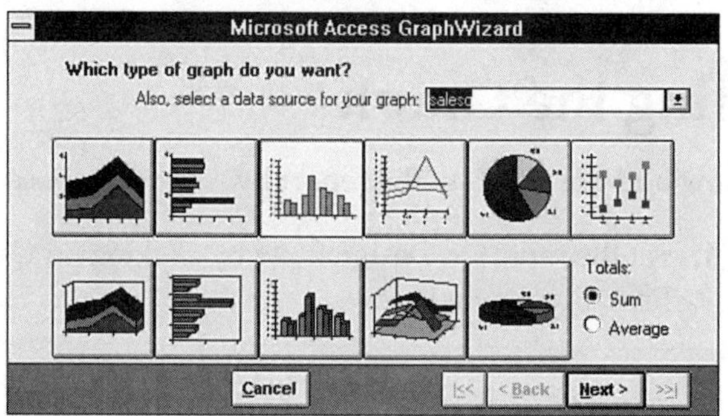

Figure 17.2 The Microsoft Access GraphWizard dialog box.

5. Now choose the data for the graph. In the text box, click on the arrow to open the list. Then choose the query on which you want to base the graph (SALESQ). Leave the default graph as two-column, and choose **Next**.
6. In the next box, select the fields for the graph. Choose **SumOfSales** and >, and then **Next**.
7. The next box asks whether to link the graph to the data; choose **No**. This means the graph won't change if the table's data is changed.
8. Enter the title on the next box, and choose the **Design** button.

Choose **Print Preview** on the **File** menu to see the report with the graph (see Figure 17.3).

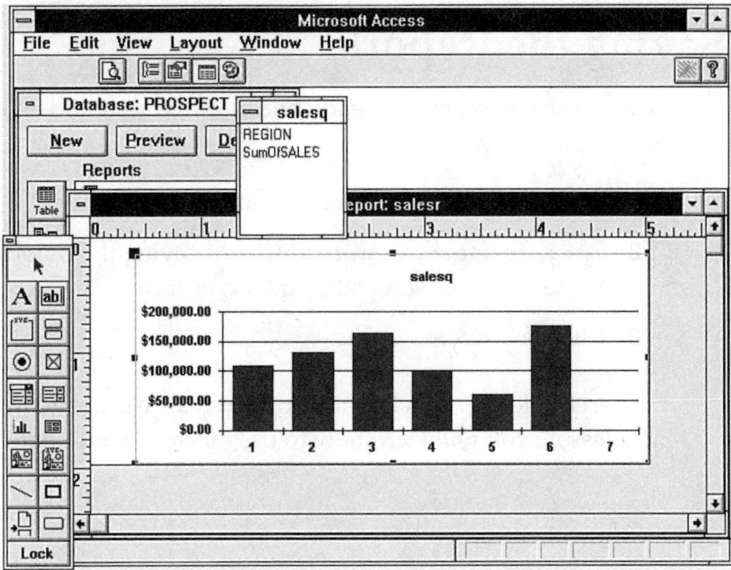

Figure 17.3 The final graph.

Editing the Graph

If you want to edit the graph, first **Cancel** any existing Print Preview window. Then double-click on the graph in Design view. This will open the graph in Microsoft Graph, a modular program that comes with Access (and resembles the chart mode of Excel, Microsoft's spreadsheet program). You can now add labels or titles, and even change the chart type, from the menu. To return to Access, choose **Exit** and **Return to Microsoft Access** from the **File** menu.

Printing the Report and Graph

You can print the report and graph by following these steps:

1. Choose the **Print** button on the Print Preview window, or choose **Print** from the **File** menu. A Print dialog box will be displayed.
2. Set the options you want.
3. Choose **OK**.

Saving the Report

After you have created the report and graph, you should save it. To save the report, follow these steps:

1. Choose **Save As** from the **File** menu.
2. Enter the name you want to use for saving the report. Do not use the name of any existing table, query, or form.
3. Choose **OK**.

In this lesson, you learned how to create a graph to use with a report. In the next lesson, you will learn how to use macros to automate your work.

18 Automating Your Work

In this lesson, you will learn how to use macros to automate your work.

What's a Macro?

After you have used Microsoft Access for a short while, you will probably find you have a few tasks you do repeatedly—for example, opening a form and going to the end of a table to enter records. Such an action can be automated, so that a single command will set up the table for data entry. You can do this with a *macro*.

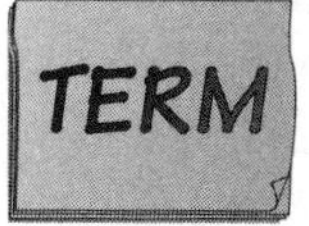

Macro A list of actions you want Microsoft Access to perform for you automatically.

Creating a Macro

Let's say you want to create a macro that will open a frequently used form (and table), and display an empty form at the end of the table for data entry. Open the database (use **Open Database** on the **File** menu), and then follow these steps:

1. Click on the **Macro** button in the Database window. Then choose **New**.
2. Click on the drop-down box in the **Action** column (see Figure 18.1) to see a list of available actions.

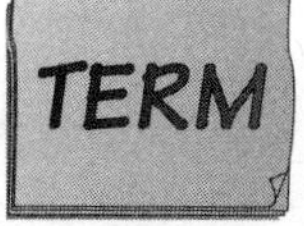

The Macro Window and Its Arguments The *Macro window* is a two-column sheet for entering the actions you want the macro to execute. Many of these actions have *arguments*, additional information that you supply to specify how you want the action carried out.

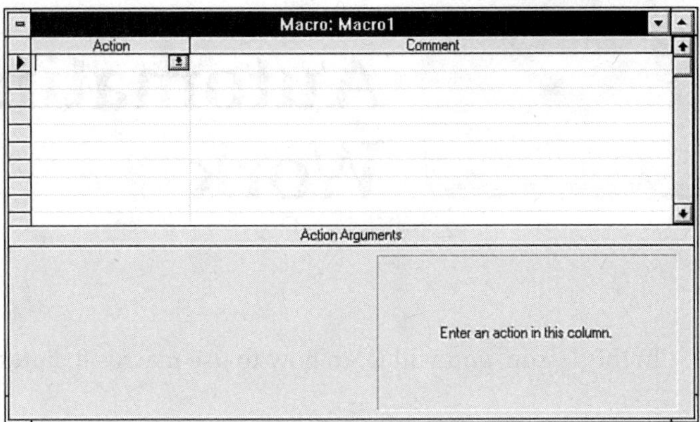

Figure 18.1 The Macro window.

3. From the Microsoft Access **Window** menu, choose **Tile** so you can see the Database window and the Macro window at the same time.
4. Choose **Form** on the Database window, and drag the desired form from the Database window to the upper left cell of the Macro window. When you release the mouse button, the word **OpenForm** will be in the cell. At the bottom of the Macro window, in an **Action Arguments** area, you can see the name of the form as the **Form Name**, one of the arguments for this command (see Figure 18.2). When the macro executes this cell, Microsoft Access will open the associated form and its table.
5. Click on the **second cell down** and then the **arrow** to open the list box. Click on **DoMenuItem** to copy it to the Macro window. This puts the second command in the macro.
6. In the Action Arguments, click on the **Menu Name** field (currently containing Edit) to see the drop-down menu items, and choose **Records** as the Menu item. In the same way click on **Command** and choose **Go To**. Click on **Subcommand** and choose **New**. This puts the arguments in the second command (see Figure 18.3).
7. Save the Macro window, using **Save As** on the **File** menu. Enter a macro name, such as **PROSPM**. Click on **OK**.
8. Close the Macro window by choosing **Close** on the **File** menu with the Macro window active. The Database window should still be open.

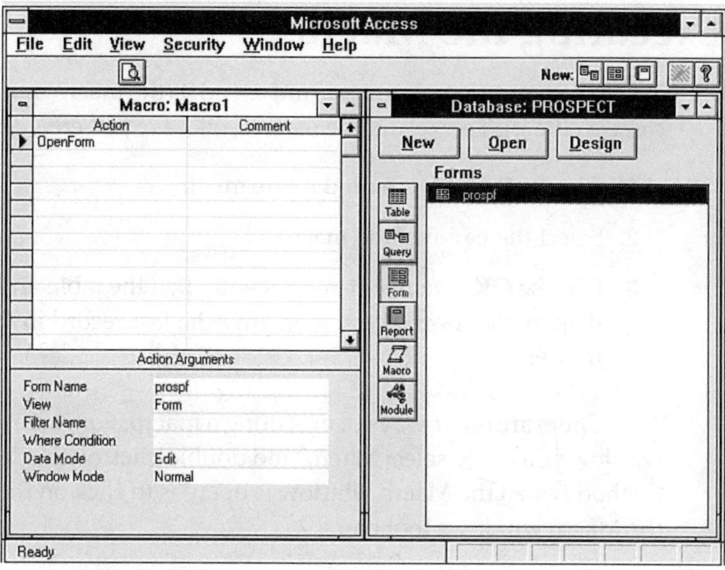

Figure 18.2 Entering the Action Arguments.

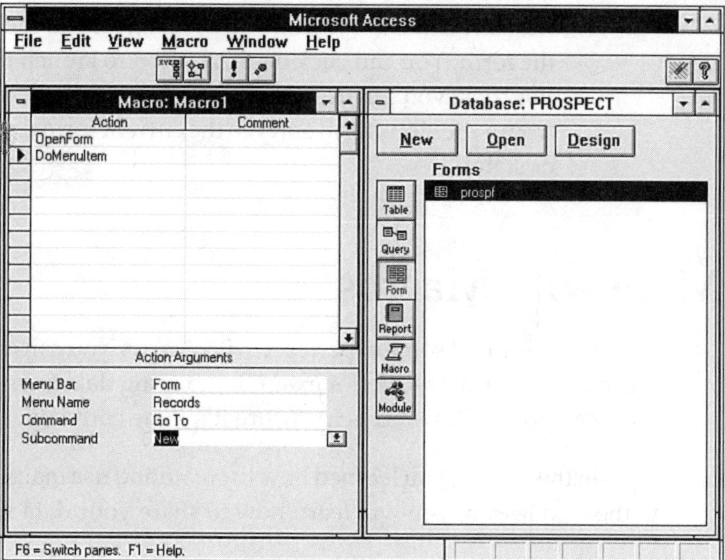

Figure 18.3 Editing the second command.

Executing the Macro

You have now created a macro and saved it (the macro must be saved before you can execute it). To execute the macro you have just created, follow these steps:

1. Choose **Run Macro** on the **File** menu.
2. Select the name of the macro.
3. Choose **OK**. Microsoft Access will open the table and form, and then display the form (positioned after the last record in the table), ready for a new entry.

There are other ways of executing a macro. For example, from the Database window you could select Macro, and double-click on the desired macro. Another method (when the Macro window is open) is to click on the exclamation point in the Macro windows tool bar.

Buttons for Launching Macros You can also use buttons to launch macro execution. For example, if you drag a macro name from the Database window to a form, you will see a new button on the form. You can click on this button to launch the macro. Using this trick, you can use a macro to open a second form, or copy data from a previous form entry to the current form entry (such as a city or state).

More with Macros

Once you have had some experience with Access, you can create macros for doing much of the routine work (for example, copying data from one form to another). They can do it faster, and help ensure it's done correctly.

In this lesson, you learned how to create and use macros in Microsoft Access. In the next lesson, you will learn how to share your data with other programs.

Sharing Data with Other Programs

In this lesson, you will learn how to share data between Microsoft Access and other programs you may be using.

Importing, Exporting, and Attaching

You may already have data files for other programs such as Microsoft Excel, Lotus 1-2-3, dBASE IV, or Paradox. This data can be used with Microsoft Access to build reports, print mailing labels, and do queries. In Microsoft Access, you can manipulate data from other programs just as you can manipulate data created in Access. You can also use your Microsoft Access data with external programs (such as spreadsheets or other databases).

- When data in a Microsoft Access database table is transferred to an *external* database (or other program), this is called *exporting* the data. Access uses a table within the other program to create an external file that is compatible with it. Both files remain static; that is, updating one does not update the other.

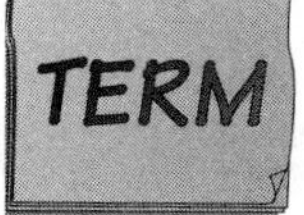

External Database When you are importing data, an *external* database is one that is not a part of your open Microsoft Access database.

- When you transfer data from an external program to Microsoft Access, you are *importing* the data. Using the external program's file, Access creates an internal table it can use. Both files remain static; that is, updating one does not update the other.
- You can attach an external database to a Microsoft Access database. Although much slower than importing files, this process allows you to view, edit, or report from the other program's data as though it were in

Microsoft Access, while staying within Access. There is a single file; users external to Access can use this file, even while you are updating or reporting from its data from within Access.

Exporting Data

When you export data, you are creating a file in the format of another program from a table in Microsoft Access. Beginning with an open database (such as PROSPECT), let's try an example: exporting a table in the format of dBASE (a Borland database product). Follow these steps:

1. Choose **Export** from the **File** menu.
2. In the **Data Destination** list box of the **Export** window, choose the destination format (see Figure 19.1). In this example, **dBASE IV** was chosen. Choose **OK**.

Figure 19.1 Choosing a format for the file to be exported.

3. In the **Select Microsoft Access Object** dialog box, choose the table name and select **OK** (see Figure 19.2). In this example, **PROSPT** was chosen.

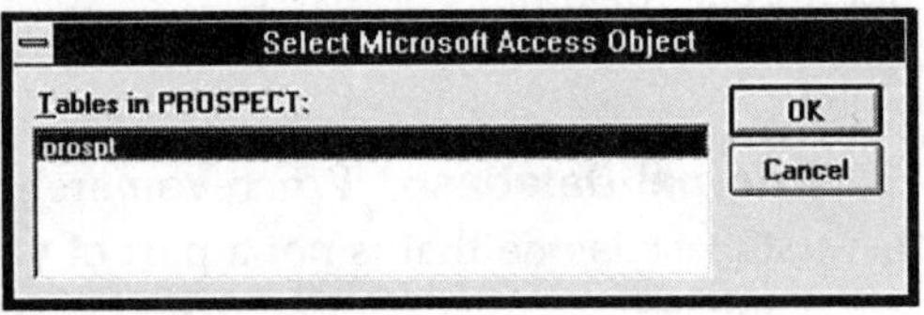

Figure 19.2 Choosing a name for the table to be exported.

4. In the **Export to File** dialog box, enter the name of the destination file (see Figure 19.3). Also select the drive and directory if necessary. Choose **OK**.

The destination file will be created in the desired format. In this case the file PROSPT.DBF (a dBASE file format) will be created.

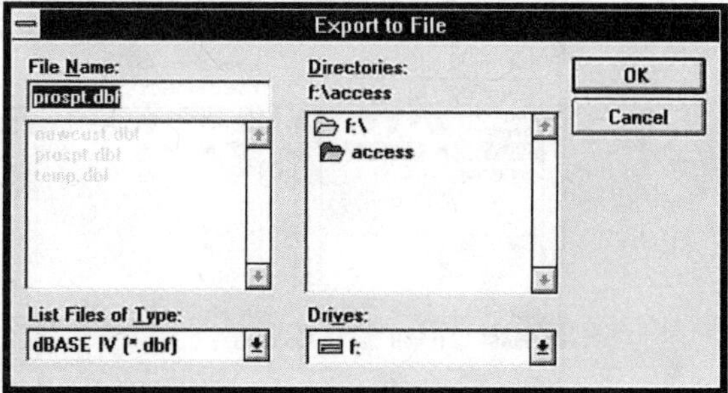

Figure 19.3 Choosing a name for the destination file.

Importing Data

When you import data, you are creating a table in Access from a file that is in another program. This external file could be in the format of Excel, Lotus 1-2-3, Paradox, dBASE IV, or even Microsoft Access (in another database). Let's see how to import the file we just created. Open a database (such as **PROSPECT**) if one is not already open.

1. Choose **Import** from the **File** menu.
2. In the **Data Source** list box of the Import dialog box, choose the type of input file to import (see Figure 19.4). Choose **OK**.

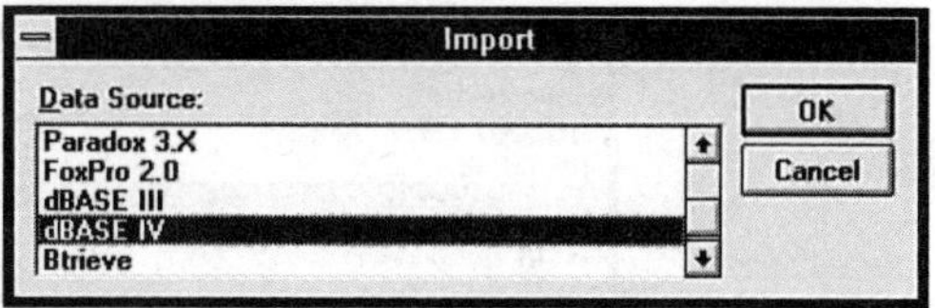

Figure 19.4 Choosing the type of file to import.

3. In the **Select File** dialog box, choose the drive and directory for the input file, and the name of the file you want to import (see Figure 19.5). Select **Import**.
4. After importing, the screen will display the message **Successfully Imported *[filename]***. Choose **OK** in the message box. The message will vary with the type of file imported.

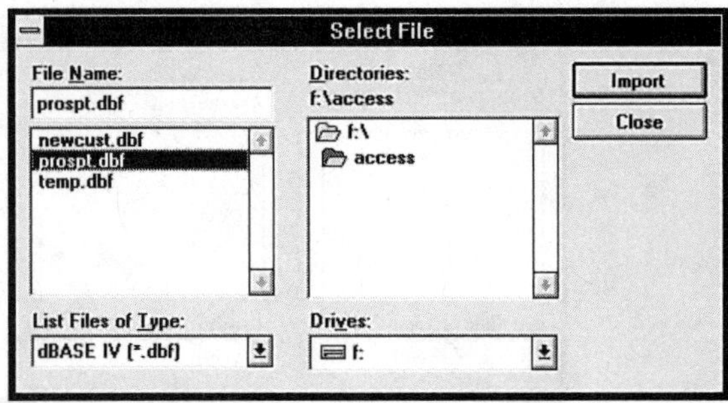

Figure 19.5 Choosing the file to import.

5. Close the **Select File** dialog box. The Database window will be displayed with the new table name.

Attaching Data

To use an external data file as if it were a table within Access, you can attach an external data file to Access. First open the desired database (such as **PROSPECT**) if it is not already open.

1. Choose **Attach Table** from the **File** menu.
2. In the **D**ata Source list box of the **Attach** dialog box, choose the type of file you want to attach (see Figure 19.6). Select **OK**.

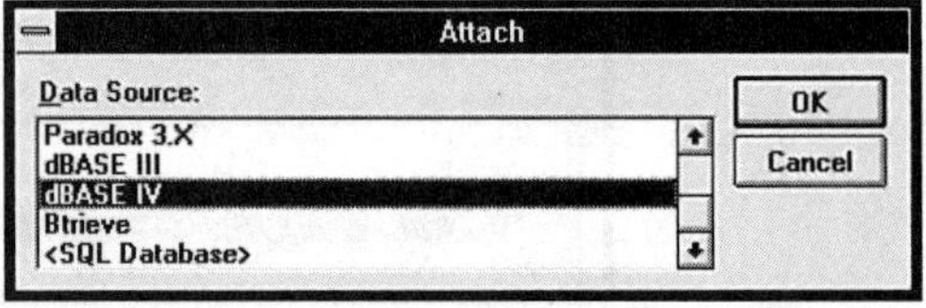

Figure 19.6 Choosing the type of table to be attached.

3. In the **Select File** dialog box, choose the drive, directory, and name of the file you are attaching (see Figure 19.7). Then select **Attach**.
4. Select any necessary index file if requested, and choose **Close** when finished.
5. Access will tell you the file was attached successfully. Choose **OK**.
6. Choose **Close** on the **Select File** dialog box.

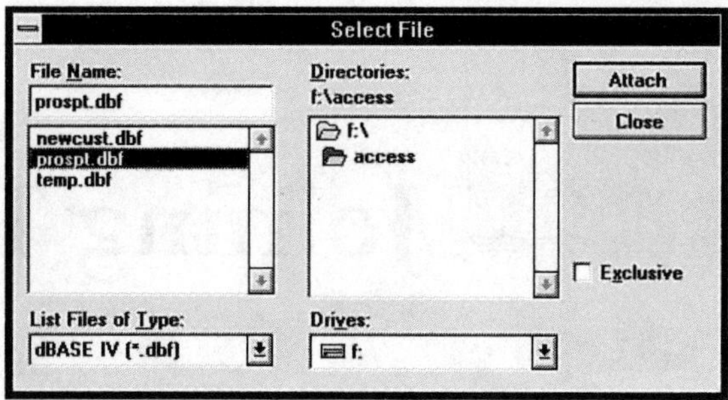

Figure 19.7 Choosing the file name for the table to be attached.

The table will be attached to your Access database, and you can use it for reports, queries, mailing labels, or graphs as you would any other table.

In this lesson you learned how to import tables to, export tables from, and attach tables to Microsoft Access. In the next lesson, you will learn how to minimize data duplication by joining tables.

Joining Tables

In this lesson you will learn how to join tables to minimize data duplication.

Why Join Tables?

In the database example used in these lessons, a REGION code identified the sales areas for the prospects. It would be better to identify regions fully with text (such as Vancouver), but all that duplicated text would make the database's main table too large. It saves space to put the region's full identification in a separate table, give each region a code, and use the region codes in the prospect table. Then we can join the two tables in a query, and have the query use the region codes to display the text that identifies each prospect. Now let's try it!

Create the Table

First, create the new table for the regions.

1. Open the database, and be sure the **Tables** button is selected. Then choose **New**. A Design view is displayed for a new table.
2. Enter **REGION** as a field, with a **Number** format.
3. Enter **REGION_NAME** as a field, with a **Text** format.
4. Select the **REGION** field, and in the Properties for this field, click on **Format**. Set the Format to **Field Size**.
5. Set the primary key by clicking in the **REGION** row, then clicking on the key in the tool bar (see Figure 20.1).
6. Save the table as **REGIONS**, using **Save As** on the **File** menu.

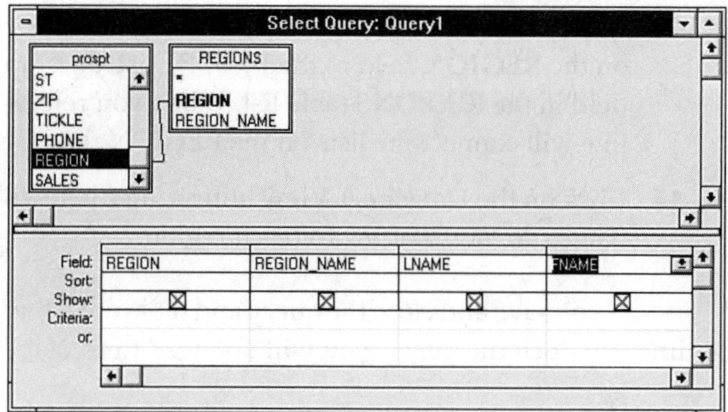

Figure 20.1 The REGIONS table.

7. Click on the **Datasheet View** button to view the datasheet; enter the data in the following way:

Under REGION:	*Under REGION_NAME:*
1	NE
2	Beaverton
3	Gresham
4	NW
5	SW
6	SE
7	Vancouver

8. Close the table to remove it from the screen.
9. In the **Database window**, select **Query**. Choose **New**.
10. In the Add Table dialog box, add the **PROSPT** and **REGIONS** tables to the query. The field list of both tables is displayed, with the primary keys in boldface. Choose **Close**.
11. Drag the desired fields to the **Field** row. Be sure both fields from the **REGIONS** table are included.
12. Click on the **Datasheet View** button. You will see the table is not correct for each region. This is because you haven't linked the tables yet.

13. Switch back to Design view by clicking on the **Design View** button. Click on the **REGION** field in the PROSPT list, and drag it to the **REGION** field in the REGIONS table list. When you release the mouse button, a line will connect the lists on the REGION field (see Figure 20.1).

14. Click on the **Datasheet View** button, and you will see that the region names are now correct for each region.

If you save and close the query and table now, the link will remain. The next time you open the query, you will not need to reestablish the link.

Link Trouble? Links can be a problem when you are editing a file from a query. If you need to do so and Microsoft Access won't let you, delete the link; reestablish it after editing.

Deleting a Link

To delete a link, click on the link to select it. Then press the **Del** key. The linking line will be deleted, and the tables will no longer be linked.

In this lesson, you learned how to create and delete links between tables. In the next lesson, you will learn how to manage your database.

21 Managing Your Database

In this lesson you will learn how to copy, delete, back up, and repair your databases.

What Is Database Management?

Database management is a collection of procedures for maintaining your databases effectively and protecting their data. These activities include copying or deleting data as necessary, backing up the system, and repairing damaged databases.

Routine File Activities

There are routine chores associated with maintaining databases, such as copying, deleting, and renaming files. Microsoft Access stores all the objects of a database in a single file; its file name has an .MDB extension.

You can use the DOS COPY command to copy the database (as a single file) to another directory or drive, or to a floppy disk. To copy the PROSPECT database from C:\ACCESS to A:\PROSPECT, for example, you would enter this command line at the DOS prompt:

COPY C:\ACCESS\PROSPECT.MDB A:\PROSPECT

For more information on the COPY command, see your DOS manual.

Whoops! I Accidentally Deleted a Database! You can rename a database from the DOS prompt with no problems, but *use caution when deleting*. If you delete a database accidentally, your only hope for recovery is using the UNDELETE command in DOS—and it may not work. See your DOS manual for more instructions on using this command.

To delete a database, use the DEL command from the DOS prompt. To delete a SALES.MDB database, for example, enter:

DEL SALES.MDB

Another Way to Delete Files You can also copy and delete files from the Windows File Manager.

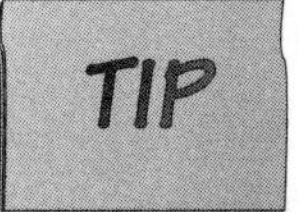

Deleting Objects To delete an object (table, report, etc.) from a database, choose the object, and then choose **Delete** from the **Edit** menu.

In the same way, you can rename a database from the DOS prompt with the REN command. For example:

REN PROSPECT.MDB SALES.MDB.

Backing Up Your Data

When using Microsoft Access, it's wise to back up your databases frequently. You should always back up a database before making important changes (such as modifying a table structure, or making design changes to queries, reports, or forms). A backup might involve nothing more than copying the current database to a file in the same directory, using a different name. This can be done quickly from the Windows File Manager.

Back Up Regularly The entire system should be backed up periodically, using software designed for this purpose. To prevent data loss from fire, flood, or other catastrophe, keep the media used for the backup somewhere else—at a separate geographic location. Do this on a regular schedule and stick to it, no matter how busy you get. The most likely time to lose data is when you are very busy, because it's harder to be careful then.

Save It Safely! Be careful not to duplicate names when you save tables, queries, and other objects in a database. *Saving a query under the same name as a table will cause the loss of the table data.*

Repairing a Database

As you use Microsoft Access, keep your databases closed unless you are using them. Display only the startup screen until you need the database open for use. Any time the database is open, it can be damaged if there is a power loss or power surge. There is the same risk if the computer locks up, forcing the user to reboot.

Microsoft Access will detect previous damage the next time you open the database. If the database is damaged, a message will appear and alert you to the need for repair. Choose the **OK** button to have Access attempt repair. Once this is done, check the last changes you made, and be sure these were completed. You may have to reenter some data, or redesign a form or report.

A database can also be damaged in a way Microsoft Access cannot detect. In this case, choose **Repair Database** from the **File** menu to force a repair of the database.

If all else fails, copy your backup database files to the hard disk again. If the Microsoft Access program becomes corrupted, it can be installed again from the floppy disks.

Congratulations! You've learned how to use Access to create databases, enter and edit data, build forms, use queries, and create reports. For more information, see the Microsoft Access *Getting Started* and *User's Guide*.

OBJECT LINKING AND EMBEDDING (OLE)

Stephen Poland

1 Using OLE to Create Links

In this lesson you'll learn what OLE is and how to use Window's OLE features to create compound documents containing dynamically linked objects.

What Is Object Linking and Embedding (OLE)?

OLE stands for Object Linking and Embedding and is a Windows standard that allows some Windows applications to transparently share information, or transfer information between applications.

For example, you may create a quarterly report in Microsoft Word that contains an Excel Chart and a list of employees created in an Access database. Each quarter the data in the chart and the employee list may change. When it comes time to generate the quarterly report, you could try to find the most up-to-date version of the Excel chart and the employee list, and copy and paste them into the report, or you could use OLE's linking and embedding features to automatically update the report with the changes made in each supporting document.

To understand how to use OLE you'll need to learn the terms listed below.

Compound Document A single document made up of parts of other Windows documents. Example: A Word document containing a Pie chart created in Excel.

Object An object is a whole document or part of a document that is produced by a Windows application. Example: a range of Excel cells.

Client Application A client application is a Windows OLE application that requests or receives information from another application. Example: Microsoft Excel.

Server Application A server application is a Windows OLE application that supplies information to another application. Example: Microsoft Word.

Source Document A source document is created by the server application and contains the information (object) that is to be copied and placed in the destination document. Example: an Excel spreadsheet containing a pie chart (the object).

Destination Document A destination document is created by the client application and is where you link or embed the information (object) created in the source document. Example: a Word document containing an Excel pie chart.

Linking Linking is the insertion of part of a source document into one or more destination documents. A link is established between the two applications by maintaining the location, name, and other pertinent information about the object in the source document. When the source document is updated, the object in the destination document(s) is also updated.

Embedding Embedding is the insertion of part of a source document created in a server application into a destination document created by a client application. Embedding allows you to access one application's features from within another application. Unlike linking, there is no connection maintained to the source document, only a tie to the server application.

To Create a Link Between Two Applications

One of the primary benefits of OLE's linking ability is its ability to change a single source document or object and update all the destination documents that contain the linked object. The following sections show you how to create a link between two OLE applications.

Creating a link between applications is quite similar to using the Windows cut and paste procedure with a few additional options at the paste step.

What Are My Options? The menu options available for creating links between documents vary among Windows applications, or may not be available at all. Be sure to check your application's documentation if you find variances in the location or names of menu options.

To create a link between two Windows applications, follow these steps:

1. Start the server application and create or open the source document.
2. Select the object you want to link. The object may be text, a range of cells, a graphic, or database records. If you create a new document in the server application, be sure to use the Save **A**s command on the **F**ile menu to save your file. You cannot link from a document that has not been saved.
3. Pull down the **E**dit menu and choose **Copy**. The object you selected is copied to the Windows Clipboard.
4. Switch to the Program Manager by selecting **Switch To ... (Ctrl+Esc)** on the Control menu. If the application you want to link the object to is already open, you can simply switch to that application and document by pressing **Alt+Esc** until it appears.
5. From the Program Manager start the client application and open the destination document. This is the document you want to paste the object into. You now have both the server application and source document and the client application and document open.
6. In the destination document, position the cursor where you want the linked object to appear.
7. Choose **Paste Special** from the **Edit** menu. A dialog box appears (Figure 1.1) showing the Data Types list of different formats in which the object can appear. If the Paste Special command is not present on the Edit menu, look for the Links or Paste Links commands.

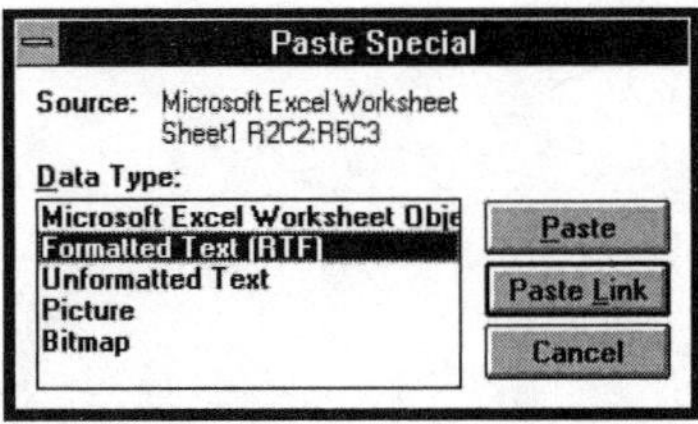

Figure 1.1 The Paste Special dialog box.

8. From the Data Type list, select the data form in which you want the object to appear. The Paste **L**ink button should be active. Do not select the Object data form—it is used for embedding an object and no link will be established with embedding.

9. Click on the Paste Link button. The object is pasted into the destination document and Windows creates an automatically updating link to the source document.

Now, each time you update the information in the source document, the changes you make can be reflected in the destination document. The links you create can be updated automatically or manually. You'll learn how to control the updating of objects in the next sections.

Peek-A-Boo! Some applications require the source document to be active for the linked object to appear. As an example, Excel must be running and the source document must be open for a range of cells pasted into a Word document to be properly displayed. If you close the Excel source document, Word places a reference to the Excel application, the source document and the Range of cells, but does not display the range of cells.

In this lesson, you learned what OLE is and how to create a link between applications. In the next lesson, you will learn how to edit and manage your links.

2 Managing Links

In this lesson, you will learn how to edit, manage, break and restore links.

Editing Linked Objects

Once you have created a linked object it is likely that you will want to edit and update the information in the object. It is at this stage that you'll realize the full benefit of an OLE link because you can edit the object one time and it will be updated in every document that it is linked to.

There are two ways to edit a linked object. The first is to start at the source document, using the server application to make changes in the object. The second is to start at the destination document and let the link information lead you to the correct source document and server application. With this method you do not have to remember the name of the source document or even what server application created it. Follow the steps below to learn how to edit linked objects using these two methods.

Editing from the Source Document

To edit a linked object from the source document, follow these steps:

1. Start the server application and open the source document that contains the object you want to edit.
2. Edit and make changes to the object.
3. Save the document and close the server application
4. Switch to or start the client application and open the destination document. If the destination document is setup to automatically update links, a dialog box appears asking if you want your document to be updated to

reflect the changes you made in the source document. If you choose **YES**, the links will be updated and the changes you made to the object will be reflected in the destination document.

Some applications enable you to edit linked objects starting from the destination document. This is convenient because you do not have to remember the exact file name and location of the source document. That information is stored as part of the link.

Now You See It, Now You Don't Some client applications let you edit or make changes directly to the object that is linked to the destination document without starting the server application. This can cause problems because the source document is not being changed, only its image is. The changes you make to the image will be wiped out when the object is updated via the source document.

Editing from the Destination Document

To edit a linked object from the destination document, follow these steps:

1. From the destination document, double-click the linked object you want to update. The server application should start and display the source document.

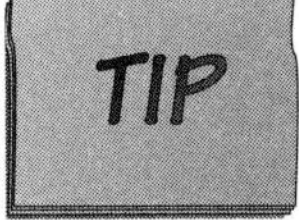

Another Way If double-clicking the object does not work, open the Links list dialog box by choosing **Links** from the **Edit** menu. Select the link you want to edit and choose the **Open Source** or **Open** button. The server application will start and display the source document.

2. Edit the object in the source document.
3. Choose **Save** from the **File** menu of the source document.
4. The destination document will now reflect the changes you made to the linked object.

Managing a Link's Update Setting

Once you have created a linked object you can control when any changes to the source document are reflected in the destination document. You can update a link manually or automatically. If a link is set to be updated manually, you must remember to follow the update steps each time you change the source document that contains the linked object.

With the automatic setting enabled (the default update setting), you will be reminded that the source document has been changed and prompted to allow the linked object to be updated in the destination document.

To set a linked object to be updated manually, follow these steps:

1. Open the destination document that contains the object link you want to update.
2. Choose the **Links** command on the **Edit** menu. (In Excel, the Links command is found on the **File** menu). The Links list dialog box will appear (Figure 2.1). For the linked objects in your document, the list indicates the Link name, the path name of the source document, and whether the link is set to update automatically or manually.

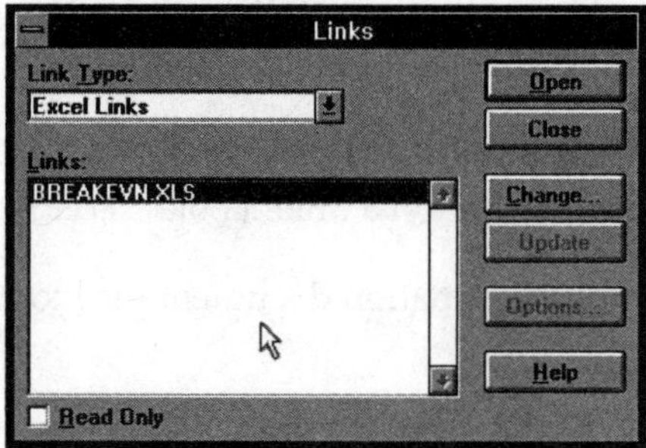

Figure 2.1 The Links list dialog box for Excel.

3. Select the link you want to update.
4. Choose the **Manual** option.
5. Update the link by choosing the **Update Now** button in the Link list dialog box.

With a link set for manual update, you must repeat step 5 of this procedure each time you want the linked object to reflect changes made in the source document.

If you set the update option for a link to Automatic in the Links list dialog box, the next time you open the destination document, you are prompted to allow the object to be updated with the changes (Figure 2.2).

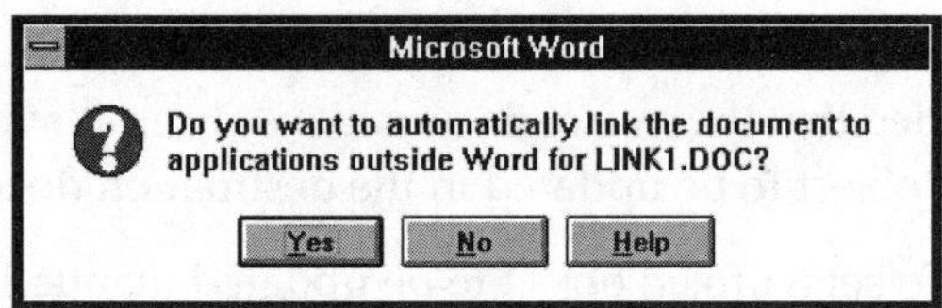

Figure 2.2 The automatic update confirmation dialog box.

Breaking Links

If at some point you decide that you want a linked object in your document to remain fixed and no longer be updated by its source document, you can break (or cancel) the link. This does not delete or alter the object, it merely removes the background information that directly ties the object to its source document. The object becomes like any other object that was placed by the Copy and Paste operation from the Windows Clipboard.

To break or cancel a linked object, follow these steps:

1. Open the destination document that contains the object whose link you want to break.
2. Select **Links** (or **Edit Link Options**) for the **Edit** menu. The Links list dialog box will appear, showing linked object information.
3. Select the link name of the object you want to break
4. Choose **Cancel Link** (or **Delete** in some applications). A warning box may appear cautioning you that you are breaking a link. Choose OK or YES to confirm your choice.

Restoring a Broken Link

It is possible to accidentally break a link to an object. If you move the source document from the directory in which the link was created, or if you change the name of the source document, Windows will not be able to find it and the link is effectively broken. You will get a warning dialog box telling you that the source document is missing or corrupted. To re-establish the broken link you must move the source document back to its original location, or tell windows where to find it in its new location.

To re-establish a broken link, follow these steps:

1. Open the destination document containing the object with a broken link. If you received an alert dialog box warning of the broken link, you have already completed this step.
2. Choose the **Links** command from the **Edit** menu. The Links list dialog box will appear, listing the objects in the destination document that are linked.
3. Select the object whose link is broken.
4. Click on the **Change Link** button. A dialog box will appear with a path name field of the linked object (Figure 2.3). It is this path name that points to the location of the source document.

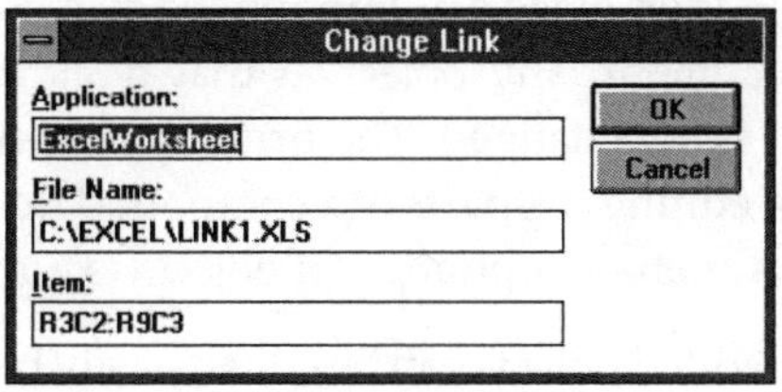

Figure 2.3 The Change Link dialog box.

5. Edit the path name or file name to reflect the new location of the source document.
6. Click on the **OK** button to complete the restoration of the link. The link is now re-established between the source and destination documents.

In this lesson you learned how to share and dynamically update your documents. In the next lesson you'll learn how to embed objects in OLE applications.

3 Embedding Objects in Windows Applications

In this lesson you'll learn the difference between linking and embedding, how to embed an object in a Windows document, and how to edit an embedded object.

Understanding OLE Embedding

The procedure for embedding objects into documents is essentially the same as that for linking objects, but the resulting connection between the source document and destination document is quite different.

Embedded objects are not linked to a source document. If you update the source document, any object in that document that is embedded in another document is not changed. The primary advantage of using embedded objects is the ease of editing the parts of a compound document. Use embedding instead of linking if automatic updating of objects is not required.

Embedded objects can be edited easily because they provide quick access to the application that created them. If you double-click on an embedded object, the application that created the object starts and allows you to edit the object. When you're finished editing the object, you exit the application by choosing Update from File menu. The application closes and you see the updated object back where you started.

There are two ways to embed an object in a document. You can create the object in the server application and embed it in the destination document, or you can start at the destination document and choose the Object command on the Insert menu to launch the server application, create the object, and embed the object in the destination document.

Creating Embedded Objects

To create an embedded object starting from a server application, follow these steps:

1. Start the server application and either open or create the document that contains the object you want to embed.
2. Select the object to be embedded.
3. Choose **Copy** from the **Edit** menu. The object will be copied to the Windows Clipboard.
4. Start or switch to the client application and open the destination document.
5. Place the insertion point where you want the object to appear.
6. Choose **Paste Special** from the **Edit** menu. This command may vary among applications. Be sure the command you choose allows you to select the Data Type of the object, and be sure not to use the Paste Link command.

A dialog box will appear (Figure 3.1) that allows you to select the data type of the object to be embedded.

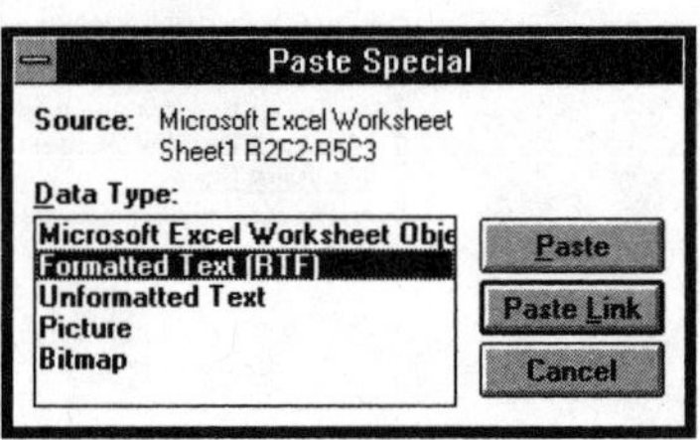

Figure 3.1 The Paste Special dialog box

7. Select the **Object data type** from the Data Type list box. The **Paste Link** button should dim (indicating you are not linking) and the **P**aste button should remain highlighted.
8. Click on the **Paste** button. The object is inserted at the insertion point, and embedded in the destination document.

9. Save the destination document. You can switch to server application and either save or discard the source document. The destination document does not need the source document to maintain the embedded object (unlike a linked destination document which needs the source document containing the linked object.)

To create an embedded object starting from the destination document, follow these steps:

1. Start the client application and open the destination document. This is the document that you want to place the embedded object into.
2. Choose the **Object** command from the **Insert** menu. A dialog box appears listing the server applications and object types that can be embedded in your document (Figure 3.2.)

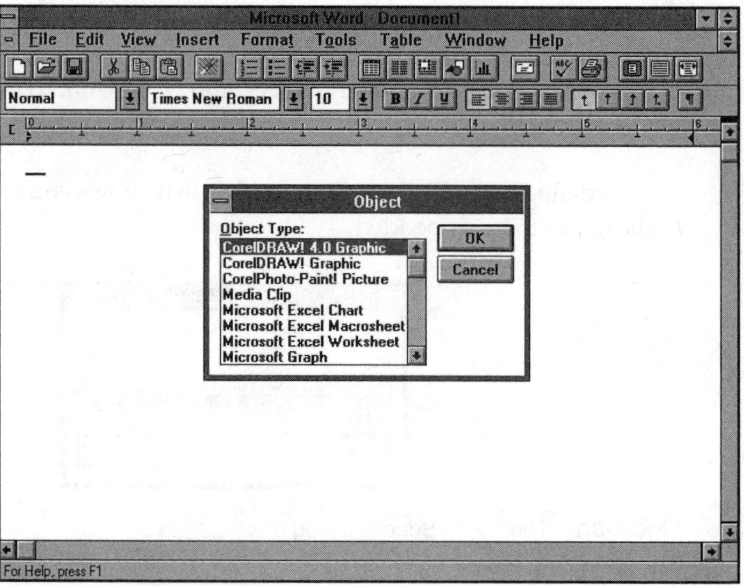

Figure 3.2 The Object Insert dialog box.

3. Choose the server application you want to use and click OK. The server application will start.
4. Either open the source document that contains the object you want to embed or create the object using the server application's tools and commands.

5. Select the object to be embedded.
6. Choose the **Update** command from the **File** menu. The server application will close and the embedded object will appear in the destination document. In some cases you might need to manually exit the server application to return to the destination document.
7. Save the destination document.

Editing Embedded Objects

Editing an embedded object is simple and straightforward. Editing an embedded object is where the prime advantage of embedding comes into play. You do not have to recall the name and location of the source document that created the embedded object. You simply double-click the object and the source application starts allowing you to edit the object.

Follow these steps to edit an embedded object:

1. Start the client application and destination document containing the embedded object you want to edit.
2. Double-click on the object. The server application of the embedded object will start.
3. Edit the object using the server application's tools and commands.
4. Select the **Update** command from the **File** menu. The server application will close and you will be returned to the destination document where the embedded object reflects the edits you made. In some cases, you might have to select the **Exit** command to close the server application.

In this lesson you learned how to use OLE embedding to create a compound document that provides easy access and editing of objects created in different Windows OLE applications.

INDEX

Symbols

A

B

C

D

E

F

G

H

J

K

M

N

O

P

S

T

U

V

W

X-Y-Z